Consumer Behavior

IMPLICATIONS
FOR
MARKETING
STRATEGY

Consumer Behavior

IMPLICATIONS FOR MARKETING STRATEGY

DEL I. HAWKINS
University of Oregon

ROGER J. BEST
University of Oregon

KENNETH A. CONEY
Late of Arizona State University

FOURTH EDITION 1989

BPI
IRWIN

HOMEWOOD, IL 60430
BOSTON, MA 02116

Cover art: Adapted from Times Mirror 1987 Annual Report

Sponsoring editor: *Elizabeth J. Schilling*
Project editor: *Ethel Shiell*
Production manager: *Carma W. Fazio*
Cover design: *Paula Lang*
Compositor: *J.M. Post Graphics, Corp.*
Typeface: 10/12 *Times Roman*
Printer: *R. R. Donnelley & Sons Company*

LIBRARY OF CONGRESS
Library of Congress Cataloging-in-Publication Data

Hawkins, Del I.
Consumer behavior: implications for marketing strategy/Del I. Hawkins, Roger J. Best, Kenneth A. Coney—4th ed.
p. cm.
Includes bibliographical references and indexes.
ISBN 0-256-06331-1
1. Consumer behavior—United States. 2. Market surveys—United States. 3. Consumer behavior—United States—Case studies. 4. Market surveys—United States—Case studies. I. Best, Roger J. II. Coney, Kenneth A. III. Title.
HF5415.33.U6H38 1989
658.8'324'0973—dc19 88-21410
CIP

Printed in the United States of America

3 4 5 6 7 8 9 0 DO 6 5 4 3 2 1 0

Preface to the First Edition

The purpose of this text is to provide the student with a usable, managerial understanding of consumer behavior. Most students in consumer behavior courses aspire to careers in marketing management. They hope to acquire knowledge and skills that will be useful to them in these careers. Unfortunately, some may be seeking the type of knowledge gained in introductory accounting classes; that is, a set of relatively invariant rules that can be applied across a variety of situations to achieve a fixed solution that is known to be correct. For these students, the uncertainty and lack of closure involved in dealing with living, breathing, changing, stubborn consumers can be very frustrating. However, if they can accept dealing with endless uncertainty, utilizing an understanding of consumer behavior in developing marketing strategy will become tremendously exciting.

The rules governing human behavior, although they do not operate like the rules developed for accounting systems, can be applied in a marketing context. Having students recognize this is a major challenge. It is our view that the utilization of a knowledge of consumer behavior in the development of marketing strategy is an art. This is not to suggest that scientific principles and procedures are not applicable. Rather, it means that the successful application of these principles to particular situations requires human judgment that we are not able to reduce to a fixed set of rules.

Let us consider the analogy with art in some detail. Suppose you want to become an expert artist. You would study known principles of the visual effects of blending various colors, of perspective, and so forth. Then you would practice applying these principles until you developed the ability to produce acceptable paintings. If you had certain "natural" talents, the right teacher, and the right topic, you might even produce a "masterpiece." The same approach should be taken by one wishing to become a marketing manager. The various factors or principles that influence consumer behavior should be thoroughly studied. Then, one should practice applying these principles until acceptable marketing strategies result. However, while knowledge and practice can in general produce acceptable strategies, "great" marketing strategies, like "masterpieces," require special talents, effort, timing, and some degree of "luck" (what if Mona Lisa had not wanted her portrait painted?).

The art analogy is useful for another reason. All of us, professors and students alike, tend to ask: "How can I use this concept of, say, social class to develop a successful marketing strategy?" This makes as much sense as an artist asking: "How can I use blue to create a great picture?" Obviously, blue alone will seldom be sufficient for a great work of art. Instead, to be successful, the artist must understand when and how to use blue in conjunction with other elements in the picture. Likewise, the marketing manager must understand when and how to use a knowledge of social class in conjunction with a knowledge of other factors in designing a successful marketing strategy.

This book is based on the premise described above. That is, it is based on the belief that a knowledge of the factors that influence consumer behavior can, with practice, be used to develop sound marketing strategy. With this in mind, we have attempted to do three things. First, we present a reasonably comprehensive description of the various behavioral concepts and theories that have been found useful for understanding consumer behavior. This is generally done at the beginning of each chapter or at the beginning of major subsections in each chapter. We believe that a person must have a thorough understanding of a concept in order to successfully apply that concept across different situations.

Second, we present examples of how these concepts have been and can be utilized in the development of marketing strategy. We have tried to make clear that these examples are *not* "how you use this concept." Rather, they are presented as "how one organization facing a particular marketing situation used this concept." The difference, while subtle, is important.

Finally, at the end of each chapter, we present new marketing situations and ask the student to apply the concepts to these situations. We view this as an important part of the learning process. To provide continuity to the class and text, we describe in some detail in the first chapter a firm that must develop a marketing strategy for an addition to its product line. We do not refer back to this firm in the content part of the text; instead, several of the discussion and project situations presented at the end of each chapter relate to this firm. By discussing these questions, the student can develop a feel for how the many concepts we discuss relate to each other in the context of a single product category.

We have attempted to write a useful and enjoyable text. The degree to which we have accomplished this goal was greatly increased by the assistance of numerous individuals and organizations. To all of them we express our gratitude. To our students, colleagues, friends, and families who suffered with us as we wrote, we express our love.

Del I. Hawkins
Roger J. Best
Kenneth A. Coney

Preface to the Fourth Edition

The boundaries of knowledge regarding consumer behavior have continued to expand since we wrote the first edition. We have tried to reflect this expansion in this edition. Otherwise, our philosophy and objective as expressed in the preface to the first edition remains intact. We hope you will take a few minutes to read that statement.

Numerous individuals and organizations helped us in the task of writing this edition. We are grateful for this assistance. Particular thanks are due our reviewers: Professors Dolores A. Barsellotti, California State Polytechnic University, Pomona; Sharon E. Beatty, University of Alabama; Joseph J. Belonax, Jr., Western Michigan University; Gordon C. Bruner, Southern Illinois University; Louis M. Capella, Mississippi State University; Kenny Chan, California State University, Chico; Howard B. Cox, Indiana University of Pennsylvania; William B. Crawford, Slippery Rock University; Calvin P. Duncan, University of Colorado, Boulder; Jack Farley, Southwest Texas State University; Richard Feinberg, Purdue University; James D. Gill, Phoenix College; Joseph P. Grunenwald, Clarion University; Kenneth H. Heischmidt, Southeast Missouri State University; Firooz Hekmat, Southeast Missouri State University; Thomas J. Hickey, State University of New York, Oswego; James B. Hunt, Baylor University; Easwar S. Iyer, University of Massachusetts; Ram Kesavan, University of Detroit; Pamela Kiecker, College of St. Thomas; William R. Lowry, Central Connecticut State College; Gerry McCready, St. Lawrence College, Kingston, Ontario, Canada; Michael Mazis, American University; Banwari Mittal, Northern Kentucky University; George Prough, University of Akron; William C. Rodgers, St. Cloud State University,; Larry W. Rottmeyer, Anderson College; W. Daniel Roundtree, Middle Tennessee State University; Claire Rowe, University of Northern Iowa; Kelly Shuptrine, University of South Carolina, Columbia; Ruth B. Smith, University of Maryland; Robert L. Thornton, Miami University.

Professor Russell Belk, University of Utah, went far beyond the call of duty in providing comments and suggestions. Likewise, our colleagues at Oregon—David Boush, Marian Friestad and Lynn Kahle—generously responded to our requests for assistance (and often when we didn't realize we needed assistance). All should be held blameless for our inability to fully incorporate their ideas.

The text would have had higher quality, been more fun to read, and much more fun to write had Ken been able to write it with us. This edition is dedicated to his memory. By his life he said to us:

Cherish your dreams
Guard your ideals
Enjoy life
Seek the best
Climb your mountains

Del I. Hawkins
Roger J. Best

Contents

SECTION FOUR Consumer Decision Process 498

Consumer Behavior

IMPLICATIONS
FOR
MARKETING
STRATEGY

SECTION ONE

Introduction

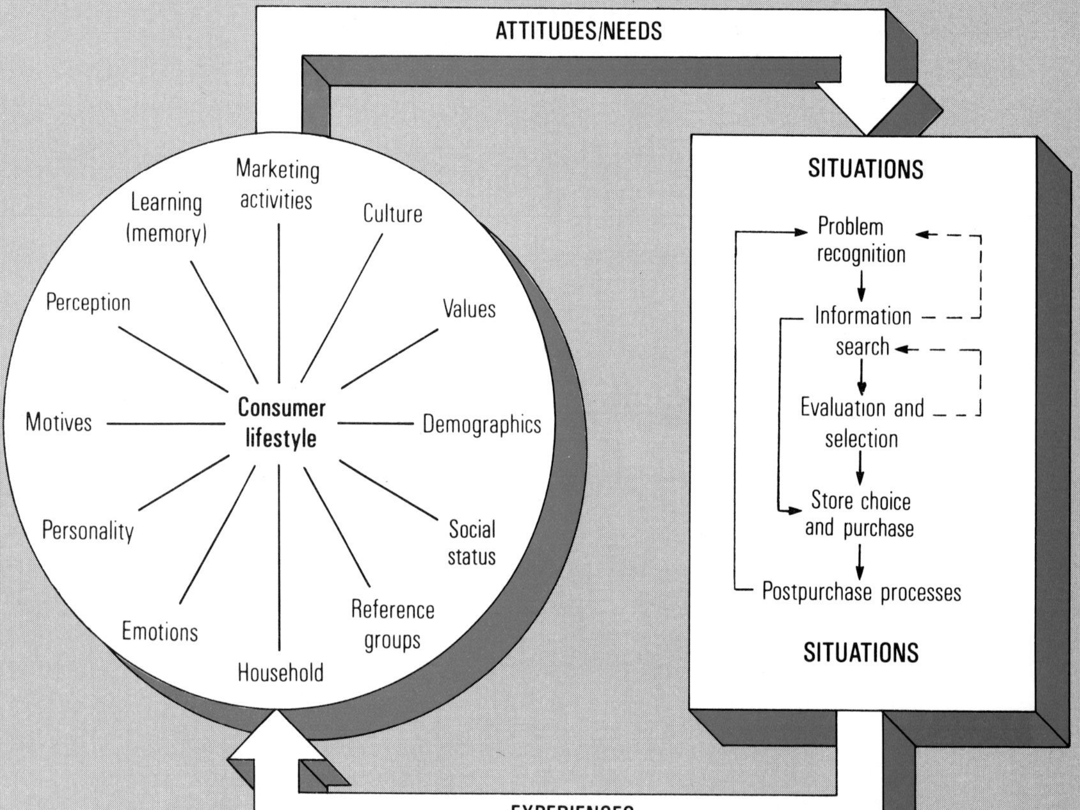

What is consumer behavior? Why should we study it? Do marketing managers actually utilize knowledge about consumer behavior in developing marketing strategy? How can we organize our knowledge of consumer behavior in order to apply it more effectively? These and a number of other interesting questions are addressed in the first chapter of the text. This chapter seeks to indicate the importance and usefulness of the material to be covered in the remainder of the text as well as provide an overview of this material. In addition, the logic underlying the model of consumer behavior shown on the facing page is presented.

CHAPTER

1 Consumer Behavior and Marketing Strategy

For the first time in two decades, the Coca-Cola Company is considering altering its labels. Working under the theory that a blue curve rolling through the trademark will sell new Coke better than a red curve, Cola-Cola USA has developed subtle changes it hopes will catch the eye of supermarket shoppers.

Discovered during consumer tests on the West Coast, the new red, white, and blue design on the new Coke can will turn up in grocery stores and vending machines across the country in early 1988. The new color scheme for the reformulated Coke, which has been losing market share since it was introduced in 1985, was designed to further differentiate the new formula from Coca-Cola Classic.

At the same time, Coca-Cola is testing graphic alterations on its six Coke brands. The testing will be conducted in Fort Wayne, Indiana, and Montgomery, Alabama. If consumers like it, the new cans will start appearing in 1989. Most consumers will know something is different about the labels; they just won't be able to put their fingers on it. Most significantly, the word *Coke* will be bigger and bolder, and it will tilt a little forward, slightly italicized, in a new look the company believes is more in harmony with the traditional Coca-Cola script label.

The company feels the new labels will give the products a uniformity that has been lost through aggressive brand extensions, and reinforce the red color of Cola-Cola's famous trademark.

Some 30,000 man-hours were spent in the redesign effort, and more than 10,000 initial designs were drafted before management "winnowed them down to a manageable 100 or so." The final designs were presented to juries of consumers before the new design package was completed.

The key to Coca-Cola's success in differentiating new Coke while adding uniformity to its extended product line is a thorough understanding of consumer behavior and its relationship to marketing strategy. The purpose of this text is to provide you with such a key. As shown in the following diagram, an understanding of consumer behavior includes observable behaviors such as amount purchased, when, with whom, by whom, and how purchases are consumed. It also includes nonobservable variables such as the consumers' values, personal needs, perceptions, what information they have in memory, how they obtain and process information, and how they evaluate alternatives.

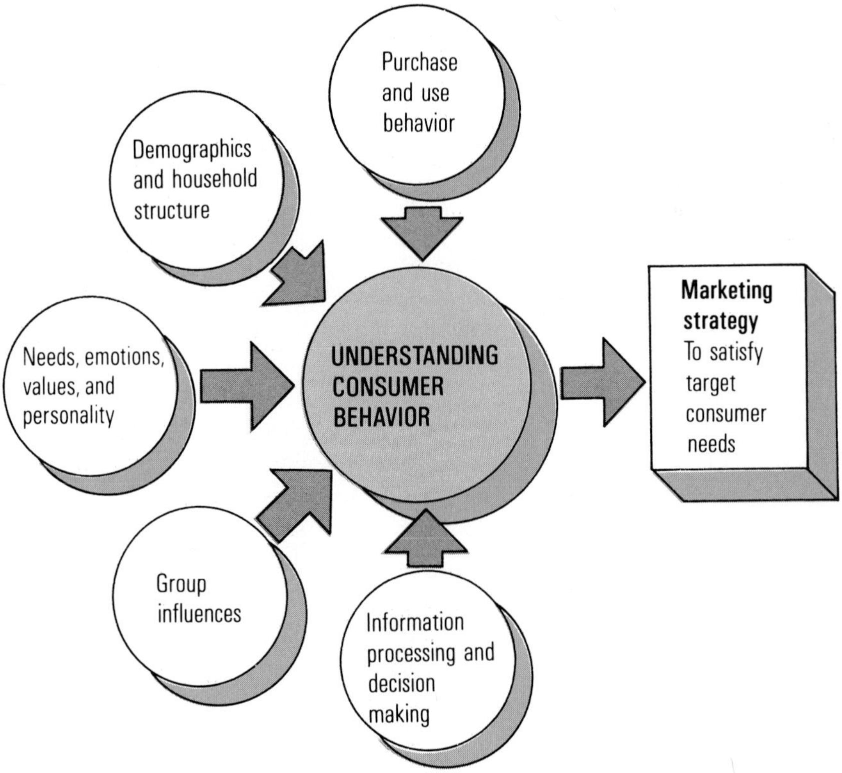

CONSUMER BEHAVIOR AND MARKETING STRATEGY

Before discussing consumer behavior and its implications for marketing strategy, it is necessary to examine the role consumer behavior plays in *developing* marketing strategy. A good way to do that is to consider the experiences of people who use a knowledge of consumer behavior in their professional lives, and to let them explain the role this knowledge plays as they develop successful marketing programs for their organizations.

Thomas S. Carroll, president and chief executive officer of the marketing-oriented Lever Brothers Company, explains the approach Lever Brothers takes to consumer behavior this way:

> Understanding and properly interpreting consumer wants is a whole lot easier said than done. Every week our marketing researchers talk to more than 4,000 consumers to find out:
>
> - What they think of our products and those of our competitors.
> - What they think of possible improvements in our products.
> - How they use our products.
> - What attitudes they have about our products and our advertising.
> - What they feel about their "roles" in the family and society.
> - What their hopes and dreams are for themselves and their families.
>
> Today, as never before, we cannot take our business for granted. That's why understanding—and therefore learning to anticipate—consumer behavior is our key to planning and managing in this ever-changing environment.[1]

Agree Creme Rinse and Agree Shampoo are both highly successful consumer products. The marketing research managers for Agree describe some of the development activities related to consumer behavior in their company as follows:

> We fielded more than 50 individual research projects before the national introduction of Agree Shampoo. . . . There were focus groups, concept studies, concept product studies, product testing, advertising testing, extended use testing, a laboratory test market, and a test market. . . . We were called upon to establish market sizes and trends and generally review the attitudes of users and nonusers. . . . We conducted many focus groups among all types of women, but increasingly we came to zero in on the young. . . . We certainly didn't stop with focus groups, we conducted quantified concept tests among target users. . . . [One] test design used a blind-paired comparison among members of a mail panel. We placed products with 400 women and had them use each for two weeks. At the end of the use period, a telephone interview determined their preferences overall and their ratings on 15 to 20 performance attributes. And we asked open-end questions for supporting diagnostics.[2]

In order to develop successful marketing strategies, marketers must understand how markets are *segmented* and how consumer behavior differs from one market

Exhibit 1–1 Brand Positioning Strategies

Courtesy Gevalia Kaffe Import Service

Upscale Positioning: Advertising from *Town & Country* magazine

Courtesy Taster's Choice Coffee

Mass Market Positioning: Advertising from *Better Homes and Gardens* magazine

segment to another. For example, in Exhibit 1–1, two brands of the same product, coffee, are advertised to two very different market segments.

As outlined in Figure 1–1, consumer behavior tends to be product and situation specific. That is, the consumer behavior that drives purchase and consumption behavior may vary from one product to another or even vary for the same product from one use to another. Thus, the insight we gain in one consumer behavior study is not always transferable from one marketing situation to another.

Exhibit 1–2 summarizes several attempts to apply an understanding of consumer behavior in order to develop effective marketing strategy. The examples cited reveal three main facts about the nature of our knowledge of consumer behavior. First, successful marketing decisions by commercial firms, nonprofit organizations, and regulatory agencies require extensive information on consumer behavior. It should be obvious from these examples that *firms are applying theories and information about consumer behavior on a daily basis*.

Each of the examples also involved the collection of information about the specific consumers involved in the marketing decision at hand. Thus, at its current

Figure 1–1
Consumer Behavior Is Product-Person-Situation Specific

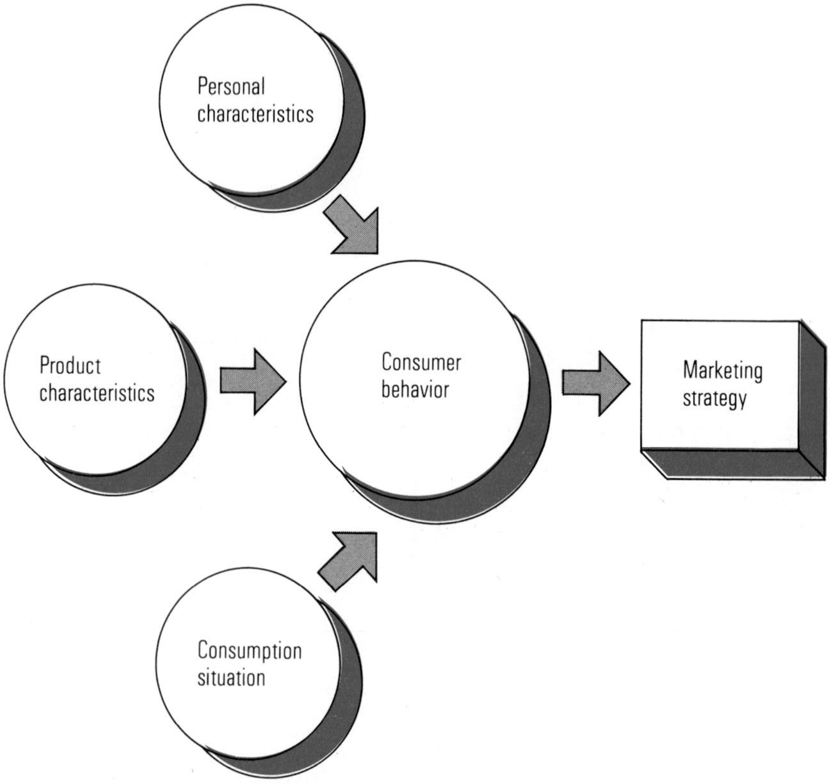

state of development, *consumer behavior theory provides the manager with the proper questions to ask*. However, given the importance of the specific situation and product category in consumer behavior, it will often be necessary to conduct research to answer these questions. Appendix A at the end of the text provides an overview of the consumer behavior research process.

Finally the examples in Exhibit 1–2 indicate that *consumer behavior is a complex, multidimensional process*. Coca-Cola has substantial evidence that consumers prefer the *taste* of new Coke to the *taste* of Classic Coke. Yet Classic Coke outsells new Coke 10 to 1. Obviously, the soft drink purchase decision involves more than just taste.

Our primary goal is to help you obtain a usable managerial understanding of consumer behavior. The key aspect of this objective is found in the phrase, *usable managerial understanding*. We want to increase your understanding of consumer behavior in order to help you become a more effective marketing manager. Our secondary goal in developing your knowledge of consumer be-

Exhibit 1–2 Successful Consumer Marketing Is Driven by a Thorough Understanding of Product Specific Consumer Behavior

THE AMERICAN RED CROSS

The American Red Cross has recently changed its annual fund-raising campaign from the passive "good neighbor" approach to the hard sell "Keep the Red Cross Ready" theme. The changes were the result of a series of research studies which indicated that previous campaigns had not effectively communicated the organization's message. Attitude research indicated widespread misconceptions about the services supplied by the Red Cross and a low level of personal identification with the organization's services.*

NEW COKE

From 1981 to 1985, Coca-Cola conducted "blind" (unbranded) taste tests comparing the formula that is now new Coke with what is now Classic Coke as well as competitive brands. Almost 200,000 consumers took part in these tests. The results indicated significant preference for the taste of the new formula. In the spring of 1985, new Coke was introduced and the old version was discontinued. Shortly thereafter, consumer pressure caused the firm to reintroduce the original formula as Coca-Cola Classic. By the end of 1987, Coca-Cola Classic was the leading soft-drink brand (19.8 percent) followed by Pepsi (18.8 percent). New Coke, with the taste most consumers appear to prefer, continued to lose market share and finished in a tie for 10th place (1.6 percent).

FEDERAL COURTS AND TRADEMARK REGISTRATION

Since 1972, Owens-Corning has spent over $60 million advertising its Fiberglas insulation with the Pink Panther as a "spokesperson" using such slogans as "Think pink," "Think more pink," and "Beat the cold with pink." Pink has no functional association with Fiberglas. The color was added years ago by Owens-Corning to differentiate a new, less itchy version from their then current version.

In the mid-1980s a new competitor made plans to enter the market with a pink insulation. Owens-Corning had not registered the color as a trademark because all previous attempts to register colors had failed. In response to the new competitor, Owens-Corning requested registration from the U.S. Trademark Trial & Appeal Board but was denied. However, a U.S. circuit court of appeals overturned the board's decision and gave Owens-Corning exclusive rights to market pink insulation. A major factor in the decision was research showing over 50 percent consumer recognition of pink insulation as Owens-Corning's brand.†

*"Red Cross Drive Result of Research," *Advertising Age,* January 15, 1979, p. 36.

†S. W. Colford, "Court to Owens-Corning: Color It Pink," *Advertising Age,* December 16, 1985, p. 31.

havior is to enhance your understanding of a major aspect of our society. Our society, as well as most developed societies, is legitimately referred to as a consumption society. Therefore, a knowlege of consumer behavior can enhance our understanding of ourselves and our environment.

Sufficient knowledge of consumer behavior currently exists to provide a usable guide to marketing practice, but the state of the art is not sufficient for us to write a cookbook with surefire recipes for success. We will illustrate how some firms were able to combine certain ingredients for success under specific conditions. However, as conditions change, the quantities and even the ingredients required for success may change. It is up to you as a student and future marketing manager to develop the ability to apply this knowledge to specific situations. To assist you, we have included example situations and questions at the end of each chapter and a series of short cases at the end of each section which can be used to develop your application skills. Also, Appendix B at the end of the text provides a list of key questions for a consumer behavior audit for developing marketing strategy.

Before outlining the consumer behavior topics to be covered, we would like to review several important aspects of marketing strategy to be used throughout this book. Each is discussed in the context of consumer behavior to reinforce the importance of understanding consumer behavior and using it to help develop marketing strategy.

Figure 1–2
Positioning of K mart

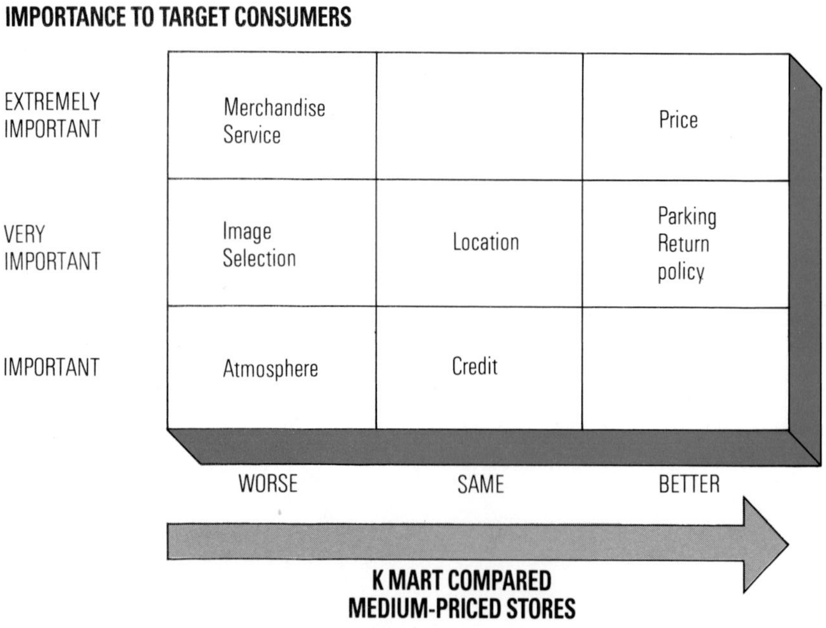

Positioning Strategy

An understanding of how your product is positioned in the minds of target consumers is important. Without knowing how your brand or store is perceived in the marketplace, it is difficult to develop effective marketing strategy. For example, K mart has evolved from a five-and-ten store in the early 60s to a discount store in the 70s and 80s. However, K mart's management now sees a different set of market conditions and would like to reposition K mart as a higher quality, higher priced store. In order to achieve this objective, they must first understand their current position.

Figure 1–2 is an example of how K mart might analyze its current position. In this example, 10 store attributes considered by *target consumers* to be im-

Figure 1–3
Consumer Perceptions of K mart

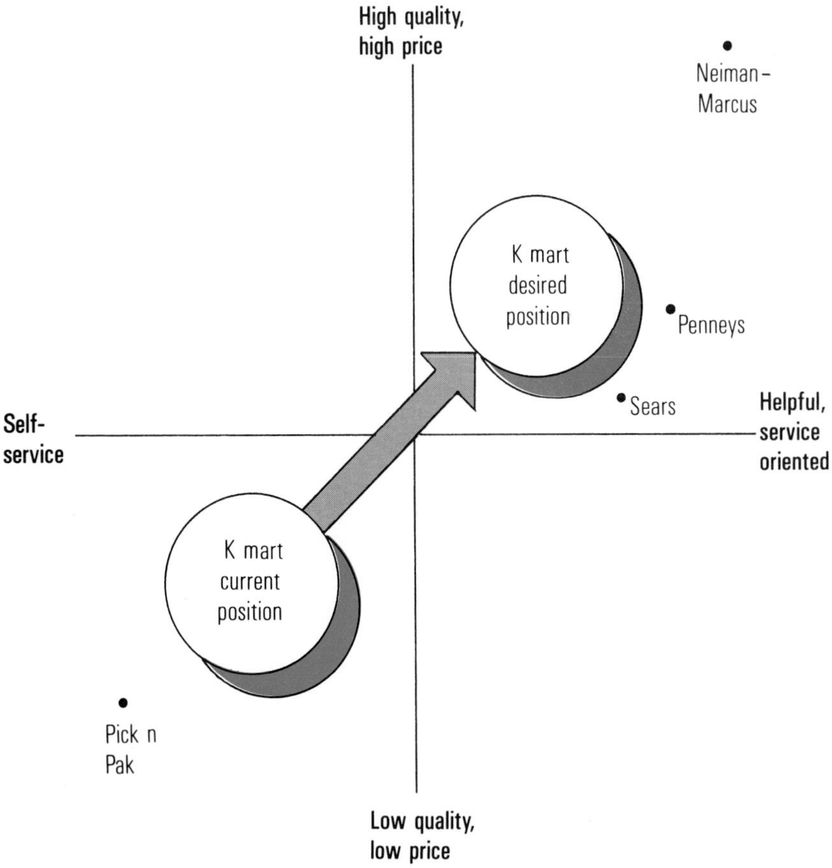

portant are used to compare K mart's current position with the company's target competitors. By using consumers to make these comparisons, K mart can learn:

- Which attributes are critical.
- Where K mart stands in comparison to competition on these critical attributes.
- The degree to which different segments of the consumer market share the same perceptions.

An alternative to constructing a positioning grid such as the one in Figure 1–2 is the creation of a perceptual map on which consumer perceptions of K mart are contrasted with those of all competing stores. In Figure 1–3 we see K mart's current positioning and the changes they must make in consumer perceptions in order to achieve their desired position. K mart's marketing strategy must focus on the information critical to their positioning, as shown in Figures 1–2 and 1–3. Exhibit 1–3 illustrates Hyundai's attempt to improve its positioning on the comfort/luxury dimension while maintaining a strong position on the practical/inexpensive dimension.

Market Segmentation

Market segmentation is the basis of most marketing strategy. It involves developing specific marketing programs targeted at consumer groups with unique needs and/or purchasing processes. Exhibit 1–4 illustrates how Scandinavian Airlines segmented the airline travel market and developed a successful marketing program for an important segment.

New Products

Thousands of new products are introduced annually into the marketplace. To be successful, these new products must solve a consumer problem. Therefore, marketers need to understand very thoroughly the needs and desires of potential consumers and the way in which product features can be combined to satisfy these needs.

Products such as GE's Space Saver microwave oven were the result of listening to homemakers complain about the counterspace their microwave ovens occupied. The success of this product has led GE to introduce several other Space Saver kitchen appliances. Exhibit 1–5 illustrates a new product developed in response to changing consumer values and attitudes toward health and diet.

Exhibit 1–3 Hyundai's Position Enhancement Strategy

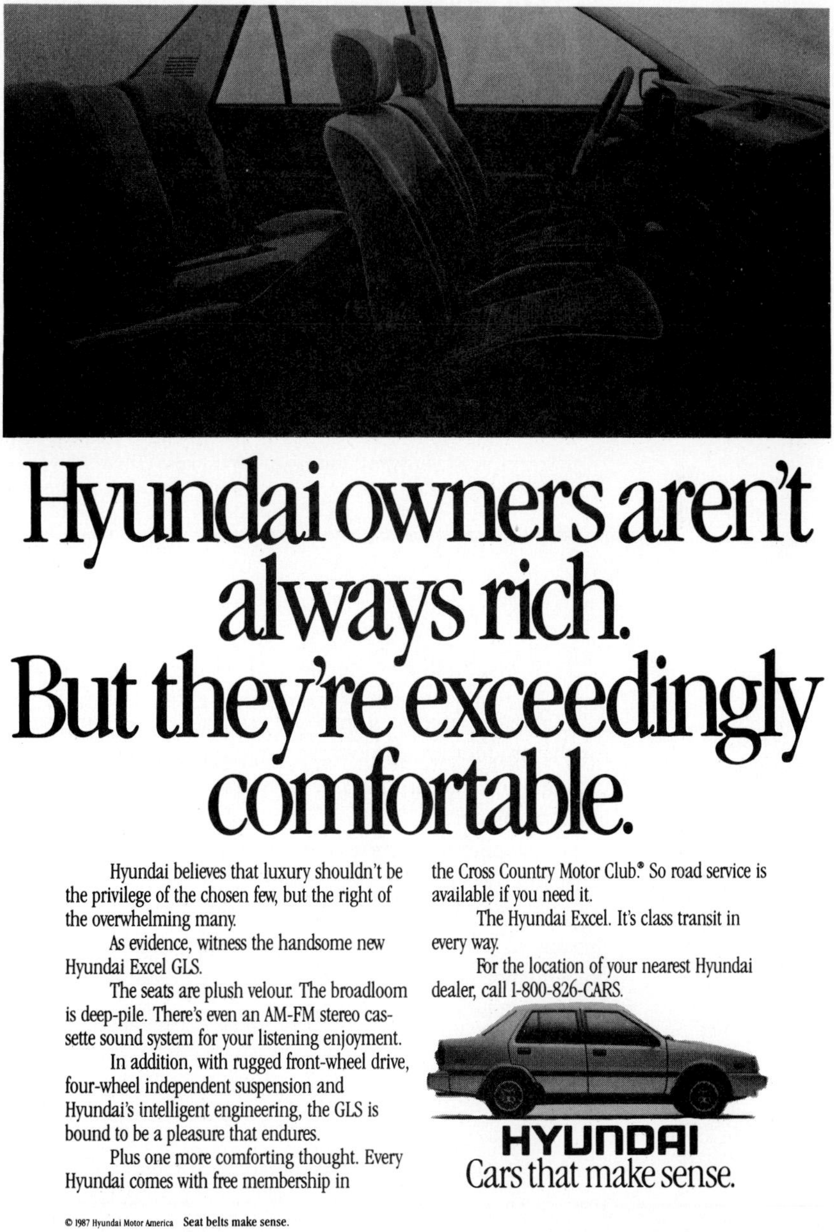

Hyundai owners aren't always rich. But they're exceedingly comfortable.
Hyundai believes that luxury shouldn't be the privilege of the chosen few, but the right of the overwhelming many.
As evidence, witness the handsome new Hyundai Excel GLS.
The seats are plush velour. The broadloom is deep-pile. There's even an AM-FM stereo cassette sound system for your listening enjoyment.
In addition, with rugged front-wheel drive, four-wheel independent suspension and Hyundai's intelligent engineering, the GLS is bound to be a pleasure that endures.
Plus one more comforting thought. Every Hyundai comes with free membership in the Cross Country Motor Club.® So road service is available if you need it.
The Hyundai Excel. It's class transit in every way.
For the location of your nearest Hyundai dealer, call 1-800-826-CARS.
HYUNDAI
Cars that make sense.
© 1987 Hyundai Motor America Seat belts make sense.

Courtesy Hyundai Motor America

Exhibit 1–4 Market Segmentation Strategy

SCANDINAVIAN AIRLINES (SAS) MARKETING STRATEGY

SAS is a cooperative venture of Norway, Sweden, and Denmark; it is a public company, government owned and operated. SAS was losing money on both its domestic and international routes because of price competition, discounts, and startup carriers.

It responded by segmenting the market in a new way; creating a business class of travel with real value-added services. Business travelers have a separate lounge area at every airport, dedicated hotel space with equipment and personnel available so that they can get their work done, the privilege of more flexible reservations and schedules, and traditional first-class amenities. The cost is less than first class, however, and higher than economy class. Business class has become, in short, a boon to business travelers and Scandinavian Airlines.

Source: J. Sheth and G. Morrison, "Winning Again in the Marketplace: Nine Strategies for Revitalizing Mature Products," *The Journal of Consumer Marketing,* no. 4 (1984), p. 19.

New Market Applications

A great many successful products can find continuing success when new markets for the product are discovered. Again, examining consumer behavior can yield insights that can produce new marketing opportunities when the right strategy is put in place.

An excellent example is the refrigerator. Refrigerators are a mature product (virtually 100 percent household penetration in the United States) with a long replacement cycle. However, several Japanese firms recently redesigned the product to a compact size (one tenth the standard size) and repositioned it as a convenience item for the office, upstairs bedroom, or deck rather than a necessity for the kitchen. Sales have boomed.

Global Marketing

Marketing your product abroad offers some exciting opportunities. A standardized marketing strategy is the easiest way to go global because it makes no changes in the elements of the marketing mix nor any changes in the nature of the population segment to whom the product is marketed. While cohesive and less expensive, standardized strategies may fail when a theme does not have universal appeal.

The global strategy has been successful, however, for Marlboro cigarettes.

Exhibit 1–5 Product Developed in Response to Changes in Consumers' Attitudes and Values toward Health and Diet

Courtesy Thomas J. Lipton Inc.

Exhibit 1–6 Global Marketing of Coca-Cola

IT PLAYED IN PHON PHAENG

. . . and Peoria, too. So-called blueprint advertising, which uses the same theme the world over, is a big part of global marketing strategy. These Coke commercials featured former Pittsburgh Steeler "Mean Joe" Green (top) in the United States and other sports figures—like Thai soccer star Niwat—elsewhere.

Courtesy Coca Cola USA, Inc.

Source: A. Fisher, "The Ad BIZ Gloms onto 'Global,' " *Fortune*, November 12, 1984.

Philip Morris gave the product a strong, masculine image with the Marlboro Cowboy. It seems that "Marlboro Country" represents a universal theme, touching a common chord in people around the world. The advertising differs little from country to country although ethnic differences are maintained in costumes and setting. The Japanese Marlboro man is a Japanese cowboy. However, the message is constant: conquest of nature without modern technology.

General Motors is also attempting a global strategy, although not with a focus on image. GM is emulating the Japanese by designing cars for the world market—making products that are always up to world standards and suitable for road conditions everywhere. GM will begin to enjoy economies of scale in all elements of the business: design, manufacturing, and marketing. It will also have the considerable advantage of being able to purchase parts from different suppliers around the world, thereby obtaining the best price available. Global thinking could make GM the world leader. Exhibit 1–6 illustrates an aspect of Coca-Cola's global marketing effort. In this case Coke felt the ad theme used in the United States had global appeal. As we will see in the next chapter, this is not always the best marketing strategy.

Marketing Mix

Products, prices, distribution, and promotion are adjusted to obtain a chosen marketing mix and resulting product position within the selected target market(s). A sound understanding of consumer behavior is necessary in order to structure the marketing mix properly. For example, a firm desiring a high-quality position for a brand *may* need to price the brand higher than the competition *if* the target market believes in a price-quality relationship.

Consider the problem faced by the Sugar Association. The association would like sugar to be positioned in such a way that "consumers appreciate its superior taste and performance as a safe and essential food, as a food that fits into everyone's lifestyle, particularly the active." However, research indicates that many consumers hold a negative image of sugar. For example, in one survey virtually no one estimated the number of calories in a teaspoon of sugar as less than 50 and some placed it as high as 1,000.[3] The actual count is 16.

Obtaining the desired product position for sugar is clearly going to require extensive promotional activities. However, the probability of success depends on the association's understanding of how consumers search for and process information, as well as the learning principles that govern what they will remember. To be successful, the marketing efforts of the Sugar Association must be based on an understanding of consumer behavior.

Exhibit 1–7 illustrates how Pine Sol's package, another element of the marketing mix, was changed in response to consumers' desire for increased ease of application.

Exhibit 1–7 The Marketing Mix Changes as Consumers' Desire for Convenience Increases

Courtesy American Cyanamid Co.

Consumerism and Consumer Behavior

Unfortunately, not all managers, politicians, doctors, educators, and others who attempt to influence consumer behavior are ethical. Further, even highly ethical individuals may occasionally engage in activities that others consider questionable. In response to real and perceived unethical marketing practices, a consumerism movement has emerged. We define consumerism as the set of activities by individuals, independent organizations, government agencies, and businesses designed to protect the consumer from unethical market conduct.

As Exhibit 1–2 indicated, efforts to protect consumers' interests require as thorough an understanding of consumer behavior as does marketing to the consumer. For example, the American Cancer Society wants teenagers to avoid smoking. Various churches would like them to attend their services. Seven-Up wants them to consume its brand. All three organizations face very similar problems and require similar types of knowledge to produce effective solutions.

The marketing decisions of nonprofit organizations such as the American Cancer Society do not differ fundamentally from the decision of a profit-oriented organization (though they generally face more constraints). Examples of applications of consumer behavior knowledge by nonprofit organizations are integrated throughout the text.

Government actions relative to consumerism and marketing generally focus on requirements (food products must list ingredients) or restraints (manufacturers may not engage in deceptive advertising). Sound regulation of marketing activities requires a thorough understanding of consumer behavior. Specific regulatory issues are discussed in relevant portions of the text.

Misleading advertising (and packaging) is discussed in conjunction with perception (Chapter 8). This includes discussion of the factors that determine how a marketing message is interpreted. *Corrective advertising,* a controversial program to undo the effects of prior misleading advertising is evaluated in the context of memory and learning theory (Chapter 9).

The issue of *sufficient information* for sound consumer decisions is covered under the information overload concept (Chapter 8), consumer information search patterns (Chapter 15), and consumer decision making (Chapter 17). The highly sensitive issue of *advertising to children* is covered under consumer socialization (Chapter 7), peer group influences (Chapter 5), and children's perception processes (Chapter 8). The role of advertising in influencing our *values and stereotyping* various groups is analyzed in the section on American values (Chapter 3).

The relationship of marketing practice to the *poverty subculture* is treated in the material on social stratification (Chapter 4). *Minority groups* and marketing are related in the coverage of subcultures (Chapter 3). Finally, the critical issues of *product safety, consumer redress,* and *consumer satisfaction* are examined as part of the postpurchase processes (Chapter 18).

Thus, consumerism issues are covered throughout the text. We believe that placing the issues in context with the relevant behavioral concepts is more effective than treating them as a distinct, separate group.

OVERVIEW OF CONSUMER BEHAVIOR

In this section we are going to do two things. First, we are going to present a model of consumer behavior. This model is *not* a predictive model. That is, it does not provide sufficient detail to allow a prediction of a particular purchase or brand choice even if we had adequate information on all the variables in the model. Instead, this model is a conceptual and organizational model. It reflects our philosophy about the nature of consumer behavior. In addition, it provides a logical means of organizing the vast quantity of information on the variables that influence consumer behavior.

Our second objective will be developed simultaneously with the first. As we present our model, we will also present a fairly detailed overview of the material that is covered in the text. Since this is a detailed overview, it is natural to ask, "Why should I be concerned with all these concepts now if I'm going to cover them in more depth in just a few days or weeks?" The answer to this question is that the factors that influence consumer behavior are all interrelated. Everything

Figure 1–4
Consumer Lifestyle and Consumer Decisions

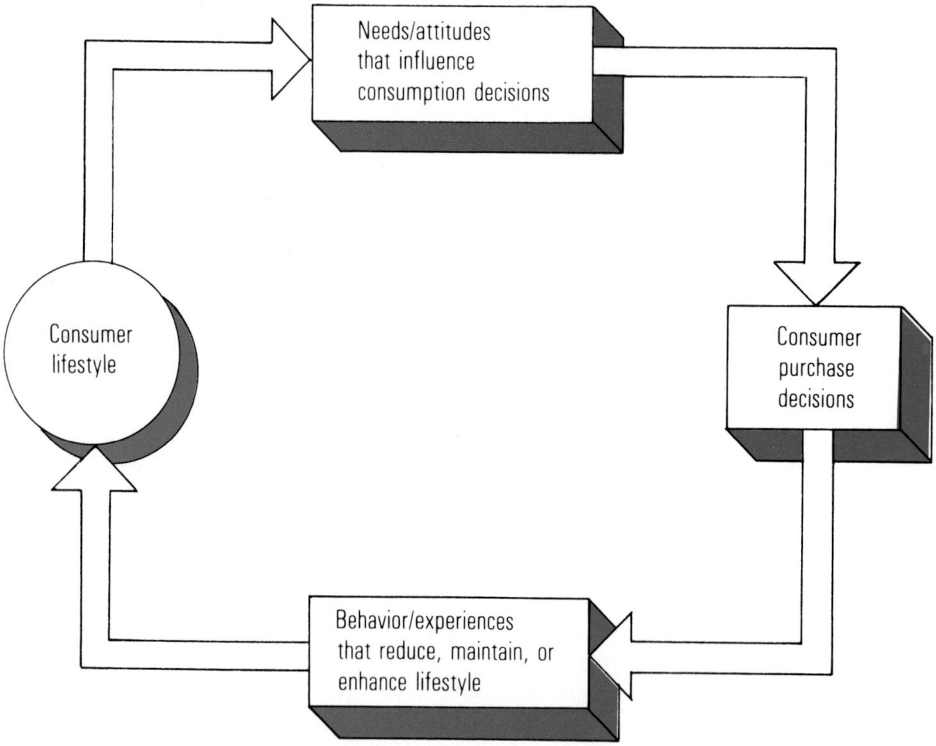

that happens affects everything else. Thus, in the next chapter, we discuss the impact cultural influences have on purchase and consumption behavior. However, it is impossible to discuss cultural influences without mentioning attitudes or the consumer decision process. This same type of problem arises in each chapter. Therefore, it is important that you develop an initial understanding of the major concepts so that their interrelationships will make sense to you.

Nature of Consumption

The marketing manager can most appropriately view the consumer as a *problem solver:*

> a decision-making unit (individual, family, household, or firm) that takes in information, processes that information (consciously and unconsciously) in light of the existing situation, and takes actions to achieve satisfaction and enhance lifestyle.

Problems arise for consumers in their attempts to develop, maintain, and/or change their lifestyle as shown in Figure 1–4. Past decisions, time-related events such as aging, and external events such as an illness or job change lead to lifestyle changes that pose additional consumption problems and result in new purchases, new attitudes, and related changes that in turn bring about further lifestyle changes. It must be stressed that most consumer problems and the resulting decisions involve very little importance or effort on the part of the consumer. Satisfying based on limited information processing is the norm.[4]

Consumer Lifestyle

What do we mean by the term *consumer lifestyle,* and why is it so vital to an understanding of how and why consumers act as they do? Quite simply, your lifestyle is *how* you live. It is the products you buy, how you use them, and what you think about them. It is the manifestations of your self-concept—the total image you have of yourself as a result of the culture you live in and the individual situations and experiences that comprise your daily existence. It is the sum of your past decisions and future plans.

Both individuals and families exhibit distinct lifestyles. We often hear of "career-oriented individuals," "outdoor families," "devoted mothers," or "swinging singles." One's lifestyle is determined by both conscious and unconscious decisions. Often we make choices with full awareness of their impact on our lifestyle, but perhaps more frequently we are unaware of the extent to which our decisions are influenced by our current or desired lifestyle.

Maintaining or changing an individual or household lifestyle often requires the consumption of products. It is our contention that thinking about products

Figure 1–5
Changing Values Have Altered Household Consumption Behavior

Traditional Mom

Today's Mom

	Traditional Mom	**Today's Mom**
Demographics:	About 42 Married with three children of high school or college age Full time homemaker—some volunteer work	About 36 Married with two children in school Works full time
Psychographics:	Enjoys her home and children Well organized—goes to all the school sports events Feels a bit behind the times	Is on top of her job and her home—her friends admire that Feels in tune with life today but there's more pressure
Market Behavior:	Brews ground coffee in morning, ground decaffeinated in the evening Lets her husband handle the finances—on vacation he gives her small-denomination traveler's checks to spend for gifts and souvenirs	Because of pressure and wanting to be healthy, has switched to decaffeinated coffee at home and at work—it's Brim, Taster's Choice, or Highpoint Takes joint responsibility for family finances, but has her own bank account and bank card

Note: From Dunham and Marcus "Life-Stages" Laboratory.

Source: A. Dunham, "New Product Marketing Is an Era of Transition," *The Journal of Consumer Marketing*, no. 4 (1984), pp. 5–16.

in terms of their relationship to consumer lifestyle is a very useful approach for managers. Therefore, managers need to understand consumer lifestyles and the factors that influence them. Consider the differences in lifestyles expressed in Figure 1–5. These two common, but distinct, lifestyles involve many different products, as well as shopping and media habits.

While the maintenance or enhancement of lifestyle is most obviously a goal when consumers purchase *high-involvement* products such as cars and fashion clothing, it also directly and indirectly affects the consumption of many *low-involvement* products such as peas or orange juice. For example, one style of

Table 1–1
Relative Consumption of High- and Low-Involvement Products

		High-Involvement Product		Low-Involvement Product	
Lifestyle	**Brief Profile of Lifestyle**	Men's Tennis	Women's Tennis	Regular Soft Drinks	Sugar-Free Soft Drinks
Sustainers	Relatively young people struggling at the edge of poverty	100	88	112	50
Belongers	Traditional, conservative, conventional, sentimental, unexperimental	38	47	82	80
Emulators	High energy, socially mobile, trying to make it big	69	171	171	90
Achievers	Successful leaders that achieve status and materialism of the good life	100	88	94	110
I-am-me	Young, zippy, impulsive, fiercely individualistic, and inventive	223	347	176	120
Experiential	Introspective and seeking inner growth, naturalism, and process over product	200	259	94	150
Societally conscious	High sense of social responsibility, supportive of environmentalism and consumerism	115	88	59	170

Note: Base index for average consumption = 100.

Source: Adapted from T. C. Thomas and S. Crocker, *Values and Lifestyles—The New Psychographics* (Menlo Park, Calif.: Stanford Research Institute, 1981), pp. 24–29.

living may lead to price-oriented decisions for low-involvement products while another style may call for brand loyalty to prestige brands. Table 1–1 illustrates the substantial consumption differences between lifestyle groups in the consumption of an apparently high-involvement product area, tennis, and an apparently low-involvement product, soft drinks.

In the following chapters, we discuss the many factors influencing our lifestyles. We focus particular attention on how marketing managers can apply what is known about each factor. Then, in Chapter 11, we return for a more complete discussion of lifestyle.

As illustrated in Figure 1–6, 12 basic factors influence consumer lifestyle: marketing activities, culture, values, demographics, social status, reference groups, households, personality, emotions, motives, perception, and learning. Information processing links the influences to the consumer and enables them to determine their desired lifestyle. These factors comprise a majority of the text and, of course, will be dealt with in detail. A brief overview of each at this point, however, will be helpful in forming your basic orientation toward consumer behavior as a marketing manager as well as providing an overview of a major portion of this text.

Figure 1–6
Factors that Determine and Influence Consumer Lifestyle

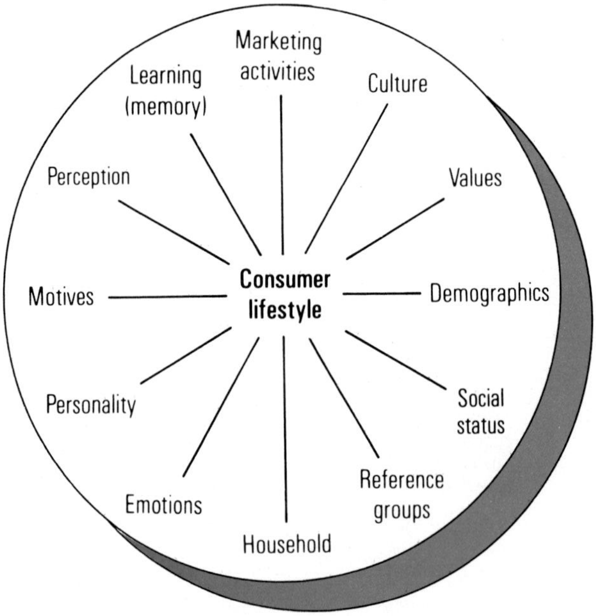

External Influences

Culture. *Culture* is viewed in the traditional sense as representing *that complex whole which includes knowledge, belief, art, morals, law, custom, and any other capabilities and habits acquired by man as a member of society*. In other words, consumer behavior is the product of a particular culture. Our culture provides us with what we know to be true. Our knowledge of how things are as consumers comes to us from our culture through our families, friends, and institutions. For instance, our particular culture has taught most of us that we should consume three meals per day with cereals, toast, eggs, bacon, or sausage being most appropriate for the morning meal. Other cultures prescribe differing numbers of meals as well as differing foods for each meal.

Probably one of the most important learned aspects of culture is a culture's *basic values*. These basic values provide us with guidelines as to what is right and wrong or good and bad in any given situation. Values vary across cultures and set broad boundaries within which lifestyles evolve. We will examine a number of important values that vary across cultures.

We will also examine cultural variations in *nonverbal communications,* a subject of particular interest to those marketing managers dealing with major subcultures in the United States and other cultures in the world markets. Cross-cultural analysis will be dealt with in order to give the reader a methodology for investigating different cultures as well as a better understanding of how our own culture functions.

Values. Our analysis of basic cultural values in Chapter 2 is continued with a discussion of our own specific American cultural values in Chapter 3. The nature of these values, the shifts occurring in them, and the implications of these shifts for marketing strategy are discussed.

Chapter 3 also contains a detailed analysis of our changing values with respect to male and female *sex roles*. Culturally defined sex roles continue to go through major changes that affect marketing management decisions. The working wife and mother is no longer an oddity. Many purchasing chores that traditionally have been carried out by women are now done by the male, either exclusively or on a shared basis. Traditional roles between husbands and wives have been substantially altered, not to mention types and kinds of products purchased and used by either sex.

Demographics. In Chapter 3, the new *demographics* of America, particularly income, geographic, and age shifts, are examined. In addition, the major American subcultures are analyzed. Subcultures are smaller, homogeneous segments of the dominant culture and are of interest to marketers when they require differential marketing activities because of unique lifestyles.

Differential marketing activities for specific market segments are expensive, and therefore managers have to be sure that they identify as different only those subcultural groups that are distinct in a meaningful way with respect to consumption. For instance, blacks were initially viewed as being a separate subcultural unit of interest to marketers simply because of differences in race. Over time it has been ascertained that while there are many differences between blacks and whites, consumption patterns are often similar and apparent differences are frequently associated more with income than with race.

Social Status. The influence of social status on consumer lifestyle has been a much debated issue. Chapter 4 examines this issue. The major questions are: (1) To what extent does our society structure and rank individuals? (2) On what characteristics is this structure built? and (3) In what ways does this structure influence consumer lifestyle and purchase decisions?

Generally, we are ranked on a number of observable characteristics representing underlying values that our culture holds to be worthwhile. For instance, one of the first questions we ask upon meeting a stranger is what he or she does for a living. Their answers allow us to define them relative to ourselves and others so that we can make an assessment of their position and how to act toward them. Sociologists have been able to group occupations and, together with other important variables, use them to identify categories that are composed of individuals holding similar jobs, values, attitudes, or, when viewed as a whole, somewhat similar lifestyles.

Marketers then can use social status as a consumer market identification tool. In fact, social status is a commonly used variable for market segment identification. There is a large body of research that reports how social classes vary in store selection, media preference, desire for assistance from retail sales personnel, and other aspects of consumer behavior.

Reference Groups. Our cultural background and social class standing—along with the value and knowledge system that comes with them—are transmitted to us, for the most part, through reference groups, often without our awareness. Certainly we also learn our culture and social class through educational and religious institutions and mass media, but the intimate groups we deal with on a daily basis have the most influence.

Reference groups and group theory are considered in Chapters 5 and 6. Most consumers belong to a large number of groups, which are defined as two or more people who have a purpose for interacting over some extended period of time. Groups serve as both a reference point for the individual and as a source of specific information. Marketing managers are particularly interested in the flow of information to and through groups. For example, 65 percent of Baileys' customers first heard about Baileys from friends or relatives.

In these chapters we examine the concept of opinion leaders within groups, and study group conformity and how group norms often prescribe certain aspects of lifestyle such as clothing fashions or the purchase of specific brands. In addition, we will analyze how new products, *innovations,* spread or diffuse through groups. Finally, *roles*—patterns of behavior expected of a position in a group rather than an individual—are discussed in light of their influence on purchasing patterns.

Household. The *household* is a very special and influential form of reference group and is the subject of Chapter 7. Three specific aspects of the household interest us as marketing managers—the composition of the household unit, household decision-making roles, and the household life cycle. Most consumers in the United States are members of households, and many of the purchases they make are made as household decisions, even though only one person in the household may do the actual purchasing. In fact, the household is the primary purchasing unit for most consumer goods. Obviously it is important for the marketing manager to be fully aware of *who* is influencing the decision within a household so that an effective information campaign can be constructed and appropriately positioned and directed. Exhibit 1–8 describes how Brown Shoe Company utilizes this type of information. Notice that two different family members are involved in the purchase decision and that two different media and creative approaches are therefore required.

Another important variable for marketers is the *household life cycle*. Most consumers in our culture grow up, physically leave their original household, and then begin a new household. In other words, the institution we call a household has a fairly regular and predictable life cycle of its own. Marketers can look at each stage of this cycle and get accurate aggregate pictures of purchase needs and desires of individuals in that stage. The chapter on households concludes Section Two of the text which focuses on external influences on lifestyle.

Internal Influences

Information Processing: Perception.

Chapter 8 describes the means by which consumers incorporate information from group influences, situations, and marketing efforts into their lifestyle and purchase decisions. Information processing

Exhibit 1–8

Household Decision Making and Buster Brown's Marketing Communication Strategy

Buster Brown advertises to parents via such magazines as *Families* and *Parents*. The message focuses on the firm's traditional name and reputation for quality.

However, research reveals that children as young as three have some influence on the brand of shoe purchased. Therefore, Buster Brown uses television advertising to reach children. A vastly different theme is used in messages aimed at children. Marilyn Popovich, divisional advertising manager for children's shoes, describes this strategy as follows: "In advertising to kids, we don't talk about quality features of the product because kids could care less. We sell the personality and fun aspect of the shoes. And we offer premiums."

Source: L. Kesler, "Buster, Baskin Robbins: If the Shoe Fits, Eat It?" *Advertising Age*, November 30, 1981, p. 28.

links various external influences and marketing practices to the consumer's decision process. It is the mechanism that makes our model function. We cover information processing at this point in the text because individual development and individual characteristics are determined in part by the information we receive and process from our culture, social class, reference groups, and households.

Information processing is particularly important in the consumer decision-making process. Information is the raw material for a decision. The consumer gathers information, processes it, discards some, stores some, combines new information with old, all to come up with solutions to problems in the form of decisions. Marketing managers are therefore vitally interested in where consumers get information, what catches their attention, why it is interpreted as it is, and how it is remembered.

Information Processing: Learning and Memory. Quite often, information processing takes place at a very low level of consumer involvement. That is, consumers process substantial amounts of information without much conscious effort, although the information thus processed may have substantial effects on subsequent behavior.

In terms of lifestyle and purchase decisions, we learn needs, tastes and preferences, and price-quality relationships. As our purchase experience increases, we learn the most effective sources of information, the best places to shop, the brand names on which to rely, and those to avoid. Thus, it is important for the marketer to understand how people learn and what must be done to affect their learning. For instance, if we can learn to like something through exposure (increased familiarity), it follows that the marketer can exert some direct influences on taste preferences through the amount and timing of promotional efforts as well as the design and characteristics of products and services offered. This critical concept, *learning,* is described in detail in Chapter 9.

Motives, Personality, and Emotion. Chapter 10 analyzes those *individual characteristics* that energize, direct, and shape a particular pattern of purchase and consumption behavior. We will first look at *motives*—the forces that initiate and direct consumer behavior. Motives may be physiologically or psychologically based. However, most consumer behavior in developed economies is guided by psychological motives. While *motives* direct behaviors toward objectives, *personality* relates to characteristic patterns of behavior. Personality is generally considered to reflect a consistent pattern of responses to a variety of situations, although the role played by the situation itself is also recognized. *Emotions* are our feelings or affective responses to situations, products, advertisements, and so forth. They affect our information processing and preferences and are of increasing interest to marketers.

Lifestyles. Chapter 11 provides a discussion of consumer *lifestyles* and how they evolve and influence consumer behavior. Personality, emotions, motives, culture, social status, reference groups, household, and individual development influence consumers in adopting a particular lifestyle that represents what they think they are and want to be. This is an ongoing process and there are continual, but generally moderate, changes in that lifestyle.

In Chapter 11 we will also discuss *self-concept* as an internal representation of lifestyle. Self-concept is basically the attitudes one holds toward oneself. Lifestyle is the outward manifestation of the self-concept. After describing the self-concept and its relationship to lifestyle, *psychographics,* the most popular method of measuring lifestyle, will be described.

Attitudes. The topic of Chapter 12, *attitudes,* represents our basic orientation for or against some object such as a product or retail outlet. Attitudes are formed out of the interrelationship between personal experience and lifestyle and the factors discussed in the preceding 11 chapters that help shape lifestyles. Attitudes are composed of cognitive (beliefs), affective (feelings), and behavioral (response tendencies) components which tend to be consistent with one another. That is, if one believes that a brand has certain desirable attributes (cognitive component), one will probably like the brand (affective component), and, should the need arise, purchase that brand (behavioral component). Marketing strategies are, therefore, frequently based on influencing one component of the attitude with the expectation that success in this endeavor will influence the remaining two components.

The basic goal of marketing strategy with respect to attitudes can take one or a combination of three forms:

- *To maintain present attitudes* by providing information to target market consumers that will help them maintain their current favorable attitude.
- *To change attitudes* from negative to positive, to further increase the strength of those that are already positive, or to change a positive competing attitude (another brand for instance) into a less favorable or negative one.
- *To create new attitudes* by introducing a new product or trying to attract consumers who are unfamiliar with an existing product.

Chapter 12 provides a detailed discussion of the various techniques available to marketing managers for achieving these goals.

Consumer Decision Process

Situations. Figure 1–7 illustrates the basic elements in the consumer decision process. As it indicates, consumers have *specific problems* that require *specific solutions,* hence the *existing situation* must always be the framework within which the decision-making process is viewed. Chapter 13 is devoted to a discussion of the role and impact of situations on the decision-making process.

Figure 1–7
Consumer Decision-Making Process

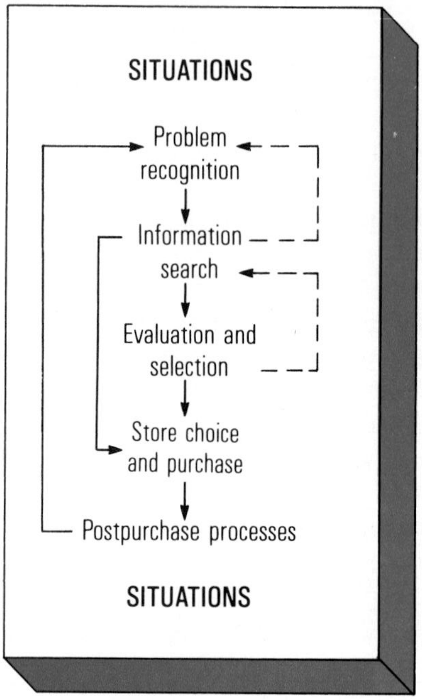

Problem Recognition. The consumer decision process begins with the recognition that a problem exists. A consumer problem is simply a difference between an existing state and a desired state. A problem which the consumer resolves by recalling one satisfactory solution and purchasing that solution without an evaluation is termed *habitual decision making*. Many consumer purchases, particularly of frequently purchased items such as detergents, soft drinks, and gasoline, are of this nature.

Other problems may be resolved by recalling several potential solutions and choosing from among them, perhaps using some additional information such as current prices. A great many consumer purchases are the result of such *limited decision making*. Problems that require thorough information searches, both internal and external, the evaluation of several alternatives along several dimensions, and considerable postpurchase evaluation produce *extended decision making*. Chapter 14 describes the factors that lead to each type of decision making. In general, the higher the degree of purchase involvement the more extensive the decision process. This is reflected in Figure 1–8 and Table 1–2.

We are interested in determining the events and situations which cause problems for consumers. In a very real sense, this is the study of the motivation

Figure 1–8
Level of Purchase Involvement and Degree of Decision Making

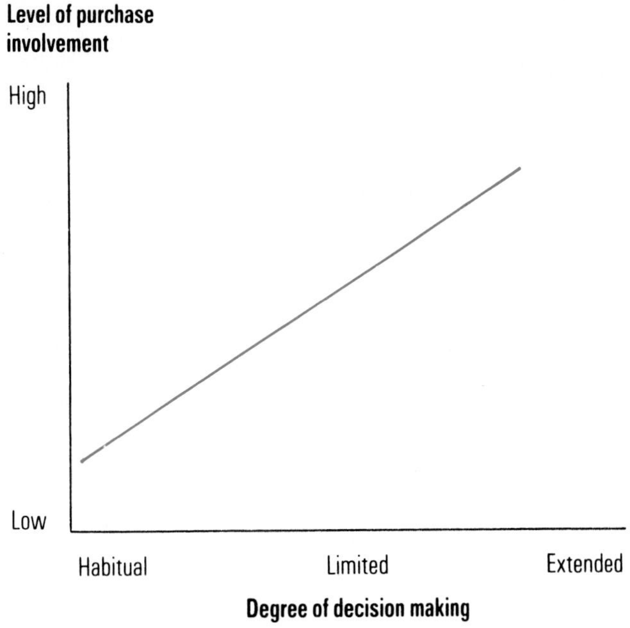

necessary for the decision-making process to begin. Managers can and do influence problem recognition, and this important aspect of marketing strategy is described in Chapter 14. Figure 1–9 illustrates this relationship and represents our completed organizational model of consumer behavior.

Information Search. Once the problem is recognized, an information search is undertaken to isolate an effective solution. As described above, the information search may be extensive, very brief, or somewhere in between. Chapter 15 provides a detailed discussion of the nature of the information search, the factors that influence the degree of information search, and marketing communication strategies based on consumers' information search patterns.

Alternative Evaluation. After information has been gathered allowing one to determine and compare the relevant and feasible alternatives, the decision can be made. Chapter 16 deals with how consumers select and evaluate relevant choice alternatives. The *evaluative criteria* (product attributes) used will be examined and we will consider such questions as: Do consumers consider all product attributes equally important or are some more critical than others? How is this information evaluated and how is a brand choice made?

Table 1–2
Consumer Decision Process for High- and Low-Involvement Purchase Decisions

	Low-Involvement Purchase Decisions	High-Involvement Purchase Decisions
Problem recognition	Trivial to minor	Important and personally meaningful
Information search	Internal to limited external search	Extensive search
Alternative evaluation	Few alternatives evaluated on few performance criteria	Many alternatives considered using many performance criteria
Store choice, purchase	One stop shopping where substitution is very possible	Multiple store visits with substitution less likely
Postpurchase activities	Simple evaluation of performance	Extensive performance evaluation, use, and disposal

Store Choice and Purchasing. Chapter 17 focuses on the selection of the retail outlet and the actual purchase of the product. The attributes that influence store choice are examined and related to the needs of particular consumer groups. The actual acquisition of the product is analyzed with particular attention given to retailers' efforts to attract and satisfy consumers in the exchange process of the consumer purchase decision.

Postpurchase Process. In Chapter 18 we examine four areas of particular concern to marketing managers that occur *after* purchase: use, evaluation, disposition, and repurchase behavior. The uses of existing products are examined by marketing managers for clues on possible product improvements or themes for promotional campaigns. Satisfaction is influenced by product performance, the purchasing process, and consumer expectations. We examine strategies that marketers can use to increase satisfaction. The disposition of products is an area of increasing concern for both public policymakers and marketing managers. In this chapter we review what is known of this process. Finally, we examine the repurchase motivation (or lack of it) for brands or products.

Industrial Buying Behavior. The primary thrust of this text is toward individual and household consumption patterns. Industrial buying behavior, purchases made on behalf of a formal organization, have many similarities with,

Figure 1–9
Overall Model of Consumer Behavior

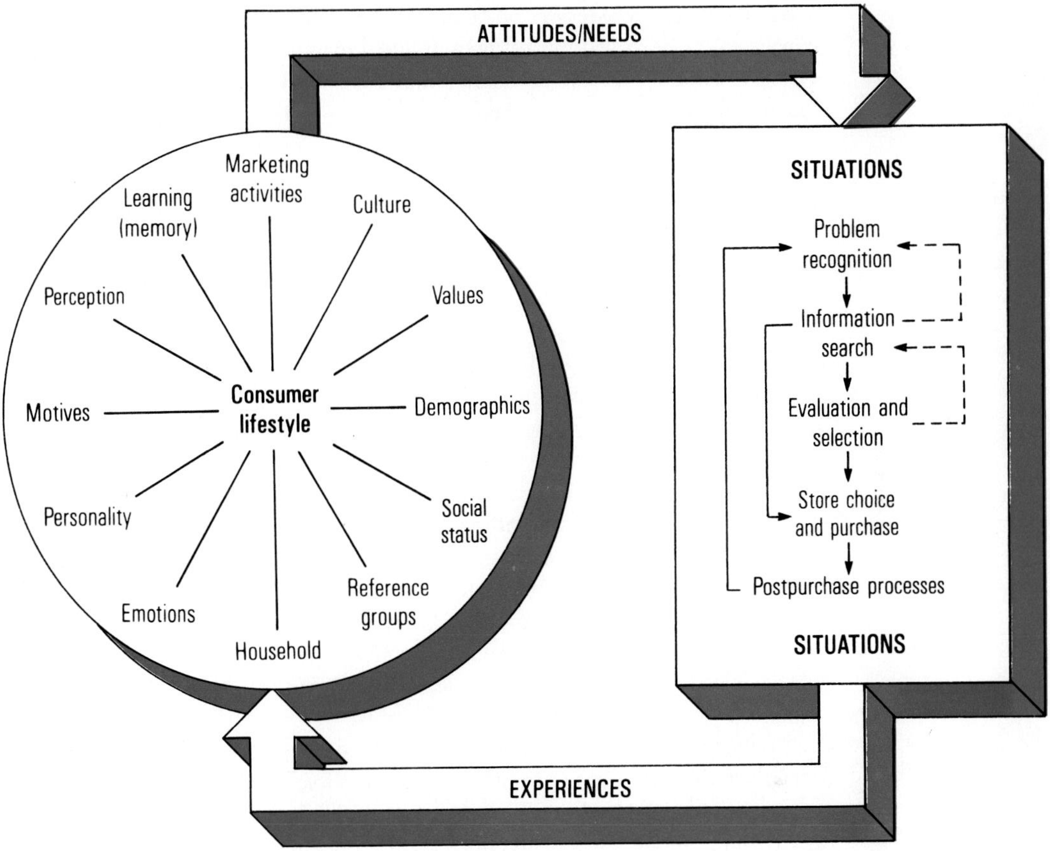

as well as differences from, consumer behavior. The final chapter of the text highlights these similarities and differences and discusses their implications for marketing strategy.

SUMMARY

Successful marketing decisions by commercial firms, nonprofit organizations, and regulatory agencies require a sound understanding of consumer behavior. Numerous examples of actual business practices make it clear that successful firms can and do apply theories and information about consumer behavior on a daily basis.

A good basic knowledge of consumer behavior at its current state of development should provide you with, at the very least, the proper questions to ask concerning a proposed marketing activity. Frequently, however, it will be necessary to conduct research to answer these questions. It is our belief that, while much remains to be discovered, sufficient knowledge of consumer behavior currently exists to provide a usable guide to marketing practice.

A knowledge of consumer behavior provides the basis for many marketing strategies such as product positioning, market segmentation, new product development, new market applications, global marketing, marketing mix decisions, and marketing actions and regulations by nonprofit organizations and government agencies. Each of these major marketing activities is more effective when based on a knowledge of consumer behavior.

The purpose of the consumer behavior model presented in this chapter is to organize the major conceptual areas of consumer behavior and illustrate their relationships with one another. This model outlines the major sources of influence that marketing managers should understand in developing marketing strategy to solve marketing problems and capitalize on marketing opportunities.

Within each major area outlined in our model of consumer behavior lies a large subset of related concepts. Because the number of these related concepts is quite large and their relative importance varies among consumers, products, and situations, a single comprehensive model of consumer behavior is not possible. Instead, for a given marketing situation a marketer must examine specific aspects of consumer behavior to develop a marketing strategy for that marketing situation.

At the hub of the consumer behavior model presented in this chapter is consumer lifestyle. In the broadest sense possible, our culture—by way of its values, norms, and traditions—is the major influence on our style of life. Within any culture, social class distinctions create differing consumer lifestyles. However, specific groups within social classes also vary due to influences created by various reference groups and household influences. Each of these influences, culture, social class, reference groups, and household, are external influences that contribute to a particular consumer lifestyle.

Those factors that influence consumer lifestyle but that are unique to the individual consumer include individual development and individual characteristics. Individual development takes place through perception, learning, and memory which contribute to the resulting lifestyle and patterns of behavior. Individual characteristics represent those motivations, personality features, and emotions that make each individual unique. The combination of these external and internal influences is manifested in consumer lifestyles and the products and services individuals consume to maintain and/or change that lifestyle.

Because of lifestyle, and indirectly all those factors that influence lifestyle, consumers establish certain attitudes toward consumption of products in various situations. The combination of a particular lifestyle, attitudes, and situational influences activates the consumer's decision process. The consumer's decision process involves some or all of the following steps, depending on the level of purchase involvement: problem recognition, information search, alternative evaluation, store choice, actual purchase and postpurchase processes.

Our model of consumer behavior may appear static since it is difficult to graphically portray the dynamic nature of consumer behavior. However, consumers are continually evolving and changing as they process new information related to their lifestyle and the outcome of past purchase decisions. Thus, underlying the entire consumer behavior process shown in our model is the assumption that information processing is a never-ceasing activity.

REVIEW QUESTIONS

1. What conclusions can be drawn from the examples presented at the beginning of this chapter?
2. How can consumer behavior influences be used in *product positioning* and *market segmentation?*
3. How can the study of consumer behavior be used to develop *new products* and discover *new market applications?*
4. What potential benefits does the study of consumer behavior provide in designing *global marketing strategies?*
5. How should marketing managers view the consumer, and how will this view of the consumer help them understand consumer purchasing behavior?
6. What is meant by a *consumer's lifestyle?*
7. What concepts make up and/or influence a consumer's lifestyle?
8. What do we mean by *culture,* and how does it relate to the study of consumer behavior?
9. What is *social stratification,* and why are marketing managers interested in this concept?
10. What are *reference groups,* and what relationship do they have to consumer behavior?
11. Why is the *household* an important reference group of interest to marketing managers?
12. What is the role of *information processing* in consumer behavior?
13. What is meant by the phrase "consumer behavior is learned behavior"?
14. What are *attitudes,* and why are they of interest to marketing managers?
15. Of what relevance is the study of the *consumer decision-making process?*
16. Why is *problem recognition* so important to consumer decision making?
17. What do we mean by *information search,* and what is its role in the decision-making process?
18. What are *evaluative criteria?*

19. What influences *consumer satisfaction?*
20. What impact does the *involvement level* have on the decision process?

DISCUSSION QUESTIONS

1. a. Why would someone buy a compact disc player? Imported wine? Tropical fish? Socks? Levi jeans? Aspirin?
   b. Why would someone else not make those purchases?
   c. How would you choose one brand over another? Would others make the choice in the same way?
2. How would a text focusing on a "broad" understanding of consumer behavior differ from the applications-oriented approach of this text?
3. Is it possible for the FTC to evaluate the "total" or nonverbal meaning of an advertisement? If so, how should they proceed?
4. Of what use, if any, are models such as the one proposed in this chapter to practicing marketing managers?
5. Of what use would the model presented in this chapter be to a manager for the products listed in Question 1?
6. What changes would you recommend in the model? Why?
7. Describe your lifestyle. Does it differ significantly from your parents' lifestyle? What causes the difference?
8. Do you anticipate any major changes in your lifestyle in the next five years? If so, what will be the cause of these changes?
9. Describe a recent, important purchase that you made. To what extent can your purchase be described by the consumer decision-making process described in this chapter? How would you explain the deviations?
10. Describe several low-involvement purchases you have made recently. How did your decision process differ from a recent high-involvement purchase?
11. F.T.D.'s flowers-by-wire sales recently totaled more than $350 million, up 11.2 percent from the previous year. However, unit sales only went up 1.8 percent, to 18,200,000.

    F.T.D. hasn't been attracting enough new customers. Aside from the economic situation, the reasons are simple. The price of the traditional flower arrangement, including delivery, has risen because of increased energy and labor costs. Even though the higher prices have been lower than the rise in the consumer price index, consumers are developing a resistance to giving flowers as a gift.

    U.S. consumers do not, as Europeans do, buy flowers just as an enhancement to daily life. Occasions, therefore, have a tremendous impact on the growth and sales of flowers. As a result, there are peaks and valleys saleswise.

    How could you use the material presented in this chapter to assist F.T.D.?

PROJECT QUESTIONS

1. Posing as a customer, visit one or more stores that sell ______. Report on the sales techniques used (point-of-purchase displays, store design, salesperson comments, and so forth). What beliefs concerning consumer behavior appear to underlie these strategies? It is often worthwhile for a male and a female student to visit the same store and talk to the same salesperson at different times. The variation in sales appeal is sometimes quite revealing.
   a. Waterbeds.
   b. Flowers.
   c. Pets.
   d. Skis.
   e. Compact disc players.
   f. Pipes.
2. Look through recent copies of a magazine such as *Advertising Age* or *Business Week* and report on three applications of consumer behavior knowledge (or questions) to marketing decisions.
3. Interview individuals who sell ____________. Try to discover their personal "models" of consumer behavior for their products.
   a. Waterbeds.
   b. Flowers.
   c. Pets.
   d. Skis.
   e. Compact disc players.
   f. Pipes.
   g. Imported wine.
   h. Art.
4. Interview three individuals who recently made a major purchase and three others who made a minor purchase. In what ways were their decision processes similar? In what ways were they different?

REFERENCES

[1] "Marketing-Oriented Lever Uses Research to Capture Bigger Dentifrice Market Shares," *Marketing News,* February 10, 1978, p. 9.

[2] For a detailed description of the entire process, see "Key Role of Research in Agree's Success Is Told," *Marketing News,* January 12, 1979, pp. 14–15.

[3] K. Higgins, "Trade Group Launches Two-Front Offensive in Fight against Aspartame," *Marketing News,* October 26, 1984, p. 9.

[4] For shortcomings of the information processing/decision-making framework, see R. W. Belk, "Happy Thought: Presidential Address," in *Advances in Consumer Research,* 14, eds. M. Wallendorf and P. Anderson (Provo: Association for Consumer Research, 1987), pp. 1–4.

SECTION TWO

External Influences

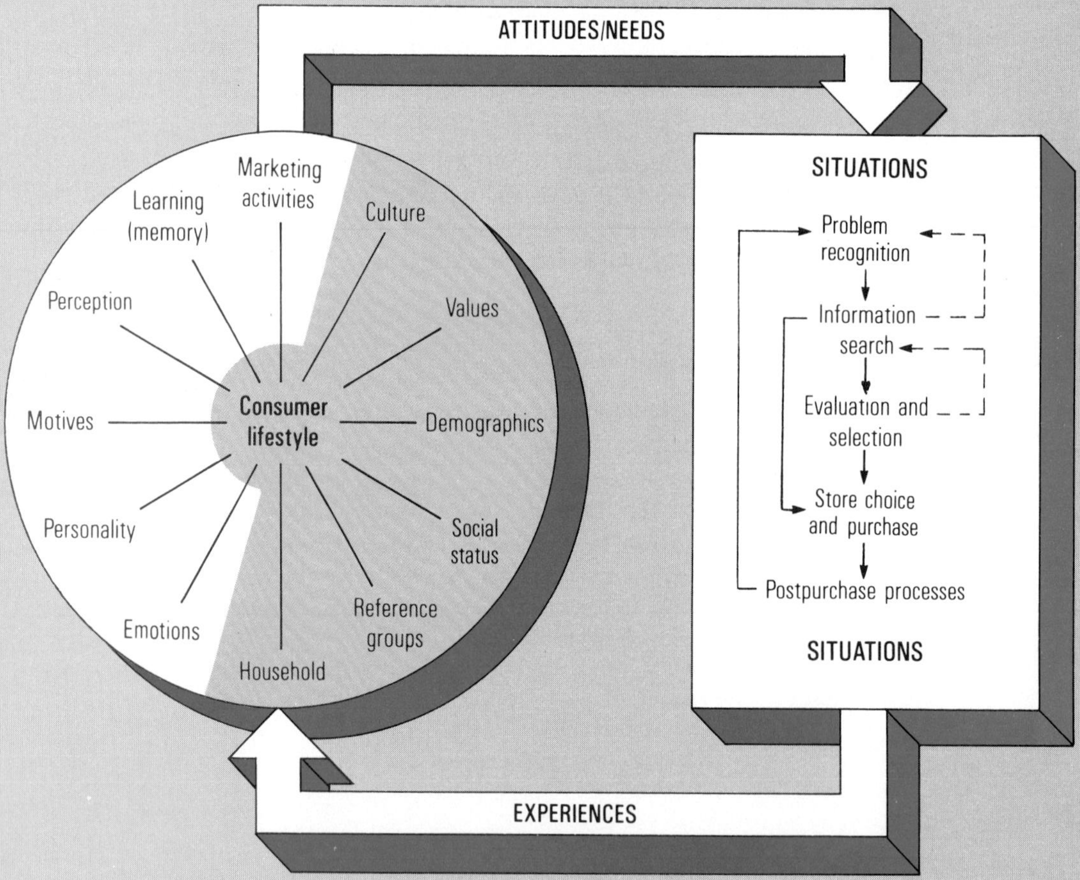

The shaded area of our model shown at left is the focal point for this section of the text. As indicated in Chapter 1, any division of the factors that influence behavior into separate and distinct categories is somewhat arbitrary. For example, we have chosen to consider learning in the next section of the text, which focuses on internal influences. However, a substantial amount of human learning involves interaction with, or imitation of, other individuals. Thus, learning also could be considered a group process. Section Two examines groups as they operate to influence consumer behavior. Our emphasis is on the functioning of the group itself and *not* the process by which the individual reacts to the group.

This section starts with large-scale, macrogroup influences and progresses to smaller, more microgroup influences. As we progress, the nature of the influence exerted by the group changes from general guidelines to explicit expectations for certain behaviors. This pattern of influence is illustrated in Figure II-1.

Figure II-1
Nature of Group Influences

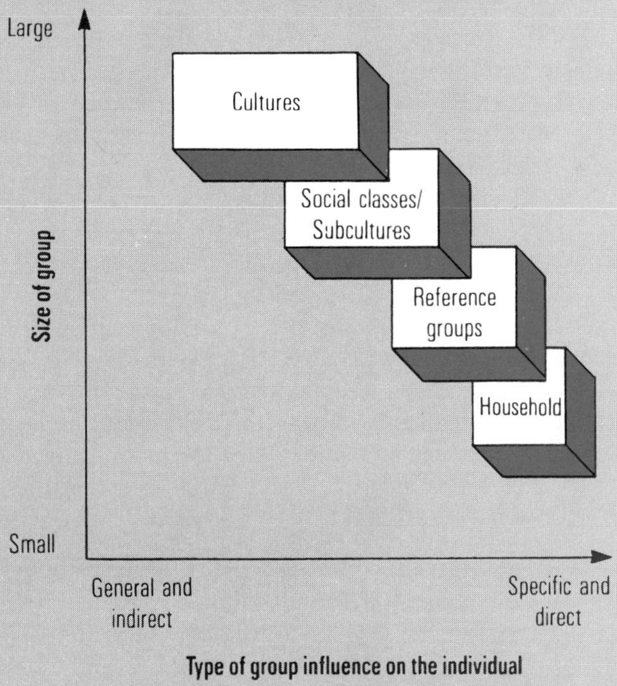

CHAPTER

2 Cross-Cultural Variations in Consumer Behavior

According to U.S. standards, Brazil should represent a major market opportunity for cereals and other breakfast foods. Brazil had a population of 119 million in 1980, with growth projected to reach 165 million by 1990. Further, the age distribution favored cereal consumption with 48 percent of the population under 20 years of age. In addition, per capita income was increasing, which would allow the purchase of ready-to-eat cereals. In examining this market, Kellogg Company noticed one additional positive feature—there was no direct competition!

Unfortunately, the absence of competition was due to the fact that Brazilians do not eat an American-style breakfast. Thus, the marketing task facing Kellogg and its ad agency, J. Walter Thompson, was to change the nature of breakfast in Brazil.

Novelas, soap operas, are very popular and influential in Brazil. Therefore, Kellogg began advertising on the novelas. The first campaign showed a boy eating the cereal out of the package. While demonstrating the good taste of the product, it also positioned it as a snack rather than as part of a breakfast meal. The campaign was soon withdrawn.

An analysis of the Brazilian culture revealed a very high value placed on the family, with the male the dominant authority. Therefore, the next campaign focused on family breakfast scenes with the father pouring the cereal into bowls and adding milk.

The second campaign was more successful than the first. Cereal sales increased, and Kellogg has a 99.5 percent market share. However, annual ready-to-eat cereal consumption remains below one ounce per capita.[1]

Variation in consumer behavior across cultures has major implications for marketing opportunities and practices. The following diagram illustrates the major variables that influence marketing strategy across countries.

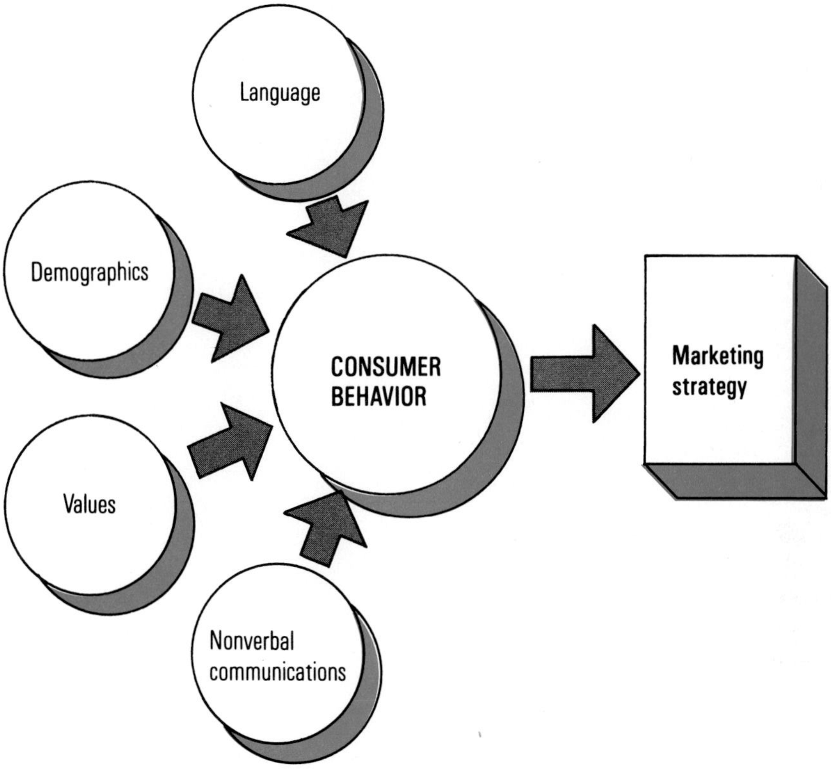

Marketing across cultural boundaries is a difficult and challenging task. As shown above, cultures differ dramatically in terms of demographics, languages, nonverbal communications, and values. Exhibit 2–1 illustrates a *demographically* based segmentation of international markets. This chapter focuses on cultural variations in *values* and *nonverbal communications*. First, we examine the general nature of culture and how culture functions to influence behavior.

Next, we analyze the variations in values that exist between cultures and the impact these variations have on marketing practice. We also evaluate the marketing implications of variations in nonverbal communications systems. Finally, a step-by-step procedure for marketing in a foreign culture is presented. Exhibit 2–2 shows how paying close attention to cross-cultural variations can lead to success in such a difficult marketing task as selling beer in a Muslim country.

THE CONCEPT OF CULTURE

Culture is that complex whole which includes knowledge, belief, art, law, morals, customs, and any other capabilities and habits acquired by man as a member

Exhibit 2–1 Segmentation of International Markets

DEPENDENTS: KENYA, BANGLADESH, ALGERIA, NEPAL, PAKISTAN, BOLIVIA, AND HONDURAS

Life expectancy in these countries is 40 years, and women generally have five or more children. They are unable to feed, clothe, house, educate, or provide medical care for themselves even at the most minimal level. One U.S. company entered this market with a program of how to use a bleach product as a disinfectant. Because literacy rates are low, the product's use is illustrated with pictures.

SEEKERS: MALAYSIA, GABON, BRAZIL, INDONESIA, VENEZUELA, TURKEY, AND SRI LANKA

Life expectancy is 60 years, and women average four or five children. These countries are identified as seekers because their livelihood depends on investments from foreign countries. These countries are progressive economically, but are having a hard time keeping up with consumer demand. While their governments encourage their residents to buy local products, the middle class is beginning to value high-quality goods.

CLIMBERS: ISRAEL, SINGAPORE, HONG KONG, GREECE, PORTUGAL, SPAIN, IRELAND, ITALY, NEW ZEALAND, AND SOUTH KOREA

Women average two or three children and there is an emerging middle class. These are countries where the sales of disposable diapers, convenience foods, and business machines are increasing. These countries use imports as status symbols, but also have a great deal of ethnic pride.

LUXURY AND LEISURE: UNITED STATES, CANADA, JAPAN, GREAT BRITAIN, AND AUSTRALIA

Population growth is slowing, and women have about two children. Families in these countries are smaller, more affluent, and spend more money on each family member and on recreation. Cable TV, specialized magazines, and unique products characterize the competition that exists as firms compete for segments within these markets.

ROCKING CHAIRS: WEST GERMANY, SWITZERLAND, LUXEMBOURG, AND THE NETHERLANDS

Women in these countries have fewer than two children, and there is a higher proportion of people in their mature years. There is more interest in social security and health care plans than in consumer goods.

Source: Adapted from D. Walsh, "Demographic Trends, Transition Phases Suggest International Marketing Opportunities, Strategies," *Marketing News*, September 16, 1983, pp. 16–17.

Exhibit 2–2 Schlitz in Saudi Arabia

Courtesy Schlitz Brewery

Schlitz has about 40 percent of the Saudi Arabian beer market. To capture this market, Schlitz uses Arabic labeling on one side of its package and English on the other (see above). The beverage looks and tastes like standard beer. However, since it contains no alcohol, it is acceptable to the prevailing values. The promotion stresses the product's American origin, which is viewed favorably in Saudi Arabia.

of society.[2] Thus, culture, as the term is used by behavioral scientists, has a meaning different from the ordinary meaning of "high brow" or "sophisticated." As one author puts it:

> National Culture is not found in museums or formed by graduate schools or universities. It is composed of common habits and patterns of living of

people in daily activities and of the common interest in entertainment, sports, news, and even advertising.[3]

Several aspects of culture require elaboration. First, culture is a *comprehensive* concept. It includes almost everything that influences an individual's thought processes and behaviors. While culture does not determine the nature or frequency of biological drives, such as hunger or sex, it does influence if, when, and how these drives will be gratified. Second, culture is *acquired*. It does not include inherited responses and predispositions. However, since most human behavior is learned rather than innate, culture does affect a wide array of behaviors.

Third, the complexity of modern societies is such that culture seldom provides detailed prescriptions for appropriate behavior. Instead, in most industrial societies, culture supplies *boundaries* within which most individuals think and act.[4]

Finally, the nature of cultural influences is such that we are *seldom aware* of them. One behaves, thinks, and feels in a manner consistent with other members of the same culture because it seems "natural" or "right" to do so. The influence of culture is similar to the air we breathe; it is everywhere and is generally taken for granted unless there is a fairly rapid change in its nature.

The Functioning of Culture

Culture operates primarily by setting rather loose boundaries for individual behavior and by influencing the functioning of such institutions as the family structure and mass media. Thus, *culture provides the framework within which individual and household life-styles evolve*.

The boundaries that culture sets on behavior are called *norms*. Norms are simply rules that specify or prohibit certain behaviors in specific situations and are based on or derived from cultural values. *Cultural values* are widely held beliefs that affirm what is desirable. It is not necessary for a culture's values to be logically consistent. In fact, some tension or strain between conflicting cultural values is probably characteristic of most advanced societies due to rapid changes in such areas as technological development. This array of abstract, and sometimes conflicting, cultural values that characterizes industrialized societies leaves room for a variety of distinct lifestyles to evolve within each society.

Violation of cultural norms results in *sanctions* or penalties ranging from mild social disapproval to banishment from the group. Conformity to norms is usually given explicit and obvious rewards only when a child is learning the culture (socialization) or an individual is learning a new culture (acculturation). In other situations, conformity is expected without reward. For example, in America we expect people to arrive on time for business and social appointments. We do not compliment them when they do arrive on time, but we tend to become angry when they arrive late. Thus, as Figure 2–1 indicates, cultural values give rise to norms and associated sanctions which in turn influence consumption patterns.

Figure 2–1
Values, Norms, Sanctions, and Consumption Patterns

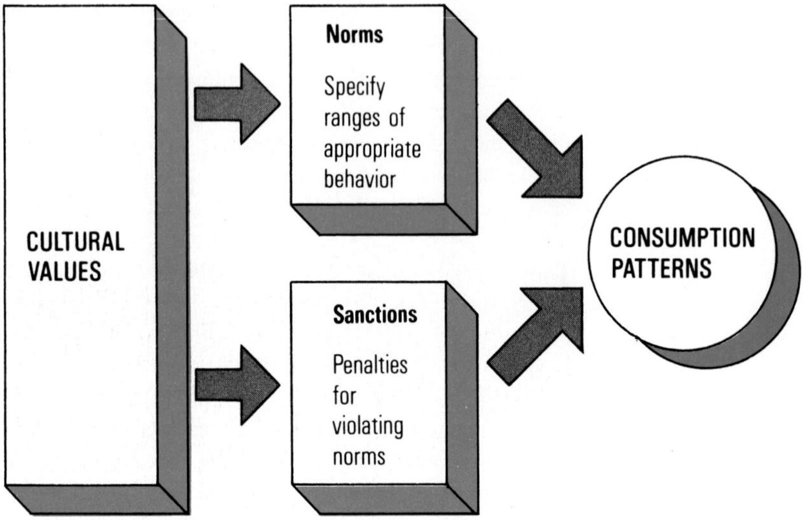

The preceding discussion may leave the impression that people are aware of cultural values and norms and that violating any given norm carries a precise and known sanction. This usually is not the case. We tend to "obey" cultural norms without thinking because to do otherwise would seem unnatural. For example, we are seldom aware of how close we stand to other individuals while conducting business. Yet, this distance is well-defined and adhered to, even though it varies from culture to culture. Nor do we consider consuming a vast array of plant and animal life that are considered delicacies in other parts of the world. In other words, we conform because it is the "natural" way to behave.

Cultures are not static. They typically evolve and change slowly over time. However, there can be major changes during relatively short time periods due to rapid technological advances, conflicts between existing values, exposure to another culture's values, or dramatic events such as a war. Marketing managers must understand both the existing cultural values and the emerging cultural values of the societies they serve.

Cross-Cultural Variations in Consumer Behavior

Why should we study foreign cultures? The five examples in Exhibit 2–3 provide a partial answer. Marketing is increasingly a global activity. Individuals and firms without cultural sensitivity are at an extreme disadvantage in today's economic environment. The following quote provides an equally important reason for examining foreign cultures:

> Culture hides much more than it reveals, and strangely enough what it hides, it hides most effectively from its own participants. Years of study have convinced me that the real job is not to understand foreign culture but to understand our own. I am also convinced that all one ever gets from

Exhibit 2–3

Cross-Cultural Marketing Mistakes

- A U.S. electronics firm landed a major contract with a Japanese buyer. The U.S. firm's president flew to Tokyo for the contract signing ceremony. Then the head of the Japanese firm began reading the contract intently. The scrutiny continued for an extraordinary length of time. At last, the U.S. executive offered an additional price discount.

  The Japanese executive, though surprised, did not object. The U.S. executive's mistake was assuming that the Japanese executive was attempting to reopen negotiations. Instead, he was demonstrating his personal concern and authority in the situation by closely and slowly examining the document.*
- Another electronics company sent a conservative American couple from the Midwest to represent the firm in Sweden. They were invited for a weekend in the country where, at an isolated beach, their Swedish hosts disrobed. The Americans misinterpreted this not uncommon Swedish behavior and their resulting attitudes destroyed a promising business relationship.*
- The average height of Brazilians is several inches less than that of Americans. Sears overlooked this important difference and built stores with "American-height" shelves. These shelves blocked Brazilian shoppers' views of the rest of the store.†
- Crest initially failed in Mexico when it used its U.S. approach of providing scientific proof of its decay prevention capabilities. Most Mexicans assign little value to the decay prevention benefit of toothpaste.
- Coca-cola had to withdraw its 2-liter bottle from the Spanish market after discovering that it did not fit local refrigerators.‡

*S. P. Galante, "U.S. Companies Seek Advice on Avoiding Cultural Gaffes Abroad," *The Wall Street Journal,* European Ed., July 20, 1984, sec. 1, p. 7.

†L. Wentz, "Marketing Errors Doomed Sears in Brazil," *Advertising Age,* May 16, 1983, p. 32.

‡P. Kotler, "Global Standardization: Courting Danger," *Journal of Consumer Marketing,* Spring 1986, p. 13.

> studying foreign culture is a token understanding (of the culture). The ultimate reason for such study is to learn more about how one's own system works.[5]

This quote provides a statement of the philosophy and objectives of this chapter. We are going to examine aspects of foreign cultures, not to become experts on a particular country, but to increase our appreciation of how culture operates. This appreciation will provide us with two advantages. First, we will better understand how culture influences consumer behavior in our own country. Second, our understanding of how culture functions will make us sensitive to the potential pitfalls that exist when we operate in a foreign culture or one of our own subcultures.[6]

Numerous American companies have awakened to the need for general cultural sensitivity. General Motors, Procter & Gamble, and Exxon recently committed $500,000 each for cross-cultural training for their employees. Red Wing Shoe Company put 21 executives through a three-day training program on the Middle East. As Red Wing's president explained: "We always give the customer what he wants. If we're playing in his ballpark, we'd better know his rules."[7]

VARIATIONS IN CULTURAL VALUES

Cultural values are widely held beliefs that affirm what is desirable. These values affect behavior through norms which specify an acceptable range of responses to specific situations. A useful approach to understanding cultural variations in behavior is to understand the values embraced by different cultures.

There are a multitude of values that vary across cultures and affect consumption. Figure 2–2 offers a classification scheme consisting of three broad forms of cultural values—*other-oriented, environment-oriented,* and *self-oriented.* The cultural values that have the most impact on consumer behavior can be classified in one of these three general categories. Individual values can affect more than one area, but their primary impact is generally in one of the three categories.

Other-oriented values reflect a society's view of the appropriate relationships between individuals and groups within that society. These relationships have a major impact on marketing practice. For example, if the society values collective activity, consumers will look toward others for guidance in purchase decisions and will not respond favorably to "be an individual" promotion appeals.

Environment-oriented values prescribe a society's relationship to its economic and technical as well as its physical environment. As a manager, you would develop a very different marketing program for a society that stressed a problem-solving, risk-taking, performance-oriented approach to its environment than you would for a fatalistic, security, and status-oriented society.

Self-oriented values reflect the objectives and approaches to life that the individual members of society find desirable. Again, these values have strong implications for marketing management. For instance, the acceptance and use

Figure 2–2
Value Orientations Influence Behavior

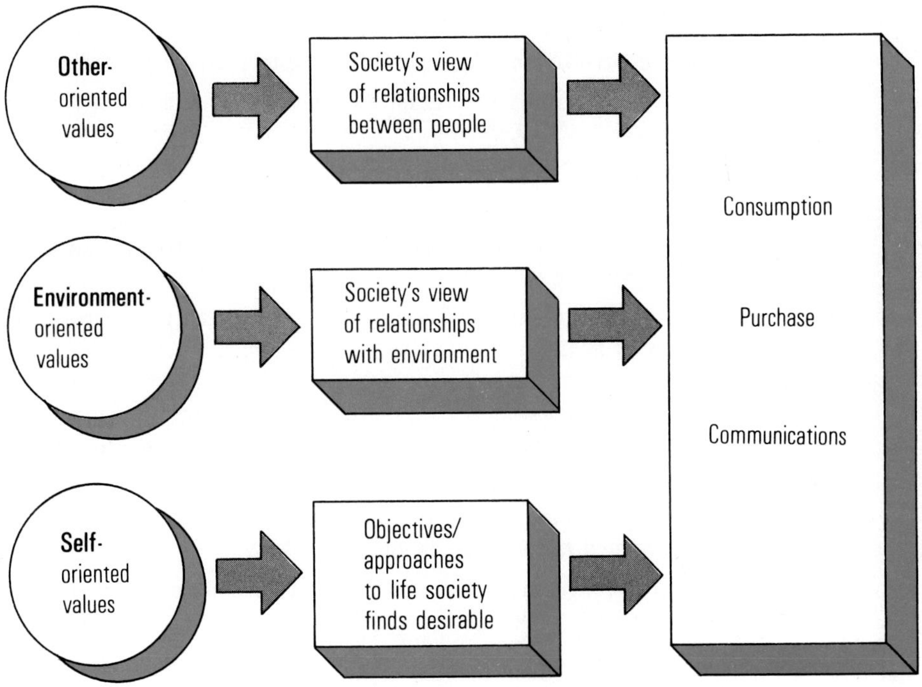

of credit is very much determined by a society's position on the value of postponed versus immediate gratification.

Table 2–1 provides a list of 18 values that are important in most cultures. The list is not meant to be exhaustive but does include the major values that are relevant to consumer behavior in industrialized societies. Most of the values are shown as dichotomies (e.g., materialistic versus nonmaterialistic); however, this is not meant to represent an either/or situation. Instead, a continuum exists between the two extremes. For example, two societies can each value tradition, but one may value it more than the other and, therefore, lies closer to the tradition end of the scale. For several of the values, a natural dichotomy does not seem to exist. For a society to place a very low value on cleanliness does not necessarily imply that it places a high value on "dirtiness." These 18 values are described in the following paragraphs.

Other-Oriented Values

Individual/Collective. Does the culture emphasize and reward individual initiative, or are cooperation with and conformity to a group more highly valued? Are individual differences appreciated or condemned? Are rewards and status

Table 2–1
Cultural Values of Relevance to Consumer Behavior

Other-Oriented Values

- *Individual/Collective*. Are individual activity and initiative valued more highly than collective activity and conformity?
- *Romantic Orientation*. Does the culture believe that "love conquers all"?
- *Adult/Child*. Is family life organized to meet the needs of the children or the adults?
- *Masculine/Feminine*. To what extent does social power automatically go to males?
- *Competition/Cooperation*. Does one obtain success by excelling over others or by cooperating with them?
- *Youth/Age*. Are wisdom and prestige assigned to the younger or older members of a culture?

Environment-Oriented Values

- *Cleanliness*. To what extent is cleanliness pursued beyond the minimum needed for health?
- *Performance/Status*. Is the culture's reward system based on performance or on inherited factors such as family or class?
- *Tradition/Change*. Are existing patterns of behavior considered to be inherently superior to new patterns of behavior?
- *Risk Taking/Security*. Are those who risk their established positions to overcome obstacles or achieve high goals admired more than those who do not?
- *Problem Solving/Fatalistic*. Are people encouraged to overcome all problems or do they take a "what will be, will be" attitude?
- *Nature*. Is nature regarded as something to be admired or overcome?

Self-Oriented Values

- *Active/Passive*. Is a physically active approach to life valued more highly than a less active orientation?
- *Material/Nonmaterial*. How much importance is attached to the acquisition of material wealth?
- *Hard Work/Leisure*. Is a person who works harder than economically necessary admired more than one who does not?
- *Postponed Gratification/Immediate Gratification*. Are people encouraged to "save for a rainy day" or to "live for today"?
- *Sensual Gratification/Abstinence*. To what extent is it acceptable to enjoy sensual pleasures such as food, drink, and sex?
- *Humor/Serious*. Is life to be regarded as a strictly serious affair or is it to be treated lightly?

given to individuals or to groups? Answers to these questions reveal the individual or collective orientation of a culture.

In Japan, compared to the United States, there is "a weaker sense of individualism and a stronger pressure to conform to and associate with one's reference groups."[8] Therefore, motivating and compensating Japanese sales personnel using individual-based incentive systems and promotions would be inappropriate. Likewise, such themes as "be yourself," "stand out," and "don't be one of the crowd" are effective in the United States but not in Japan. However, these generalizations are less accurate today than in the recent past. Evidence indicates that the Japanese, particularly the younger generation, are becoming more individualistic.[9] Japanese advertising themes are reflecting this change.[10]

As the following quote indicates, Marlboro adjusts its advertising strategy to reflect the collective orientation of its Hong Kong market:

> In Asia, popularity, perceived or real, sells goods. Asian people are not individualists. They prefer to be harmonious with their social group rather than stand out through individual choice. For this reason, the most popular products tend to remain the most popular products.
>
> For several years, Marlboro has appealed to the Chinese (Hong Kong) by citing the brand's dominant market share in the United States, as tabulated by the Maxwell Report. Despite their complete lack of familiarity with John Maxwell and his U.S. cigarette market survey, "the people began to accept this obviously authoritative Maxwell Report to the point where now Marlboro . . . sends a personality to New York to announce by satellite telecast the latest Maxwell [figures]."[11]

Romantic Orientation. Is the "boy meets girl, overcomes obstacles, marries, and lives happily ever after" theme common in popular literature? Is there freedom of choice in the selection of mates? A Listerine ad in Thailand showing a boy and girl, obviously fond of each other, failed. It was changed to two girls discussing Listerine and was judged successful.[12] Advertisements portraying courtship activities are not effective in India where many marriages are still arranged by parents. In contrast, Unilever's female body spray, Impulse, is successfully marketed in 31 countries using a straightforward romantic theme.[13]

Adult/Child. To what extent do the primary family activities focus on the needs of the children instead of those of the adults? What role, if any, do children play in family decisions? What role do they play in decisions that primarily affect the child?

The results of using child-centered promotional themes in an adult-oriented society can be seen in General Mills's experience in England. General Mills tried to capture a share of the English breakfast cereal market with a package and promotional theme similar to several that had proven successful in the United States. In this case, the theme was a picture of a boy saying, "See kids, it's great." The campaign was unsuccessful because British mothers and fathers, unlike American parents, were not accustomed to taking advice from children on food selection.[14] This is confirmed by a study which found that 71 percent of American respondents, compared to 57 percent of British respondents, agreed with the statement: "My children are the most important thing in my life."[15] Japanese children tend to be indulged even more than American children in terms of granting their requests for products.[16]

Masculine/Feminine. Are rank, prestige, and important social roles assigned primarily to men? Can a female's life pattern be predicted at birth with a high degree of accuracy? Does the husband or wife, or both, make important family decisions? Basically, we live in a masculine-oriented world, yet the degree of masculine orientation varies widely.

Both obvious and subtle aspects of marketing are influenced by this dimension. Obviously, you would not portray women executives in advertisements in Muslim countries. Nor would you show Japanese women as executives in Japanese advertisements. However, suppose you were going to portray a furniture or household appliance purchase decision for a Dutch market. Would you show the decision to be made by the husband, the wife, or made jointly? A joint decision process would probably be used.[17] Or suppose you had an office in a Muslim country. Would you follow the common American practice of hiring a female secretary? To do so would be an affront to many of your Muslim clients.

Competition/Cooperation. Is the path to success found by outdoing other individuals or groups, or is success achieved by forming alliances with other individuals and groups? Does everyone admire a winner? Variation on this value can be seen in the way different cultures react to comparative advertisements. For example, Mexico and Spain ban such ads while the United States encourages them. Market share objectives, sales force compensation and motivation policies, and comparative advertising themes are among the decisions that would be affected by a culture's competition-cooperation orientation.

Youth/Age. Are prestige, rank, and important social roles assigned to younger or older members of society? Are the behavior, dress, and mannerisms of the younger or older members of a society imitated by the rest of the society? While American society is clearly youth-oriented, the Confucian concept practiced in Korea emphasizes age. An advertising campaign for Reyno (Salem) failed in Germany because the young models in the ads were perceived as being inexperienced rather than persons to imitate.[18]

Environment-Oriented Values

Cleanliness. Is cleanliness "next to Godliness," or is it a rather minor matter? Is one expected to be clean beyond reasonable health requirements? In the United States, a high value is placed on cleanliness. In fact, many Europeans consider Americans to be paranoid on the subject of personal hygiene. Figure 2–3 illustrates this difference.

Figure 2–3
Culture Differences in the Use of Deodorant

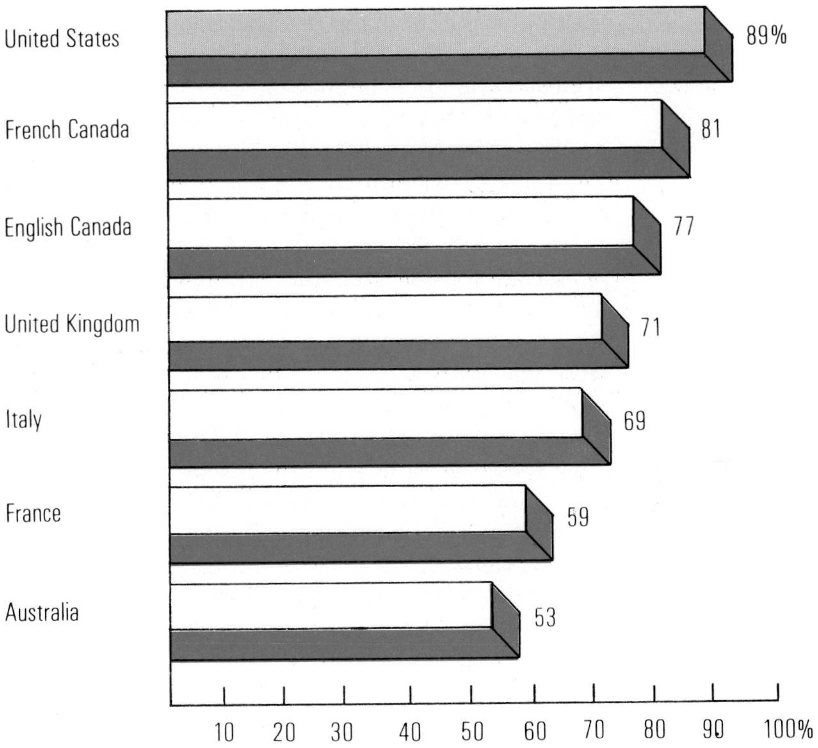

Source: Adapted from J. T. Plummer, "Consumer Focus in Cross-National Research," *Journal of Advertising* (Spring 1977), p. 10.

In an impressive reflection of the impact of this value, Gleem toothpaste's promotional theme, "For people who can't brush after every meal," was very successful in the United States. However, it did poorly in much of Europe, where brushing after every meal would be considered strange.[19] Likewise, people in parts of Southeast Asia respond negatively to toothpaste promises of sparkling white teeth since black and discolored teeth are considered desirable.[20]

Performance/Status. Are opportunities, rewards, and prestige based on an individual's performance or on the status associated with the person's family, position, or class? Do all people have an equal opportunity economically, socially, and politically at the start of life, or are certain groups given special privileges? A status-oriented society is more likely to prefer "quality" or established brand names and high-priced items over functionally equivalent items with unknown brand names or lower prices. This is the case in Japan, Hong Kong, Singapore, the Philippines, Malaysia, Indonesia, Thailand, and most Arabic countries, where consumers are attracted by prestigious, known brands. This makes it very difficult for new brands to gain market share.[21]

Tradition/Change. Is tradition valued simply for the sake of tradition? Is change or "progress" an acceptable reason for altering established patterns? Societies that place a relatively high value on tradition tend to resist product changes. One study found that American women stated more of a preference for trying new grocery products and retail services than did French women.[22] Associated with this are more rapid changes in grocery products and retailing institutions in the United States than in France. "All innovation is the work of the devil" is a quote attributed to Muhammad.[23] Is it little wonder that economic development and modern business and marketing practices often produce turmoil in Muslim cultures?

Risk Taking/Security. Do the "heroes" of the culture meet and overcome obstacles? Is the person who risks established position or wealth on a new venture admired or considered foolhardy? This value has a strong influence on entrepreneurship and economic development. The society that does not admire risk taking is unlikely to develop enough entrepreneurs to achieve economic change and growth. New product introductions, new channels of distribution, and advertising themes are affected by this value.

Problem Solving/Fatalistic. Do people react to obstacles and disasters as challenges to be overcome, or do they take a "what will be, will be" attitude? Is there an optimistic "we can do it" orientation? In the Dominican Republic, difficult or unmanageable problems are dismissed with the expression "no problem." This actually means: "There is a problem, but we don't know what to do about it—so don't worry!"[24]

Mexico also falls toward the fatalistic end of this continuum. As a result, Mexican customers are less likely to express formal complaints when confronted with an unsatisfactory purchase.[25]

This attitude affects advertising themes and the nature of products that are acceptable. For example, Japanese advertising does not stress control over the environment to the same extent that American ads do.[26]

Nature. Is nature assigned a positive value, or is it viewed as something to be overcome, conquered, or tamed? Americans historically considered nature as something to be overcome or improved. In line with this, animals were either destroyed as enemies or romanticized and made into heroes and pets. Horses and dogs, for example, are romanticized in the United States, and few Americans would feel comfortable consuming either as food. However, they are a common food source in much of the rest of the world.

In Thailand, animals are regarded as a lower form of creation and Thais are not attracted to advertising using animal themes. This rejection of animal themes included even the almost universally successful "Put a tiger in your tank" campaign by ESSO. A culture's attitudes toward nature can influence advertising themes as well as product and package designs.

Self-Oriented Values

Active/Passive. Are people expected to take a physically active approach to work and play? Are physical skills and feats valued more highly than less physical performances? Is emphasis placed on doing? A recent study identified American and French women who were socially active outside the home. The French women were characterized by agreement with the statement: "Fireside chats with friends are my favorite ways of spending an evening." In contrast, American women tended to agree with: "I like parties where there is lots of music and talk."[27] On a different dimension, Norwegian women spend two to four times more time participating in sports than do American women.[28] Vastly different products and advertising themes are required by these differing approaches to outside activities.

Material/Nonmaterial. Is the accumulation of material wealth a positive good in its own right? Does material wealth bring more status than family ties, knowledge, or other activities? A desire for material items can exist and grow despite official government attempts to reduce it, such as in the Soviet Union. As one observer of Russian society noted:

> It was apparent [in Russia] that while American bourgeois materialism might be officially censured, the American middle-class way of life embodied the aspirations of a growing number of Russians, especially in the cities. People wanted their own apartments, more stylish clothes, more swinging music, a television set and other appliances, and for those lucky enough, a private car.[29]

There are two types of materialism. *Instrumental materialism* is the acquisition of things to enable one to do something. For example, skis can be acquired to allow one to ski. *Terminal materialism* is the acquisition of items for the sake of owning the item itself. Cultures differ markedly in their relative emphasis on these two types of materialism. For example, a substantial percentage of advertisements in both the United States and Japan have a materialistic theme. However, instrumental materialism is most common in U.S. advertising while terminal materialism is predominant in Japanese ads.[30]

A further description of cultural variation in the meaning of material items is presented in the section on nonverbal communications.

Hard Work/Leisure. Is work valued for itself, independent of external rewards, or is work merely a "means to an end"? Will individuals continue to work hard even when their minimum economic needs are satisfied, or will they opt for more leisure time? In parts of Latin America, work is viewed as a necessary evil. However, Swiss women "reject commercial appeals emphasizing time and effort saved in performing household tasks."[31] Likewise, an American brand of instant coffee was unsuccessful in Germany until its instructions were altered to add an element of work to the preparation (i.e., boil, steep, then stir the coffee).[32]

A General Foods executive stated the marketing strategy implications of this value quite clearly when discussing marketing Tang in Brazil (a country with a copious supply of fresh fruit):

> I suppose the only reasonable reason to buy Tang is that it's convenient, but God forbid we should try to sell it as being easier than squeezing your own oranges.[33]

Instead of promoting convenience, Tang (made sweeter to suit Brazilian tastes) promotes a selection of flavors and fun (contests, give-aways, and coupons). Exhibit 2–4 provides a discussion of the problems that ignoring this value has caused the Campbell Soup Company and Gerber Foods in Brazil.

Postponed Gratification/Immediate Gratification. Is one encouraged to "save for a rainy day," or should one "live for today"? Is it better to secure immediate

Exhibit 2–4 Campbell Soup's Marketing Failure in Brazil

Campbell Soup entered the Brazilian market in 1978 with a large capital investment in plant and a major marketing effort that won two national awards. By 1981, Campbell was forced to withdraw from the consumer market due to poor sales.

What happened? Campbell packed its soups in extra large cans with a variant of the familiar red and white label. After it was clear that the product was in trouble, in-depth interviews by a company-retained psychologist "revealed that the Brazilian housewife felt she was not fulfilling her role as a homemaker if she served her family a soup she could not call her own." Brazilian housewives prefer dehydrated soups which they can use as a start but still add their own special ingredients. Campbell's soups were generally saved for "emergencies," when housewives felt very rushed.

Gerber withdrew its line of prepared baby foods from the Brazilian market for similar reasons.

Source: Adapted from "Campbell Soup Fails to Make It to the Table," *Business Week*, October 12, 1981, p. 66; A. Heiming, "Culture Shocks," *Advertising Age*, May 17, 1982, p. M-9; and "Gerber Abandons a Baby-Food Market," *Business Week*, February 8, 1982, p. 45.

benefits and pleasures, or is it better to suffer in the short run for benefits in the future (or in the hereafter or for future generations)?

This value has implications for distribution strategies, efforts to encourage savings, and the use of credit. For example, one study found that some Americans, as compared to Germans, have an overriding concern with buying the product that is available now.[34] In Germany and the Netherlands, buying on credit is widely viewed as living beyond one's means. In fact, the word for debt in German (*schuld*) is the same word used for "guilt." A large mail-order company in Holland which specializes in credit sales uses unmarked packaging and unidentifiable trucks to make its deliveries![35]

Sensual Gratification/Abstinence. Is it acceptable to pamper oneself, to satisfy one's desires for food, drink, or sex beyond the minimum requirement? Is one who foregoes such gratification considered virtuous or strange? Muslim cultures are very, very conservative in all values. Advertisements, packages, and products must carefully conform to Muslim standards. For example, one company used Muhammad Ali, who is very popular among Arabians, as a spokesperson. However, advertisements in which he used his famous "I am the greatest" line were offensive "because only God is great."

Polaroid's instant cameras gained rapid acceptance because they allowed Arab men to photograph their wives and daughters without fear that a stranger in a film laboratory would see the women unveiled.[36] In contrast, Brazilian advertisements contain nudity and blatant (by U.S. standards) appeals to sensual gratification. Consider the following prime-time television ad for women's underwear:

> A maitre d' hands menus to a couple seated at a restaurant table. When the man opens his menu to the "chef's suggestion," he has a "vision" of a woman's bare torso and arms. She then pulls on a pair of panties.
>
> "What a dish!" he exclaims, only to have another "vision," this time of a women unclasping her front-closing bra to fully expose her breasts.
>
> The man slumps under the table to the consternation of both his wife and the waiter.[37]

Humor/Serious. Is life a serious and frequently sad affair, or is it something to be taken lightly and laughed at when possible? Cultures differ in the extent to which humor is accepted and appreciated and in the nature of what qualifies as humor. Americans see little or no conflict between humor and serious communication. Latin Americans and Continental Europeans do see a conflict. In their view, if a person is serious, the talk is completely serious; when a person tells jokes or funny stories, the entire situation is to be taken lightly.[38] Personal selling techniques and promotional messages should be developed with an awareness of a culture's position on this value dimension.

Clearly, the preceding discussion has not covered all of the values operating in the various cultures. However, it should suffice to provide a feel for the importance of cultural values and how cultures differ along value dimensions.

CULTURAL VARIATIONS IN NONVERBAL COMMUNICATIONS

Differences in verbal communication systems are immediately obvious to anyone entering a foreign culture. An American traveling in Britain or Australia will be able to communicate, but differences in pronunciation, timing, and meaning will be readily apparent. For example, to "table a report or motion" in the United States means to postpone discussion, while in England it means to give the matter priority. These differences are easy to notice and accept because we realize that language is an arbitrary invention. The meaning assigned to a particular group of letters or sounds is not inherent in the letters or sounds. A word means what a group of people agree that it will mean.

Attempts to translate marketing communications from one language to another can result in ineffective communications, as Ford Motor Company is painfully aware:

> Fiera (a low-cost truck designed for developing countries) faced sales problems since *fierra* means "ugly old woman" in Spanish. The popular Ford car Comet had limited sales in Mexico where it was named Caliente. The reason—*caliente* is slang for a streetwalker. The Pinto was briefly introduced in Brazil without a name change. Then it was discovered that *pinto* is slang for a "small male sex organ." The name was changed to Corcel which means horse.[39]

Exhibit 2–5 indicates that Ford is not the only company to encounter translation problems. The problems of literal translations and slang expressions are compounded by symbolic meanings associated with words, the absence of certain words from key languages, and the difficulty of pronouncing certain words:

- Taco Time recently expanded into the Japanese market but had to position its menu as American Western rather than Mexican, because the Japanese have a negative image of Mexico.
- Mars addressed the problem of making the M&M's name pronounceable in France, where neither ampersands nor the apostrophe "s" plural form exists, by advertising extensively that M&M's should be pronounced "aimainaimze."[40]
- In the Middle East, consumers often refer to a product category by the name of the leading brand. Thus, all brands of vacuum cleaners are referred to as Hoovers and all laundry detergents are Tide.[41]
- To market its Ziploc food storage bags in Brazil, Dow Chemical had to use extensive advertising to create the word "zipar," meaning to zip, since there was no such term in Portuguese.[42]

Nonetheless, verbal language translations generally do not present major problems as long as we are careful. What many of us fail to recognize, however, is that each culture also has nonverbal communication systems or languages that,

Exhibit 2–5

Translation Problems in International Marketing

- An American airline operating in Brazil advertised the plush "rendezvous lounges" on its jets only to discover that *rendezvous* in Portuguese means a room hired for lovemaking.*
- General Motors' "body by Fisher" was translated as "corpse by Fisher" in Flemish.†
- Colgate's Cue toothpaste had problems in France as *cue* is a crude term for "butt" in French.‡
- In Germany, Pepsi's advertisement, "Come alive with Pepsi," was presented as "Come alive out of the grave with Pepsi."§
- Sunbeam attempted to enter the German market with a mist-producing curling iron named the Mist-Stick. Unfortunately, *mist* translates as "dung" or "manure" in German.
- Pet milk encounters difficulties in French-speaking countries where *pet* means, among other things, "to break wind."
- Fresca is a slang word for "lesbian" in Mexico.
- Esso found that its name phonetically meant "stalled car" in Japanese.||
- Kellogg's Bran Buds translates to "burned farmer" in Swedish.

*D. A. Ricks, J. S. Arpan, and M. Y. Fu, "Pitfalls in Advertising Overseas," *Journal of Advertising Research,* December 1974, p. 48.

†E. M. Mazze, "How to Push a Body Abroad without Making It a Corpse," *Business Abroad,* August 10, 1964, p. 15.

‡H. Martin, *International Business: Principles and Problems* (New York: Macmillan, 1964), p. 78.

§K. Lynch, "Adplomacy Faux Pas Can Ruin Sales," *Advertising Age,* January 15, 1979, p. S-2.

||D. A. Ricks, *Big Business Blunders* (Homewood, Ill.: Dow Jones-Irwin, 1983), pp. 39–46.

like verbal languages, are specific to each culture. Unlike verbal languages, most of us think of our nonverbal languages as being innate or natural rather than learned. Therefore, when we encounter a foreign culture, we tend to assign our own culture's meanings to the nonverbal signs being utilized by the other culture. The problem is compounded by the fact that the "foreigner" is interpreting our nonverbal cues by the "dictionary" used in his or her own culture. The frequent result is misunderstanding, unsuccessful sales calls and advertising campaigns, and, on occasion, long-lasting bitterness.

The following discussion examines seven variables (shown in Figure 2–4) we consider to be nonverbal languages: time, space, friendship, agreements, things, symbols, and etiquette.[43] Since nonverbal languages, like verbal ones, evolve over time, the specific examples cited should be interpreted as illustrative of the *nature* of nonverbal communications, not as accurate descriptors of particular cultures.

Figure 2–4
Factors Influencing Nonverbal Communications

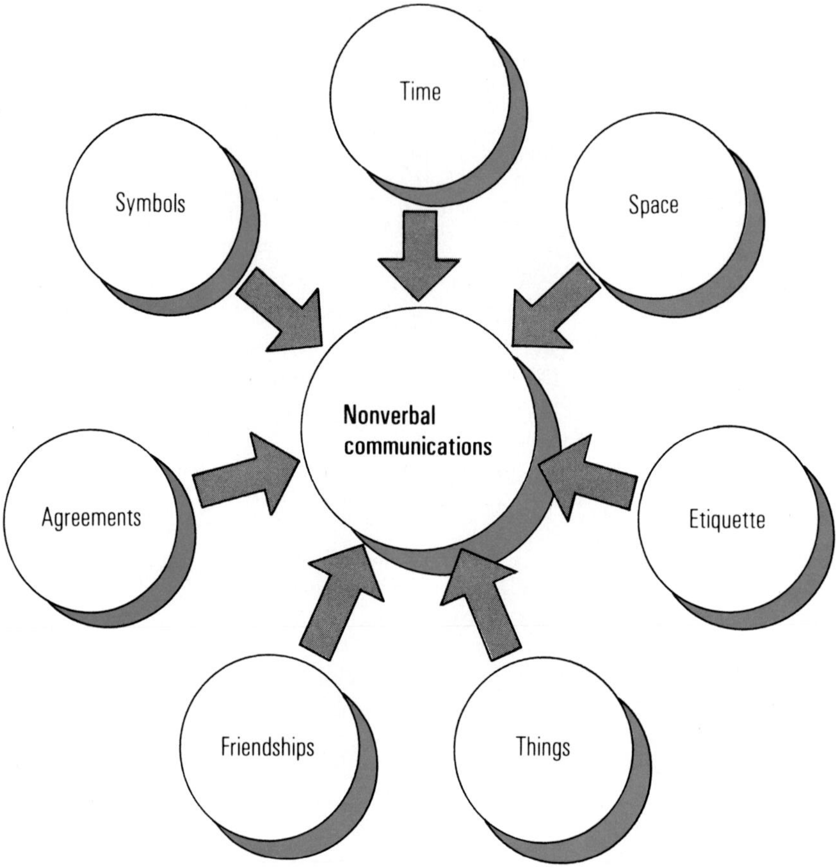

Time

The meaning of time varies between cultures in two major ways. First is what we call time perspective; this is a culture's overall orientation toward time. The second is the interpretations assigned specific uses of time.[44]

Time Perspective. Americans tend to view time as inescapable and fixed in nature. It is a road reaching into the future with distinct, separate sections (hours, days, weeks, and so on). Time is seen almost as a physical object: we can schedule it, waste it, lose it, and so forth. We have a strong orientation toward the future and consider the future to be anywhere from 5 to 25 years.

These views affect our lives and business practices in many ways. The scheduling of time for store hours, classes, construction projects, and so forth is based on our view of time. Individuals and business firms plan for the future within this time perspective.

Other cultures have different time perspectives. Latin Americans tend to view time as being less discrete and less subject to scheduling. This orientation leads to a different set of expectations concerning appointments and meetings. Southeast Asians think of the future in terms of hundreds or even thousands of years. This can lead to a different outlook on investments as well as on the urgency of current activities. After all, if one is thinking in terms of several hundred years, today's events are not as important.

As the following examples illustrate, time perspectives affect marketing practice in a variety of ways:

- An American firm introduced a filter-tip cigarette into an Asian culture. However, it soon became evident that the venture would fail. One of the main advertised advantages of filter cigarettes was that they would provide future benefits in the form of reduced risks of lung cancer. However, future benefits were virtually meaningless in this particular society which was strongly oriented to the present.[45]
- The high value Americans place on "saving" time is not shared by all other cultures. This has made convenience or timesaving products less valued in many cultures. For example, fast-food outlets including Wimpy, Kentucky Fried Chicken, Jack in the Box, and McDonald's have found the Latin American markets difficult to penetrate.[46]
- Likewise, canned soups have faced difficulties in Italy. More than 99 percent of a sample of Italian housewives responded *no* to the following question posed in a study by Campbell Soup: "Would you want your son to marry a canned soup user?"[47]
- In contrast, the high value assigned to time by the Japanese has made them very receptive to many Western timesaving convenience goods.

Meanings in the Use of Time. Specific uses of time have varying meanings in different cultures. In much of the world, the time required for a decision is proportional to the importance of the decision. Americans, by being well prepared with "ready answers," may adversely downplay the importance of the business being discussed. Likewise, both Japanese and Middle Eastern executives are put off by Americans' insistence on coming to the point directly and quickly in business transactions.[48] Greek managers find the American habit of setting time limits for business meetings to be insulting. Consider the following advice from a business consultant:

> In many countries we are seen to be in a rush; in other words, unfriendly, arrogant, and untrustworthy. Almost everywhere, we must learn to wait patiently and never to push for deadlines. Count on things taking a long time, the definition of "a long time" being at least *twice* as long as you would imagine.[49]

Exhibit 2–6

Variations in Waiting Times between Cultures

Arriving a little before the hour (the American respect pattern), he waited. The hour came and passed; 5 minutes—10 minutes—15 minutes. At this point he suggested to the secretary that perhaps the minister did not know he was waiting in the outer office . . . 20 minutes—25 minutes—30 minutes—45 minutes (the insult period)!

He jumped up and told the secretary that he had been "cooling his heels" in an outer office for 45 minutes and he was "damned sick and tired" of this type of treatment.

The principal source of misunderstanding lay in the fact that in the country in question, the five-minute delay interval was not significant. Forty-five minutes, on the other hand, instead of being at the tail end of the waiting scale, was just barely at the beginning. To suggest to an American's secretary that perhaps her boss didn't know you were there after waiting 60 seconds would seem absurd, as would raising a storm about "cooling your heels" for five minutes. Yet this is precisely the way the minister registered the protestations of the American in his outer office.

Source: Adapted from E. T. Hall, *The Hidden Dimension* (Garden City, N.Y.: Doubleday Publishing, 1966).

The lead time required for scheduling an event varies widely. One week is the minimum lead time for most social activities in America. However, a week represents the maximum lead time in many Arabic countries.

Promptness is considered very important in America. Furthermore, promptness is defined as being on time for appointments, whether you are the person making the call or the person receiving the caller. Exhibit 2–6 indicates the variation in waiting time between cultures.

Space

The use people make of space and the meanings they assign to their use of space constitute a second form of nonverbal communication. In America, "bigger is better." Thus, office space in corporations generally is allocated according to rank or prestige rather than need. The president will have the largest office, followed by the executive vice president, and so on. The fact that a lower echelon executive's work may require a large space seldom plays a major role in office allocation.

American sales personnel and others learn to evaluate the prestige of those with whom they are dealing by the relative size of the individual's office, among other things. However, Arabic and Latin American cultures have a different perception of what is large. An office that seems large to a member of one of these cultures might easily appear small to an American. Unless Americans are attuned to culture differences, they may underestimate the standing of their contact.

Americans tend to separate the offices of supervisors from the work space of subordinates. The French tend to place supervisors in the midst of subordinates. In the United States, the chief executive offices are on the top floor, and production, maintenance, or "bargain basements" are located on the lowest floor. In Japanese department stores, the bargain basement is located on the top floor.

A second major use of space is *personal space*. It is the nearest that others can come to you in various situations without your feeling uncomfortable. In the United States normal business conversations occur at distances of 5 to 8 feet and highly personal business from 18 inches to 3 feet. In parts of northern Europe the distances are slightly longer, while in most of Latin America, they are substantially shorter.

An American businessperson in Latin America will tend to back away from a Latin American counterpart in order to maintain his or her preferred personal distance. In turn, the host will tend to advance toward the American in order to maintain his or her personal space. The resulting "chase" would be comical if it were not for the results. Both parties generally are unaware of their actions or the reasons for them. Furthermore, each assigns a meaning to the other's actions based on what the action means in his or her own culture. Thus, the North American considers the Latin American to be pushy and aggressive. The Latin American, in turn, considers the North American to be cold, aloof, and snobbish.

Friendship

The rights and obligations imposed by friendship are another nonverbal cultural variable. Americans, more so than most other cultures, make friends quickly and easily and drop them easily also. In large part, this may be due to the fact that our society has always had a great deal of both social and geographic mobility. People who move every few years must be able to form friends in a short time period and depart from them with a minimum of pain. In many other parts of the world, friendships are formed slowly and carefully because they imply deep and lasting obligations.

Consider the contrast presented in the following description of Chinese and American attitudes:

> At the inception of a negotiation, the sort of Dale Carnegie charm and charisma that the individualistic American bestows alike on friends, strangers, and the world strikes the Chinese as insincere and superficial. The American, ready to be "friends" with everyone, does not limit his sales techniques and man-to-man approach to any particular relationship. With the Chinese, the relationship must be genuine; long-range and deep attitudes and procedures will flow from it even in trade and business.[50]

Attempts to imitate Avon's American success in Europe were unsuccessful. Avon's use of homemakers to sell beauty products to their friends and neighbors was not acceptable in much of Europe in part because of a strong reluctance to sell to friends at a profit.[51] However, in Mexico the approach was very successful as the Mexican homemaker found the sales call an excellent opportunity to socialize.

Friendship often replaces the legal or contractual system for ensuring that business and other obligations are honored. In countries without a well-established and easily enforceable commercial code, many people insist on doing business only with friends. For example, in the Middle East, "the caliber of the executive team from the standpoint of its personal acceptability (or lack of it) to a prospective customer can be crucial in winning or losing an opportunity, hence the need for tailoring the team to the assignment."[52] Likewise, friendship ties with small retailers have slowed the spread of the less personal supermarket in many countries.[53]

An international business consultant offers the following advice on this point:

> Product and pricing and clear contracts are not as important as the *personal relationship and trust* that is developed carefully and sincerely over time. The marketer must be established as simpatico, worthy of the business, and dependable *in the long run*. Contracts abroad often do not mean what they do here, so interpersonal understanding and bonds are important. Often business is not discussed until after *several* meetings, and in any one meeting business is only discussed after lengthy social conversation. The American must learn to sit on the catalog until the relationship has been established.[54]

Agreements

Americans rely on an extensive and, generally, highly efficient legal system for ensuring that business obligations are honored and for resolving disagreements. Many other cultures have not evolved such a system and rely instead on friendship and kinship, local moral principles, or informal customs to guide business conduct. For example, "in China the business relationship is always subsumed under the moralistic notion of a friendship."[55] Under the American system, we would examine a proposed contract closely. Under the Chinese system, we would examine the character of a potential trading partner closely.

When is an agreement concluded? Americans consider the signing of a contract to be the end of negotiations. However, to many Greeks such a signing is merely the signal to begin serious negotiations that will continue until the project is completed. At the other extreme, presenting a contract for a signature can be insulting to an Arab who considered the verbal agreement to be completely binding.

We also assume that, in almost all instances, prices are uniform for all buyers, related to the service rendered, and reasonably close to the going rate. We order many products such as taxi rides without inquiring in advance about the cost.

In many Latin American and Arab countries the procedure is different. Virtually all prices are negotiated *prior* to the sale. If a product such as a taxi ride is consumed without first establishing the price, the customer must pay whatever fee is demanded by the seller.

Things

The two quotes in Exhibit 2–7 demonstrate the vastly different meanings that housing has in two economically similar cultures. Such findings are common. Items conveying dependability and respectability to the English would often seem out-of-date and backward to Americans. Japanese homes would seem empty and barren to many Americans. In addition to assigning different meanings to the possession of various objects, cultures differ in the degree to which they value the acquisition of goods as an end in itself (terminal materialism) or as a means to an end, such as acquisition of a graphite racket to play tennis (instrumental materialism).[56] Such differences lead to problems in determining salary schedules, bonuses, gifts, product designs, and advertising themes.

The differing meanings that cultures attach to things, including products, make gift-giving a particularly difficult task. The business and social situations

Exhibit 2–7

Variations in the Meaning of Housing

- At my house he could talk freely and he impressed me with his knowledge and abilities; I was not invited back to his house. I only later found out where it was and realized how incongruous it was for him. Having a house of European type was clearly a necessity for ToNori (a native of New Britain), given the current fashion of house buying and given his own status aspirations.
- I asked Juan Navarro (a Mexican peasant) what were his major economic concerns. He answered very quickly, "Food and clothes." "How about housing?" I asked. "That is never a problem," he said, "for I can always make a house." . . . For Musio, Juan, and the others, a house is not a prestige symbol but simply a place to sleep, a place to keep dry in, a place for family privacy, and a place in which to store things. . . . It seems difficult to overestimate the importance of clothing. A clean set of clothes is a pass into town, or a fiesta. Clothes are the mark of a man's self-respect, and the ability of a man to clothe his family is in many ways the measure of a man.

Source: R. F. Salisbury, "ToNori Buys a House"; and J. E. Epstein, "A Shirt for Juan Navarro," in *Foundations for a Theory of Consumer Behavior*, ed. W. T. Tucker (New York: Holt, Rinehart & Winston, 1967), p. 38, and pp. 74–75.

that call for a gift, and the items that are appropriate gifts, vary widely. For example, a gift of cutlery is generally inappropriate in Russia, Taiwan, and West Germany.[57] In Japan, small gifts are required in many business situations, yet in China they are inappropriate.

Symbols

If you were to see a baby wearing a pink outfit, you would most likely assume the child is female. If the outfit were blue, you would probably assume the child is male. These assumptions would be accurate most of the time in the United States but would not be accurate in many other parts of the world such as Holland. Failure to recognize the meaning assigned to a color or other symbols can cause serious problems. For example, a manufacturer of water-recreation products lost heavily in Malaysia because the company's predominant color, green, was associated with the jungle and illness.

A leading U.S. golf ball manufacturer was initially disappointed in its attempts to penetrate the Japanese market. Its mistake was packaging its golf balls in sets of four. Four is a symbol for death in Japanese.[58] Pepsi-Cola lost its dominant market share in Southeast Asia to Coke when it changed the color of its coolers and vending equipment from deep "regal" blue to light "ice" blue. Light blue

Exhibit 2–8 The Meaning of Numbers, Colors, and Other Symbols

White:	Symbol for mourning or death in the Far East; happiness, purity in United States.
Purple:	Associated with death in many Latin American countries.
Blue:	Connotation of femininity in Holland; masculinity in Sweden, United States.
Red:	Unlucky or negative in Chad, Nigeria, Germany; positive in Denmark, Rumania, Argentina. Brides wear red in China but it is a masculine color in the United Kingdom and France.
Yellow flowers:	Sign of death in Mexico; infidelity in France.
White lilies:	Suggestion of death in England.
7:	Unlucky in Ghana, Kenya, Singapore; lucky in Morocco, India, Czechoslovakia, Nicaragua, United States.
Triangle:	Negative in Hong Kong, Korea, Taiwan; positive in Colombia.
Owl:	Wisdom in United States; bad luck in India.

is associated with death and mourning in Southeast Asia.[59] Exhibit 2–8 presents additional illustrations of varying meanings assigned to symbols across cultures.

Etiquette

Etiquette represents generally accepted ways of behaving in social situations. Assume that an American firm is preparing a commercial which shows people eating an evening meal, with one person about to take a bite of food from a fork. The person will have the fork in the right hand, and the left hand will be out of sight under the table. To an American audience this will seem natural. However, in many European cultures, a well-mannered individual would have the fork in the left hand and the right hand on the table! Likewise, portraying the American custom of patting a child on the head would be inappropriate in the Orient where the head is considered sacred.

Behaviors considered rude or obnoxious in one culture may be quite acceptable in another. The common and acceptable American habit (for males) of crossing one's legs while sitting, such that the sole of a shoe shows, is extremely insulting in many Eastern cultures. In these cultures, the sole of the foot or shoe should never be exposed to view. Yet, many American ads show managers with their feet on the desk, soles exposed!

President Reagan bought some souvenirs during his visit to China. He gave the shopkeeper 10 yuan ($4.35) for a 5-yuan purchase and told him to keep the change as he walked away. Humiliated, the shopkeeper dashed after the president and returned the change. Tipping isn't allowed in China and is considered an insult by many.[60]

As American trade with Japan increases, we continue to learn more of the subtle aspects of Japanese business etiquette. For example, a Japanese executive will seldom say no directly during negotiations, as this would be considered impolite. Instead, he might say, "That will be very difficult," which would mean no. An example of another aspect of Japanese business etiquette, *meishi,* is provided in Exhibit 2–9.

The importance of proper, culture-specific etiquette for sales personnel and advertising messages is obvious. Although people are apt to recognize that etiquette varies from culture to culture, there is still a strong emotional feeling that "our way is natural and right."

Conclusions on Nonverbal Communications

Can you imagine yourself becoming upset or surprised because people in a different culture spoke to you in their native language, say Spanish, French, or German, instead of English? Of course not. We all recognize that verbal languages vary around the world. Yet we generally feel that our nonverbal languages are natural or innate. Therefore, we misinterpret what is being "said" to us because we think we are hearing English when in reality it is Japanese, Italian, or Russian. It is this error that marketers must and can avoid.

Exhibit 2–9 The Exchange of Meishi (MAY-shee) in Japan

"Your meishi is your face."
"Meishi is most necessary here. It is absolutely essential."
"A man without a meishi has no identity in Japan."

The exchange of meishi is the most basic of social rituals in a nation where social ritual matters very much. It solidifies a personal contact in a nation where personal contacts are the indispensable ingredient for success in any field. The act of exchanging meishi is weighted with meaning. Once the social minuet is completed, the two know where they stand in relation to each other, and their respective statures within the hierarchy of corporate or government bureaucracy.

What is this mysterious "exchange of meishi"? It is the exchange of business cards when two people meet! A fairly common, simple activity in America, it is an essential, complex social exchange in Japan.

Adapted from S. Lohr, "Business Cards: A Japanese Ritual," *The New York Times*, September 13, 1981, pp. D1–D2.

CROSS-CULTURAL MARKETING STRATEGY

Our primary goal for examining foreign cultures is to gain a better understanding of how our own culture operates. The remainder of this chapter pursues our secondary goal of developing sufficient cultural sensitivity to avoid major pitfalls in international marketing. Exhibit 2–10 illustrates the success that cultural sensitivity can bring.

A Standardized International Marketing Strategy?

Since the late 1960s, there has been continuing controversy over the extent to which cross-cultural marketing strategies, particularly advertising, should be standardized.[61] Standardized strategies can result in substantial cost savings. Although a study of consumers in the United States, France, India, and Brazil found significant differences in the importance attached to 18 of 24 soft drink attributes, Coca-Cola has recently moved toward a single worldwide commercial.[62]

Like Coca-Cola, Levi Strauss & Company and Y Confecciones Europeas (the world's fourth largest jeans maker) recently moved toward a more consistent, worldwide image. In contrast, Blue Bell International (Wrangler jeans) decided against a more standardized approach after a major six-month review of its international advertising.[63] Exhibit 2–11 provides an illustration of a nonstandard approach.

Exhibit 2–10 Barbie Goes to Japan

Courtesy Mattel, Inc.

Barbie, the popular toy by Mattel, has been sold in Japan for decades. However, sales have been less than spectacular. At the suggestion of its Japanese partner, Mattel recently altered the American Barbie and created the Japanese version shown above. As can be seen, she is slightly smaller, less curvaceous and busty, with brown rather than blue eyes, and less vividly blonde hair.

In the two years since the change, sales have gone from near zero to 2 million. Including clothing sales, the Japanese have spent almost $13 million on the "Japanese" Barbie.

The critical decision is whether utilizing a standardized marketing strategy, in any given market, will result in a greater return on investment than would an individualized campaign. Thus, the consumer response to the standardized campaign and to potential individualized campaigns must be considered in addition to the cost of each approach. Ford of Europe now follows a "pattern standardization" strategy whereby the overall strategy is designed from the outset to be

Exhibit 2–11

Stick Ups in England

Stick Ups, a room deodorizer, quickly achieved success in the United States and shortly thereafter in England. However, research produced the following changes before Stick Ups were introduced in England:

1. The strength of the product's fragrance was greatly increased to meet British preferences.
2. The U.S. cardboard twin-pack was changed to a single blister pack. The higher costs associated with the increased fragrance made this necessary to encourage trial.
3. The advertisements showed the product in less conspicuous places than had the American ads, since the British preferred an unobtrusive product.
4. The media mix was shifted away from radio and into print media and billboards.

Adapted from "European Insist Pretesting," *Advertising Age*, August 24, 1981, p. 38. 38.

susceptible to extensive modification to suit local conditions while maintaining sufficient common elements to minimize the drain on resources and management time.[64]

Considerations in Approaching a Foreign Market

Table 2–2 provides a listing of seven key considerations for each geographic market that a firm is contemplating. An analysis of these seven variables provides the background necessary to decide whether or not to enter the market and to what extent, if any, an individualized marketing strategy is required.[65] A small sample of experts, preferably native to the market under consideration, often will be able to provide sufficient information on each variable.[66]

Is the Geographic Area Homogeneous or Heterogeneous with Respect to Culture? Marketing efforts are generally directed at defined geographic areas, primarily political and economic entities. Legal requirements and existing distribution channels often encourage this approach. However, it is also supported by the implicit assumption that geographical or political boundaries coincide with cultural boundaries. This assumption is incorrect more often than not.

Canada provides a clear example. Many American firms treat the Canadian market as though it were a single cultural unit despite the fact that they must make adjustments for language differences. However, studies have found French Canadians to differ from English Canadians in attitudes toward instant foods[67] and spending money;[68] in spending patterns toward expensive liquors, clothing,

Table 2–2
Key Areas for Developing a Cross-Cultural Marketing Strategy

1. Is the geographic area homogeneous or heterogeneous with respect to culture?
   Are there distinct subcultures in the geographic area under consideration? How narrow are the behavioral boundaries or norms imposed by the culture(s)?
2. What needs can this product fill in this culture?
   What needs, if any, does this product currently meet in this culture? Are there other needs it could satisfy? What products are currently meeting these needs? How important are these needs to the people in the culture?
3. Can enough of the group(s) needing the product afford the product?
   How many people need the product and can afford it? How many need it and cannot afford it? Can financing be obtained? Is a government subsidy possible?
4. What values are relevant to the purchase and use of the product?
   Is the decision maker the husband or wife? Adult or child? Will use of the product contradict any values, such as hard work as a positive good? Will ownership of the product go against any values such as a nonmaterial orientation? Will the purchase of the product require any behavior, such as financing, that might contradict a value? What values support the consumption of the product?
5. What is the distribution, political, and legal structure concerning this product?
   Where do consumers expect to buy the product? What legal requirements must the product meet? What legal requirements must the marketing mix meet?
6. In what ways can we communicate about this product?
   What language(s) can we use? What forms of nonverbal communications will affect our salespeople, packages, and advertisements? What kinds of appeals will fit with the culture's value system?
7. What are the ethical implications of marketing this product in this manner in this country?
   Might the use of this product impair the health or well-being of those using it? Will the consumption of this product divert resources from beneficial uses? Might the use or disposition of this product have negative side effects on the environment or economy?

personal care items, tobacco, soft drinks, candy, and instant coffee; in television and radio usage patterns; and in eating patterns.[69] Exhibit 2–12 describes Anheuser-Busch's successful responses to cultural pluralism in Canada.[70]

Exhibit 2–12 Anheuser-Busch's Response to Cultural Pluralism

Anheuser-Busch has successfully introduced Budweiser throughout Canada, including Quebec. It has achieved an equal penetration among both English and French Canadians. However, two distinct marketing approaches were used to reach the two cultural groups.

Since Budweiser was well known among the English-speaking Canadians (due in large part to American television viewing), the theme "This Bud's for You" was used in a manner very similar to the American campaign. The main differences were the inclusion of a Canadian flag, social references to Quebec, and stress on the fact that Canadian Bud has 5 percent alcohol (stronger than American beers but standard for Canada).

Budweiser was relatively unknown among French-speaking Canadians. Therefore, a strategy was built which tied Bud to "the positive values of American society." Since French Canadians view rock'n'roll as a positive aspect of America, the classic song, "Rock Around the Clock," is the theme for the two French commercials. One is a *Happy Days*-type scene with young adults dancing to "Rock Around the Clock" with the words "rock, rock, rock" replaced by "Bud, Bud, Bud."

Source: Adapted from B. Dunn, "Quebec, This Bud's for You," *Advertising Age*, October 5, 1981, p. S–13.

What Needs Can This Product or a Version of It Fill in This Culture? While not exactly in accordance with the marketing concept, most firms examine a new market with an existing product or product technology in mind. The question they must answer is what needs their existing or modified product can fill in the culture involved.[71] For example, bicycles and motorcycles serve primarily recreational needs in the United States, but provide basic transportation in many other countries. Sewing machines fulfill different needs in economically developed and economically undeveloped countries. Many people sew largely for pleasure in developed cultures such as ours and, therefore, must be approached differently than in countries where sewing is a necessary aspect of a homemaker's job.

General Foods has successfully positioned Tang as a substitute for orange juice at breakfast in the United States. However, in analyzing the French market, they found that the French drink little orange juice and almost none at breakfast. Therefore, a totally different positioning strategy was used; Tang was promoted as a new type of refreshing drink for any time of the day.[72]

Can Enough of the Group(s) Needing the Product Afford the Product? This requires an initial demographic analysis to determine the number of individuals or households that might need the product and the number that can probably afford it. In addition, the possibilities of establishing credit, obtaining a government subsidy, or making a less expensive version should be considered.

For example, Levi Strauss de Argentina launched a trade-in campaign in which consumers receive a 50,000 peso (about $7) "reward" for turning in an old pair of jeans with the purchase of a new pair.[73] A strong recession in Argentina prompted the action.

What Values or Patterns of Values Are Relevant to the Purchase and Use of This Product? The first section of this chapter focused on values and their role in consumer behavior. The value system should be investigated for influences on purchasing the product, owning the product, using the product, and disposing of the product. Much of the marketing strategy will be based on this analysis.

What Are the Distribution, Political, and Legal Structures for the Product? The legal structure of a country can have an impact on each aspect of a firm's marketing mix. For example, the Mexican government requested Anderson Clayton & Co. to "tone down" its commercials for Capulla mayonnaise because the advertisements were "too aggressive." The aggression involved direct comparisons with competing brands (comparative advertising), which is not acceptable in Mexico.[74] Regulation of marketing activities, particularly advertising, is increasing throughout the world.[75] Unfortunately, uniform regulations are not emerging. This increases the complexity and cost of international marketing.

In addition to regulatory activities, the political climate in a society will influence the types of products and activities that will succeed. For example, the Mexican government helped the Coca-Cola Company to develop a low-priced, nutritious soft drink aimed at improving the diets of Mexico's low-income children.[76]

The distribution channels and consumer expectations concerning where to secure products vary widely across cultures. In the Netherlands, drugstores do not sell prescription drugs (they are sold at an *apotheek* or apothecary, which sells nothing else). Existing channels and consumer expectations generally must be considered as fixed, at least in the short run.

In What Ways Can We Communicate the Product? This question requires an investigation into (1) available media and who attends to each type, (2) the needs the product fills, (3) values associated with the product and its use, and (4) the verbal and nonverbal communications system of the culture(s). All aspects of the firm's promotional mix (including packaging, nonfunctional product design features, personal selling techniques, and advertising) should be based on these four factors.[77]

For example, BSR Ltd. of Japan, an importer of phonograph turntables and changers from Britain, initially was unsuccessful because of its packaging strategy. The Japanese consumer uses a product's package as an important indicator of product quality. Thus, the standard shipping carton used by BSR, while it protected the product adequately, did not convey a high-quality image. To overcome this problem, BSR began packaging its phonograph equipment in two cartons: one for shipping and one for point-of-purchase display.[78]

What Are the Ethical Implications of Marketing This Product in This Country? All marketing programs should be evaluated on ethical as well as financial dimensions. However, the ethical dimension is particularly important and complex in marketing to Third World and developing countries.[79] Consider the opening illustration of this chapter. The following questions represent the type of ethical analysis that should go into the decision:

> If we succeed, will the average nutrition level be increased or decreased?
>
> If we succeed, will the funds spent on cereal be diverted from other uses with more beneficial long-term impact for the individuals or society?
>
> If we succeed, what impact will this have on the local producers of currently consumed breakfast products?

Understanding and acting on ethical considerations in international marketing is a difficult task. However, it is also a necessary one.

Conclusions on Cross-Cultural Marketing Strategy

Most of the examples we have cited deal with problems firms have had in international marketing. However, as billions of dollars in foreign trade indicate, cross-cultural marketing strategy can and does work. The formula for success is relatively simple. To succeed in a foreign culture, the marketing manager must first evaluate each of the seven areas which may influence the success of marketing in a foreign culture and then adjust the marketing mix accordingly.[80]

SUMMARY

Culture is defined as that complex whole which includes knowledge, beliefs, art, law, morals, custom, and any other capabilities acquired by humans as members of society. Culture includes almost everything that influences an individual's thought processes and behaviors.

Culture operates primarily by setting boundaries for individual behavior and by influencing the functioning of such institutions as the family structure and mass media. The boundaries or *norms* are derived from *cultural values*. Values are widely held beliefs that affirm what is desirable. Cultures change when values change, the environment changes, or when dramatic events occur.

Cultural values are classified into three categories: other, environment, and self. *Other-oriented values* reflect a society's view of the appropriate relationships between individuals and groups within that society. Relevant values of this nature include *individual/collective, romantic orientation, adult/child, masculine/feminine, competition/cooperation,* and *youth/age*.

Environment-oriented values prescribe a society's relationships with its economic, technical, and physical environments. Examples of environment values are *cleanliness, performance/status, tradition/change, risk taking/security, problem solving/fatalistic,* and *nature.*

Self-oriented values reflect the objectives and approaches to life that individual members of society find desirable. These include *active/passive, material/nonmaterial, hard work/leisure, postponed gratification/immediate gratification, sensual gratification/abstinence,* and *humor/serious.*

Differences in *verbal* communication systems are immediately obvious across cultures and must be taken into account by marketers wishing to do business in those cultures. Probably more important, however, and certainly more difficult to recognize are *nonverbal communication differences.* Major examples of nonverbal communication variables that affect marketers are *time, space, friendship, agreement, things, symbols,* and *etiquette.*

Seven questions are relevant for developing a cross-cultural marketing strategy. First, is the geographic area homogeneous with respect to culture? Second, what needs can this product fill in this culture? Third, can enough people afford the product? Fourth, what values are relevant to the purchase and use of the product? Fifth, what are the distribution, political, and legal structures concerning this product? Sixth, how can we communicate about the product? Seventh, what are the ethical implications of marketing this product in this country?

REVIEW QUESTIONS

1. What is meant by the term *culture?*
2. Is a country's culture more likely to be reflected in its art museums or its television commercials? Why?
3. Does culture provide a detailed prescription for behavior in most modern societies? Why or why not?
4. What does the statement "Culture sets boundaries on behaviors" mean?
5. Are we generally aware of how culture influences our behavior? Why or why not?
6. What is a *norm?* From what are norms derived?
7. What is a *cultural value?*
8. What is a *sanction?*
9. How do cultures and cultural values change?
10. Why should we study foreign cultures if we do not plan to engage in international or export marketing?
11. Cultural values can be classified as affecting one of three types of relationships—other, environment, or self. Describe each of these and differentiate each one from the others.
12. How does a ________ orientation differ from a ________ orientation?
    a. Individual/Collective.
    b. Performance/Status.
    c. Tradition/Change.
    d. Active/Passive.
    e. Material/Nonmaterial.
    f. Hard Work/Leisure.

g. Risk Taking/Security.
h. Masculine/Feminine.
i. Competitive/Cooperation.
j. Youth/Age.
k. Problem Solving/Fatalistic.
l. Adult/Child.
m. Postponed Gratification/Immediate Gratification.
n. Sensual Gratification/Abstinence.
o. Humor/Serious.

13. What is meant by *nonverbal communications?* Why is this such a difficult area to adjust to?
14. What is meant by ________ as a form of nonverbal communications?
    a. Time.
    b. Space.
    c. Friendship.
    d. Agreements.
    e. Things.
    f. Symbols.
    g. Etiquette.
15. Give an example of how each of the variables listed in question 14 could influence marketing practice.
16. What are the advantages and disadvantages of standardized international advertising?
17. What are the seven key considerations involved in deciding whether or not to enter a given international market?
18. What is meant by determining if a geographic area or political unit is "homogeneous or heterogeneous with respect to culture"? Why is this important?
19. What is the difference between *instrumental* and *terminal* materialism?

DISCUSSION QUESTIONS

1. The text provides a seven-step procedure for analyzing a foreign market. Using this procedure, analyze the U.S. market for:
    a. Korean wine.
    b. German bicycles.
    c. Japanese perfume.
2. What are the most relevant cultural values affecting the consumption of ________? Describe how and why these values are particularly important.
    a. Toothpaste.
    b. Perfume.
    c. Beer.
    d. Personal computers.
    e. Bicycles.
    f. VCRs.
3. What variations between the United States and other societies, *other than cultural variations,* may affect the relative level of usage of ________?
    a. Toothpaste.
    b. Perfume.
    c. Beer.
    d. Personal computers.
    e. Bicycles.
    f. VCRs.
4. What, if any, nonverbal communication factors might be relevant in the marketing of ________?

a. Toothpaste.
b. Perfume.
c. Beer.
d. Personal computers.
e. Bicycles.
f. VCRs.

5. The text lists 18 cultural values of relevance to marketing practice. Describe and place into one of the three categories four additional cultural values that have some relevance to marketing practice.
6. Are the cultures of the world becoming more similar or more distinct?
7. Select two cultural values from each of the three categories. Describe the boundaries (norms) relevant to that value in American society and the sanctions for violating those norms.
8. If you have visited a foreign culture, describe any experiences you can recall involving variations in nonverbal communications.
9. Why do Japanese ads focus more on terminal materialism while American ads focus more on instrumental materialism?
10. Why do values differ across cultures?
11. Why do nonverbal communication systems vary across cultures?
12. What are the major ethical issues in introducing new products to Third World countries?

PROJECT QUESTIONS

1. Interview two students from two different cultures. Determine the extent to which ________ are used in those cultures and the variations in the values of those cultures that relate to the use of ________.
   a. Toothpaste.
   b. Perfume.
   c. Beer.
   d. Personal computers.
   e. Bicycles.
   f. VCRs.
2. Interview two students from two different foreign cultures. Report any differences in nonverbal communications they are aware of between their culture and the U.S. culture.
3. Interview two students from two different foreign cultures. Report their perceptions of the major differences in cultural values between their culture and the U.S. culture.
4. Imagine you are a consultant working with your state's tourism agency. You have been asked to advise the state on the best promotional themes to use to attract foreign tourists to the state. What would you recommend if Japan and Germany were the two target markets selected by the state?
5. Analyze a foreign culture of your choice and recommend a marketing program for an American brand of ________.
   a. Toothpaste.
   b. Perfume.
   c. Beer.
   d. Personal computers.
   e. Bicycles.
   f. VCRs.

6. Examine foreign magazines and newspapers in your library or bookstore.
   a. Comment on any general difference you notice in advertising from various countries. What causes this difference?
   b. Copy or describe ads from the same company that differ across countries. Explain the differences.
7. Read the articles listed in footnote 80. Prepare a report on the common elements in each case.

REFERENCES

[1] S. C. Jain, *International Marketing Management* (Boston: Kent Publishing, 1987), 403–6.

[2] See J. F. Sherry, Jr., "The Cultural Perspective in Consumer Research," in *Advances in Consumer Research, XIII,* ed. R. J. Lutz (Chicago: Association for Consumer Research, 1986), pp. 573–75.

[3] Loevinger, "There Need Be No Apology, No Lament," *TV Guide Magazine,* April 6, 1968, pp. 8–9.

[4] R. W. Belk, "Cultural and Historical Differences in Concepts of Self," in *Advances in Consumer Research, XI,* ed. T. C. Kinnear (Chicago: Association for Consumer Research, 1984), pp. 753–60.

[5] E. T. Hall, *The Silent Language* (New York: Fawcett World Library, 1959), p. 39.

[6] For a treatment of the role of culture in international business, see V. Terpstra and K. David, *The Cultural Environment of International Business* (Cincinnati: South-Western Publishing, 1985); and D. A. Ricks, *Big Business Blunders* (Homewood, Ill.: Dow Jones-Irwin, 1983).

[7] S. P. Galante, "Clash Courses," *The Wall Street Journal,* European ed., July 20, 1984, p. 1.

[8] B. Granner, "Cross-Cultural Adaptation in International Business," *Contemporary Business,* no. 3, 1980, p. 106.

[9] L. Armstrong and B. Buell, "The Rise of the Japanese Yuppie," *Business Week,* February 16, 1987, pp. 54–55; and R. W. Belk and R. W. Pollay, "Materialism and Status Appeals in Japanese and U.S. Print Advertising," in *Comparative Consumer Psychology,* A. Woodside and C. Keown.

[10] B. Mueller, "Reflections of Culture," *Journal of Advertising Research,* June/July 1987, pp. 57–58.

[11] J. Roddy quoted in J. Levine, "Hard Sell Falls Flat for S.E. Asians," *Advertising Age,* June 21, 1982, p. 35.

[12] Ricks, *Big Business Blunders,* p. 63.

[13] B. Oliver, "A Little Romance," *Advertising Age,* June 24, 1985, p. 39.

[14] E. A. McCreary, *The Americanization of Europe* (Garden City, N.Y.: Doubleday Publishing, 1964), p. 131.

[15] J. T. Plummer, "Consumer Focus in Cross-National Research," *Advertising,* Spring 1977, p. 10.

[16] S. Ward et al., "Children's Purchase Requests and Parental Yielding," in Lutz, *Advances, XIII.*

[17] B. J. Verhage and R. T. Green, "Purchasing Roles in the Family: An Analysis of Instrumental and Expressive Decision Making," *European Research,* January 1981, p. 6; see also R. T. Green et al., "Societal Development and Family Purchasing Roles," *Consumer Research,* March 1983, pp. 436–42.

[18] McCreary, *Americanization of Europe,* p. 131.

[19] McCreary, *Americanization of Europe,* pp. 131–32.

[20] D. Ricks, "Boo-boos Abroad," *Weight Watchers,* May 1981, p. 10.

[21] "Europeans Insist on Pretesting," *Advertising Age,* August 24, 1981, p. 38; Belk and Pollay, "Materialism"; and M. Field, "Despite Recession, Import Market Still Strong," *Advertising Age,* January 30, 1986, p. 10.

[22] R. T. Green and E. Langeard, "A Cross-National Comparison of Consumer Habits and Innovator Characteristics," *Journal of Marketing,* July 1975, p. 38.

[23] Terpstra and David, *The Cultural Environment,* p. 133.

[24] J. Cerruti, "The Dominican Republic: Caribbean Comeback," *National Geographic,* October 1977, p. 545.

[25] A. Villarreal-Camacho, "Consumer Complaining Behavior," in *1983 AMA Educators' Proceedings,* ed. P. E. Murphy et al. (Chicago: American Marketing Association, 1983), pp. 68–73.

[26] R. W. Belk and W. J. Bryce, "Materialism and Individual Determinism," in Lutz, *Advances, XIII.*

[27] S. P. Douglas and C. D. Urban, "Life-Style Analysis to Profile Women in International Markets," *Journal of Marketing,* July 1977, p. 49.

[28] D. K. Hawes, S. Gronmo, and J. Arndt, "Shopping Time and Leisure Time: Some Preliminary Cross-Cultural Comparisons of Time-Budget Expenditures," in *Advances in Consumer Research V,* ed. H. K. Hunt (Chicago: Association for Consumer Research, 1978), pp. 151–59.

[29] H. Smith, *The Russians* (New York: Quadrangle, 1976), p. 55.

[30] Belk and Pollay, "Materialism"; and Belk and Bryce, "Materialism."

[31] S. Douglas and B. Dubois, "Looking at the Cultural Environment for International Marketing Opportunities," *Columbia Journal of World Business,* Winter 1977, p. 103.

[32] R. F. Roth, "Research Foreign Markets for Marketing Communication Planning," in *International Market Report* (International House, 1976).

[33] L. Wentz, "How Big Advertisers Flopped in Brazil," *Advertising Age,* July 5, 1982, pp. 17–25.

[34] R. Anderson and J. Engledow, "A Factor Analysis Comparison of U.S. and German Information Seekers," *Journal of Consumer Research,* March 1977, p. 196.

[35] G. Katona, B. Strumpel, and E. Zahn, "The Sociocultural Environment," in *International Marketing Strategy,* ed. H. B. Thorelli (New York: Penguin Books, 1973), p. 145.

[36] Field, "Despite Recession," p. 10.

[37] J. Michaels, "Nudes Dress Up Brazil Undies Ads," *Advertising Age,* August 3, 1987, p. 42.

[38] W. F. Whyte, "Must You Tell a 'Funny Story,'" *Columbia Journal of World Business,* July–August 1968, p. 86.

[39] Ricks, *Big Business Blunders,* p. 39.

[40] L. Wentz, "M&M's Continues Global Roll," *Advertising Age,* September 14, 1987, p. 90.

[41] Field, "Despite Recession," p. 10.

[42] J. Michaels and R. Turner, "Ziploc Bags Open in Brazil," *Advertising Age,* August 17, 1987, p. 30.

[43] See Hall, *The Silent Language;* and E. T. Hall, "The Silent Language in Overseas Business," *Harvard Business Review,* May–June 1960, pp. 87–96.

[44] See R. J. Graham, "The Role of Perception of Time in Consumer Research," *Journal of Consumer Research,* March 1981, pp. 335–42.

[45] J. A. Lee, "Cultural Analysis in Overseas Operations," in *World Marketing,* ed. J. K. Ryons, Jr., and J. E. Baker (New York: John Wiley & Sons, 1967), p. 59.

[46] J. R. Penteado, Jr., "U.S. Fast-Foods Move Slowly," *Advertising Age,* May 25, 1981, p. S–8.

[47] W. J. Keegan, *Multinational Marketing Management* (Englewood Cliffs, N.J.: Prentice-Hall, 1980), p. 92.

[48] M. E. Metcalfe, "Islam, Social Attitudes Heart of Arab Business," *Advertising Age,* August 18, 1980, p. S–16.

[49] L. Copeland, "Foreign Markets: Not for the Amateur," *Business Marketing,* July 1984, p. 116.

[50] H. P. Hoose, "How to Negotiate with the Chinese of PRC," in *Doing Business with China,* W. Whitson (New York: Praeger Publishers, 1974).

[51] "Avon on Products: Is Its Beauty Only Skin Deep?" *Forbes,* July 1, 1973, pp. 20–27.

[52] Metcalfe, "Islam, Social Attitudes."

[53] A. Goldman, "Transfer of a Retailing Technology into the Less Developed Countries: The Supermarket Case," *Journal of Retailing,* Summer 1981, p. 22.

[54] Copeland, "Foreign Markets." See also D. Ford, "Buyer/Seller Relationships in International Industrial Markets," *Industrial Marketing Management,* 2d Quarter 1984, pp. 101–12; and J. L. Graham, "Cross-Cultural Marketing Negotiations," *Marketing Science,* Spring 1985, pp. 130–45.

[55] R. Sheng, "Outsiders' Perception of the Chinese," *Columbia Journal of World Business,* Summer 1979, p. 20.

[56] Belk, "Cultural and Historical"; and Belk and Pollay, "Materialism."

[57] W. J. Stanton, *Fundamentals of Marketing* (New York: McGraw-Hill, 1981), p. 479. See also S. B. Hitchings, "Beware When Bearing Gifts in Foreign Lands," *Business Week,* December 6, 1976, pp. 91–92.

[58] "Adapting Export Packaging to Cultural Differences," *Business America,* December 3, 1979, p. 3.

[59] M. M. Lomont, "Ten Commandments Guide Multinational Packaging," *Marketing News,* December 23, 1983, p. 3.

[60] Galante, "Clash Courses," p. 7.

[61] See T. Levitt, "The Globalization of Markets," *Harvard Business Review,* May–June 1983, pp. 92–102; F. Simon-Miller, "World Marketing"; J. Sheth, "Global Markets or Global Competition?"; P. Kotler, "Global Standardization"; and Y. Wind, "The Myth of Globalization," all in *Journal of Consumer Marketing,* Spring 1986; J. U. Farley, "Are There Truly International Products?", *Journal of Advertising*

Research, October/November 1986, pp. 17–20; and J. A. Quelch and E. J. Hoff, "Customizing Global Marketing," *Harvard Business Review,* May/June 1986, pp. 59–68.

[62] R. T. Green, W. H. Cunningham, and I. C. M. Cunningham, "The Effectiveness of Standardized Global Advertising," *Journal of Advertising,* Summer 1975, pp. 25–29; and N. Giges, "Bergin's Job: Coke Consistency," *Advertising Age,* August 18, 1980, pp. 1, 62.

[63] D. Chase and E. Bacot, "Levi Zipping Up World Image," *Advertising Age,* September 14, 1981, pp. 34, 36. See also T. Keane, "How GE Medical Systems Coordinate Sophisticated International Promotion," *Business Marketing,* October 1983, pp. 118–20; and J. A. Lawton, "Kodak Penetrates the European Copier Market," *Marketing News,* August 3, 1984, pp. 1, 6.

[64] M. Colvin, R. Heeler, and J. Thorpe, "Developing International Advertising Strategy," *Journal of Marketing,* Fall 1980, pp. 73–79.

[65] See E. Kaynak and L. A. Mitchell, "Analysis of Marketing Strategies Used in Diverse Cultures," *Journal of Advertising Research,* June 1981, pp. 25–32.

[66] See J. Hornik and S. C. Rubinow, "Expert-Respondents' Synthesis for International Advertising Research," *Journal of Advertising Research,* June 1981, pp. 9, 16; and S. P. Douglas and C. S. Craig, *International Marketing Research* (Englewood Cliffs, N.J.: Prentice-Hall, 1983).

[67] G. W. Lane and G. L. Watson, "A Canadian Replication of Mason Haire's 'Shopping List' Study," *Journal of the Academy of Marketing Science,* Winter 1975, pp. 48–59.

[68] R. G. Wyckham, "Spending Attitudes of Consumers: Pilot Studies in French and English Canada," *Journal of the Academy of Marketing Science,* Winter 1975, pp. 109–18.

[69] C. M. Schaninger, J. C. Bourgeois, and W. C. Buss, "French-English Canadian Subcultural Consumption Differences," *Journal of Marketing,* Spring 1985, pp. 82–92.

[70] For details on dealing with this problem, see R. D. Tamilia, "Cultural Market Segmentation in a Bilingual and Bicultural Setting," *European Journal of Marketing,* 4th Quarter 1981, pp. 223–31.

[71] N. W. McGuinness and B. Little, "The Influence of Product Characteristics on the Export Performance of New Industrial Products," *Journal of Marketing,* Spring 1981, pp. 110–22; and J. S. Hill and R. R. Still, "Adapting Products to LDC Tastes," *Harvard Business Review,* March/April 1984, pp. 92–101.

[72] R. Alsop, "Efficacy of Global Ad Projects Is Questioned in Firm's Survey," *The Wall Street Journal,* September 13, 1984, p. 29.

[73] M. O'Reilly, "Argentina Economy Ravages Ad Climate," *Advertising Age,* September 28, 1981, p. 68.

[74] S. Donner, "Capullo Labeled Too Aggressive," *Advertising Age,* August 14, 1978, p. 54.

[75] J. J. Boddewyn, "The Global Spread of Advertising Regulation," *MSU Business Topics,* Spring 1981, pp. 5–13; J. J. Boddewyn, "Advertising Regulation in the 1980s: The Underlying Global Forces," *Journal of Marketing,* Winter 1982, pp. 27–35; and J. K. Ryans, Jr., S. Samiee, and J. Wills, "Consumerist Movement and Advertising Regulation in the International Environment," *European Journal of Marketing,* no. 1 (1985), pp. 5–11.

[76] Donner, "Coke Launches Samson Nutritional Drink in Mexico," *Advertising Age,* August 14, 1978, p. 57.

[77] See C. S. Madden, M. J. Caballero, and S. Matsukubo, "Analysis of Information Content in U.S. and Japanese Magazine Advertising," *Journal of Advertising,* no. 3 (1986), pp. 38–45; and J. W. Hong, A. Muderrisoglu, and G. M. Zinkhan, "Cultural Differences and Advertising Expression," *Journal of Advertising,* no. 1 (1987), pp. 55–62.

[78] M. Tharp, "Getting Oriented," *The Wall Street Journal,* March 9, 1977, p. 1.

[79] R. W. Belk and Zhou, "Learning to Want Things," in *Advances in Consumer Research XIV,* ed. M. Wallendorf and P. Anderson (Provo: Association for Consumer Research, 1987), pp. 478–81; N. Dholakia and J. F. Sherry, Jr., "Marketing and Development" in *Research in Marketing IX,* ed. J. N. Sheth (Greenwich, Conn.: JAI Press, 1987), pp. 119–43; and R. W. Belk, "Variations in Consumer Wants Across Times and Cultures," in *Proceedings of the 1988 Winter AMA Educators' Conference* (forthcoming).

[80] Examples of successful strategies can be found in H. D. Manjies, "Westinghouse Takes Aim at the World," *Fortune,* January 14, 1980, pp. 48–53; G. D. Harrell and R. O. Kiefer, "Multinational Strategic Market Portfolios," *MSU Business Topics,* Winter 1981, pp. 5–15; "Bud is Making a Splash in the Overseas Beer Market," *Business Week,* October 22, 1984, pp. 52–53; and R. DeRose, "The Critical Communication Link-Up in Global Marketing," *Journal of Consumer Marketing,* Summer 1984, pp. 81–9.

CHAPTER

3 The Changing American Society

Until recently, the prevailing stereotype of an automobile purchase involved a male making the purchase alone. If accompanied by his wife or girlfriend, she only offered suggestions concerning color and interior features.

Today, research indicates that women influence 80 percent of all automobile purchases and are the predominant buyers of many models including Nissan Pulsars, Cadillac Cimarrons, Toyota SR5s, Pontiac Fieros, and Ford Escort EXPs. Marketers who have clung to the outdated stereotype by either ignoring women purchasers or by focusing on excessively "feminine" themes have lost substantial sales opportunities. For example, one of Chevrolet's first ads aimed at women backfired because it contained limited product feature information but showed lots of pinks and lavenders. Likewise, Chrysler failed with a model named "La Femme" that was designed for the stereotyped woman of yesterday.

Cars have traditionally been designed by and for males. Although surveys consistently indicate that women want the same basic features in a car as males, there are subtle differences. For example, many automobiles have radios, heaters, and other accessories that are difficult to operate with long fingernails. Likewise, women find unrealistic role portrayals in automobile advertising offensive and are frequently frustrated in their attempts to deal with dealer sales personnel who don't treat them seriously.[1]

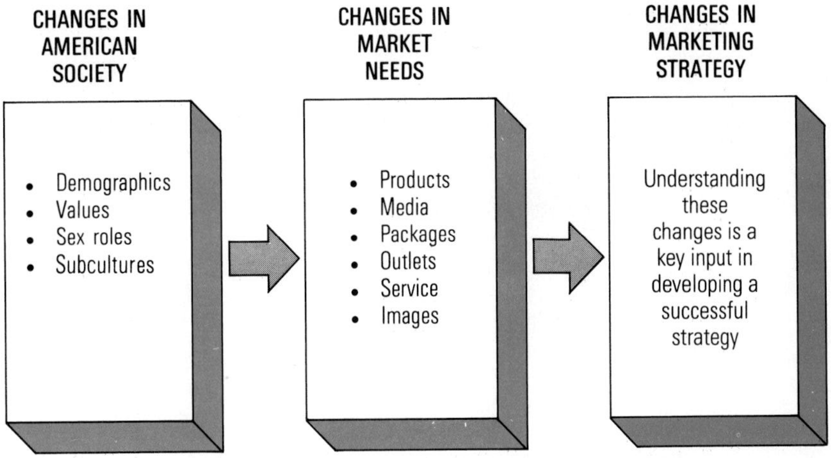

In the previous chapter, we discussed how variations in values influenced consumption patterns across cultures. As the opening example illustrates, changes in key American values are producing changes in our consumption patterns as well. We begin this chapter with a discussion of American values and how their evolution is affecting consumer behavior and thus marketing strategy.

Other forces are also evolving and influencing our society. We will examine two of the additional forces—demographics and subcultures—in the balance of this chapter.

CHANGING AMERICAN VALUES

> The great currents of history are rarely depicted in media headlines. Headlines record the behavioral eruptions that reflect the deeper forces at work in the core of the national psyche. Examining the hidden forces is not as exciting as watching the visible explosions, but it is essential to understanding the problem and seeking its solution.[2]
>
> Indeed, so far-ranging are these changes that each time I encounter them a recurring image comes to mind, the image of the earth moving deep beneath the surface and so transforming the landscape that it loses its comfortable familiarity.[3]

These statements make two major points. First, observable shifts in behavior, including consumption behavior, often reflect underlying shifts in values. Second, it is necessary to understand the underlying *value shifts* in order to deal effectively with current and future behavior. Exhibit 3–1 illustrates how advertisements are often based on a society's values.

Figure 3–1 presents our estimate of how American values are changing. These

Focus on Security

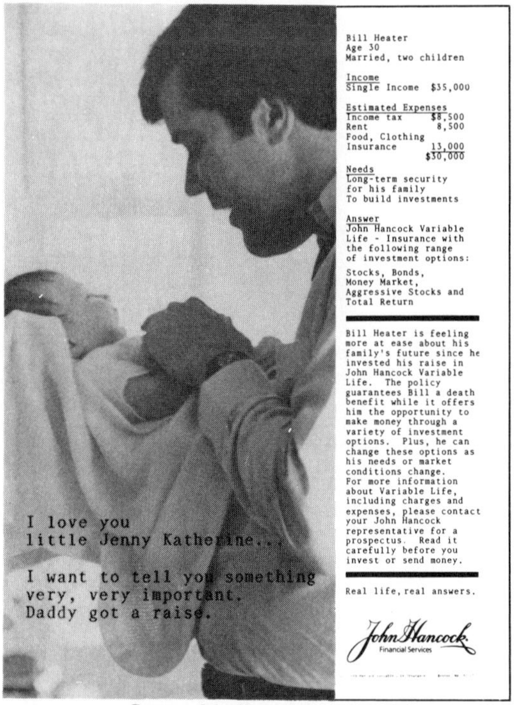

Bill Heater
Age 30
Married, two children
Income
Single Income $35,000
Estimated Expenses
Income tax $8,500
Rent 8,500
Food, Clothing
Insurance 13,000
$30,000
Needs
Long-term security
for his family
To build investments
Answer
John Hancock Variable Life - Insurance with the following range of investment options:
Stocks, Bonds, Money Market, Aggressive Stocks and Total Return
Bill Heater is feeling more at ease about his family's future since he invested his raise in John Hancock Variable Life. The policy guarantees Bill a death benefit while it offers him the opportunity to make money through a variety of investment options. Plus, he can change these options as his needs or market conditions change.
For more information about Variable Life, including charges and expenses, please contact your John Hancock representative for a prospectus. Read it carefully before you invest or send money.
Real life, real answers.
John Hancock
Financial Services
I love you
little Jenny Katherine...
I want to tell you something
very, very important.
Daddy got a raise.

Courtesy John Hancock Variable Life Insurance Co.

Focus on Performance

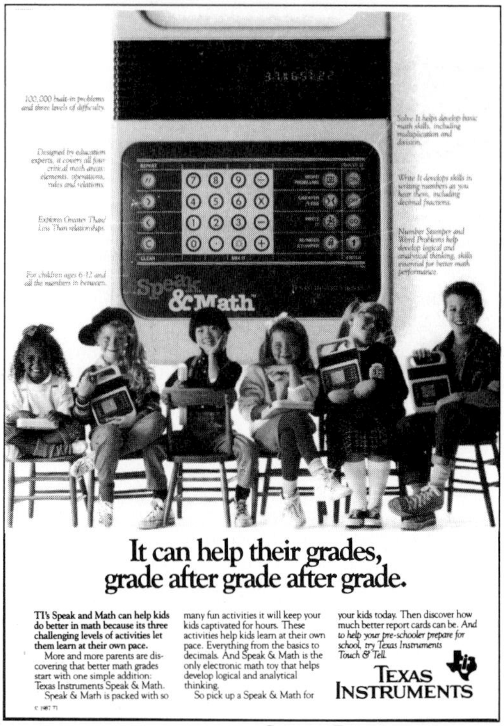

Speak & Math
It can help their grades,
grade after grade after grade.
TI's Speak and Math can help kids do better in math because its three challenging levels of activities let them learn at their own pace.
More and more parents are discovering that better math grades start with one simple addition: Texas Instruments Speak & Math.
Speak & Math is packed with so many fun activities it will keep your kids captivated for hours. These activities help kids learn at their own pace. Everything from the basics to decimals. And Speak & Math is the only electronic math toy that helps develop logical and analytical thinking.
So pick up a Speak & Math for your kids today. Then discover how much better report cards can be. And to help your pre-schooler prepare for school, try Texas Instruments Touch & Tell.

Courtesy Texas Instruments Inc.

Focus on Individual Orientation

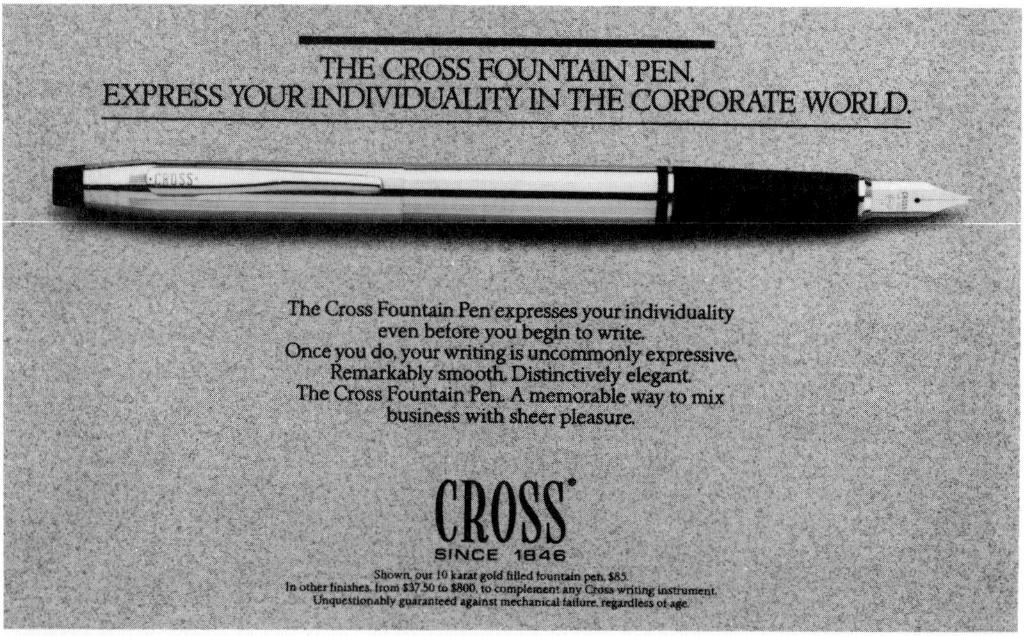

THE CROSS FOUNTAIN PEN.
EXPRESS YOUR INDIVIDUALITY IN THE CORPORATE WORLD.
The Cross Fountain Pen expresses your individuality even before you begin to write.
Once you do, your writing is uncommonly expressive.
Remarkably smooth. Distinctively elegant.
The Cross Fountain Pen. A memorable way to mix business with sheer pleasure.
CROSS®
SINCE 1846
Shown, our 10 karat gold filled fountain pen, $85.
In other finishes, from $37.50 to $800, to complement any Cross writing instrument.
Unquestionably guaranteed against mechanical failure, regardless of age.

Courtesy A.T. Cross

Figure 3–1
Traditional, Current, and Emerging American Values

Self-Oriented

Active	ECT							Passive
Material	T	CE						Nonmaterial
Hard work	T	E				C		Leisure
Postponed gratification	T					E	C	Immediate gratification
Sensual gratification		C		E			T	Abstinence
Humorous		ECT						Serious

Environment-Oriented

Maximum cleanliness		TCE						Minimum cleanliness
Performance	T	E	C					Status
Tradition					E	C	T	Change
Risk taking	T	E		C				Security
Problem solving	T	CE						Fatalistic
Admire nature				E C			T	Overcome nature

Other-Oriented

Individual	T	E	C					Collective
Romantic			T	CE				Nonromantic
Adult			T	E	C			Child
Competition	T	CE						Cooperation
Youth	T			C		E		Age
Masculine	T	C	E					Feminine

T = Traditional
E = Emerging
C = Current

are the same values used to describe different cultures in Chapter 2. The estimates provided are based upon our subjective interpretation of background material examined. Therefore, we must emphasize that Figure 3–1 represents the opinions of the authors. You should feel free to challenge these judgments.

Self-Oriented Values

Self-oriented values exhibiting the biggest change include values related to hard work and gratification. Although less than in the past, there is substantial evidence that hard work is still highly valued by most Americans. A 1983 survey of 2,000 Americans found that over 75 percent associated hard work with success, and more than half categorized themselves as success oriented.[4] However, less than one fourth of the same respondents agreed with the statement "work is the center of my life," while 60 percent agreed that "self-fulfillment can only be achieved within myself, not through work."

Although the evidence is mixed, it appears that the shift to immediate gratification is reversing.[5] This reversal may reflect recent economic conditions. However, it appears to be associated with a general shift toward our traditional value structure.

Figure 3–2 reflects this trend with respect to the use of credit and various types of savings programs. The effect of the consumer plans shown in the figure will extend far beyond financial institutions. A noticeable retreat from the use of consumer credit would have an immediate, negative impact on the sales of most consumer goods. Manufacturers, as well as retailers, must be prepared to cope with this trend.

Figure 3–2
Savings and Credit Plans Reflect a Shift toward Postponed Gratification

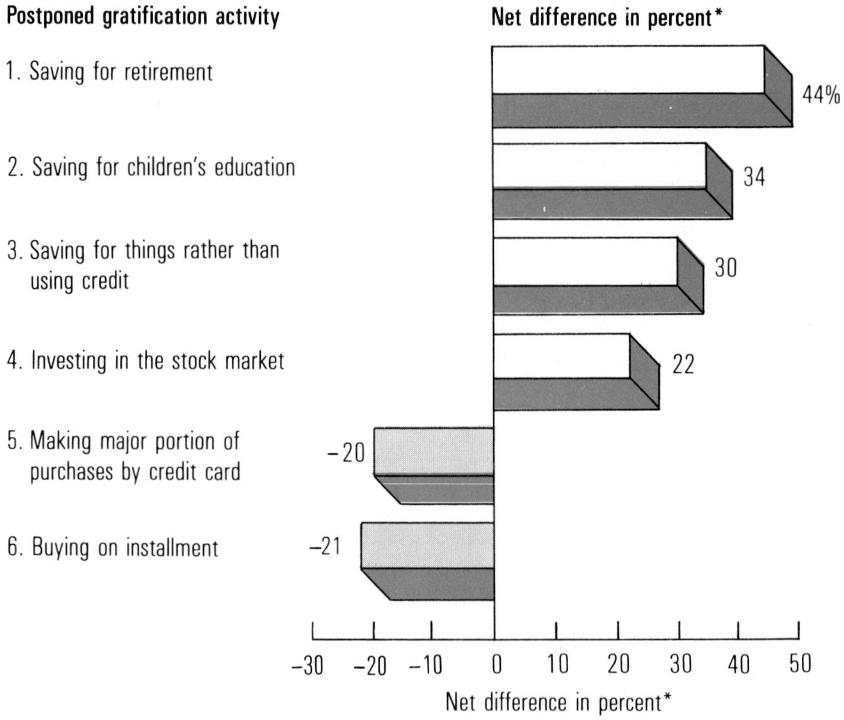

*Difference between those who plan to start or increase and those who plan to stop or decrease.

Source: "Increase in Optimism Accompanied by Focus on Self-Improvement," *Soundings*, April 1984, p. 2.

A value similar to immediate versus postponed gratification is sensual gratification versus abstinence. Traditionally, the American culture prescribed that not only should one postpone gratification, but also one should abstain from those activities that delight the senses—eating, drinking, sex, and other activities that provide sensual bodily pleasure. Our culture has historically considered these as relatively sinful, especially when done in excess (excess being defined as anything beyond minimum requirements). Over time, particularly during the 1960s and 1970s, this value changed. It became quite acceptable to do things simply because they "felt good." While it appears that this value is now shifting back in the more traditional direction,[6] people still find acceptable products that allow for and, in fact, encourage sensual gratification, as well as advertising themes that emphasize sensual gratification and a focus on serving oneself.[7]

Environment-Oriented Values

Environment-oriented values prescribe a society's relationship with its economic, technical, and physical environments. Americans have traditionally admired cleanliness, change, performance, risk taking, problem solving, and the conquest of nature. While this cluster of values remains basically intact, there are some significant shifts occurring.

Our risk-taking orientation seems to have changed somewhat over time. There is an increasing emphasis on security. Perhaps this is because many of the risks we took for granted have become too large, with consequences too critical. Recent near-miss accidents involving nuclear power plants, experiences with a "stagflation" economy, and an extended recession reinforced this trend for security. Despite this shift, risk taking remains prominent and appears to be regaining popularity as we look to entrepreneurs for economic growth.

Traditionally, nature has been viewed as an obstacle. We have attempted to bend nature to our wants and desires. We have felt that we should reshape nature to make for a more perfect world. However, this orientation has shifted. Now we are more prone to admire nature, to coexist with it, and to learn from it. This shift affects us as marketers and consumers in many ways. For example, packaging materials have changed in response to this value shift. Biodegradable material is in higher demand and returnable packages are frequently desired. Natural foods and cosmetics are increasingly popular.

Other-Oriented Values

Other-oriented values reflect a society's view of the appropriate relationships between individuals and groups within that society. Historically, America was an individualistic, competitive, romantic, masculine, youth, and parent-oriented society. As we will see, several aspects of this orientation are undergoing change.

Children have always played an important role in our society and have been

Exhibit 3–2 Child-Centered Advertising

Courtesy American Motors Corporation

and received more prestige and importance. In the 20th century this changed and the child became more and more the focus of the family unit. Exhibit 3–2 illustrates how one marketer has used this value orientation.

Traditionally, age has been highly valued in almost all cultures. Older people were considered wiser than young people and were, therefore, looked to as

Exhibit 3–3 Levi's Approach to the Middle-Age Market

Levi's Womenswear Division will spend $6 million on a TV and print campaign for its Bend Over line aimed at women 35 to 64. The campaign describes the female shown in the ads as "old enough to know what she wants and young enough to get it." The magazine ads feature sketches of mature women (in at least one case realistically rendered with a slight paunch) commenting on the style and comfort of the line.

The Menswear Division is approaching the older male market with a campaign utilizing mature models on Monday Night Football. One theme is, "The comfort you loved as a boy, the fit you need as a man."

Source: "Levi's Targets Older Market," *Advertising Age,* June 8, 1981, p. 102; and J. Dance, "Business Doesn't Send Cards but It Still Remembers Birthdays," *Knight-Ridder Newspapers,* October 13, 1981.

models and leaders. This has never been true in American culture, probably because it required characteristics such as physical strength, stamina, youthful vigor, and imagination to transform a wilderness into a new type of producing nation. This value on youth continued as we became an industrial nation. Since World War II, it has increased to such an extent that products such as cars, clothing, cosmetics, and hairstyles seem designed for and sold only to the young!

However, there is a slow reversal of this currently held value on youth. Because of their increasing numbers and disposable income, older citizens have developed political and economic clout and are beginning to use it. Retirement communities excluding younger people are being developed in large numbers. Cosmetics, medicines, and hair care products are being marketed specifically to older consumers. Middle-aged consumers will soon constitute the largest single market segment, and this segment will most likely develop and maintain lifestyles distinct from the youth market. For example, a survey conducted for a major retail chain found that the "person in the middle" group (aged 29–40) had developed clothing preferences independent of and different from those of younger consumers.[8] Exhibit 3–3 describes Levi's attempt to reach the middle-aged market. Note that these attempts are *not* based on the premise that middle-aged persons desire to emulate youth.

American society, like most others, has reflected a very masculine orientation for a long time. This chapter's opening story indicates how radically this orientation is changing. The marketing implications resulting from changes in this value are so vast that the next section of this chapter is devoted to this topic.

SEX ROLES IN AMERICAN SOCIETY

The behaviors considered appropriate for males and females have undergone massive changes over the past 20 years. The general nature of this shift has been

Exhibit 3–4 Attitude Segments among Married Males

1. **CLASSIC (25 percent).** View themselves as sharing decisions with their wives but feel they have the final say on most issues. Do not approve of women working. Tend to be in all but the lowest income groups, all occupation groups, and older than average.
2. **NEW BREED (32 percent).** View marriage as a shared responsibility. Support their wives working for noneconomic reasons. Tend to be somewhat younger than average and in all income and education groups.
3. **RETIRED (16 percent).** Independent of age, they have withdrawn from many aspects of life. Remote from their families, they do not view themselves as the strong head of the family, though they feel that "a woman's place is in the home." Tend to be older with low income and lower status occupations.
4. **BACHELOR HUSBAND (15 percent).** Place less importance on their families but view themselves as having the final say in family matters. Very supportive of a wife working, but also demand that she fulfill the traditional role. Tend to be younger, fairly well educated, and in all income and occupation groups.
5. **STRUGGLING (12 percent).** View themselves as running a tight ship at home, demanding a neat, clean house in which they have the final say. Prefer a traditional role for women. Tend to be middle-aged, in blue-collar occupations, and having a difficult time financially.

HOUSEHOLD BEHAVIORS OF THE SEGMENTS

Behavior	Total United States	Classic	New Breed	Retired	Bachelor	Strug-gling
Prepare complete meals	45%	38%	61%	27%	51%	32%
Prepare one or more meals per week	22	14	37	13	24	10
Wife pays bills	50	54	45	42	45	71
Do many household tasks	26	22	36	22	24	13
Do major shopping with wife	63	66	64	64	55	61
Help prepare shopping list	27	17	38	33	15	22
Buy brands wife wants	24	24	23	34	11	23

Source: Adapted from *Husbands as Homemakers—II* (Cunningham & Walsh, 1980).

for behaviors previously considered appropriate primarily for men to be acceptable for women, too.

Sex roles are *ascribed roles*. An ascribed role is based on *an attribute over which the individual has little or no control*. This can be contrasted with *achievement roles* which are based on *performance criteria over which the individual has some degree of control*. Individuals can, within limits, select their occupational roles (achievement roles), but they cannot influence their sexual category (ascribed role).

Researchers categorize women into traditional or modern orientations based on their preference for one or the other of two contrasting lifestyles:

> *Traditional:* A marriage with the husband assuming the responsibility for providing for the family, and the wife running the house and taking care of the children.
> *Modern:* A marriage where husband and wife share responsibilities for both—each works and shares homemaking and child responsibilities.[9]

In a 1975 nationwide survey, 45 percent of the female respondents expressed a preference for a traditional lifestyle, while 54 percent opted for a modern orientation.[10] A 1980 study found 65 percent of the women (and 62 percent of the men) preferring the modern lifestyle. This preference was highest (74 percent) among the youngest respondents (age 14–20), and lowest among those over 65 (54 percent).[11]

Another survey found that approximately 80 percent of both males and females approved of a woman working, "even if she has a husband who is capable of supporting her." However, the same survey found over 70 percent of both sexes agreeing that a "woman with young children should not work outside the home."[12] Similarly, studies consistently find that many men resent and resist spending time on household chores, though this is changing.[13]

Thus, we find a pattern typical of a changing value: growing acceptance of the value, but not for all aspects of it, and substantial resistance to the new behaviors from the more traditional groups. Exhibit 3–4 describes five segments of adult males based on their attitude/behavior toward sex roles. Clearly, acceptance of the modern value is not even across segments. We are now going to examine some of the marketing implications of this value shift.

Market Segmentation. Neither the women's nor the men's market is as homogeneous as it once was. Exhibit 3–4 illustrates various male market segments in relationship to sex roles. At least four significant female market segments exist:

1. *Traditional Housewife:* Generally married. Prefers to stay at home. Very home- and family-centered. Desires to please husband and/or children. Seeks satisfaction and meaning from household and family maintenance as well as volunteer activities. Experiences strong pressures to work outside the home and is well aware of foregone income opportunity. Feels supported by family and is generally content with role.

2. *Trapped Housewife:* Generally married. Would prefer to work, but stays at home due to small children, lack of outside opportunities, or family pressure. Seeks satisfaction and meaning outside the home. Does not enjoy most household chores. Has mixed feelings about current status and is concerned about lost opportunities.
3. *Trapped Working Woman:* Married or single. Would prefer to stay at home, but works for economic necessity or social/family pressure. Does not derive satisfaction or meaning from employment. Enjoys most household activities, but is frustrated by lack of time. Feels conflict about her role, particularly if younger children are home. Resents missed opportunities for family, volunteer, and social activities. Is proud of financial contribution to family.
4. *Career Working Woman:* Married or single. Prefers to work. Derives satisfaction and meaning from employment rather than, or in addition to, home and family. Experiences some conflict over her role if younger children are at home, but is generally content. Views home maintenance as a necessary evil. Feels pressed for time.

While the above descriptions are oversimplified, they indicate the diverse nature of the adult female population. Clearly, a single brand positioning strategy for a household cleaner that would appeal to all four segments would be difficult to achieve.

Product Strategy. Many products are losing their traditional sex typing. Liqueurs, cars, cigarettes, motorcycles, and many other once-masculine products are now being designed with the woman in mind. However, this is not to suggest a desire for a "unisex" world by either males or females. For example, males tend to prefer masculine brand names for their brands while females prefer feminine brand names.[14] Being "attractive" remains important for both traditional and modern women.[15]

Working women, and modern women in general, are taking a more active approach to leisure. Competitive sports, once primarily a male domain, are rapidly gaining popularity with women. This has opened substantial new markets for a wide variety of products ranging from sports bras to special magazines.

The workwife with a full-time job has a minimum of 40 hours a week less time to devote to household chores and other activities than does a nonworking wife. Shifting chores to the children and husband still detracts from the total "free" time available to the family unit. Therefore, to workwife families, convenience is a critical variable, often more important than price. For example, Heinz found it necessary to reposition its line of prepared gravies to appeal specifically to working women since homemakers would not accept its convenience orientation.[16] Chef Boyardee appears to be positioning its frozen foods particularly for the trapped workwife segment as it stresses convenience and family approval:

How, you might wonder, can a woman spend all day at work and still make her family a dinner that looks like she spent all day working in the kitchen?

It's easy. With some help from Chef Boyardee.

The latest Barbie doll clearly reflects the changing role of women. Introduced with the theme, "We girls can do anything, right, Barbie?" Home & Office Barbie represents the working woman. The new Barbie has a calculator, business card, credit card, newspaper, and business magazines. A dollhouse-like accessory package provides an office desk with a personal computer terminal. However, her business suit is a feminine pink with white accents.

Marketing Communications. As sex roles have changed, both males and females have been increasingly fragmented into segments that require different communications strategies. Exhibit 3–5 provides Doyle Dane Bernbach's approach to creating ads showing men using household products. It appears that their approach to appealing to males would also work with the career working woman and the trapped housewife segments, but not with the traditional housewife or trapped working women segments.

Venkatesh found major differences in advertising perceptions and preferences between traditional and feminist market segments. For example, only 10 percent of the traditional women agreed that "I would like to see boys playing with dolls just the way girls do." In contrast, 66 percent of the feminists agreed with this view.[17] Clearly, communicating with one group without offending the other is a difficult task.[18] The problem is partially alleviated because of differing media

Exhibit 3–5 Doyle Dane Bernbach's Approach to Portraying Males Using Household Products

The advertising of household products to husbands is appropriate because many men are now engaged in such tasks. However, it is important to keep in mind that most men, while they do some housework, resent having to do it. Therefore, the houseworking husband should be shown as a no-nonsense person knocking off a job because it has to be done. The pleasure is in the completion of the task, not in the act of doing it.

The husband should not be shown as doing the wife a favor by helping her out. While this might appeal to the husband, it may well alienate the wife. As more and more women pursue careers, they will expect the sharing of household tasks as a right and obligation, not as a favor on the part of their mates.

Source: Adapted from "Males Don't Like New Women: DDB," *Advertising Age*, October 20, 1980, p. 60.

Exhibit 3–6

American Express's Strategy to Penetrate the Female Market

The American Express "Do you know me?" campaign is one of the most popular and successful advertising campaigns of the past 10 years. Successful, that is, in terms of male response. However, it has not been successful in the female market.

The company has been wooing women for years. A magazine ad in the early 1970s showed a cigar-smoking man, described as a "former male chauvinist pig," saying: "It's time women got their own American Express card and started taking me to dinner." More women (actress Barbara Feldon, conductor Sara Caldwell) were shown in "Do you know me?" commercials.

Such efforts have accomplished little. American Express estimates that its 2.5 million female cardholders represent only about 20 percent of the women that meet its financial, occupational, and lifestyle criteria.

Marketing research revealed that while women were familiar with American Express and laudatory about it, they didn't see the American Express card as something for them. The sort of prestige promoted in "Do you know me?" ads appealed mostly to men.

Ogilvy & Mather, the company's ad agency, was assigned to write ads geared to women. The result is a campaign that is running in 16 national women's magazines and on TV in seven cities that make up about one fourth of the U.S. population. Although "Do you know me?" continues to dominate the advertising there, it is accompanied by a campaign that does away with celebrities.

Instead, the TV commercials feature confident, independent women using their American Express cards. In one ad, a briefcase-toting woman takes her husband to dinner to celebrate her first American Express card. In another, a mother—her marital status undisclosed—trades wisecracks with her kids in a restaurant. A third ad shows a young woman in a bookstore playfully fending off a flirtatious man. The American Express card, a female announcer says in each spot, is "part of a lot of interesting lives."

That slogan also is carried in all the print ads. All other copy has been eliminated. One shows a woman cross-country skiing, her infant in a carrier on her front. Another features a dress-for-success woman leaving a sporting goods shop, carrying her briefcase in one hand and a lacrosse stick in the other.

In cities where the commercials have been shown, American Express has found the number of women who say they feel the company is interested in them has nearly tripled. The number who plan to apply for a card has doubled.

Source: B. Abrams, "American Express Is Gearing New Ad Campaign to Women," *The Wall Street Journal,* August 4, 1983, p. 23.

preferences. However, both groups respond negatively to advertisements portraying women in insulting ways.[19]

Exhibit 3–6 illustrates a dual campaign strategy with one set of ads appealing primarily to males and the other to modern-oriented females.

Retail Strategy. Males have different expectations and needs in terms of retail outlets. As they become increasingly involved in shopping for groceries, children's clothes, and so forth, store layout, advertising, product assortments, and sales force training will need to be adapted to the needs of the male shopper. Many supermarkets have responded as follows:

> Supers have increased space devoted to specialty departments particularly appealing to men, such as automotive supplies, hardware, and gardening equipment. Another lure for the male shopper is later store hours. Many men interviewed said they hated crowds and preferred shopping at odd hours to avoid congested stores.[20]

Not only husbands, but also children, are becoming more involved in household activities. A recent survey found that over a third of all teenagers shop once a week or more for *family* food in supermarkets. These teenagers spend 15 percent of the family food budget and make both product and brand decisions.[21] Their preferences must also be accommodated.

Conclusions on America's Value Structure

Our discussion of American values has focused on "mainstream," middle-American values. We must reemphasize that the many groups that make up American society hold these values to differing degrees. Subcultures such as religious, ethnic, and nationality groups may differ dramatically from the larger society with respect to individual values.

For the past 35 years, America's values have been shifting away from their traditional foundations. This trend accelerated during the 1960s and 1970s. However, it now appears that the pendulum has begun to swing the other way.

DEMOGRAPHICS

Just as our value structure is changing, so are our demographics. Demographics are used to describe a population in terms of its size, structure, and distribution. *Size* means the number of individuals in a population, while *structure* describes the population in terms of age, income, education, and occupation. Naturally, the size and income associated with a certain age-group of the U.S. population (say 25 to 34) will directly affect the market demand for products commonly consumed by individuals in that age-group. *Distribution* of the population describes the location of individuals in terms of geographic region and rural, urban,

- *Clearasil* has traditionally had a single focus on the acne problems of teens. In July 1984, they introduced Clearasil Adult Care which is targeted at the skin problems in the growing adult market. Peter Wilston, marketing vice president of skin care products, explains, "We're following the baby boomers up."*

Courtesy Richardson-Vick, Inc.

- *Coca-Cola* thinks that diet brands could account for half of the $20 billion soft drink market by1990 when baby boomers are over 28. That would be almost three times today's market demand for diet soft drinks. This trend has influenced Coca-Cola's need for more diet brands as it competes for this growing market.†
- *Fisher-Price* estimates that by 1990 more than 8 million babies will be crawling around, an increase of 11 percent from 1983. Within this market, Fisher-Price found mothers especially interested in clothing that will enable children to dress themselves at an earlier age. To capitalize on this consumer research, Fisher-Price has introduced a line of children's clothing that is advertised as "The Children's Clothing Mothers Helped Design."‡
- *General Foods's* efforts to serve the growing market for decaffeinated coffee involves two brands of decaffeinated coffee. Sanka is positioned mainly for older coffee drinkers. Brim, the other GF decaffeinated brand, is positioned for the younger consumer.§

*"What the Baby Boomers Will Buy Next," *Fortune*, October 15, 1984, p. 30.

†Ibid., p. 30.

‡*The Wall Street Journal*, August 2, 1984, p. 23.

§"Coffee and Tea Cup Runneth Under," *Marketing & Media Decisions*, October 1983, p. 182.

or suburban location. Each of these factors influences the behavior of consumers and contributes to the overall demand for various products and services.

As Exhibit 3–7 illustrates, demographics play an important role in market demand, segmentation, and marketing mix decisions.[22] In this section we examine:

- Changes in size, distribution, and age of the American population.
- Changes in income characteristics of the population.
- Changes in educational attainment of the population.
- Changes in occupational distribution of the population.[23]

Population Size

As shown in Figure 3–3, the size of the U.S. population has grown steadily and is projected to continue growing in the immediate future. This continued and steady growth allowed some industries to survive and others to grow. For example, coffee consumption has declined steadily from 3.5 cups per day in the 1960s to an average of less than 1.5 cups. However, the addition of over 50 million people during this period enabled the industry to maintain its total sales.

Thus, population growth can have dramatic effects on an industry. If the growth of the U.S. population slows or stops, many industries will face stable

Figure 3–3
U.S. Population: 1950–2000

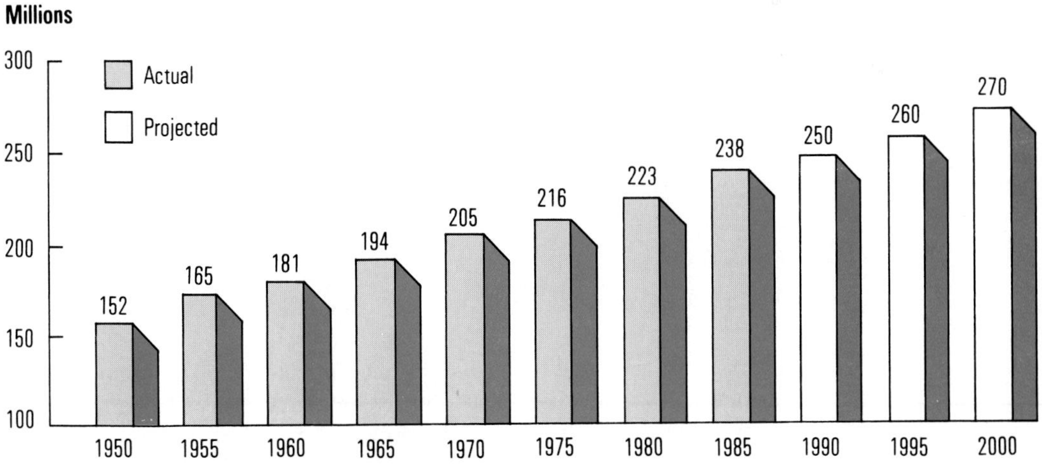

Source: *Current Population Reports: Population Estimates and Projections,* U.S. Bureau of the Census, Series P–25 (1984).

or declining demand. This could lead to the failure of firms, increased diversification, a more competitive environment, and increased emphasis on export sales.

Age Structure

"Age is a powerful determinant of consumer behavior. A person's age affects his or her interests, tastes, purchasing ability, political preferences, and invest-

Exhibit 3–8 Positioning to Serve Two Demographic Segments

	Teen Market	Mature Market
Product feature stressed	Cleansing capabilities	Moisturizing properties
Celebrity spokeswoman	Mariel Hemingway	Meredith Baxter Birney
Typical print medium	*Teen* magazine	*Cosmopolitan*

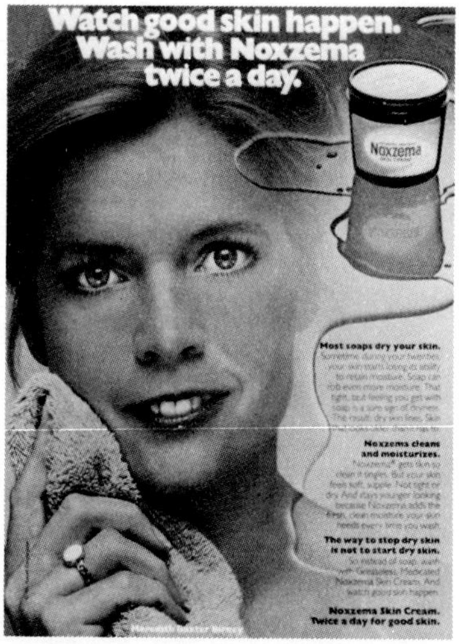

Noxzema discovered that the market for their product could be segmented demographically. They found that younger women and teens had a greater need for cleansing capabilities, while women in their thirties and forties wanted moisturizing capabilities. Because the product offered both attributes, it became a matter of positioning Noxzema differently in each segment to better serve the needs of each.

ment behavior."[24] Age has been found to affect the consumption of products ranging from beer and bourbon to toilet paper.[25] Demographic trends that will be of key concern to marketers throughout the rest of the 20th century include:

- A slight baby boom in the 1980s, followed by a baby bust in the 1990s.
- A drastic decrease in the percentage of teenagers and young adults.
- Fewer people in their 50s and early 60s, but a significant increase in affluent, well-educated, middle-aged Americans.

Thus, the age structure of a population impacts on the demand for certain products and the marketing strategies most appropriate for those products. Exhibit 3–8 illustrates how Noxzema developed two distinct marketing strategies to serve two age-groups with the same product.

In Figure 3–4, we can see how the U.S. population will be structured across age-groups in 1990. This structure has several important marketing implications. First, the largest segments of our population will be in age-groups under 14 and from 45 to 64. This means that demand for products consumed by individuals in these age-groups will be large compared to the demand for products consumed by other groups.

As important to marketers as the *size* of the various age groups are *changes* in the size of the groups over time. Exhibit 3–9 shows the changes predicted to occur in the various age groups between 1990 and 2000. The exhibit also lists some of the more obvious implications of these changes. As can be seen, rapid growth is predicted for one of the most affluent age groups in our society. This has major implications for many businesses.

Figure 3–4
Age Structure of the U.S. Population: 1990

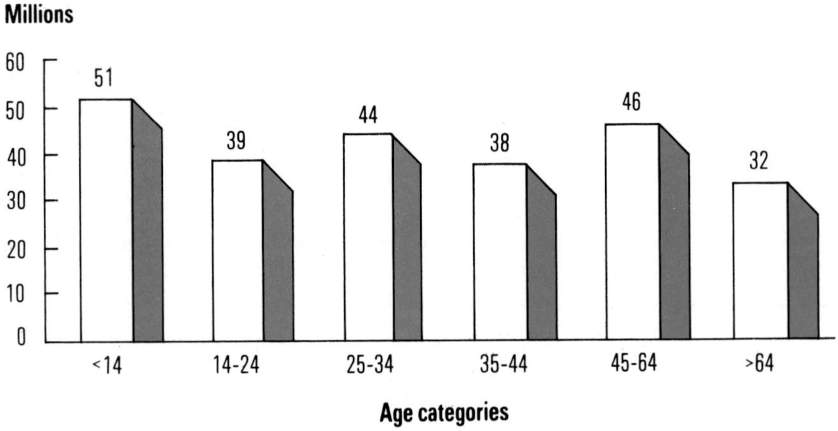

Exhibit 3–9 Changes in Population Age and Market Demand

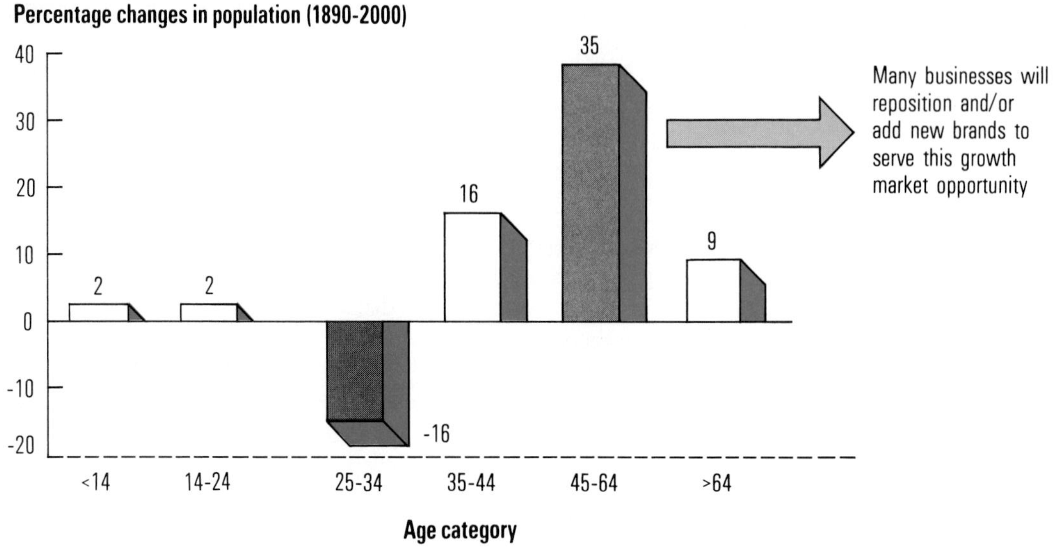

MARKETING IMPLICATIONS FOR 1990 TO 2000

- Demand for youth-based products such as toys, bicycles, and breakfast cereals will slow.
- Demand for first-time purchases of household durables, stereos, and some models of automobiles will drop as population in the 25-to-34 age-group drops by 7 million (16%).
- Products predominantly consumed by individuals in the 35-to-44 age-group will increase by 16 percent.
- The biggest market opportunity will be for goods sold to those in the 45-to-64 age-group. Leisure products, vacation packages, and health-oriented products should experience increased demand.
- Finally, a 9 percent growth in the population over 64 will increase demand for health-related medicines and leisure-time products and services that cater to those over 64.

Source: *Current Population Reports: Population Estimates and Projections*, U.S. Bureau of the Census, Series P–25 (1984).

In our society, we attach a high value to youth and, as shown in Figure 3–5, most people over 30 perceive themselves to be younger than they actually are. As we get older, the number of years we perceive ourselves to be younger than our actual age increases. This has tremendous importance in the positioning of products for various age-groups. For example, a product targeted at the 50-

Figure 3–5
Perceived Age versus Actual Age

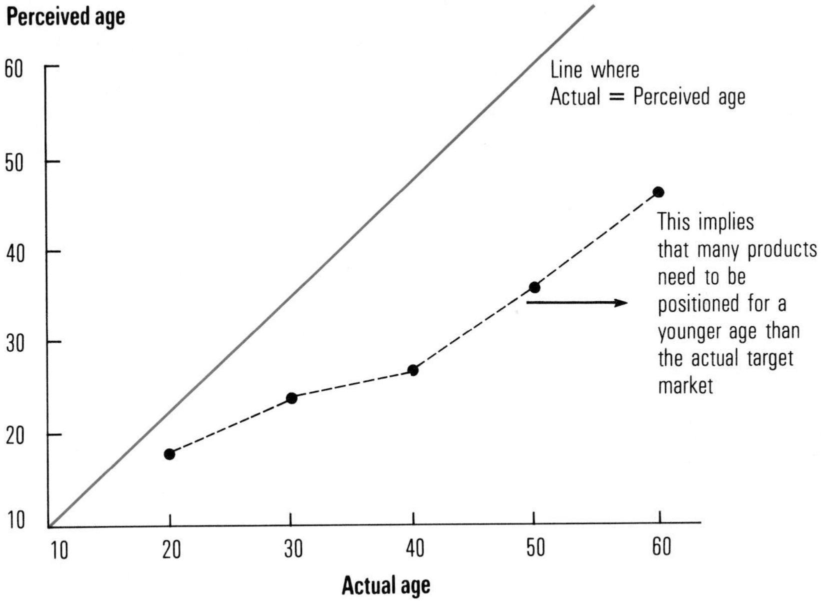

Source: L. Underhill and F. Caldwell, "What Age Do You Feel: Age Perception Study," *Journal of Consumer Marketing*, Summer 1983, p. 19.

to-60 age-group would be more successful if portrayed in terms of *the age people in this group feel,* rather than their actual age.

Population Distribution

In addition to growth of a population, it is important for marketers to know where this growth is likely to take place. For example, Florida is predicted to grow in population 79 percent from 1980 to 2000.[26] This creates a tremendous marketing opportunity for those who understand the needs of people likely to make up this population growth. Likewise, California and Texas are expected to grow in population while New York will decrease.

However, the size and growth of a regional population must be combined with regional consumption patterns when developing a regional marketing program. As shown below, consumption patterns and marketing strategies vary widely across regions.

- Anheuser-Busch developed separate marketing strategies for different regions of Texas. In the North they positioned with a strong western cowboy image, while in the South they positioned with a strong Hispanic identity. Market share rose from 23 percent to 37 percent. They have begun to apply the same approach in other regions.[27]

- When Campbell Soup's pork and beans did not sell well in the Southwest, they cut out the pork and added some chili pepper and ranchero beans. Sales increased from virtually nothing to 75,000 cases in the Southwest. In a similar way, a Campbell's subsidiary developed Zesty Pickles for consumers in the Northeast who like sourer pickles than most Americans.[28]
- General Foods is creating a fresh-prepared dinner line to compete against restaurants and gourmet takeouts. While improved quality and freshness are key features of the product, the brand will be tailored to regional tastes as GF rolls out this new product line.[29]

Income

While population plays a major role in both the overall and localized demand for products and services, income plays an equally important role for many products and services. For example, even the consumption of such "stable" items as margarine, detergents, and shampoo is affected by income level. Changes in disposable income (income after taxes) can be directly linked to changes in market demand for many durable products and nonessential services. For ex-

Figure 3–6
Household Incomes: 1980–1995

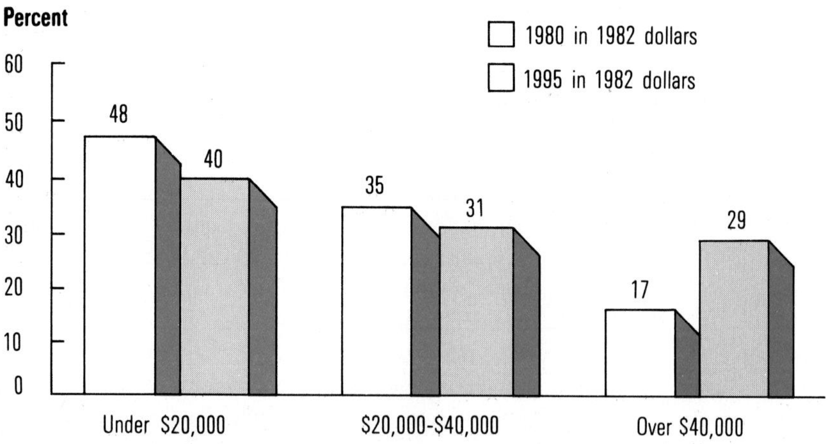

Source: Adapted from "Households and Income in 1995," *American Demographics*, April 1984.

ample, the total demand for housing, automobiles, and recreational equipment will drop when disposable income drops independent of population growth. As a result, long-run trends and short-range changes in income are extremely important to the market demand for many products and services.

As shown in Figure 3–6, disposable income is expected to grow in the 1980s and early 1990s. By 1995, 43 percent of the population will have household incomes of $30,000 and over.[30] This increased buying power will directly affect purchases of an assortment of durable and nondurable products.

Exhibit 3–10 Using the Buying Power Index to Estimate Market Demand

Trading Area	Population (millions)	Buying Income (billions)	Retail Sales (billions)	Buying Power Index (percent)	BPI Economy Priced Products	BPI Moderate Priced Products	BPI Premium Priced Products
Cincinnati, Ohio	1.41	13.60	6.62	0.61%	0.57%	0.59%	0.61%
Austin, Tex.	.59	5.82	3.26	0.27	0.27	0.26	0.27
Orlando, Fla.	.86	9.98	4.16	0.36	0.35	0.37	0.30
Chicago, Ill.	6.03	64.20	29.34	2.80	2.23	2.35	3.13
Denver, Colo.	1.54	16.93	8.64	0.75	0.64	0.72	0.83
San Francisco, Calif.	1.50	19.32	9.33	0.83	0.67	0.71	0.92
Phoenix, Ariz.	1.65	15.40	7.63	0.71	0.71	0.75	0.74
Little Rock, Ark.	.49	4.31	2.45	0.21	0.21	0.23	0.21
New York, N.Y.	8.12	83.36	30.61	3.45	3.20	3.24	3.86

Source: 1983 Survey of Buying Power, *Sales & Marketing Management*, 1983.

BUYING POWER INDEX (BPI) AND MARKET DEMAND

The Buying Power Index is an index for a given trading area based on size of population, buying income, and retail sales. The BPI for Cincinnati, Ohio, is 0.614 percent. This means that we would expect 0.00614 of the total demand for a product to occur in Cincinnati.

PRICE INFLUENCE ON MARKET DEMAND

Because some trading areas are more sensitive to price and quality differences, the Buying Power Index is also computed for products sold in three price categories—economy, moderate, and premium. Note that in Orlando, Florida, the BPI is highest for economy-priced products (0.350%) and lowest for premium-priced products (0.308%). In San Francisco, the BPI is highest for premium-priced products (0.92%).

Income, like population, is distributed across regions of the United States as well as across metropolitan and rural areas within regions. The combination of an area's population, income, and value of retail purchases is used to create what is called a "buying-power index." Each year a buying-power index is computed by *Sales and Marketing Management* magazine for each state, major metropolitan areas within that state, and each county or township in the state. This is very useful in estimating the market demand for an area and is often used in allocating sales force efforts and advertising expenditures to market areas. Because this is a useful index that is sensitive to population, income, and buying behavior, we have provided an example of how it can be used in Exhibit 3–10.

Occupation

The number of white-collar workers grew three times faster than the number of blue-collar workers over the past 25 years. And within the white-collar segment, professionals and technicians grew approximately 130 percent, from 8 million in the early sixties to 18 million in the eighties. Because our occupation influences

Figure 3–7
Changing Education Level of U.S. Population

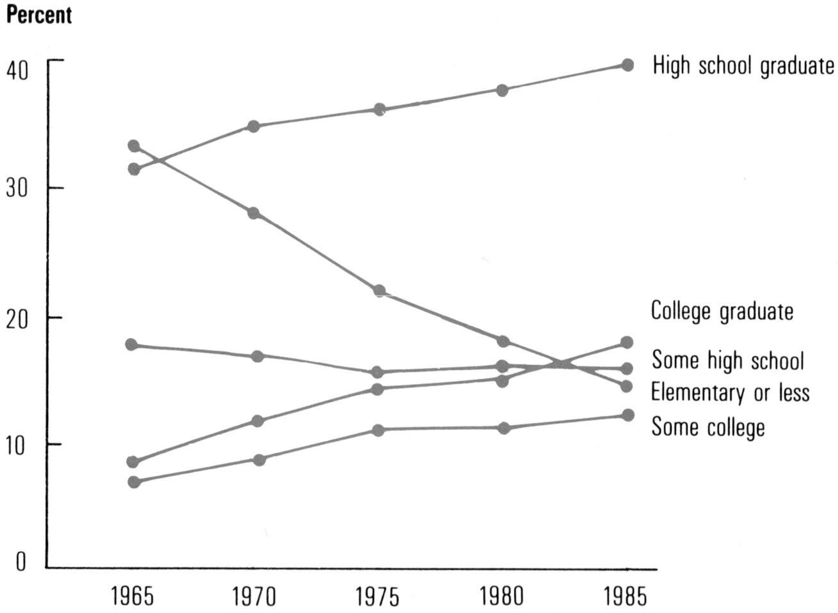

Source: Adapted from F. Linden, "From Here to 1985," *Across the Board,* September 1977.

the clothes we wear, cars we drive, and foods we eat, products that serve the white-collar worker have experienced greater growth in demand than those targeted at the blue-collar worker.

Differences in consumption between occupational classes have been found for products such as beer, cake mixes, soft drinks, detergents, dog food, shampoo, hair spray, and paper towels.[31] These implications are discussed in depth in the next chapter.

Education

Like income, the level of education in the United States continues to rise. As Figure 3–7 shows, the percentage of the population age 25 and over completing high school and college is going up, while the percentage with some high school or elementary or less education is decreasing.

As education levels increase, we can expect to see many changes in preference to occur in the demand for beverages, automobiles, media (print versus electronic), and home computers. Marketers will have to recognize the education level of target markets to effectively reach and communicate with them.

SUBCULTURES

The U.S. population has numerous subcultures. We will describe three: blacks, Hispanics, and senior citizens. As shown in Figure 3–8, each of these subcultures is significant in size and is projected to have continued growth. The important point, however, is not their size but the fact that they often have distinct needs. It is to these needs that marketers must be sensitive in order to best serve the interests of these consumer segments.

A subculture is a segment of a culture that shares distinguishing patterns of behavior. There are two important features in this definition. First is the emphasis that needs to be placed on *distinguishing patterns of behavior*. For a group to constitute a subculture, its members must share behaviors that *differ* from those of the larger or dominant culture of a society. Thus, a group unique in skin color, religion, or nationality will constitute a subculture only if they have distinctly different behavior patterns.

A second important point is that members of a subculture are *also members of the larger culture*. As illustrated in Figure 3–9, members of a subculture generally have more behaviors that coincide with those of the larger culture than behaviors that differ from it. In fact, our society is composed of a vast number of subcultures, and an individual may exist simultaneously in more than one subculture. For example, older (65 years and over) blacks would belong to both the black subculture and a subculture characterized by age (senior citizens).

Figure 3–8
Size and Growth of Major U.S. Subcultures

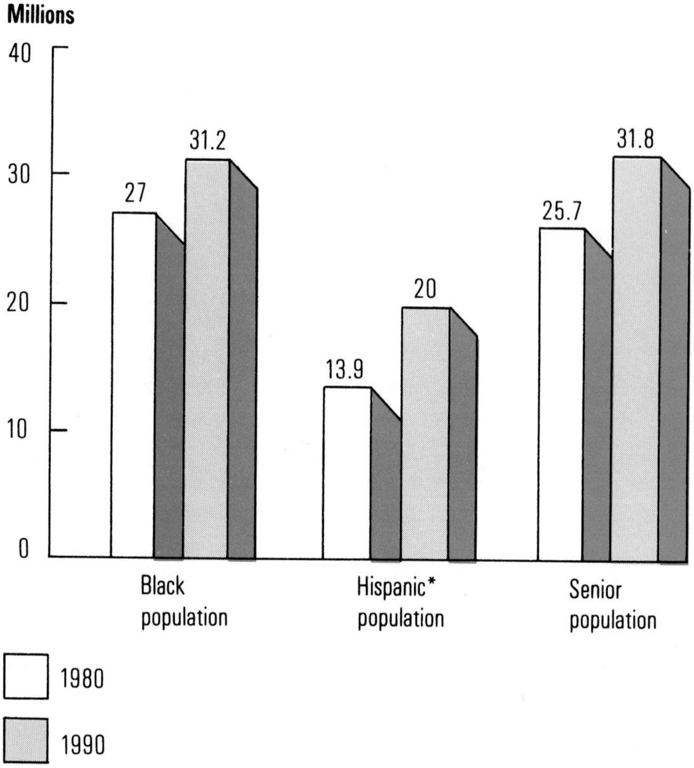

*Does not include illegal aliens.

Marketers are interested in subcultures to the extent that they can serve their unique needs. For example, Norelco has a rotary razor called the "Black Pro Tripleheader," a specially engineered razor for the shaving problems encountered by black males.

Thus, if the needs or behaviors of a group, such as the shaving needs of black males, differ from those of the general population, a marketing opportunity exists. If the members of a subculture, no matter how distinct from the dominant culture, do not differ in their needs and behaviors associated with a particular product area, the subculture does not require recognition as a separate group or market segment. In addition, to serve any subculture with a specific marketing program requires that the subculture be sufficiently large to enable the marketing program to operate at an acceptable level of profitability (or effectiveness for nonprofit organizations).

Figure 3–9
Subcultures Share Many of the Behaviors of the Dominant Culture While Also Having a Set of Unique Behaviors

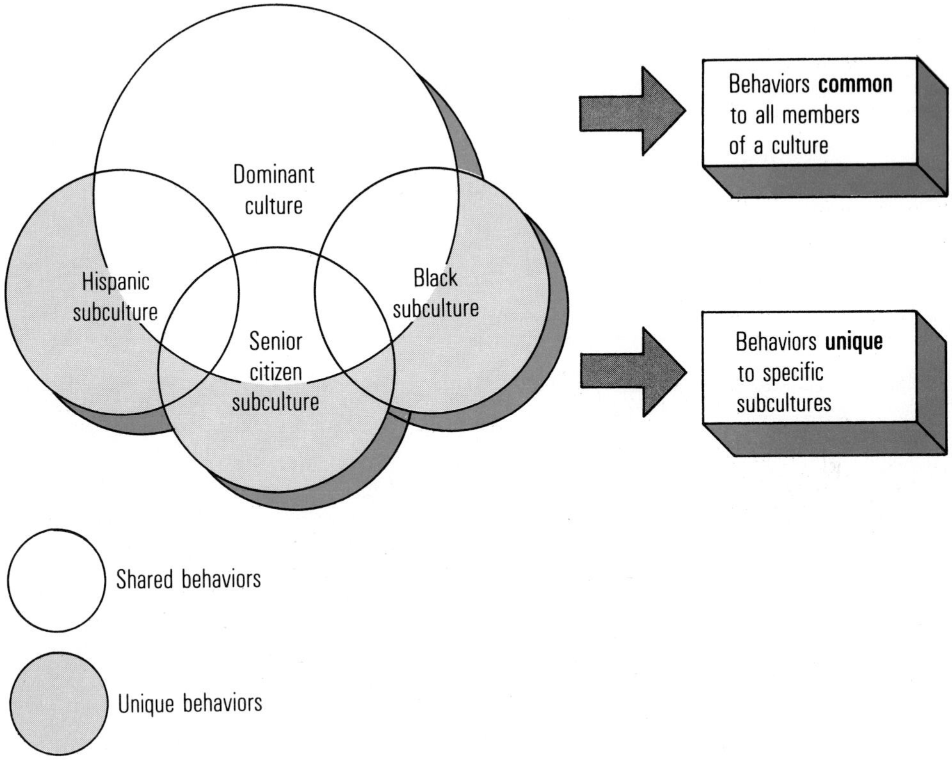

Subcultures Based on Race

Major subcultures based on race in the United States include blacks, Orientals, and American Indians. Because the black subculture is the largest of these, we will focus our discussion on this group. Before starting, it should be emphasized that the black subculture is not a homogeneous group, any more than is the white subculture.[32]

Black demographics, product needs, and media usage are often distinct and as a result, product positioning and market communications strategies must also be different. For example, the director of marketing for cosmetics at Johnson Products points out:

> Product innovations in the cosmetics area for many years ignored the needs of the black female. Such products as moisturizing lipstick and eye makeup were generally not marketed in shades appropriate for darker skin tones. In response, Johnson Products revamped its UltraSheen Cosmetics

> line to include products targeted at the more fashion-conscious black female (over 30% of black females).[33]

While some products need to be created or modified to meet unique needs of blacks, others require only positioning as appropriate for blacks as well as whites. Exhibit 3–11 illustrates both approaches.

An example of repositioning is Liquid Brown Sugar. Liquid Brown Sugar was introduced in late 1977 by the Amstar Corporation, based on the assumption that consumers disliked the hardened lumps in granulated brown sugar. Amstar fully expected consumers to switch to a lumpless liquid product. The firm spent more than $1 million to introduce the product but consumers did little more than sample it.

Exhibit 3–11 Product Formulation and Product Positioning for the Black Market

Courtesy M&M Products Company

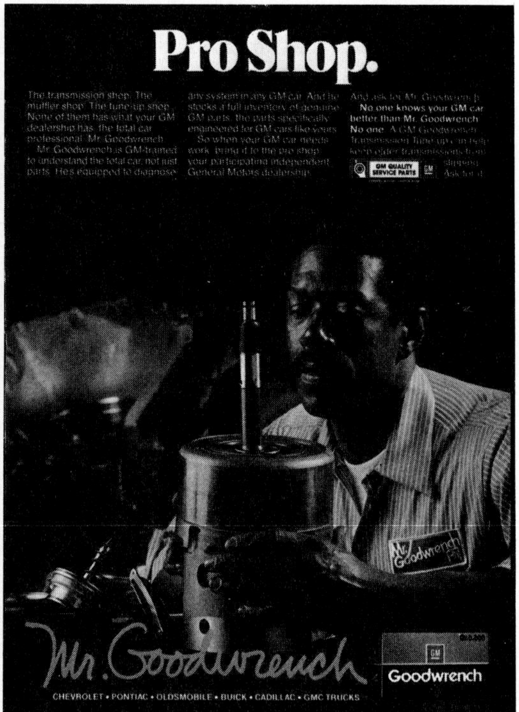

Reprinted with permission from General Motors Corporation, April 1988

Product Design

Product attributes are formulated specifically for blacks' hair characteristics.

Product Positioning

The product is unchanged but is promoted as appropriate for blacks as well as whites.

Amstar's consumer research revealed that the general population used Liquid Brown Sugar only for dishes associated with liquids, such as barbeque sauce and baked beans. Black consumers had a much wider range in using Liquid Brown Sugar, and 20 percent of its black consumers used it as a tabletop sweetener. Their research also showed that 12 percent of all blacks were using Liquid Brown Sugar without the product ever having been advertised specifically to blacks. Of the 12 percent, 20 percent were heavy users, using one or more bottles per household per month.

Amstar's new strategy is to reposition Liquid Brown Sugar and target it at black consumers. According to the product manager, "We're going to give Liquid Brown Sugar a black identity and a black identity only." The new black targeting involves heavy TV advertising featuring black actors using the product in a variety of dishes.[34]

Blacks prefer to read black magazines such as *Ebony, Essence,* and *Jet,* but can also be reached with more general magazine publications such as *Good Housekeeping* and *Sports Illustrated.* With respect to radio, blacks prefer black-oriented radio stations and listen to AM radio more than whites.[35] Black households account for 10 percent of the televisions and 15 percent of TV viewing. However, it is black females who watch considerably more hours of television per week than white females, as there is no difference in the amount of television watched between black and white males.

Subcultures Based on Nationality

Nationality forms a basis for a subculture when members of that nationality group identify with it and base at least some of their behaviors on the norms of the national group. In the United States, Mexican-Americans, Puerto Ricans, Scandinavians, Italians, Poles, Irish, Japanese, and Chinese constitute important nationality subcultures. This subcultural influence tends to be strongest in cases where a significant number of the group members are geographically grouped together, such as Chinese in Chinatown in San Francisco, the Mexican population in the southwestern states (Arizona, California, Colorado, New Mexico, and Texas), and Cuban and Puerto Rican populations located in Florida and New York.

Each of these subcultures has unique traditions and behaviors that are a potential influence on product preferences and consumption behavior. Therefore, marketers can often find opportunities to serve their unique needs. Because the Hispanic subculture is the largest of this type of subculture (14 million in 1980 and growing toward 20 million in 1990), we will examine a few of its unique features. However, we must keep in mind that like the black subculture, the Hispanic subculture is heterogeneous with multiple subgroups.[36]

Hispanic Subculture. While the size of the Hispanic subculture was reported to be 15 million in 1984, another 8 million illegal alien Hispanics are also estimated to live in the United States. In 1980, the buying power of this subculture was $53 billion. By 1990, it is predicted to be over $150 billion. This purchasing power, combined with the unique characteristics of this group, creates substantial opportunities for alert marketers.

As a group, the Hispanic subculture differs from the white in several demographic areas. In comparison to whites, Hispanics have lower incomes, are more likely to live in cities, have less education, have larger families, and are less likely to be white-collar workers. These kinds of differences create different expectations and purchasing power and thus a different pattern of behavior. For example, Hispanics compared to the U.S. population are more brand loyal, buy popular brands, and are less likely to think store brands are better than nationally advertised brands.[37]

However, the most unique feature of the Hispanic subculture is its use of the Spanish language. It is an enduring characteristic of the subculture and has many subtle variations.[38] Twenty-three percent of Hispanics speak *only* Spanish, and another 20 percent speak Spanish and just enough English to get by.[39] This requires that marketers targeting programs at this segment first give special attention to both the importance of the Spanish language and subtle differences created by this language. This is a difficult task since the language varies somewhat between the various Hispanic groups. Exhibit 3–12 outlines several classic blunders that occurred when marketers did not pay attention to the translated meaning of their advertising copy.

Less obvious than the language difference that exists between many Hispanics and whites are differences in values. A study of Hispanic values revealed that compared to whites, Hispanics are:

> Less active in problem-solving style; less dynamic, less technological, and more internal; more family centered; less complex in "cognitive structures"; more cooperative in interpersonal activities; more fatalistic and pessimistic in outlook on life; and more present-time oriented.[40]

Exhibit 3–12 Hispanic Positioning Requires Careful Understanding of Translated Ad Copy

- Frank Perdue's chicken slogan, "It Takes a Tough Man to Make a Tender Chicken," was directly translated and read, "It Takes a Sexually Excited Man to Make a Chick Affectionate."
- Budweiser's slogan ended up being, "The Queen of Beers," while another brand was "Filling; Less Delicious."
- A candy marketer wanted to print a statement on its package, bragging about its 50 years in the business. When a tilde did not appear over the appropriate "n," the package claimed it contained 50 anuses.
- One food company's burrito became *burrada,* a colloquialism for "big mistake."

Source: "Marketing to Hispanics," *Advertising Age,* February 8, 1987, p. S–23.

Obviously, these subtle differences must also be recognized along with differences in language, demographics, and product preferences when marketing to the Hispanic market. Outlined below are the experiences of several firms targeting marketing programs at the Hispanic subculture.[41]

- Pepsi-Cola has overtaken Coca-Cola among Hispanics in Florida by using Hispanic backgrounds in its ads.
- After 10 months of targeting the Hispanic population, Scott Paper found its brand preference among targeted Hispanics rose from 15 percent (prior to advertising) to 40 percent.
- Sears, Roebuck appeals to Hispanics by portraying family closeness. In a baby furniture advertisement, Sears uses two ads. . . . The ad targeted at the non-Hispanic population shows a husband and wife picking out the furniture, while the Hispanic ad includes not only the expectant couple, but teenage daughter and grandparents.
- Coors beer targets the non-Hispanic population with "Come to the High Country," which presents the good life of skiing in Colorado. Hispanics are targeted with "Another Cold One, Another Coors."

Exhibit 3–13 illustrates other marketing efforts aimed at this subculture.

Subcultures Based on Age

The senior citizen market is a subculture that exists because of a discernible age difference. While age alone is not important, people in this age-group typically take on unique behaviors and lifestyles that directly impact their preference for and consumption of products.

There are 61 million people in the United States age 50 and over, and the number over 65 for the first time exceeds the number of teenagers. This segment, whose annual discretionary income is $100 billion, will double in number over the next 40 years. Senior citizens own 43 percent of all domestic cars and control nearly 80 percent of all assets in savings and loan institutions. However, it is important to recognize that there are subsegments within this subculture, as shown below:

- *PRERETIREMENT SEGMENT (50–64)*. This group consists of the most active and affluent consumers of this subculture. Most are still working and many are in their peak earning years.
- *EARLY RETIREES (65–74)*. Also an active group, but with more time to engage in activities such as travel, continuing education, hobbies, sports, physical fitness, and volunteer work.
- *LESS ACTIVE (75 and up)*. This group is more likely to need health-care products and service. Its members are independent but less active

Exhibit 3–13 Marketing Efforts Directed at a Hispanic Market

OUTDOOR BILLBOARD

This McDonald's outdoor billboard was created for Hispanic neighborhoods in order to deliver McDonald's familiar message ("Nobody can do it like McDonald's can") in a language familiar to Hispanic consumers.

Source: Reprinted with permission from "Outdoor Gets Boost in Minority Market," *Advertising Age,* April 7, 1980, pp. 5–8. Copyright 1980 by Crain Communications, Inc.

TV SPOTS

Pepsi-Cola initially ran into trouble when translating its campaign "Catch that Pepsi Spirit" into Spanish. According to Pepsi's ad agency manager, "You can't use that slogan in the Spanish market because the spirit relates to something dead." Instead, the agency came up with "Pepsi Saluda!" in a series of TV spots (shown below) featuring neighborhood bodegas (grocery stores) and their owners.

Source: "Flavors of Spanish," *Advertising Age,* April 6, 1981, p. S–18. Copyright 1981 by Crain Communications, Inc.

Exhibit 3–13 *(concluded)*

DIRECT MAIL COUPONS

Shown below are Viceroy cigarette and Tylenol coupons in Spanish that were mailed to 6 million Hispanic households.

Source: "Donnelly to Mail Spanish-Language Coupons to Two Million Upscale Hispanic Households," *Marketing News,* February 20, 1981, p. 1.

than younger consumers over 50. However, this is the fastest growing 50-and-over segment, and by the year 2000 they will represent half of this subculture.[42]

In general, this segment of our population has less household income, has smaller households, shops at fewer grocery stores, spends more time shopping, has further to travel to shop, is less likely to shop for groceries after 5 P.M., and is more likely to read store ads, use coupons, and pay with cash. This group represents a significant new market opportunity as described below:

> More companies need to recognize that older people aren't saving their money the way they once did to leave behind a big inheritance. Market researchers estimate that consumers over 55 account for more than $400 billion of income annually and have about twice the discretionary funds of people under 35.[43]

Exhibit 3–14 Periodical Targeted at the Upscale Senior Citizen

50 Plus is a magazine targeted at the older consumer. It provides access to this growing segment of the American population. Some unique characteristics of this readership are described below:

- 44 percent of readers have incomes above national average.
- 88 percent own their homes; 71 percent have savings accounts; 56 percent own corporate stocks and bonds.
- 90 percent will travel within the United States this year; 15 percent, to Canada; 12 percent, to Europe; 8 percent, to the Carribbean.
- 84 percent carry American Express or MasterCard; 79 percent, VISA; 49 percent use traveler's checks.
- 70 percent buy wine regularly; 60 percent take vitamins; 82 percent buy cosmetics.
- 54 percent own instant cameras; 34 percent own 35 mm cameras; 25 percent own movie cameras and projectors.

In addition to products targeted at this group, several product and service innovations have begun to evolve. For example:

- Roman Meal Company introduced the half loaf (10 to 12 slices instead of 22 to 24) to better serve smaller size households.
- Selchow & Right Co. brought out a version of the game *Scrabble* with letter tiles 50 percent larger than normal.
- Sears formed a club called the Mature Outlook which offers discounts to people over 55.
- Johnson & Johnson introduced a special shampoo for people over 40.

The media habits of senior citizens are also quite different. Older consumers watch about 60 percent more television than younger Americans and 25 percent more than those who are middle-aged; they spend more time reading newspapers, but listen to the radio less often than people under 65.

Specialized magazines such as *50 Plus* target their circulation at the older segment of our population. As shown in Exhibit 3–14, *50 Plus* reaches a fairly upscale segment of the older population, allowing certain marketers an important channel for communications directed at this segment. For example, Ralston Purina places coupons for Bran Chex in magazines aimed at older consumers since older consumers are more likely to consume bran cereals.

SUMMARY

American society is described in part by its demographic makeup, which includes a population's size, distribution, and structure. The structure of a population refers to the population's demographics based on gender, age, income, education, and occupation. Because individuals differ in their needs and preferences for products that fulfill their needs, population demographics have been and continue to be important variables in market segmentation and the management of marketing programs.

Population demographics, however, are not static. At present, the rate of population growth is slowing, average age is increasing, southern and western regions are growing, movement out of urban to suburban areas is slowing, and the work force contains more women and white-collar workers than ever before. These changes must be recognized by marketers to best serve existing markets and new market segments that may evolve with the changing demographics of a population.

A subculture is a segment of a culture that shares distinguishing patterns of behavior. Because unique needs and preferences often exist within subcultures, marketers of many products may find marketing opportunities in serving their specialized needs and preferences. Members of subcultures are also members of the broader culture, which means that, though they differ in some behaviors, most behaviors coincide with the predominant culture.

Though we often identify a subculture on the basis of race, nationality, or religion, other subcultures exist on the basis of age, geographic location, gender, and social class. Marketing managers are interested in subcultures only to the extent that subcultures influence the consumption process for their products.

American society has changed in its value orientation and will continue to change as new values emerge. In terms of those values that influence an individual's relationship with *others,* Americans are slightly less individualistic than in the past. We have substantially less of a masculine orientation now than in the past. We also place a greater value on older persons and on cooperation. Families appear to be returning to a parent-centered orientation.

Values that affect our relationship to our *environment* have become somewhat less performance oriented and less oriented toward change and risk taking. There is more of a tendency to coexist with nature.

Self-oriented values have also undergone change. In particular, hard work is regaining respect as an end in itself. We also place slightly less emphasis on sensual gratification and we are more content to delay our rewards than in the recent past.

One aspect of American society that has undergone dramatic change in the past 10 years is the role of women. Roles are prescribed patterns of behavior expected of a person in a situation. *Sex roles* are *ascribed roles* based on the sex of the individual rather than on characteristics the individual can control. In contrast, an *achievement role* is acquired based on performance over which an individual does have some degree of control.

Because sex roles are changing in American society, marketers must understand how they affect preferences for their products and the marketing programs they develop to market those products. The emergence of the workwife and her role in American society has created new needs, product and store preferences, and attitudes that marketers must understand to serve target markets in contemporary American society.

REVIEW QUESTIONS

1. What are *demographics?*
2. What trend(s) characterizes the size of the American population?
3. What trend(s) characterizes the geographic distribution of the American population?
4. What trend(s) characterizes the age distribution of the American population?
5. Why is *population growth* an important concept for marketers?
6. What trend(s) characterizes the level and distribution of income in the United States?
7. What trend(s) characterizes the level of education in the United States?
8. What trend(s) characterizes the occupational structure of the United States?
9. What is a *subculture?* When are subcultures important to marketing managers?
10. How does black product usage differ from white product usage?

11. How does black media usage differ from white media usage?
12. How do overall Hispanic demographics differ from white demographics?
13. How do the demographics of consumers 65 and over differ from those under 65? What kinds of opportunities and problems are created when serving the over-65 consumer?
14. Are subcultures homogeneous? Give an example to support your answer.
15. What is a *cultural value*? Are cultural values shared by all members of a culture?
16. Do American cultural values provide explicit guides to specific behaviors? Explain.
17. What is meant by *other-, environment-,* and *self-oriented values?*
18. Describe the current American culture in terms of the following values:
    a. Individual/Collective.
    b. Performance/Status.
    c. Tradition/Change.
    d. Masculine/Feminine.
    e. Competition/Cooperation.
    f. Youth/Age.
    g. Active/Passive.
    h. Material/Nonmaterial.
    i. Hard work/Leisure.
    j. Risk taking/Security.
    k. Problem solving/Fatalistic.
    l. Admire nature/Overcome nature.
    m. Adult/Child.
    n. Postponed gratification/ Immediate gratification.
    o. Sensual gratification/ Abstinence.
    p. Humorous/Serious.
    q. Romantic/Nonromantic.
    r. Cleanliness.
19. How does an *ascribed role* differ from an *achievement role*?
20. What is a *sex role?*
21. What is happening to male and female sex roles?
22. Are housewives a homogeneous group with respect to future work plans, spending patterns, and so forth? Explain your answer.
23. What are some of the major marketing implications of the changing role of women?

DISCUSSION QUESTIONS

1. Which demographic shifts, if any, do you feel will have a noticeable impact on the market for ________ in the next 10 years? Justify your answer.
    a. Soft drinks.
    b. Compact disc players.
    c. Blood donations.
    d. Television viewing.
    e. Mouthwash.
    f. Art.
2. Examine each of the major subcultures described in this chapter. Do any of them constitute a unique market segment for ________? Justify your answer.

a. Soft drinks.
b. Compact disc players.
c. Blood donations.
d. Television viewing.
e. Mouthwash.
f. Art.

3. Given the shift in population shown in Exhibit 3–9, name five product areas that will face increasing demand and five that will face declining demand.
4. What are five specific marketing implications of differences in the rate of state population growth?
5. Will the increasing median age of our population affect the general "tone" of our society? In what ways?
6. Discuss the marketing strategy used by Noxzema to market its product to two different age-groups. Would it have been wiser to develop a new name and formula for the teen market rather than try to serve two segments with one product?
7. Use the buying power index in Exhibit 3–10 to compute the expected 1990 wine consumption of San Francisco. Assume that U.S. consumption in 1990 was 550 million gallons.
8. Referring to question 7, assume wine is a premium-priced product. How would you change your estimate of wine market demand for the San Francisco area?
9. Referring to senior citizens as a subculture, list five characteristics they have in common with the main culture and five characteristics unique to senior citizens.
10. Discuss the positioning of Liquid Brown Sugar in the black market. What other strategies are possible? What is the best strategy?
11. How should differences in values held by Hispanics be utilized in developing ad copy for a vacation ad targeted at this group?
12. Describe one or more unique consumption patterns associated with a religious subculture with which you are familiar.
13. If you have lived in a different region of the country, describe some of the variations in consumption patterns between that region and the region you are currently in.
14. How will the projected household income changes affect the market and appropriate marketing strategies for vacations, bicycles, and toothpaste?
15. What marketing strategy implications are there based on the relationship between perceived and actual age shown in Figure 3–5?
16. Which values are most relevant to the purchase and use of a __________? Are they currently favorable or unfavorable for __________ ownership? Are they shifting at all? If so, is the shift in a favorable or unfavorable direction?

    a. Blood donation.
    b. Compact disc player.
    c. Toothpaste.
    d. Diet soft drink.
    e. Foreign travel.
    f. Luxury watch.

17. In what way, if any, can the current shifts in sex roles be used to develop marketing strategy for __________?

a. Blood donations.
b. Toothpaste.
c. Automobiles.
d. Furniture stores.
e. Fast food outlets.
f. Television programs.

18. Describe additional values you feel could (or should) be added to Figure 3–1. Describe the marketing implications of each.
19. Pick the three values you feel the authors were most inaccurate about in describing the *current* American values. Justify your answer.
20. Pick the three values you feel the authors were most inaccurate about in describing the *emerging* American values. Justify your answer.
21. Pick the three values you feel are undergoing the most rapid rate of change. How will these changes affect marketing practice?
22. Do you think housewives may become "defensive" or "sensitive" about not having employment outside of the home? If so, what implications will this have for marketing practice?
23. Develop an advertisement for each of the market segments in Exhibit 3–4 for __________
    a. Vacuum cleaner.
    b. Detergent.
    c. Vacation.
    d. Furniture store.
    e. Grocery store.
    f. Bank.
24. Repeat question 23, but for the four female market segments identified in the section on market segmentation (traditional housewife, trapped housewife, trapped working woman, career working woman).
25. Name five products that are now primarily associated with the:
    a. Male role but will increasingly be used by females.
    b. Male role but will *not* increasingly be used by females.
    c. Female role but will increasingly be used by males.
    d. Female role but will *not* increasingly be used by males.

PROJECT QUESTIONS

1. Interview a salesperson at a hot tub outlet and obtain a description of the "average" purchaser in demographic terms. Are the demographic shifts predicted in the text going to increase or decrease the size of this average-purchaser segment?
2. Interview three members of one of the following subcultures. Identify the major ways, if any, that their consumption-related behaviors are unique because of their membership in that subcultural group.
    a. Black.
    b. Hispanic.
    c. Senior citizen.
3. Examine ads in magazines aimed at __________. Describe differences in

the types of products advertised and the nature of the advertisements compared to ads in a similar magazine aimed at the main culture.

a. Blacks.

b. Hispanics.

c. Senior citizens.

4. Examine ads in magazines aimed at ________. Select one ad you feel will be very effective and one you feel is ineffective. Justify your selection.

a. Blacks.

b. Hispanics.

c. Senior citizens.

5. Interview a ________ salesperson. Ascertain the interest shown in ________ by males and females. Determine if males and females are concerned with different characteristics of ________ and if they have different purchase motivations.

a. Automobile.

b. Ski.

c. Watch.

d. Wine.

e. Furniture.

f. Art.

6. Interview 10 male and 10 female students. Ask each to describe a typical ________ owner or consumer. If they do not specify, ask for the sex of the typical owner. Then probe to find out why they think the typical owner is of the sex they indicated. Also determine the perceived marital and occupational status of the typical owner and the reasons for these beliefs.

a. Pipe.

b. Cat.

c. "Cooler" drinks.

d. *Business Week*.

e. Moped.

f. Personal computer.

7. Examine a magazine directed to males such as *Playboy*, one oriented toward upper income females such as *Cosmopolitan*, and one oriented toward lower income females such as *True Romance*. Do the sex roles portrayed in the advertisements differ among these three magazine types? Speculate on the reasons for this.

8. Interview a salesperson that has been selling automobiles for at least 10 years. See if this individual has noticed a change in the purchasing roles of women over time. Also interview the following salespersons:

a. Jewelry salesperson.

b. Art salesperson.

c. Waterbed salesperson.

d. Book salesperson.

9. Interview a career-oriented workwife and a traditional housewife of a similar age. Report on differences in attitudes toward shopping, products, and so forth.

10. Find one advertisement you think is particularly appropriate for each of the female market segments identified in the market segmentation section (traditional housewife, trapped housewife, trapped working woman, career working woman.)

REFERENCES

[1] Boredon J. Snyder and R. Serafin, "Auto Makers Set New Ad Strategy to Reach Women," *Advertising Age,* September 23, 1985, pp. 3, 80; "Women and the Auto Market," *Advertising Age,* September 15, 1986, sec. S; and "Women Help Select Cars," *Marketing News,* October 9, 1987, p. 18.

[2] R. C. Chewning, "Can Free Enterprise Survive Ethical Schizophrenia?" *Business Horizons,* March 1984, p. 5.

[3] D. Yankelovich, *New Rules* (New York: Random House, 1981), pp. xiii–xiv.

[4] B. I. Brown, "Baby Boom Generation Now Mirrors the Values and Attitudes of Its Elders," *Marketing News,* April 13, 1984, p. 9; and A. Furnham and A. Lewis, *The Economic Mind* (New York: St. Martin's Press, 1986).

[5] For a differing view, see R. W. Belk, "Yuppies as Arbiters of the Emerging Consumption Style," in *Advances in Consumer Research 13,* ed. R. J. Lutz (Provo, Utah: Association for Consumer Research, 1986), pp. 514–19.

[6] See S. P. Sherman, "America's New Abstinence," *Fortune,* March 18, 1985, pp. 20–23; and J. Adler, "The Year of the Yuppie," *Newsweek,* December 31, 1984, pp. 18–24.

[7] See D. O. Jorgenson, "Agency and Communion Trends in Consumer Goods Advertising," *Personality and Social Psychology Bulletin,* September 1981, pp. 410–14.

[8] "Men's Clothiers Zero In on Ages 29 through 40," *United Press International,* March 22, 1978.

[9] F. D. Reynolds, M. R. Crask, and W. D. Wells, "The Modern Feminine Life Style," *Journal of Marketing,* July 1977, pp. 38–45. For other ways of defining the "modern" woman, see R. Bartos, "The Moving Target: The Impact of Women's Employment on Consumer Behavior," *Journal of Marketing,* July 1977, pp. 31–37; and A. Venkatesh, "Changing Roles of Women—A Life-Style Analysis," *Journal of Consumer Research,* September 1980, pp. 189–97.

[10] Reynolds et al., "Modern Feminine Life Style," p. 39.

[11] *The Connecticut Mutual Life Report on American Values in the 80s: The Impact of Belief* (Connecticut Mutual Life Insurance Co., 1981), p. 151.

[12] Ibid., pp. 153, 156.

[13] "Males Don't Like New Women: DDB," *Advertising Age,* October 20, 1980, p. 60; and C. M. Schaninger and W. C. Buss, "The Relationship of Sex-Role Norms to Household Task Allocation," *Psychology and Marketing,* Summer 1985, 93–104.

[14] R. P. Leone, "The Effect of an Individual's Sex on Preference for Brand Names," in *The Changing Marketing Environment: New Theories and Applications,* ed. K. Bernhardt et al. (Chicago: American Marketing Association, 1981), pp. 187–200.

[15] "Looks Still Count for Women, DDB Study Finds," *Advertising Age,* March 10, 1980, p. 67; P. Lang, "Women Executives Discuss Dressing the Part in Focus Group Sessions," *Marketing Today*. First Quarter 1981, pp. 1, 3; and S. Douglas and M. Soloman, "Clothing the Female Executive," *1983 Educators Conference Proceedings* (Chicago: American Marketing Association, 1983), pp. 127–32.

[16] N. Giges, "Smooth and Easy Brand's Short Life Was Anything But," *Advertising Age,* September 10, 1979, p. 33. Empirical studies have been mixed. See R. W. Jackson, S. W. McDaniel, and C. P. Rao, "Food Shopping and Preparation," *Journal of Consumer Research,* June 1985, pp. 110–13; D. Bellante and A. C. Foster, "Working Wives and Expenditures on Services," *Journal of Consumer Research,* September 1984, pp. 700–707; and M. D. Reilly, "Working Wives and Convenience Consumption," *Journal of Consumer Research,* March 1982, pp. 407–18.

[17] A. Venkatesh, "Changing Roles of Women—A Life-Style Analysis," *Journal of Consumer Research,* September 1980, p. 192. See "Ads Glorifying Career 'Superwomen' Can Alienate Full-Time Homemakers," *Marketing News,* May 1, 1981, p. 1; and J. Alter, "Working Women 'Neglected'—Study," *Advertising Age,* May 4, 1981, p. 50.

[18] See T. E. Barry, M. C. Gilly, and L. E. Doran, "Advertising to Women with Different Career Orientations," *Journal of Advertising Research,* April/May 1985, pp. 26–35.

[19] J. V. Petrof and P. Vlahopoulos, "Advertising and Stereotyping of Women," in *1984 AMA Educators' Conference Proceedings,* ed. R. W. Belk et al. (Chicago: American Marketing Association, 1984), pp. 6–9.

[20] "The Men who Man the Shopping Carts," *Shopper Behavior Kit* (Progressive Grocer, 1979), p. 2. See also H. F. Ezell and W. H. Motes, "Differentiating between the Sexes," *Journal of Consumer Marketing,* Spring 1985, pp. 29–40.

[21] R. Kreisman, "Teens' Role Grows in Family's Grocery Purchases," *Advertising Age,* May 17, 1982, p. 68.

[22] J. M. Jones and F. S. Zufryden, "An Approach for Assessing Demographics and Price Influences on Brand Purchase Behavior," *Journal of Marketing,* Winter 1982, pp. 36–46; and M. F. Utsey and V. J. Cook, Jr. "Demographics and the Propensity to Consume," in *Advances in Consumer Research,* ed. T. C. Kinnear, (Chicago: Association for Consumer Research, 1984), pp. 718–23.

[23] Similar information for Canada can be found in the most recent edition of *Canada Year Book* (Canada Year Book Section, Information Division, Statistics, Canada).

[24] "The Year 2000: A Demographic Profile of the Consumer Market," *Marketing News,* May 25, 1984, pp. 8–10.

[25] Utsey and Cook, Jr., "Demographics."

[26] U. S. Bureau of the Census, *Current Population Report,* 1983.

[27] T. Moore, "Different Folks, Different Strokes," *Fortune,* September 16, 1985, p. 68.

[28] Ibid.

[29] J. Dagnoli, "GF Tests Regional Tastes," *Advertising Age,* June 22, 1987, p. 3.

[30] "Households and Income in 1995," *American Demographics,* April 1984, p. 50.

[31] Utsey and Cook, Jr., "Demographics."

[32] "New Survey Reveals Five Lifestyle Segments of Age 18–49 Black Women," *Marketing News,* April 21, 1981, p. 6.

[33] N. Millman, "Ultra Sheen Cosmetics Revamped," *Advertising Age,* June 9, 1980, p. 7.

[34] L. Rozen, "Amstar Redirects Liquid Brown Sugar Effort," *Advertising Age,* November 10, 1980, p. 40.

[35] G. J. Glasser and G. D. Metzger, "Radio Usage by Blacks: An Update," *Journal of Advertising Research,* April 1981, pp. 47–52.

[36] J. Saegert, R. J. Hoover, and M. T. Hilger, "Characteristics of Mexican-American Consumers," *Journal of Consumer Research,* June 1985, pp. 104–9.

[37] L. Adkins, "New Strategies to Sell Hispanics," *Dunn's Business Month,* July 1983, pp. 64–69. See also R. W. Wilkes and H. Valencia, "Shopping Orientations of Mexican-Americans," in *1984 AMA Educators Proceedings,* ed. R. W. Belk et al. (Chicago: American Marketing Association, 1984), pp. 26–31; and R. Deshpande, W. D. Hoyer, and N. Danthu, "The Intensity of Ethnic Affiliation," *Journal of Consumer Research,* September 1986, pp. 214–20.

[38] A. Guernica, "The Hispanic Market: A Profile," *Theme,* May/June 1981, pp. 4–7.

[39] *Spanish USA* (SIN National Spanish Television Network, 1981), p. 7.

[40] B. A. Brusco, "Hispanic Marketing: New Application for Old Methodologies," *Theme,* May/June 1981, pp. 8–9.

[41] Adkins, "New Strategies."

[42] A. Sutherland, Jr., "Misdirected Advertising Prevents Marketers from Taking Bite from 'Golden Apple' Maturity Market," *Marketing News,* October 26, 1984, p. 19.

[43] R. Alsop, "Firms Try New Ways to Tap Growing Over-50 Population," *The Wall Street Journal,* August 23, 1984, p. 21.

CHAPTER

4 Social Stratification

The positioning of many products is based on existing or desired social status. For example, the Lenox China advertisement shown facing is positioned to appeal to both those high in social status and those aspiring to reach a higher social status. For those high in social status, the ad reinforces the association of Lenox China with high social status. For those striving for higher social status, Lenox China is shown as a means of acquiring aspects of this lifestyle.

Other products such as Tree Top apple juice are positioned with a strong blue-collar identity. Not all consumers are striving to be members of higher social status groups. Many blue-collar workers, while preferring more money or wealth, are uncomfortable with a higher social status and prefer their blue-collar identity. In some cases the identification is so strong that they consciously disdain products consumed by upper social strata. The Tree Top ad copy has a stronger appeal to the blue-collar worker than the Lenox China ad copy.

Product Positioning Using Social Class

Courtesy Lenox, Inc.

Courtesy Tree Top, Inc.

We are all familiar with the concept of social class, but trying to explain it to a foreigner emigrating to the United States would be difficult. Americans use the words *social class* and *social standing* interchangeably to mean *societal rank*. When asked to explain in their own words what social class means, Americans say that "social class means differences between people in their social standing."[1]

How do we obtain a social standing? Your social standing is a result of characteristics you possess that others in society desire and hold in high esteem. Your education, occupation, ownership of property, and source of income influence your social standing as shown in Figure 4–1. Social standing ranges from the lower class, those with few or none of the socioeconomic factors desired by society, to the upper class, who possess many of the socioeconomic characteristics considered by society as desirable and high in status. Individuals with different social standings tend to have different needs and consumption patterns.

Because individuals with different social standings are likely to live their lives differently, a social class system can be defined as:

> A hierarchical division of a society into relatively distinct and homogeneous groups with respect to attitudes, values, and lifestyles.

Figure 4–1
Social Standing Is Derived and Influences Behavior

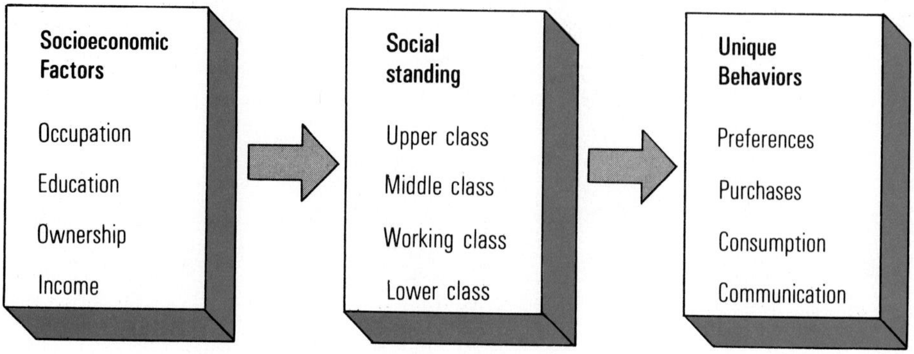

The fact that members of each social class have a set of unique behaviors makes the concept relevant to marketers. For example, the lifestyle and social standing of the couple portrayed in the Lenox China ad copy fits the user of expensive china and crystal. Although apple juice is consumed by all social classes, the Tree Top ad is targeted at the working class. While both strategies may be effective, the strength of the relationship between social class behavior and product usage is stronger in the Lenox China ad copy since the product has a more distinct meaning in expressing social standing.

It is important for marketers to understand when social class is an influencing factor and when it is not. As shown in Figure 4–2, not all behaviors differ between social strata; many are shared. Therefore, we should recognize that the applicability of social class in the formulation of marketing strategies is product specific (e.g., expensive china and crystal) and often situation specific (e.g., entertaining).

In this chapter we are going to examine the characteristics of social class, the various methods of measuring social status, and the nature of American social classes. Throughout the chapter we emphasize the impact social stratification can have on purchase and consumption, and hence the opportunities it may present for the development of marketing strategy.

THE CONCEPT OF SOCIAL CLASS

For a social class system to exist in a society, the individual classes must meet five criteria (as shown in Figure 4–3): they must be (1) bounded, (2) ordered, (3) mutually exclusive, (4) exhaustive, and (5) influential.[2] *Bounded* means that there are clear breaks between each social class that separate one class from another. In other words, it is necessary that a rule be devised for each class that

Figure 4–2
Not All Behaviors within a Social Class Are Unique

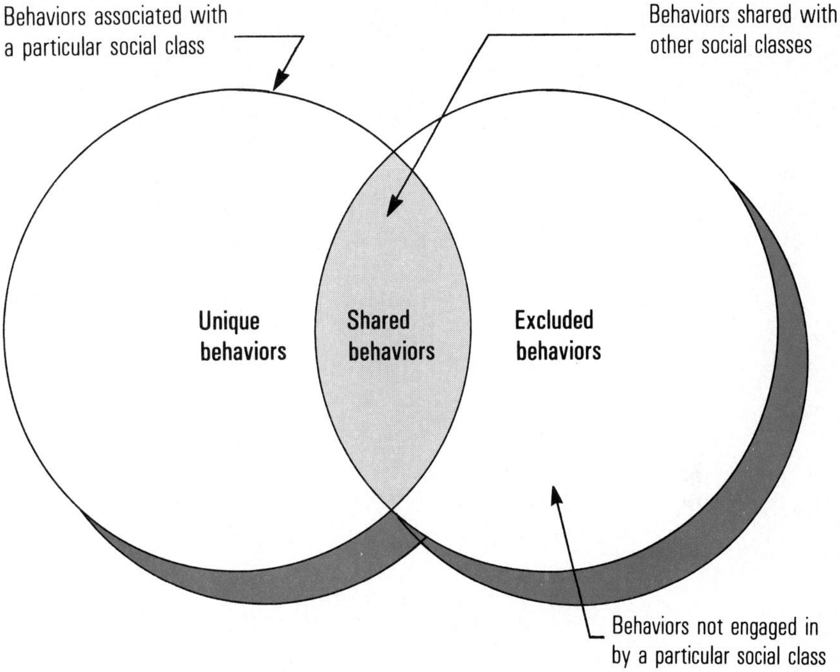

will include or exclude any particular individual. *Ordered* means that the classes can be arrayed or spread out in terms of some measure of prestige or status from highest to lowest. *Mutually exclusive* means that an individual can only belong to one social class (though movement from one class to another over time is possible). This requires that there be a generally accepted rule or rules in use to assign the same individual to the same social class.

Requiring social classes to be *exhaustive* means that every member of a social system must fit into some class. There must be no "undefined" individuals. Finally, the social classes must be *influential*. That is, there must be behavioral variations between the classes. This is closely related to the degree of class awareness or class consciousness by members of the society.

Based on these five criteria, it is clear that a strict and tightly defined social class system does not exist in the United States or most other industrialized nations. The first criteria, that the classes be distinctly bounded, obviously is not so in the United States. The two classic studies of social class in America developed differing numbers of classes (and other researchers have reported yet other breakdowns).[3] If there were indeed firm boundaries, reasonably careful researchers would always identify the same number of classes. Likewise, various

Figure 4–3
Requirements for a Social Class System

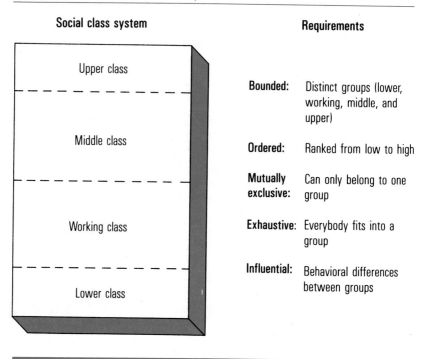

Social class system

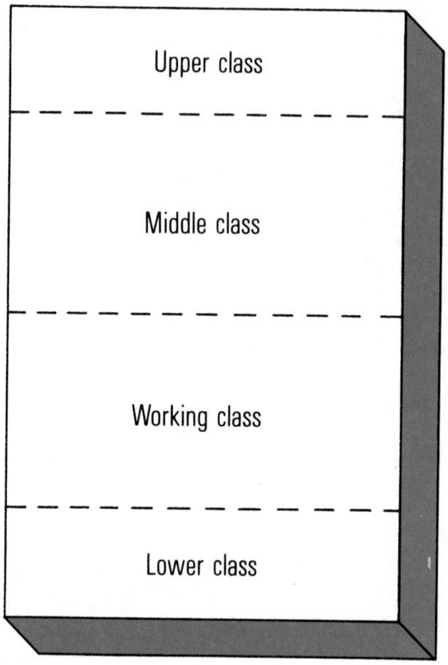

Requirements

Bounded:	Distinct groups (lower, working, middle, and upper)
Ordered:	Ranked from low to high
Mutually exclusive:	Can only belong to one group
Exhaustive:	Everybody fits into a group
Influential:	Behavioral differences between groups

criteria of social class will place individuals into different categories. That is, a person may be considered upper middle class if education is the placement criterion but upper lower if income is used. This casts doubt on the ability to construct mutually exclusive social classes.

Social classes can be made exhaustive by simply constructing appropriate rules. However, these rules may distort the internal consistency of the various classes if substantial numbers of individuals clearly do not fit into one class. This is a common problem when families are assigned to social classes based on the husband's characteristics while ignoring those of the wife. As we saw in Chapter 3, working wives contribute as much or more financial resources and prestige to the family as the husband.

Status Crystallization

"Pure" social classes do not exist in the United States or most other industrialized societies. However, it is apparent that these same societies do have hierarchical groups of individuals and that individuals in those groups do exhibit some unique behavior patterns that are different from other groups. The following quote clearly represents the vague nature of social class in current American society:

> I would suppose social class means where you went to school and how far. Your intelligence. Where you live. The sort of house you live in. Your general background, as far as clubs you belong to, your friends. To some degree the type of profession you're in—in fact, definitely that. Where you send your children to school. The hobbies you have. Skiing, for example, is higher than the snowmobile. The clothes you wear . . . all of that. These are the externals. It can't be (just) money, because nobody ever knows that about you for sure.[4]

What exists is *not a set of social classes,* but a *series of status continua.*[5] These status continua reflect various dimensions or factors that the overall society values. In an achievement-oriented society such as the United States, achievement-related factors constitute the primary status dimensions. Thus, education, occupation, income, and, to a lesser extent, quality of residence and place of residence are important status dimensions in the United States. Race, age, and sex are *ascribed* dimensions of social status that are not related to achievement.[6] Likewise, the status characteristics of a person's parents are an ascribed status dimension that appears to exist in the United States. However, heritage is a more important dimension in a traditional society such as England.

The various status dimensions are related to each other both functionally and statistically. In a functional sense, the status of one's parents or one's race

Figure 4–4
Status Crystallization Depends on Consistency across Status Dimensions

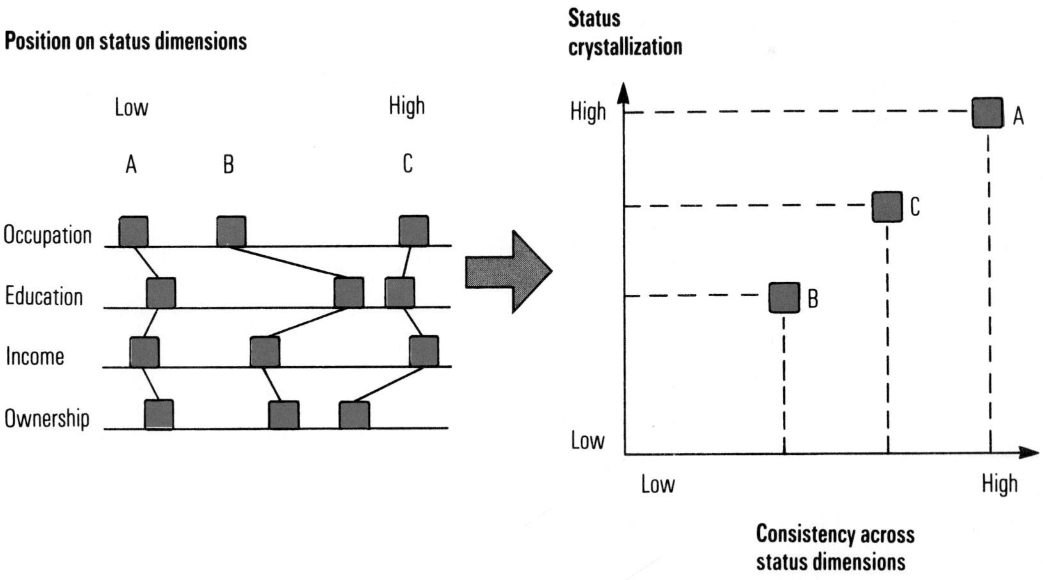

influences one's education, which in turn influences occupation that generates income which sets limits on one's lifestyle. Does this mean that an individual with high status based on one dimension will have high status based on the other dimensions? This is a question of *status crystallization*.

The more consistent an individual is on all status dimensions, the greater the degree of status crystallization for the individual. For example, in Figure 4–4, Person A is low on most status dimensions but has a relatively high degree of status crystallization because of this consistency. Likewise, Person C has a fair degree of status crystallization because of consistency across status dimensions. Person B has a low degree of status crystallization since there are major inconsistencies across the four dimensions.

Status crystallization is relatively low in the United States. One study found correlations of approximately 0.6 between education and occupation ratings, 0.33 between education and income ratings, and 0.4 between occupation and income ratings (where 1 indicates a perfect correlation and 0 indicates no correlation).[7]

SOCIAL STRUCTURE IN THE UNITED STATES

The low degree of status crystallization in the United States is support for the contention that a social class system is not a perfect categorization of social position. However, this does not mean that the population cannot be subdivided into status groups that share similar lifestyles, at least with respect to particular product categories or activities. Furthermore, there are many people with high levels of status crystallization who exhibit many of the behaviors associated with a class system. It is useful for the marketing manager to know the characteristics of these relatively pure class types, even though the descriptions represent a simplified abstraction from reality.[8]

Functional Approach

Social class structures can be defined in a variety of ways. Gilbert and Kahl use a "functional" approach that focuses on occupational role, income level, living conditions, and identification with a possibly disadvantaged ethnic or racial group. In the functionalist approach:

> We pay more attention to capitalist ownership and to occupational division of labor as the defining variables . . . then treat prestige, association, and values as derivatives."[9]

The Gilbert-Kahl social class structure is present in Table 4–1. In their system, the *upper class* (15 percent) is divided into the capitalist class (1 percent) and upper-middle class (14 percent). The *middle class* (65 percent) is divided between the middle level white-collar (33 percent) and middle level blue-collar worker

Table 4–1
Functional Approach to Social Class Structures

The Gilbert-Kahl New Synthesis Class Structure: A situations model from political theory and sociological analysis*

Upper Americans

- Capitalist Class (1%). Their investment decisions shape the national economy; income mostly from assets, earned/inherited; prestige university connections.
- Upper-Middle Class (14%). Upper managers, professionals, medium businessmen; college educated; family income is nearly twice the national average.

Middle Americans

- Middle Class (33%). Middle level white-collar, top level blue-collar; education past high school typical; income somewhat above the national average.
- Working Class (32%). Middle level blue-collar; lower level white-collar; income runs slightly below the national average; education is also slightly below.

Marginal and Lower Americans

- Working Poor (11–12%). Below mainstream America in living standard, but above the poverty line; low-paid service workers, operatives; some high school education.
- Underclass (8–9%). Depend primarily on welfare system for sustenance; living standard below poverty line; not regularly employed; lack schooling.

*Abstracted by Coleman from D. Gilbert and J. A. Kahl, "The American Class Structure: A Synthesis," in *The American Class Structure: A New Synthesis* (Chicago: Dorsey Press), 1982, chap. 11.

(32 percent). The *lower class* (20 percent) is composed of working poor (11.5 percent) and the underclass (8.5 percent).

Reputational Approach

Coleman and Rainwater base their social class structure on "reputation," relying heavily on the "man in the street" imagery.[10] A reputationalist approach:

> is designed to reflect popular imagery and observation of how people interact with one another—as equals, superiors, or inferiors. Personal and group prestige is at its heart.[11]

In their system, which is shown in Table 4–2, the upper class (14 percent) is divided into three groups primarily on differences in occupation and social affiliations. The middle class (70 percent) is divided into the middle class (32 percent), average income white- and blue-collar workers living in better neighborhoods, and working class (38 percent), which are also average income blue-collar workers but who lead a "working-class lifestyle." The lower class (16 percent) is divided into two groups, one living just above the poverty level and the other visibly poverty-stricken.

While the "Functionalist" and "Reputationalist" approaches are based on different conceptual frameworks, there is a high degree of similarity between the

Table 4–2
Reputational Approach to Social Class Structure

The Coleman-Rainwater Social Standing Class Hierarchy: A reputational, behavioral view in the community study tradition.*

Upper Americans

- Upper-Upper (0.3%). The "capital S society" world of inherited wealth, aristocratic names.
- Lower-Upper (1.2%). The newer social elite, drawn from current professional, corporate leadership.
- Upper-Middle Class (12.5%). The rest of college graduate managers and professionals; lifestyle centers on private clubs, causes, and the arts.

Middle Americans

- Middle Class (32%). Average pay white-collar workers and their blue-collar friends; live on "the better side of town," try to "do the proper things."
- Working Class (38%). Average pay blue-collar workers; lead "working-class lifestyle" whatever the income, school background, and job.

Lower Americans

- Upper-Lower (9%). "A lower group of people but not the lowest"; working, not on welfare; living standard is just above poverty; behavior judged "crude," "trashy."
- Lower-Lower (7%). On welfare, visibly poverty-stricken, usually out of work (or have "the dirtiest jobs"); "bums," "common criminals."

*This condensation of the Coleman-Rainwater view is drawn from chapters 8, 9, and 10 of R. P. Coleman and L. P. Rainwater, with Kent A. McClelland, *Social Standing in America: New Dimensions of Class* (New York: Basic Books), 1978.

Source: R. P. Coleman, "The Continuing Significance of Social Class to Marketing," *Journal of Consumer Research* (December 1983), p. 267.

Table 4–3
The Coleman-Rainwater Social Standing Class Hierarchy

	Typical Profile			
Social Class	Percent	Income	Education	Occupation
Upper Americans				
Upper-upper	.3%	$600,000	Master's degree	Board chairman
Lower-upper	1.2	450.000	Master's degree	Corporate president
Upper-middle	12.5	150,000	Medical degree	Physician
Middle Americans				
Middle class	32.0	28,000	College degree	High school teacher
Working class	38.0	15,000	High school	Assembly worker
Lower Americans				
Upper-lower	9.0	9,000	Some high school	Janitor
Lower-lower	7.0	5,000	Grade school	Unemployed

two social structures. This similarity is particularly true in the approximate size of the three major partitions in social class shown in Tables 4–1 and 4–2—upper, middle, and lower.

While each social class structure offers a useful way to examine social class differences, we will focus on the class structure developed by Coleman and Rainwater. Table 4–3 presents the Coleman and Rainwater social class structure, along with a brief profile of each class in terms of income, education, and occupation. The remainder of this section is devoted to a discussion of each major social class and how the behavioral and lifestyle characteristics of each social class create unique marketing opportunities.

UPPER AMERICANS (14 PERCENT)

The Upper-Upper Class

Members of the upper-upper social class are often depicted as the old rich of aristocratic families who are small in number and generally make up the social elite. Members with this level of social status generally are the nucleus of the best country clubs and sponsors of major charitable events. They provide leadership and funds for community and civic activities and often serve as trustees for hospitals, colleges, and civic organizations. The upper-upper class is similar to Gilbert and Kahl's "capitalist class."

The Lower-Upper Class

The lower-upper class is often referred to as "new rich—the current generation's new successful elite." These families are relatively new in terms of upper-class social status and have not yet been accepted by the upper crust of the community. In some cases, their income is greater than those of families in the upper-upper social strata. However, their consumption is often more conspicuous and acts as an important symbol of their social status.

Families in the lower-upper social strata are major purchasers of large homes, luxury automobiles, and more expensive clothing, food, vacations, and furniture. Together, the upper-upper and lower-upper constitute less than 2 percent of the population. However, because they are a visible symbol of social status, their

Exhibit 4–1 Advertisement Aimed at the Upper-Middle Class

To meditate on life's rewards,
relax in one.
Success may be its own reward, but it brings other pleasant things into your life along with it. We feel it's simply your duty now and then to lean back in a Tropitone chair and reflect on the good things of life —Tropitone, of course, being one of them. There's probably no other outdoor furniture made with such exacting care in design and construction. That's why we can offer a 15-year, "No Fine Print" warranty, which makes Tropitone a reward of lasting pleasure.
tropitone
Probably the finest.
Write for our color catalog. Only $1.00. P.O. Box 3197, Sarasota, FL 33578; 5 Marconi, Irvine, CA 92718.

Courtesy Tropitone Co.

behavior and lifestyle can influence individuals in lower social strata. Residence often plays a role in the social status of members in these two upper social class groups since it is an overt symbol of their status.

The Upper-Middle Class

The upper-middle class is comprised of families who possess neither family status derived from heritage nor unusual wealth. Their social position is achieved primarily by their occupation and career orientation. Occupation and education are key aspects of this social strata as it consists of successful professionals, independent businesspeople, and corporate managers. As shown in Table 4–3, members of this social class are typically college graduates, many of whom have professional or graduate degrees. Education and occupation are, therefore, two important factors that contribute to the social status and position of these families.

The upper-middle-class members are well-paid, highly educated professionals who buy fine homes, expensive automobiles, quality furniture, good wines, and so forth. Exhibit 4–1 contains an advertisement aimed at this group.

While this segment of the U.S. population is small (approximately 12.5 percent), it is highly visible and many Americans would like to belong to it. Because it is aspired to by many, it is an important positioning variable for some products.

Figure 4–5 illustrates this "upward pull" strategy. This pull strategy works well for the manufacturer of expensive fashion items such as Gucci. Gucci, high in social status, is attractive to those middle-class consumers wishing to improve their social status or to enjoy elements of the upper-middle-class lifestyle. However, as we will see later, this "upward pull strategy" does not apply to all products or all social classes.

Figure 4–5
"Upward Pull Strategy" Targeted at Middle Class

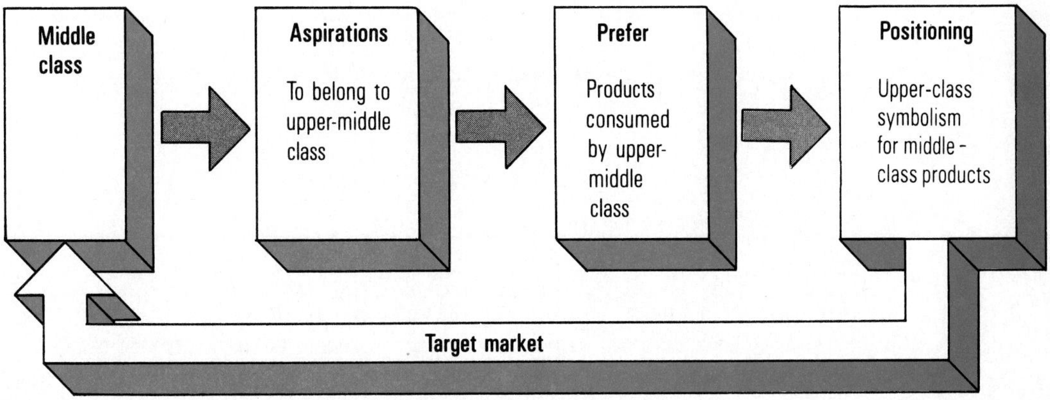

MIDDLE AMERICANS (70 percent)

The Middle Class

The middle class is relatively large (approximately 32 percent of the population) and is composed of white-collar workers (office workers, school teachers) and high-paid blue-collar workers (plumbers, factory supervisors). Thus, the middle class represents the majority of the white-collar group and the top of the blue-collar group.

Members of the middle class have respectable incomes and often college educations and some management responsibility. The middle-class core is typically a college-educated, white-collar worker or a factory supervisor with average income. They generally live in modest suburban homes, avoid elegant furniture, and are likely to get involved in do-it-yourself projects. They represent the primary target market for the goods and services of home improvement centers, garden shops, automotive parts houses, as well as for mouthwashes and deodorants.

With limited incomes, they must balance their desire for current consumption with aspirations for future security as well as limited cash flow. Music, particularly rock 'n' roll, is important to this group. Bruce Springsteen currently symbolizes many of the values held by this class. Chevrolet, Coors, Coke, McDonald's and many other firms use music to reach this group. Examples of campaigns that have succeeded with these individuals include:

- Miller beers' "American Way" TV commercials that combine patriotism with images of comradarie, hard work, and good times among workers.
- A Subaru ad showing a son surprising his cost-conscious father by buying a very sporty but nonetheless practical car.
- A McDonald's commercial showing a young woman who pumps gas in the morning to work her way through college and barely has enough time to eat an Egg McMuffin for breakfast.
- Levitz furniture stores which use a warehouse-showroom format with brands and prices appropriate for this group. A major appeal is instant access to the desired brand and color without a delay of several months for ordered furniture.[12]

The Working Class

The working class (38 percent) is the largest social-class segment in the U.S. population, although it is declining in relative size. It is solidly blue collar and consists of skilled and semiskilled factory workers. Though some households in this social stratum seek advancement, members of this stratum are more likely to seek security for and protection of what they already have.

As illustrated in Figure 4–6, many "working-class aristocrats" dislike the

Figure 4–6
Positioning within Social Class

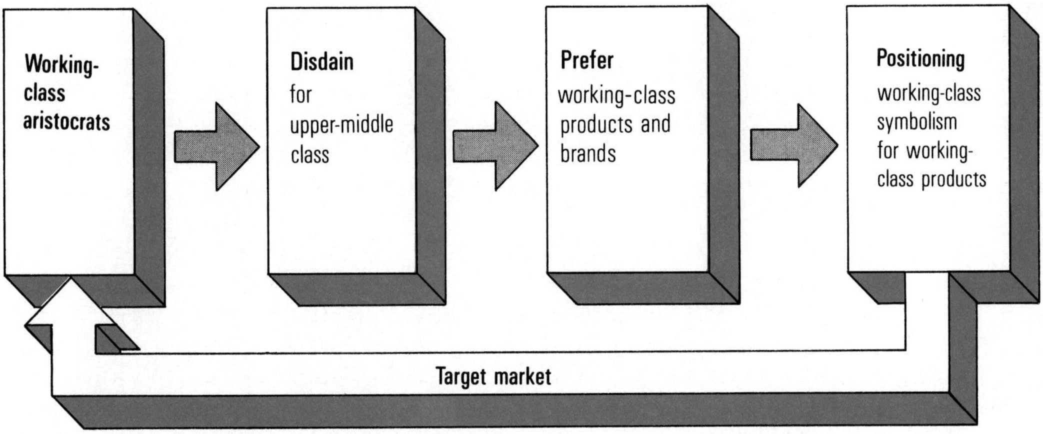

Source: Adapted from F. LeMasters, *Blue Collar Aristocrats: Life Style at a Working Class Tavern* (University of Wisconsin Press, 1975).

upper-middle class and prefer products positioned at their social-class level. They are heavy consumers of pickups and campers, hunting equipment, power boats, and beer. The working class is also more likely to belong to Christmas Clubs at banks and to make major purchases on installment. The ad in Exhibit 4–2 is very appropriate for this social class.

LOWER AMERICANS (16 PERCENT)

The Upper-Lower Class

Approximately 9 percent of the U.S. population can be categorized as members of the upper-lower class. The upper-lower class consists of individuals who are poorly educated, have very low incomes, and work as unskilled laborers (janitor, laborer in a bottling plant, and so on).

Because of their limited education, members in this social stratum have a difficult time moving up in occupation, and hence, social status. Painfully aware of the lifestyle of the class below them, they strive to avoid slipping into the ranks of the society-dependent, lower-lower class. Yet, without sufficient education or occupational training, they are unable to move up. As one author put it: "They are in bondage—to monetary policy, rip-off advertising, crazes and delusions, mass low culture, fast foods, consumer schlock."[13] However, sophisticated chain retailers such as Dollar General Corporation have begun to meet the unique needs of this segment.[14]

Exhibit 4–2 An Ad Appealing to Working-Class Values

Courtesy Lee Company

The Lower-Lower Class

The lower-lower social stratum (7 percent), the poverty class, or the "bottom layer" as Coleman and Rainwater have categorized them, has the lowest social standing in society. They have very low incomes and minimal education. This segment of society is often unemployed for long periods of time and is the major recipient of government support and services provided by nonprofit organizations.

The poor represent a problem for public policymakers attempting to eliminate or at least minimize poverty.[15] Likewise, serving the poor has been viewed as a problem for the marketing system as a whole and for individual firms. As the income, and thus expenditures, of the nonpoverty groups grows, it will be increasingly easy to ignore the low-income segment of the market. To ignore this segment completely is to forgo a large and potentially profitable market segment. Marketers should at least examine the possibility of developing marketing strategies for this market segment. The motive for such decisions can be profit instead of, or in addition to, social responsibility.

Conclusions on Social Structure in the United States

The descriptions provided above are brief. In part, this reflects our belief that it is relatively unproductive to attempt to provide very specific descriptions for social classes. The complexity and variety of behaviors and values involved precludes doing a thorough job. Rather, marketing managers must investigate the various status dimensions to determine which, if any, affect the consumption process for their products. In the next section, we discuss how this can be done.

THE MEASUREMENT OF SOCIAL STATUS

As described earlier, education, occupation, income, and, to a lesser extent, place of residence are the primary achievement-based status dimensions used to determine social standing. Race, age, gender, and parents' status are ascribed (nonachievement) status dimensions. How do we measure these dimensions in the most useful manner? There are two basic approaches:

1. A single dimension: a single-item index.
2. A combination of several dimensions: a multi-item index.

Single-Item Indexes

Single-item indexes estimate social status based on a single dimension. Since an individual's overall status is influenced by several dimensions, single-item indexes are generally less accurate at predicting an individual's social standing or position in a community than are well-developed multi-item indexes. However, single-item indexes allow one to estimate the impact of specific status dimensions on the consumption process. The three most common single-item indexes are (1) education, (2) occupation, and (3) income.

Education. Education has traditionally been highly valued in our culture. It has served as the primary path for upward social mobility. Thus, education is a direct measure of status and is used as a component in several of the multiple-item indexes. In addition, education may influence an individual's tastes, values, and information-processing style. For example, Figure 4–7 indicates the impact that education has on television viewing. It is also associated with variation in

Figure 4–7
Male-Female TV Viewing Varies by Education Level

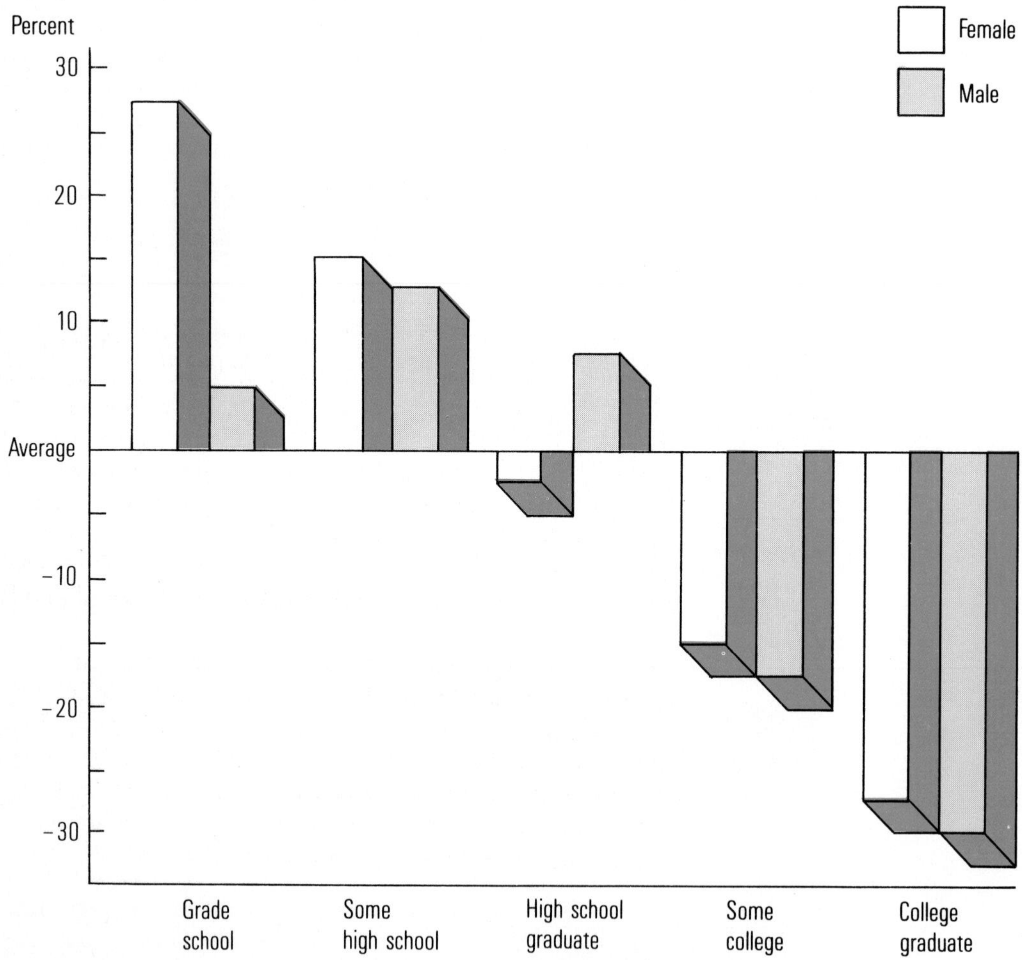

consumption of such common products as margarine, cereal, and paper towels,[16] as well as discount store patronage.[17]

Education is relatively simple to measure. It is generally broken into categories much like those described in Chapter 3:

- College graduate.
- Some college.
- High school graduate.
- Some high school.
- Elementary school or less.

Education level is correlated with both occupation and income. In addition, it influences the lifestyle and, therefore, consumption patterns of individuals in a direct manner. However, education seldom provides a complete explanation for consumption patterns. For example, college graduates earning $30,000 per year probably have different lifestyles than college graduates earning $80,000 per year, despite similar educational backgrounds.

Occupation. Occupation is the most widely used single-item index in marketing studies. In fact, occupation is probably the most widely used single cue that allows us to evaluate and define individuals we meet. That this is true should be obvious when you stop to think of the most common bit of information we seek from a new acquaintance. "What do you do?" Almost invariably we need to know someone's occupation to make inferences about his/her probable lifestyle. Occupation is associated with education and income, although the association is not as strong as it once was.[18] The type of work one does and the types of individuals one works with directly influence one's preferred lifestyle. This influence has been shown to affect the consumption of products such as frozen orange juice, beer, cake mix, and dog food.[19]

A number of approaches are used to assign scores or rankings to the hundreds of occupational categories that exist in an industrial society. By far the most widely used today is the socioeconomic index (SEI) orginally developed by Duncan.[20] Noting the relationship of education and income to status, Duncan developed an occupational scale based on the educational attainments and income of individuals in that occupation. The weight given each component was derived so that the score given each occupation was similar to the "standing" assigned that occupation by a large sample of the public. Once the appropriate weights were derived, any occupation could be ranked.

This scale has been revised several times and is the most up-to-date scale available. Table 4–4 provides the SEI scores for a number of job titles.

Income. Income has traditionally been used as a measure of both purchasing power and status. Historically, the association between income and status has been high. However, this association is not as strong today as in the past. Correlations between income and education of 0.33 and income and occupational

Table 4–4
SEI Scores for Selected Occupations

Occupation	SEI Score	Occupation	SEI Score
Accountant	65	Marketing manager	58
Aerospace engineer	84	Marketing professor	83
Athlete	49	Mail carrier	28
Auto mechanic	21	Plumber	27
Bartender	24	Police	38
Chemist	78	Registered nurse	46
Dentist	89	Sales, apparel	25
Elementary school teacher	70	Sales, engineer	78
Housekeeper	15	Stevedore	22

Source: G. Stevens and J. H. Cho, "Socioeconomic Indices," *Social Science Research* 14, 1985, pp. 142–68.

category of 0.4 have been reported (where a 1.0 represents a perfect association and a 0 represents no association between the variables).[21]

Using income directly poses a number of measurement problems. Basically, the researcher must decide which income to measure. This involves such decisions as:

- Individual or family income.
- Before or after taxes.
- Salary or total income.

Table 4–5
Income and Consumption*

	Income				
Food Item	$25,000 and Over	$20,000 to $24,999	$15,000 to $19,999	Below $15,000	**Significant Difference**
Ground coffee	4.24	3.98	4.25	3.52	No
Instant coffee	5.20	5.42	5.05	5.71	No
Frozen juice	5.71	5.08	4.58	4.65	Yes
Kool-Aid	1.62	2.27	1.95	1.87	No
Tonic water	2.65	1.90	1.65	1.81	Yes
Imported red wine	3.41	2.88	2.13	1.90	Yes
Liqueurs	2.45	2.24	1.83	1.50	Yes
Potato chips	2.88	2.88	3.27	2.71	No
Luncheon meat	3.53	3.48	4.17	3.27	No

*Frequency of consumption.

Source: Adapted from C. Schaninger, "Social Class versus Income Revisited: An Empirical Investigation," *Journal of Marketing Research*, published by the American Marketing Association, May 1981, pp. 197–201.

Many individuals may not have accurate knowledge of their incomes as defined by the researcher (i.e., total family pre-tax income). In addition, individuals are often reluctant to reveal their income, and if they do respond, they may not provide an accurate answer.

Income is clearly necessary to maintain a lifestyle. Likewise, there is a higher status attached to higher incomes than to lower incomes. Still, income does not explain lifestyles completely. A college professor or lawyer may have the same income as a truck driver or plumber. Nonetheless, it is likely that their consumption process for a variety of products will differ. As we will see shortly, income relative to other variables such as occupation may be quite useful, and a number of studies have found it useful when used alone. Table 4–5 shows the impact of income on the consumption of several product categories.

Relative Occupational Class Income

Thus far we have been discussing the relative merits of one status dimension over another. However, in some cases it may be more productive to consider using one status dimension *in conjunction with another*. This is what the concept of Relative Occupational Class Income (ROCI) involves. ROCI is the "relationship of a family's total income to the median income of other families in the same occupational class."[22] Thus, occupational class is viewed as setting the basic lifestyle, while relative income provides (1) excess funds, (2) neither excess nor deficient funds, or (3) deficient funds for the desired lifestyle. The three categories are referred to as overprivileged, average, and underprivileged, respectively.

Figure 4–8 shows the results of one study using this concept. The study used 10 occupational categories. The authors concluded that with respect to automobiles, "the buying behavior of relatively well-off, blue-collar workers is more like that of affluent, white-collar and professional workers than that of less well-off, blue-collar workers."[23]

Another study found ROCI to be associated with the purchase of high-priced versus lower-priced coffee.[24] Other combinations of status dimensions such as *relative income class education* may prove very useful for other product categories.

Multi-Item Indexes

The use of social class as an explanatory consumer behavior variable has been heavily influenced by two studies, each of which developed a multi-item index to measure social class.[25] The basic approach in each of these studies was to determine, through a detailed analysis of a relatively small community, the classes into which the community members appeared to fit. Then, more objective and measurable indicators or factors related to status were selected and weighted in a manner that would reproduce the original class assignments.

Figure 4–8
Difference (in Percent) of Actual Ownership Share from Expected Share of Each Automobile Class by Each Income Status Group

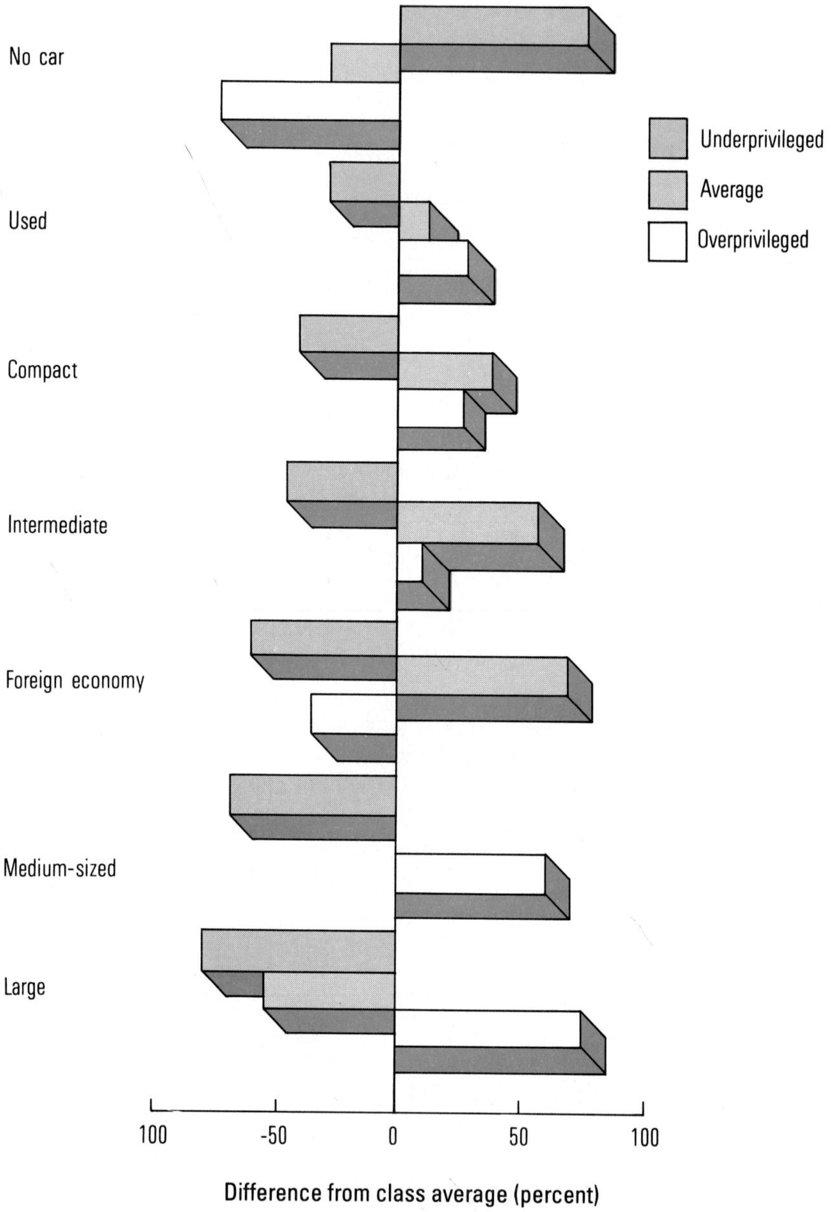

Source: Adapted from W. H. Peters, "Relative Occupational Class Income: A Significant Variable in the Marketing of Automobiles," *Journal of Marketing*, April 1970, p. 76.

Figure 4–9
Hollingshead Index of Social Position (ISP)

- **Occupation Scale (Weight of 7)**

Description	**Score**
Higher executives of large concerns, proprietors, and major professionals	1
Business managers, proprietors of medium-sized businesses, and lesser professionals	2
Administrative personnel, owners of small businesses, and minor professionals	3
Clerical and sales workers, technicians, and owners of little businesses	4
Skilled manual employees	5
Machine operators and semiskilled employees	6
Unskilled employees	7

- **Education Scale (Weight of 4)**

Description	**Score**
Professional (M.A., M.S., M.E., M.D., Ph.D., LL.B., and the like)	1
Four-year college graduate (B.A., B.S., B.M.)	2
One to three years college (also business schools)	3
High school graduate	4
Ten to 11 years of school (part high school)	5
Seven to nine years of school	6
Under seven years of school	7

ISP score = (Occupation score × 7) + (Education score × 4)

Classification System

Social Strata	**Range of Scores**	**Population Breakdown**
Upper	11–17	3.0%
Upper-middle	18–31	8.0
Middle	32–47	22.0
Lower-middle	48–63	46.0
Lower	64–77	21.0

Source: Adapted from A. B. Hollingshead and F. C. Redlich, *Social Class and Mental Illness* (New York: John Wiley & Sons, 1958).

Hollingshead Index of Social Position. One of these scales, the Hollingshead Index of Social Position (ISP), is a two-item index that is well developed and widely used. The item scales, weights, formulas, and social class scores are shown in Figure 4–9. Using Hollingshead's Index of Social Position, significant differences in the rates of consumption are shown for seven of the nine food items in Table 4–6.

Differences in consumption of tonic water, imported red wine, and liqueurs are clearly discernible as these products are more readily consumed by upper and upper-middle social classes. While the same is true for ground coffee all social classes have approximately the same rate of instant coffee consumption. Other products, such as Kool-Aid and potato chips, are more frequently consumed by families lower in social status.

It is important to note that this scale, like most multi-item indexes, was designed to measure or reflect an individual family's overall social position within a community. Because of this, it is possible for a high score on one variable to offset a low score on another. Thus, the following three individuals would all be classified as middle class: (1) someone with an eighth-grade education who is a successful owner of a medium-sized firm; (2) a four-year college graduate working as a salesperson; and (3) a graduate of a junior coilege working in an administrative position in the civil service. All of these individuals may well have similar standing in the community. However, it seems likely that their consumption processes for at least some products will differ, pointing up the fact that overall status may mask or hide potentially useful associations between individual status dimensions and the consumption process for particular products.

Table 4–6
Consumption Differences across Hollingshead Index of Social Position Strata*

	Social Strata					
Food Item	Upper	Upper-Middle	Middle	Lower-Middle	Lower	**Significant Difference**
Ground coffee	4.07	4.79	4.17	3.93	2.61	Yes
Instant coffee	5.30	4.82	5.25	5.44	6.15	No
Frozen juice	5.48	6.00	5.35	4.83	3.58	Yes
Kool-Aid	1.19	1.74	1.96	2.14	2.12	Yes
Tonic water	3.07	2.31	1.79	1.69	1.58	Yes
Imported red wine	4.22	3.00	2.77	2.20	1.52	Yes
Liqueurs	2.44	2.18	2.19	1.90	1.42	Yes
Potato chips	1.96	2.58	3.15	3.08	3.30	Yes
Luncheon meat	2.67	3.65	3.58	3.70	4.00	No

*Frequency of consumption.

Source: Adapted from C. Schaninger, "Social Class versus Income Revisited: An Empirical Investigation," *Journal of Marketing Research*, published by the American Marketing Association, May 1981, pp. 197–201.

Figure 4–10 Warner's Index of Status Characteristics (ISC)

Score	Occupation	Source of Income	House Type	Dwelling Area
	Characteristics			
1	Professionals and proprietors of large businesses	Inherited wealth	Excellent houses	Very high: Gold Coast, North Shore, etc.
2	Semiprofessionals and officials of large businesses	Earned wealth	Very good houses	High: better suburbs and apartment house areas
3	Clerks and kindred workers	Profits and fees	Good houses	Above average: areas all residential, space around houses, apartments in good condition
4	Skilled workers	Salary	Average houses	Average: residential neighborhoods, no deterioration
5	Proprietors of small businesses	Wages	Fair houses	Below average: area beginning to deteriorate, business entering
6	Semiskilled workers	Private relief	Poor houses	Low: considerably deteriorated, run down and semi-slum
7	Unskilled workers	Public relief and nonrespectable income	Very poor houses	Very low: slum

ISC score = (Occupation × 4) + (Income source × 3) + (House type × 3) + (Dwelling area × 2)

Classification System

Social Strata	Range of Scores	Population Breakdown
Upper-upper	12–17	1.4%
Lower-upper	18–24	1.6
Upper-middle	25–37	10.2
Lower-middle	38–50	28.8
Upper-lower	51–62	33.0
Lower-lower	63–84	25.0

Source: W. L. Warner, M. Meeker, and K. Eels, *Social Class in America: Manual of Procedure for the Measurement of Social Status* (Chicago: Science Research Associates, 1949).

Warner's Index of Status Characteristics. Another widely used multi-item scale of social status is Warner's Index of Status Characteristics (ISC).[26] Warner's system of measurement is based on four socioeconomic factors: occupation, source of income, house type, and dwelling area. As shown in Figure 4–10, each of these dimensions of status is defined over a range of seven categories and each carries a different weight. This system classifies individuals into one of six social status categories.

Census Bureau's Index of Socioeconomic Status. A three-factor social status index based on occupation, income, and education is used by the U.S. Bureau of the Census.[27] This scale, which is presented in Figure 4–11, is referred

Figure 4–11
Census Bureau Index of Socioeconomic Status (SES)

Income Category	Income Score	Education Category	Education Score	Occupation Category	Occupation Score
Under \$3,000	15	Some grade school	10	Laborers	20
\$3,000–\$4,999	31	Grade school graduate	23	Students	33
\$5,000–\$7,499	62	Some high school	42	Service workers	34
\$7,500–\$9,999	84	High school graduate	67	Operators	45
\$10,000–\$14,999	94	Some college	86	Craftsmen	58
\$15,000–\$19,999	97	College graduate	93	Clerical sales	71
\$20,000–\$29,999	99	Graduate school	98	Managers	81
\$30,000 and over	100			Professionals	90

$$\text{SES score} = \frac{(\text{Income}) + (\text{Education}) + (\text{Occupation})}{3}$$

Classification System

Social Strata	Range of SES Scores	Population Breakdown
Upper	90–99	15.1%
Upper-middle	70–89	34.5
Middle	45–69	34.1
Lower-middle	0–44	16.3

Note: Income levels should be adjusted by consumer price index before using.

Source: U.S. Bureau of the Census, *Methodology and Scores of the Socioeconomic Status.* Working Paper No. 15 (Washington, D.C.: U.S. Government Printing Office, 1963).

Exhibit 4–3 AT&T's Use of Social Class to Better Understand Differences in Customer Needs (percent agreeing with statement)

Product-Specific Statements	Upper	Upper-Middle	Lower-Middle	Lower
1. Phones should come in patterns and designs as well as colors.	58%	63%	80%	60%
2. A telephone should improve the decorative style of a room.	77	73	82	47
3. Telephones should be modern in design.	89	83	85	58
4. A home should have a variety of telephone styles.	51	39	46	8
5. You can keep all those special phones; all I want is a phone that works.	56	68	67	83
6. The style of a telephone is unimportant to me.	51	58	54	86

From this information AT&T should be better able to serve its many and diverse customers. Using this information, AT&T could structure its efforts targeted at the upper and middle classes by focusing on more decorative phones (statement 2) and more modern phone design (statement 3). The lower-middle class, while also favoring more decorative, modern designs, also favors more colors (statement 1). Families in the lower social strata are more concerned with reliability (statement 5) and less concerned with style (statement 6). Naturally, these insights are valuable in developing different marketing programs for each social strata.

Source: Adapted from A. M. Roscoe, Jr., A. LeClaire, Jr., and L. G. Schiffman, "Theory and Management Applications of Demographics in Buyer Behavior," in *Consumer and Industrial Buying Behavior*, ed. A. G. Woodside, J. N. Sheth, and P. D. Bennett (New York: American Elsevier, 1977), pp. 74–75.

to as the Socioeconomic Status scale (SES). Exhibit 4–3 presents a discussion of what AT&T learned from the opinions of telephone customers across the four social strata created by using the SES method of measuring social status.

Which Scale Should Be Used?

The selection of a measure of social status or prestige is not as complex a problem as it might appear. What must be realized is that there is no one, unidimensional status or class continuum. Thus, the problem is not one of selecting the best measure. Rather, it is to select the most appropriate prestige or status dimension for the problem at hand. When an individual's total personal status is the dimension of concern, perhaps in a study of opinion leadership, a multi-item index such as the Warner or Hollingshead index would be most appropriate. Studies of taste and intellectually oriented activities such as magazine readership or television viewing should consider education as the most relevant dimension. Occupation might be most relevant for studies focusing on leisure-time pursuits.

The task of the marketing manager is to think the problem through and select the measure of social stratification that is conceptually most relevant to the problem. Given this perspective, it is not surprising that studies attempting to determine the single best measure of social class have been inconclusive.[28]

Social Stratification and Marketing Strategy

While social stratification does not explain all consumption behavior, it is certainly relevant for some product categories. For clear evidence of this, visit a furniture store in a working-class neighborhood and then an upper-class store such as Ethan Allen Galleries.

Figure 4–12 indicates the steps involved in using social stratification to develop marketing strategy. The first task managers must perform is to determine, for their product categories, which aspects of the consumption process are affected by social status. This will generally require research in which relevant measures of social class are taken and associated with product/brand usage, purchase motivation, outlet selection, media usage, and so forth.

Figure 4–12
Using Social Stratification to Develop Marketing Strategy

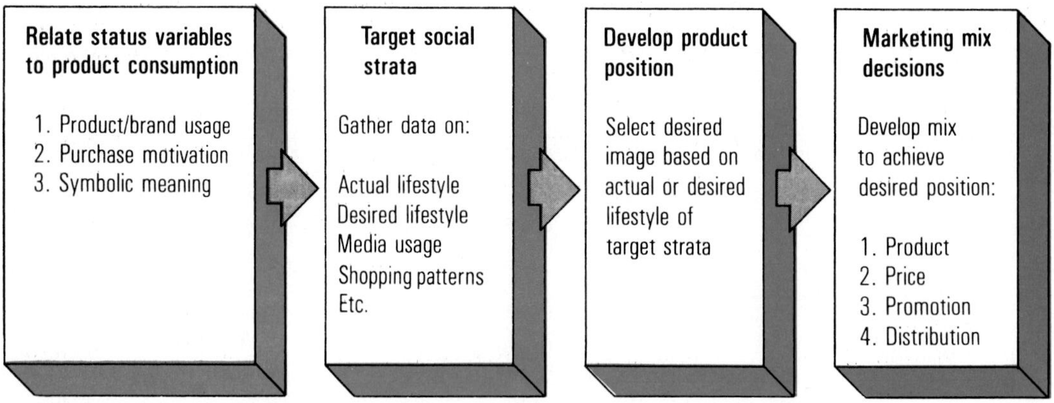

13. Name five products for which the "upward pull" strategy shown in Figure 4–5 would be appropriate. Name five for which it would be inappropriate. Justify your answer.
14. What are the marketing implications of Figure 4–6?
15. What are the marketing implications of Figure 4–7?
16. What are the marketing implications of Figure 4–8 for automobile manufacturers?
17. What are the marketing implications of Figure 4–12?
18. Discuss the similarities and differences between multi-item measures of social status shown in Figures 4–9, 4–10, and 4–11.
19. Select a product and develop a marketing mix using Figure 4–12 as a model. Make assumptions that are justified by material in the chapter.
20. Discuss the marketing strategy implications for marketing home telephones based on the preferences expressed in Exhibit 4–3.

PROJECT QUESTIONS

1. Interview salespersons from stores carrying differing quality levels of furniture. Determine the social class or status characteristics of his or her customers, and the marketing strategies used by the store.
2. Using Standard Rate and Data, pick three magazines that are oriented toward different social classes. Comment on the differences in content and advertising.
3. Interview two salespersons from one of the following product categories. Ascertain their perceptions of the social classes or status of their customers. Determine if their sales approach differs with differing classes.
   a. Used cars.
   b. Real estate.
   c. Stereos.
   d. Dresses.
   e. Insurance.
4. Examine a variety of magazines/newspapers and clip or describe an advertisement which positions a product as appropriate for five of the seven social classes described in the text.
5. Using Figures 4–5 and 4–6, find advertisements that are examples of these marketing strategies. Explain the strategy of each ad in terms of the target market, product positioning, and periodical used to reach this target market.
6. Interview an established professor, grocery checker, car salesperson, and plumber. Measure their social status using one of the multi-item measurement devices. Evaluate their status crystallization, unique and similar consumer behaviors.

REFERENCES

[1] R. P. Coleman and L. Rainwater, *Social Standing in America: New Dimensions of Class* (New York: Basic Books, 1978), p. 18.

[2] W. R. Hodge and P. M. Siegel, "The Measurement of Social Class," *International Encyclopedia of the Social Sciences* (New York: Free Press, 1968), pp. 316–17.

[3] See A. B. Hollingshead, *Elmstown's Youth* (New York: John Wiley & Sons, 1949); and W. L. Warner, M. Meeker, and K. Eels, *Social Class in America: A Manual of Procedure for the Measurement of Social Status* (Chicago: Science Research Associates, 1949).

[4] Coleman and Rainwater, *Social Standing in America.*

[5] J. E. Fisher, "Social Class and Consumer Behavior," in *Advances in Consumer Research XIV,* ed. M. Wallendorf and P. Anderson (Provo, Utah: Association for Consumer Research, 1987), pp. 492–96.

[6] A. Foner, "Ascribed and Achieved Bases of Stratification," *American Review of Sociology,* 1979, pp. 219–42.

[7] O. D. Duncan, D. L. Featherman, and B. Duncan, *Socioeconomic Background and Achievement* (New York: Seminar Press, 1972), p. 38.

[8] P. Hugstad, "A Reexamination of the Concept of Privilege Groups," *Journal of the Academy of Marketing Science,* Fall 1981, p. 399.

[9] D. Gilbert and J. Kahl, *The American Class Structure: A New Synthesis* (Chicago: Dorsey Press, 1982), p. 354.

[10] R. Coleman and L. Rainwater, *Social Standing in America.*

[11] R. Coleman, "The Continuing Significance of Social Class in Marketing." *Journal of Consumer Research,* December 1983, p. 265.

[12] K. T. Walsh, "The New-Collar Class," *U.S. News & World Report,* September 16, 1985, p. 62.

[13] P. Fussell, *Class* (New York: Ballantine Books, 1984), p. 38.

[14] W. Dunn, "In Pursuit of the Downscale," *American Demographics,* May 1986, pp. 26–33.

[15] W. O'Hare, "The Eight Myths of Poverty," *American Demographics,* May 1986, pp. 22–25.

[16] M. F. Utsey and V. J. Cook, Jr., "Demographics and the Propensity to Consume," in *Advances in Consumer Research XI,* ed. T. C. Kinnear (Chicago: Association for Consumer Research, 1984), pp. 718–23.

[17] S. Dawson and M. Wallendorf, "Associational Involvement," in *Advances in Consumer Research XII,* ed. E. C. Hirschman and M. B. Holbrook (Provo, Utah: Association for Consumer Research, 1985), pp. 586–91.

[18] R. M. Hauser and D. L. Featherman, *The Process of Stratification* (New York: Academic Press, 1977), p. xxiv.

[19] Utsey and Cook, Jr., "Demographics."

[20] G. Stevens and J. H. Cho, "Socioeconomic Indexes," *Social Science Quarterly,* Winter 1985, pp. 142–68.

[21] Duncan et al., *Socioeconomic Background,* p. 38.

[22] W. H. Peters, "Relative Occupational Class Income: A Significant Variable in the Marketing of Automobiles," *Journal of Marketing,* April 1970, p. 74.

[23] Ibid.

[24] R. E. Klippel and J. F. Monoky, "A Potential Segmentation Variable for Marketers: Relative Occupational Class Income," *Journal of the Academy of Marketing Science,* Spring 1974, pp. 351–56; and Hugstad, "A Reexamination."

[25] A. B. Hollingshead and F. C. Redlich, *Social Class and Mental Illness* (New York: John Wiley & Sons, 1985); and Warner et al., *Social Class in America.*

[26] Warner et al., *Social Class in America.*

[27] U.S. Bureau of the Census, *Methodology and Scores of the Socioeconomic Status,* Working paper no. 15 (Washington, D.C.: U.S. Government Printing Office, 1963).

[28] Recent reviews of this evidence are C. Schaninger, "Social Class Versus Income Revisited," *Journal of Marketing Research,* May 1981, pp. 197–201; and L. Dominguez and A. Page, "Stratification in Consumer Behavior Research: A Re-Examination," *Journal of the Academy of Marketing Science,* Summer 1981, pp. 250–73.

CHAPTER

5 Group Influence on Consumer Behavior

Reebok is one of the most successful, rapidly growing shoe firms in the world. Sales in America grew from $12.5 million in 1983 to $307 million in 1985. How did the firm accomplish this dramatic growth during a time when shoe sales, particularly sales of athletic shoes, were flat?

A large part of the firm's initial success was due to its association with aerobics. In 1983, aerobics was a minor sport with limited participation and no custom products such as shoes. Paul Fireman, who had U.S. distribution rights for Reebok, recognized the potential appeal of aerobics to women, particularly younger, upscale, active women. Equally important, Fireman recognized that group pressures would strongly influence the clothing worn during aerobics sessions and that style as well as function would be important.

Therefore, in addition to developing a functional shoe designed specifically for aerobics, Reebok's were stylish, trendy, and unique. Reebok also helped develop the sport of aerobics by publishing newsletters, sponsoring seminars, developing an aerobics teacher-certification program, and providing a clearinghouse for information on injury prevention. Sales of Reebok shoes grew rapidly as aerobics gained popularity. They became "the" shoe to wear for aerobics and, increasingly, in other contexts as well.

Reebok's strategy clearly involved aspects of the group influences shown below.[1]

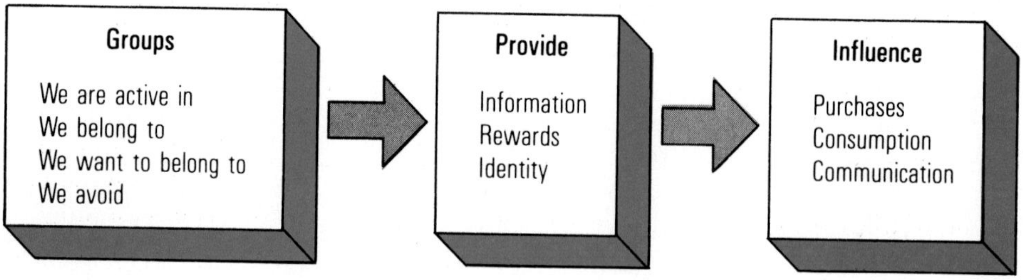

When you decided what to wear to the last party you attended, you probably based your decision in part on the anticipated responses of the other individuals at the party. Likewise, your behavior at an anniversary celebration for your grandparents probably would differ from your behavior at a graduation party for a close friend. These behaviors are responses to group influences.

The term *group*, considered in its broadest sense, refers to *two or more individuals who share a set of norms, values, or beliefs and have certain implicitly or explicitly defined relationships to one another such that their behaviors are interdependent.*[2] Almost all consumer behavior takes place within a group setting. In addition, groups serve as one of the primary agents of consumer socialization and learning.[3] Therefore, understanding how groups function is essential to understanding consumer behavior. As the Reebok example illustrates, marketers use knowledge of group influences when developing marketing strategy.

This chapter examines the manner in which groups function. Our first concern is with the various ways groups can be classified. Next, we analyze the impact reference groups have on the consumption process and how marketers can develop strategies based on these influences. Roles—behaviors associated with a position in a group—are then described and their implications for marketing strategy discussed.

TYPES OF GROUPS

The terms *group* and *reference group* need to be distinguished. A group was defined earlier as two or more individuals who share a set of norms, values, or beliefs and have certain implicitly or explicitly defined relationships to one another such that their behaviors are interdependent. A reference group is *a group whose presumed perspectives or values are being used by an individual as the basis for his or her current behavior.*[4] Thus, a reference group is simply a group that an individual uses as a guide for behavior in a specific situation.

Most of us belong to a number of different groups and perhaps would like to belong to several others. When we are actively involved with a particular group, it generally functions as a reference group. As the situation changes we may base our behavior on an entirely different group which then becomes our reference group. We may belong to many groups simultaneously, but we generally use only one group as a point of reference in any given situation. This is illustrated in Figure 5–1.

Groups may be classified according to a number of variables. Marketers have found three classification criteria to be particularly useful: membership, type of contact, and attraction.

The *membership* criterion is dichotomous: either one is a member of a particular group or one is not a member of that group. Of course, some members are more secure in their membership than others are. That is, some members feel they really "belong" to a group while others lack this confidence. However, membership is generally treated as an either/or criterion for classification purposes.

Figure 5–1
Reference Groups Change as the Situation Changes

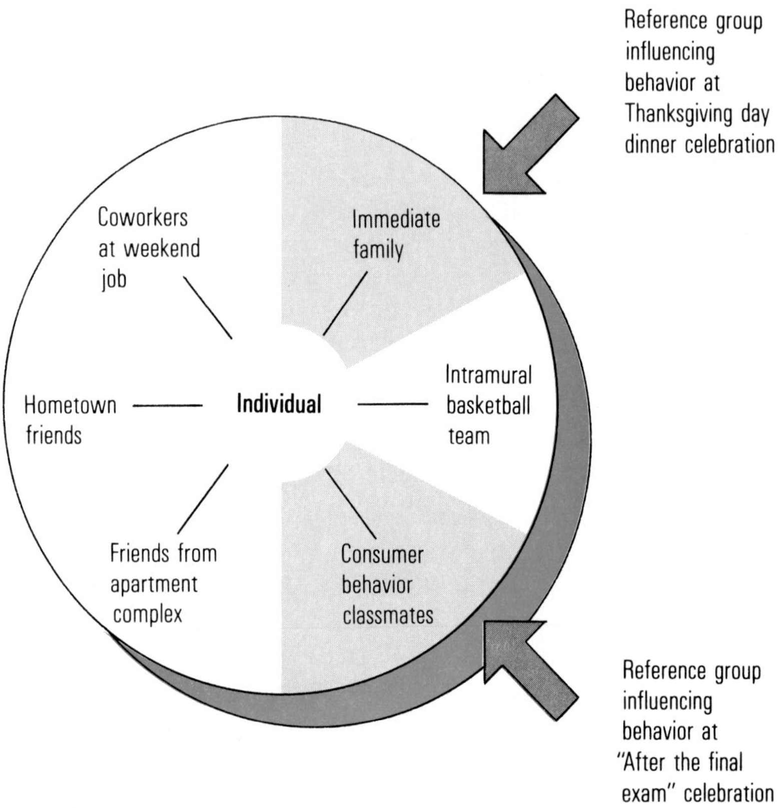

Degree of contact refers to how much interpersonal contact the group members have with each other. As group size increases, interpersonal contact tends to decrease. For example, you probably have less interpersonal contact with all other members of the American Marketing Association or your university than you have with your family or close friends. Degree of contact is generally treated as having two categories. Groups characterized by frequent interpersonal contact are called *primary* groups. Groups characterized by limited interpersonal contact are referred to as *secondary* groups.

Attraction refers to the desirability that membership in a given group has for the individual. This can range from negative to positive. Groups with negative desirability can influence behavior just as do those with positive desirability. For example, at one time motorcycles in the United States became associated with disreputable groups such as the Hell's Angels. Sales of motorcycles were limited because many people did not want to use a product associated with such groups.

Thus, motorcycle gangs served as negative reference groups for those individuals. (However, they were a positive reference group for individuals identifying with the Hell's Angels.) It took extensive advertising by firms such as Honda ("You meet the nicest people on a Honda") to change this image and increase market acceptance of motorcycles.

Attraction is often a more important determinant of group influence than membership. For example, *aspiration reference groups,* which are nonmembership groups with a positive attraction, have been found to exert a strong influence on desired products.[5] That is, individuals may purchase products thought

Figure 5–2
Types of Groups

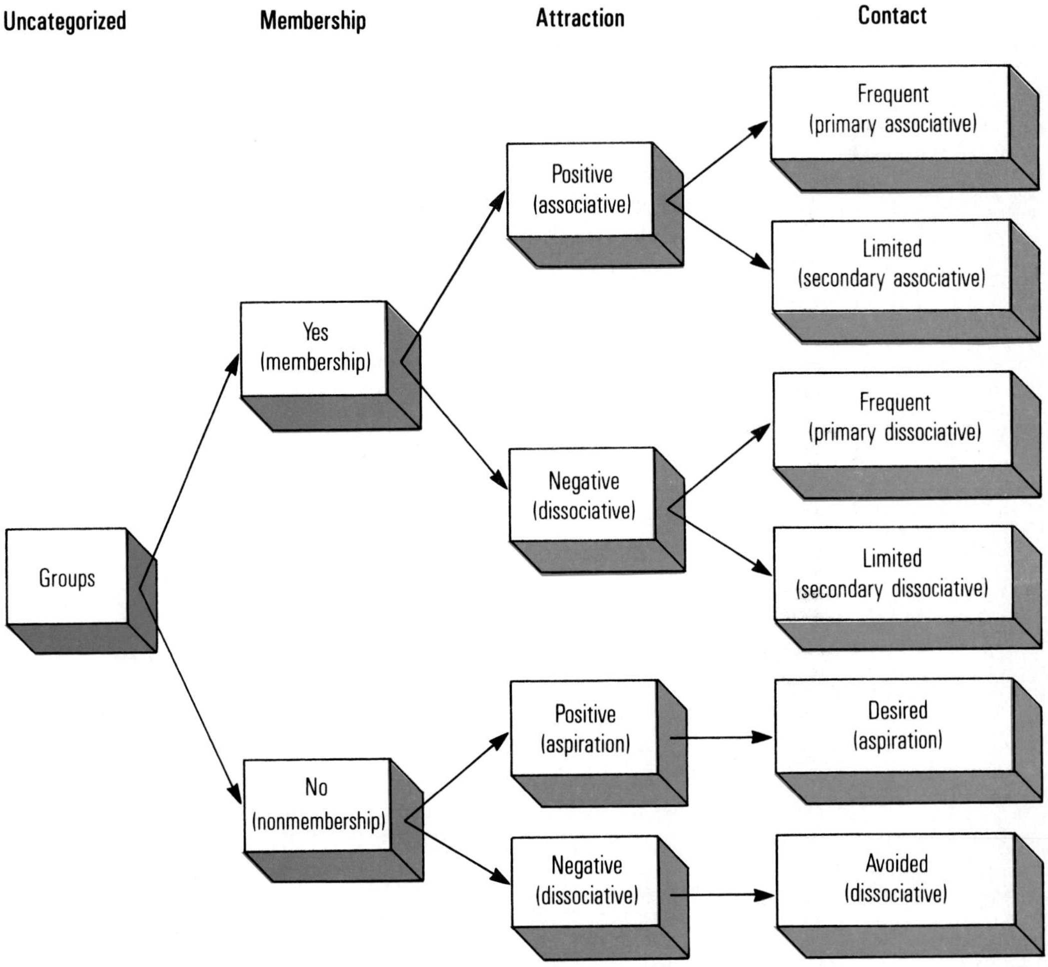

to be used by the desired group in order to achieve actual or symbolic membership in the group. The following theme from an ad for *Financial World* illustrates this:

> Surveys show that one of four *Financial World* readers is a millionaire. Our average reader is worth over $628,000. Join this select group who rely on *Financial World* for investment news, information, and insights.

Figure 5–2 illustrates the various types of groups that commonly influence consumer behavior. The ways they influence behavior are described below.

REFERENCE GROUP INFLUENCES ON THE CONSUMPTION PROCESS

Discussions of group influences or conformity to group expectations frequently give rise to negative feelings. Conformity is often viewed as following the crowd, not acting and thinking as an individual. It is important that we achieve a more realistic view of conformity, for it is the mechanism that makes groups influential. Conformity is the tendency to want to be like relevant and significant others.

We all conform in a variety of ways to numerous groups. By conforming, we make our lives more pleasant. For example, the fact that we wear clothes when attending class is conforming to a basic societal norm. By the same token, shorts, sandals, and no shirt would be inappropriate to wear to church on Sunday. Note that we, as individuals, do not generally consider these behaviors to constitute conformity. Normally, we conform without even being aware of doing so, though we also frequently face conscious decisions on whether or not to go along with the group. When we respond to group expectations, we are reacting to either *role expectations* (discussed in the next section) or *group norms*.

Norms are general expectations about behaviors that are deemed appropriate for all persons in a social context, regardless of the position they hold.[6] Norms arise quickly, often without verbal communication or direct thought, anytime a group exists. Norms tend to cover all aspects of behavior relevant to the group's functioning, and violation of the norms can result in sanctions. For example, in most classrooms in which the teacher does not use a seating chart, students select and maintain one seat throughout the term. As an experiment, try sitting in "someone else's seat" in such a class. Chances are you will receive a mild social sanction such as a stare.

Reference groups have been found to influence a wide range of consumption behaviors.[7] Before examining the marketing implications of these findings, we need to examine the nature of reference group influence more closely.

The Nature of Reference Group Influence

Conformity is not a unidimensional concept. Three types of group influence are illustrated in Figure 5–3. It is important to distinguish among these types since the marketing strategy required depends on the type of influence involved.[8]

Figure 5–3
Three Types of Group Influence

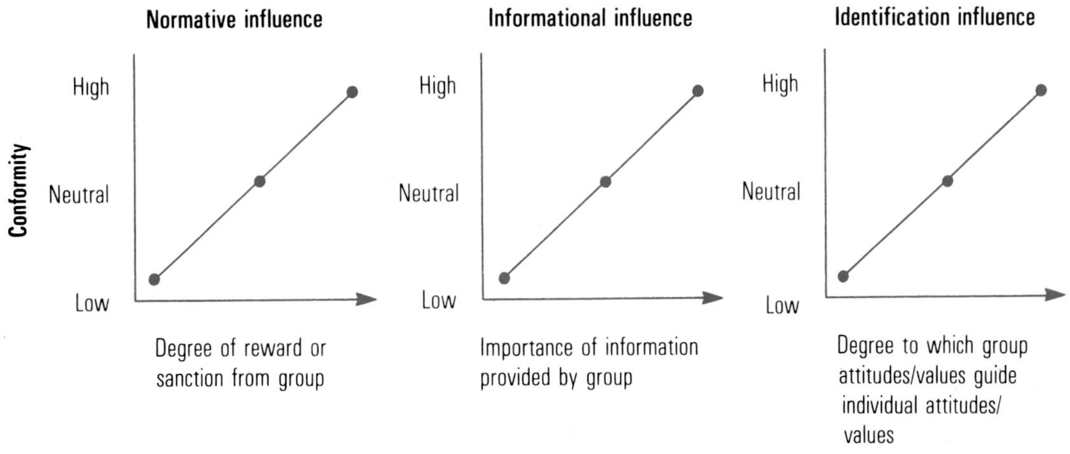

Informational influence occurs when an individual uses the behaviors and opinions of reference group members as potentially useful bits of information. Thus, a person may notice several members of a given group using a particular brand of coffee. He or she may then decide to try that brand simply because there is evidence (its use by friends) that it may be a good brand.[9] Or, one may decide to see a particular movie because a friend with similar tastes in movies recommends it. In these cases, conformity is simply the result of information shared by the group members.

Normative influence, sometimes referred to as *utilitarian* influence, occurs when an individual fulfills group expectations to gain a direct reward or to avoid a sanction. You may purchase a given brand of coffee to win approval from a spouse or a neighborhood group. Or you may refrain from wearing the latest fashion for fear of teasing by friends.

Identification influence, also called *value-expressive* influence, occurs when individuals use the perceived group norms and values as a guide for their own attitudes or values. Thus, the individual is using the group as a reference point for his or her own self-image.[10] Peer reference groups appear to have a particularly important identification influence on adolescents.[11]

Table 5–1 illustrates a series of consumption situations and the type of reference group influence that is operating in each case. While this table indicates the wide range of situations in which groups influence the consumption process, there are other situations in which groups have at most a limited, indirect effect.[12] For example, purchasing a particular brand of aspirin or noticing a billboard advertisement generally are not subject to group influence.

Table 5–1
Consumption Situations and Reference Group Influence

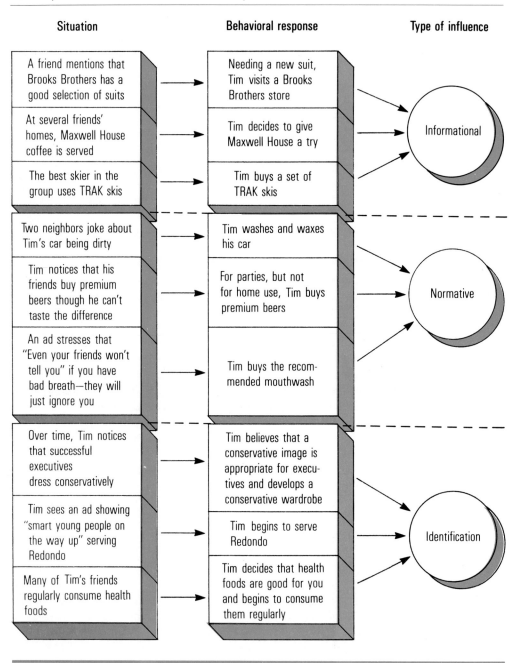

Situation	Behavioral response	Type of influence
A friend mentions that Brooks Brothers has a good selection of suits	Needing a new suit, Tim visits a Brooks Brothers store	Informational
At several friends' homes, Maxwell House coffee is served	Tim decides to give Maxwell House a try	Informational
The best skier in the group uses TRAK skis	Tim buys a set of TRAK skis	Informational
Two neighbors joke about Tim's car being dirty	Tim washes and waxes his car	Normative
Tim notices that his friends buy premium beers though he can't taste the difference	For parties, but not for home use, Tim buys premium beers	Normative
An ad stresses that "Even your friends won't tell you" if you have bad breath—they will just ignore you	Tim buys the recommended mouthwash	Normative
Over time, Tim notices that successful executives dress conservatively	Tim believes that a conservative image is appropriate for executives and develops a conservative wardrobe	Identification
Tim sees an ad showing "smart young people on the way up" serving Redondo	Tim begins to serve Redondo	Identification
Many of Tim's friends regularly consume health foods	Tim decides that health foods are good for you and begins to consume them regularly	Identification

Degree and Type of Reference Group Influence

Reference groups may have no influence in a given situation or they may influence usage of the product category, the type of product used, and/or the brand used. Brand influence is most likely to be a category influence rather than a specific brand. That is, a group is likely to approve (or disapprove) a range of brands such as imported beers or luxury automobiles.

In addition, the nature of the influence—informational, normative, or identification—may vary across situations. Therefore, it is useful to understand the conditions that are associated with various types and levels of reference group influence.

Determinants of the Type of Reference Group Influence. Any marketing attempt to utilize reference group influence requires an understanding of the *type* of influences operating. Therefore, it is important to be able to predict the relevant type of influence for a particular consumption situation. Table 5–2 summarizes the association between three product characteristics and types of reference group influence.

This table represents a useful starting point when considering the type of influence relevant to a specific product. For example, a manager dealing with a complex, conspicuous product with a substantial variation among brands, such as skis or sports cars, would expect to find a high level of both normative and identification reference group influence. This in turn suggests appropriate advertising themes.

Determinants of the Degree of Reference Group Influence. Figure 5–4 shows how two consumption situation characteristics—necessity/nonnecessity and visible/private consumption—combine to influence the degree of reference

Table 5–2
Product Characteristics and Type of Reference Group Influence

	Reference Group Influence		
Product Characteristics	Informational	Normative	Identification
High product complexity	+	0	0
High product conspicuousness	+	+	+
Low distinction among brands	+	+	+

\+ indicates the presence of reference group influence.

0 indicates the absence of reference group influence.

Source: Adapted from V. P. Lessig and C. W. Park, "Motivational Reference Group Influences," *European Research,* April 1982, p. 98.

Figure 5–4
Two Consumption Situation Characteristics and Product/Brand Choice

Consumption	**Degree Needed**	
	Necessity Weak reference group influence on product	Nonnecessity Strong reference group influence on product
Visible Strong reference group influence on brand	*Public necessities* Influence: Weak product and strong brand Examples: Wristwatch Automobile	*Public luxuries* Influence: Strong product and brand Examples: Snow skis Sailboat
Private Weak reference group influence on brand	*Private necessities* Influence: Weak product and brand Examples: Mattress Refrigerator	*Private luxuries* Influence: Strong product and weak brand Examples: TV game Trash compactor

Source: Adapted from W. D. Bearden and M. J. Etzel, "Reference Group Influence on Product and Brand Purchase Decision," *Journal of Consumer Research,* September 1982, p. 185.

group influence likely to operate in a specific situation. In the following paragraphs we will discuss these and three additional determinants of reference group influences.[13]

Group influence is strongest *when the use of product or brand is visible to the group*. For a product such as aerobic shoes, the product category (shoes), product type (aerobic), and brand (Reebok) are all visible. A dress is visible in terms of product category and product type (style), but the brand is less obvious. The consumption of other products such as vitamins is generally private. Reference group influence typically affects only those aspects of the product (category, type, or brand) that are visible to the group.

In Figure 5–4, the influence of the visibility dimension on brand selection is shown for necessities and nonnecessities. Automobiles and snow skis are consumed in highly visible situations, and reference groups are likely to influence the brand consumed. In contrast, mattresses and trash compactors are less visible and the brand is less subject to reference group influences.

Reference group influence is higher *the less of a necessity an item is*. Thus, reference groups have strong influence on the ownership of nonnecessities such as sailboats and stereo systems, but much less influence on necessities such as wristwatches and refrigerators.

In general, *the more commitment an individual feels to a group, the more the individual will conform to the group norms*. We are much more likely to consider group expectations when dressing for a dinner with a group we would like to join (stay with) than for dinner with a group that is unimportant to us.

The fourth factor influencing the impact of a reference group on an individual's behavior is *the relevance of the behavior to the group*. The more relevant a particular activity is to the group's functioning, the stronger the pressure to conform to the group norms concerning that activity. Thus, style of dress may be important to a social group that frequently eats dinner together at nice restaurants and unimportant to a reference group that meets for basketball on Thursday nights.

The final factor that affects the degree of reference group influence is *the individual's confidence in the purchase situation*. One study found the purchase of color televisions, automobiles, home air conditioners, insurance, refrigerators,

Figure 5–5
Consumption Situation Determinants of Reference Group Influence

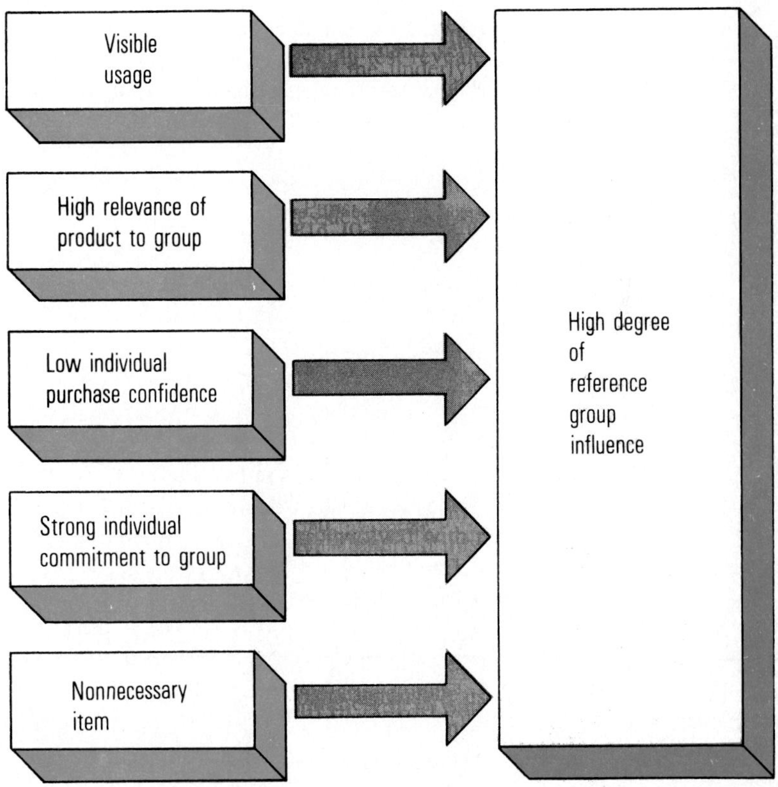

medical services, magazines or books, clothing, and furniture to be particularly susceptible to reference group influence. Several of these products such as insurance and medical services are neither visible nor important to group functioning. Yet they are important to the individual and are products about which most individuals have limited information. Thus, group influence is strong because of the individual's lack of confidence in purchasing these products. In addition to confidence in the purchase situation, there is evidence that individuals differ in their tendency to be *influenced by reference groups.*[14]

Figure 5–5 summarizes the manner in which these factors influence product and brand usage. Marketing managers can use this structure to determine the likely degree of group influence on the consumption of their brand.[15]

MARKETING STRATEGIES BASED ON REFERENCE GROUP INFLUENCES

Reference group influence is used by marketers primarily in the areas of advertising and personal selling. While it can be used to help make a price acceptable, reference group influence is seldom used in setting a price level. Nor does it provide much help for product design decisions. It does play a role in distribution decisions, but these are more closely related to personal selling.

The first task the manager faces in using reference group influences is to determine the degree and nature of reference group influence that exists, *or can be created,* for the product in question. Table 5–2 and Figure 5–5 provide the starting point for this analysis.

Personal Sales Strategies

The power of group norms has been demonstrated in a series of studies now generally referred to as the Asch experiments or the Asch phenomenon. The basic Asch study is described in Exhibit 5–1.

This study has been repeated in a variety of formats and has generally achieved the same results. Interviews with respondents after the experiments found that many changed their beliefs concerning which answers were correct. Thus, more than verbal conformity occurs. In addition, many respondents who expressed correct judgments indicated doubts about their own accuracy afterward. Note that the conformity being obtained was among strangers with respect to a discrete, physical task that had an objective, correct answer. Imagine how much stronger the pressures to conform are among friends or when the task is less well defined, such as preferring one brand or style over another.

Exhibit 5–1 also illustrates one way that the Asch phenomenon has been used by marketers in a personal selling situation.

Tupperware and other firms using "party" sales situations rely on situations in which reference group behavior encourages sales. Tupperware products are ones for which we would not normally predict a strong level of reference group influence—private usage, limited relevance to the group, fairly high individual

Exhibit 5–1

Utilization of the Asch Phenomenon in Personal Selling

THE CLASSIC ASCH EXPERIMENT

Eight subjects are brought into a room and asked to determine which of a set of three unequal lines are closest to the length of a fourth line shown some distance from the other three. The subjects are to announce their judgments publicly. Seven of the subjects are working for the experimenter, and they announce incorrect matches.

The order of announcement is arranged so that the naive subject responds last. In a control situation, 37 naive subjects performed the task 18 times each without any information about others' choices. Two of the 37 subjects made a total of three mistakes. However, when another group of 50 naive subjects responded *after* hearing the unanimous but *incorrect* judgment of the other group members, 37 subjects made a total of 194 errors, all of which were in agreement with the mistake made by the group.*

THE ASCH FORMAT IN PERSONAL SELLING

A group of potential customers—owners and salesmen of small firms—are brought together in a central location for a sales presentation. As each design is presented, the salesman scans the expressions of the people in the group, looking for the one who shows approval (e.g., head nodding) of the design. He then asks that person for an opinion, since the opinion is certain to be favorable. The person is asked to elaborate. As he does so, the salesman scans the faces of the other people, looking for more support. He then asks for an opinion of the next person now showing most approval. He continues until he reaches the person who initially showed the most disapproval. In this way, by using the first person as a model, and by social group pressure on the last person, the salesman gets all or most of the people in the group to make a positive public statement about the design.†

*Adapted from S. E. Asch, "Effects of Group Pressure upon the Modification and Distortion of Judgments," in *Readings in Social Psychology,* ed. E. E. MacCoby et al. (New York: Holt, Rinehart & Winston, 1958), pp. 174–83.

†P. Zimbardo and E. Ebbesen, *Influencing Attitudes and Changing Behavior* (Reading, Mass.: Addison-Wesley Publishing, 1970), pp. 114–22.

purchase skills, and a necessary item. However, by making the *purchase itself* part of a party *at a friend's home,* the situation is dramatically changed. Now the *purchase act* is the focus of attention, and it is visible and highly relevant to the party group to which the individual usually has a fair degree of commitment.

A very successful insurance agent obtains the names of next year's new faculty members each spring. During the summer, he sends them information on the town and offers to assist them with their insurance needs. In his letter he mentions several faculty members in their department who have insurance with him. After the new faculty arrive on campus, the agent arranges a meeting with them. The major goal of this meeting is to establish a relationship with the new faculty members and to provide a more complete list of existing faculty who currently use his services. Thus, this agent makes effective use of informational influence. Similar strategies can be applied in a variety of sales situations for both consumer and industrial products.

Exhibit 5–2 Identification and Information Influence Advertisements

Courtesy Fortune Magazine

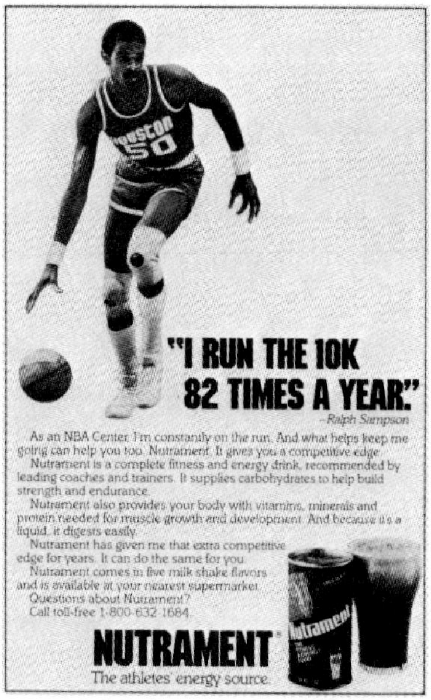

Courtesy the Drackett Co.

The *Fortune* advertisement describes an aggressive, business-oriented entrepreneur. It is based in part on the belief that many potential subscribers will identify with this type of person. In contrast, the Ralph Sampson advertisement, which appeared in *Runner's World,* is primarily providing information. Few runners would identify with Sampson. Instead, he is saying, "I engage in sport very similar to yours and you know I am good at it. Nutrament helps me and it will help you too." Thus, informational conformity seems to be the goal.

Exhibit 5–3

Group Pressure in Advertising to Children

Hasbro Industries, Inc., developed the Sno-Man Sno-Cone Machine and promoted it with television commercials that featured the lyric, "Who's the kid with all the friends hanging round? The kid with the Sno-Man Sno-Cone." The children's unit of the National Advertising Division (NAD) of the Council of Better Business Bureaus questioned this copy as using undue peer (group) pressure to sell a product to children.

In response, Hasbro conducted research designed to reveal children's perceptions of the advertisement. Fifty children between the ages of 5 and 10 were interviewed using a standard communications testing method. Twenty-eight percent of the children interviewed gave responses which related to the questioned part of the advertising copy. Most children stated that they wanted the toy so they could share it with friends. Only 4 percent stated acquiring "friends" as the *only* reason for wanting the product. NAD felt the responses indicated that children did not perceive the message as one of peer pressure at a sufficiently high level to warrant modification or discontinuance of the ad. However, Hasbro was requested to communicate an "ambience of sharing" as clearly as possible in the future.

Source: *A Four-Year Review of the Children in Advertising Review Unit, June 1974 through June 1978* (National Advertising Division, Council of Better Business Bureaus, Inc., undated), p. 14.

Advertising Strategies

Marketers use all three types of reference group influence when developing advertisements. Exhibit 5–2 contains an advertisement that relies on an informational approach and another that uses identification.

Advertising and, to a lesser extent, personal selling using group influence is controversial. This is particularly true when sanctions for not using the product or brand are implied. Exhibit 5–3 illustrates the NAD's rule against using "undue" peer pressure in advertising to children. Similar concerns have been raised about advertisements designed to create or enhance insecurities in adults. Thus, the marketing manager must consider the ethics as well as the probable effectiveness of this type of advertisement.

ROLES

Roles are defined and enacted within groups. A *role is a prescribed pattern of behavior expected of a person in a given situation by virtue of the person's position in that situation.*[16] Thus, while an individual must perform in a certain way, the expected behaviors are based on the position itself and not on the individual involved. For example, in your role as a student, certain behaviors are expected of you such as attending class and studying. The same general behaviors are expected of all other students. Roles are based on positions, not individuals.

While all students in a given class are expected to exhibit certain behaviors, the manner in which these expectations are fulfilled varies dramatically from individual to individual. Some students arrive at class early, take many notes, and ask numerous questions. Others come to class consistently, but never ask questions. Still others come to class only occasionally. *Role style* refers to these *individual variations in the performance of a given role*. *Role parameters* represent the *range of behavior acceptable within a given role*. The role of college student has wide parameters while the role of a private in the U.S. Marines carries very narrow parameters.

Sanctions are punishments imposed on individuals for violating role parameters. Thus, a student who fails to attend class or disrupts the conduct of the class generally is subject to sanctions ranging from mild reprimands to dismissal from school. The most severe sanction for most role violations is disqualification from that role. Therefore, an individual's *role commitment* or desire to continue in the role position is an important determinant of the effectiveness of the sanctions and the likelihood that the individual will remain within the role parameters.

All of us fulfill numerous roles, which is known as *role load*. When an individual attempts to fill more roles than the available time, energy, or money allows, *role overload* occurs. Occasionally two roles demand different behaviors. Consider the individual represented in Figure 5–6. In numerous situations, this fairly typical student will face incompatible role demands. For example, the basketball team member role may require practice one evening while the student role requires library research. This is known as *role conflict*.[17] Most career-oriented individuals experience conflicts between their role as family member (husband, wife, father, or mother) and their career.

The set of roles that an individual fulfills over time is not static. Individuals acquire new roles, *role acquisition,* and drop existing roles, *role deletion*. Since roles often require products, individuals must learn which products are appropriate for their new roles. For example, the student in Figure 5–6 may soon drop her roles as college student, intramural basketball player, and bookstore employee. She may acquire additional roles such as assistant brand manager, wife, and tennis club member. To be effective in her new roles, she will have to learn new behaviors and consume different products.

Roles themselves are not static over time. *Role evolution* occurs. The behaviors and products appropriate for a given role change with time. For example, in Chapter 3 we discussed the changes associated with sex role evolution.

A *role stereotype* is a shared visualization of the ideal performer of a given role.[18] Most of us share a common view of the physical and behavioral characteristics of a doctor, lawyer, or grade school teacher. Close your eyes and imagine any of these occupational types. Chances are that your mental image is similar to the image held by your classmates. The fact that large numbers of people share such common images is quite useful to marketing managers.

Figure 5–6
One Student's Role Set

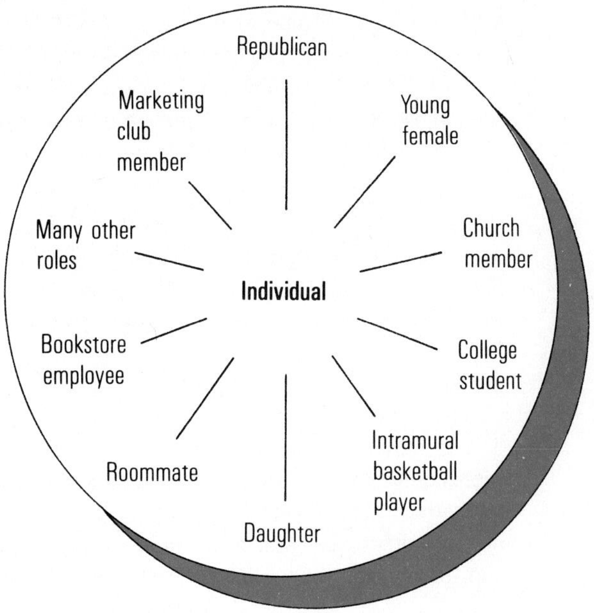

Application of Role Theory in Marketing Practice

Role-Related Product Cluster. *A role-related product cluster* is *a set of products generally considered necessary to properly fulfill a given role.*[19] The products may be functionally necessary to fulfill the role or they may be symbolically important. For example, the boots associated with the cowboy role originally were functional. The pointed toe allowed the foot to enter the stirrup quickly and easily while the high heel prevented the foot from sliding through the stirrup. The high sides of the boot protected the rider's ankles from thorns. Today, the "cowboy" role still calls for boots, although few urban cowboys spend much time in the saddle. The boot now is symbolically tied to the cowboy role.

Role-related clusters are important because they define both appropriate and inappropriate products for a given role. Since many products are designed to enhance role performance, marketing managers must be sure that their products fit with existing and evolving roles. Consider a key theme of Apple Computer's campaign for Macintosh:

If you have a desk, you need a Macintosh.

The advertisements go on to describe how the Macintosh is appropriate for the student role, the small business owner role, and the corporate employee role.

The advertisement for *Fortune* in Exhibit 5–2 is using identification influence with a role stereotype to indicate that *Fortune* is part of the successful entrepreneur role-related product cluster. It is one of a series of similar ads each of which features a different successful entrepreneur. Dewar's has used a very similar campaign to position their brand of scotch.

Evolving Roles. As roles evolve and change, challenges and opportunities are created for marketers. For example, the shifting role of women now includes active sports. In response, numerous apparel companies have introduced sports bras. In fact, the market is already segmented into special bras for various types of sports, such as casual running versus marathon running.[20] These products involve more than name and advertising changes. They are functionally different products based on the differing physiological requirements of active sports.

The successful entrepreneur shown in the *Fortune* advertisement in Exhibit 5–2 is female. Such an ad would not have appeared 15 years ago. Today it seems quite normal. The location and operating hours of many retail outlets now reflect the changed shopping patterns caused by widespread female participation in the work force. Marketers must be prepared to adjust product, promotion, and distribution to stay in tune with evolving roles.

Role Conflict and Role Overload. As roles evolve and change, new types of role conflicts come into existence. These role conflicts offer opportunities for marketers. For example, many airlines have altered their pricing policies and promote, "take your spouse along on your business trip," in an attempt to capitalize on conflicts between career and family roles. Students are frequently advised of the existence of speed-reading courses which promise to improve classroom performance and reduce conflict between the student role and other roles, by reducing the time required for studying. The following advertising copy from an Evelyn Wood Reading Dynamics' bulletin reflects this theme:

> **Why let the responsibilities that college demands deprive you of enjoying the college life? With Reading Dynamics you can handle both all the reading you're expected to do and know, plus still have time to do what you want to do.**

Role Acquisition. Role acquisitions present marketers with the opportunity to associate their products or brands with the new role.[21] Myers Rum uses this concept when it advertises:

> **So if you're ready to move up in life, maybe it's time you graduated to the flavor of Myers Jamaican Rums.**

This is a particularly useful approach when major role changes occur for significant numbers of people. For example, the role change from young single

Exhibit 5–4 Role Acquisition Advertisement

Why more wise newlyweds invest in John Hancock's Variable Life.
The special people in your life deserve special attention and care. This is true today and will be true in the future. John Hancock's Variable Life Insurance will help you provide both care and protection immediately and in the future.
Unlike traditional policies, John Hancock's Variable Life lets you invest some of your premiums in stock, bond or money market accounts. It's a sound approach. Not only is the face value of your policy guaranteed, but you can add to this amount without paying additional premiums.
Small wonder, that within the past year, over 35% of the life insurance policies we've sold have been our new Variable Life Insurance. It's a smart way to begin a program of family protection. It's also an ideal means of purchasing additional coverage at a reasonable cost.
Care for those close to you can take on many forms. One of the newest and best is John Hancock's Variable Life Insurance. Send in our coupon and learn more today.
I need to review my life insurance program.
Please send me more complete information and a Prospectus, including charges and expenses. I'd like to read the materials carefully before investing or forwarding funds.
Name
Address
City
State
Zip
Phone (optional)
☐ Check here if you are an insurance agent or broker.
Mail to: John Hancock Variable Life Insurance Co.
John Hancock Place, T-54, P.O. Box 111
Boston, MA 02117
John Hancock
Variable Life Insurance Company
We can help you here and now. Not just hereafter.
11011900084

to young married person happens to most people in our society and requires a significant shift in role-related behaviors. Exhibit 5–4 is an insurance advertisement from *Bride's* magazine. The ad describes a product the company feels is particularly appropriate for people moving from the single to the married role.

With increasing participation of women in the work force, role overload has become more common for both females and males. This presents marketers with the opportunity and challenge to provide time-saving products and shopping opportunities.[22]

SUMMARY

A *group* in its broadest sense includes two or more individuals who share a set of norms, values, or beliefs and have certain implicit or explicit relationships such that their behaviors are interdependent. Groups may be classified on the basis of membership, nature of contact, and attraction.

Some groups require *membership*; others (e.g., aspiration groups) do not. The *nature of contact* is based on the degree of interpersonal contact. Groups that have frequent personal contact are called *primary groups,* while those with limited interpersonal contact are called *secondary groups. Attraction* refers to the degree of positive or negative desirability the group has to the individual.

Norms are general expectations about behaviors that are deemed appropriate for all persons in a social context, regardless of the position they hold. Norms arise quickly and naturally in any group situation. The degree of conformity to group norms is a function of: (1) the visibility of the usage situation, (2) the level of commitment the individual feels to the group, (3) the relevance of the behavior to the functioning of the group, (4) the individual's confidence in his or her own judgment in the area, and (5) the necessity/nonnecessity nature of the product.

Group influence varies across situations. *Informational influence* occurs when individuals simply acquire information shared by group members. *Normative influence* is stronger because an individual conforms to group expectations to gain approval or avoid disapproval. *Identification conformity* is still stronger since an individual uses the group norms and identifies with them as a part of his or her self-concept and identity.

A *role* is defined as a prescribed pattern of behavior expected of a person in a given situation by virtue of the person's position in that situation. Thus, roles are based on positions and situations and not on individuals. Many characteristics affect role behavior, such as *role style* and *parameters,* one's *commitment* to a certain role, and *role conflict.* An important use of role theory in marketing revolves around the fact that there is usually a set of products considered necessary to properly fulfill a given role—in other words, a *role-related product cluster.* Marketers also structure strategies around *role conflict, role acquisition, role evolution,* and *role overload.*

REVIEW QUESTIONS

1. What is a *negative attraction reference group*? In what way can negative attraction reference groups influence consumer behavior?

2. What criteria are used by marketers to classify groups?
3. What is an *aspiration reference group*? How can an aspiration reference group influence behavior?
4. How does a *group* differ from a *reference group*?
5. What is the *Asch phenomenon*?
6. What factors determine the degree of influence a reference group will have on a given consumer decision?
7. What types of group influence exist? Why must a marketing manager be aware of these separate types of group influence?
8. What product characteristics appear to influence the type of reference group influence that will exist in a given situation?
9. How can personal sales strategies use a knowledge of reference group influence?
10. How can a marketer use a knowledge of reference group influences to develop advertising strategies?
11. What is a *role*?
12. How does *role style* relate to *role parameters*?
13. How does a *role sanction* relate to a *role parameter*?
14. How does *role commitment* relate to *role sanctions*?
15. What is *role conflict*? How can marketers use role conflict in product development and promotion?
16. What is a *role stereotype*? How do marketers use role stereotypes?
17. What is a *role-related product cluster*? Why is it important to marketing managers?
18. How does a *group norm* differ from a *role*?
19. What is meant by *role acquisition*? How can marketers use this phenomenon?
20. What is *role evolution*? Why is this concept important to marketing managers?
21. What is *role load*? *Role overload*?

DISCUSSION QUESTIONS

1. Using college students as the market segment, describe the most relevant reference group(s) and indicate the probable degree of influence for each of the following decisions:
   a. Purchase of health insurance.
   b. Type of shoes to wear to class.
   c. Brand of skis to buy when taking up skiing.
   d. Decision to stop eating red meat.
   e. Type of clothing to wear to a job interview.

f. Brand of mouthwash.

g. Brand of aspirin.

2. Answer the following questions for: (1) blood donation, (2) compact disc player, (3) clothing store, (4) skis, (5) socks, or (6) beer.
   a. How important are reference groups to the purchase of ________? Would their influence also affect the brand or model? Would their influence be informational, normative, or identification? Justify your answers.
   b. What reference groups would be relevant to the decision to purchase a ________ (based on students on your campus)?
   c. What are the norms of the social groups of which you are a member concerning ________?
   d. Could an Asch-type situation be used to sell ________?
   e. How could ________ be associated with the student role on your campus?
3. Describe five groups to which you belong and give two examples of purchase instances when each served as a reference group.
4. Describe two groups that serve as aspiration reference groups for you. In what ways, if any, have they influenced your consumption patterns?
5. Describe two groups to which you belong. For each, give two examples of instances when the group has exerted (*a*) informational, (*b*) normative, and (*c*) identification influence on your behavior.
6. Why is reference group influence weak on product ownership (use) of necessities and strong on nonnecessities?
7. Describe the role-related product cluster for students in your major on your campus. In what ways will this product cluster change when you begin your career?
8. Describe three situations in which you have experienced role conflict.
9. Describe a situation in which you have violated a group norm with respect to product ownership or use. What sanctions, if any, were applied?
10. Describe a recent role acquisition that you have engaged in. What new functional products were required? Were any symbolic products required?
11. Describe your role load. Do you experience role overload? How do you deal with role overload?

PROJECT QUESTIONS

1. Find three advertisements that use reference groups in an attempt to gain patronage.
   a. Describe the advertisement.
   b. Describe the type of reference group being used.
   c. Describe the type of conformity being sought.
2. Find three advertisements that use role stereotypes and describe the type of role being portrayed.

3. Find and describe an advertisement, product, or other use of the marketing mix based on role conflict.
4. Perform the following activities for: (1) blood donation, (2) compact disc player, (3) clothing store, (4) skis, (5) socks, or (6) beer.
   a. Develop an advertisement using an informational reference group influence.
   b. Develop an advertisement using a normative reference group influence.
   c. Develop an advertisement using an identification reference group influence.
   d. Develop an advertisement using a role-related product cluster approach.
   e. Develop an advertisement using a role conflict approach.
   f. Develop an advertisement using a role acquisition approach.
5. Interview: (*a*) 5 students, (*b*) 5 working women, or (*c*) 5 working men with children at home to determine the types of role conflicts they face. What marketing opportunities are suggested by your results?
6. Interview 5 recently married males and 5 recently married females to determine how their consumption patterns have changed as a result of their role change. What marketing opportunities are suggested by your results?
7. Interview 5 recent college graduates now employed in a management or sales position to determine how their consumption patterns have changed as a result of their role change. What marketing opportunities are suggested by your results?
8. Find two advertisements that use the role-related product cluster approach. What role is being used? Is the advertisement effective? Why?

REFERENCES

[1] Adapted from G. Lazaras, *Marketing Immunity* (Homewood, Ill.: Dow Jones-Irwin, 1988), pp. 48–49.

[2] L. E. Ostlund, "Role Theory and Group Dynamics," in *Consumer Behavior: Theoretical Sources,* ed. S. Ward and T. S. Robertson (Englewood Cliffs, N.J.: Prentice-Hall, 1973), p. 232.

[3] G. P. Moschis, "Socialization Perspectives and Consumer Behavior," *Review of Marketing 1981,* ed. B. M. Enis and K. J. Roering (Chicago: American Marketing Association, 1981), pp. 43–56; and W. R. Darden et al., "Consumer Socialization Factors in a Patronage Model of Consumer Behavior," in *Advances in Consumer Behavior VII,* ed. K. B. Monroe (Chicago: Association for Consumer Research, 1981), pp. 655–61.

[4] An overview of reference group theory is found in J. E. Stafford and A. B. Cocanougher, "Reference Group Theory," in *Perspectives in Consumer Behavior,* ed. H. H. Kassarjian and T. S. Robertson (Glenview, Ill.: Scott, Foresman, 1981), pp. 329–43.

[5] A. B. Cocanougher and G. D. Bruce, "Socially Distant Reference Groups and Consumer Aspiration," *Journal of Marketing Research,* August 1971, pp. 379–81.

[6] L. S. Wrightsman, *Social Psychology* (Monterey, Calif.: Brooks/Cole Publishing, 1977), p. 17.

[7] D. I. Hawkins and K. A. Coney, "Peer Group Influences on Children's Product Preferences," *Journal of the Academy of Marketing Science,* Spring 1974, pp. 322–31; J. D. Ford and E. A. Ellis, "A Reexamination of Group Influence on Member Brand Preference," *Journal of Marketing Research,* February 1980, pp. 125–32; and G. P. Moschis and L. G. Mitchell, "Television Advertising and Interpersonal Influences" in *Advances in Consumer Research XIII,* ed. R. J. Lutz (Provo, Utah: Association for Consumer Research, 1986), pp. 181–85.

[8] V. P. Lessig and C. W. Park, "Promotional Perspectives on Reference Group Influence: Advertising Implications," *Journal of Advertising,* Spring 1978, pp. 41–47; and V. P. Lessig and C. W. Park, "Motivational Reference Group Influences," *European Research,* April 1982, pp. 91–101.

[9] See R. E. Burnkrant and A. Cousineau, "Informational and Normative Social Influence in Buyer Behavior," *Journal of Consumer Research,* December 1975, pp. 206–15.

[10] See B. P. Moschis, "Social Comparison and Informal Group Influence," *Journal of Marketing Research,* August 1976, pp. 237–44.

[11] G. A. Churchill, Jr., and G. P. Moschis, "Television and Interpersonal Influences on Adolescent Consumer Learning," *Journal of Consumer Research,* June 1979, pp. 23–35; and R. L. Moore and G. P. Moschis, "Social Interaction and Social Structural Determinants in Adolescent Consumer Socialization," in *Advances in Consumer Research VII,* ed. J. C. Olson (Chicago: Association for Consumer Research, 1980), pp. 757–89.

[12] P. W. Miniard and J. P. Cohen, "Modeling Personal and Normative Influences on Behavior," *Journal of Consumer Research,* September 1983, pp. 169–80.

[13] See Lessig and Park, "Promotional Perspectives"; and D. W. Hendon, "A New and Empirical Look at the Influence of Reference Groups on Generic Product Category and Brand Choice," *Proceedings of the Academy of International Business* (College of Business, University of Hawaii, 1979), pp. 752–61; and Ford and Ellis, "A Reexamination."

[14] R. C. Becherer, W. F. Morgan, and L. M. Richard, "Informal Group Influence among Situationally/Dispositionally Oriented Customers," *Journal of the Academy of Marketing Science,* Summer 1982, pp. 269–81.

[15] A technical approach to measuring conformity is presented by S. J. Garfunkel, L. G. Schiffman, T. Madden, and W. R. Dillon, "Assessing Group Conformity: A Test of an Individualized Measurement Approach," in *The Changing Marketing Environment,* ed. K. Bernhardt et al. (Chicago: American Marketing Association, 1981), pp. 229–32.

[16] For a theoretical discussion of roles see G. Zaltman and W. Wallendorf, *Consumer Behavior* (New York: John Wiley & Sons, 1983), pp. 197–229.

[17] See S. Onkvisit and J. J. Shaw, "Multiplicity of Roles, Role Conflict Resolution and Marketing Implications," in *Developments in Marketing Science VII,* ed. J. D. Lindquist (Academy of Marketing Science, 1984), pp. 57–61.

[18] See J. M. Munson and W. A. Spivey, "Product and Brand-User Stereotypes among Social Classes," *Journal of Advertising Research,* August 1981, pp. 37–46.

[19] Other uses of role theory in marketing are discussed in D. T. Wilson and L. Bozinoff, "Role Theory and Buying-Selling Negotiations: A Critical Overview," in

Marketing in the 1980s, ed. R. P. Bagozzi et al. (Chicago: American Marketing Association, 1980), pp. 118–21.

[20] Sloan, "Bra Makers Sprint to Fill Sports Market," *Advertising Age,* December 25, 1978, p. 4.

[21] See M. Solomon and P. Anand, "Ritual Costumes and Status Transition," in *Advances in Consumer Research 12,* ed. E. Hirschman and M. Holbrook (Provo, Utah: Association for Consumer Research, 1985), pp. 315–18.

[22] M. D. Reilly, "Working Wives and Convenience Consumption," *Journal of Consumer Research,* March 1982, pp. 407–18; E. Foxman and A. C. Burns, "Role Load in the Household," in *Advances in Consumer Research XIV,* ed. M. Wallendorf and P. Anderson (Provo, Utah: Association for Consumer Research, 1987), pp. 458–62; and J. A. Belliggi and R. E. Hite, "Convenience Consumption and Role Overload," *Journal of the Academy of Marketing Science,* Winter 1986, pp. 1–9.

CHAPTER

6 Group Communications

Two high school friends, Michael Crete and Stuart Bewley, pooled their savings and, at age 27, started a company in an abandoned farm labor camp. Four years later their sales hit $100 million! The product, California Cooler, is a mixture of lightly carbonated wine and fruit juice. Their impressive sales were obtained at a time when U.S. wine and beer sales were showing virtually no growth.

The entrepreneurs began with a 15-gallon keg of the cooler made from a recipe Crete had used for beach parties during his college days. In their first year, the two claimed to represent an established firm and sold 700 cases from the back of a pickup. The second year, several Coors distributors agreed to handle the product and sales increased to 80,000 cases. In the third year, 5.4 million gallons ($25 million wholesale) were sold. Numerous competitors began entering the market in year four.

Crete and Bewley did a number of innovative things. First, the product itself was new, though wine coolers were often mixed and served at parties. Second, California Cooler was packaged in 12-ounce bottles and sold 4 to the pack or 24 to the case. Third, the product was generally sold chilled in the cold beer racks of retail outlets. Thus, the cooler is a wine-based product, but is packaged and sold much like a beer product. Unlike either the beer or wine industries, California Cooler relied on word-of-mouth communications rather than advertising to spread the news of the product. However, when strong competition entered the market, Crete and Bewley added a substantial advertising budget.[1]

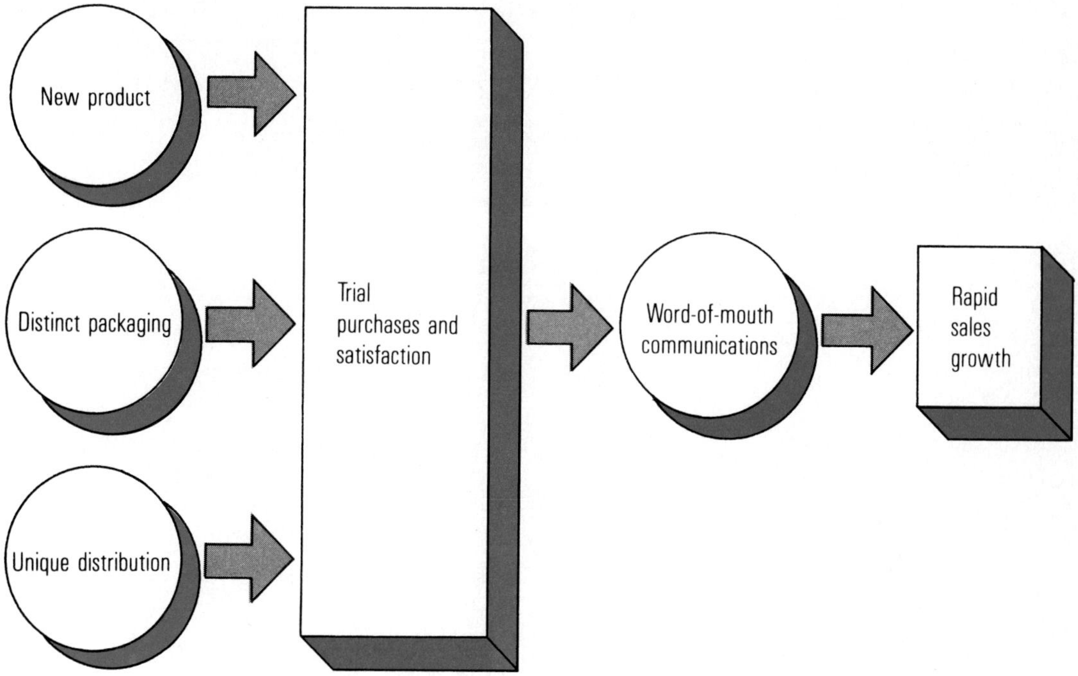

As the above example indicates, new products—*innovations*—are an important and exciting part of our economic life. It also shows the tremendous power of word-of-mouth communications—5.4 million gallons of California Cooler were sold in one year without advertising. This chapter examines both of these critical concepts.

COMMUNICATION WITHIN GROUPS

Since California Cooler was not advertised, consumers could only learn about it through in-store exposure or from other individuals. While many consumers undoubtedly tried the product after seeing it in a store, most learned about it from friends. We learn about new products from our friends and other reference groups by (1) observing or participating with them as they use the product, or (2) by seeking or receiving advice and information from them.

Figure 6–1 illustrates the relative importance of various information sources to purchasers of home video game hardware.[2] Several findings shown in this table are noteworthy. First, a variety of information sources was considered important. However, reference group sources were as important as all other sources combined. This is not unusual in situations involving a major purchase.

A second common finding is that the relative importance of information

Figure 6–1
Relative Importance of Information Sources for Purchasers of Home Video Game Hardware

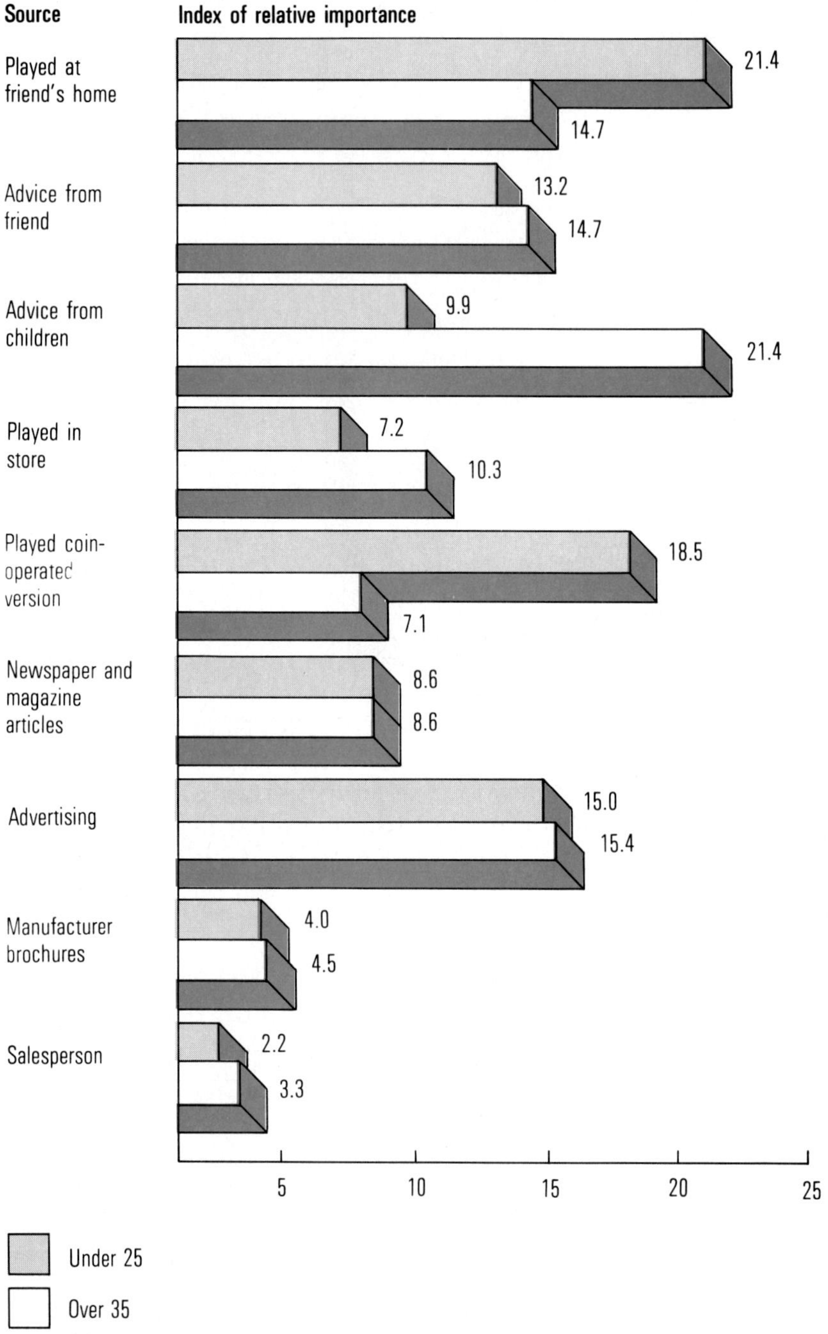

Source: Derived from "1982–83 Newsweek Study of Home Video Game Hardware Purchasers," *Newsweek Magazine*, 1983.

sources is not the same for all groups. Not surprisingly, children have a much smaller influence on young adults than on older adults (who are likely to have more and older children at home). Obviously, different sources of information are used for different products. For example, children are not likely to be an information source for life insurance.

Another key aspect shown in Figure 6–1 is the fact that using the product at a friend's home was an important source of information. This information source no doubt was vital for California Cooler as well.

Figure 6–1 indicates the clear importance that personal sources of information have in at least some purchase decisions. Individuals who supply consumption-related information to others are referred to as *opinion leaders*.

OPINION LEADERSHIP

Information is the primary tool marketers use to influence consumer behavior. While information is ultimately processed by an individual, in a substantial number of cases one or more group members filter, interpret, or provide the information for the individual. The person who performs this task or role is known as an *opinion leader*. The process of one person receiving information from the mass media or other marketing sources and passing that information on to others is known as the *two-step flow* of communications. The two-step flow explains some aspects of communication within groups, but it is too simplistic to account for most communication flows. What usually happens is a multistep flow of communication.[3] Figure 6–2 contrasts the direct flow with a multistep flow of mass communications.

The multistep flow involves opinion leaders for a particular product area who actively seek relevant information from the mass media as well as other sources. These opinion leaders process this information and transmit their interpretations of it to some members of their groups. These group members also receive information from the mass media as well as from group members who are not opinion leaders. The figure also indicates that these nonopinion leaders often initiate requests for information and supply feedback to the opinion leaders.[4]

Situations in Which Opinion Leadership Occurs

The exchange of advice and information between group members can occur when: (1) one individual seeks information from another; (2) when one individual volunteers information; and (3) as a by-product of normal group interaction.

Imagine that you are about to make a purchase in a product category with which you are not very familiar. Further imagine that the purchase is important to you—perhaps a new stereo system, skis, a bicycle, or jogging shoes. How would you go about deciding what type and brand to buy? Chances are you would, among other things, consult someone you know who you believe to be

Figure 6–2
Mass Communication Information Flows

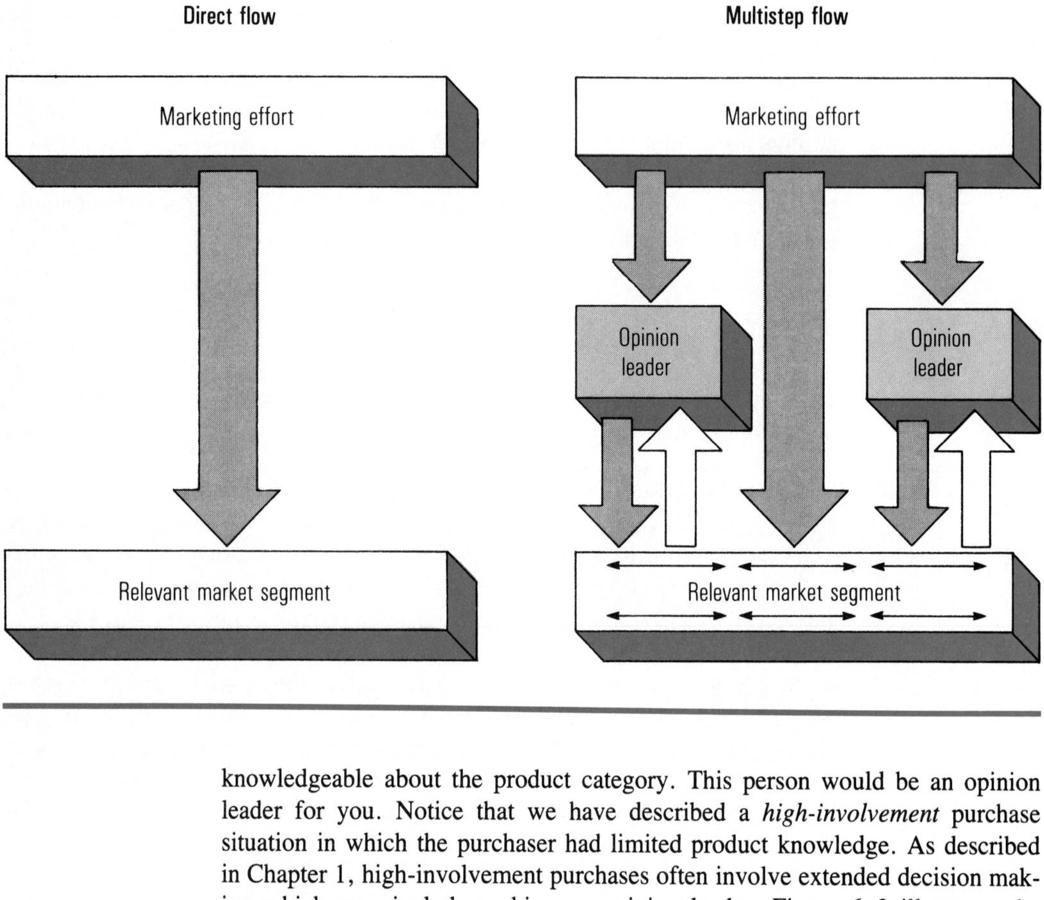

knowledgeable about the product category. This person would be an opinion leader for you. Notice that we have described a *high-involvement* purchase situation in which the purchaser had limited product knowledge. As described in Chapter 1, high-involvement purchases often involve extended decision making which may include seeking an opinion leader. Figure 6–3 illustrates the factors that would lead to this situation. Of course, both product involvement and knowledge will vary across consumers.

Industrial and retail buyers behave in a manner similar to consumers when seeking information from members of their reference groups (other purchasing agents and businesspeople). For example, one study found such personal information sources to be significantly more important for retail buyers when purchasing a complex item than when purchasing a relatively simple item.[5]

In a low-involvement purchase, one is less likely to seek an opinion leader. (Imagine seeking out a friend and asking which brand of wood pencil is best!) However, opinion leaders may well volunteer information on low-involvement products. Of course, such products and purchases would not be low involvement for the opinion leader. For example, most of us would consider canned peas an unimportant (low-involvement) purchase. However, a person concerned with health might be highly involved with food purchases. Such a person might well

Figure 6–3
Likelihood of Seeking an Opinion Leader

Product/purchase involvement	Product knowledge	
	High	Low
High	Moderate	High
Low	Low	Moderate

seek out information and provide unsolicited opinions on the salt content of various brands of canned peas.

In addition to *explicitly* seeking or volunteering information, group members provide information to each other through observable behaviors. For example, suppose you visit a friend's house and are served a California Cooler and play a video game. Obviously, you have learned that your friend likes these products and you have gained personal experience with them.

Opinion Leader Characteristics

What characterizes opinion leaders? The most salient characteristics are greater involvement with and knowledge of the product category than the nonopinion leaders in the group. Thus, an individual tends to be an opinion leader only for specific product or activity clusters.[6] Opinion leaders are exposed to more mass media, particularly to mass media oriented toward their area of leadership than are nonopinion leaders.[7]

Opinion leadership functions primarily through interpersonal communications and observation. These activities occur most frequently among individuals with similar demographic characteristics. Thus, it is not surprising that opinion leaders are found within all demographic segments of the population and seldom differ significantly on demographic variables from the people they influence. For certain product categories, such as fashions, movies, or foods, some demographic groups are more informed and thus are more likely to serve as opinion leaders. Opinion leaders tend to be more gregarious and outgoing than nonopinion leaders.[8]

These findings can be summarized as follows:

Characteristic	Opinion Leader Compared to Nonopinion Leaders
Product knowledge	Greater
Relevant media exposure	Greater
Demographics	Similar
Personality	More gregarious

In addition to the above individual characteristics associated with opinion leadership, a very important situational characteristic has been identified: product (or store) dissatisfaction. Substantial research evidence indicates that dissatisfied consumers are highly motivated to tell others about the reasons for their dissatisfaction, and these negative messages influence the recipients' attitudes and behaviors.[9] This phenomenon makes imperative both consistent product quality and quick, positive responses to consumer complaints.

The Market Maven. Opinion leaders are generally product or activity specific. However, some individuals appear to have information about many kinds of products, places to shop, and other aspects of markets. They both initiate discussions with others about products and shopping and respond to requests for market information. They are referred to as *market mavens*.[10]

Market mavens appear to play a particularly important role in providing information about retail outlet characteristics, price and product changes, and low-involvement products. Unfortunately, it is difficult to target messages to this group as they do not appear to have unique demographics. However, market messages can be structured to appeal specifically to their interests.

Marketing Strategy and Opinion Leadership

The importance of opinion leadership varies radically from product to product and from target market to target market. Therefore, the initial step in using opinion leaders is to determine—through research, experience, or logic—the role opinion leadership has in the situation at hand. Once this is done, marketing strategies can be devised to make use of opinion leadership.

Identifying Opinion Leaders. Utilizing knowledge of opinion leadership and the multistep flow of communication is complicated by the fact that opinion leaders are difficult to identify. They tend to be similar to those they influence. While opinion leaders can be identified using sociometric techniques, key informants, and self-designating questionnaires, these methods are seldom practical for marketing applications.

The fact that opinion leaders are heavily involved with the mass media, particularly media that focus on their area of leadership, provides a partial solution to the identification problem. For example, Nike could assume that many subscribers to *Runners World* serve as opinion leaders for jogging and running shoes. Likewise, the fact that opinion leaders are gregarious and tend to belong to clubs and associations suggests that Nike could also consider members, and particularly officials, of local running clubs to be opinion leaders.

Some product categories have professional opinion leaders. For products related to livestock, county extension agents are generally very influential. Barbers and hairstylists serve as opinion leaders for hair care products. Pharmacists are important opinion leaders for a wide range of health care products. Computer science majors may be natural opinion leaders for other students considering purchasing a personal computer.

Thus, for many products it is possible to identify individuals who have a high probability of being an opinion leader. Once these individuals are identified, what should the marketer do?

Marketing Research. Since opinion leaders receive, interpret, and relay marketing messages to others, marketing research should focus on opinion leaders rather than "representative" samples in those product categories and groups in which opinion leaders play a critical role. Thus, product-use tests, pretests of advertising copy, and media preference studies should be conducted on samples of individuals likely to be opinion leaders. It is essential that these individuals be exposed to, and respond favorably to, the firm's marketing mix. Of course, for those product categories or groups in which opinion leadership is not important, such a strategy would be unwise.

Product Sampling. Sampling—sending a sample of a product to a group of potential consumers—is an effective means of generating interpersonal communications concerning the product. In one study, 33 percent of a randomly selected group of women who received a free sample of a new brand of instant coffee discussed it with someone outside their immediate family within a week.[11] Instead of using a random sample, a marketer should attempt to send the product to individuals likely to be opinion leaders.

Retailing/Personal Selling. Numerous opportunities exist for retailers and sales personnel to use opinion leadership. Clothing stores can create "fashion advisory boards" composed of likely style leaders from their target market. An example would be cheerleaders and class officers for a store catering to teenagers. Restaurant managers can send special invitations, 2-for-1 meal coupons, and menus to likely leaders in their target markets, such as officers in Junior League, League of Women Voters, and Rotary.

Retailers and sales personnel can encourage their current customers to pass along information to potential new customers. For example, an automobile salesperson, or the dealership, might provide a free car wash or oil change to current customers who send friends in to look at a new car. Real estate agents might send a coupon good for a meal for two at a nice restaurant to customers or other contacts who send them new clients.

Advertising. Advertising attempts to both *stimulate* and *simulate* opinion leadership. Stimulation involves themes designed to encourage current owners to talk about the product/brand or prospective owners to ask current owners for their impressions.[12] Before such a campaign is used, the firm needs to be certain that there is a high degree of satisfaction among existing owners.

Simulating opinion leadership involves having an acknowledged opinion leader—such as Florence Joyner or Carl Lewis for running equipment—endorse a brand. Or, it can involve having an apparent opinion leader recommend the product in a "slice of life" commercial. These commercials involve an "overheard" conversation between two individuals in which one provides brand advice to the other.

Exhibit 6–1 Creation of High School Opinion Leaders for Rock Records

PROCEDURE

1. Social leaders (presumably gregarious) such as class presidents, secretaries, sports captains, and cheerleaders were selected from geographically diverse high schools in test cities. Research indicated that few of those selected were currently opinion leaders for records.
2. These individuals were asked to join a panel composed of "leaders" who "should be better able to identify potential rock-and-roll hits." In return for participation, the student would receive free records.
3. Information about the record and singing star were provided for each record the student was to evaluate. In addition, the students were encouraged to investigate other sources of information such as *Billboard* magazine and record stores.
4. The students were also encouraged to discuss each record with their friends before voting.

RESULTS

Several test records reached the top 10 in the cities with the student panels. None of these records reached the top 10 in other cities. Thus, the firm was apparently successful in creating opinion leaders who, in turn, influenced sales.

Source: Adapted from J. R. Mancuso, "Why Not Create Opinion Leaders for New Product Introductions," *Journal of Marketing*, July 1969, p. 21.

Creating Opinion Leaders. Rather than identify current opinion leaders, it is sometimes possible to create them. Remember that opinion leaders are characterized by gregariousness, interest in the product category, and knowledge about the product. Sometimes a firm can identify gregarious individuals and stimulate their interest and knowledge about a particular product. Exhibit 6–1 illustrates the way one record company went about this. Versions of this technique have been used in the electronics and metalworking industries. Glenmore Distilleries used a modification of this approach in the introduction of a new liqueur,[13] and Canada Dry has used it with their club soda.

DIFFUSION OF INNOVATIONS

The manner by which a new product is accepted or spreads through a market is basically a group phenomenon. In this section, we will examine this process in some detail.[14]

Nature of Innovations

An innovation is an idea, practice, or product perceived to be new by the relevant individual or group. Whether or not a given product *is* an innovation is determined by the perceptions of the potential market, not by an objective measure of technological change. Polaroid's 600 System camera, which will "automatically blend strobe light and existing light to a degree previously impossible," represents a major engineering accomplishment. Yet, unless consumers interpret it as a change, they will not respond to it as an innovation. One analyst states Polaroid's problem as follows: "The average instant photographer does not understand what is going on to begin with, so how is he going to understand the significance of these technical improvements?"[15]

A product does not have to be new in terms of the length of time it has been in existence to be an innovation. Yogurt, like many other health foods, has been used for hundreds of years. Recent marketing efforts have introduced these products to market segments that were not familiar with them. To these market segments, the products were innovations and were responded to as such.

Categories of Innovations

Try to recall new products that you have encountered in the past two or three years. As you reflect on these, it may occur to you that there are degrees of innovation. For example, an electric razor was more of an innovation than a double-blade safety razor. We can picture any given product as falling somewhere on a continuum ranging from no change to radical change depending on the target market's response to the item. This is shown in Figure 6–4.

Behavior change in Figure 6–4 refers to changes required in the consumer's

Figure 6–4
Categories of Innovations

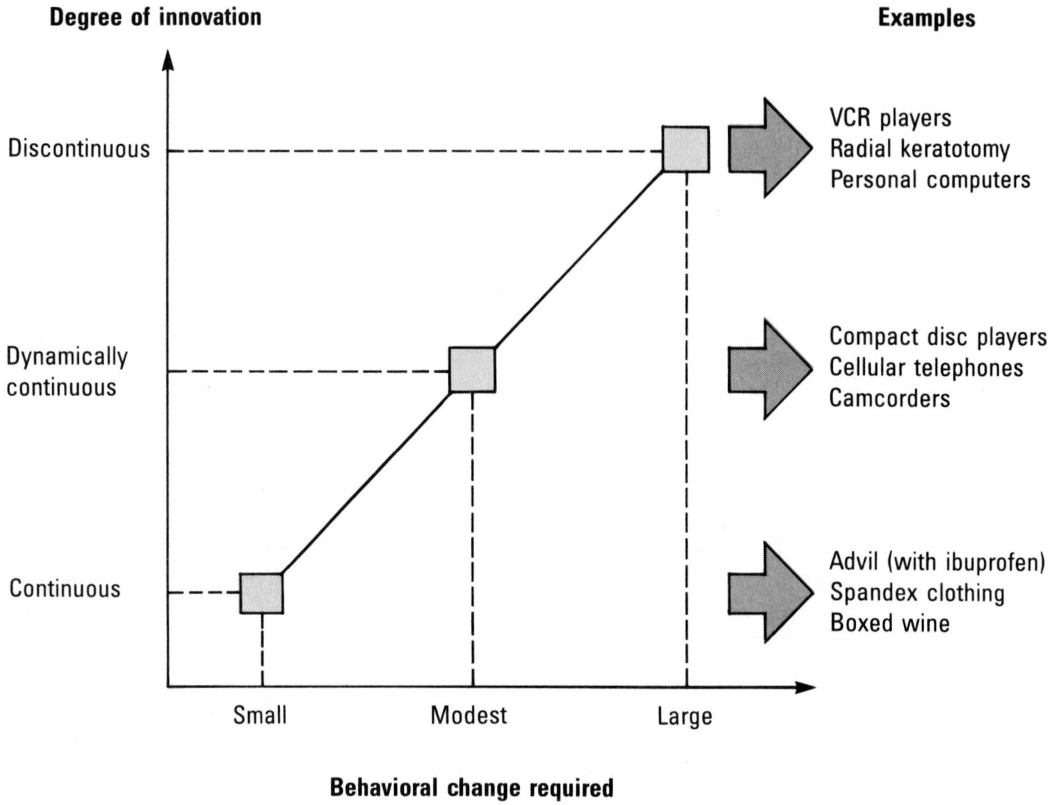

behavior (including attitudes and beliefs) if the innovation is adopted or utilized. It does not refer to technical or functional changes in the product. Thus, shifting to LA or another brand of low-alcohol beer from a regular beer would not require a significant change in most drinkers' behaviors. However, purchasing a home computer requires significant behavior changes.

Also indicated in Figure 6–4 are three categories into which it is useful to classify a given innovation as viewed by a specific market segment. Each of these categories is described below. Note that no boundaries are shown between the categories. This is because there are no distinct breaks between each category.

1. **Continuous Innovation.** Adoption requires relatively minor changes in behavior. Examples include Spandex clothing, Almaden boxed wines, Showermate liquid shower soap, and Advil with ibuprofen.

2. **Dynamically Continuous Innovation.** Adoption requires a major change in an area of behavior that is relatively unimportant to the individual. Examples would include compact disc players, cellular telephones, camcorders, and home shopping programs.
3. **Discontinuous Innovation.** Adoption requires major changes in behavior in an area of importance to the individual or group. Examples would include microwave ovens, personal computers, water beds, and radial keratotomy (eye surgery).

Figure 6–5
Adoption Process and Extended Decision Making

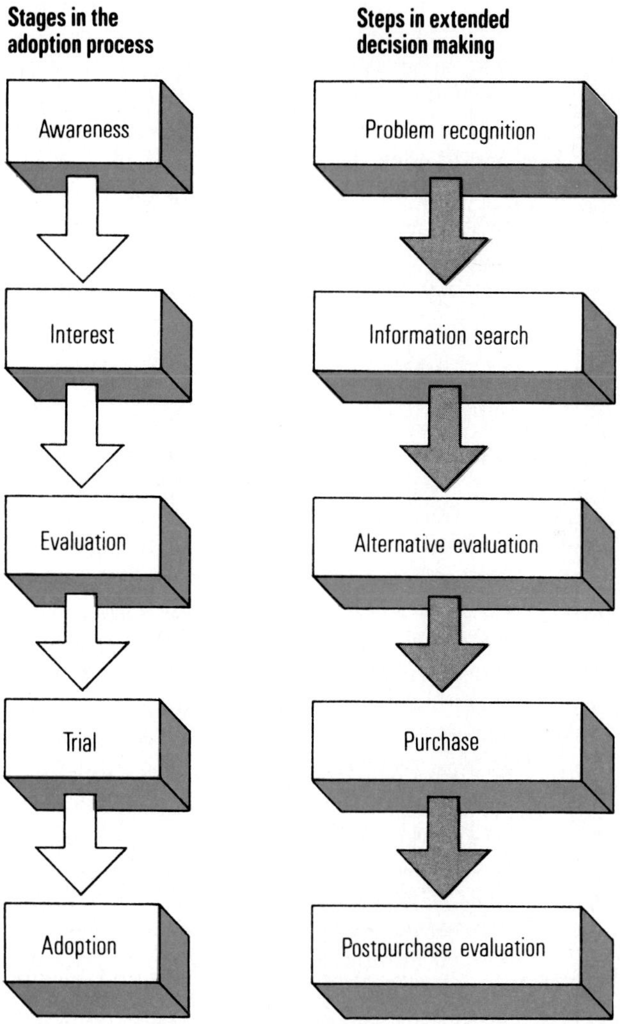

Most of the thousands of new products or alterations introduced each year tend toward the no-change end of the continuum. Much of the theoretical and empirical research, however, has been based on discontinuous innovations. For example, individual consumers presumably go through a series of very distinct steps or stages known as the *adoption process* when purchasing a new innovation. These stages are shown in Figure 6–5.

Figure 6–5 also shows the steps in extended decision making as described in Chapter 1. As can be seen, *the adoption process* is basically a term used to describe extended decision making when a new product is involved. As we saw in Chapter 1 (and will discuss in detail in Chapter 14), extended decision making occurs when the consumer is *highly involved* in the purchase. High purchase involvement is likely for discontinuous innovations, and most studies of innovations of this nature have found that consumers use extended decision making.

However, it would be a mistake to assume that all innovations are evaluated using extended decision making (the adoption process). In fact, most continuous innovations probably trigger limited decision making. That is, as consumers we generally don't put a great deal of effort into deciding to purchase such innovations as Hershey Foods' new Marabou Milk chocolate rolls or Heublein's new bottled drink, Espree.

Thus, we have a situation where diffusion theory and research have focused on discontinuous innovations while most new consumer products are continuous innovations. The following material is most valid for discontinuous innovations and least applicable for continuous innovations.

Diffusion Process

The diffusion process is the manner in which innovations spread to the members of a social system. From a marketing context, the term *spread* refers to purchase behavior in which the members of the social system purchase the product with some degree of continuing regularity; that is, they adopt the product. The social system for a marketer refers to the target market. The target market can range from virtually the entire American society (for a new soft drink perhaps) to the students at a particular junior high (for an automated fast-food and snack outlet).

No matter which innovation is being studied or which social group is involved, the diffusion process appears to follow a similar pattern over time: a period of relatively slow growth, followed by a period of rapid growth, followed by a final period of slower growth. This pattern is shown in Figure 6–6. However, there are exceptions to this pattern. In particular, it appears that for continuous innovations such as new ready-to-eat cereals, the initial slow-growth stage may be skipped.

An overview of innovation studies reveals that the time involved from introduction until a given market segment is saturated (i.e., sales growth has slowed or stopped) varies from a few days or weeks to years. This leads to two interesting questions: (1) *What determines how rapidly a particular innovation will spread through a given market segment?* and (2) *In what ways do those who purchase innovations relatively early differ from those who purchase them later?*

Figure 6–6
Diffusion Rate of an Innovation Over Time

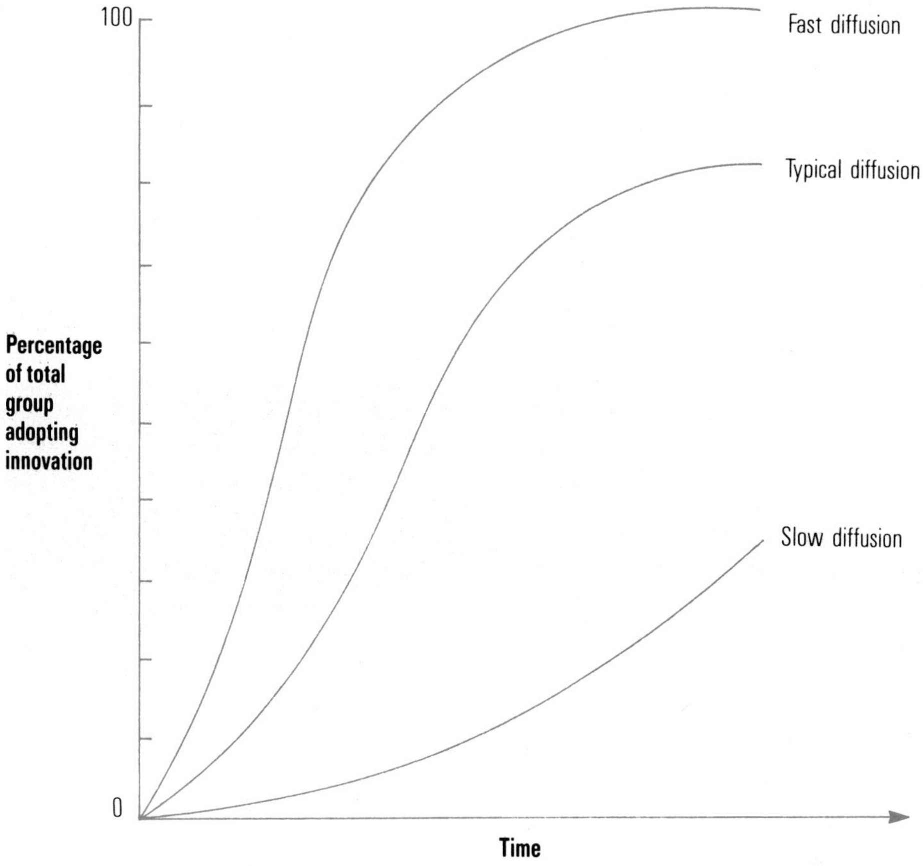

Factors Affecting the Spread of Innovations. The rate at which an innovation is diffused is a function of ten factors:

1. Type of group. Some groups are more accepting of change than others. In general, young, affluent, and highly educated groups accept change, including new products, readily. Thus, the target market for the innovation is an important determinant of the rate of diffusion.

2. Type of decision. The type of decision is basically an individual versus collective dimension. The fewer individuals involved in the decision, the more rapidly the innovation will spread. Therefore, innovations likely to involve two or more household members will generally spread slower than innovations that affect primarily one individual.

3. Marketing effort. The rate of diffusion is influenced by the extent of marketing effort involved. That is, the rate of diffusion is not completely beyond the control of the firm. A good example of this is provided by Apple Computer's expenditure of $180 million on advertising and sales promotion in 1984, largely to promote the Macintosh computer which became a huge success.[16] Without such major expenditures as a $2 million superbowl commercial, the acceptance of this innovative new computer would have been much slower.

4. Fulfillment of felt need. The more manifest or obvious the need that the innovation satisfies, the faster the diffusion. One of the difficulties the Polaroid 600 System (described earlier) faced was the fact that consumers did not feel a strong need for the performance improvement the system offered.

5. Compatability. The more the purchase and use of the innovation is consistent with the individual's and group's values or beliefs, the more rapid the diffusion. VCRs are quite compatible with the existing values of large segments of the American society, while boxed or canned wine is not.

6. Relative advantage. The better the innovation is perceived to meet the relevant need compared to existing methods, the more rapid the diffusion. For example, a Weed Eater appears to offer substantial advantages over hand trimming a lawn. Included in relative advantage is *price*. Thus, while a Weed Eater enjoys a tremendous advantage over hand trimming in terms of effort involved, this aspect of relative advantage is somewhat offset by the higher cost.

7. Complexity. The more difficult the innovation is to understand and use, the slower the diffusion. The key to this dimension is ease of use, *not* complexity of product. For example, compact disc players, while very complex products, are very simple for most stereo owners to use. Complexity involves both attribute complexity and trade-off complexity.[17] *Attribute complexity* deals with the difficulty encountered in understanding or using the attributes of a product. A home computer has a high level of attribute complexity for many older consumers. *Trade-off complexity* refers to the degree and number of conflicting benefits. A microwave oven has a high degree of trade-off complexity for many consumers because it contains such conflicting attributes as speed of cooking versus quality of cooking, cost of purchase versus economy of operation, and convenience versus space requirements.

8. Observability. The more easily consumers can observe the positive effects of adopting an innovation, the more rapid its diffusion will be. Cellular telephones are relatively visible. Radial keratotomy and compact disc players, while less visible, are often the topic of conversation. On the other hand, headache remedies such as Advil are less obvious and generally less likely to be discussed.

9. Trialability. The easier it is to have a low-cost or low-risk trial of the innovation, the more rapid its diffusion. The diffusion of such products as radial keratotomy and cellular telephones has been hampered by the difficulty of trying out the product. This is much less of a problem with low-cost items such as headache remedies, or such items as VCRs or compact disc players that can be rented, borrowed, or tried at a retail outlet.

10. Perceived risk. The more risk associated with trying an innovation, the slower the diffusion. Risk can be financial, physical, or social. It is a function of three dimensions: (1) the probability that the innovation will not perform as

Figure 6–7
Determinants of a Rapid Rate of Diffusion

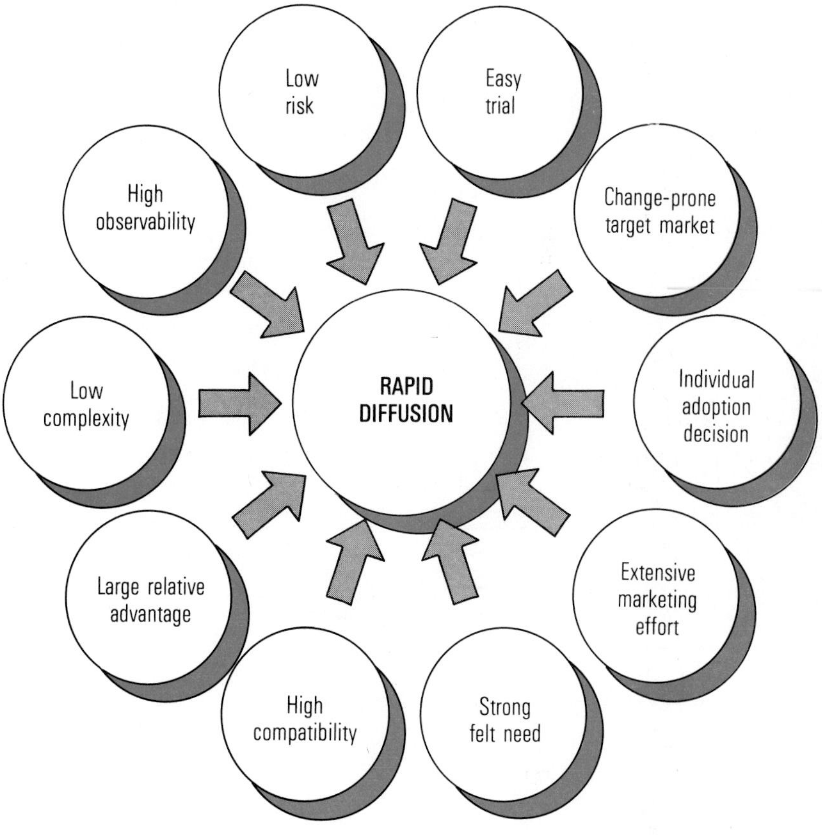

expected; (2) the consequences of its not performing as expected; and (3) the ability to reverse, and the cost of reversing, any negative consequences. Thus, many consumers feel a need for the benefits offered by a radial keratotomy and view the probability of its working successfully as being quite high. However, they perceive the consequences of failure as being extreme and irreversible and therefore do not adopt this innovation.

Figure 6–7 summarizes the impact of these determinants on the rate of diffusion when all are favorable.

Characteristics of Individuals Who Adopt an Innovation at Varying Points in Time. The curves shown in Figure 6–6 are cumulative curves that illustrate the increase in the percentage of adopters over time. If we change those curves from a cumulative format to one that shows the percentage of a market that

Figure 6–8
Adoptions of an Innovation Over Time

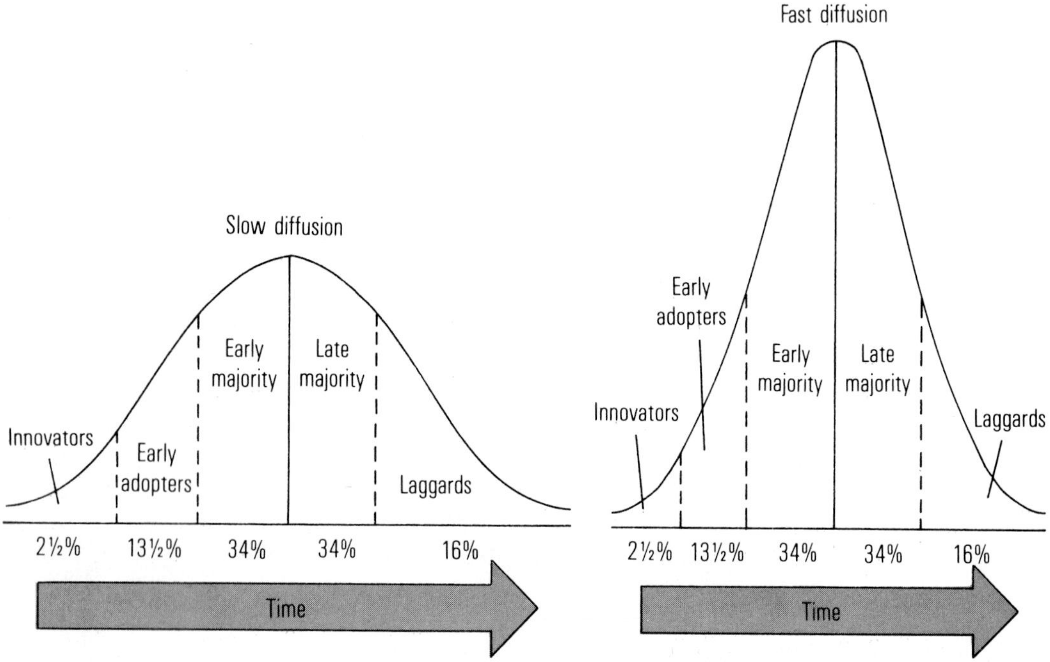

adopts the innovation at any given point in time, we will have the familiar bell-shaped curves shown in Figure 6–8.

Figure 6–8 reemphasizes the fact that a few individuals adopt an innovation very quickly, another limited group is very reluctant to adopt the innovation, and the majority of the group adopts at some time in between the two extremes. As shown, the total time involved varies by product.

Researchers have found it useful to divide the adopters of any given innovation into five groups based on the relative time at which they adopt. These groups, called *adopter categories,* are shown in Figure 6–8 and are defined below:

Innovators:	The first 2.5 percent to adopt an innovation.
Early adopters:	The next 13.5 percent to adopt.
Early majority:	The next 34 percent to adopt.
Late majority:	The next 34 percent to adopt.
Laggards:	The final 16 percent that adopt.

How do these five groups differ? The first answer is: It depends on the product category being considered. Table 6–1 illustrates the rather dramatic differences

Table 6–1
Early Purchasers of Home Computers and VCRs

	Home Computer	VCR
Age*		
18–24	103	163
25–34	113	91
35 +	94	84
Education*		
College graduate	179	152
Attended college	125	86
High school	77	92
Marital status*		
Married	209	92
Single	107	136
Products owned†		
Tennis clothing	0	+
Squash racquet	0	–
Water skis	–	+
Target gun	–	+
Bowling ball	–	+
Ski boots	–	0
Luxury car	–	0
Men's diamond ring	–	+
Classical folk records/tapes	0	–
Contemporary jazz records/tapes	–	0
Book club	0	–
Solar heating	+	–
Food dehydrator	+	–
Electric ice cream maker	–	+

*Results are index numbers where 100 equals average consumption.

†+ = Heavy consumption; 0 = Moderate consumption; and – = Light consumption.

Source: A. J. Kover, "Somebody Buys New Products Early—But Who? Unpublished paper prepared for Cunningham & Walsh, Inc.

between early purchasers of home computers and VCRs.[18] Thus, while we propose some broad generalizations, they may not hold true for a particular product category. Indeed, they should be treated as hypotheses or ideas to test for the product category you are involved with rather than as established facts.

Innovators are venturesome risk-takers. They are capable of absorbing the financial and social costs of adopting an unsuccessful product. They are cosmopolitan in outlook and use other innovators rather than local peers as a reference group. They tend to be younger, better educated, and more socially mobile than their peers. Innovators make extensive use of commercial media, sales personnel, and professional sources in learning of new products.

Early adopters tend to be opinion leaders in local reference groups. They tend to be successful, well educated, and somewhat younger than their peers. They are willing to take a calculated risk on an innovation but are concerned

with failure. Early adopters also use commercial, professional, and interpersonal information sources, and they provide information to others.[19]

Early majority consumers tend to be cautious with respect to innovations. They adopt sooner than most of their social group but also after the innovation has proven successful with others. They are socially active but seldom leaders. They tend to be somewhat older, less well educated, and less socially mobile than the early adopters. The early majority relies heavily on interpersonal sources of information.

Late majority members are skeptical about innovations. They often adopt more in response to social pressures or a decreased availability of the previous product than because of a positive evaluation of the innovation. They tend to be older and have less social status and mobility than those who adopt earlier.

Laggards are locally oriented and engage in limited social interaction. They

Figure 6–9
Generalized Relationships of Selected Variables with Adopter Categories

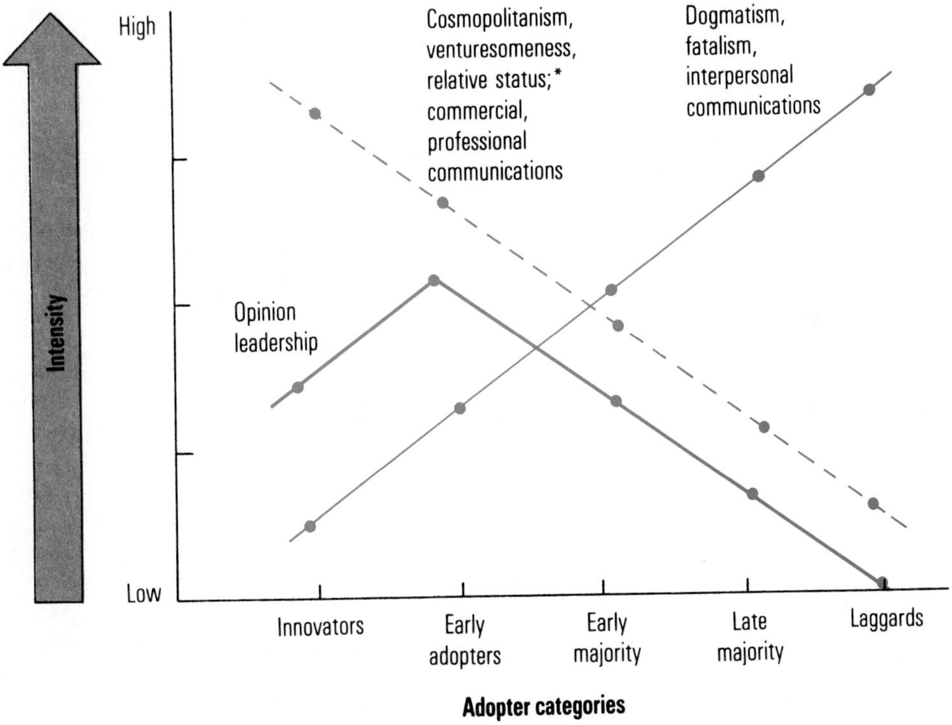

*Measured in a variety of ways, such as income, occupation, education, and lifestyle.

tend to be relatively dogmatic and oriented toward the past. Innovations are adopted only with reluctance.

Figure 6–9 illustrates some of the generalizations just described. Again, it must be emphasized that the ideal types presented above and the generalizations shown in Figure 6–9 are summary profiles that may not hold true for a particular product category.

In conclusion, we can say that, for most innovations:

- Adopter categories exist.
- They differ from each other on a number of dimensions.
- They are relatively stable over time.
- They are product-category or activity-cluster specific.

Marketing Strategies and the Diffusion Process

Market Segmentation. The fact that earlier purchasers of an innovation differ from later purchasers suggests a "moving target market" approach. That is, after a general target market is selected, the firm should initially focus on those individuals within the target market most likely to be innovators and early adopters. As the product gains acceptance, the focus of attention should shift to the early and late majority. This means that both media and advertising themes may need to change as a product gains market acceptance.

Diffusion Enhancement Strategies. Table 6–2 provides a framework for developing strategies to enhance the market acceptance of an innovation. The critical aspect of this process is to analyze the innovation *from the target market's perspective*. This analysis will indicate potential obstacles—*diffusion inhibitors*—to rapid market acceptance. The manager's task is then to overcome these inhibitors with *diffusion enhancement strategies*. Table 6–2 lists a number of possible enhancement strategies. Many others are possible.

Suppose a proposed innovation scores high (favorably) on all attributes except compatibility. What marketing strategy does this suggest? The firm's communications, particularly advertising, will have to minimize this problem. For example, "light" (diet) beers were introduced successfully by relating them to active, masculine individuals and avoiding direct references to diet, which many "real beer drinkers" felt to be for women and sissies. Likewise, the fact that the relative advantage of Polaroid's 600 System was not readily observable meant that its introductory advertising budget was "twice as much as any other previous Polaroid product introduction."[20]

Conclusions on the Diffusion of Innovations. There have been over 2,000 published studies of the diffusion process. From this volume of research, a

Table 6–2
Innovation Analysis and Diffusion Enhancement Strategies

Diffusion Determinant	Diffusion Inhibitor		Diffusion Enhancement Strategies
1. Nature of group	Conservative	→	Search for other markets Target innovators within group
2. Type of decision	Group	→	Choose media to reach all deciders Provide conflict reduction themes
3. Marketing effort	Limited	→	Target innovators within group Use regional rollout
4. Felt need	Weak	→	Extensive advertising showing importance of benefits
5. Compatibility	Conflict	→	Stress attributes consistent with values and norms
6. Relative advantage	Low	→	Lower price Redesign product
7. Complexity	High	→	Distribute through high service outlets Use skilled sales force Use product demonstrations Extensive marketing efforts
8. Observability	Low	→	Use extensive advertising
9. Trialability	Difficult	→	Use free samples to early adopter types Special prices to rental agencies Use high service outlets
10. Perceived risk	High	→	Success documentation Endorsement by credible sources Guarantees

number of useful generalizations have emerged as described in the preceding sections. Despite our knowledge in this area, many new consumer products are commercial failures. The primary reason for this high failure rate is not a lack of knowledge, but a failure to apply what is known. Executives too often utilize their own evaluation of the attributes of the innovation rather than those of the relevant market segments, or the initial introduction is aimed at the average consumer. However, the average consumer often is not the innovator or early adopter who must try the product first. Exhibit 6–2 provides an analysis of the successful diffusion of a recent innovation—microwave ovens.

Exhibit 6–2

The Diffusion of Microwave Ovens

Amana introduced the first countertop microwave oven for consumer use in 1965. Litton followed suit with private label versions in 1969, and its own brand in the 1970s. Five years after the first consumer microwave was introduced, only 0.1 percent of the U.S. households had one. Now, 25 years after introduction, about 75 percent of U.S. households have a microwave oven. An examination of the diffusion of this product illustrates many of the concepts discussed in the text.

I. **Category of innovation.** Purchasers viewing the microwave as their primary cooking device probably perceived it as a discontinuous innovation since it would require a major behavioral change in an important activity. Most early marketing efforts encouraged this view. However, most purchasers actually use the product as a supplement for thawing frozen items, heating leftovers, or cooking parts of a meal. Thus, word-of-mouth communications encouraged a perception of a dynamically continuous innovation.

II. **Diffusion process.** Microwave oven sales have followed the typical diffusion curve shown in Figure 6–6.
   A. *Group.* Initial efforts were targeted at middle- to upper-income households. This should speed diffusion.
   B. *Type of decision.* A microwave oven purchase would generally involve both spouses. This should slow diffusion.
   C. *Extent of marketing effort.* Marketing effort was limited initially as Amana was the only firm in the market. The growth of competition has increased total marketing effort which has accelerated acceptance.
   D. *Felt need.* A faster way to prepare meals was a recognized need by a significant group of consumers.
   E. *Compatibility.* While convenience and speed are now widely accepted values, the belief that slow cooking and taking time with a meal produce better results is still held by many people. Some traditional homemakers find this type of product inappropriate for their perceived roles.
   F. *Relative advantage.* Speed and convenience are major advantages. However, cost, safety concerns, limited counter space, and a limited range of cooking somewhat offset these advantages.
   G. *Complexity.* Microwaves are simple to operate, but successfully cooking with them requires additional learning.
   H. *Observability.* Microwaves are relatively easy to observe in others' homes and are a frequent topic of conversation.
   I. *Trialability.* A microwave can be tested in a store; a substantial amount of marketing effort was devoted to encouraging this type of trial.

Exhibit 6–2 *(concluded)*

J. *Perceived risk.* A microwave oven is an expensive purchase (financial risk) for most households, and many consumers felt there was a considerable health risk.

III. **Adopters.** Initial adopters tended to be younger, middle to upper income, and urban. These adopters used mass media and sales personnel for information. As the product has spread through the early and into the late majority, the characteristics of the purchasers are about the national norm and personal sources of information (friends and family) are more important.

SUMMARY

Communication within groups is a major source of information about certain products. It is a particularly important source when an individual has a high level of *purchase involvement* and a low level of *product knowledge*. In such cases, the consumer is likely to seek information from a more knowledgeable group member. This person is known as an *opinion leader*. Opinion leaders are sought out for information, and they also volunteer information. Of course, substantial product information is exchanged during normal group interactions.

Opinion leaders are product-category or activity-group specific. They tend to have greater product knowledge, more exposure to relevant media, and more gregarious personalities than their followers. They tend to have demographics similar to their followers. A situational variable, product dissatisfaction, motivates many individuals to become temporary opinion leaders. The term *market maven* is used to describe individuals who are opinion leaders about the shopping process in general.

Marketers attempt to identify opinion leaders primarily through their media habits and social activities. Identified opinion leaders then can be used in marketing research, product sampling, retailing/personal selling, and advertising. It is also possible to create opinion leaders.

Groups, because of their interpersonal interaction and influence, greatly affect the diffusion of innovations. *Innovations* vary in degree of behavioral change required and the rate at which they are diffused. The first purchasers of an innovative product or service are termed *innovators;* those who follow over time are known as *early adopters, early majority, late majority,* and *laggards*. Each of these groups differs in the time of adoption of an innovation and in terms of personality, age, education, and reference group membership. These characteristics help marketers identify and appeal to different classes of adopters at different stages of an innovation's diffusion.

The time it takes for an innovation to spread from innovators to laggards is affected by several factors:

1. Nature of the group involved.
2. Type of innovation decision required.
3. Extent of marketing effort.
4. Strength of felt need.
5. Compatibility of the innovation with existing values.
6. Relative advantage.
7. Complexity of the innovation.
8. Ease in observing usage of the innovation.
9. Ease in trying the innovation.
10. Perceived risk in trying the innovation.

REVIEW QUESTIONS

1. What is an *opinion leader?* How does an opinion leader relate to the *multistep flow of communication?* How does an opinion leader differ from a *market maven?*
2. What characterizes an opinion leader?
3. What determines the likelihood that a consumer will seek information from an opinion leader?
4. How can marketing managers identify opinion leaders?
5. How can marketers utilize opinion leaders?
6. How could one "create" opinion leaders?
7. How do the information sources for video game equipment differ between younger and older purchasers?
8. How can opinion leaders be used in personal selling?
9. What is an *innovation?* Who determines whether a given product is an innovation?
10. What are the various categories of innovations? How do they differ?
11. What is the *diffusion process?* What pattern does the diffusion process appear to follow over time?
12. Describe the factors that affect the diffusion rate for an innovation. How can these factors be utilized in developing marketing strategy?
13. What are *adopter categories?* Describe each of the adopter categories.
14. How can a marketer use a knowledge of adopter categories?

DISCUSSION QUESTIONS

1. Answer the following questions for: (1) Spandex clothing, (2) canned wine, (3) low-alcohol beer, (4) Planters Lite peanuts (one-third fewer calories than regular peanuts), or (5) compact disc record players.
   a. Is ________ an innovation? Justify your answer.

b. Assume ______ becomes widely used on your campus. Speculate on the characteristics of the adopter categories.

c. Using the student body on your campus as a market segment, evaluate the perceived attributes of ______.

d. Who on your campus would serve as opinion leaders for ______?

e. Will the early adopters of ______ use the adoption process (extended decision making), or is a simpler decision process likely?

f. Describe how you would "create" opinion leaders for ______ on your campus.

2. Describe two situations in which you have served as an opinion leader. Are these situations consistent with the text?

3. Describe two situations in which you have sought information from an opinion leader. Are these situations consistent with the text?

4. The figure below approximates the diffusion rate for television sets and automatic washers in the Milwaukee area. On an after-the-fact basis, analyze the attributes of each product to see if such an analysis would predict their relative rates of diffusion.

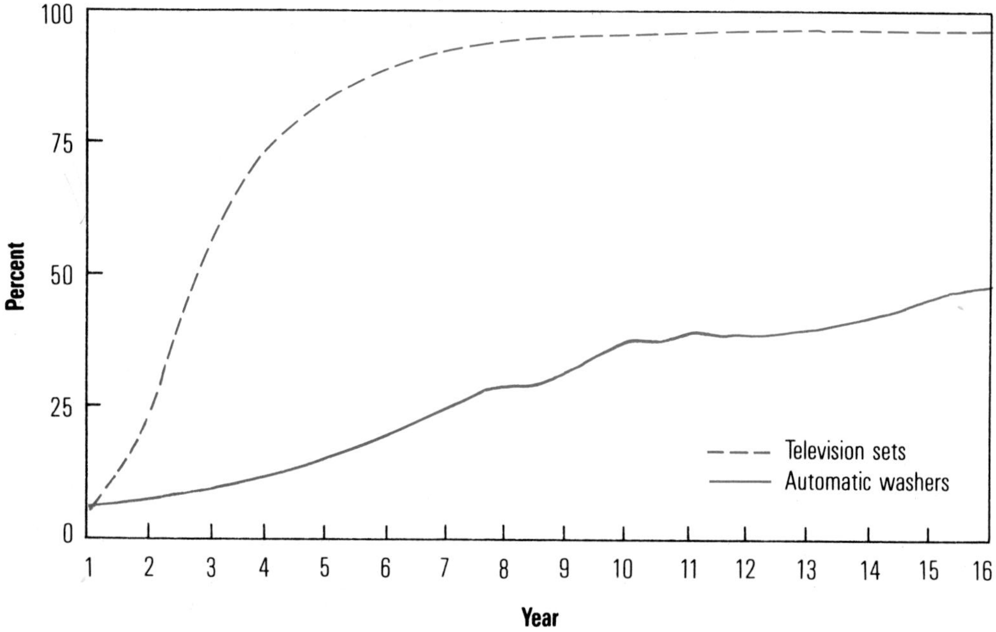

5. Assume that you are a consultant to firms with new products. You have members of the appropriate market segments rate the innovation on the 10 characteristics described in the chapter. Based on these ratings you develop marketing strategies. Assume that a rating of 9 is extremely favorable (strong relative advantage or a lack of complexity), and 1 is extremely unfavorable. Develop appropriate strategies for each of the following products.

Attribute	Product A	B	C	D	E	F	G	H	I
Fulfillment of felt need	7	3	8	8	5	7	8	9	9
Compatibility	8	8	8	9	2	8	9	8	8
Relative advantage	2	8	9	7	8	9	8	8	9
Complexity	9	9	9	9	3	8	8	7	9
Observability	8	9	1	9	4	8	8	8	8
Trialability	9	8	9	9	2	9	2	9	8
Nature of group	8	7	7	9	9	7	7	3	3
Type of decision	7	8	8	6	7	7	3	7	3
Marketing effort	7	8	7	8	6	3	8	7	6
Perceived risk	8	7	7	3	7	8	8	5	3

6. Identify two recent (*a*) continuous innovations, (*b*) dynamically continuous innovations, and (*c*) discontinuous innovations. Justify your selections.
7. Describe an innovation you adopted and for which you went through each of the steps in the adoption process. Describe another for which you did not explicitly use each step. Why did you use differing processes in the two situations?
8. Are you aware of market mavens on your campus? Describe their characteristics, behaviors, and motivation.

PROJECT QUESTIONS

1. Identify and interview several innovators on your campus for:
   a. Camcorders.
   b. Radial keratotomy.
   c. Spandex clothing.
   d. Canned wine.

   To what extent do they match the "ideal profile" of an innovator?
2. Repeat question 1 for early adopters.
3. Find and interview two opinion leaders for one of the product categories listed in Discussion Question 1. To what extent do they match the description provided in the chapter?
4. Interview three clothing salespersons. Determine the role that opinion leaders play in the purchase of their product. To what extent, if any, do they utilize opinion leaders?
5. Look in the first issue of a recent month's *Advertising Age* at the section entitled "New Products." Categorize the new products as continuous, dynamically continuous, or discontinuous innovations. Interpret the results.
6. Using the source in question 5 above or your own knowledge, pick a dynamically continuous or discontinuous innovation. Perform a diffusion enhancement analysis (Table 6–2) and recommend appropriate strategies.

7. As 6 above, but use (*a*) canned wine, (*b*) radial keratotomy, (*c*) camcorders, (*d*) cellular telephones, or (*e*) Spandex clothing.

REFERENCES

[1] "The Concoction That's Raising Spirits in the Wine Industry," *Business Week,* October 8, 1984, pp. 182, 186.

[2] For another approach to this issue, see M. B. Taylor and A. M. Mathias, "The Impact of TV Advertising versus Word-of-Mouth on the Image of Lawyers," *Journal of Advertising,* Fourth Quarter 1983, pp. 42–49.

[3] P. H. Reingen and J. B. Kernan, "Analysis of Referral Networks in Marketing," *Journal of Marketing Research,* November 1986, pp. 370–78.

[4] L. F. Feick, L. L. Price, and R. A. Higie, "People Who Use People," in *Advances in Consumer Research XIII,* ed. R. J. Lutz (Provo, Utah: Association for Consumer Research, 1986), pp. 301–5; and P. H. Reingen, "A Word-of-Mouth Network," in *Advances in Consumer Research XIV,* ed. M. Wallendorf and P. Anderson (Provo, Utah: Association for Consumer Research, 1987), pp. 213–17.

[5] G. D. Upah, "Product Complexity Effects on Information Source Preference by Retail Buyers," *Journal of Business Research,* First Quarter 1983, pp. 107–26.

[6] L. F. Feick and L. L. Price, "The Market Maven," *Journal of Marketing,* January 1987, pp. 83–97.

[7] G. M. Armstrong and L. P. Feldman, "Exposure and Sources of Opinion Leaders," *Journal of Advertising Research,* August 1976, pp. 21–27. Contradictory findings are reported in J. H. Myers and T. S. Robertson, "Dimensions of Opinion Leadership," *Journal of Marketing Research,* February 1972, pp. 41–46.

[8] J. N. Sheth, "Word-of-Mouth in Low-Risk Innovations," *Journal of Advertising Research,* June 1971, pp. 15–18; and L. G. Schiffman and V. Gaccione, "Opinion Leaders in Institutional Markets," *Journal of Marketing,* April 1974, pp. 49–53.

[9] R. W. Mizerski, "An Attribution Explanation of the Disproportionate Influence of Negative Information," *Journal of Consumer Research,* December 1982, pp. 301–10; M. L. Richens, "Negative Word-of-Mouth by Dissatisfied Customers," *Journal of Marketing,* Winter 1983, pp. 68–78; and M. L. Richins, "Word-of-Mouth Communications as Negative Information," in *Advances in Consumer Research XI,* ed. T. C. Kinnear (Provo, Utah: Association for Consumer Research, 1984), pp. 697–702.

[10] Feick and Price, "The Market Maven." See also H. H. Kassarjian, "Low Involvement," in *Advances in Consumer Research,* ed. K. B. Monroe (Ann Arbor, Michigan: Association for Consumer Research, 1981), pp. 31–34; and M. E. Slama and A. Tashchain, "Selected Socioeconomic and Demographic Characteristics Associated with Purchasing Involvement," *Journal of Marketing,* Winter 1985, pp. 72–82.

[11] J. H. Holmes and J. D. Lett, Jr., "Product Sampling and Word of Mouth," *Journal of Advertising Research,* October 1977, pp. 35–40.

[12] B. L. Bayus, "Word of Mouth: The Indirect Effects of Marketing Efforts," *Journal of Advertising Research,* June/July 1985, pp. 31–35.

[13] N. F. Millman, "Glenmore Moves to Follow Up Amaretto Success," *Advertising Age,* June 25, 1979, p. 4.

[14] L. A. Brown, *Innovation Diffusion* (Methuen, 1981); and A. M. Kennedy, "The Adoptions and Diffusion of New Industrial Products," *European Journal of Marketing,* Third Quarter 1983, pp. 31–85; E. M. Rogers, *Diffusion of Innovations* (New York: The Free Press, 1983); and H. Gatignon and T. S. Robertson, "A Propositional Inventory for New Diffusion Research," *Journal of Consumer Research,* March 1985, pp. 849–67.

[15] L. A. Fanelli, "Polaroid Shows, but Can It Tell (and Sell)?" *Advertising Age,* June 6, 1981, p. 3, p. 86.

[16] J. R. Evans and B. Berman, *Marketing* (New York: Macmillan Publishing Co., 1987), p. 743.

[17] K. Derow, "Classify Consumer Products with Perceptual Complexity, Observation, Difficulty Model," *Marketing News,* May 14, 1982, p. 16.

[18] See also M. D. Dickerson and J. W. Gentry, "Characteristics of Adopters and Non-Adopters of Home Computers," *Journal of Consumer Research,* September 1983, pp. 225–35; and W. D. Danko and J. M. MacLachlon, "Research to Accelerate the Diffusion of a New Innovation," *Journal of Advertising Research,* June/July 1983, pp. 39–43.

[19] L. L. Price, L. F. Feick, and D. C. Smith, "A Re-examination of Communication Channel Usage by Adopter Categories," in *Advances in Consumer Research XIII,* ed. R. J. Lutz (Provo, Utah: Association for Consumer Research, 1986), p. 409.

[20] Fanelli, "Polaroid Shows," p. 3.

CHAPTER

7 Household Structure and Consumption Behavior

With the increase in working mothers and single-parent households, teenagers, particularly females, are actively involved in household decision making. In one study, half the teenage daughters of working mothers did most of the grocery shopping, and 24 percent said they made most brand decisions. The study also found that 86 percent preferred supermarkets while only 8 percent preferred convenience stores and 6 percent neighborhood markets.

Teens also influence where families take vacations (60%) and the type of magazines read at home (55%). They influence the purchase of VCRs (59%) and spend $239 million on movie rentals. Overall, teens spent $70 billion in 1986, $30 billion of which was their own money. The other $40 billion was supplied by their parents.[1] Exhibit 7–1 indicates how one magazine views a segment of this market.

As the American household changes in structure, the roles of different household members are also changing. Marketers have to be sensitive to these changes in order to effectively target their communications and position their products (see facing page).

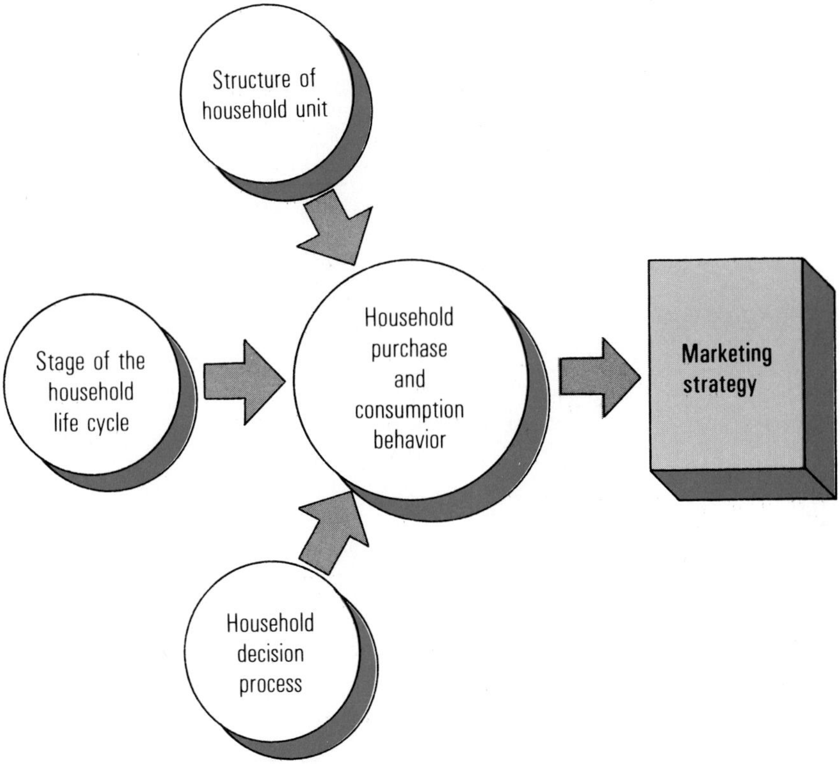

In many instances, the purchaser of a product is not its primary consumer. This is particularly true for presweetened cereals, which are targeted at children. As illustrated in Exhibit 7–2, the parent is an information gatherer, decision maker, and purchaser, yet the parent is influenced by children, who are the primary consumers. In a case where each has different desires (parents want less sugar; children want the cereals because they like the cartoon characters used to promote them), the marketer has to focus both on adult and child members of the household to affect the household decision process. Quaker Oats is one company that attempts to serve both parents and children and has developed unique communications for each.

The household is the basic consumption unit for most consumer goods in the American society. Major items such as food, housing, automobiles, and appliances are consumed more by household units than by individuals. Furthermore, the consumption patterns of individual household members seldom are independent from those of other household members. For example, deciding to grant a child's request for a bicycle may mean spending discretionary funds that could have been used to purchase an evening out for the parents, new clothing for a sister or brother, or otherwise used by another member of the household. Therefore, it is essential that marketers understand the household as a consumption unit.[2]

Exhibit 7–1 Reaching a Key Member in Many Household Purchase Decisions

Courtesy Triangle Publications

Exhibit 7–2 Targeting Communications at "Influencers" and "Information Gatherers"

In 1981, the Quaker Oats Company conducted test markets in three cities for a new product called Halfsies. Halfsies, which contain half as much sugar as presweetened cereals, was the result of extensive consumer research at the Quaker Oats Company. This research verified that "parents feel they are 'in a bind' about presweetened cereals. Children want the ones they see advertised on TV, and parents find it difficult to refuse their wishes all the time."

To market Halfsies, Quaker Oats developed adult- and children-directed advertising. Adult-directed advertising talks in a serious way about the new product by stressing that it will meet parents' concerns about sugar yet will appeal to their children. Children-directed advertising and packaging features the "Land of Half" in which everything is in half. Quaker's consumer research showed that it is essential that Halfsies have the same appeal to children as presweetened brands; "it's important that kids ask for it by name."

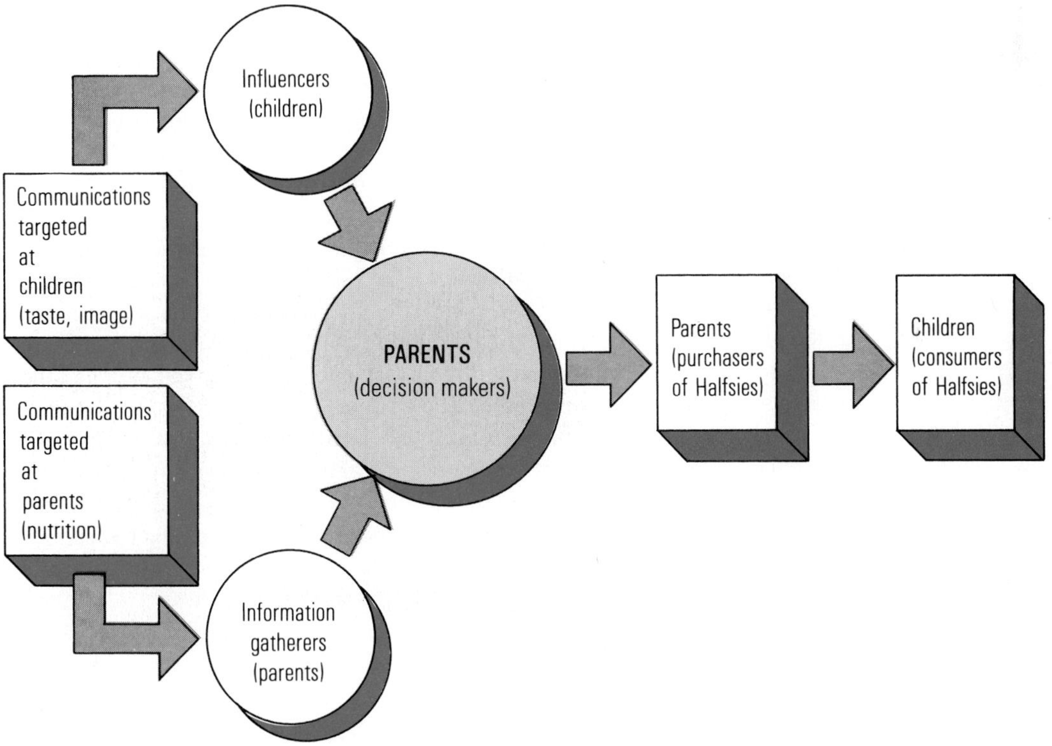

Source: "Quaker Evaluating Halfsies Test," *Advertising Age*, April 20, 1981, p. 69.

Households are important not only for their direct role in the consumption process, but also for the critical role they perform in socializing children. The family household is the primary mechanism whereby cultural and social class values and behavior patterns are passed on to the next generation. Purchasing and consumption patterns are among those attitudes and skills strongly influenced by the family household unit.

This chapter examines: (1) the nature and importance of households in contemporary American society; (2) the household life cycle; (3) the nature of the household decision process; and (4) consumer socialization.

THE NATURE OF AMERICAN HOUSEHOLDS

Types of Households

The term *household* designates a variety of distinct social groups. This variety can cause confusion unless each type of household unit is distinguished clearly. The Census Bureau defines a *family* household as *a household unit that consists of two or more related persons, one of whom (i.e., the householder) owns or rents the living quarters*. The *nuclear family* consists of two adults of opposite sex, living in a socially approved sex relationship with their own or adopted children. The nuclear family is important in virtually every culture.

The nuclear family described above represents the *prescriptive* (culturally desirable) and *descriptive* (most common) version of the nuclear family. In 1986 there were 61 million nuclear-family households in the United States. However, there are several variations of the nuclear family. The most common variation in the United States is the single-parent family household created by the death of one spouse or, more commonly, divorce. In either case, the children and the mother are likely to remain together as a nuclear family.

The *extended family* is a household that includes the nuclear family plus additional relations. The most common form of the extended family involves the inclusion of one or both sets of grandparents. In addition, aunts, uncles, cousins, in-laws, and other relatives may be included. By combining the various types of family households, you can see in Figure 7–1 that nearly three fourths of all households in 1986 were family households.

Household units that are not families also have several variations. The Census Bureau defines a *nonfamily* household as *households made up of householders who either live alone or with others to whom they are not related*. In 1986, 28 percent of all households were classified as nonfamily.

Changes in Household Structure

Households, family or nonfamily, are important to marketing managers because they constitute consumption units, and therefore represent the proper unit of

Figure 7–1
Family and Nonfamily American Households: 1986

Type of Household	Number (000)	Percentage	Median Income
• Family Households (72%)			
Married couples			
With children <18 at home	24,630	28%	$32,400
Without children <18 at home	26,304	30	29,400
Female head of household			
With children <18 at home	6,105	7	11,000
Without children <18 at home	4,106	5	18,900
Male head of household	2,414	3	24,500
• Nonfamily Households (28%)			
Persons living alone			
Male householder	8,285	9	15,000
Female householder	12,893	15	8,700
Persons living with nonrelatives			
Male householder	2,363	3	30,000
Female householder	1,359	1	27,300
All households	88,459	100%	$23,600

Source: T. Exter, "Where the Money Is," *American Demographics*, March 1987, p. 28.

analysis for many aspects of marketing strategy. The fact that the number of household units is growing and is projected to continue to grow, as shown in Figure 7–2, is more important than population growth for marketers of refrigerators, stoves, telephones, and other items purchased primarily by household units. Equally as important to home builders, appliance manufacturers, and automobile manufacturers are the *structure* and *size* of households. Between 1970 and 1986, changes such as those cited below had a major impact on a wide variety of marketing practices.

- Family households grew by 10.6 million, but 90 percent of that growth (9.4 million) was in single-parent households.
- Nonfamily households grew by 12.8 million, doubling from 12 million in 1970 to 24.9 million in 1986.

These changes in household structure are reflected in the reduced average size of households, as shown in Figure 7–3. This decline has been caused by an

Figure 7–2
Household Growth, 1950-1990

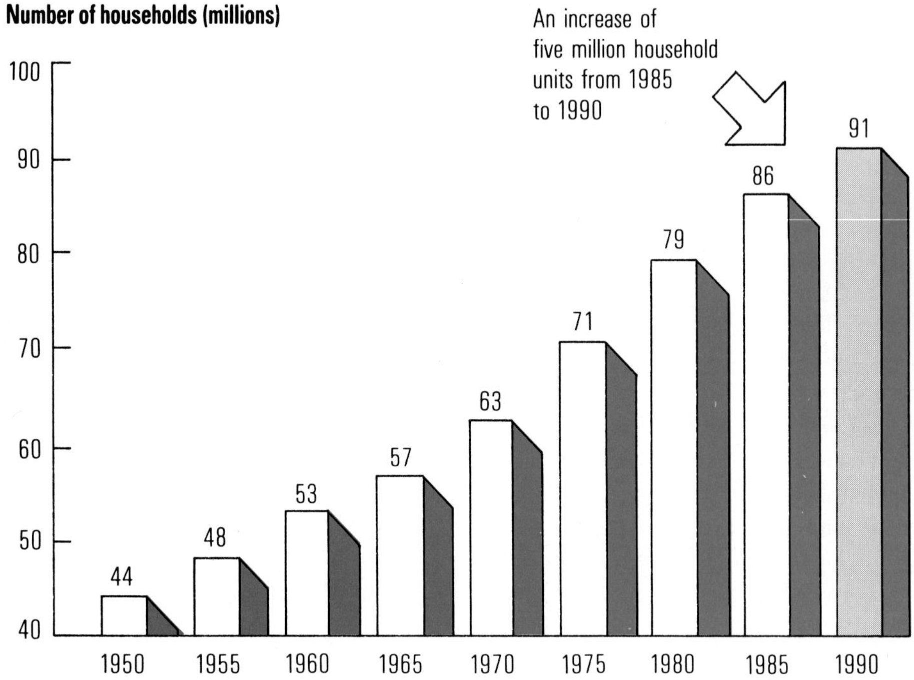

Source: Adapted from U.S. Department of Commerce, "Households, Families, Marital Status, and Living Arrangements: March 1984," *Population Characteristics,* Series P-20, no. 391 (August 1984), pp. 6–9.

increase in single-parent and single-person households as well as by a decline in the birth rate.

While continued growth in the number, structure, and size of households is important, the age of the householder also plays a role in purchase and consumption behavior. The greatest gain in household growth during the 1990s will occur in the 45 to 64 age category.[3] The kinds of household products this age-group consumes are different from products consumed by younger and older households and represent a prime opportunity for sales expansion. The consumption of household products by the under-35 age-group is projected to have very limited growth in the 1990s. This trend will require some firms to shift their emphasis and perhaps realign their product lines to appeal more to households in the 45 to 64 age-group.

What are the marketing implications of these shifts? The rapid growth of established households implies a strong demand for upgraded household fur-

Figure 7–3
Average Size of Household and Family Units

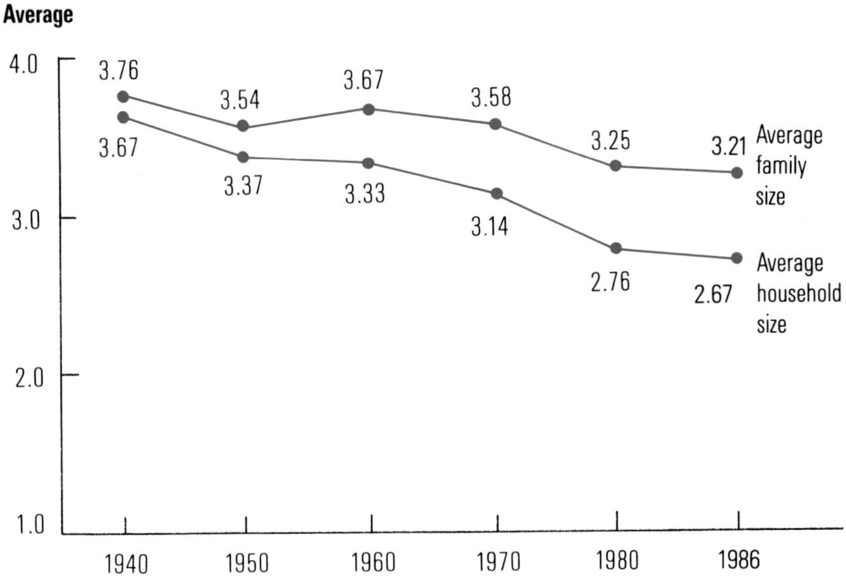

Source: Adapted from U.S. Department of Commerce, "Households, Families, Marital Status, and Living Arrangements: March 1986," *Population Characteristics,* Series P–20, no. 412 (November 1986), p. 3.

nishings, vacations, luxury items, and sports and entertainment items targeted at a more mature market. The fact that much of this growth is coming from single-person households suggests that apartments, appliances, and food containers should be produced in sizes appropriate for the single individual.

The growth in single-parent families also implies a need for convenience items, day-care centers, and appliances which relatively young children can operate. The timing and content of advertising aimed at singles and single-parent families may need to differ from those aimed at the traditional nuclear families. As with most variables affecting consumer behavior, the marketing manager must examine the shifts in the American family structure for specific product category implications.

The combination of rapid household growth in the 30 to 40 age category along with shifts in household structure and the cost of housing produced what some observers termed "the condo craze" during the 1980s; demand reached an annual level of 300,000 units in 1985, compared to approximately 100,000 in 1980. The factors driving the growth of this housing alternative and the household demographics of its primary buyers are described below:

Figure 7–4
Stages in the Household Life Cycle

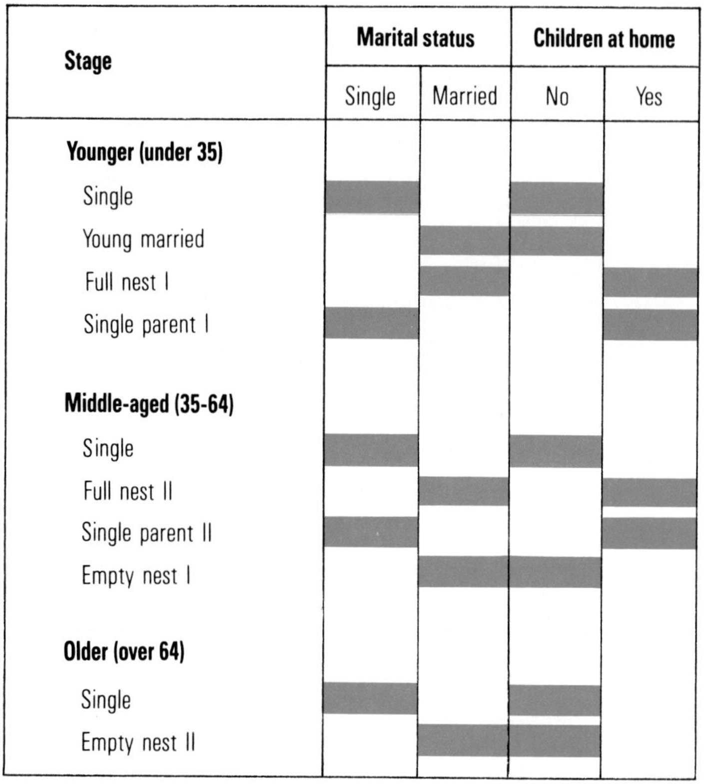
Stage
Marital status
Children at home
Single
Married
No
Yes
Younger (under 35)
Single
Young married
Full nest I
Single parent I
Middle-aged (35-64)
Single
Full nest II
Single parent II
Empty nest I
Older (over 64)
Single
Empty nest II

- The number of people in the home-buying ages of 25 to 40 grew by 10 million in the 1980s. Because the average price of a new, single-family home was over $60,000 in 1980, and continued to rise, there was increased demand for alternative homes such as the condominium.
- Those living in condominiums (condos) are younger (48 percent under 36), more affluent (63 percent have incomes over 20,000), and occupationally upscale (65 percent are professionals or managers) than those living in single-family homes.
- Household size is quite different, also; 57 percent of the condo households have one person, 38 percent have two people, while only 8 percent have three or more. Single women make up more than a third of condo owners.[4]

THE HOUSEHOLD LIFE CYCLE

The structure of most family and nonfamily households changes over time. As you move from being single to married, then through various stages of child rearing, you move through discernible changes in family structure. To better understand and describe these structural differences, the concept of *family life cycle* was developed.[5] The basic assumption underlying the family life cycle approach is that most families pass through an orderly progression of stages, each with its own characteristics, financial situation, and purchasing patterns. However, since 30 percent of the households in 1990 are projected to be nonfamily households, it is important to extend the family life cycle concept to a *household life cycle*. This is shown in Figure 7–4.

The household life cycle (HLC) applies to both *family* and *nonfamily households*. It assumes that these entities, like individuals, move through a series of relatively distinct and well-defined stages with the passage of time. Each stage in the household life cycle poses a series of problems which household decision

Figure 7–5
Average Monthly Long-Distance Telephone Expenditures by Household Life Cycle Stages

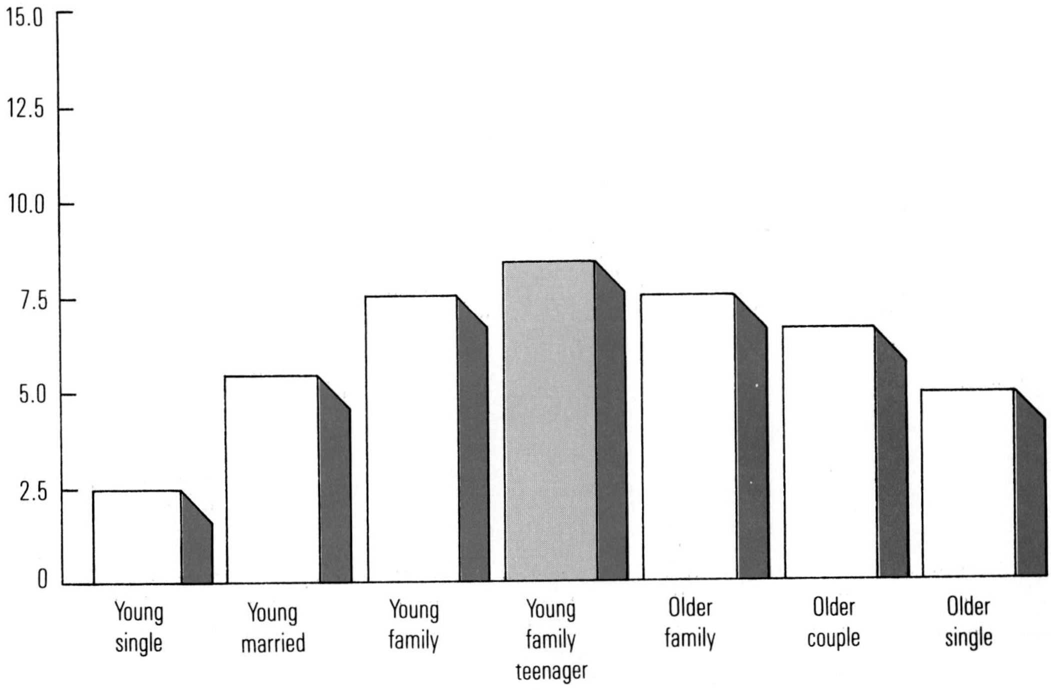

Source: A Marvin Roscoe, Jr., and Jagdish N. Sheth, "Demographic Segmentation of Long-Distance Behavior: Data Analysis and Inductive Model Building," in *Third Annual Conference of the Association for Consumer Research*, ed. M. Venkatesen (1972), p. 262. Also, courtesy of the American Telephone & Telegraph Company.

makers must solve. The solution to these problems is bound intimately to the selection and maintenance of a lifestyle and, thus, to product consumption.[6] For example, all young married couples with no children face a need for relaxation or recreation. Solutions to this common problem differ. Some couples opt for an outdoors-oriented lifestyle and consume camping equipment and related products. Others choose a sophisticated urban lifestyle and consume tickets to the theater and opera, restaurant meals, and so forth. As these families move into another stage in the HLC, generally the "full nest I" stage, the problems they face also change. The amount of time and resources available for recreation usually diminishes. New problems related to raising a family become more urgent.

Each stage presents unique needs and wants as well as financial conditions and experiences. Thus, the HLC provides marketers with relatively homogeneous household segments that share similar needs with respect to household-related problems and purchases. The HLC is a tool that marketing managers can use to better understand their potential market segments. Like all tools, however, the HLC is not universally applicable. Managers also must be sure to establish whether the purchase and use of their product is in any significant way affected by stages in the HLC before trying to force the product to fit the tool.

One example of how consumer behavior differs at various stages of the HLC is illustrated in Figure 7–5. In this application, you can readily see that young families with teenagers make more than three times the number of long-distance telephone calls that young singles make. This fact, in turn, should guide the thinking of those promoting household use of long-distance telephone calls. The HLC has also been found to influence the consumption of such diverse products as beer, cake mixes, colas, shampoo, detergents, and paper towels.[7]

The remainder of this section describes each stage of the household life cycle shown in Figure 7–4, and some of the consumption problems unique to households in each stage. Exhibit 7–3 contains ads focusing on different stages in the HLC.

Young Single

The young single is characterized by age (under 35) and marital status (single). This group makes up approximately 9 percent of America's adult population and is the primary target for many products and services. Outdoor sporting goods, sports cars, fashion clothing, and entertainment and recreation services are consumed heavily by young singles. On the other hand, young singles are below-average consumers of products such as encyclopedias, pianos, and furniture. Because this group is significant in numbers and unique in its lifestyle, many marketers develop specific marketing programs for the young single. For example, Chevrolet developed a special sequence of Chevy Citation advertisements targeted at the young single. In these advertisements, the lifestyle of the young single was depicted by a cartoon-type character called "super single."

Courtesy Heublein, Inc.

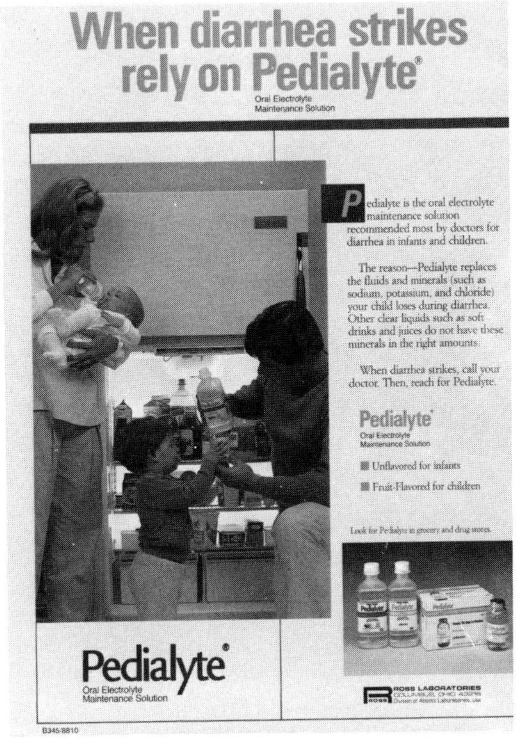

Reprinted with permission of Ross Laboratories, Columbus, Ohio

Courtesy International Games, Inc.

© 1989 American Express Travel Related Services Company, Inc. Reprinted with permission.

Young Married: No Children

The decision to marry (or to live together) brings about a new stage in the household life cycle. The lifestyles of two young singles are generally altered as they develop a joint lifestyle. Joint decisions and shared roles in household responsibilities are in many instances new experiences. Savings, household furnishings, major appliances, and more comprehensive insurance coverage are among the new areas of problem recognition and decision making to which a young married couple must give serious consideration.

Though this stage of the household life cycle is generally short, approximately 3 percent of the nation's adult population is in this stage. Like the young single stage, the time spent by a young couple in this stage of the HLC has grown as couples either delay their start in having children or choose to remain childless. Eighty-five percent of all households in this group have dual incomes and are thus relatively affluent. Compared to full nest I families, this group spends heavily on theater tickets, expensive clothes, luxury vacations, restaurant meals, and alcoholic beverages.[8]

Full Nest I: Young Married with Children

The addition of a child to the young married family creates many changes in lifestyle and consumption. This group represents approximately 20 percent of the adult population. Naturally, new purchases in the areas of baby clothes, furniture, food, and health care products occur in this stage. Lifestyles are also greatly altered. The couple may have to move to another place of residence since many apartments do not permit children. Likewise, choices of vacations, restaurants, and automobiles must be changed to accommodate young children. McDonald's, for example, attempts to occupy children in a restaurant environment by providing recreational equipment at their outlets that cater heavily to families with young children. Income tends to decline as one spouse often stays home with the young children (only 61% have dual incomes). Discretionary funds are also reduced by the need to spend on child-related necessities. However, the increasing average age of parents before the birth of the first child and the smaller families common today have reduced this impact.[9]

Single Parent I: Young Single Parents

Divorce continues to be a significant part of American society, so marketers cannot ignore the needs of young single parents. One in every three marriages will end in divorce, and this occurs most frequently at earlier points in a marriage.[10] While most divorced individuals eventually remarry, more than 2 percent of the U.S. adult population can be categorized as young single with children, and 20 percent of U.S. children live in single parent households.[11] This type of family situation creates many unique needs in the areas of child care, easy-to-prepare foods, and residence. Individuals in this situation often face severe financial difficulties which greatly intensify the problems associated with purchasing the products and services needed to support their families' desired lifestyles. Financial burdens are intensified by the need for child care and time shortages if the household head works.

Middle-Aged Single

The middle-aged single category is made up of those who were never married, and individuals who are divorced and have no child-rearing responsibilities. These individuals are in the 35 to 64 age category. This group is relatively small, comprising about 2 percent of the U.S. adult population. The needs of middle-age singles in many ways reflect those of young singles. But middle-age singles are likely to have more money to spend on their lifestyles. Thus, they may live in nice condominiums, frequent expensive restaurants, and travel often.

Empty Nest I: Middle-Aged Married with No Children

The lifestyle changes in the 1970s and 1980s influenced many young couples either to not have children or to delay having children. As a result, about 12 percent of American households are middle-aged married couples without children. In many cases, these households may represent second marriages in which children from a first marriage are not living with the parent. This group also includes those married couples whose children have left home. Both adults typically will have jobs, so they will be short on time but have money to spend on dining out, expensive vacations, and time-saving services such as housecleaning, laundry, and shopping.

Full Nest II: Middle-Aged Married with Children

This group, the largest, accounts for 40 percent of the adult population. Because it includes people 35 to 64, in most cases the children of this group are over six years old and are less dependent than the children of the young married couple. However, the fact that the children are older creates another set of unique consumption needs. Families with children six and older are the primary consumers of lessons of all types (piano, dance, gymnastics, and so on), dental care (orthodontics, braces, fillings), soft drinks, presweetened cereals, and a wide variety of snack foods. Greater demands for space create a need for larger homes and cars. This, coupled with heavy demand for clothing, places a considerable financial burden on households in this stage of the household life cycle.

As described at the beginning of this chapter, the teenage members of this segment, as well as those in the single parent II segment, are important consumers. Marketers target them as individual consumers and as purchasers for the household. Nabisco, Quaker Oats, Kellogg, and Procter and Gamble advertise household products to teens on MTV, while Chef Boy-Ar-Dee's canned pasta, Swiss Miss Cocoa Mix, Mazola Cooking Oil, and Gorton's Frozen Seafood are advertised on "American Bandstand."[12] In 1983, teens aged 16 to 19 spent the following amounts per week on products for themselves (and they earned 60 percent of the money):[13]

Product	Males	Females
Clothing	$ 8.15	$13.30
Movies/entertainment	8.90	4.30
Gasoline/auto	8.50	4.40
Food/snacks	6.60	3.90
Records	.90	1.45
Savings	10.15	9.30
Other	10.25	17.95
Total	$53.45	$54.60

Single Parent II: Middle-Aged Single with Children

Single individuals in the 35 to 64 age-group who have children (more than 2 percent of adult population) often are faced with tremendous financial pressures. The same demands that are placed on the middle-aged married couple with children are present in the life of a middle-aged single with children—except that the single person generally is the sole supporter and completely responsible for all household duties. Besides financial stress, a tremendous time burden is placed on this segment of the population. Many individuals in this position are thus inclined to use time-saving alternatives, such as ready-to-eat food, and are likely to eat at fast-food restaurants.

Empty Nest II: Older Married Couples

This group represents married individuals with the head of household more than 64 years of age. The head of household may still be working, but for the most part couples in the over-64 age-group are either fully or partially retired from full-time employment. Because of age, social orientation, and weakening financial status (due to retirement), the older married couple has unique needs in the areas of health care, housing, food, and recreation. For example, this group has a great deal of time but not a great deal of money. This has made the sale of travel trailers and group vacations very attractive to many older married couples (a popular bumper sticker on the back of travel vehicles reads: "I'm spending my children's inheritance").

Figure 7–6
Household Life Cycle/Social Stratification Matrix

Stage of Household	Blue Collar	White Collar	Managerial-Professional	Retired	Student
Younger (<35) Single					
Young married					
Married (children)					
Single parent					
Middle-aged (35–64) Single					
Married/children					
Single parent					
Married (no children)					
Older (>**64**) Single					
Married					

CONSUMPTION DIFFERENCES

Store choice, the use of credit, method of savings, vacations, food and entertainment preferences, and leisure-time activities differ significantly for different combinations of household structure and social class.

Older Single

The older single represents more than 2 percent of our adult population. Older singles typically are female, since females tend to outlive males. Again, the conditions of being older (over 64), single, and generally not working create many unique needs for housing, socialization, travel, and recreation. Many financial firms have set up special programs to work with these individuals. They often have experienced a spouse's death and now are taking on many of the financial responsibilities once cared for by the other person.

HOUSEHOLD LIFE CYCLE/SOCIAL STRATIFICATION MATRIX

The household life cycle can be combined with social class to create a matrix of households that differ in structure and social status. The household structure/social class matrix shown in Figure 7–6 uses the stages of household life cycle and five occupational categories: blue collar, white collar, managerial-professional, retired, and student. As stated earlier, stage in the HLC sets many consumption-related problems. As we saw in Chapter 4, social class provides accepted solutions for many of these problems. Thus, the combination of occupational categories with different stages of the HLC provides a useful way for marketers to understand naturally occurring consumption differences.

Figure 7–7
Different Roles in a Toy Purchase

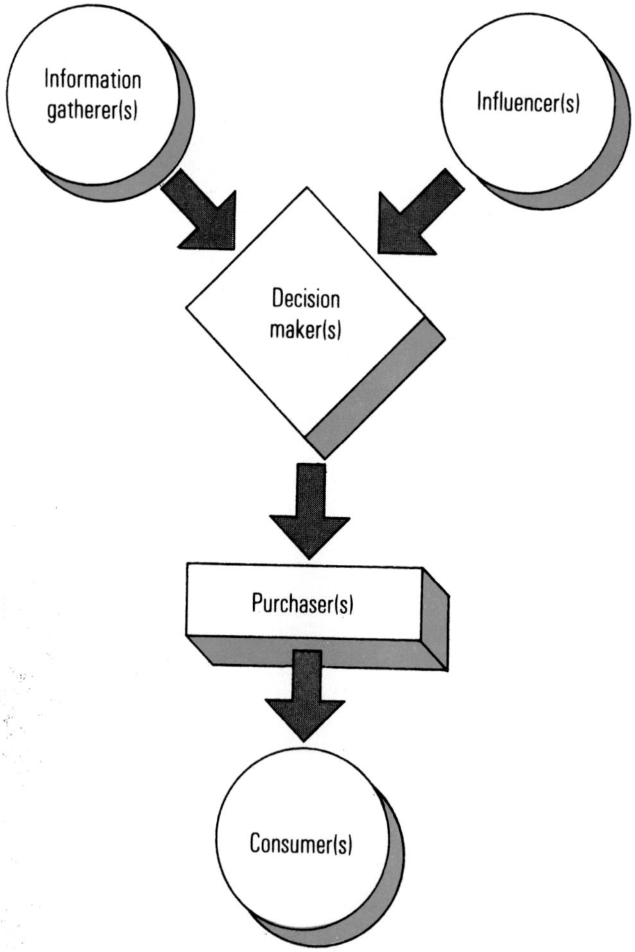

Figure 7–7 *(concluded)*

- **Information gatherer(s).** The individual who has expertise and interest in a particular purchase. In a toy purchase, both parents and children gather information, even though they may be interested in different criteria.
- **Influencer(s).** The person most likely to influence the alternatives evaluated. In a toy purchase, the child will be most instrumental in deciding which toys are considered.
- **Decision maker(s).** The individual who makes the final decision. Of course, joint decisions also are likely to occur. In a toy purchase, parents are generally the final decision makers. But joint decisions in compromise situations are common.
- **Purchaser(s).** The family member who actually purchases the product. This is typically an adult. In a toy purchase, it would be the child's mother or father or both.
- **Consumer(s).** The user of the product. While there often can be many users, in a toy purchase the child is the primary user of the product.

HOUSEHOLD DECISION MAKING

Decision making by a group such as a household differs in many important respects from decisions that are completely individual. For example, recall the purchasing of cereal described at the beginning of this chapter in which the child uses the product but the parents make the purchase and are involved in problem recognition and alternative evaluation. Since marketers frequently wish to influence the decisions made by household units, it is essential that they understand how consumption decisions are made within the household unit.

In this section we will examine household roles and influences, joint decision making, and conflict resolution in household decision making.

Household Roles and Influences

In many household purchase decisions, the primary consumers are neither the decision maker nor the purchaser. For example, women (wives and girlfriends) purchase 70 percent of the fragrances used by men.[14] Figure 7–7 outlines the various roles a household member could play in the purchase of a toy. In this example, information is gathered by one or both parents and the child, but the parents (the decision makers) are influenced by the child. Though the final decision and purchase generally is made by the parents, the child is the consumer or user of the product.

Exhibit 7–4 Crayola® Advertisement Targeted at Mothers

Source: Used with permission. CRAYOLA is a registered trademark of Binney & Smith Inc.

Exhibit 7–5

Targeting Parents with a Product Used by Children

COMM'L NO.: CLCX 9373
LENGTH: 30 SECONDS
SMALL GIRL: This is my very own puppy...
everyday, I take him for a walk.
These are my new boo-boos... 'cause yesterday, he took me for a walk.
So my mom put on a Curad.
Mom says Curads are "ouchless" and helps boo-boos heal fast.
Curad
ouchless pad
See, Curad sticks to my skin,
SUPER: CURAD OUCHLESS PAD
Curad
ouchless pad
not to my sore.
SUPER: CURAD OUCHLESS PAD
curad
Helps boo-boos heal fast.
SMALL GIRL: Mom likes Curad, 'cause it helps boo-boos heal fast.
SUPER: HELPS BOO-BOOS HEAL FAST.
SMALL GIRL: I like Curad 'cause it won't ouch me.

Used with permission from Curad

The storyboard above outlines the ad copy displayed in a 30-second TV advertisement targeted at parents. The Curad ad copy stresses to parents the primary benefit of its plastic bandage, in the hope that they will purchase it for their children's use. By heavy promotion on adult television programs such as Dynasty, Curad is able to reach 70 percent of the parents of heavy users at least four times per month.

Thus, marketers must decide who in the household plays which role before they can affect the household decision process. For example, after careful examination of the household decision process, Crayola® shifted its advertising budget from children's television to women's magazines. Their research revealed that mothers rather than children were more likely to recognize the problem, evaluate alternatives, and make the purchase. Exhibit 7–4 illustrates an example of their advertising strategy. For this product category, a household member other than the user is the primary decision maker. Exhibit 7–5 describes similar marketing strategy for Curad plastic bandages.

Another example of household member influence at different stages of the decision process is illustrated in Figure 7–8. You can see readily that the decision to eat at a fast-food restaurant is very likely to be a joint household decision, from initiation of the purchase to final decision. While a family trip is also likely to be a joint husband-wife-child decision, a good percentage of the time it will be a husband-wife-only decision process.

Marketing researchers have only recently begun considering the household as a decision-making unit. To date, most studies have focused not on household decision making but on husband-wife decision making. The influence of children has been largely ignored. Yet, children often exert a substantial influence on the consumption process.[15] Furthermore, most studies have focused on direct influence and ignored indirect influence. For example, a wife might report purchasing an automobile without discussing it with any member of her family. Yet she might purchase a blue station wagon to meet her perceptions of the demands of the family rather than the red sports car that she personally would prefer. Most research studies would classify the above decision as strictly wife-dominated. Clearly, however, other household members influenced the decision.[16]

Household decision making allows different household members to become involved at different stages of the process. It also allows different members to make specific subdecisions of the overall decision. When an individual makes a decision, he or she evaluates all the relevant attributes of each alternative and combines these evaluations into a single decision. In a family decision, different members often focus on specific attributes. For example, a child may evaluate the color and style of a bicycle while one or both parents evaluate prices, warranty, and safety features.

Joint Decision Making

Household decision making can be categorized as husband-dominant, wife-dominant, joint-decision (syncretic), or individualized decisions (autonomic).[17] Husband-dominant decisions generally occur with the purchase of such products as automobiles,[18] liquor,[19] and life insurance.[20] Wife-dominant decisions are more likely to occur in the purchase of furniture,[21] food,[22] and small appliances.[23] Joint decisions are likely to occur when buying a house,[24] living room furniture,[25] and vacations.[26] These areas will undoubtedly change as marital roles continue to evolve. Finally, some decisions are simply made individually (autonomic) because the product may be more related to a specialized role one spouse plays in the household.

How household members interact in a purchase decision is largely dependent on the *role specialization* of different household members and the degree of *involvement* each has in the product area of concern.

Figure 7–8
Relative Influence on Household Members in Purchase Decision Process

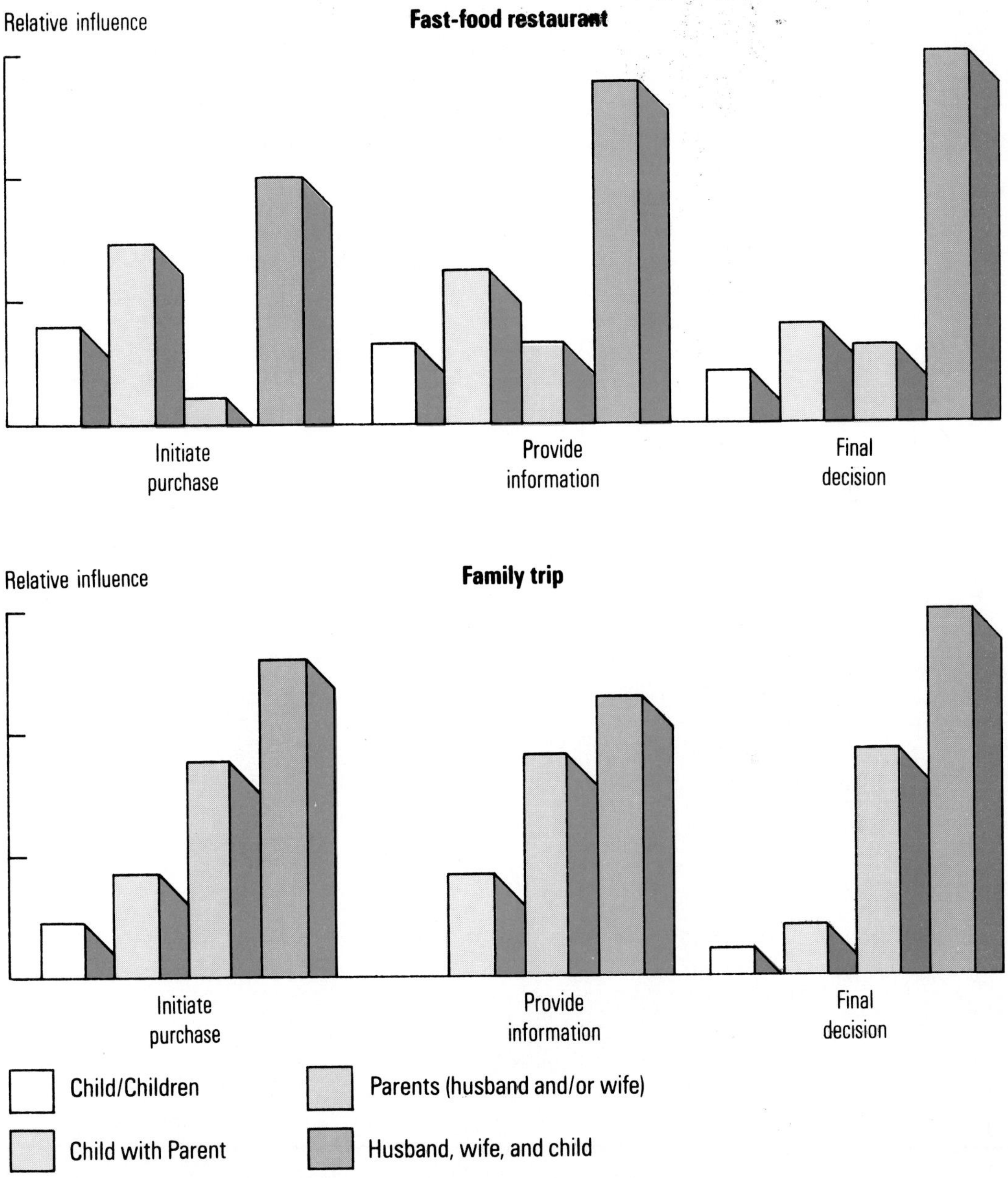

Source: Adapted from G. J. Szybillo and A. Sosanie, "Family Decision Making: Husband, Wife and Children," in *Advances in Consumer Research IV*, ed. W. D. Perreault, Jr. (Chicago: Association for Consumer Research, 1977), p. 47.

Over time, each spouse develops more specialized roles as a part of their household lifestyle and household responsibilities. Husbands are often expected to play a more significant role in automotive repairs and maintenance and, therefore, have a more specialized role in establishing criteria and evaluating alternatives in an automobile purchase. Wives often have a more specialized role in certain aspects of child rearing and, as a result, have a more specialized role in buying children's clothing and food. Because role specialization within any household takes time to develop, younger couples often engage in greater degrees of joint decision making than more established households.[27] The greater the role specialization and the more closely related the product is to the area of specialization, the less likely a shared or syncretic decision will be made.

Involvement in a product area is another major factor that has an impact on how a household purchase decision will be made.[28] Naturally, the more involved a spouse is with a product area, the more likely he or she will be to exert influence over other family members during a purchase in that product area. For example, a spouse very interested in electronics as a hobby probably would greatly influence the purchase of a stereo, television, or home computer.

Exhibit 7–6 Changing Role of Males in Child Rearing

Courtesy the Dial Corporation

While involvement and role specialization are major influences that affect husband-wife decision making, the nature of this involvement and role specialization will often be different between families and change within families over time.[29] For example, in a household where the wife is a banker and the husband is a history teacher, an insurance purchase would most likely be wife-dominant. This would stem from the wife's involvement in the area of finance and the greater likelihood of her playing a more specialized role in household financial matters. Likewise, as more household responsibilities are shared by males, the more likely there will be a change in traditional areas of household involvement and role specialization. Exhibit 7–6 reflects the changing role of males in child rearing.

Household Influences by Stage of the Decision Process

Up to now we have described husband-wife decision making as husband dominant, wife dominant, syncretic, or autonomic, depending on product involvement and role specialization. Actually, involvement and role specialization can vary throughout the decision process. Hence, a mixture of decision-making styles may occur at each stage of the decision process. For example, the recognition of a problem may be initiated by one spouse because of role specialization and product involvement. But information search and evaluation may be shared (a joint decision process) and final purchase made by the other spouse.

Figure 7–9 shows how household decision making changes at different stages of the decision process to buy an automobile and a rug. The automobile purchase, while predominantly husband dominant in the early stages of the decision process, is a more shared decision for many couples during evaluation. The final decision, however, generally is husband dominant. In the purchase of a rug, the wife is more likely to dominate problem recognition and guide the selection of decision criteria. However, as the decision process progresses, it becomes more syncretic. Marketers must understand how these roles vary through the decision process.

Conflict Resolution

Conflicts between household members may arise at any stage of the decision process. Perhaps the most frequent areas of conflict are (1) whether or not a problem is of sufficient magnitude to require a solution, and (2) the evaluative criteria to be used in reaching a decision. Despite the opportunities for conflict, agreement appears to be more common than disagreement.[30]

When conflict in the household decision process does arise, there are three basic ways of resolving it: problem solving, bargaining, or persuasion. In Table 7–1, you can see that family *discussion* (problem solving) was the predominant mode of resolution in family decision conflicts involving television and vacations. However, the resolution of conflict over cereals most often was achieved in a problem-solving manner where the decision was made by the family member most knowledgeable about cereals.

Figure 7–9
Husband-Wife Roles at Different Stages of the Decision Process

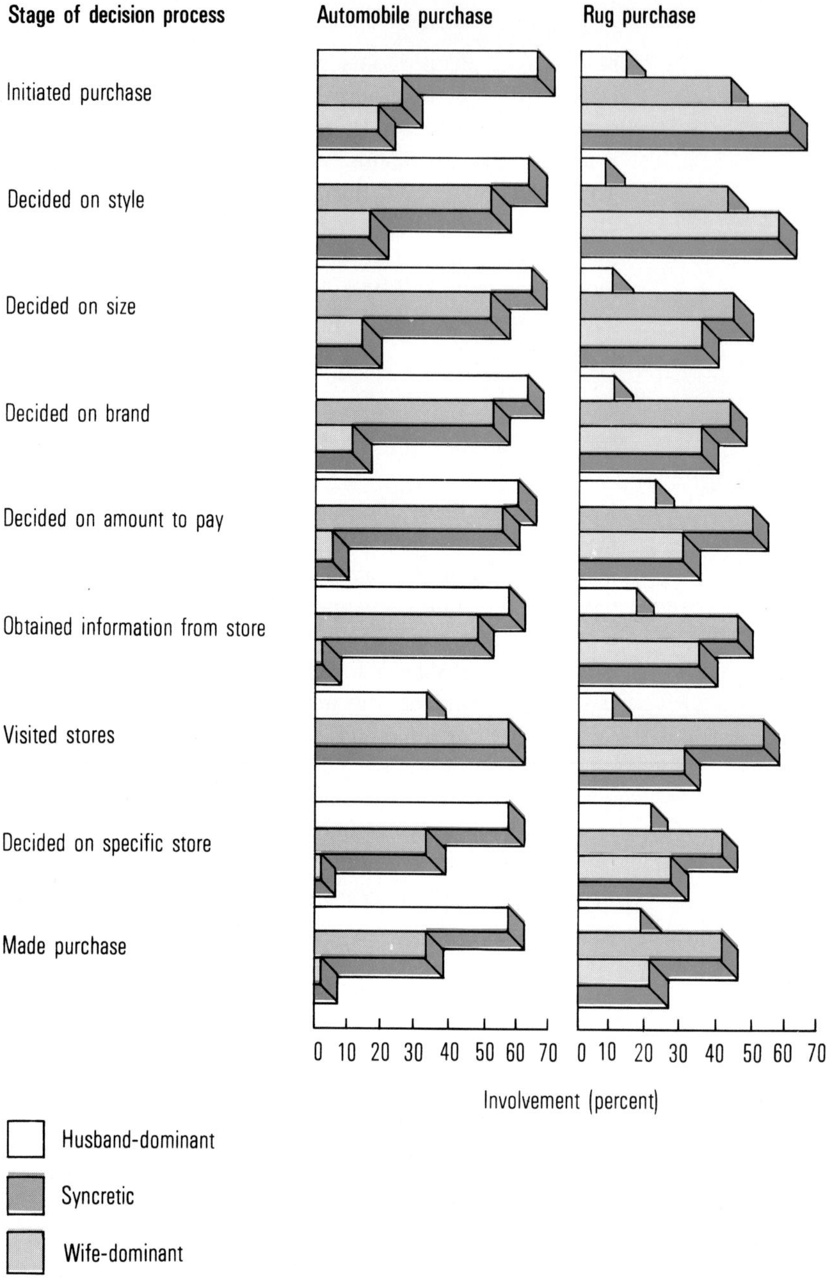

Source: Adapted from A. Woodside and W. Motes, "Husband and Wife Perceptions of Marital Roles in Consumer Decision Processes for Six Products," in *1979 Educator's Conference Proceeding,* ed. N. Beckwith et al. (Chicago: American Marketing Association, 1979), pp. 215–16.

Table 7–1
Household Members' Perceptions of Conflict Resolution Modes (rank ordered from 1 to 7 by each member)

	Television			Vacation			Cereal		
	Husband	Wife	Child	Husband	Wife	Child	Husband	Wife	Child
Problem solving:									
• More information gathered	3	1	2	2	2	2	4	5	4
• Family discussion	1	2	1	1	1	1	3	3	3
• Decisions made by knowledgeable member	2	3	3	4	3	4	1	1	1
Bargaining:									
• Promise of future consideration for agreement	7	7	7	7	7	6	6	6	5
• Delaying of decision	5	6	6	6	6	7	7	7	7
Persuasion:									
• Coalition formation	6	5	5	5	5	5	5	4	6
• Exertion of authority	4	4	4	3	4	3	2	2	2

Source: Adapted from M. Belch, G. Belch, and D. Schiglimpaglia, "Conflict in Family Decision Making: An Exploratory Investigation," in *Advances in Consumer Research VII,* ed. J. Olson (Chicago: Association for Consumer Research, 1980), pp. 477–78.

Conclusions on Household Decision Making

Much remains to be learned about household decision making. But we can offer five general conclusions:

1. Different household members may be involved at different stages of the decision process.
2. Different household members may evaluate different attributes of a product or brand.
3. The direct involvement of household members in each stage of the decision process represents only a small part of the picture. Taking into account the desires of other household members is also important, though seldom studied.
4. Who participates at each stage of the decision process and the method by which conflicts are resolved are primarily a function of the product category, and secondarily a function of the characteristics of the individual household members and the characteristics of the household. The product category is important because it is closely related to who uses the product.
5. Overt conflicts in decision making are less common than agreement. Conflicts are most frequently resolved through problem solving.

Table 7–2
Managerial Framework for Evaluating Household Decision Process

Product ________

Stage in the Decision Process	Household Members Involved	Household Members' Motivation and Interests
Problem recognition		
Information search		
Alternative evaluation		
Purchase		
Use/consumption		
Disposition		
Evaluation		

These conclusions are too broad to provide specific guidelines to the marketing manager. However, they do give you the framework necessary to guide research for specific products. This framework is presented in Table 7–2. There is substantial variation across product categories, so a separate analysis is required for each product category. But once the cells in the table have been completed, the marketing manager is in a position to make informed decisions on product design, media selection, advertising copy, and related factors.

CONSUMER SOCIALIZATION

The household unit provides the basic framework in which *consumer socialization* occurs. Consumer socialization is defined as *the processes by which young people acquire skills, knowledge, and attitudes relevant to their functioning as consumers in the marketplace.*[31] Learning, including acquiring consumption-related knowledge, is a lifelong process.[32] However, the quantity and nature of learning that take place before early adulthood (around 18), as well as its impact on subsequent learning, are sufficiently unique to justify focusing on this time period.

We are concerned with understanding both what behaviors children learn and how those behaviors are associated with the purchase and use of goods and services. The *what* of consumer learning refers to the content of learning, and the *how* refers to the methods by which that content is acquired.

The content of consumer learning can be broken down into two categories:

directly relevant and *indirectly relevant*.[33] *Directly relevant* aspects of consumer behavior are those necessary for purchase and use to actually take place. In other words, a person has to learn particular skills, such as how to shop, how to compare similar brands, how to budget available income, and so forth.[34] Knowledge and attitudes about stores, products, brands, salespeople, clearance sales, advertising media, and coupons are examples of directly relevant consumer learning content.

Indirectly relevant consumer learning content refers to everything that has been learned which motivates purchase and use behavior. In other words, it is the knowledge, attitudes, and values which cause people to want certain goods or services and allow them to attach differential evaluations to products and brands. For example, some consumers know (have learned) that Calvin Klein is a prestigious brand name, and they may respond positively to various products carrying this name. This information about Calvin Klein's prestige is not necessary to carry out the actual purchase (directly relevant). But it is extremely important in deciding *to* purchase and *what* to purchase (indirectly relevant).

Consumer Socialization and Advertising

While the household unit is where most consumer socialization occurs, advertising also is an important means by which children learn consumption-related behaviors and attitudes. Advertising, in fact, often produces conflict between adults and children.

In 1980, Quebec's Consumer Protection Act went into effect. This act directly prohibits commercial advertising to persons under 13 years of age. The United States Federal Trade Commission, meanwhile, has backed away from numerous proposals to eliminate all advertisements to young children and advertisements for sugared food products aimed at older children.[35]

The American advertising industry's primary self-regulatory body, the National Advertising Division of the Council of Better Business Bureaus, maintains a special unit to review advertising aimed at children—the Children's Advertising Review Unit (CARU).[36]

The widespread concern with the impact of television on children stems in part from the substantial amount of time American children spend viewing television. Children between 2 and 11 years of age spend more than 30 hours per week during the winter watching television.[37] This viewing is spread throughout the week, though prime time (Monday–Sunday, 7:30–11:00 P.M.) is most popular.

The large amount of time children devote to watching television, including commercials, gives rise to four major areas of concern:

- The potential for commercial messages to generate intrafamily conflict.
- The impact of commercial messages on children's values.
- The impact of commercial messages on children's health and safety.

- The ability of children to understand and evaluate persuasive commercial messages.[38]

Family conflict, health/safety issues, and values are discussed below. A discussion of the fourth issue is featured in the chapter on information processing (Chapter 8).

Family Conflict. Advertising can generate family conflict by encouraging children to want products their parents do not want them to have or cannot afford to buy. CARU rules clearly encourage advertisers to minimize this potential: "Children should not be urged to ask parents or others to buy any products." One study of family conflict found that:

- A majority of children were stimulated by television commercials to ask for toys and cereals.
- Nearly half of these children argued with their parents over denials of their requests.
- More than half became angry with their mothers when the request was denied.[39]

Such conflict is natural and is not necessarily bad. It can, in fact, lead to useful learning experiences. But the concern is that the level of conflict induced by consistent viewing of advertising is unhealthy.

Health and Safety. Concern also has risen that advertising may promote unsafe or dangerous behavior. In many instances, advertising directed at adults is viewed by children and the consequences are potentially harmful, as described in Exhibit 7–7.

Ensuring that advertisements portray only safe uses of products is sometimes difficult, but it is not a controversial area. Advertising of health-related products, particularly snack foods and cereals, is much more controversial.[40] The bulk of the controversy focuses on the heavy advertising emphasis placed on sugared products. Advertising sugared products does increase their consumption. However, this same advertising may also increase the consumption of related products, such as milk. What is not known (and probably cannot be determined) are the eating patterns that would exist in the absence of such advertising. That is, if children did not know about cereals such as Cap'n Crunch, would they eat a more nutritious breakfast, a less nutritious breakfast, or perhaps no breakfast at all?

Values. Advertising is frequently criticized as fostering overly materialistic, self-focused, and short-term values in children. It has also been charged with portraying undesirable stereotypes of women and minority groups. Unfortunately, we do not have sound evidence on the impact of advertising on children's values. However, CARU guidelines are clear: "Advertising should emphasize positive social and moral values and enrich the dignity of human life, and should

Exhibit 7–7

Child Safety and Advertising

A television commercial for Calgonite automatic dishwasher detergent showed a woman inside an automatic dishwasher. The commercial was withdrawn voluntarily after CARU received a complaint that a three-year-old child had climbed into a dishwasher shortly after viewing the commercial. The problem caused by the Calgonite commercial illustrates the difficulty of complying with the safety guideline. This commercial was not aimed at children nor shown during a children's program. The fact that children watch prime time television extensively places an additional responsibility on marketers. You must ensure that all of your commercials are appropriate for children from a safety standpoint.

Source: "B-M Drops Spots after Query by NAD," *Advertising Age*, April 20, 1981, p. 10.

avoid portrayals of violence, appeals to fear, or prejudice of any kind." About 10 percent of CARU's cases involve the area of values. Exhibit 5–3 (page 173) provides an example of one such case.

The Role of the Household in Consumer Socialization

Advertising and other marketing activities influence consumer socialization, and the family unit exerts both *direct* and *mediational* influences.[41]

Direct Influences. Family members directly influence consumer socialization through *direct instrumental training* and *modeling*. Direct instrumental training occurs when a parent, or sibling, specifically and directly attempts to bring about certain responses through reasoning or reinforcement. In other words, a parent may try directly to teach a child which snack foods should be consumed by explicitly discussing nutrition. Or, rules may be established which limit the consumption of some snack foods and encourage the consumption of others.

A more common direct influence, modeling, occurs when a child learns appropriate (or inappropriate) consumption behaviors by observing others. Modeling frequently, though not always, occurs without direct instruction from the role model and even without conscious thought or effort on the part of the child. Modeling is an extremely important way for children to learn relevant skills, knowledge, and attitudes. For instance, for many young boys, the process of learning to shave is developed through imitation of their fathers. Dad is seen shaving, and shaving is seen as one of the things a grown-up does. The manual or electric shaving equipment a child is first exposed to by this very important role model will undoubtedly affect his own learning of what is a proper shaving device. However, when he becomes old enough to buy his own shaving equipment, other factors also will influence the young man's final choice.

Mediation. The role of family in mediation can easily be seen in the following example:

CHILD: Can I have one of those? See, it can walk!

PARENT: No. That's just an advertisement. It won't really walk. They just make it look like it will so kids will buy them.

The advertisement illustrated a product attribute and triggered a desire, but the parent altered the belief in the attribute and in the believability of advertising in general.[42] This is not to suggest that family members mediate all commercials, or for all product categories, or even for all children.[43] However, children generally learn about the purchase and use of products during interactions with other family members. Thus, the firm wishing to influence children must do so in a manner consistent with the values of the rest of the family.

SUMMARY

The household is the basic purchasing and consuming unit in American society and is, therefore, of great importance to marketing managers of most products. Family households also are the primary mechanism whereby cultural and social class values and behavior patterns are passed on to the next generation.

The family household consists of two or more related persons living together in a dwelling unit. Nonfamily households are dwelling units occupied by one or more unrelated individuals.

The household life cycle is the classification of the household into stages through which it passes over time. Households, family and nonfamily, change over time at relatively predictable intervals based largely on demographic (and thus readily measurable) variables. The household life cycle is, therefore, a very valuable marketing tool because its stages provide marketers with segments that face similar consumption problems.

The demographic variables most frequently used to define household life cycle are age, marital status of the head of the household, and the presence and age of children. Using these variables, specific stages can be determined and described. One common form of the life cycle lists the following stages: young single, young married, full nest I, single parent I, middle-aged single, empty nest I, full nest II, single parent II, empty nest II, and older single.

Household decision making involves consideration of some very important and very complex questions. Who buys, who decides, and who uses are only a few of the questions that marketers must ask when dealing with products purchased and used by and for households.

Marketing managers must analyze the household decision process separately for each product category within each target market. Household member involvement in the decision process varies by involvement with the specific product as well as by stage in the decision process. Role specialization within the family also influences which household members are most likely to be directly involved in a purchase decision.

Conflict between household members with respect to purchase and consumption decisions may arise at any stage of the decision process. There are three common ways that households resolve such conflicts: problem solving, bargaining, and persuasion.

Consumer socialization deals with the processes by which young people (from birth until 18 years of age) learn how to become functioning consumers. How children become socialized (learn their own culture with respect to consumption) is very important to marketers interested in selling products to young people now or in the future. Consumer socialization deals with the learning of both directly relevant purchasing skills (budgeting, shopping) and indirectly relevant skills (symbols of quality and prestige, for example).

Public policy officials, parents, and marketing managers have become concerned about the effects that television advertising can have on children's learning and consumption activities. Recent attention has focused on four areas: (1) the potential for commercial messages to generate intrafamily conflict, (2) the impact of commercial messages on children's values, (3) the effect of advertising on children's health and safety, and (4) the ability of children to understand and evaluate persuasive commercial messages.

While marketing activities have a substantial impact on consumer socialization, this impact is mediated by the family. Families also assist consumer socialization through direct instrumental teaching and by providing role models.

REVIEW QUESTIONS

1. The household is described as "the basic consumption unit for consumer goods." Why?
2. What is a *nuclear family*? Can a single-parent family be a nuclear family?
3. How does a *nonfamily household* differ from a *family household*?
4. What is an *extended family household*?
5. Why are households important to marketing managers?
6. How has the distribution of household types in the United States been changing? What are the implications of these shifts?
7. What is meant by the *household life cycle*? How do family and nonfamily households progress through this cycle?
8. What is meant by the statement: "Each stage in the household life cycle poses a series of problems which household decision makers must solve?"
9. Describe the general characteristics of each of the following stages in the household life cycle:
   a. Young single.
   b. Young married.
   c. Full nest I.
   d. Single parent I.

e. Middle-aged single.
f. Full nest II.
g. Single parent II.
h. Empty nest I.
i. Older single.
j. Empty nest II.

10. Which stage of the HLC is the heaviest user of long distance telephone?
11. What is *consumer socialization*? How is knowledge of it useful to public policy officials as well as marketing managers?
12. What do we mean when we say that children learn *directly relevant* and *indirectly relevant* consumer skills and attitudes?
13. How do children learn to become consumers?
14. In what ways does the family influence children's consumption learning?
15. Describe the HLC/Social Stratification Matrix.
16. What is meant by *household decision making*? How can different members of the household be involved with different stages of the decision process?
17. The text states that "the marketing manager must analyze the household decision process separately for each product category within each target market." Why?
18. What factors influence involvement by a household member in a purchase decision?
19. What is meant by *role specialization* with respect to household purchase decisions?
20. Describe the three basic ways of resolving conflict within the household decision process.
21. What is meant by *consumer socialization*? What role does advertising play in consumer socialization?
22. Describe the role of teenagers in the household consumption process.

DISCUSSION QUESTIONS

1. Rank the stages of the household life cycle (starting at young single) in terms of their probable purchase of ____________. Justify your answer.
   a. Piano.
   b. Skis.
   c. Waterbed.
   d. Compact disc player.
   e. Instant coffee.
   f. Vacation.
2. Pick two stages in the HLC. Describe how your marketing strategy for condos would differ depending on which group was your primary target market.
3. Do you think the trend toward nonfamily households will continue? Justify your response.
4. What are the primary marketing implications of the household structure and income shown in Figure 7–1?
5. Based on Figure 7–4 and the text material related to it, describe how the

marketing strategies for the following products would vary with each stage in the HLC (starting with young single).

a. Toothpaste.
b. Restaurant.
c. Pet store.
d. Camcorder.

6. Create two different household structure/social status matrixes using different measures of structure and status. How would the segments identified by these matrixes differ from each other and from the ones in the text?
7. How could the information in Figure 7–8 be used by the management of a chain of fast-food restaurants?
8. What are the marketing implications of buying a rug versus buying an automobile, as shown in Figure 7–9?
9. What effects do television commercials aimed at children under seven have on their socialization process? How do these effects contribute to their behavior as teenagers and young adults? What role should the government play in regulating television advertisements aimed at children seven and younger?
10. Answer Question 9 for children aged 7–10.
11. Complete Table 7–2 for the products listed in Question 1.

PROJECT QUESTIONS

1. Interview a high school student who owns a car. Determine and describe the household decision process involved in the purchase.
2. Interview two appliance salespersons from different outlets. Try to ascertain which stages in the household life cycle constitute their primary markets and why this is so.
3. Interview one individual from each stage in the household life cycle. Determine and report the extent to which these individuals conform to the descriptions provided in the text.
4. Interview a family with at least one child at home. Interview both the parents and the child, but interview the child separately. Try to determine the influence of each family member on the following products for the child's use. In addition, ascertain what method(s) of conflict resolution are used.

   a. Toothpaste.
   b. Fruit.
   c. Shoes.
   d. Restaurants.
   e. Shampoo.
   f. Candy.

5. Interview a couple that has been married between 10 and 15 years. Ascertain and report the degree and nature of role specialization that has developed with respect to their purchase decisions.
6. Examine five different magazines and count the ads that appear to portray each stage of the HLC. What do you conclude?
7. Find and copy or describe an ad for each stage of the HLC.

REFERENCES

[1] "Teenagers Are Often the Bread Buyers," *Marketing News,* February 13, 1987, p. 5.

[2] See J. Grashoff and D. Dixon, "The Household: The Proper Model for Research into Purchasing and Consumption Behavior," in *Advances in Consumer Research VII,* ed. J. Olson (Chicago: Association for Consumer Research, 1980), pp. 486–91.

[3] See Exhibit 3–9.

[4] C. Russell, "The Condo Craze," *American Demographics,* May 1981, p. 44.

[5] W. Wells and G. Gubar, "Life Cycle in Marketing Research," *Journal of Marketing Research,* November 1966, pp. 335–63; E. P. Cox III, "Family Purchase Decision Making and the Process of Adjustment," *Journal of Marketing Research,* May 1975, pp. 189–95; and P. Murphy and W. Staples, "A Modernized Family Life Cycle," *Journal of Consumer Research,* June 1979, pp. 13–14.

[6] A. Andreasen, "Life Status Changes and Changes in Consumer Preferences and Satisfaction," *Journal of Consumer Research,* December 1984, pp. 784–94.

[7] M. F. Utsey and V. J. Cook, Jr., "Demographics and the Propensity to Consume," in *Advances in Consumer Research XI,* ed. T. C. Kinnear (Association for Consumer Research, 1984), pp. 718–23.

[8] D. Bloom, "Childless Couples," *American Demographics,* August 1986, pp. 23–25.

[9] Ibid.; and J. Langer, "The New Mature Mothers," *American Demographics,* July 1985, pp. 29–31.

[10] P. C. Gliele, "How American Families Are Changing," *American Demographics,* January 1984, pp. 21–25.

[11] S. M. Bianche and J. A. Seltzer, "Life without Father," *American Demographics,* December 1986, pp. 42–47.

[12] G. Hauser, "How Teenagers Spend the Family Dollar," *American Demographics,* December 1986, pp. 38–41.

[13] D. L. Walsh, "Targeting Teens," *American Demographics,* February 1985, pp. 21–25.

[14] P. Sloan, "Matchabelli Name Readied for Men's Fragrance Line," *Advertising Age,* April 21, 1980, p. 69.

[15] W. R. Swinyard and C. P. Sim, "Perception of Children's Influence on Family Decision Processes," *Journal of Consumer Marketing,* Winter 1987, pp. 25–37.

[16] R. Spiro, "Persuasion in Family Decision Making," *Journal of Consumer Research,* March 1983, pp. 393–402.

[17] See M. Lavin, "Husband-Wife Decision Making," in *1985 AMA Educators' Proceedings,* ed. R. F. Lusch (Chicago: American Marketing Association, 1986), pp. 21–25.

[18] A. Woodside and W. Motes, "Husband and Wife Perceptions of Marital Roles in Consumer Decision Process for Six Products," in *1979 Educators' Conference Proceedings,* ed. N. Beckwith et al. (Chicago: American Marketing Association, 1979), pp. 215–16.

[19] Haley, Overholser and Associates, Inc., *Purchase Influence: Measures of Husband/Wife Influence on Buying Decisions* (Overholser, Inc., 1975).

[20] A. Burns and S. DeVere, "Four Situations and Their Perceived Effects on Husband and Wife Purchase Decision Making," in *Advances in Consumer Research VIII,* ed. K. Monroe (Association for Consumer Research, 1981), pp. 736–41.

[21] R. Baran, "Patterns of Decision-Making Influence for Selected Products and Services," in *The Changing Marketing Environment: New Theories and Applications,* ed. K. Bernhardt et al. (Chicago: American Marketing Association, 1981), pp. 139–42.

[22] Haley, *Purchase Influence.*

[23] Burns, "Four Situations."

[24] G. Munsinger, J. Weber, and R. W. Hansen, "Joint Home Purchasing Decisions by Husbands and Wives," *Journal of Consumer Research,* March 1975, pp. 60–65.

[25] Baran, "Patterns of Decision-Making."

[26] M. Belch, G. Belch, and D. Sciglimpaglia, "Conflict in Family Decision Making: An Exploratory Investigation," in *Advances,* ed. Olson, pp. 477–78.

[27] R. Ferber, "Applications of Behavioral Theories to the Study of Family Marketing Behavior," in *Behavioral Models for Market Analysis,* ed. F. N. Nicosia and Y. Wind (Hinsdale, Ill.: Dryden Press, 1977), p. 89.

[28] A. C. Burns, "Spousal Involvement and Empathy in Jointly Resolved and Authoritatively Resolved Purchase Subdecisions," in *Advances in Consumer Research III,* ed. B. B. Anderson (Association for Consumer Research, 1976), pp. 199–207. See also S. Mehrotra and S. Torges, "Determinants of Children's Influence on Mother's Buying Behavior," in *Advances in Consumer Research IV,* ed. W. D. Perreault, Jr. (Association for Consumer Research, 1977), pp. 56–60.

[29] H. Davis and B. Rigaux, "Perceptions of Marital Roles in the Decision Process," *Journal of Consumer Research,* June 1974, pp. 51–61.

[30] J. Sheth, "A Theory of Family Buying Decisions," in *Models of Buyer Behavior: Conceptual, Quantitative, and Empirical,* ed. J. Sheth (New York: Harper & Row, 1974), pp. 17–33; H. Davis, "Decision Making within the Household," *Journal of Consumer Research,* March 1976, pp. 241–60.

[31] S. Ward, "Consumer Socialization," *Journal of Consumer Research,* September 1974, p. 2.

[32] G. P. Moschis, "Socialization Perspectives and Consumer Behavior," in *Review of Marketing 1981,* ed. B. M. Enis and K. J. Roering (Chicago: American Marketing Association, 1981), pp. 43–56.

[33] Ward, "Consumer Socialization."

[34] B. B. Reece and T. C. Kinnear, "Indices of Consumer Socialization for Retailing Research," *Journal of Retailing,* Fall 1986, pp. 267–80; and B. B. Reece, "Children and Shopping," *Journal of Public Policy and Marketing,* vol. 5 (1986), pp. 185–94.

[35] Federal Trade Commission, *FTC Staff Report on Television Advertising to Children,* February 1978. See also P. Turk, "Children's Television Advertising: An Ethical Morass for Business and Government," *Journal of Advertising,* Winter 1979, pp. 4–8; H. J. Rotfeld and L. N. Reid, "Potential Secondary Effects of Regulating Children's Television Advertising," *Journal of Advertising,* Winter 1979, pp. 9–14; B. M. Enis, D. R. Spencer, and D. R. Webb, "Television Advertising and Children: Regulatory versus Competitive Perspectives," *Journal of Advertising,* Winter 1980, pp. 21–26.

[36] G. M. Armstrong, "An Evaluation of the Children's Advertising Review Unit," *Journal of Public Policy and Marketing,* vol. 4 (1984), pp. 38–55.

[37] S. Banks, "Children's Television Viewing Behavior," *Journal of Marketing,* Spring 1980, pp. 48–55. See also W. K. Bryant and J. L. Gerner, "Television Use by Adults and Children: A Multivariate Analysis," *Journal of Consumer Research,* September 1981, pp. 154–61.

[38] A more detailed breakdown is provided by A. J. Resnik, B. L. Stern, and B. Alberty, "Integrating Results from Children's Television Advertising Research," *Journal of Advertising,* Summer 1979, pp. 3–12.

[39] C. K. Atkin, *The Effects of Television Advertising on Children,* report submitted to Office of Child Development, 1975. See also S. Ward and D. Wackman, "Children's Purchase Influence Attempts and Parental Yielding," *Journal of Marketing Research,* August 1972, pp. 316–19; and S. C. Cosmos and N. Yannopoulos, "Advertising Directed to Children: A Look at the Mother's Point of View," *Journal of the Academy of Marketing Science,* Summer 1981, pp. 174–90.

[40] See D. L. Scammon and C. L. Christopher, "Nutrition Education with Children via Television: A Review," *Journal of Advertising,* Second Quarter 1981, pp. 26–36.

[41] See G. P. Moschis, "The Role of Family Communication in Consumer Socialization," *Journal of Consumer Research,* March 1985, pp. 898–913.

[42] Reid, "The Impact," E. T. Popper, "Mothers Mediation of Children's Purchase Requests," and D. B. Wackman, "Family Processes in Children's Consumption," in *1979 Educator's Conference Proceedings,* ed. N. Beckwith et al. (Chicago: American Marketing Association, 1979), pp. 645–48 and 649–52.

[43] See J. R. Rossiter and T. S. Robertson, "Children's Independence from Parental Mediation in Learning about OTC Drugs," in *1979 Educators,* ed. Beckwith, pp. 653–57.

CASES

CASE 2–1 WHITMAN'S CHOCOLATES*

A marketing strategy is developed to attract women candy buyers and to persuade women to give boxed chocolates to men as a Valentine's gift.

In the 1940s Whitman Chocolates used Elizabeth Taylor and Bing Crosby to encourage men to buy chocolates for women. While this approach was successful, sales of Whitman Chocolates are highly seasonal and regarded as an impulse purchase. Their consumer research shows that men tend to be last-minute shop-

Figure A
Whitman's Traditional Positioning

Elizabeth Taylor was very effective in attracting males to buy chocolates for females in the 1940s.

Whitman's biggest opportunity for future growth is in attracting female chocolate buyers who will give chocolate as a gift to males.

*Based on material supplied by Whitman's Chocolates.

pers which adds further to a concentration of shopping days around specific seasons of the year. Their research also shows that women buyers generally shop earlier than men.

The candy market in the United States is $12 billion per year, with the largest portion occurring for gift-giving situations. The Christmas season is the largest and longest selling season for boxed chocolates, with sales in this period beginning in late November. Valentine's Day is the second largest buying period for boxed chocolates, making up $1 billion or 8.3 percent of total annual sales. However, Valentine's Day sales are tightly compressed into a few busy days.

To increase demand, as well as expand the buying population, Whitman Chocolates is trying to induce women to buy chocolates for men. Male-oriented Valentine's Day chocolates feature the traditional heart-shaped box of chocolates, but dressed up in black tie or flannel pinstripes. The research revealed a growing trend of women giving what they had traditionally received. "The idea of women giving Valentine's Day gifts to their sweethearts has become popular in more recent years. It's romantic. Women are becoming more sophisticated, and it's hard to find a Valentine's Day gift for men" (marketing manager for Godiva Chocolates). However, love does not come cheaply at Godiva Chocolates, which markets its gray-flannel pinstripe heart for $40 per 14-ounce box. Brach Chocolates features a full-dress tuxedo box of chocolates, complete with red silk carnation and velvet lapels, for $10.95 for a one-pound box.

Other boxed chocolate marketers are trying other marketing tactics to increase sales. For example, a regional marketer in the East is testing a "hearts and flowers" promotion in selected New Jersey supermarkets. They are offering $1-off coupons for the in-store florist with the purchase of a 13-ounce box of their Claridge Chocolates.

Questions

1. How does the situation influence consumer behavior with respect to the purchase of boxed chocolates?
2. Should Whitman try to differentiate its marketing program from others attempting to get women to buy chocolates for men, or follow the same theme of black tie and flannel pinstripes? What other options are available?
3. How could Whitman increase its nonseasonal sales to women and men buyers? Are different strategies needed?
4. In what other channels of distribution could Whitman distribute its boxed chocolates?
5. How would you segment the women's market to focus on the groups most likely to buy chocolates as a gift for men? Describe the segments you feel are most appropriate and develop product concept, packaging, advertising theme, and media to reach them.

CASE 2–2 ADVANCED MICRO DEVICES, INC.*

An American semiconductor firm develops advertising to position the firm and its products in Japan in a culturally acceptable manner.

In 1982, Advanced Micro Devices, Inc. (AMD) had worldwide sales of $329,000 in the highly competitive semiconductor market. By 1987 their worldwide sales will be near the billion dollar mark making them among the larger producers in the world. Because the markets and competition are international in scope, AMD knew it would have to compete in each of the world markets. As shown in Figure A, over half the world market for semiconductors is outside the United States. And while the United States possessed 11 of the top 25 worldwide producers of semiconductors, the Japanese with 9 and Europe with 5 presented stiff competition.

Market entry was easier in Europe where semiconductor competition was less established. However, to gain entry and success in Japan would require an unusual effort due to protective government practices and well-established, price-aggressive Japanese semiconductor manufacturers. Though AMD was known for its technological leadership and innovation, they knew that to gain sustained success in Japan they had to have more than the right product with the latest technology. They had to fit in culturally as well. To accomplish this, AMD hired Japanese managers to help them adapt culturally. A major aspect of this cultural adaptation was a radical change to the way they communicated through advertising.

Figure A
World Semiconductor Market and Competition

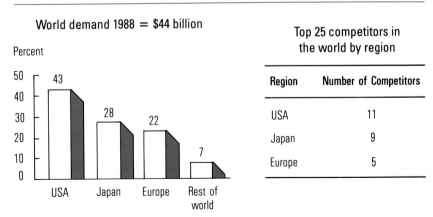

World demand 1988 = $44 billion

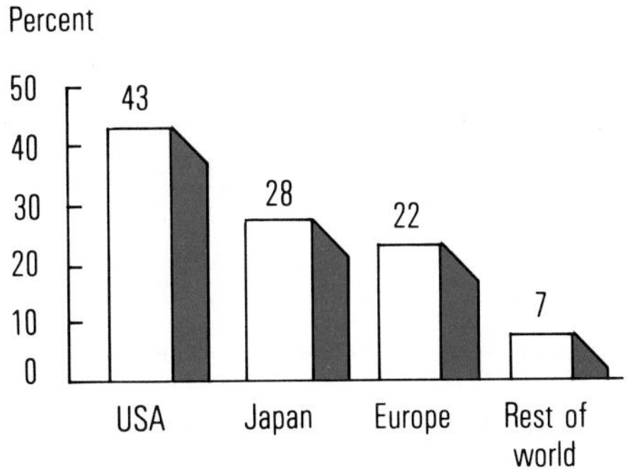

Top 25 competitors in the world by region

Region	Number of Competitors
USA	11
Japan	9
Europe	5

*Used with permission from Advanced Micro Devices, Inc.

AMD Japanese Advertising

While hi-tech advertising in the United States is very technical and benefit driven, appealing to the Japanese hi-tech buyer through advertising requires emotion and feeling. In the Japanese market, advertising is used to create an image, a feeling, a mood. It attempts to create an atmosphere that feels comfortable. When successful, this creates a positive association between the prospective buyer and seller of the advertised product. By contrast, advertising in the United States is supposed to communicate a compelling reason as to why one should want the advertised product. Therefore, AMD developed several Japanese advertisements that focused on food images (see Figure B). There is, for example, a small circuit card popping out of the toaster with the title, "Have a Little Toast with Your Morning Chips." The ad sought to make a subtle but important link between a desirable breakfast setting and AMD's chips on a circuit card. The ad copy simply tried to create a feeling, with little information provided.

A second theme also focused on food. This time, however, the theme is "A Delightful Dinner." The ad shows a polished place-setting complete with AMD chips and cherry blossoms. The setting is elegant and the message once again subtle and created by an association of pleasant feelings along with the AMD products.

Finally, there is dessert. This advertisement features AMD-Monolithic Memories, Inc., along with a pineapple and banana fused together to create a hybrid fruit called a "Pineana." The message in this advertisement is even more subtle. Monolithic Memories, Inc., is a subsidiary of AMD acquired in late-1986. The ad copy attempts to communicate that this new relationship between AMD and Monolithic Memories is like the creation of a new hybrid fruit such as the pineana.

These advertisements have been well received in Japan and are considered the best in the Japanese semiconductor industry. According to Mr. Shinn, AMD's general manager in Japan, the breakfast ad includes a compact circuit board card that can control four disk drives. It is so small that it fits into a toaster. The cultural translation is, "High levels of integration make a tastier product," according to Mr. Shinn.

The elegant dinner ad promotes new lower power, complementary metal-oxide semiconductor circuits. Mr. Shinn translates this as a high-quality food theme in which the flavor, of course, is AMD. Finally, the hybrid fruit represents the merger of two delightful entities and the "birth of a new variety."

Questions

1. Discuss the differences between the advertising approach taken in Japan and one that would be typically taken for a highly technical product in the United States.
2. How do cultural differences and values contribute to these two distinct orientations?

Figure B
AMD's Japanese Ads for Semiconductors

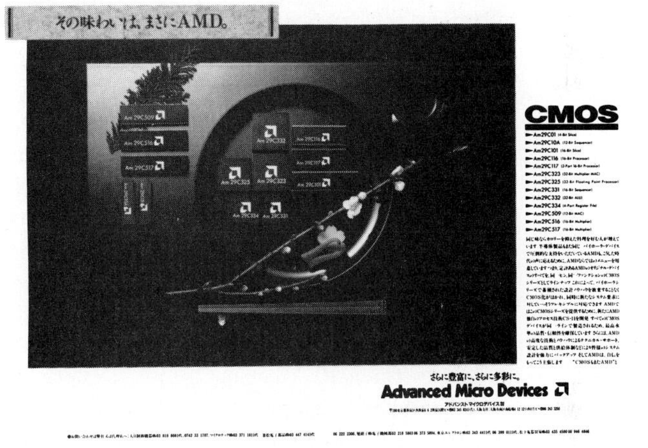

3. Would AMD be successful without this advertising approach? Explain.
4. Would the approach taken in Japan work in the United States? Explain.

CASE 2–3 GENERAL MOTORS

Differences in personal values are measured and related to car preferences and potential advertising themes.

Approximately 12 million automobiles are purchased in the United States each year. The competition for these purchases is fierce, and consumer needs are fragmented and complex. The purchase of an automobile is a great deal more than simply satisfying a transportation need. All the competing cars fulfill this need with varying degrees of longevity and reliability. However, a variety of other factors come into play in developing a preference for one car over another.

Basic needs for reliable, fuel-efficient, safe transportation are easily determined, as are key demographics that influence car preferences—such as family status, age, income, occupation, and education. Yet even with excellent research input—such that basic demographics and basic product needs are well known, and the media schedule is carefully matched with the media habits of the target customers—car advertisements often deliver low levels of likeability.

While there are many potential causes for ad failure, one cause is that the ad portrays values inconsistent with the values of its target customers. For example, an automobile ad that stresses a "sense of belonging" may appeal to some consumers who consider this value relatively important. Others motivated more by a "sense of accomplishment," may see the ad as less appealing. And, because our values influence our needs and help shape our attitudes, values influence product preference.

To learn more about how values interact with car preferences, General Motors sponsored a study to (1) uncover differences in values between consumers, and (2) to see if those differences related to preferences for different cars when positioned with different values as advertising themes.

Values Research Study

Eighty-nine car owners participated in the study. They varied in age from 18 to 70, with 40 percent under 25, 32 percent between 25 and 30, and 28 percent over 30 years of age. Fifty-five percent were male.

The participants were asked to evaluate three basic values, taken from the LOV value components, each at three degrees of importance to the individual. Participants were also asked to rank alternative sets of primary car needs and to rank order their preference for three automobiles. The three automobiles were presented in the form of an advertisement, each stressing a particular value that best matched the positioning of that automobile. For example the station wagon, a family car, was positioned with a strong "sense of belonging" theme, while an upscale four-door sedan embodied a "sense of accomplishment" theme. The third ad copy featured a sporty two-door coupe and emphasized "fun and enjoyment." Demographic information was also collected from each participant.

Results

After the importance rating of different values was done individually, participants with identical or very similar value importance ratings were grouped together. This grouping produced four distinct segments based on differences in the importance assigned to different values, as shown in Figure A. Group I placed heavy importance on "fun and enjoyment," while Group II valued a "sense of belonging" as most important. Groups III and IV both considered a "sense of accomplishment" as their most important value, but differed on which value was of secondary importance to them.

Group I preferred the two-door coupe, whose ad copy stressed "fun and enjoyment." Thus, there was consistency between their values and the values projected in the car ad they preferred. This group comprised 30 percent of the sample. Its members were predominantly younger (median age 24), and both male (52%) and female (48%).

Group II preferred the station wagon, whose ad copy stressed a "sense of belonging." Again, there was consistency between the importance of underlying values and the values projected in the preferred car ad. This group, which made up 23 percent of the sample, was older and predominantly male (71%).

Group III preferred the two-door coupe which stood for "fun and enjoyment." This preference was not consistent with their expressed values, since Group III placed a great deal of importance on a "sense of accomplishment." This group comprised 14 percent of the sample; its members were younger (median age 24) and predominantly male (71%).

Group IV was also somewhat inconsistent, as these car owners preferred the station wagon, but their second choice was the four-door sedan. This group made up 33 percent of the sample, was younger (median age 24), and was a mix of males (58%) and females (42%).

Overall, the study did demonstrate that car owners view the importance of

Figure A
Differences in Value Importance

Group	Sample Percent	Fun and Enjoyment	Sense of Belonging	Sense of Accomplishment
I	30%	70%	18%	12%
II	23	20	64	16
III	14	9	22	69
IV	33	29	6	65

values differently, and in many instances preferred cars that were positioned with values that matched values important to them. It appears, however, that a variety of other factors have to be taken into account to fully understand car owner preferences.

Questions

1. Why would someone's values influence their car preference or the degree to which they like or dislike a car advertisement?
2. Independent of their values, what other factors might cause a car owner to prefer one car and car advertisement over another?
3. Would the results have shown more consistency between values and preferences if a particular type of car had not been shown in the ads, or if the same type of car had been shown in all the ads?
4. Design an advertisement for any of the three values used in the study for a car that would project a similar set of values. Discuss how the values presented in the ad copy and projected by the automobile should influence a target car buyer with similar values.
5. Would values as a part of product positioning be more important in high- or low-involvement products? Explain your position.

CASE 2–4 RINCON RACQUET CLUB

A proposed new racquet club determines market demand on the basis of geographic concentration of population, area demographics, and the location of competing racquet clubs.

A city whose population is over 500,000 is currently served by four private racquet clubs. The northwest sector of the city has grown disproportionately faster than the rest of the city. In addition, this area is upscale economically, with houses among the most expensive in the city. However, those of its residents interested in racquet sports such as tennis, racquetball, and squash must drive from twenty minutes to three quarters of an hour to reach one of the four existing racquet clubs. Thus, there appeared to be a market opportunity for a new racquet club located within this area.

A major study of racquet clubs shows that members come from a 15-minute driving radius. Beyond this radius the probability of attracting a member is drastically reduced. Shown in Figure A are the driving radii for the four existing racquet clubs and the location of a proposed racquet club. As one can see, the proposed location (A) is likely to encounter limited competition, since its trading radius has limited overlap with competing clubs. As one might imagine, the competition among clubs C, D, and E is considerable. Based on the trading radius shown for the proposed club, census data was used to determine that approximately 75,000 people lived in its primary drawing area.

Figure A
Fifteen-Minute Driving Radius to Existing and Proposed Racquet Clubs

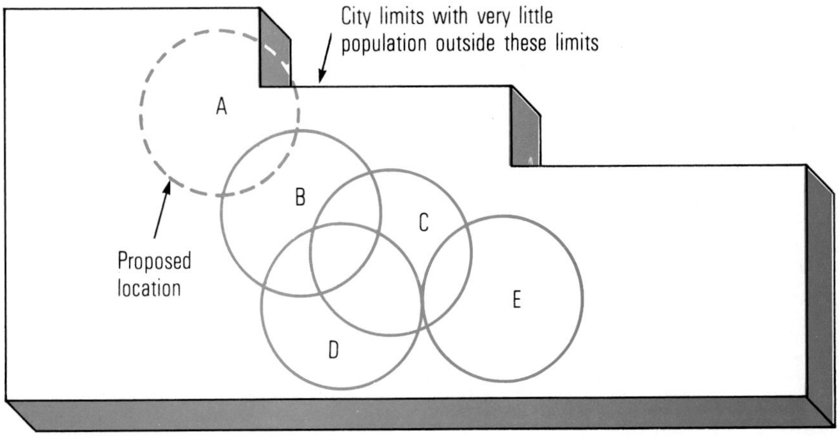

Of course, population size is not the only force affecting membership in a racquet club. The demographics of the trading area are also critical. Studies of racquet clubs show that age and income are important factors in estimating potential memberships. Those between 21 and 45, with head of household incomes greater than $30,000 per year, are the primary users of racquet clubs.

Within the target market area for the proposed racquet club, approximately 40 percent of the households fall into this combined category of age and income.

Figure B
Target Market Segment within Trading Area

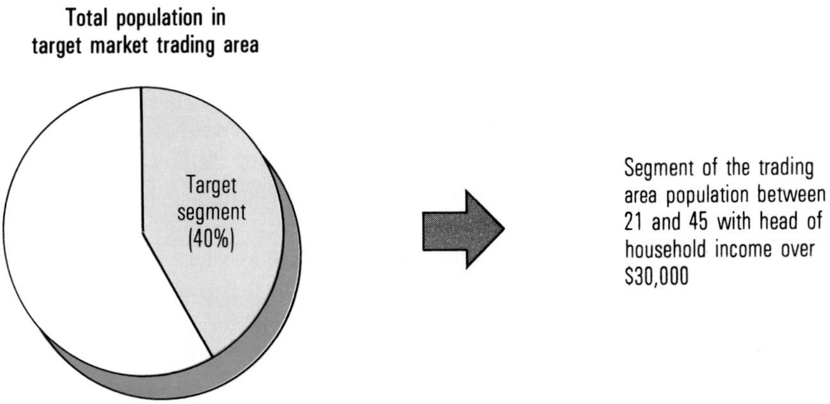

Thus, of the 75,000 living in the target market area, 30,000 meet the demographic criteria for membership in a racquet club.

Of course, not everyone between the ages of 21 and 45 with head of household incomes over $30,000 is inclined to join a racquet club. Prior studies also show that of this demographic segment, only 5 percent join a racquet club. Therefore, when we take into account the population size of the trading area, target demographics based on age and income, and a 5 percent attraction factor the following estimate of membership is obtained:

$$\begin{aligned}\text{Number of members} &= (\text{Area population}) \times (\text{Target demographics}) \times (\text{Attraction})\\ &= (75{,}000) \times (.40) \times (.05)\\ &= 1{,}500\end{aligned}$$

Thus, based on these factors, it is predicted that the proposed racquet club would attract 1,500 members. Based on estimated fixed and variable costs and the proposed monthly membership fee, the club could break even at 867 members. Thus, Rincon Racquet Club would begin to make money after attracting their 868th member. With an estimated membership of 1500 this seems to be an attractive venture.

Questions

1. What other factors might act to lower the estimated number of members attracted to the Rincon Racquet Club?
2. What future demographic changes would be important to take into consideration?
3. What would cause individuals outside the trading area to join the proposed racquet club?
4. How would you advertise the opening of this new racquet club? Be specific as to what benefits would attract individuals in your trading area to become members? What channels of market communications would you recommend to best reach this target? How does each channel affect the quality of the message sent?

CASE 2–5 JOHNSON PRODUCTS—EUROPE*

A unique package design is combined with individual country branding to position a toilet bowl cleaner in each of the culturally distinct countries of Western Europe.

There are 320 million consumers in Western Europe, approximately 80 million more people than in the United States. However, Western Europe is divided into 13 separate and culturally distinct nations. This makes marketing to these 320 million consumers considerably more difficult than marketing in the United

*Based on material supplied by Johnson Products.

Figure A
Package Design and Consumer Benefits

Package Design	**Benefits**
	• Functional . . . the lip of the dispenser fits under the lip of the toilet bowl to make dispensing the liquid easy and more sanitary. • Pleasant . . . the packaging was friendly and the scented liquid cleaner created a pleasant feeling. • Easy to find . . . among the many household cleansers often stored under the sink, this one was easy to spot.

States. Obvious differences in language and less obvious differences in culture have to be understood and incorporated into marketing strategies designed to serve more than a single European country. Marketing consumer products in Europe is further complicated by the fact that some 5,000 new products enter the European consumer market each year.

Johnson Products is a worldwide marketer of a variety of household nondurables. Products such as Johnson Wax and other household cleansers are well known and used throughout the world. Recognizing the need to grow through new product development and product line extension, Johnson is constantly in search of new product opportunities. One such opportunity was presented to them in the mid-1980s by a Swiss engineer who had developed a new package design for liquid toilet bowl cleaners. The package design shown in Figure A is in the shape of a swan or duck. It offers some tangible benefits over conventional packaging of liquid toilet bowl cleaners.

While the package offered promotable functional benefits, its unique shape made it friendly and memorable. The swanlike shape softened the harsh association with an unpleasant-smelling chemical used in an unpleasant household task. Furthermore, its unique shape made it stand out on cluttered supermarket shelves. These are powerful advantages to marketing a low-involvement household product such as a toilet bowl cleaner. While the new package design offered many pluses to both the consumer and the merchandiser of this product, the question of how to handle individual country differences needed to be resolved before a final strategy could be agreed upon.

International Marketing Strategy

While the product itself did not have to be modified, the answer as to whether this concept in packaging would have universal appeal was not known. To what degree would the package design have to be altered to ensure appeal in each of the countries Johnson hoped to serve? Once this was decided, modifications in country-specific advertising could also be incorporated into the overall marketing strategy.

Consumer research revealed that the swan-shaped packaging had universal appeal, as most people viewed both swans and ducks as pleasant. The name "Toilet Duck" was also well received. But the strategy to launch sequentially, country by country, was viewed as a hedge against potential consumer dislike for the package or the name. While the package, the promoted benefits, and advertising message would be the same for each country, the name of the product and information presented would always be in the native language of that country.

The branding decision was critical to the success of the marketing effort since the name had to draw a strong association between the package design and brand name. While "Toilet Duck" was a good name for England, many countries used the term "Water Closet" or "WC" when referring to the toilet. Thus, the package would carry the name "Toilet Duck" in England and other countries where the word toilet was appropriate. However, in France it would be branded "WC Canard," and in Spain "Pato WC." Shown in Figure B is the complete line of

Figure B
Package Design Modifications Used to Reach 22 Distinct European Cultures

package designs developed for distinct differences in the countries Johnson had targeted in its marketing strategy.

Results

The new product was first launched in England where after eight months it had captured a 25 percent market share. After six months in France it was the market share leader. In Holland it captured a 75 percent market share, while in Switzerland this Johnson product enjoyed a 40 percent market share. The package design, the message, and the benefits were the same for each country. The only difference was adaptation to local language and custom in terms of how one refers to a toilet.

Questions

1. Discuss the cultural values that would make this package design and branding strategy have such universal appeal across distinctly different European cultures.
2. Discuss how a low-involvement product such as a toilet bowl cleaner could be perceived, correctly interpreted, and remembered without extensive repeat advertising exposure.
3. Discuss the advantages this package design offered in terms of being recognized among the 5,000 new products introduced into the European market each year.
4. While this package design distinctly differentiates itself from conventional packaging for such items as liquid detergent and toilet bowl cleaners, what will happen if competitors respond with similar designs featuring other likeable animals or characters?
5. Will this product succeed as dramatically in the United States? In Japan?

CASE 2–6 OREGON DEPARTMENT OF ENERGY*

How can the Oregon Department of Energy encourage and assist restaurants to convert to more energy-efficient equipment and achieve substantial energy savings?

In an effort to reduce energy consumption, the Oregon Department of Energy (ODOE) evaluated 16 technologies as they applied to 15 commercial and industrial energy markets. Using the criteria shown in Figure A, the restaurant industry was targeted as a market which offered considerable energy-savings

---

*Based on materials supplied by the Oregon Department of Energy.

Figure A
Criteria for Selecting Target Industries for Energy Savings

Criteria	Description of Criteria
Resource potential	Number of BTUs per year that could be conserved
Commercial feasibility	Degree technology is developed and proven
Flexibility	Lead time needed to adopt technology
Adoption rate	Current level of market adoption of technology
Payback period	Number of years to earn back investment
Environmental impact	Degree to which environmental problems are created
Impactable by ODOE	Degree to which ODOE can affect adoption
Widely acceptable	Number of applicable businesses

potential if the state could influence these restaurants to convert to more energy-efficient equipment. The technologies available and the potential savings possible suggested that restaurants could achieve a very quick payback and hence derive greater profits from their business while consuming less energy.

To promote the conversion to energy-efficient equipment, the state was pre-

Figure B
Technology Awareness and Reception of Adequate Information

Awareness of heat recovery systems

32%. . .Dishwasher heat recovery
42%. . .Refrigeration heat recovery
41%. . .Heat recovery from exhaust hoods
47%. . .Efficient grills and ovens

Do you receive adequate information?

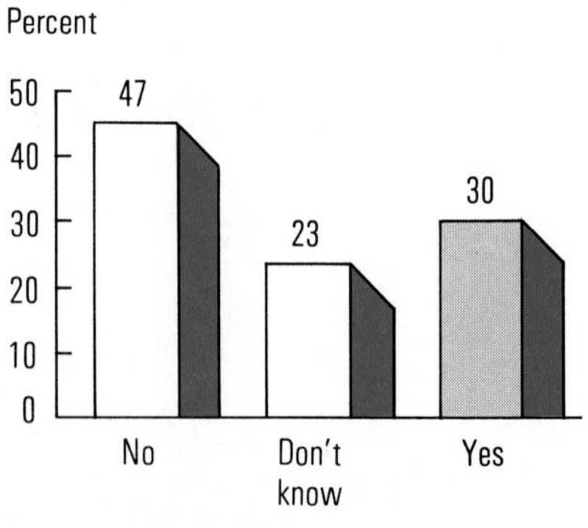

pared to offer tax credits and energy loans under the Small Energy Loan Program (SELP). However, these programs are of little value if the restaurant owners are unaware of them. Furthermore, these tax credits and energy loans have no meaning if the restaurant managers do not understand how converting to more energy-efficient equipment can make them more money. Therefore, ODOE had to effectively communicate and market the concept of profitable energy-savings equipment purchases to restaurant owners. To begin, they conducted a market research study that would provide them the information needed to develop a marketing strategy targeted at this business sector.

Market Research

Due to a variety of disqualifying reasons, not all of the many restaurants located in the state would be eligible. However, an estimated 2,000 would be eligible and these are the target market for this program. To understand the needs and key issues concerning a purchase decision of the type to be promoted, ODOE started its market research effort with depth interviews with trade association officials, vendors, and known opinion leaders in the restaurant industry. Using this information they were able to construct a survey that was administered by telephone to 112 full-service restaurant operators.

Results of Market Survey

Of the 112 restaurants contacted, 28 percent had installed heat-recovery equipment. However, awareness of heat-recovery equipment was low, as shown in Figure B. When asked if they were receiving adequate information on energy-saving equipment, almost half responded "No," while 30 percent felt they were receiving adequate information. This corresponded very closely to the 28 percent that had adopted energy-savings equipment in their restaurants. Thus, there seemed to be an obvious information void.

A second area of importance was awareness of and interest in the tax credit program. As shown in Figure C, only 7 percent could accurately recall the tax credit program. While 47 percent said they were aware of the program, this group could not give sufficient details to suggest they understood the program or its benefits. Further, 44 percent were not aware of the program. However, when the program was explained, 70 percent said they "Definitely Would" apply for it if they were investing in energy-savings equipment. Only 7 percent said they would not apply for the program, and the remaining 23 percent indicated that they "Probably Would" apply.

When asked what sources they used in acquiring information related to energy savings, survey respondents listed equipment vendors and the media as the two most used sources. Only 7 percent listed ODOE as a source of information.

Figure C
Awareness of and Interest in the Tax Credit Program

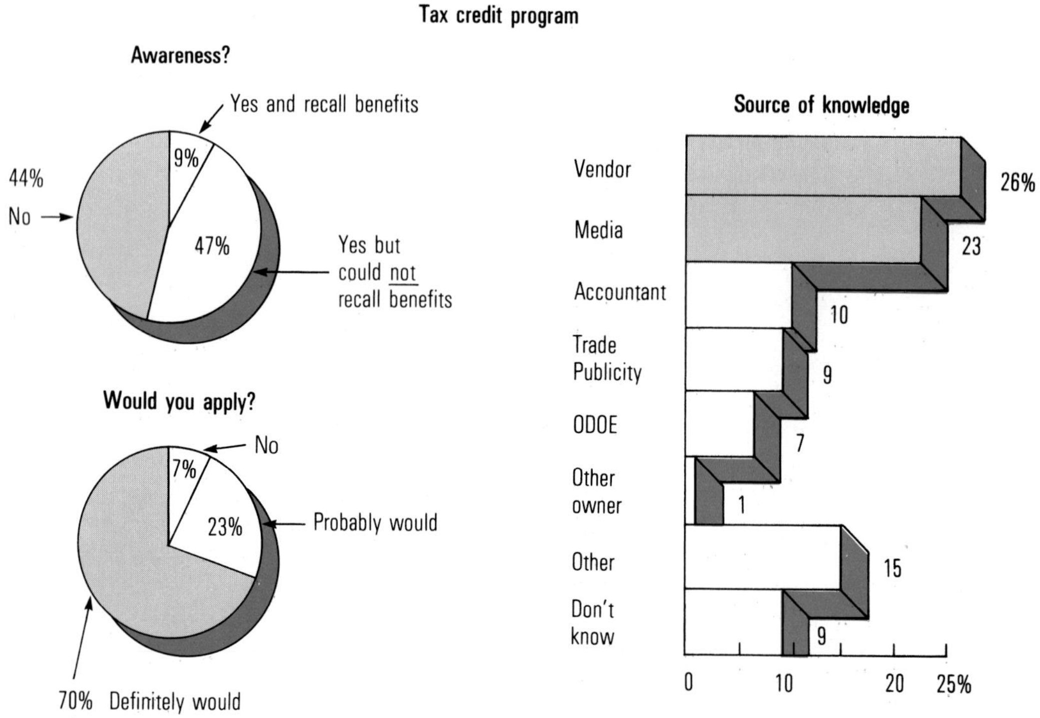

Questions

1. Discuss the diffusion process and the factors that may accelerate or slow the adoption of heat-recovery technology equipment in this market.
2. What role would opinion leaders play in the adoption of the desired energy-savings equipment? What kind of opinion leaders might exist and how would you recommend using them?
3. What could ODOE do to help accelerate the adoption of energy-savings equipment?
4. Develop a marketing strategy to increase the number of restaurants adopting energy-savings equipment.
5. How could ODOE use intermediaries such as vendors, accountants, and trade association personnel to promote energy-savings equipment investments? In comparison to direct communications from ODOE, how effective would indirect communications be?

CASE 2–7 MERRILL-LYNCH FINANCIAL SERVICES*

The female market for investor services is segmented into three distinct segments on the basis of different needs, demographics, and lifestyles.

Though the financial holdings of female investors are enormous, it was not until recently that financial services companies such as Merrill Lynch recognized the unique needs of different female investors. Some facts were well known. The financial wealth controlled by females was in the billions of dollars and larger than that held by males. In addition to financial assets controlled throughout the lifecycle, women outlive men and acquire a large quantity of stocks, bonds, mutual funds, certificates of deposit, and so on in the latter stages of the household life cycle.

However, until recently the female investor market was largely ignored and was not targeted as an important market opportunity. Consumer analysis of the female investor market uncovered a variety of differences with respect to needs, demographics, lifestyles, income, and awareness and knowledge of investment alternatives. Other differences such as media habits pointed out the fact that there is tremendous diversity among this group of investors. A quantitative analysis of this information uncovered the existence of three market segments, each unique in terms of needs for financial services, demographics, consumer lifestyle, awareness and knowledge of financial services, and media habits.

Each of these female investor segments represents a unique market opportunity. In order to design an effective marketing strategy for any or all of these segments, it is first necessary to understand the unique aspects of each female investor segment.

The Career Woman

This segment of the female investor market is the smallest but is growing rapidly. These investors are younger (30–40), college educated, and actively pursuing a career. Their incomes are high relative to other working women and growing as they progress in their careers. This group includes single and married females, but the majority did not have children living in their households.

While their demographics are unique, equally important differences exist in their needs for financial services. Women in this segment have higher incomes and pay considerable taxes because they are single or, if married, have two sources of income. As a result, their needs focus on ways to increase their financial holdings without incurring additional tax obligations. Also, because they do not need current income, they have a greater need for long-term capital appreciation rather than current interest or dividend income.

*Based on material supplied by Merrill Lynch.

Figure A
Summary of Female Investor Segmentation

Segment	Basic Needs	Experience	Key Demographics
Career woman	Tax avoidance, long-term growth	Limited to average	Educated, working at career, between 25 and 40
Single parent	Security, future income	None to limited	Unmarried with children, between 35 and 55
Older investor	Current income, security	Limited to extensive	Typically single, 55 and older

The Single Parent

This segment is the second largest in size and also growing. These female investors are middle aged (35–45), unmarried, but have children living at home. Their single-parent status could be the result of divorce or death of a spouse. Because these events tend to happen more often at middle age, this particular female investor is often thrust into managing money without much experience. Current income is generally under pressure and money affairs have to be carefully budgeted.

For this segment, security is first. With parental responsibility and limited income they want to make sure their money will be there in the future. As a result, they prefer investments that offer secure growth. This investment will be a source of income later in life and/or used for their children's education. In either case these consumers do not want to risk their futures.

The Older Investor

This segment is the largest of the female market for financial services. These female investors are older (55 and up) and typically single. Unlike the "Single Parent," these female investors do not have children at home and often have more discretionary income. Also, many of these investors have considerable knowledge and experience with the many financial alternatives that exist.

A need for current income makes this segment of female investors different from the other two segments. In many instances, these women support themselves from interest and dividends on their investments. Because investments are often their sole source of income, they seek safety and minimum risk in the investments they hold. Thus, their ideal investment portfolio would include a variety of secure investments that yield good current income.

While many differences exist among the many female investors, these three female investor segments capture important differences in basic needs, demographics, and lifestyle as summarized in Figure A. Based on these differences, individualized marketing strategies could be developed for each segment. The degree to which such strategies will succeed will depend on how well each strategy satisfies the specific needs of each segment in terms of both product offerings and market communications.

Questions

1. Discuss how different demographic situations (i.e., age, income, marital status, etc.) contribute to different financial needs among female investors.
2. How might each of these segments be further segmented demographically? What would be the advantages and disadvantages of further segmentation of this market?
3. For the three segments described, prepare an ad concept for each, such that the ad copy communicates products that fit the target segments' financial needs and also matches their demographics and lifestyles. Also specify which print media you would recommend to reach each target segment.
4. How could the channels of distribution for presenting and selling financial services be designed to best meet the needs of each target segment?

SECTION THREE

Internal Influences

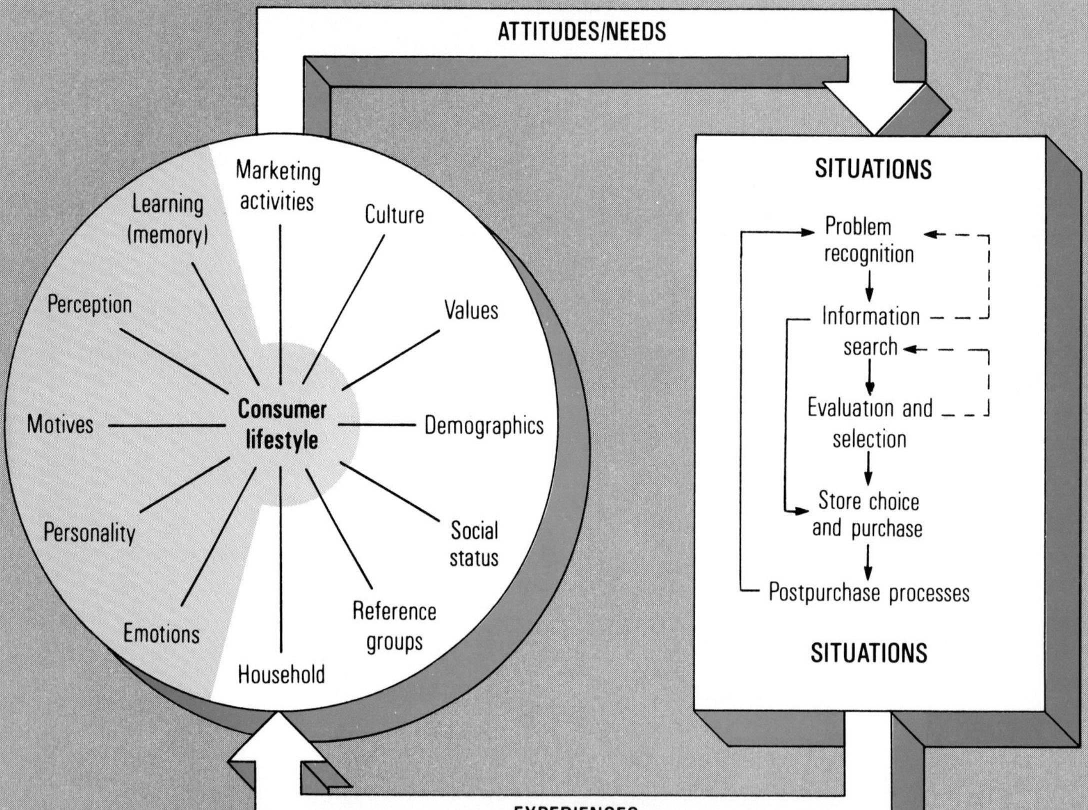

The shaded area of our model shown at left is the focal point for this section of the text. That is, our attention now shifts from group influence to the processes by which *individuals* react to group influences, environmental changes, and marketing efforts.

The perception and processing of information for consumer decision making is the subject of Chapter 8. Then the learning process necessary for consumer behavior is discussed in Chapter 9. Next we examine motivation, personality, and emotion in Chapter 10. Consumer lifestyle is the topic of Chapter 11. All of the previous topics tie together to influence a consumer's actual and desired lifestyle. Attitudes are the focus of Chapter 12, and we look at them as representing our basic orientations about products and marketing activities. Attitudes are brought out at this stage in the text because they are the actual manifestations of our learning about products and are the basic concept that marketers can measure and use to predict purchase tendencies. They are relatively stable clusters of knowledge, feelings, and behavioral orientations that we bring to specific purchase situations.

CHAPTER

8 Information Processing: Perception

The Federal Crop Insurance Corporation (FCIC) spent $13.5 million over a four-year period on an advertising campaign to increase awareness and knowledge among farmers of the federal crop insurance program. The campaign included "direct mailings to millions of producers of crops covered by the farmers' disaster program and to FCIC policyholders; national and local news releases; feature stories in national magazines, including most state publications; a radio campaign; publication of several brochures; and formal training programs for independent agents, insurance company officials, and FCIC employees."

However, "farmers ended up knowing no more about this program after the ad campaign than they did before." J. W. Ellis, director of public affairs for the FCIC, described the problem with the program thusly: "It was very good and very effective advertising. The trouble is that we had a hard time getting people to read it."[1]

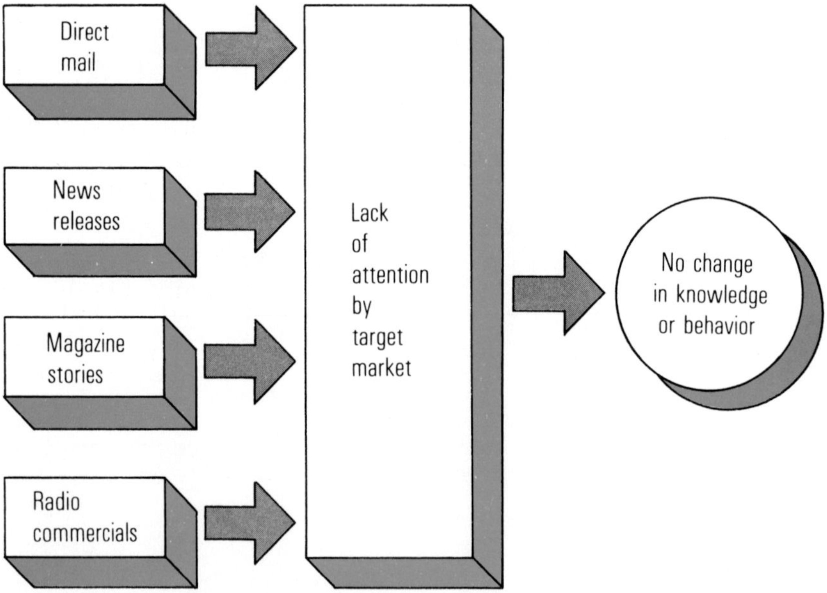

No organization wants to run $13.5 million dollars worth of "very good and very effective advertising" that people do not read. A sound knowledge of information processing is essential to avoid this and other problems encountered when communicating with various target audiences. *Information processing is the critical activity that links the individual consumer to group, situation, and marketer influences.*[2]

This chapter discusses three major aspects of consumer information processing: (1) the nature of information, (2) the perception process, and (3) the use of perception principles in the development of marketing activities. The next chapter completes the discussion of information processing by examining learning and memory.

NATURE OF INFORMATION

Information Defined

Information consists of all *facts, estimates, predictions,* and *generalized relationships* that affect a decision maker's perceptions of the nature and extent of a given consumer problem or opportunity. Facts, estimates, predictions, and generalized relationships are defined as follows:

- *Facts.* The simplest kind of information, a fact is an event or condition that is directly observed or that is believed by the individual to be an accurate representation of an event, including internal events such as emotions.
- *Estimates.* Estimates differ from facts in that they are based on inference (either logical or statistical) rather than on direct observation. We would prefer to have facts, but frequently must use estimates due to time and cost constraints.
- *Predictions.* Facts and estimates deal with the past and the present, while predictions deal with the future. They are beliefs about what will exist in the future.
- *Generalized relationships.* To obtain estimates and predictions, particularly for complex problems, specific facts concerning specific situations must be related to each other (cause and effect) and generalized to other similar situations and facts.

Exhibit 8–1 illustrates each of these four components for a consumer deciding between two brands of aspirin. Note that the various components of information serve as the raw material for the decision. Marketing managers must understand the differences between these types of information, since the appropriate marketing strategy depends on the type of information required. For example, assume that the consumer described in Exhibit 8–1 is typical of a market segment. That segment will not buy the generic brand even though many experts would consider

Exhibit 8–1 Components of Information for a Specific Consumer Decision

Decision:	Should I purchase a 100-aspirin bottle of Bayer aspirin or should I purchase a 200-aspirin bottle of generic aspirin?
1. Facts:	The Bayer aspirin costs $1.39 per bottle while the generic aspirin costs $0.68 per bottle. According to the labels, each aspirin contains five grains.
2. Estimates:	The Bayer aspirin costs about four times as much as the generic aspirin on a per aspirin basis. (Note: This could be computed and become a fact. However, because of time pressures while shopping, an estimate is used.)
3. Predictions:	My roommate and I will probably use about 20 aspirins a month unless one of us gets a cold. If that happens, we may use 30 aspirins, but I don't think either of us will get a cold.
4. Generalized relationships:	I believe that you usually get what you pay for, particularly with health care items. Therefore, since Bayer aspirins cost more, they are probably better.

it a better buy. Note that most of the information used by the segment is accurate. Only the generalized relationship, perhaps acquired through a low-involvement learning process, is (possibly) incorrect.

Now that we have an idea of the nature of information and its importance to the marketing manager, let us examine the ways consumers process information.

INFORMATION PROCESSING ACTIVITIES

Information processing is a series of activities by which stimuli are transformed into information and stored.

Figure 8–1 illustrates a useful information processing model. This model views information processing as having four major steps or stages: exposure, attention, interpretation, and memory. The first three of these are generally known as *perception*. *Exposure* occurs when a stimulus such as a billboard comes within range of a person's sensory receptor nerves—vision for example.

Attention occurs when the receptor nerves pass the sensations on to the brain for processing. *Interpretation* is the assignment of meaning to the received sensations. *Memory* is the short-term use of the meaning for immediate decision making or the longer-term retention of the meaning.

Figure 8–1 and the above discussion suggest a linear flow from exposure to memory. However, these processes occur virtually simultaneously and are clearly

Figure 8–1
Information Processing for Consumer Decision Making

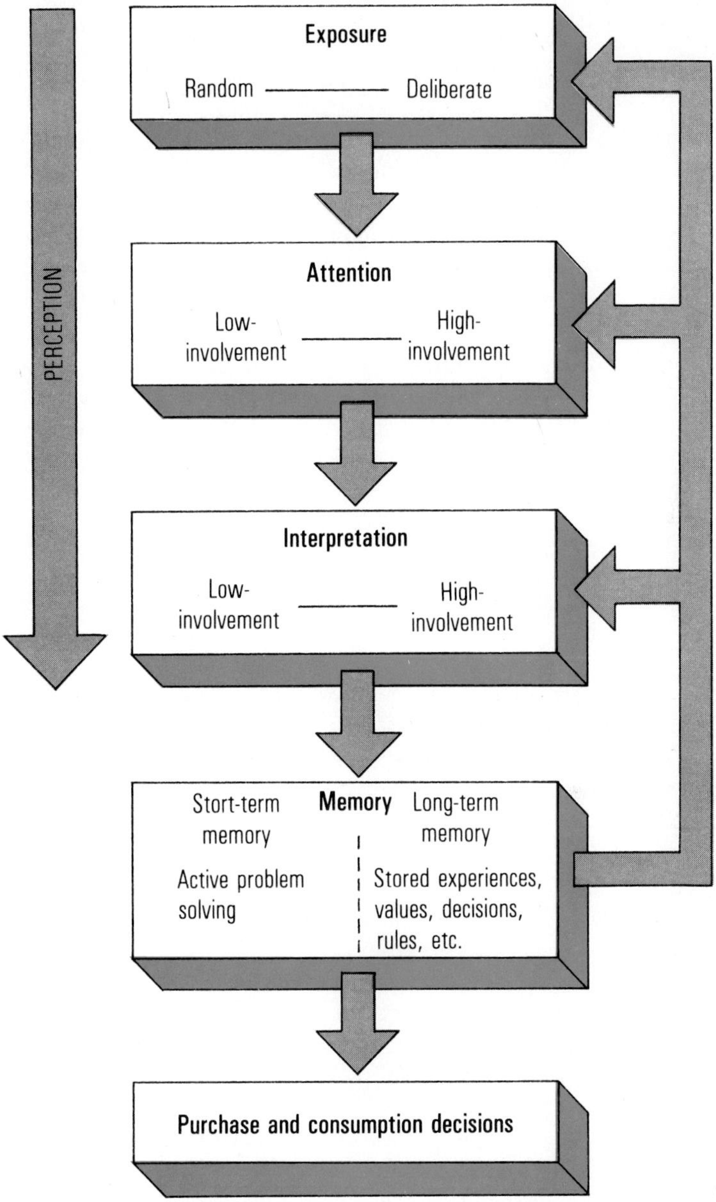

interactive. That is, our memory influences the information we are exposed to, attend to, and the interpretations we assign. At the same time, memory itself is being shaped by the information it is receiving.

PERCEPTION

Perception, the first three of the information processing stages, is described in some depth in the following pages. The final stage, memory, is described in the next chapter. Both perception and memory are extremely selective. Of the massive amount of information available, an individual can be exposed to only a limited amount. Of the information to which the individual is exposed, only a relatively small percentage is attended to and passed on to the central processing part of the brain for interpretation.

Much of the interpreted information will not be available to active memory when the individual needs to make a purchase decision. This is illustrated in Figure 8–2. Clearly, the marketing manager faces a challenging task when communicating with consumers.

Figure 8–2
Information Processing Is Selective

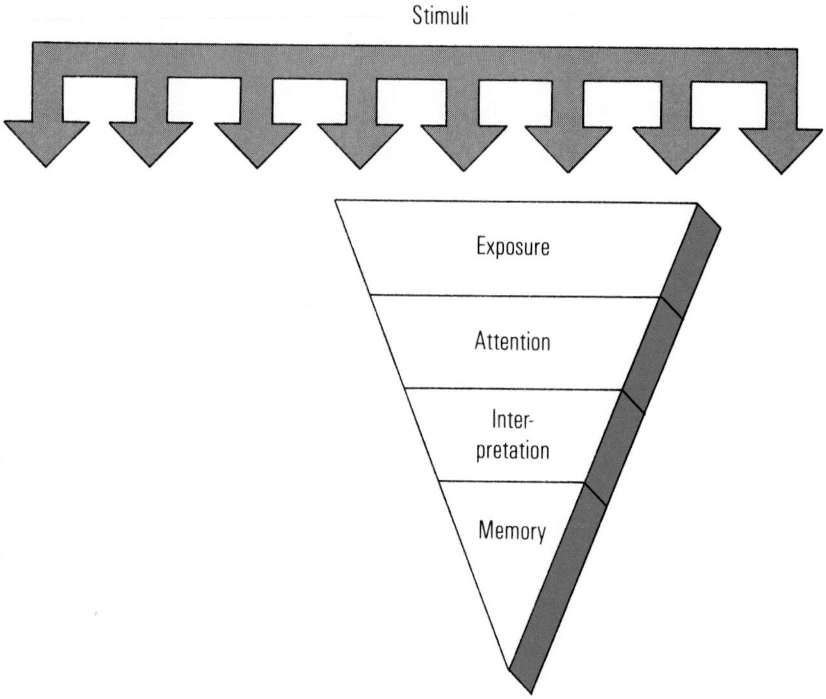

Exposure

Exposure occurs *when a stimulus comes within range of our sensory receptor nerves*. For an individual to be exposed to a stimulus requires only that the stimulus be placed within the person's relevant environment. The individual need not receive the stimulus for exposure to have occurred.

As the model in Figure 8–2 shows, an individual is generally exposed to no more than a small fraction of the available stimuli. One normally watches only one television station at a time, reads one magazine, newspaper, or book at a time, and so forth. What determines which specific stimulus an individual will be exposed to? Is it a random process or purposeful?

Why are you reading this text? Clearly you are doing so for a reason. Most of the stimuli to which an individual is exposed are "self-selected." That is, we deliberately seek out exposure to certain stimuli and avoid others.

Evidence of the active, self-selecting nature of exposure can be seen in "zapping." Zapping occurs when television viewers switch channels, or fast-forward (if watching a prerecorded show) when commercials occur on television. The advent of remote-controlled television sets and VCRs has made this easy to do and most consumers with this equipment actively avoid commercials.[3]

What influences us as to which types of stimuli we will seek out? Generally, we seek *information that we think will help us achieve our goals*. These goals may be immediate or long-range. Immediate goals could involve seeking stimuli such as a television program for amusement, an advertisement to assist in a purchase decision, or a compliment to enhance our self-concept. Long-range goals might involve studying this text in hopes of passing the next exam, obtaining a degree, becoming a better marketing manager, or all three. An individual's goals and the types of information needed to achieve those goals are a function of the individual's existing and desired lifestyle and such short-term motives as hunger or curiosity.

Of course, we are also exposed to a large number of stimuli on a more or less random basis during our daily activities. While driving, we may hear commercials, see billboards and display ads, and so on, that we did not purposefully seek out. Likewise, even if we have remote control, we do not always "zap" commercials.

Attention

Attention occurs when *the stimulus activates one or more sensory receptor nerves, and the resulting sensations go to the brain for processing*. We are constantly exposed to thousands of times more stimuli than we can process. The average supermarket has 10,000 individual items. It would take hours to attend to each of them. Therefore, we have to be selective in attending to marketing as well as other messages. It is estimated that consumers consciously attend to only 5 to 25 percent of the advertisements to which they are exposed.[4]

This selectivity has major implications for marketing managers and others

Figure 8–3
Attention to Prime-Time Television Commercials

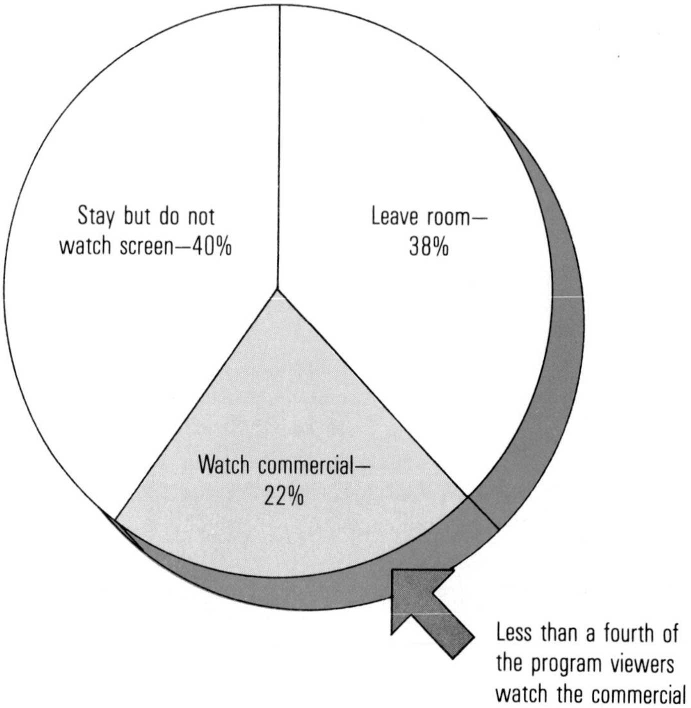

Total program audience = 100%.
Source: "Eyes on Television, 1980," *Newsweek* (1980).

concerned with communicating with consumers. For example, a Federal Trade Commission staff report indicates that fewer than 3 percent of those reading cigarette ads ever notice the health warning.[5] Figure 8–3 illustrates the results of a study for *Newsweek,* which found that during the average prime-time commercial break, only 62 percent of the audience remains in the room and only a third of those (22 percent of the total audience) watch the screen through the commercial.[6] Obviously, anyone wishing to communicate effectively with consumers must understand how to obtain attention after obtaining exposure.

Exhibit 8–2 illustrates how diligently companies are working to capture our attention. What determines or influences attention? At this moment you are attending to these words. If you shift your concentration to your feet, you will most likely become aware of the pressure being exerted by your shoes. A second shift in concentration to sounds will probably produce awareness of a number of background noises. These stimuli are available all the time but are not processed until a deliberate effort is made to do so. However, no matter how hard

Exhibit 8–2

Recent Attempts To Attract Attention to Television Commercials

Apple Computer Inc. spent $400,000—four times the average cost of a 30-second commercial—to produce an introductory commercial for the Macintosh computer. Facing a major struggle with **IBM's PC** (with a $40 million advertising budget), Apple created an elaborate vision of George Orwell's *1984*, with hundreds of dronelike characters and a big-screen Big Brother. The ad was shown during the Super Bowl at a cost of $600,000. Apple's director of marketing communications justified the expenditure thusly:

> **We felt that we had to do something that dramatic and impactful to get the average viewer interested.**

Diet Pepsi's $35 million introductory campaign for Diet Pepsi with NutraSweet broke with traditional advertising approaches. Instead of upbeat music, dancing, and active sport and play scenes, the firm used a series of sexy mini-dramas that included "intimate" conversations between a man and a woman. A Pepsi executive explains the logic:

> **There are 17 cola advertisers. Unless we wanted to become part of that wallpaper, we had to create advertising that was very different.**

Source: "The New TV Ads Try to Wake Up Viewers," *Business Week*, March 19, 1984, p. 46.

you are concentrating on this text, a loud scream or a sudden hand on your shoulder would probably get your attention. Attention, therefore, is determined by two factors—*stimulus* and *individual*. Of course, attention always occurs within the context of a situation. The *same individual* may devote different levels of attention to the *same stimulus* in *different situations*.

Stimulus Factors. Stimulus factors are physical characteristics of the stimulus itself. The stimulus has the ability to make us pay attention due to the effects it (the stimulus) has on our nervous systems. Let us look at a few examples more closely.[7]

Contrast. *Contrast* refers to our tendency to attend more closely to stimuli that contrast with their background than to stimuli that blend with it.[8] This principle appears to underlie Pizza Inn's advertising shift from jingles and interior views showing happy employees and customers to a mystical, humorous campaign. Pizza Inn's marketing vice president explains their logic as follows: "There's a lot of air noise," and Pizza Inn has "less bucks to spend than a Pizza Hut or McDonald's." Therefore, "it's time to be unique."[9] Contrast has been

Exhibit 8–3

What Happened to the Culligan Man?

For almost a quarter of a century, Culligan, a water treatment company, had run the same advertising campaign. It featured a "shrewish housewife screeching, 'Hey, Culligan man!' " when she experienced water problems. During the 1960s, the woman's extremely shrill voice was very effective in attracting attention. However, by the 1980s some customers began asking, "What happened to the Culligan man?" Research indicated that company name recognition had dropped from 64 percent in the late 1960s to 34 percent in the mid-1980s. Yet, the company was doing more advertising than ever!

Consumers had apparently adapted to the shrill tactics of the advertisement and no longer attended to it. In 1984, the company dropped the old campaign and began an entirely new one.

Source: R. Alsop, "Culligan Drops Familiar Voice to Broaden Appeal of Its Ads," *The Wall Street Journal*, August 9, 1984, p. 27.

found to be a primary component of award-winning headlines.[10] Likewise, the name Apple Computer is widely regarded as a stroke of genius, in part because it contrasts with the technologically oriented names usually associated with this product category.

Over time we adjust to the level and type of stimulus to which we are accustomed. Thus, an advertisement that stands out when new will eventually lose its contrast effect. There is a body of knowledge called *adaptation level theory* that deals with this phenomenon. Exhibit 8–3 provides an illustration of adaptation to a marketing mix element.

Adaptation level theory is advanced as a major explanation for a decline in the impact of television advertising. (In 1965, 18 percent of television viewers could correctly recall the brand in the last commercial aired; that figure dropped to 7 percent by the 1980s.) Viewers have adapted to the presence of television and increasingly use it as "background" while doing other things.[11]

Size and intensity. The *size* of the stimulus influences the probability of paying attention.[12] Larger stimuli are more likely to be noticed than smaller ones. Thus, a full-page advertisement is more likely to be noticed than a half-page advertisement. Figure 8–4 indicates the relative attention-attracting ability of various sizes of magazine ads. Ads with longer copy have been found to be more effective in attracting the attention of industrial buyers than ads with shorter copy.[13] *Insertion frequency,* the number of times the same ad appears in the same issue of a magazine, has an effect similar to ad size. Three insertions generate more than twice the impact of one insertion.[14] The *intensity* (e.g., loudness, brightness) of a stimulus operates in much the same manner as size.

Color and movement. Both *color* and *movement* serve to attract attention with brightly colored and moving items being more noticeable. A brightly colored

Figure 8–4
The Impact of Size on Advertising Readership*

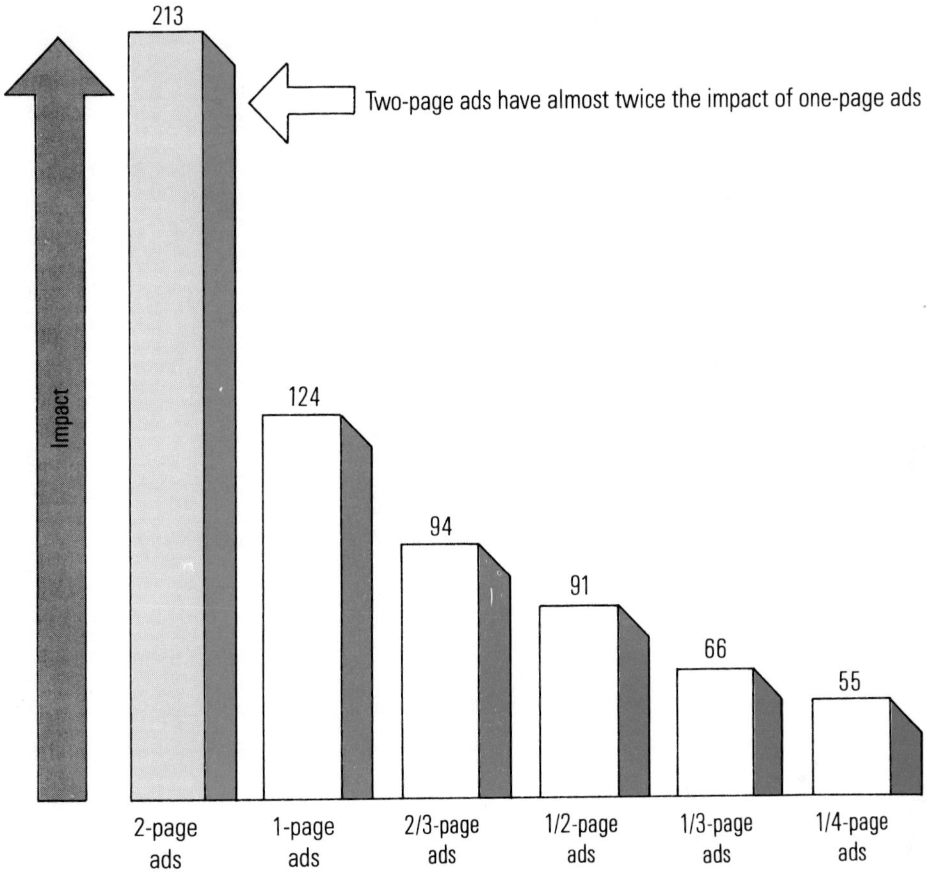

*Based on an analysis of 2,353 ads. Average readership for all ads studied was set equal to 100.
Source: CARR Report No. 110.1 (Boston: Cahners Publishing, 1979).

package is more apt to receive attention than a dull package. A recent study on the impact of color in newspaper advertising concluded that "median sales gains (on reduced-price items) of approximately 41 percent may be generated by the addition of one color to black-and-white in retail newspaper advertising."[15] Figure 8–5 shows the relative attention-attracting ability of black-and-white, two-color, and four-color magazine ads. However, the impact of contrast can reverse this. That is, if all the ads in a magazine are in color, a black-and-white ad may attract substantial attention.

Position. *Position* refers to the placement of an object in a person's visual field. Objects placed near the center of the visual field are more likely to be

Figure 8–5
The Impact of Color on Advertising Readership*

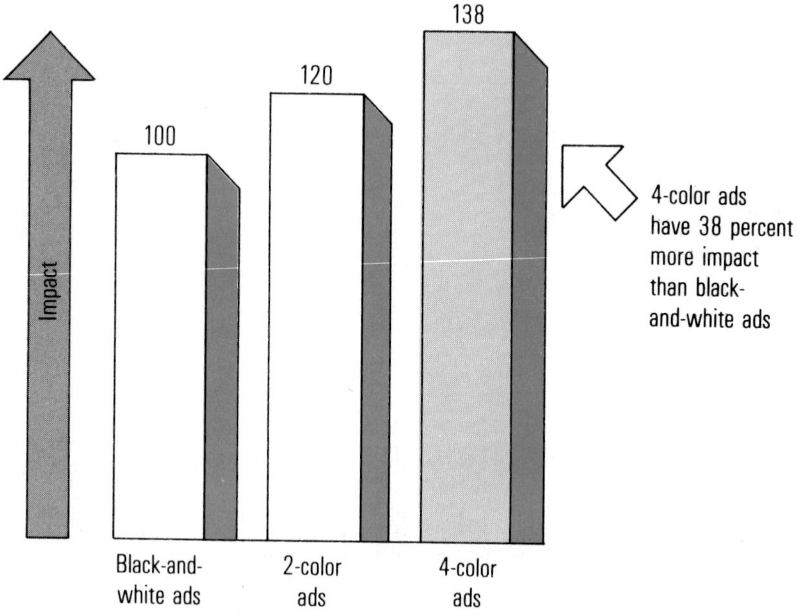

*Based on an analysis of 2,531 ads. Average readership for black-and-white ads was set at 100.

Source: CARR Report No. 112.1A (Boston: Cahners Publishing, 1980).

noticed than those near the edge of the field. This is a primary reason why consumer goods' manufacturers compete fiercely for eye-level space in grocery stores. In one study, the simple addition of a mobile over the dairy case improved the sales of cheese 30 percent, as long as the mobile was at the right height. If it was too high or too low, no improvement in sales resulted.[16]

Isolation. *Isolation* is separating a stimulus object from other objects. The use of "white space" (placing a brief message in the center of an otherwise blank or white advertisement) is based on this principle. Christian Dior recently introduced a major shift in the manner in which its magazine ads for cosmetics are presented. It now uses substantial amounts of "white" space to create a contrast between its advertisements and those of its competitors. A company executive explains:

> Practically every major cosmetics company has the same concept. There's a pretty girl on the right and the product on the left or dropped into a box on a double-page spread. If you hide the name of the company, you won't know whose visual it is.[17]

Compressed messages. Initial research indicated that speeding up a message may increase attention. Such messages are termed *compressed messages.* In one experiment, 30-second commercials were reduced to 24 seconds via a device that does not produce sound distortions. The compressed commercials were found to be more interesting and to generate at least the same level of product recall as standard commercials. Thus, there appears to be potential to accelerate all or selected parts of advertisements presented via broadcast media.[18] In fact, 18 of the top 20 advertising agencies reportedly have used or tested compressed commercials.[19]

Unfortunately, recent research suggests a more complex pattern. In general, we can say that compressed commercials do not distract from attention and may increase attention. However, attention level will vary with the type of message, the product, and the nature of the audience. The interpretation assigned the content of a compressed message will also vary and is not always favorable.[20]

Information overload. A final stimulus factor, information overload, relates more to the total stimulus field than to any particular item in that field. Although there is substantial variation among individuals,[21] all consumers have limited capacities to process information. Despite the fact that these capacities can be expanded by training, both marketing managers and regulatory agencies recognize the potential dangers of information overload. *Information overload* occurs when consumers are confronted with so much information that they cannot or will not attend to all of it.[22] Instead, they become frustrated and either postpone or give up the decision, make a random choice, or utilize a suboptimal portion of the total information available.

There are no general rules or guidelines concerning how much information consumers can or will use. Marketers, the federal government, and various consumer groups want product labels, packages, and advertisements to provide *sufficient* information to allow for an informed decision. One approach is to provide all potentially relevant information. This approach is frequently recommended by regulatory agencies and is required for some product categories such as drugs. Problems with this approach can arise, however. For example, a relatively simple, one-page advertisement for ModiCon oral contraceptive required a second full page of small type telling of dosage, precautions, and warnings in order to comply with federal full-disclosure regulations.

The assumption behind the full-disclosure approach is that each consumer will utilize those specific information items required for the particular decision. Unfortunately, consumers frequently do not react in this manner, particularly for low-involvement purchases. Instead, they may experience information overload and ignore all or most of the available data.

Thus, public policy should be concerned with the *likelihood* that information will be attended to rather than simply its availability. Marketers will generally try to present the key bits of information and use message structures that make complete processing easy. Exhibit 8–4 provides clear evidence of how ineffective excess information can be.

Individual Factors. *Individual factors* are characteristics of the individual. *Interest* or *need* seems to be the primary individual characteristic that influences

Exhibit 8–4

Impact of Excess Consumer Information

A recent federal act required banks belonging to the Federal Reserve to explain to their customers the detailed protections built into money transfer systems available in electronic banking. Thus, Northwestern National Bank of Minneapolis was forced to create and mail a pamphlet explaining Amended Regulation E to its 120,000 customers. At a cost of $69,000 the bank created and mailed the 4,500-word pamphlet.

In 100 of the pamphlets, the bank placed a special paragraph that offered the reader $10 just for finding that paragraph. The pamphlets were mailed in May and June. As of August, not one person had claimed the money!

Source: "$10 Sure Thing," *Time,* August 4, 1980, p. 51.

attention. Interest is a reflection of overall lifestyle as well as a result of long-term goals and plans (e.g., becoming a sales manager) and short-term needs (e.g., hunger). Short-term goals and plans are, of course, heavily influenced by the situation. In addition, individuals differ in their *ability* to attend to information.[23]

Individuals seek out (exposure) and examine (attend to) information relevant to their current situation. For example, an individual contemplating a vacation is likely to attend to vacation-related advertisements. Individuals attending to a specialized medium such as *Runners World* or *Business Week* are particularly receptive to advertisements for related products.[24] Parents with young children are more likely to notice and read warning labels on products such as food supplements than are individuals without young children.[25]

Nonfocused Attention. Thus far, we have been discussing a fairly high-involvement attention process in which the consumer deliberately and consciously focuses attention on some aspect of the environment due to stimulus, individual, or situational factors. However, information may be attended to without deliberate or conscious focusing of attention.

Hemispheric lateralization. *Hemispheric lateralization* is a term applied to activities that take place on each side of the brain. The left side of the brain is primarily responsible for verbal information, symbolic representation, sequential analysis, and the ability to be conscious and report what is happening. It controls those activities we typically call rational thought. The right side of the brain deals with pictorial, geometric, timeless, and nonverbal information without the individual being able to verbally report it. It works with images and impressions.[26]

The left brain needs fairly frequent rest. However, the right brain can easily scan large amounts of information over an extended time period. This has led Krugman to suggest that "it is the right brain's picture-taking ability that permits the rapid screening of the environment—to select what it is the left brain should focus on."[27]

While it is a difficult area to research, the evidence indicates that there is some validity to this approach.[28] This suggests that advertising, particularly advertising repeated over time, will have substantial effects that traditional measures of advertising effectiveness cannot detect. The nature of these effects is discussed in more detail in the next chapter. At this point, we need to stress that applied research on this topic is just beginning and much remains to be learned.[29]

Subliminal stimuli. There is also some evidence to indicate that some stimuli or messages, called *subliminal messages,* are attended to without awareness even if the individual tries to focus attention on them. A message is subliminal if it is presented so fast or so softly or so masked by other messages that one is not aware of "seeing" or "hearing" it.

Public interest in masked subliminal stimuli has been enhanced by two books.[30] The author "documents" numerous advertisements which, once you are told where to look and what to look for, appear to contain the word *sex* in ice cubes, phalli in mixed drinks, and nude bodies in the shadows. Most, if not all, of these symbols are the chance result of preparing thousands of print ads each year (a diligent search could no doubt produce large numbers of religious symbols, animals, or whatever). Such masked symbols (deliberate or accidental) have been shown to have very mild effects on performance on subsequent tests of imagery or imagination.[31] However, they do not appear to affect standard measures of advertising effectiveness or influence consumption behavior.[32]

Research on messages presented too rapidly to elicit awareness indicates that, *at most,* subliminal messages produce *very* limited effects.[33] Thus, though the general public is concerned about subliminal messages,[34] such messages do not appear to present a threat to the general public nor do they offer a potentially effective communications device.[35]

Interpretation

Interpretation is the assignment of meaning to sensations. It is a function of the Gestalt or pattern formed by the characteristics of the stimulus, the individual, and the situation, as illustrated in Figure 8–6.

It is the individual's interpretation, not objective reality, that will influence behavior. For example, a firm may introduce a high-quality new brand at a lower price than existing brands because the firm has a more efficient production or marketing process. If consumers interpret this lower price to mean lower quality, the new brand will not be successful regardless of the objective reality.

Interpretation is a process whereby stimuli are placed into existing categories of meaning.[36] This is an interactive process. The addition of new information to existing categories also alters those categories and their relationships with

Figure 8–6
Determinants of Interpretation

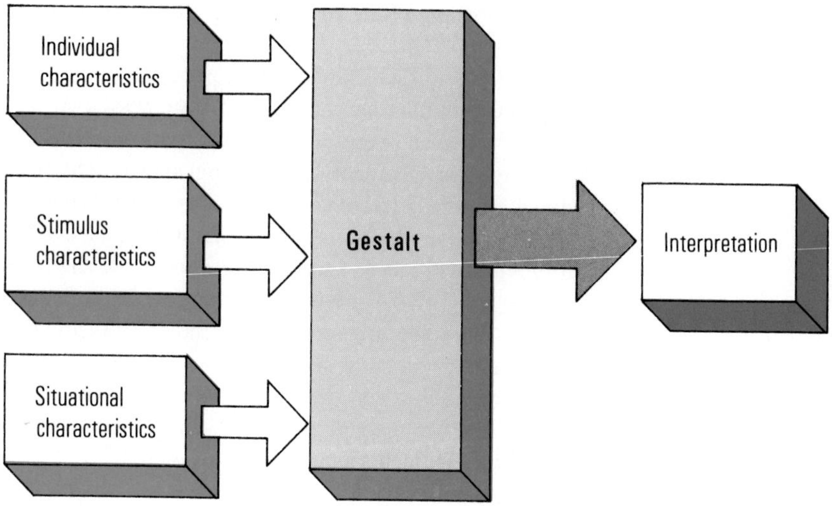

other categories. When the microwave oven was first introduced to consumers, most undoubtedly grouped it in the general category of ranges, ovens, and cookers in order to be able to evaluate it. With further experience and information, many consumers have gained detailed knowledge about microwaves and perhaps have several subcategories for classifying the various brands or types of microwaves.[37] The interpretation given a particular product or brand relative to similar products or brands is known as its *product* (brand) *position*.

Individual Characteristics. A number of *individual characteristics* influence interpretation. For example, gender and social class affect the meaning assigned to owning various products.[38] The two major personal variables affecting interpretation are *learning* and *expectations*.

Learning. We saw in Chapter 2 that the meanings attached to such "natural" things as time, space, friendship, and colors are learned and vary widely across cultures. Even within the same culture, different subcultures assign different meanings to similar stimuli. For example, "dinner" refers to the noon meal for some social classes in some geographic regions of the United States, and to the evening meal for other social classes and geographic regions. Marketers must be certain that the audience has learned the same meanings that they wish to portray.

Expectations. Individuals tend to interpret stimuli consistently with their *expectations*. For example, we expect dark brown pudding to taste like chocolate, not vanilla, because dark pudding is generally chocolate flavored and vanilla pudding is generally cream colored. In a recent taste test, 100 percent of a sample of college students accepted dark brown *vanilla* pudding as chocolate. Further, in comparing three versions of the vanilla pudding that differed only in degree of darkness, the students rated the darkest as having the best chocolate flavor.[39] Thus, their expectations, cued by color, lead to an interpretation that was inconsistent with "objective" reality.

Consumers will frequently evaluate the performance of a well-known brand or a more expensive brand as higher than an identical product with an unknown brand name or a lower price. Before Coca-Cola introduced "new" Coke, consumers consistently expressed a preference for Pepsi in blind (unlabeled) taste tests, but preferred Coke when the labels were attached.[40] Consumers also frequently attribute advertisements for new or unknown brands to well-known brands. Even an "objective" product feature like price is sometimes interpreted to be closer to an expected price.[41]

Situational Characteristics. A variety of situational characteristics influence interpretation. Temporary characteristics of the individual, such as hunger or loneliness, influence the interpretation of a given stimulus, as do moods.[42] The amount of time available also affects the meaning assigned to marketing messages. Likewise, physical characteristics of the situation such as temperature, the number and characteristics of other individuals present,[43] the nature of the material surrounding the message in question,[44] and the reason the message is being processed,[45] affect how the message is interpreted.

Stimulus Characteristics. The stimulus sets the basic structure to which an individual responds. The structure and nature of the product, package, advertisement, or sales presentation has a major impact on the nature of the mental processes that are activated and on the final meaning assigned the message.[46]

In recognition of the critical importance of the meaning associated with stimuli, marketers are beginning to use *semiotics*. Semiotics is the *science of how meaning is created, maintained, and altered*. It focuses on *signs*, which are anything that conveys meaning including words, pictures, music, smells, gestures, products, and so forth.[47] General principles of how meanings are learned are discussed in the next chapter. In the next paragraphs we describe several specific aspects of signs that influence how they are interpreted.

Proximity refers to a tendency to perceive objects or events that are close to one another as being related. The principle of proximity is being applied when soft drinks are shown in social settings. Both Coca-Cola and General Foods refuse to advertise some products during news broadcasts because they believe that "bad" news might affect the interpretation of their products. According to William Sharp, vice president of advertising for Coca-Cola, USA:

> It's a Coca-Cola corporate policy not to advertise on TV news because there's going to be some bad news in there, and Coke is an upbeat, fun product.[48]

The source[49] of the message affects the interpretations of the message as does the medium[50] in which the message appears. Likewise, the nature of the product influences how promotional claims are interpreted.[51] Previous experiences with the same or competing products or firms, and relevant external factors such as the state of the economy, also influence the interpretation of a message.

Not only is a message interpreted in the context of its situation, but all aspects of the message itself influence our interpretation. This can include our reaction to the overall style, visual and auditory background, and other nonverbal and verbal aspects of the message,[52] as well as its explicit content and even lack of content.[53] The National Advertising Division of the Council of Better Business Bureaus used an overall interpretation when it requested Bic Pen Corp. to change a comparative television commercial because, "*In the context of the whole commercial* (italics added), the claim could be construed as an absolute fact rather than the opinion of the people tested."[54]

Misinterpretation of Marketing Messages. Both marketing managers and public policy officials want consumers to interpret messages accurately, that is, in a manner consistent with what others or experts would consider to be the "true" or "objective" meaning of the messages. Having read the previous material on interpretation, you probably suspect that widespread agreement on, or accurate interpretation of, mass media messages is difficult to obtain. Two major studies indicate that this is indeed the case. A study of both commercial and noncommercial television communications reached the following conclusions:

- A large proportion of the audience miscomprehends communications broadcast over commercial television.
- No communication (program content or advertisement) is immune from miscomprehension.
- An average of 30 percent of the total information was miscomprehended.
- Nonadvertising communications had higher levels of miscomprehension than did advertising messages.
- Some demographic variables appear to be slightly associated with miscomprehension.[55]

While the methodology of the study has been criticized,[56] there is no doubt that substantial miscomprehension of television messages, including marketing messages, does occur. The second study, which focused on editorial and advertising content in general-circulation magazines, reached essentially the same conclusions.[57] Evidence also indicates that package information, including FTC-mandated disclosures, is subject to miscomprehension.[58] Neither the consumer nor the marketer benefits from such miscomprehension.

We are just beginning to learn about methods to minimize miscomprehension and it is a complex task. For example, repetition does not appear to reduce miscomprehension.[59] And while very simple television messages are less subject to miscomprehension, the same is not true for print messages.[60] Television messages containing both print and visual elements appear to increase miscomprehension. Older, less educated, lower-income consumers are somewhat more likely to misinterpret either print or television messages.[61]

At this time we have ample evidence that even relatively simple television, magazine, and package messages are subject to miscomprehension. Unfortunately, we do not yet have a workable set of guidelines for eliminating this problem. Thus, marketers, public officials, and others wishing to communicate with the public should carefully pretest their messages to ensure that they are being interpreted correctly.

Memory

Memory plays a critical role in guiding the perception process. As Figure 8–1 indicates, memory has a long-term storage component and a short-term active component. These are not distinct entities; active memory is simply that portion of total memory that is currently activated or in use. In the next chapter, we provide a more detailed discussion of the nature of memory and the factors that influence our ability to retrieve items from long-term memory for use in consumption decisions.

CHILDREN'S INFORMATION PROCESSING

Thus far we have been discussing information processing from an adult perspective. However, there is evidence that younger children have limited abilities to process certain types of information.[62] Table 8–1 shows a widely accepted

Table 8–1
Piaget's Stages of Cognitive Development

1. *The period of sensorimotor intelligence (0–2 years).* During this period, behavior is primarily motor. The child does not yet "think" conceptually, though "cognitive" development is seen.
2. *The period of preoperational thought (3–7 years).* This period is characterized by the development of language and rapid conceptual development.
3. *The period of concrete operations (8–11 years).* During these years the child develops the ability to apply logical thought to concrete problems.
4. *The period of formal operations (12–15 years).* During this period the child's cognitive structures reach their greatest level of development and the child becomes able to apply logic to all classes of problems.

Source: B. J. Wadsworth, *Piaget's Theory of Cognitive Development* (New York: David McKay, 1971).

set of stages of information processing or cognitive development. Piaget's approach is basically developmental. It suggests naturally occurring stages that change primarily with physiological maturation. Other researchers have suggested different stages, with learning rather than maturation as the underlying cause of observed differences.[63] However, the general pattern of less ability to deal with abstract, generalized, unfamiliar, and/or large amounts of information by younger children is common to all approaches.[64]

PERCEPTION AND MARKETING STRATEGY

Information is the primary raw material the marketer works with in influencing consumers. Therefore, a knowledge of the perception process is an essential guide to marketing strategy. In the following sections, we discuss seven areas where it is particularly useful:

1. Media strategy.
2. Retail strategy.
3. Advertising and package design.
4. Regulation of advertising and packaging.
5. Brand name selection.
6. Advertising evaluation.
7. Regulation of advertising aimed at children.

Media Strategy

The fact that the exposure process is selective rather than random is the underlying basis for effective media strategies.[65] If the process were random, a broad approach of trying to place messages randomly in the environment would make sense. Since exposure is not random, the proper approach is to determine to which media consumers in the target market are most frequently exposed and then place the advertising messages in those media. Donald Peterson, of Ford Motor Co., has expressed this idea clearly:

> We must look increasingly for matching media that will enable us best to reach carefully targeted, emerging markets. The rifle approach rather than the old shotgun.[66]

For some products and target markets, consumers are highly involved with the product category itself and will go to considerable trouble to secure product-relevant information. This occurs most frequently among heavy users of hobby and luxury items, such as skis and mountaineering equipment or for fashion items.

Table 8–2
Selective Exposure to Magazines Based on Demographic Characteristics

Demographic Characteristics	United States	*Play-boy*	*National Geo-graphic*	*Family Circle*	*Forbes*
Total adults	100%	100%	100%	100%	100%
Men	47	75	51	19	67
Women	53	25	49	81	33
Age:					
18–24 years	18	30	17	16	16
25–34 years	22	37	24	25	25
35–49 years	23	22	26	27	27
50–64 years	22	10	22	24	23
65+ years	15	1	10	9	9
Graduated college	15	21	28	17	51
Head of household income:					
$35,000+	11	15	19	14	36
$25,000–$35,000	15	21	22	20	22
$20,000–$25,000	14	16	15	16	12
$15,000–$20,000	15	18	14	15	13
<$15,000	45	30	31	34	17

Source: Adapted from "Average Issue Audience of Nineteen Selected Magazines," *Newsweek Marketing Report: MR 80-5, Newsweek.*

For other products and target markets, consumers have limited involvement with the product category. Products such as salt or detergents are examples. In a situation such as this, the marketer must find media that the target market is interested in and place the advertising message in those media. As we learned earlier, potential target markets as defined by age, ethnic group, social class, or stage in the family life cycle have differing media preferences. Table 8–2 illustrates selective exposure to several magazines based on demographic characteristics.

Many magazine advertisers go even further and insist that their ads appear opposite certain articles or columns. Television advertisers are concerned about where within the commercial break their ad appears and the interest level aroused by the program[67]

Retail Strategy

Most retail environments contain a vast array of information. Given the fact that consumers cannot process all of this information, retailers need to be concerned about information overload. That is, they do not want consumers to become frustrated or minimize their in-store information processing.

Retailers often use exposure very effectively. Store interiors are designed with frequently sought out items (canned goods, fresh fruits/vegetables, meats) separated so that the average consumer will travel through more of the store. This increases total exposure. High-margin items are often placed in high traffic areas to capitalize on increased exposure.

Shelf position and amount of shelf space influence which items and brands are allocated attention. Point-of-purchase displays also attract attention to sale and high-margin items. Stores are designed with highly visible shelves and overhead signs to make locating items (an information processing task) as easy as possible. Stores provide reference prices to increase consumers' ability to accurately interpret price information. Unit price information by brand may be displayed on a separate sign in ascending or descending order to facilitate price comparisons. Nutrition information provided in a similar manner enhances consumers' abilities to choose nutritious brands.[68]

The total mix of in-store information cues (brands, layout, point-of-purchase displays, etc.), external building characteristics, and advertising combine to form the meaning or store image assigned the store.

Advertisement and Package Design

Advertisements and packages must perform two critical tasks—capture attention and convey meaning. Unfortunately, the techniques appropriate for accomplishing one task are often counterproductive for the remaining task.

What should a manager do to attract attention to a package or advertisement? As with most aspects of the marketing process, it depends on the target market, the product, and the situation. If the target market is interested in the product category, or in the firm or brand, attention will not constitute much of a problem.[69] Once consumers are exposed to the message, they will most likely attend to it. Unfortunately, most of the time consumers are not actively interested in a particular product. Interest in a product tends to arise only when the need for the product arises. Since it is difficult to reach consumers at exactly this point, marketers have the difficult task of trying to communicate with them at times when their interest is low or nonexistent.

Assume that you are responsible for developing a campaign designed to increase the number of users for your firm's toilet bowl freshener. Research indicates that the group you wish to reach has very little interest in the product. What do you do? Two strategies seem reasonable. One is to *utilize stimulus characteristics* such as full-page ads, bright colors, animated cartoons, or surrealism to attract attention to the advertisement.[70] The second is to *tie the message to a topic the target market is interested in*. Celebrities are often used in advertisements in part for this reason, as is humor.[71] Sex, in the form of attractive models, is also frequently used.[72] For example, Black Velvet whiskey used "sexy" women in black velvet dresses in its advertising. Sales increased from 150,000 cases a year to almost 2 million, in part because "those slinky women have given it an extremely high brand awareness among men."[73]

Black Velvet illustrates how successful advertisements can be by using consumer interests unrelated to the product. However, using either stimulus characteristics or consumer interest unrelated to the product category to attract attention presents two dangers. The first danger is that the strategy will be so successful in attracting attention to the stimulus object that it will reduce the attention devoted to the sales message. The reader may observe an attractive member of the opposite sex in an advertisement and not attend to the sales message or copy. This occurred with ads for Lincoln-Mercury which featured Catherine Deneuve in a "revealing" gown, and for RCA Colortrack ads using Linda Day George.[74]

Exhibit 8–5 is an ad that makes use of stimulus factors and sex appeal. The photograph of the model is extremely high quality with brown skin, a dark blue background, a yellow bikini, and an off-white bottle. The suggestive headline is in bright white letters. The balance of the ad uses limited copy and ample white space. It will definitely attract attention. However, will those who read the ad notice the brand name? Will they associate any product benefits with Aloe Butter? Will the target market respond favorably to the implicit associations contained in the ad?

Attention-attracting features of the advertisement can also focus attention on specific parts of the ad.[75] Corporate advertising—advertising which talks about a company rather than the company's products—tends to generate a relatively high level of attention. Yet a study of more than 2,000 such advertisements has shown that about half of all people exposed to the ads do not notice the single most important bit of information in the ad—the company name. The same study found that the simplest way to avoid this problem is to place the name in the most prominent part of the ad—the headline. The following results for a Motorola corporate ad are typical:[76]

	No Name in Headline	Name in Headline
Magazine readership	4,600,000	4,500,000
Involved with ad	91% = 4,186,000	84% = 3,780,000
Involved and saw Motorola name	43% = 1,978,000	70% = 3,150,000

The second risk associated with using stimulus characteristics or unrelated consumer interests to attract attention is that the *interpretation* of the message will be negatively affected. For example, the use of humor to attract attention to a commercial for beer may result in the brand being viewed as appropriate only for very light-hearted, casual situations. The use of a second color (red) with large yellow-page ads, while a proven attention-attracting device, has been found to actually deter consumers from calling that advertiser.[77] Thus, caution must be used to ensure that attention-attracting devices do not have a negative impact on attention to, or interpretation of, the main message.

Exhibit 8–5 Use of Stimulus Items and Sexual Content to Attract Attention

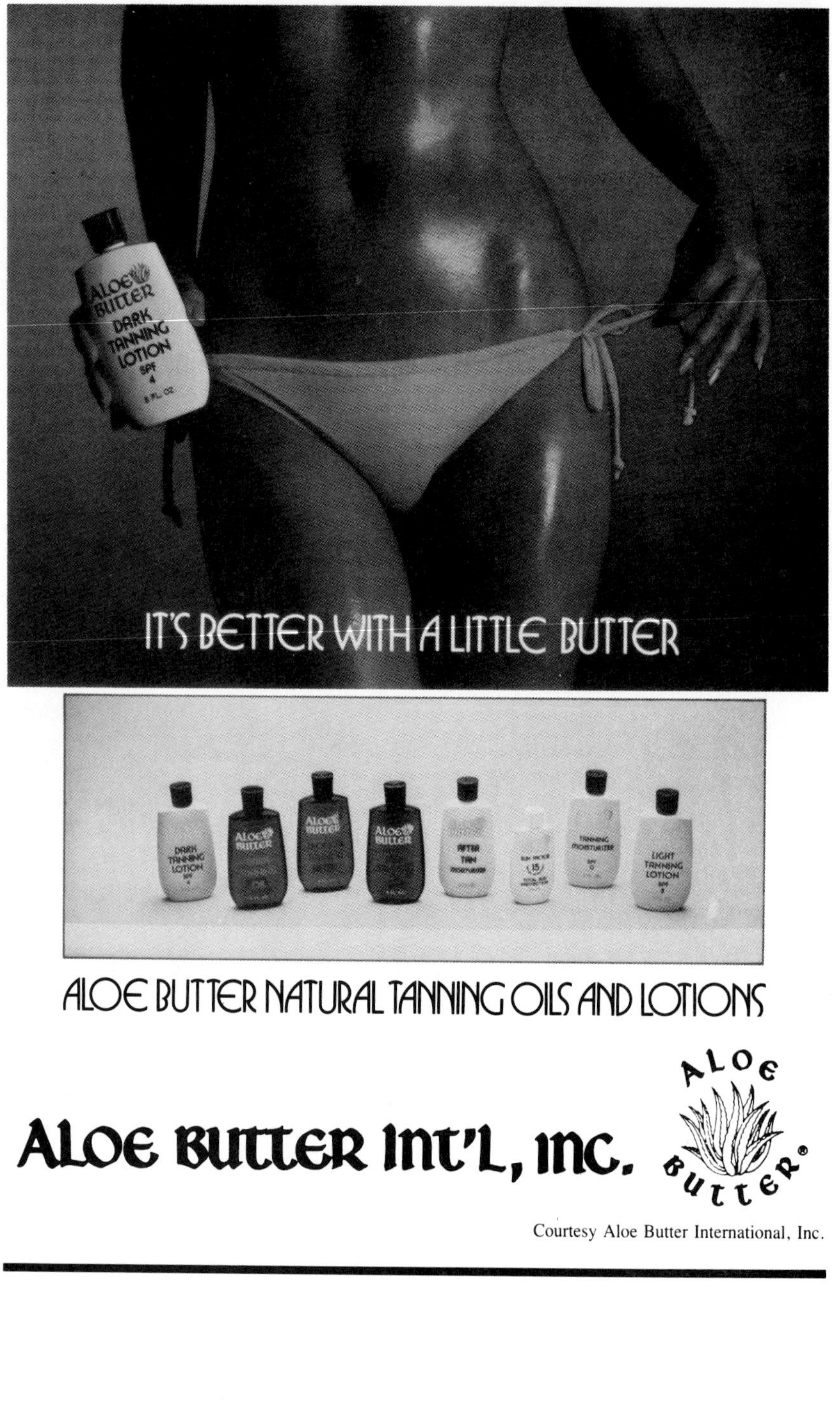

Courtesy Aloe Butter International, Inc.

Regulation of Marketing Messages

Suppose you saw a snorkel or swim fins with the National Association of Scuba Diving Schools' "Seal of Approval" on the package. What would this mean to you? Many of us would interpret it to mean that the product had been tested by the association or was manufactured to conform to a set of standards established by the association. However, the FTC charged that the seal was *sold* for use on diving products *without tests or standards*.[78]

Because of such problems, various regulatory agencies are deeply concerned with the interpretation of marketing messages.[79] The Bureau of Consumer Protection, a division of the FTC, has considered focusing on the total advertisement rather than just the verbal portions in assessing whether or not an ad is misleading. As an example, the bureau's deputy director cited an ad for Belair cigarettes which is "dominated by a full-page color photograph of a happy couple frolicking in the surf." The words used in the ad were not misleading. However, if the message (interpretation) of the entire ad is that smoking Belairs will make you "healthy" and "happy," it might be considered deceptive.[80]

In fact, the FTC has begun taking action based on the total impression conveyed by an advertisement or package. For example, General Mills was fined $90,000 for an advertisement which allegedly implied that a toy horse could stand upright by itself when in fact it required support. In addition, they were fined $10,000 for certain model kits which the FTC claimed were packaged in oversized containers or with pictures or written material that created a false idea of the toy's size.[81]

However, determining the exact meaning of a marketing message is not a simple process.[82] Exhibit 8–6 illustrates some of the areas where controversy over the interpretation of various marketing messages has existed.

Obtaining accurate assignments of meaning is made even more difficult by the variation in information processing skills among differing population groups.[83] For example, this warning was ruled inadequate in a product liability case:

> Always inflate tire in safety cage or use a portable lock ring guard. Use a clip-on type air chuck with remote valve so that operator can stand clear during tire inflation.

The court held that (1) "There is a duty to warn *foreseeable* users of all hidden dangers" and (2) "in view of the unskilled or semiskilled nature of the work and the existence of many in the work force who do not read English, warnings *in the form of symbols* might have been appropriate since the employee's ability to take care of himself was limited."[84] Thus, marketers must often go to considerable lengths to provide messages that the relevant audience will interpret correctly. Fortunately, we are developing considerable knowledge on effectively presenting such difficult messages as product risks, nutrition, and affirmative disclosures, as well as standard messages.[85] Nonetheless, thorough pretesting of messages to consumers is recommended.

Exhibit 8–6

Regulation and the Interpretation of Marketing Messages

- The 4th U.S. Circuit Court of Appeals ruled that meat from a turkey thigh can be called a "turkey ham" even if it contains no pork. A lower court had reached the opposite conclusion. The ruling appeared to rely heavily on a technical definition of the term *ham*.
- Maximum Strength Anacin's claim that it is "the maximum strength allowed" was ruled illegal because it "implies that an appropriate authority has authorized the sale of products like Maximum Strength Anacin." No such authorization exists.*
- An advertisement for the Holly Hobby oven with the statement "assembly required" was challenged by the Children's Advertising Review Unit of the Council of Better Business Bureaus. According to the children's unit, "research has shown that the average child does not understand 'assembly required.' " Instead, a simpler phrase such as "you have to put it together before you can play with it" is recommended. The manufacturer agreed.
- The Association of Petroleum Re-Refiners petitioned the FTC to reconsider its Trade Regulation Rule which requires all re-refined oil products to "clearly and conspicuously" label the origin of the product. This has meant that "made from used oil" appears on all labels. The association feels that this disparages the quality of such lubricants, and they want to use the phrase "recycled oil product" instead.†
- The National Advertising Division (NAD) of the Council of Better Business Bureaus stated that ads which contained statements like "savings up to *X* percent" should have at least 10 percent of the total sale items reduced by the maximum shown in the ad.
- The Florida Citrus Commission is challenging the right of Procter & Gamble's Citrus Hill Plus Calcium and Coca-Cola Foods' Minute Maid Calcium Fortified orange juices to use the label "100% juice" or "100% pure" or "juice." If *anything* is added to the natural product, the Florida commission requires that it be labeled a beverage or drink, not a juice. The FDA has a more liberal regulation.‡

*N. Giges, "Anacin Ad Claims Struck by Judge," *Advertising Age*, July 28, 1980, p. 3.

†"Can 'Recycled Oil' Replace 'Used Oil' on Labels?" *FTC News Summary*, August 22, 1980, p. 3.

‡J. Dagnoli and L. Freeman, "Citrus Group Slams 'Pure' Claims," *Advertising Age*, November 16, 1987, p. 12.

Brand Name Development

Shakespeare notwithstanding, marketers do not believe that "a rose by any other name would smell the same."[86] Would you rather have a soft drink sweetened with NutraSweet or with aspartame? Lincoln-Mercury recently named a new model the Merkur XR4T. The name is supposed to suggest the car's German

Exhibit 8–7 Sears' New Logo

Sears SEARS

Courtesy Sears Roebuck & Co.

The old Sears' logo had been used for 20 years. As Sears moved to modernize its image, the logo was examined to determine whether it conveyed the more contemporary image of Sears. The company spent a year testing the old logo and developing various new formats. The old logo was very well known but was limited in terms of the size, colors, and symbols that could be placed with it. The new typeface was designed to be versatile, bold, and progressive. The all-capital letters are to display strength and boldness. They were italicized "to suggest a sense of controlled forward motion." Since the logo must go on products ranging from dresses to tractors, it was given a line that can carry color which adds to its versatility.

Source: "Sears Writes Its Name Differently," *The Register-Guard*, July 1, 1984, p. 5E.

origins, but it is difficult to pronounce (Mare-Coor) and does not convey much of a visual image.

Brand names are important for both consumer and industrial products. An adhesive named *RC 601* was marketed for a number of years to equipment designers. Marketing research led to a redefinition of the target market to maintenance workers and reformulation of the product to make it easier to use. Equally important was a name change from the meaningless *RC 601* to the image-rich *Quick Metal*. Sales which were projected to be $320,000 under the old approach jumped to $2,200,000.[87]

Until recently, computers were generally "named" numbers—the IBM 360 or the HP 3000. However, when a new company entered the personal and small business market, it wanted a less intimidating name. Its choice—Apple. A large part of its success is associated with the name. And it is staying with this approach. Would you feel more comfortable with Apple's Macintosh or an IBM PC XT?

Companies such as NameLab use linguists and computers to create names that convey the appropriate meaning for products. For example, NameLab created "Compaq" for a portable computer that was originally to be called "Gateway." The focus of NameLab is the total meaning conveyed by the interaction of the meanings of the name's parts. For Compaq, *com* means computer and communications while *paq* means small. The unique spelling attracts attention and gives a "scientific" impression.[88] In general, concrete terms with relevant, established visual images such as Mustang, Apple, or Cup-a-Soup are easier to recognize and recall than are more abstract terms.[89]

The impact of the image conveyed by a name was vividly demonstrated in a recent study. Three groups of consumers evaluated the same sporting goods product. The *only* difference among the three groups was the name associated with the product. The perceptual differences caused by the name include:[90]

	Percent Attributing Feature to Product		
Feature	Name A	Name B	Name C
For all surfaces	11	26	17
Easy to see	8	34	19
For professionals	42	53	30
Large	38	53	18

Clearly, name selection influences how consumers interpret product features.

Name changes are at least as difficult as new name selection. When changing a name, the firm generally wants to maintain the loyalty and benefits attached to the old name, while updating the brand. The manner in which the name is presented also influences consumer perceptions of the firm. Exhibit 8–7 illustrates Sears' recent logo change.

Advertising Evaluation

A successful advertisement (or any other marketing message) must accomplish four tasks:

1. **Exposure:** It must physically reach the consumer.
2. **Attention:** It must be attended to by the consumer.
3. **Interpretation:** It must be properly interpreted.
4. **Memory:** It must be stored in memory in a manner that will allow retrieval under the proper circumstances.

Advertising research covers all of these tasks. However, most of the effort is focused on attention and, to a lesser extent, on memory.

Measures of exposure. Exposure to print media is most frequently measured in terms of circulation. Data on circulation are provided by a variety of commercial firms. The major difficulty with this data is that it frequently is not broken down in a manner consistent with the firm's target market. Thus, a firm may be targeting the lower-middle social class but circulation data may be broken down by income rather than social class. Further, circulation measures are generally based on households and do provide data on who within a household is exposed to the magazine or newspaper.

Measuring exposure to electronic media is even more difficult. As we saw earlier in the chapter, leaving a television on as "background" noise without "watching" it is common, as is "zapping" commercials. Diary reports, in which respondents record their daily listening patterns, and telephone interviews are the two methods used to determine radio listening.

Television viewing is measured primarily by *meters,* which are electronic devices that automatically determine if a television is turned on and, if so, to which channel. Unfortunately, traditional meters do not indicate who, if anyone, is watching a turned-on television set. A new meter, called a *people meter,* has been developed to take care of this problem. It allows each household member to "log on" when viewing, by punching an identifying button. The demographics of each potential viewer are stored in the central computer so viewer profiles can be developed. Although there is considerable controversy over this methodology, it is now the primary technique in use. Initial results appear to confirm earlier findings that television shows have far fewer viewers than suggested by the number of sets in use.[91]

Measures of attention. The attention-attracting powers of commercials or packages can be partially measured in a direct manner using the techniques described in Exhibit 8–8.[92] Of these techniques, eye tracking appears to offer the greatest potential. A recent application involved analyses of commercials for RCA Colortrack TV sets and Lincoln-Mercury cars. Both commercials used attractive celebrity presenters (Linda Day George and Catherine Deneuve) in "revealing" gowns. The eye-tracking test revealed that the audience focused on the celebrities and did not attend to the product.[93]

Indirect tests of attention (they also tap at least some aspects of memory) include theater tests, day-after recall, recognition tests, and Starch scores. *Theater tests* involve showing commercials along with television programs in a theater. Viewers complete questionnaires designed to measure which commercials (and what aspects of those commercials) attracted their attention. *Day-after recall* (DAR) is the most popular method of measuring the attention-getting power of television commercials. Individuals are interviewed the day after a commercial is aired on a program they watched. Recall of the commercial and recall of specific aspects of the commercial are interpreted as a reflection of the amount of attention.

Day-after recall measures of television commercials have been criticized as favoring rational, factual, "hard sell" type ads and high involvement products while discriminating against "feeling," emotional, "soft-sell" ads. However, for many product/target market combinations the latter approach may be superior.[94] In response, substantial work has been done to develop recognition measures for television commercials.[95] *Recognition tests* are tests in which the commercial of interest, or key parts of it, along with other commercials are shown to target-market members. Recognition of the commercial, or key parts of the commercial, is the measure. This technique appears to work better than standard recall measures.[96] It seems particularly appropriate for low-involvement products which are selected in a store situation.

Starch scores are the most popular technique for evaluating the attention-attracting power of print ads. The respondents are shown advertisements from magazine issues they have recently read. For each advertisement, they indicate

Exhibit 8–8 Direct Measures of Attention

I. **Eye Pupil Dilation.** Changes in the size of the pupil of the eye appear to be related to the amount of attention that a person is giving a message. A pupilometer can measure these changes accurately.

II. **Eye Tracking.** An eye camera can track movements of the eyes relative to the ad being read or watched. The paths of the eyes can then be mapped to determine: (1) what parts of the message were attended to, (2) what sequence was used in viewing the message, and (3) how much time was spent on each part.

III. **Tachistoscopic Test.** A tachistoscope is a slide-projector with adjustable projector speeds and levels of illumination. Thus, ads can be shown very rapidly and/or dimly. Ads are tested to determine at what speeds elements such as the product, brand, and headline are recognized. Speed of recognition of various elements in the ads and readership (attention) are highly correlated.

IV. **Theater Tests.** Theater tests involve showing commercials along with television shows in a theater. Some, such as the one maintained by ASI Market Research, have dials at each seat which viewers use to constantly indicate their interest (attention) in the show or commercial.

V. **Brain Wave Analysis.** There is some evidence that electroencephalographs can indicate the amount and type of attention given to an advertisement or package.

which parts (headlines, illustrations, copy blocks) they recall reading. Three main "scores" are computed:

1. ***Noted.*** The percent who recall seeing the ad in that issue.
2. ***Seen-associated.*** The percent who recall reading a part of the ad that clearly identifies the brand or advertiser.
3. ***Read most.*** The percent who recall reading 50 percent or more of the copy.

Starch scores allow an indirect measure of attention to the overall ad and to key components of the ad.[97] Unfortunately, the scores are generally based on the responses of a random sample of subscribers to the magazine, *not* a sample of target market members. As you might suspect from knowledge that attention is focused on topics of interest, this can cause a serious misinterpretation of the effectiveness of an ad.

Measures of interpretation. Marketers investigate *interpretation* primarily through the use of focus groups, theater tests, and day-after recall. *Focus groups* involve a group of 5 to 15 members of the target audience who have a relatively free-form discussion of the meaning conveyed by the advertisement. *Theater* and *day-after recall* tests measure interpretation, as well as memory, by asking respondents to recall the meaning as well as the content of the advertisement.

One of the problems of these techniques, particularly the last two, is their tendency to produce a restatement of the verbal content of the advertisement rather than subtle meanings conveyed by the total ad. However, it is clear that consumers utilize all of the advertisement, including nonverbal visual and auditory imagery, in forming an impression of the product. In low-involvement learning situations, affect (liking) may be the only thing learned, and this is not reflected in currently used recall measures.

The Regulation of Advertising Aimed at Children

Quebec's Consumer Protection Act prohibits commercial advertising to persons under 13 years of age. The United States Federal Trade Commission has considered proposals to eliminate all advertisements to young children and advertisements for sugared food products aimed at older children. The American advertising industry's primary self-regulatory body, the National Advertising Division of the Council of Better Business Bureaus, maintains a special unit to review advertising aimed at children—the Children's Advertising Review Unit (CARU). Some of the special rules relating to information processing which guide CARU's policing of children's advertising are shown in Exhibit 8–9. As was discussed in Chapter 7, CARU and others are interested in the impact that the *content* of children's advertising has, as well as the ability of children to process advertising messages. However, our concern in this chapter is limited to children's abilities to *comprehend* advertising messages. There are two components to this concern: (1) Can children discern the difference between program and commercial? and, (2) Can children understand specific aspects of commercials, such as comparisons?

Adults are well aware that commercials are not "entertainment" in the same sense that the program is, and that the purpose of a commercial is generally to sell a product. They are able to evaluate commercial messages in this light. However, children may not distinguish commercials from programs and may not assign a sales intent to the commercials (Exhibit 8–9, guideline 4). In fact, an FTC administrative law judge listed this question as a "disputed area": "To what extent can children between the ages of 2 and 11 distinguish between children's commercials and children's programs to the point that they comprehend the selling purpose of television advertising?"[98]

Most research indicates that younger children (under seven) have at least some difficulty in distinguishing commercials from programs (either not noticing the change or thinking of commercials as another program).[99] It also

Exhibit 8–9

Selected Rules Guiding the Children's Advertising Review Unit

1. Since younger children have a limited capability for evaluating the credibility of what they watch, they place a special responsibility on advertisers to protect them from their own susceptibilities.
2. It is recognized that advertising which compares the advertised product to another product may be difficult for children to understand and evaluate and may, therefore, be misunderstood. Therefore, advertisers are urged to present products on their merits without reference to competition.
3. All price representations should be clearly and concisely set forth in a manner so as not to exert undue pressure to purchase, and price minimizations such as "only" or "just" should not be used in any advertising directed to children.
4. Program personalities or characters, either live or animated, on children's programs should not be used to promote products, premiums, or services in or adjacent to any program(s) in which the personality or character appears. Similarly, when a product resembling the program personality or character is advertised within a program in which the person or character appears, care should be taken to clearly differentiate between the content of the advertisement and the content of the program.

Source: *An Eye on Children's Advertising Self-Regulation* (Children's Advertising Review Unit, National Advertising Division, Council of Better Business Bureaus, undated.)

appears that younger children are less able to determine the selling intent of commercials.[100] However, there is some evidence that young children are aware of the selling intent but cannot verbalize this intent.[101] Currently, the advertising industry strives to separate children's commercials from the programs by prohibiting overlapping characters and by using *separators* such as: "We will return after these messages." This problem is growing in intensity as children's products are increasingly the "stars" of animated children's television programs.[102]

The second aspect of comprehension involves specific words or types of commercials that children might misunderstand. For example, research indicates that disclaimers such as "Part of a nutritious breakfast," "Each sold separately," and "Batteries not included," are ineffective with preschool children.[103] Thus, CARU discourages comparison advertising and prohibits price minimizations such as "only" or "just" (Exhibit 8–9, guidelines 2 and 3). In addition, it suggests specific phrasing for certain situations, such as "you have to put it together" instead of "Assembly required." Exhibit 8–10 describes several cases in which CARU investigated advertisements aimed at younger consumers.

Exhibit 8–10 CARU and Advertising Aimed at Children

LJN TOYS. A television commercial for its Photon electronic target game showed the guns appearing to shoot red laser beams. The commercial included a visual disclaimer: "Red beam for illustration only." Because the commercial ran during children's programming, the CARU challenged the adequacy of the disclaimer.

MATTEL TOYS. A TV commercial showed Monstroid, a figure in its Masters of the Universe line, apparently grabbing other figures automatically. Copy said, "Now, a raging terror grabs hold of the universe. . . . When Monstroid gets wound up, it grabs. . . ." CARU challenged the ad on the basis that children would not understand that Monstroid's grip is manually operated.*

WALT DISNEY MUSIC CO. An ad stating that a record album plus a poster, read-along book, and stickers were offered "all for only $12.95" was challenged for using a price minimization such as "only." CARU also questioned "the sense of urgency" in the ad as possibly "overwhelming" younger viewers.†

*"VLI Is Challenged," *Advertising Age*, February 16, 1987, p. 12.

†"Ads Aimed at Kids Get Tough NAD Review," *Advertising Age*, June 17, 1985, p. 12.

SUMMARY

Information consists of facts, estimates, predictions, and generalized relationships that are used by consumers to recognize and solve problems. *Information processing* consists of those activities by which an individual acquires and assigns meaning to stimuli. *Perception* begins with *exposure:* this occurs when a stimulus comes within range of one of our primary sensory receptors. We are exposed to only a small fraction of the available stimuli and this is usually the result of "self-selection."

Attention occurs when the stimulus activates one or more of the sensory receptors and the resulting sensations go into the brain for processing. Because of the amount of stimuli we are exposed to, we selectively attend to those stimuli that physically attract us (stimulus factors) or personally interest us (individual factors). *Stimulus factors* are physical characteristics of the stimulus itself, such as contrast, size, intensity, color, and movement. *Individual factors* are characteristics of the individual, such as interests and needs.

Interpretation is the assignment of meaning to stimuli that have been attended to. Interpretation is a function of the individual as well as stimulus characteristics. Interpretation appears to involve a process whereby new stimuli are placed into existing categories of meaning.

In general, children under age 12 or so have less developed information processing abilities than older individuals. To protect children, a variety of formal and informal advertising guidelines have been developed.

Marketing managers use their knowledge of information processing in a variety of ways. The fact that media exposure is selective is the basis for *media strategy*. *Retailers* can enhance their operations by viewing their outlets as information environments. Both stimulus and personal interest factors are used to attract attention to *advertisements* and *packages*. Characteristics of the target market and the message are studied to ensure that accurate interpretation occurs. The meaning that consumers assign to words and parts of words is the basis for selecting *brand names*. Information processing theory guides a wide range of *advertising evaluation techniques*. Likewise, information processing theory is a basis for *regulating advertising*.

REVIEW QUESTIONS

1. What is *information?* What does it consist of?
2. Why is information important to the consumer?
3. Why is information important to the marketing manager?
4. What is *information processing?*
5. What is meant by *exposure?* What determines which stimuli an individual will be exposed to? How do marketers utilize this knowledge?
6. What is meant by *attention?* What determines which stimuli an individual will attend to? How do marketers utilize this?
7. What stimulus factors can be used to attract attention? What problems can arise when stimulus factors are used to attract attention?
8. What is *adaptation level theory?*
9. What is an *accelerated* or *compressed message?*
10. What is *information overload?* How should marketers deal with information overload?
11. What is meant by *nonfocused attention*?
12. What is meant by *hemispheric lateralization?*
13. What is meant by *subliminal perception?* Is it a real phenomenon? Is it effective?
14. What is meant by *interpretation?*
15. What determines how an individual will interpret a given stimulus?
16. What is meant by the term *Gestalt* as it relates to interpretation? Why is it important?
17. What is meant by *misinterpretation of a marketing message?* Is it common?
18. In what ways, if any, do children process information differently than adults?
19. Describe Piaget's stages of cognitive development.

20. How does a knowledge of information processing assist the manager in:
    a. Formulating media strategy?
    b. Formulating retail strategy?
    c. Designing advertisements and packages?
    d. Developing brand names?
    e. Evaluating advertising?
    f. Regulating advertising?
21. What is the underlying basis of media strategy?
22. Explain the differences between an eye camera, a tachistoscope, and a pupilometer.
23. What is a *Starch score?*
24. What is a *focus group?*
25. What is meant by *day-after recall?*
26. What is meant by *recognition tests*?
27. What is a *people meter?*
28. How is exposure measured? What problems are encountered in this process?
29. What are the main issues in regulating advertising to children?

DISCUSSION QUESTIONS

1. How could a marketing manager for (*a*) salt, (*b*) bicycles, (*c*) a politician, (*d*) children's toothpaste, or (*e*) skis use the material in this chapter on perception to guide the development of a national advertising campaign? To assist local retailers in developing their promotional activities? Would the usefulness of this material be limited to advertising decisions? Explain your answer.
2. Anheuser-Busch test-marketed a new soft drink for adults called Chelsea.[104] The product was advertised as a "not-so-soft drink" that Anheuser-Busch hoped would become socially acceptable for adults. The advertisements featured no one under 25 years of age, and the product contained one half of 1 percent alcohol (not enough to classify the product as an alcoholic beverage).

   The reaction in the test market was not what the firm expected or hoped for. The Virginia Nurses Association decided to boycott Chelsea, claiming that it "is packaged like a beer and looks, pours, and foams like beer, and the children are pretending the soft drink is beer." The Nurses Association claimed the product was an attempt to encourage children to become beer drinkers later on. Secretary of Health, Education and Welfare, Joseph Califano, urged the firm to "rethink their marketing strategy." Others made similar protests. Although Anheuser-Busch reformulated the product and altered the marketing mix substantially, the product could not regain momentum and was withdrawn.

   Assuming Anheuser-Busch was in fact attempting to position Chelsea as an adult soft drink (which it appears was their objective), why do you think it failed?

3. A television advertisement for General Mills's Total cereal made the following claim: "It would take 16 ounces of the leading natural cereal to equal the vitamins in 1 ounce of fortified Total." The Center for Science in the Public Interest filed a petition against General Mills claiming that the advertisement is deceptive. It was the center's position that the claim overstated Total's nutritional benefits because the cereal is not 16 times higher in other factors important to nutrition.[105]
   a. Is the claim misleading? Justify your answer.
   b. How should the FTC proceed in cases such as this?
   c. What are the implications of cases such as this for marketing management?
4. In recent years, manufacturers of meat products have introduced a product labeled as "turkey ham." The product looks like ham and tastes like ham but it contains no pork; it is all turkey. A nationwide survey of consumers showed that most believed that the meat product contained both turkey and ham. The USDA approved this label based on a dictionary definition for the technical term ham: the thigh cut of meat from the hind leg of any animal. Using Figure 8–1, discuss how consumers processed information concerning this product and used this information in purchasing this product. (One court ruled the label to be misleading but was overruled by a higher court.)
5. Develop a brand name for (*a*) an expensive domestic automobile, (*b*) a nonalcoholic wine, (*c*) a diet dessert, or (*d*) a chain of retail pet stores located near college campuses. Justify your selection.
6. Is the ad in Exhibit 8–5 successful? Why or why not?
7. Will Sears' logo change be successful? Explain.
8. To what extent, if any, and how should the government regulate advertising seen by children?
9. How would a television commercial designed to ________ change for the following age-groups: (1) 3–7, (2) 8–11, (3) 12–15, (4) 15–18? Why?
   a. Encourage sound nutrition.
   b. Sell Super Pop (a soft drink).
10. What is the best way to evaluate an advertising campaign?
11. Why might Starch scores based on a random sample of *Seventeen* magazine subscribers/readers mislead advertisers evaluating an ad for contact lens solution (assume the firm's target market is young females)?
12. What problems do you see with the new people meters?

PROJECT QUESTIONS

1. Find examples of marketing promotions that specifically use stimulus factors to create attention. Look for examples of each of the various factors discussed

earlier in the chapter, and try to find their use in a variety of promotions (e.g., point-of-purchase, billboards, print advertisements). For each example, evaluate the effectiveness of the stimulus factors used.

2. Repeat question 2 above, but this time look for promotions using individual factors.
3. Read *Symbolic Seduction* by Wilson Bryan Key. Is the author really describing subliminal perception? Do you feel he makes a valid point?
4. Read J. E. Russo, B. L. Metcalf, and D. Stephens, "Identifying Misleading Advertising," *Journal of Consumer Research,* September 1981, pp. 119–31. Create various types of misleading and corrective ads and test them using the procedure they recommend.
5. Complete Discussion Question 5 and test your name on a sample of students. Justify your testing procedure.
6. Watch 10 TV commercials aimed at children under 9, and 10 aimed at adults. Analyze the differences, if any, between the commercials from an information processing perspective.
7. Develop a short questionnaire to measure children's depth of awareness and understanding of television commercials shown on Saturday mornings. Interview four children, two in the 5-to-7 age-group, and two in the 8-to-10 category. Discuss the results in terms of differences between the two groups in number of commercials recalled, specific information recalled, and ability to differentiate between commercials and programs.
8. Visit a children's toy store and examine various types of toys that seem to be marketed to specific age-groups. Do you find any correspondence between these age-groups and those postulated by Piaget? How do marketers of toys such as these appeal to their consumers?
9. Find two ads that you think are potentially misleading and two that you think are likely to be misinterpreted (but are not misleading). Justify your selections.
10. Keep a diary of your TV viewing and radio listening for two weeks. How accurate do you feel the results are?
11. Interview 10 students about their behavior during television and radio commercial breaks. What do you conclude?
12. Answer question 11, but use a focus group.

REFERENCES

[1] "Farm Ads Win Golden Fleece," *The Stars and Stripes,* July 10, 1984, p. 6.

[2] See R. J. Harris, *Information Processing in Advertising* (Lawrence Erlbaum Associates, 1983).

[3] See B. M. Kaplan, "Zapping"; C. Heeter and B. S. Greenberg, "Profiling the Zappers"; and D. A. Yorke and P. J. Kitchen, "Channel Flickers and Video Speeders." All in *Journal of Advertising Research,* April/May 1985, pp. 9–12; 15–19; and 21–25.

[4] R. A. Bauer and S. A. Greyser, *Advertising in America: The Consumer View* (Cambridge, Mass.: Harvard University Press, 1968); and D. W. Hendon, "How Mechanical Factors Affect Ad Perception," *Journal of Advertising Research,* August 1973, p. 43.

[5] "Tobacco Industry Spent More Than $1 Billion in 1979 to Promote Cigarette Sales," *FC News Summary,* September 11, 1981, p. 1.

[6] "Eyes on Television, 1980," *Newsweek* (1980). See also L. Bogart and C. Lehman, "The Case of the 30-Second Commercial," *Journal of Advertising Research,* March 1983, pp. 11–19.

[7] For overviews, see M. B. Holbrook and D. R. Lehmann, "Form versus Content in Predicting Starch Scores," *Journal of Advertising Research,* August 1980, pp. 53–59; J. R. Rossiter, "Predicting Starch Scores," *Journal of Advertising Research,* October 1981, pp. 63–68; and L. C. Soley and L. N. Reid, "Predicting Industrial Ad Readership," *Industrial Marketing Management,* July 1983, pp. 201–6.

[8] See P. S. Schindler, "Color and Contrast in Magazine Advertising," *Psychology & Marketing,* Summer 1986, pp. 69–78.

[9] H. R. Bernstein, "Taco Pizza Joins Pizza Inn Line," *Advertising Age,* April 1979, p. 3.

[10] R. F. Beltramini and V. J. Blasko, "An Analysis of Award-Winning Headlines," *Journal of Advertising Research,* April/May 1986, pp. 48–51.

[11] Bogart and Lehman "The Case of the 30-Second Commercial."

[12] See J. R. Rossiter, "Visual Imagery," in *Advances in Consumer Research,* vol. 9, ed. A. Mitchell, (Chicago: Association for Consumer Research, 1982), pp. 101–6; and Soley and Reid, "Predicting Industrial."

[13] L. C. Soley, "Copy Length and Industrial Advertising Readership," *Industrial Marketing Management,* 1986, pp. 245–51.

[14] P. H. Chook, "A Continuing Study of Magazine Environment, Frequency, and Advertising Performance," *Journal of Advertising Research,* August/September 1985, pp. 23–33.

[15] R. Sparkman, Jr., and L. M. Austin, "The Effect on Sales of Color in Newspaper Advertisement," *Journal of Advertising,* Fourth Quarter 1980, p. 42.

[16] "How to Turn P-O-P into Sales Dollars," *Progressive Grocer,* June 1977, pp. 83–100.

[17] "Dior Sees the Whites of Its Ads," *Advertising Age,* October 5, 1981, p. 65.

[18] J. MacLachlan and P. LaBarbera, "Time-Compressed TV Commercials," *Journal of Advertising Research,* August 1978, pp. 11–15.

[19] P. A. LaBarbera, "Time-Compressed Tapes Increase Learning Efficiency of Students," *Marketing News,* July 25, 1980, p. 7.

[20] See J. MacLachlan and M. H. Siegel, "Reducing the Cost of TV Commercials by Use of Time Compressions," *Journal of Marketing Research,* February 1980, pp. 52–57; J. MacLachan, "Listener Perception of Time-Compressed Spokespersons," *Journal of Advertising Research,* April/May 1982, pp. 47–51; C. B. Riter et al., "Time Compression: New Evidence," *Journal of Advertising Research,* January 1983, pp. 39–43; M. J. R. Schlinger et al., "Effects of Time Compression on Attitudes and Information Processing," *Journal of Marketing,* Winter 1983, pp. 79–85; G. S. Nickell and J. N. Pinto, "The Effects of Compressed Speech on Listener Attitudes," *Psychology & Marketing,* Spring 1984, pp. 49–58; D. L. Moore, D. Hausknecht, and K. Thamodaran, "Time Compression, Response Opportunity, and Persuasion," *Journal*

of Consumer Research, June 1986, pp. 85–99; and J. W. Vann, R. D. Rogers, and J. P. Penrod, "The Cognitive Effects of Time-Compressed Advertising," *Journal of Advertising*, no. 2, 1987, pp. 10–19.

[21] W. A. Henry, "The Effect of Information-Processing Ability on Processing Accuracy," *Journal of Consumer Research*, June 1980, pp. 42–48; and D. Roedder John and C. A. Cole, "Age Differences in Information Processing," *Journal of Consumer Research*, December 1986, pp. 297–315.

[22] See J. Jacoby, "Perspectives on Information Overload," and N. K. Malhotra, "Reflections on the Information Overload Paradigm in Consumer Decision Making," both in *Journal of Consumer Research*, March 1984, pp. 432–35 and 436–40; and N. K. Malhotra, "Information and Sensory Overload," *Psychology & Marketing*, Fall/Winter 1984, pp. 9–21.

[23] S. Calcich and E. Blair, "The Perceptual Task in Acquisition of Package Information," in *Advances in Consumer Research*, vol. 10, ed. R. P. Bagozzi and A. M. Tybout (Chicago: Association for Consumer Research, 1983), pp. 221–25.

[24] H. M. Cannon, "A New Method for Estimating the Effect of Media Context," *Journal of Advertising Research*, November 1982, pp. 41–48. See also, H. E. Krugman, "Television Program Interest and Commercial Interruption," *Journal of Advertising Research*, March 1983, pp. 21–23. For conflicting results see Chook, "A Continuing Study."

[25] G. R. Funkhouser, "Consumers' Sensitivity to the Wording of Affirmative Disclosure Messages," *Journal of Public Policy and Marketing*, vol. 3, 1984, pp. 26–37.

[26] F. Hansen, "Hemispheral Lateralization: Implications for Understanding Consumer Behavior," *Journal of Consumer Research*, June 1981, pp. 23–36.

[27] H. E. Krugman, "Sustained Viewing of Television," *Journal of Advertising Research*, June 1980, p. 65; and H. E. Krugman, "Low Recall and High Recognition of Advertising," *Journal of Advertising Research*, February/March 1986, pp. 79–86.

[28] See ibid.; S. Weinstein, V. Appel, and C. Weinstein, "Brain-Activity Responses to Magazine and Television Advertising," *Journal of Advertising Research*, June 1980, pp. 57–63; J. R. Rossiter, "Brain Hemisphere Activity," *Journal of Advertising Research*, October 1980, pp. 75–76; and S. Weinstein, C. Weinstein, and R. Drozdenko, "Brain Wave Analysis," *Psychology & Marketing*, Spring 1984, pp. 18–42.

[29] W. A. Katz, "A Critique of Split-Brain Theory," *Journal of Advertising Research*, May 1983, pp. 63–66; D. W. Stewart, "Physiological Measurement of Advertising Effects," *Psychology and Marketing*, Spring 1984, pp. 43–47; J. S. Nevid, "Methodological Considerations in the Use of Electroencephalographic Techniques," *Psychology & Marketing*, Summer 1984, pp. 5–19; and M. L. Rothschild, "Hemispheric Lateralization," in *Advances in Consumer Research XIV*, ed. M. Wallendorf and P. Anderson (Provo, Utah: Association for Consumer Research, 1987), pp. 54–56.

[30] W. B. Key, *Subliminal Seduction* (Signet Books, 1974); and W. B. Key, *Media Sexploitation* (Signet Books, 1977).

[31] C. A. Fowler et al., "Lexical Access with and without Awareness," *Journal of Experimental Psychology*, Third Quarter 1981, pp. 341–62.

[32] J. S. Kelly, "Subliminal Embeds in Print Advertising," *Journal of Advertising*, Summer 1979, pp. 20–24; and M. Gable, H. T. Wilkens, L. Harris, and R. Feinberg, "An Evaluation of Subliminally Embedded Sexual Stimuli," *Journal of Advertising*,

no. 1, 1987, pp. 26–31. Conflicting results are in W. E. Kilbourne, S. Painton, and D. Ridley, "The Effect of Sexual Embedding," *Journal of Advertising*, no. 2, 1985, pp. 48–56.

[33] H. Shervin and S. Dickman, "The Psychological Unconscious," *American Psychologist*, May 1980, pp. 421–34; T. E. Moore, "Subliminal Advertising: What You See Is What You Get," *Journal of Marketing*, Spring 1982, pp. 38–47; and R. Cuperfain and T. K. Clarke, "A New Perspective on Subliminal Perception," *Journal of Advertising*, no. 1, 1985, pp. 36–41.

[34] E. J. Zanot, J. D. Pincus, and E. J. Lamp, "Public Perceptions of Subliminal Advertising," *Journal of Advertising*, First Quarter 1983, pp. 39–45; and M. P. Block and B. G. Vanden Bergh, "Can You Sell Subliminal Messages to Consumers?" *Journal of Advertising*, no. 3, 1985, pp. 59–62.

[35] J. Saegert, "Why Marketing Should Quit Giving Subliminal Advertising the Benefit of the Doubt," *Psychology & Marketing*, Summer 1987, pp. 107–20.

[36] See J. B. Cohen and K. Basu, "Alternative Models of Categorization," *Journal of Consumer Research*, March 1987, pp. 455–72.

[37] See T. K. Srull, "The Role of Prior Knowledge in the Acquisition, Retention, and Use of New Information," and J. W. Alba, "The Effects of Product Knowledge on the Comprehension, Retention, and Evaluation of Product Information," both in *Advances*, ed. Bagozzi and Tybout, pp. 572–76, 577–80; and E. J. Johnson and J. E. Russo, "Product Familiarity and Learning New Information," *Journal of Consumer Research*, June 1984, pp. 542–50.

[38] R. Belk, R. Mayer, and K. Bahn, "The Eye of the Beholder," in *Advances*, ed. Mitchell, pp. 523–30. See also P. L. Alreck, R. B. Settle, and M. A. Belch, "Who Responds to 'Gendered' Ads, and How?" *Journal of Advertising Research*, May 1982, pp. 25–32; and N. Capon and R. Davis, "Basic Cognitive Ability Measures as Predictors of Consumer Information Processing Strategies," *Journal of Consumer Research*, June 1984, pp. 551–63.

[39] G. Tom et al., "Cueing the Consumer," *Journal of Consumer Marketing*, Spring 1987, pp. 23–27.

[40] J. Sculley, *Odyssey* (New York: Harper & Row, 1987).

[41] J. G. Helgeson and S. E. Beatty, "Price Expectation and Price Recall Error," *Journal of Consumer Research*, December 1987, p. 379.

[42] A. Horowitz and R. S. Kaye, "Perception and Advertising," *Journal of Advertising*, June 1975, pp. 15–21; and G. H. Bower, "Mood and Memory," *American Psychologist*, February 1981, pp. 129–48.

[43] R. P. Hill, "The Impact of Interpersonal Anxiety on Consumer Information Processing," *Psychology & Marketing*, Summer 1987, pp. 93–105.

[44] S. N. Singh and G. A. Churchill, Jr., "Arousal and Advertising Effectiveness," *Journal of Advertising*, no. 1, 1987, pp. 4–10.

[45] M. Brucks, A. A. Mitchell, and R. Staelin, "The Effect of Nutritional Informational Disclosure in Advertising," *Journal of Public Policy & Marketing*, vol. 3, 1984, pp. 1–25.

[46] See J. R. Rossiter and L. Percy, "Visual Communications in Advertising," in *Information Processing*, ed. Harris, pp. 83–126; M. B. Holbrook, "Some Further Dimensions of Psycholinguistics, Imagery and Consumer Response," and L. Percy, "Psycholinguistic Guidelines for Advertising Copy," both in *Advances*, ed. Mitchell, pp. 112–17, 107–11; M. B. Holbrook, "Product Imagery and the Illusion of Reality,"

in *Advances,* ed. Bogozzi and Tybout, pp. 65–71; and J. A. Edell and R. Staelin, "The Information Processing of Pictures in Print Advertisements," *Journal of Consumer Research,* June 1983, pp. 45–61.

[47] D. G. Mick, "Consumer Research and Semiotics," *Journal of Consumer Research,* September 1986, pp. 196–213; and R. D. Zakia and M. Nadin, "Semiotics, Advertising and Marketing," *Journal of Consumer Marketing,* Spring 1987, pp. 5–12. See also G. McCracken, "Culture and Consumption," *Journal of Consumer Research,* June 1986, pp. 71–84.

[48] "GF, Coke Tell Why They Shun TV News," *Advertising Age,* January 28, 1980, p. 39.

[49] R. M. Sparkman, Jr., "The Discounting Principle in the Perception of Advertising," in *Advances 9,* ed. Mitchell, pp. 277–80; and R. W. Cook and W. B. Joseph, "Effect of Sponsor Advocacy on Message Perception and Attitude Change," *Journal of the Academy of Marketing Science,* Spring 1982, pp. 140–53.

[50] Cannon, "A New Method," and Krugman, "Television Program."

[51] R. G. Wyckam, "Implied Superiority Claims," *Journal of Advertising Research,* February/March 1987, pp. 54–63.

[52] A. A. Mitchell and J. C. Olson, "Are Product Attribute Beliefs the Only Mediator of Advertising Effects on Brand Attitude?" *Journal of Marketing Research,* August 1981, pp. 318–32; A. A. Mitchell, "Cognitive Processes Initiated by Exposure to Advertising," in *Information Processing,* ed. Harris, pp. 13–42; and A. J. Bush and R. P. Bush, "Should Advertisers Use Numbers-Based Copy?" *Journal of Consumer Marketing,* Summer 1986, pp. 71–79.

[53] D. W. Finn, "Inferential Belief Formation through the Use of Non-Information: An Example," in *Advances in Consumer Research VIII,* ed. Monroe (Chicago: Association for Consumer Research, 1981), pp. 344–48.

[54] L. A. Fanelli, "Bic's Comparative Spots Get a Trimming by NAD," *Advertising Age,* August 20, 1979, p. 6.

[55] J. Jacoby and W. D. Hoyer, "Viewer Miscomprehension of Televised Communications," *Journal of Marketing,* Fall 1982, pp. 12–31.

[56] G. T. Ford and R. Yalch, "Viewer Miscomprehension of Televised Communication—A Comment," R. W. Mizerski, "Viewer Miscomprehension Findings Are Measurement Bound," and J. Jacoby and W. D. Hoyer, "On Comprehending Televised Communication: A Rejoinder," all in *Journal of Marketing,* Fall 1982, pp. 32–43; D. C. Schmittlein and D. G. Morrison, "Measuring Miscomprehension for Televised Communications Using True-False Questions," *Journal of Consumer Research,* September 1983, pp. 147–56; and F. R. Gates, "Further Comments on the Miscomprehension of Televised Advertisements," *Journal of Advertising,* no. 1, 1986, pp. 4–9.

[57] *The Comprehension and Miscomprehension of Print Communications* (New York: The Advertising Educational Foundation, Inc., 1987).

[58] Funkhouser, "Consumers' Sensitivity."

[59] M. D. Alpert, L. L. Golden, and W. D. Hoyer, "The Impact of Repetition on Advertisement Miscomprehension and Effectiveness," in *Advances,* ed. Bagozzi and Tybout, pp. 130–35.

[60] M. C. Macklin, N. T. Bruvold, and C. L. Shea, "Is It Always As Simple As 'Keep It Simple!'?" *Journal of Advertising,* no. 4, 1985, pp. 28–35.

[61] W. D. Hoyer, R. K. Srivastava, and J. Jacoby, "Sources of Miscomprehension in Television Advertising," *Journal of Advertising,* Second Quarter 1984, pp. 17–26; and *Comprehension and Miscomprehension,* pp. 10–11.

[62] See K. D. Bahn, "How and When Do Brand Perceptions First Form?" *Journal of Consumer Research,* December 1986, pp. 382–93; Roedder John and Cole, "Age Differences"; J. Bryant and D. R. Anderson, *Children's Understanding of Television* (New York: Academic Press, 1986); D. L. Roedder, "Age Differences in Children's Responses to Television Advertising: An Information-Processing Approach," *Journal of Consumer Research,* September 1981, pp. 144–53; and R. P. Adler et al., *The Effects of Television Advertising on Children* (Lexington, Mass.: Lexington Books, 1980).

[63] C. L. Costley and M. Brucks, "Product Knowledge As an Explanation for Age-Related Differences," in *Advances XIV,* ed. Wallendorf and Anderson; and in D. Roedder John and J. C. Whitney, Jr., "The Development of Consumer Knowledge in Children," *Journal of Consumer Research,* March 1986, pp. 406–17.

[64] G. F. Soldow, "The Processing of Information in the Young Consumer," *Journal of Advertising,* Third Quarter 1983, pp. 4–14; M. C. Macklin, "Do Children Understand TV Ads?" *Journal of Advertising Research,* March 1983, pp. 63–70; M. C. Macklin, "Verbal Labeling Effects in Short-Term Memory for Character/Product Pairings," in *Advances in Consumer Research II,* ed. T. Kinnear (Chicago: Association for Consumer Research, 1984), pp. 343–47; G. F. Soldow, "The Ability of Children to Understand the Product Package," *Journal of Public Policy and Marketing,* vol. 4, 1985, pp. 55–68; and M. A. Fischer, "A Developmental Study of Preference for Advertised Toys," *Psychology & Marketing,* Spring 1985, pp. 3–12.

[65] See W. O. Bearden et al., "Attentive Audience Delivery of TV Advertising Schedules," *Journal of Marketing Research,* May 1981, pp. 187–91.

[66] "Ford Boss Outlines Shift to 'Rifle' Media," *Advertising Age,* October 26, 1981, p. 89.

[67] S. Emmrich, "Magazines Pressed on Positioning of Ads," *Advertising Age,* September 28, 1981, p. 3; H. E. Krugman, "Television Program Interest and Commercial Interruption," *Journal of Advertising Research,* February/March 1983, pp. 21–23; C. J. Cobb, "Television Clutter and Advertising Effectiveness," in *1985 AMA Educators' Proceedings,* ed. R. F. Lusch et al. (Chicago: American Marketing Association, 1985), pp. 41–47; and S. N. Singh and G. A. Churchill, Jr., "Arousal and Advertising Effectiveness," *Journal of Advertising,* no. 1, 1987, pp. 4–10.

[68] T. E. Muller, "Structural Information Factors Which Stimulate the Use of Nutrition Information," *Journal of Marketing Research,* May 1985, pp. 143–57.

[69] M. A. Sewall and D. Sarel, "Characteristics of Radio Commercials and Their Recall Effectiveness," *Journal of Marketing,* January 1986, pp. 52–60.

[70] P. M. Homer and L. R. Kahle, "A Social Adaptation Explanation of the Effects of Surrealism on Advertising," *Journal of Advertising,* no. 2, 1986, pp. 50–54.

[71] T. J. Madden and M. G. Weinberger, "The Effects of Humor on Attention in Magazine Advertising," *Journal of Advertising,* Third Quarter 1982, pp. 8–14.

[72] D. Richmond and T. P. Hartman, "Sex Appeal in Advertising," *Journal of Advertising Research,* November 1982, pp. 53–61; L. N. Reid and L. C. Soley, "Decorative Models and the Readership of Magazine Ads," *Journal of Advertising Research,* May 1983, pp. 27–32; D. C. Bello, R. E. Pitts, and M. J. Etzel, "The Communication Effects of Controversial Sexual Content in Television Programs and

Commercials," *Journal of Advertising,* Third Quarter 1983, pp. 32–42; R. E. Reidenbach and K. W. McCleary, "Advertising and Male Nudity," *Journal of the Academy of Marketing Science,* Fall 1983, pp. 444–54; M. J. Caballero and P. J. Solomon, "Effects of Model Attractiveness on Sales Response," *Journal of Advertising,* First Quarter 1984, pp. 17–24; and M. J. Caballero and W. M. Pride, "Selected Effects of Salesperson Sex and Attractiveness in Direct Mail Advertisements," *Journal of Marketing,* Winter 1984, pp. 94–100.

[73] C. Goldschmidt, "Many Marketing Success Stories Are Due to Mutual Respect between Ad Agencies, Clients," *Marketing News,* February 19, 1982, p. 8.

[74] B. Whalen, "Eye Tracking Technology to Replace Day-After Recall by '84," *Marketing News,* November 27, 1981, p. 18.

[75] S. B. MacKenzie, "The Role of Attention in Mediating the Effect of Advertising on Attribute Importance," *Journal of Consumer Research,* September 1986, pp. 174–95.

[76] J. Treistman, "Will Your Audience See Your Name?" *Business Marketing,* August 1984, pp. 88–94.

[77] D. R. Berdie and E. M. Hauff, "Surprises Are Found in Consumer Reactions to Ads in Yellow Pages," *Marketing News,* September 11, 1987, p. 8.

[78] "Diving Association May Not Use 'Seal of Approval' Unless Based on Tests," *FTC New Summary,* May 21, 1982, p. 1.

[79] G. T. Ford and J. E. Calfee, "Recent Developments in FTC Policy on Deception," *Journal of Marketing,* July 1986, pp. 82–103.

[80] S. Crock, "FTC Is Seeking Way to Decide if Pictures in Advertising Convey False Impressions," *The Wall Street Journal,* August 11, 1978, p. 4.

[81] "Biggest FTC Ad Fine Hits General Mills," *Advertising Age,* May 28, 1979, p. 2.

[82] K. G. Grunet and K. Dedler, "Misleading Advertising," *Journal of Public Policy and Marketing,* vol. 4, 1985, pp. 153–65.

[83] G. J. Gaeth and T. B. Heath, "The Cognitive Processing of Misleading Advertising," *Journal of Consumer Research,* June 1987, pp. 43–54.

[84] B. Reid, "Adequacy of Symbolic Warnings," *Marketing News,* October 25, 1985, p. 3.

[85] Funkhouser, "Consumers' Sensitivity"; M. Brocks, A. A. Mitchell, and R. Staelin, "The Effect of Nutritional Information Disclosure in Advertising," *Journal of Public Policy and Marketing,* vol. 3, 1984, pp. 1–25; J. R. Bettman, J. W. Payne, and R. Staelin, "Cognitive Considerations in Designing Effective Labels for Presenting Risk Information"; and M. Venkatesan, W. Lancaster, and K. W. Kendall, "An Empirical Study of Alternate Formats for Nutritional Information Disclosure," both in *Journal of Public Policy & Marketing,* vol. 5, 1986, pp. 1–28, and pp. 29–43.

[86] See B. Rigaux-Bricmont, "Influences of Brand Name and Packaging on Perceived Quality," in *Advances,* ed. Mitchell, pp. 472–77; and G. M. Zinkhan and C. R. Martin, Jr., "New Brand Names and Inferential Beliefs," *Journal of Business Research,* 15, 1987, pp. 157–72.

[87] B. Abrams, "Consumer-Product Techniques Help Lactile Sell to Industry," *The Wall Street Journal,* April 2, 1981, p. 29.

[88] R. A. Mamis, "Name-Calling," *Inc,* July 1984, pp. 28–33. See also J. M. McNealand and L. M. Zeren, "Brand Name Selection for Consumer Products," *MSU Business Topics,* Spring 1981, pp. 35–39; G. M. Zinklam and C. R. Martin, Jr., "The

Attitudinal Implications of a New Brand's Name," in *Advances,* ed. Mitchell, pp. 467–71; and T. A. Swartz, "Brand Symbols and Message Differentiation," *Journal of Advertising Research,* November 1983, pp. 59–64.

[89] K. R. Robertson, "Recall and Recognition Effects of Brand Name Imagery," *Psychology & Marketing,* Spring 1987, pp. 3–15.

[90] J. N. Axelrod and H. Wybenga, "Perceptions That Motivate Purchase," *Journal of Advertising Research,* June/July 1985, pp. 19–21.

[91] V. Gay, "Nielsen's Meter Tally Rocks Nets," *Advertising Age,* December 1, 1986, p. 1; "People Meters To Be Sole Tool," *Marketing News,* January 30, 1987, p. 1; V. Gay, "Make-Goods Stagger Networks," *Advertising Age,* December 21, 1987, pp. 1, 34; and V. Gay, "Nielsen Strikes Back at CBS," *Advertising Age,* January 25, 1988, pp. 3, 76.

[92] J. T. Cacioppo and R. E. Petty, "Physiological Responses and Advertising Effects," *Psychology & Marketing,* Summer 1985, pp. 115–26.

[94] Whalen, "Eye Tracking."

[94] Krugman, "Low Recall."

[95] H. A. Zielske, "Does Day-After Recall Penalize 'Feeding' Ads?" *Journal of Advertising Research,* no. 1, 1982, pp. 19–22; J. H. Leigh and A. Menon, "A Comparison of Alternative Recognition Measures of Advertising Effectiveness," *Journal of Advertising,* no. 3, 1986, pp. 4–20; S. N. Singh and G. A. Churchill, Jr., "Response-Bias-Free Recognition Tests to Measure Advertising Effects," *Journal of Advertising Research,* June/July 1987, pp. 23–36; G. M. Zinkhan, W. B. Locander, and J. H. Leigh, "Dimensional Relationships of Aided Recall and Recognition," *Journal of Advertising,* no. 1, 1986, pp. 38–46.

[96] S. N. Singh, M. L. Rothschild, and G. A. Churchill, Jr., "Recognition vs Recall as Measures of Television Commercial Forgetting," *Journal of Marketing Research,* February 1988, pp. 72–80.

[97] R. Manville, "Readership Scores Get a Failing Grade," *Marketing News,* January 3, 1986, p. 75; and G. M. Zinkhan and B. D. Gelb, "What Starch Scores Predict," *Journal of Advertising Research,* August/September 1986, pp. 45–50.

[98] "Cognitive Ability of Children a Disputed Issue in Kidvid Proceedings," *Washington Report* (American Advertising Federation, August 21, 1979), pp. 3–4.

[99] M. G. Hoy, C. E. Young, and J. C. Mowen, "Animated Host-Selling Advertisements," *Journal of Public Policy and Marketing,* vol. 5, 1986, 171–84.

[100] A. Stutts, D. Vance, and S. Hudleson, "Program-Commercial Separators in Children's Television," *Journal of Advertising,* Second Quarter 1981, pp. 16–48.

[101] T. R. Donohue, L. L. Henke, and W. A. Donohue, "Do Kids Know What TV Commercials Intend?" *Journal of Advertising Research,* October 1980, pp. 51–56; and M. C. Macklin, "Preschoolers' Understanding of the Informational Function of Television Advertising," *Journal of Consumer Research,* September 1987, pp. 229–39.

[102] "NAD Slams Spot from Mattel," *Advertising Age,* October 19, 1987, p. 6.

[103] M. A. Stutts and G. G. Hunnicutt, "Can Young Children Understand Disclaimers?" *Journal of Advertising,* no. 1, 1987, pp. 41–46.

[104] This problem is based on "Nurses Foaming over Chelsea," *Advertising Age,* October 23, 1978, p. 8.

[105] "FTC Urged to Review Total Spots," *Advertising Age,* October 23, 1978, p. 114.

CHAPTER

9 Information Processing: Learning and Memory

Sewer sludge is the solid matter remaining after municipalities have processed the sewage and disposed of the effluent, generally through dumping it into rivers or oceans. The amount of sludge produced annually is growing dramatically with population increases and enhanced antipollution regulations.

Sludge is used as a soil enhancer, fertilizer, and compost. Sludge is treated by the utilities and is not a health hazard as it was in the past. However, citizen groups frequently oppose the application of sludge to farmlands or other properties. As one official stated after a citizens' group had blocked plans to apply sludge to 6,000 acres near their town: "We kind of walked into that one blindfolded. We now realize that the public is not knowledgeable about sludge and its disposal."

To deal with problems posed by such citizens' groups, the utilities are launching public relations campaigns to educate the public about the attributes of sludge. That is, they want the public to learn new information about sludge in the belief that such learning will lead to behavior changes.[1]

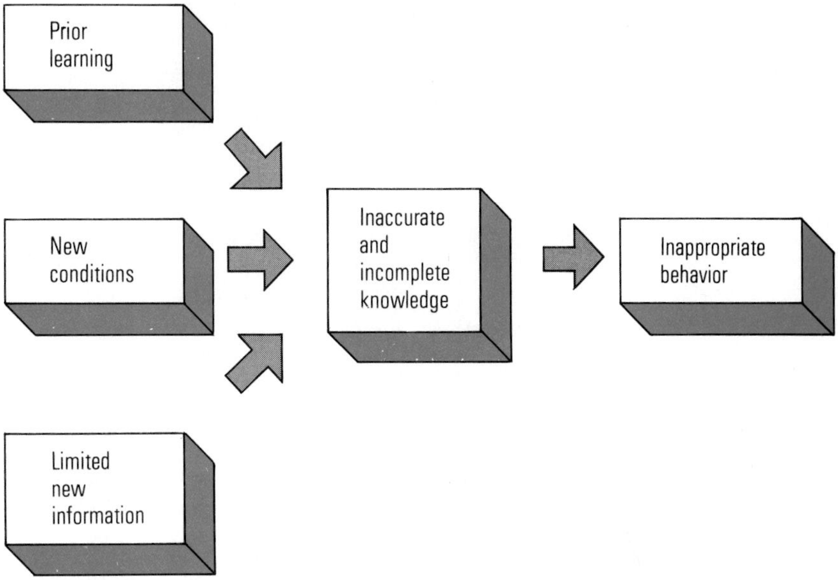

As the opening example illustrates, organizations are interested in teaching consumers and others about the nature of their products and services. In this chapter, we discuss the nature of learning and memory, conditioning and cognitive theories of learning, and general characteristics of learning. Implications for marketing managers also are examined within each section. The outcome of consumer learning about a brand and product category—product position—is discussed in the final section.

NATURE OF LEARNING

Learning is essential to the consumption process. In fact, consumer behavior is largely *learned* behavior. As illustrated in Figure 9–1, we acquire most of our attitudes, values, tastes, behaviors, preferences, symbolic meanings, and feelings through learning. Our culture and social class, through such institutions as schools and religious organizations, as well as our family and friends, provide learning experiences that greatly influence the type of lifestyle we seek and the products we consume. Marketers expend considerable effort to ensure that consumers learn of the existence and nature of their products.

Think for a moment of the many things you have had to learn in order to make consumption decisions. For example, one consumer might have learned the following:

Figure 9–1
Learning Is a Key to Consumer Behavior

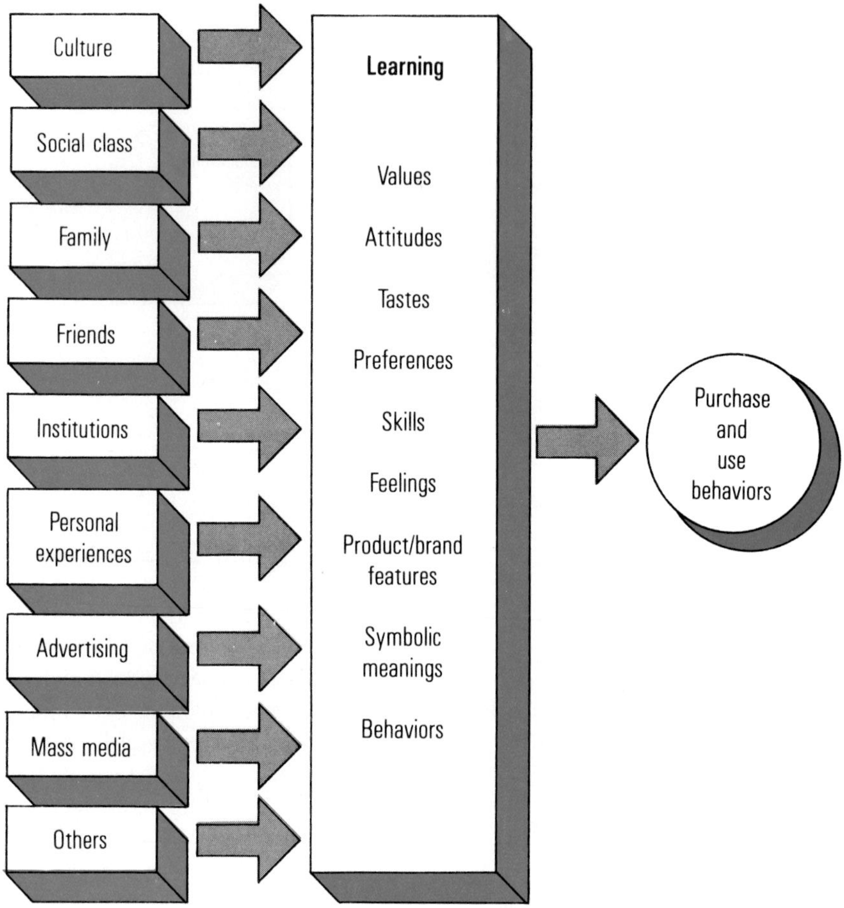

- In the purchase of durable goods such as compact disc players, a national brand is a safer buy than a retailer's private brand.
- A price of $5.99 is too much to pay for a six-pack of beer brewed in America.
- The best values for small appliances are found in discount stores rather than in full-service department stores.
- All brands of aspirin are really the same, regardless of advertised claims.
- When buying a new suit to wear to work, disregard bright colors and the latest style and consider only styles similar to those worn by the other people at the office.

- Escargot should not be ordered as an appetizer at a restaurant because it tastes bad.
- The food advertising in the newspaper should be read very closely on Wednesday because that is when all the good buys are advertised.

Of course, this consumer would have learned thousands of other things such as store locations and hours, and such general skills as how to read and drive. The situations and behaviors leading to the learning of the material shown above probably varied widely. Learning to dislike escargot probably involved a behavior (trying it) and a reaction (dislike). Learning that all aspirin are the same may have required seeking out and reading relevant material and applying a logical reasoning process. Learning to avoid brightly colored suits may have involved the deliberate observation that success at work and conservative dress seem to go together. The belief that national brands are better than private brands may have more or less "seeped in" over years of exposure to television commercials that were only "half" watched.

Learning Defined

Learning is any change in the content or organization of long-term memory.[2] Thus, learning is the result of information processing as described in the last chapter. Recall from Chapter 8 that information processing may be conscious and deliberate in high-involvement situations. Or, it may be nonfocused and even nonconscious in low-involvement situations. In either case, learning results *from* information processing and *causes* changes in memory as shown below.

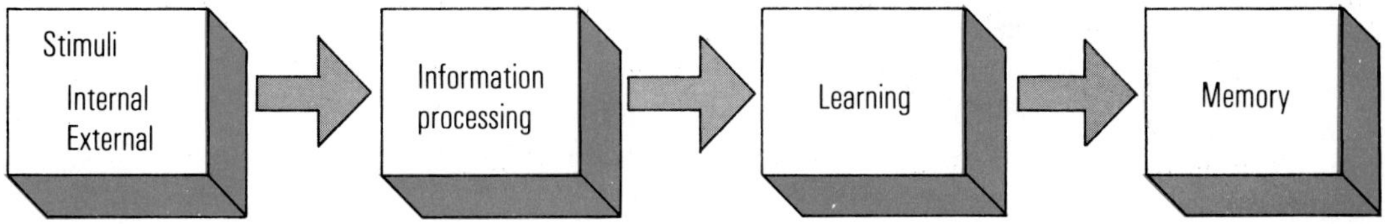

NATURE OF MEMORY

Memory is the total accumulation of prior learning experiences.[3] It consists of two interrelated components: short-term and long-term memory. These are *not* distinct physiological entities. Instead, *short-term memory* is that portion of total memory that is currently activated or in use. In fact, it is often referred to as *working memory*.

The concept of short-term memory as active problem solving, and its relationship to long-term memory is analogous to the use of a desk:

> When working on a problem, an individual may assemble materials related to the topic from various files and books and place them on the desk top.

When he is finished, he may stuff the materials placed on the desk into a drawer and keep them as a unit. Or he may return the items to their original locations, perhaps storing the problem solution.[4]

Long-Term Memory

Long-term memory is viewed as an unlimited, permanent storage. It can store numerous types of information such as concepts, decision rules, processes, affective (emotional) states, and so forth. Marketers are particularly interested in *schematic memory* (frequently termed *semantic memory*), which is the stored

Figure 9–2
Schematic Memory for California Cooler

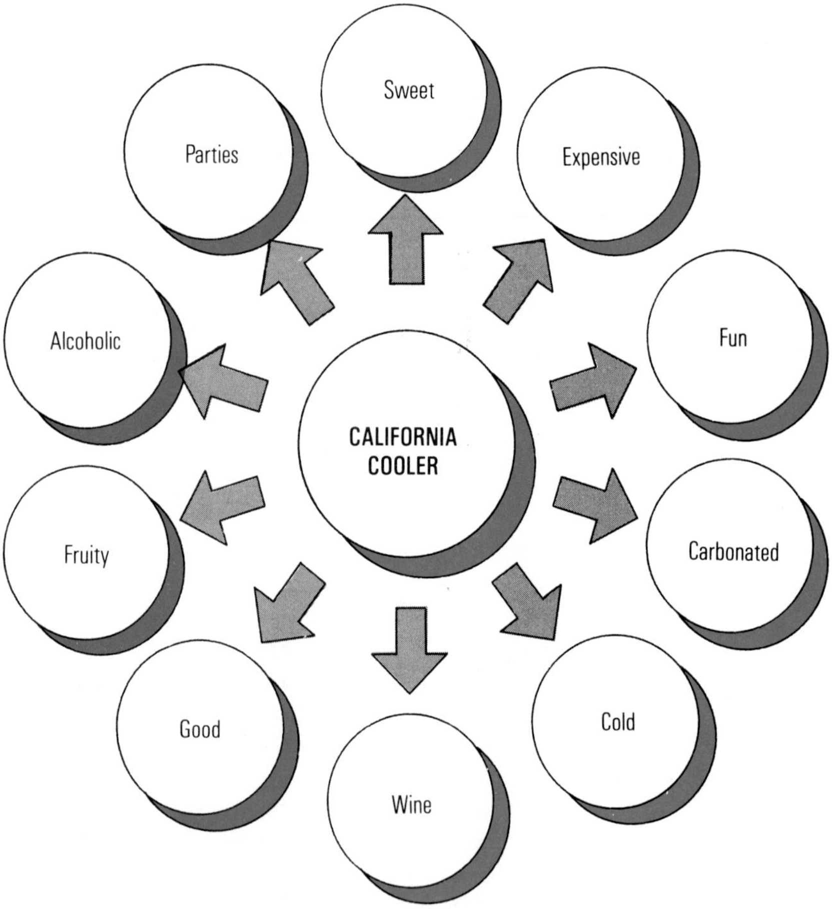

representations of our generalized knowledge about the world we live in.[5] It is this form of memory that is concerned with the association and combinations of various "chunks" of information.

Figure 9–2 provides an example of a schema by showing how one might associate various concepts with California Cooler to form a complete network of meaning for that brand. Notice that our hypothetical schema contains *product characteristics, usage situations,* and *affective reactions*. The schematic memory of a brand is the same as the brand image or product position. It is what the consumer thinks of and feels when the brand name is mentioned.

What do you think of when you see the word *thirst*? The various things, including brands, that come to mind constitute the schema for thirst. Pepsi-Cola exerts substantial marketing effort in an attempt to become part of the schema associated with thirst. Brands in the schematic memory for a consumer problem such as thirst are known as the *evoked set*. We will discuss the way consumers and marketers use the evoked set in Chapter 15.

Memory of an action sequence, such as purchasing and drinking a soft drink in order to relieve thirst, is a special type of schemata known as a *script* (sometimes referred to as *episodic memory*). Marketers and public policy officials want consumers to develop scripts for appropriate product acquisition, use, and disposal behavior.

Current opinion holds that long-term memory has unlimited capacity for information storage. The problem of forgetting is really one of being unable to retrieve information that is there. Retrieval is the process of obtaining information from long-term memory for use in elaborative operations or problem-solving in short-term memory. In other words, "retrieval is the process by which information stored in long-term memory is activated to recognize new input or solve a problem."[6] We will examine the conditions that enhance one's ability to retrieve information from long-term memory in the next section of this chapter.

Short-Term Memory

Short-term or working memory has been described in terms of two basic kinds of information processing activities—maintenance rehearsal and elaborative activities.[7] *Maintenance rehearsal* is the continual repetition of a piece of information in order to hold it in current memory for use in problem solving or transferral to long-term memory. While extensive rehearsal generally strengthens retention in long-term memory, it is not essential for a strong long-term memory.

Elaborative activities are the use of previously stored experiences, values, attitudes, beliefs, and feelings to interpret and evaluate information in *working* memory as well as add relevant previously stored information. Elaborative activities serve to redefine or add new elements to memory. Thus, the interpretation process described in Chapter 8 is based on elaborative activities.

Short-term memory is closely analogous to what we normally call thinking. It is an active, dynamic process, not a static structure.

Our previous discussion of long-term memory implies that working memory operates primarily by activating and processing schemata in a discursive or descriptive manner—that is, by *symbol* manipulation. While this accounts for a significant amount of the activities in working memory, *imagery* is also important.[8] Imagery involves concrete sensory representations of ideas, feelings, and objects. It permits a direct recovery of past experiences. Thus, imagery processing involves the recall and mental manipulation of sensory images including sight, smell, taste, and tactile situations. The two tasks below will clarify the distinctions between schema and imagery in working memory:

- Write down the first ten *words* that come to mind when I say "romantic evening."
- Imagine a "romantic evening."

Obviously, marketers often want to elicit imagery responses rather than verbal ones. While we are just beginning to study imagery responses, they are a significant part of consumers' mental activities. We describe the role of imagery in vicarious learning in the next section of this chapter. Techniques to enhance imagery-processing activities are described in the following section.

LEARNING UNDER CONDITIONS OF HIGH AND LOW INVOLVEMENT

Learning may occur in either a high-involvement or a low-involvement situation.[9] A *high-involvement learning* situation is one in which the consumer is motivated to learn the material. For example, an individual reading *Consumer Reports* prior to purchasing a personal computer is probably highly motivated to learn the material dealing with the various computer brands. A *low-involvement learning* situation is one in which the consumer has little or no motivation to learn the material. A consumer whose television program is interrupted by a commercial for a product he or she doesn't currently use has little motivation to learn the material presented in the commercial. Obviously, learning involvement is not an either/or situation. Rather, it is one of degree.

Much, if not most, consumer learning occurs in a relatively low-involvement context. Unfortunately, we do not have a complete understanding of low-involvement learning. In the previous chapter, we indicated that different mental processes—the left brain versus the right brain—*may* be involved in high- versus low-involvement information processing. It appears that high- and low-involvement learning are based on similar learning principles. However, certain types of learning are more likely to occur in high-involvement situations and other types are more likely in low-involvement situations.

Figure 9–3 shows the two general situations and the five specific learning theories that we are going to consider. The solid lines in the figure indicate that operant conditioning, vicarious/modeling learning, and reasoning are commonly used learning strategies in high-involvement situations. Classical conditioning, iconic rote learning, and vicarious/modeling learning tend to occur in low-involvement situations. Each of these specific theories is described in the following pages.

Figure 9–3
Learning Theories in High- and Low-Involvement Situations

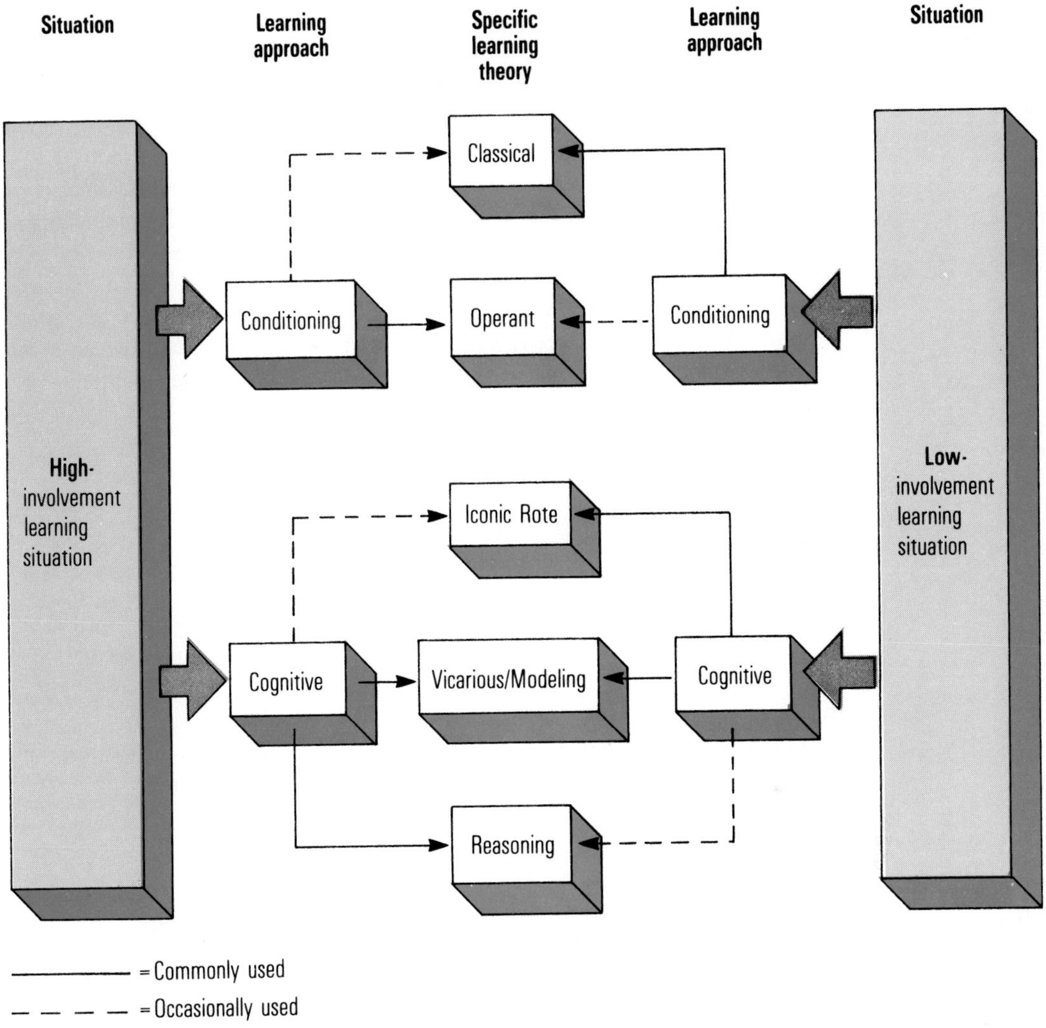

Conditioning

Conditioning refers to learning based on *association of stimulus (information) and response (behavior or feeling)*. The word *conditioning* has a negative connotation to some and brings forth images of robotlike humans. However, conditioned learning simply means that through exposure to some stimulus and a corresponding response, one learns that they go together (or do not go together). There are two basic forms of conditioned learning—classical and operant.[10]

Classical Conditioning. Classical conditioning is *the process of using an established relationship between a stimulus and response to bring about the learning of the same response to a different stimulus*. Figure 9–4 illustrates this type of learning.

Hearing popular music (unconditioned stimulus) elicits a positive emotion (unconditioned response) in many individuals. If this music is consistently paired with a particular brand of pen or other product (conditioned stimulus), the brand itself will come to elicit the same positive emotion (conditioned response).

Although the ability of commercials to form associations by classical conditioning is controversial, this approach is widely used.[11] For example, Vantage cigarettes are advertised in full-page magazine ads that consist primarily of a beautiful winter snow scene, the brand name, and a picture of the cigarette package. Part of the objective of such ads is to associate the positive emotional response to the outdoor scene with the brand. This in turn will increase the likelihood that the individual will try and like the brand. Other marketing applications include:[12]

- Consistently advertising a product on exciting sports events may result in the product itself generating an "excitement" response.
- An unknown political candidate may come to elicit "patriotic feelings" by consistently playing patriotic background music in his/her commercials and appearances.

Figure 9–4
Consumer Learning through Classical Conditioning

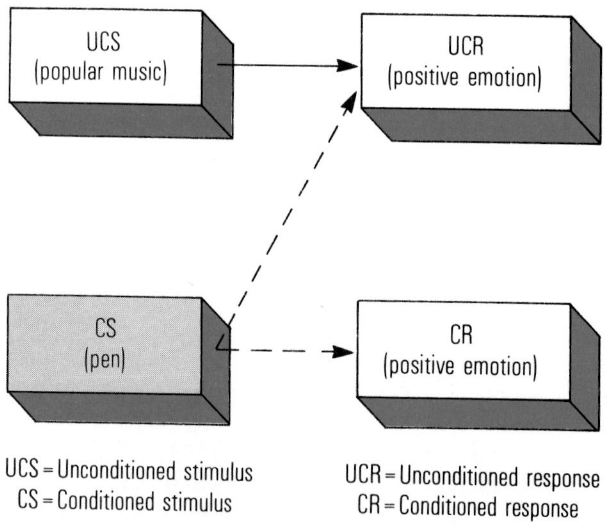

- Christmas music played in stores may elicit emotional responses associated with giving and sharing, which in turn may increase the propensity to purchase.

Classical conditioning is most common in low-involvement situations. In the Vantage example described above, it is likely that many consumers devote little or no focused attention to the advertisement since cigarette ads are low-involvement messages even for most smokers. However, after a sufficient number of low-involvement "scannings" or "glances at" the commercial, the association may be formed. It is important to note that what is learned is generally not information but emotion or an affective response. If this affective response leads to learning about the product or leads to a product trial, we have the following situation:

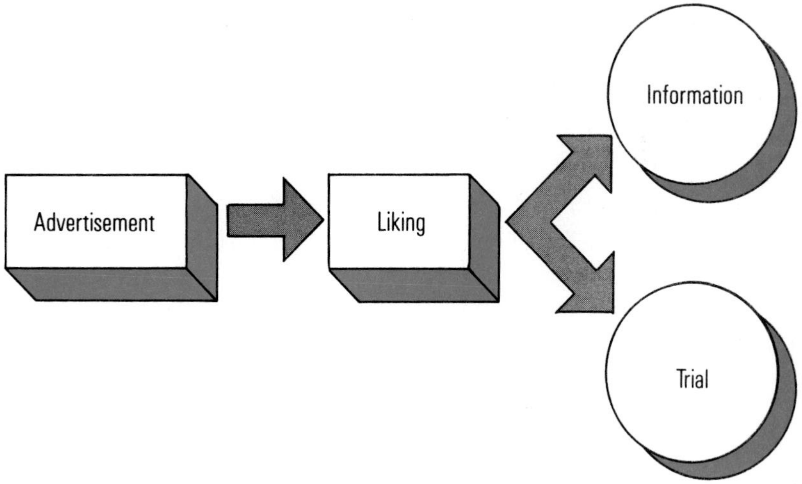

Operant Conditioning. Operant conditioning, also known as instrumental learning, differs from classical conditioning primarily in the role and timing of reinforcement.[13]

Suppose you are the product manager for American Chicle's new Spring Menthol mint gum. You believe your product has a light, fresh taste that consumers will like. How can you influence them to learn to consume your brand? One approach would be to distribute a large number of free samples through the mail. American cultural values against waste would cause many consumers to chew the gum (desired response). To the extent that the taste of the gum is indeed pleasant (reinforcement), the probability of continued consumption is increased. This is shown graphically in Figure 9–5.

Notice that reinforcement plays a much larger role in operant conditioning than it does in classical conditioning. Since no automatic stimulus-response relationship is involved, the subject must first be induced to engage in the desired behavior. Then, this behavior must be reinforced. The sequence of events in-

Figure 9–5
Consumer Learning by Operant Conditioning

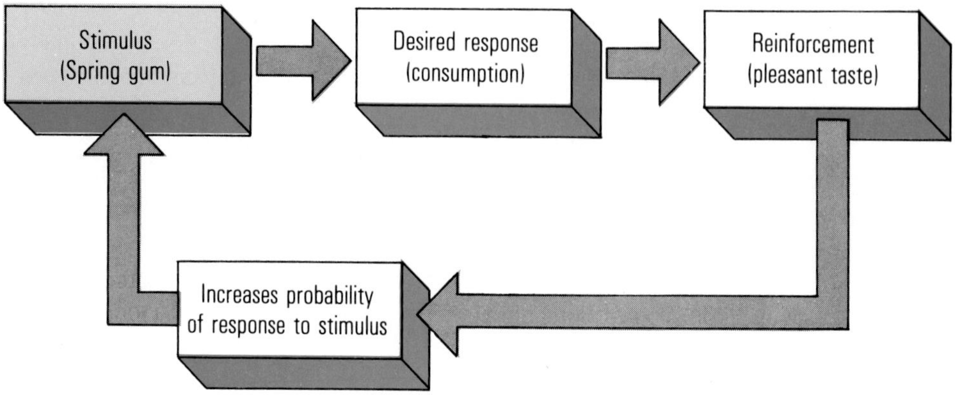

volved in operant conditioning is different from that associated with classical conditioning. For operant conditioning, trial precedes liking. The reverse is often true for classical conditioning.

Operant conditioning often involves the actual usage of the product. Thus, a great deal of marketing strategy is aimed at securing an initial trial. Free samples (at home or in the store), special price discounts on new products, and contests all represent rewards offered to consumers to try a particular product or brand. If they try the brand under these conditions and like it (reinforcement), they are likely to take the next step and purchase it in the future. This process of encouraging partial responses leading to the final desired response (consume a free sample → purchase at a special introductory price → purchase at full price) is known as *shaping*. This process is illustrated in Figure 9–6.

While reinforcement increases the likelihood of behavior such as a purchase being repeated, a negative consequence (punishment) has exactly the opposite effect. Thus, the purchase of a brand that does not function properly greatly reduces the chances of future purchases of that brand. This underscores the critical importance of consistent product quality.

Operant conditioning is widely used by marketers. The most common application is to have consistent quality products so that the use of the product to meet a consumer need is reinforcing. Other applications include:

- Direct mail or personal contacts after a sale that congratulate the purchaser for making a wise purchase.
- Giving "extra" reinforcement for shopping at a store, such as trading stamps, rebates, or prizes.
- Giving "extra" reinforcement for purchasing a particular brand, such as rebates, toys in cereal boxes, or discount coupons.

Figure 9–6
The Process of Shaping in Purchase Behavior

- Giving free product samples or introductory coupons to encourage product trial (shaping).
- Making store interiors, shopping malls, or downtown areas pleasant (reinforcing) places to shop by providing entertainment, controlled temperature, exciting displays, and so forth.
- Advertising, which reinforces product ownership or use: "The best people own. . . ."

The power of operant conditioning is demonstrated by an experiment conducted by a Midwest insurance company. Over 2,000 consumers who purchased life insurance over a one-month period were randomly divided into three groups. Two of the groups received reinforcement after each monthly payment in the form of a nice "thank-you" letter or telephone call. The third group received no such reinforcement. Six months later, 10 percent of the members of the two groups receiving reinforcement had terminated their policies while 23 percent of those not receiving reinforcement had done so! Clearly, reinforcement (being thanked) lead to continued behavior (sending in the monthly premium).[14]

Operant conditioning is most likely to occur in high-involvement situations. Using a particular product implies at least some involvement. Most high-involvement purchases are followed by a conscious evaluation of the degree of reward obtained. A person who purchases a new suit is likely to devote at least some deliberate effort to evaluating both the symbolic and functional outcome of the purchase. Reinforcement (positive or negative) will have a strong impact in such a situation.

Lower-involvement purchases are generally given a deliberate evaluation only if the product performs far below expectations. Thus, while satisfactory perfor-

Exhibit 9–1

Operant and Classical Conditioning in Advertising

Courtesy J. C. Penney Co.

Courtesy Jantzen, Inc.

Operant Conditioning

Direct compliment to current users of Penney's suits

Classical Conditioning

Pairing the positive emotional response to the scene with the Jantzen name

mance is rewarding for low-involvement purchases, it's much less rewarding than in high-involvement situations.

Exhibit 9–1 shows two advertisements. The Jantzen advertisement associates the positive emotional response to an attractive, admired young woman with the firm's brand name. J. C. Penney provides a direct reinforcement (a compliment) to current users of Penney's suits.

Cognitive Learning

The *cognitive* approach to learning encompasses all the mental activities of humans as they work to solve problems or cope with situations. It involves learning ideas, concepts, attitudes, and facts that contribute to our ability to reason, solve problems, and learn relationships without direct experience or reinforcement. Cognitive learning can range from very simple information acquisition to complex, creative problem solutions.

Iconic Rote Learning. Iconic rote learning involves learning the *association between two or more concepts in the absence of conditioning.*[15] For example, one may see an ad that states, "Advil is a headache remedy," and associate the new concept Advil with the existing concept "headache remedy." There is neither an unconditioned stimulus nor a direct reward involved.

A substantial amount of low-involvement learning involves iconic rote learning. Numerous repetitions of a simple message may result in the essence of the message being learned, probably at weak level, as a result of the consumer scanning the environment. Through iconic rote learning, consumers may form beliefs about the characteristics or attributes of products without being aware of the source of the information. When the need arises, a purchase may be made based on those beliefs.

Vicarious/Modeling Learning. *Vicarious learning* or *modeling* is another important manner by which consumers learn.[16] It is not necessary for consumers to directly experience a reward or punishment to learn. Instead, we can observe the outcomes of others' behaviors and adjust our own accordingly. Likewise, we can use imagery to anticipate the outcome of various courses of action.

This type of learning is common in both low- and high-involvement situations. In a high-involvement situation such as purchasing a new suit shortly after taking a job, a consumer may deliberately observe the styles worn by others at work or by role models from other environments, including advertisements.

A substantial amount of modeling also occurs in low-involvement situations. Throughout the course of our lives we observe people using products and behaving in a great variety of situations. Most of the time we pay limited attention to these behaviors. However, over time, we learn that certain behaviors (and products) are appropriate in some situations while others are not.

Marketers make extensive use of vicarious learning. Advertisements promise rewards for using products or, more commonly, show consumers receiving re-

Exhibit 9–2 Use of Vicarious Learning and Reasoning in Advertising

Courtesy Hanes Hosiery, Inc.

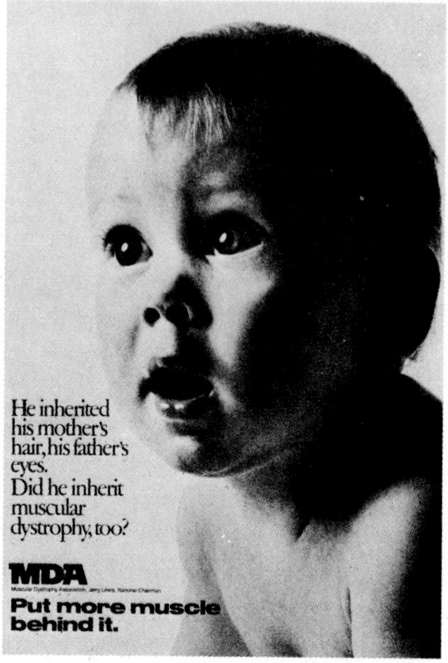

Courtesy Muscular Dystrophy Association

Vicarious Learning

Consumer observes a person in an ad receiving a reward for using a product and can imagine receiving the same reward.

Reasoning

Ad requires the reader to think about the relationship between muscular dystrophy and inherited characteristics.

wards for using a product. The Hanes ad in Exhibit 9–2 shows a woman receiving positive reinforcement (admiring glance) because she is wearing Hanes Alive. The potential consumer can imagine similar results if she uses the product.

Reasoning. *Reasoning* represents the most complex form of cognitive learning. In reasoning, individuals engage in creative thinking to restructure and recombine existing information as well as new information to form new associations and concepts. Most high-involvement purchases generate at least some learning by reasoning.

The MDA advertisement in Exhibit 9–2 requires the reader to think about the relationship between muscular dystrophy and inherited characteristics. This thought will hopefully result in a series of conclusions: "It is not known if muscular dystrophy is inherited; therefore more research is required; therefore I should support MDA." These conclusions are not mentioned in the advertisement. The reader must use reasoning to reach them.

Summary on Learning Theories

Theories of learning help us understand how consumers learn across a variety of situations. We have examined five specific learning theories: operant conditioning, classical conditioning, iconic rote learning, vicarious/modeling learning, and reasoning. Each of these learning theories can operate a high- or a low-involvement situation. Table 9–1 summarizes these theories and provides examples from both high- and low-involvement contexts.

GENERAL CHARACTERISTICS OF LEARNING

Regardless of which approach to learning is applicable in a given situation, several general characteristics of learning are relevant and of interest to marketing managers. Five of the most important are strength of learning, extinction (or forgetting), stimulus generalization, stimulus discrimination, and the response environment.

Strength of Learning

What is required to bring about a strong and long-lasting learned response? How can the promotion manager of Pepsi teach you the advantages of this brand so that you will not quickly forget them? The *strength of learning* is heavily influenced by four factors: *importance, reinforcement, repetition,* and *imagery*. Generally, learning comes about more rapidly and lasts longer (*a*) the more important the material to be learned, (*b*) the more reinforcement (or punishment) received during the process, (*c*) the greater the number of stimulus repetitions (or practice) that occurs, and (*d*) the more imagery contained in the material.

Importance. Importance refers to the value that the consumer places on the information to be learned. The more important it is for you to learn a particular behavior or piece of information, the more effective and efficient you become in the learning process.[17]

Importance is the dimension that separates high-involvement learning situations from low-involvement situations. Therefore, high-involvement learning tends to be more complete than low-involvement learning. As we will see, high involvement with the learning situation reduces need for reinforcement, repetition, imagery, and optimal presentation formats. Unfortunately, marketers are most often confronted with consumers in a low-involvement learning situation.

Reinforcement. While learning frequently occurs in the absence of *reinforcement* (or punishment), reinforcement has a significant impact on the speed at

Table 9–1
Summary of Learning Theories with Examples of Involvement Level

Theory	Description	High-Involvement Example	Low-Involvement Example
Classical conditioning	A response elicited by one object will be elicited by the second object if both objects frequently occur together.	The favorable emotional response elicited by the word *America* comes to be elicited by the brand Chrysler after a consumer reads that Chrysler plans to use only American-made parts.	The favorable emotional response elicited by a picture comes to be elicited by a brand name that is consistently shown with that picture, even though the consumer does not "pay attention" to the advertising.
Operant conditioning	A response that is given reinforcement is more likely to be repeated when the same situation arises in the future.	A suit is purchased and the purchaser finds that it does not wrinkle and generates several compliments. A sport coat made by the same firm is then purchased.	A familiar brand of peas is purchased without much thought. They taste "all right." The consumer continues to purchase this brand.
Iconic rote learning	Two or more concepts become associated without conditioning.	A jogger learns about various brands of running shoes as a result of closely reading many shoe advertisements which he/she finds enjoyable.	A consumer learns that Apple makes home computers, without ever really "thinking" about Apple advertisements or products.
Vicarious or modeling learning	Behaviors are learned by watching the outcomes of others' behaviors or by imagining the outcome of a potential behavior.	A consumer watches the reactions people have to her friend's new short skirt before deciding to buy one.	A child learns that men don't wear dresses without ever really "thinking" about it.
Reasoning	Individuals use thinking to restructure and recombine existing information and new information to form new associations and concepts.	A consumer believes that baking soda removes odors from the refrigerator. Noticing an unpleasant aroma in the carpet, the consumer decides to sweep some baking soda into the carpet.	Finding that the store is out of black pepper, a consumer decides to substitute white pepper.

which learning occurs and the duration of its effect.[18] We define reinforcement as anything which increases the likelihood that a given response will be repeated in the future.

A *positive reinforcement* is a pleasant or desired consequence. A thirsty person purchases and consumes a Tab, which quenches the thirst. Tab is now more likely to be purchased and consumed the next time the person is thirsty. A *negative reinforcement* involves the removal or the avoidance of an unpleasant consequence. Clerz 2 eye drops are positioned as a means of avoiding eye discomfort from wearing contact lenses too long. *Punishment* is the opposite of reinforcement. It is any consequence which decreases the likelihood that a given response will be repeated in the future.

Marketers attempt to teach us that their products have attributes that will satisfy one or more of our goals. Eventually, if their promotional campaigns are successful and the goal or need the product can satisfy is sufficiently important, we will try the product. To the extent that it satisfies our goal(s), we will be reinforced and the probability of our purchasing that brand again increases. To the extent that the product does not fulfill our goal(s), we will not be reinforced and the probability of our purchasing that brand again will decrease.

From the above discussion, we can see that there are two very important reasons for marketers to determine precisely what reinforces specific consumer purchases. First, to obtain repeat purchases the product must satisfy the goals sought by the consumer. Second, to induce the consumer to make the first purchase, the promotional messages must promise the appropriate type of reinforcement; that is, satisfaction of the consumer's goals.[19]

Repetition. *Repetition* (or practice) increases the strength and speed of learning. Quite simply, the more times we are exposed to information or practice a behavior, the more likely we are to learn it. The effects of repetition are, of course, directly related to the importance of the information and the reinforcement given. In other words, less repetition of an advertising message is necessary for us to learn the message if the subject matter is very important or if there is a great deal of relevant reinforcement. Since many advertisements do not contain information of current importance to consumers or direct rewards for attention, repetition plays a critical role in the promotion process for low-involvement products and messages.

Figure 9–7, based on a study of 16,500 respondents, shows the impact of various levels of advertising repetition over a 48-week period on brands that had either high or low levels of initial awareness. Several features stand out. First, the initial exposure has the largest impact. Second, frequent repetition (once a week) outperforms limited repetition (once every other week or every four weeks). This advantage grows the longer the campaign lasts. Finally, relative gains are much greater for unknown brands.

Both the number of times a message is repeated and the timing of those repetitions affect the extent and duration of learning.[20] Figure 9–8 illustrates the relationship between repetition timing and product recall for a food product. One group of homemakers, represented by the curved line in the figure, was exposed to a food product advertisement once a week for 13 consecutive weeks. For this

Figure 9–7
Impact of Repetition on Brand Awareness for High- and Low-Awareness Brands

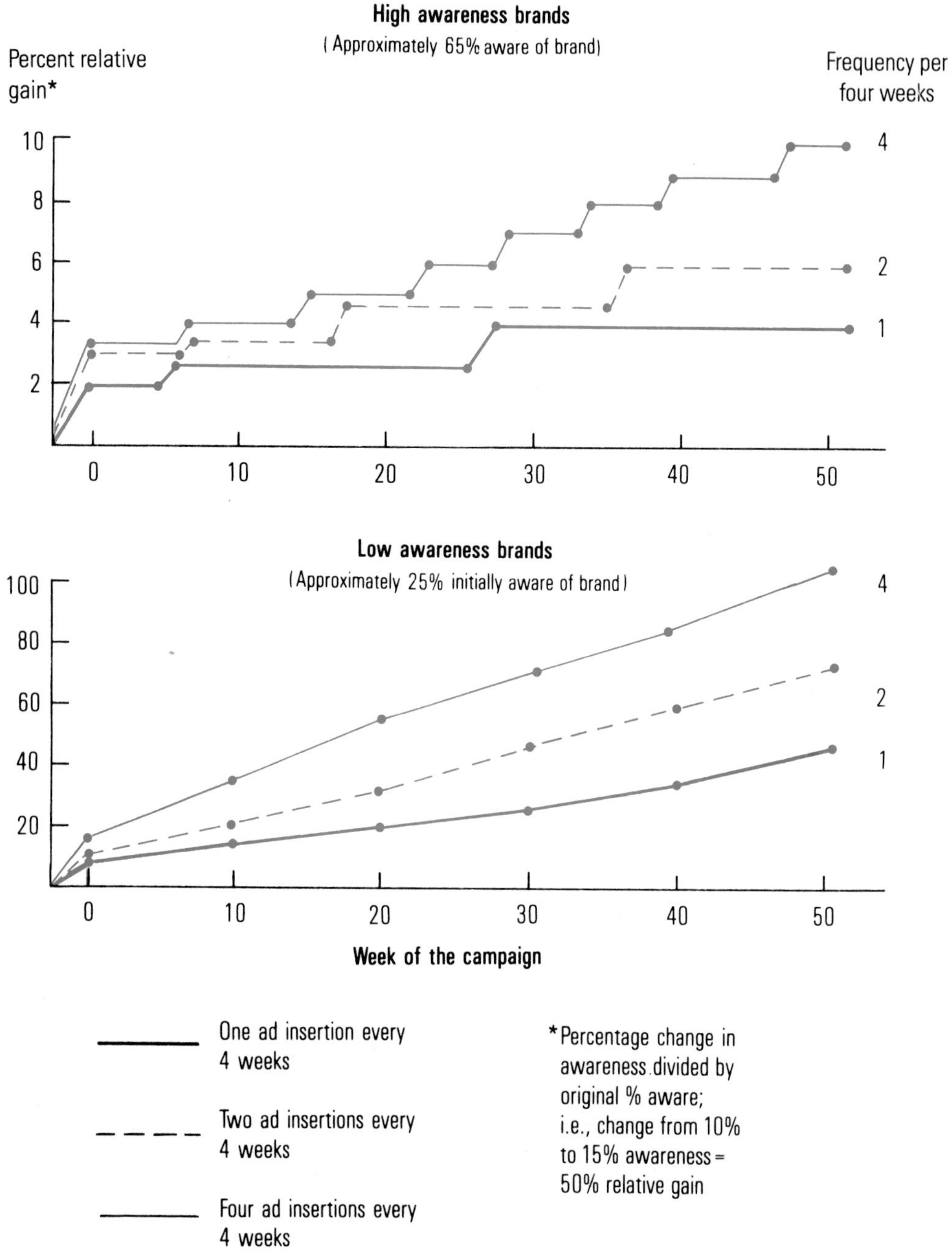

Source: *A Study of the Effectiveness of Advertising Frequency in Magazines* (Time Inc., 1982).

Figure 9–8
Repetition Timing and Advertising Recall

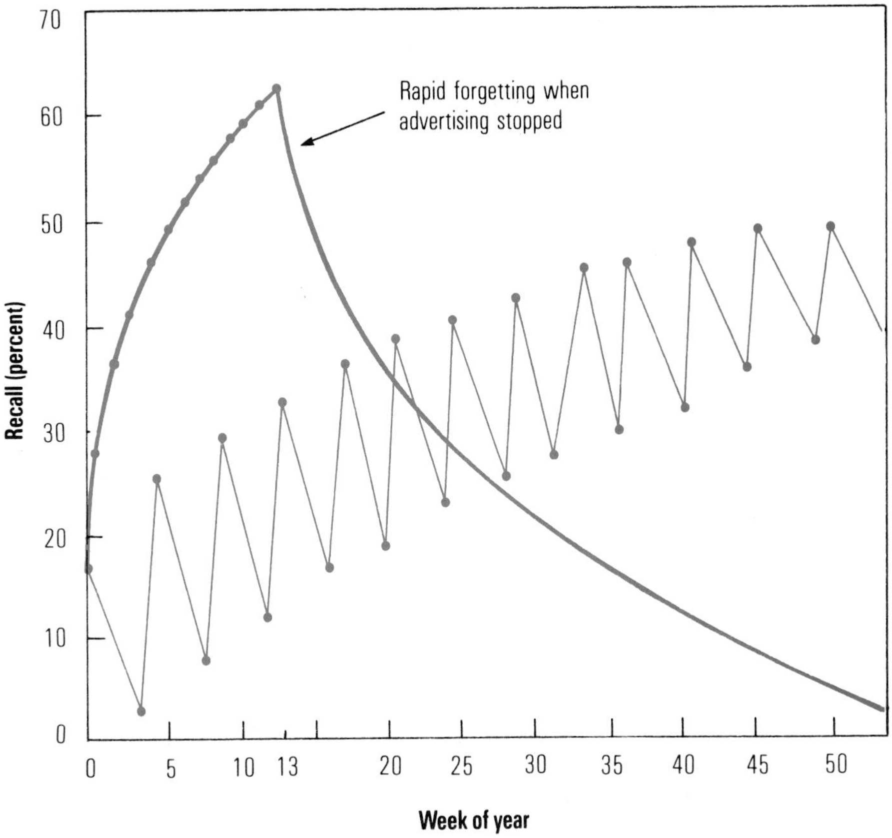

Source: Reprinted from H. J. Zielske, "The Remembering and Forgetting of Advertising." *Journal of Marketing*, January 1959, p. 240, with permission from the American Marketing Association. The actual data and a refined analysis are in J. L. Simon, "What Do Zielski's Data Really Show about Pulsing," *Journal of Marketing Research*, August 1979, pp. 415–20.

group, product recall (learning) increased rapidly and reached its highest level during the 13th week, forgetting occurred rapidly, and recall was virtually zero by the end of the year.

A second group of homemakers was exposed to the same 13 direct-mail advertisements. However, they received one ad every four weeks. The recall pattern for this group is shown by the zigzag line in the figure. Here learning increased throughout the year, but with substantial forgetting between message exposures.

Placing multiple insertions of the same ad in the single issue of a magazine enhances learning. Three insertions generate more than twice the impact of one insertion.[21] Concentrating one's messages during a single television broadcast has a similar effect. Compared to one showing of a Miller Lite Beer commercial, three showings during a championship baseball game produced two and a third times the recall, with 20 percent more positive attitudes and 50 percent fewer negative attitudes.[22] The results below are based on the number of times another commercial appeared during an NFC championship game:

Number of Times Commercial Shown	Average Recall (percent)
1	28
2	32
3	41
4	45

The A. C. Gilbert Company, a toy manufacturer, spread its entire advertising budget equally over a year by appearing on the same cartoon show every Saturday morning.[23] Was this the most effective repetition schedule? Since most toy purchases occur at Christmas, concentrating the firm's advertising during this time period would probably be more effective.

Any time it is important to produce widespread knowledge of the product rapidly, frequent (close together) repetitions should be used. This is referred to as *pulsing*. Thus, political candidates frequently hold back a significant proportion of their media budgets until shortly before the election and then use a "media blitz" to ensure widespread knowledge of their desirable attributes. More long-range programs, such as store image development, should use more widely spaced repetitions.

Consumers frequently complain about repetition in advertising, and some even declare that because of excess repetition, "I will never buy that brand!" Thus, there is a fine line for the marketer to balance in terms of repetition. Too much repetition can cause people to actively shut out the message, evaluate it negatively, or pay no attention to it.[24]

Imagery. Words, whether a brand name or corporate slogan, create certain images.[25] For example, brand names such as Camel and Rabbit evoke sensory images or well-defined mental pictures. As a result these words possess a high degree of imagery or mental visibility. This aids learning, as words high in imagery are substantially easier to learn and remember than low-imagery words. The theory behind the imagery effect is that high-imagery words leave a dual code since they can be stored in memory on the basis of both verbal and pictorial dimensions, while low-imagery words can only be coded verbally.[26] Since imagery greatly enhances the speed and nature of learning, the imagery of a brand name represents a critical marketing decision.

Pictures *are* images and thus, by definition, have a high level of imagery.

Compared to verbal content, pictorial components of advertisements appear to enhance learning.[27] Pictures enhance the consumer's visual imagery, which is a particularly effective learning device. They also appear to assist consumers in encoding the information into relevant chunks. Thus, the key communication points of an ad should be in the images elicited by its pictorial component, as this is what will be learned most quickly and firmly.

There is also evidence that *echoic memory,* memory of sounds including words, has characteristics distinct from visual memory. However, we are just beginning to research this area.[28]

Extinction

Liggett & Myers's share of the cigarette market slid from 20 percent to less than 4 percent. Much of this decline appears to have resulted from limited marketing activities. As one executive stated:

> Some time after the company moved away from advertising and marketing, it became clear that people would quickly forget about our products if we didn't support them in the marketplace.[29]

The above quote emphasizes that marketers want consumers to learn *and* remember positive features, feelings, and behaviors associated with their brands. However, *extinction,* or forgetting as it is more commonly termed, occurs when the reinforcement for the learned response is withdrawn, or the learned response is no longer used.

Figure 9–9 illustrates a commonly found rate-of-forgetting (decay) curve for advertising. In this study, aided and unaided recall of four advertisements from *American Machinist* magazine were measured. As can be seen, recall dropped rapidly after five days, then stabilized.

The rate at which extinction occurs is inversely related to the strength of the original learning. That is, the more important the material, the more reinforcement, the more repetition, and the greater the imagery, the more resistant the learning is to extinction.

At times, marketers or regulatory groups desire to accelerate extinction. For example, the American Cancer Society and other organizations offer programs designed to help individuals "unlearn" smoking behavior. Manufacturers want consumers to forget unfavorable publicity or outdated product images.[30] For example, a recent national study found that American automobiles are seen as bland, less prestigious than their European competitors and less reliable than Japanese cars. They were rated low on "sporty," "fun," and "innovative" dimensions.[31] Clearly, American car manufacturers need to help consumers "unlearn" these negative aspects of their image and learn new, positive material.

Corrective advertising is the most controversial area in extinction or "unlearning." The idea is straightforward. If a commercial or series of commercials

Figure 9–9
Forgetting over Time: Magazine Advertisement

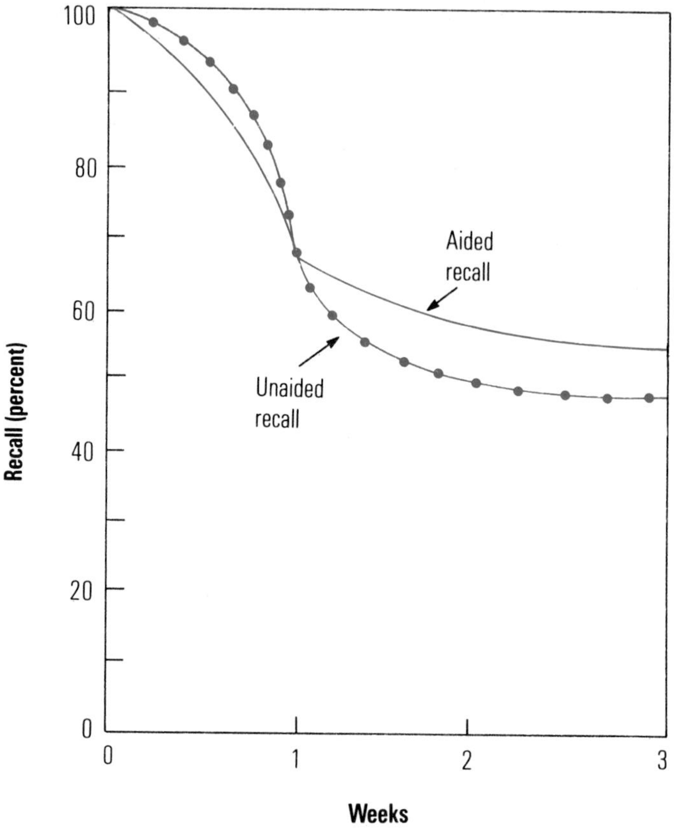

Source: LAP Report #5260.1 (New York: Weeks McGraw-Hill, undated. Used with permission.

causes a group of consumers to learn false information about a brand, a second series of commercials can be designed to speed extinction of the incorrect information. Research indicates that corrective commercials can achieve their objective but they are less than completely effective. The inclusion of the corrective message does not appear to have a negative effect on the other communications objectives of the commercial.[32] Exhibit 9–3 illustrates corrective advertising in the Listerine case.

Stimulus Generalization

At the end of a pitch to sell a jet engine to an airframe manufacturer, a GE executive asked if his company could be of any further help. "Well, now that

Exhibit 9–3

The Listerine Corrective Advertising Case

From September 4, 1978, through February 1, 1980, Warner-Lambert Co. was required to include the following statement in all television advertisements for Listerine: "Listerine will not help prevent colds or sore throats or lessen their severity." This requirement was in response to an FTC finding that Listerine had been deceptively advertised as a cold remedy.

Studies of the interpretation of the corrective ads by Burke Marketing Research found that the corrective Listerine statement was understood by the viewers. That is, viewers were not detracted from the commercial's sales message by the inclusion of the corrective message.

A study of the impact of the corrective campaign found that there was a 40 percent drop in the amount of mouthwash used for colds and sore throats. Likewise, the number of people who considered a mouthwash's ability to prevent colds or sore throats dropped from 31 percent before the corrective campaign to 25 percent afterward. However, the study also found that "while 22 percent of Listerine users associated the corrective message with Listerine advertising, 42 percent still believe colds and sore throat effectiveness is a principle Listerine advertising theme." In addition, about 40 percent of Listerine users use mouthwash to relieve or prevent a cold or sore throat.

Clearly, once a message or behavior is thoroughly learned, extinction is difficult to obtain.

Source: "Listerine Corrective Ads Change Consumer Awareness of Product's Effectiveness," *FTC News Summary* (Federal Trade Commission, October 30, 1981), pp. 1–2.

you brought it up," replied the executive in charge, "I've got a problem with my GE TV set, and my washing machine doesn't work too well, either." The GE executive quickly phoned his service people to get the problem fixed. But several months later, when asked if the appliances were giving more trouble, the airframe manufacturer answered, "No, I've gotten rid of all my GE appliances."[33]

The danger the above situation presents to GE is not the loss of an appliance customer. Rather, the danger is that the airframe company executive will assume that GE aircraft engines have the same performance characteristics that his GE appliances had. This is termed *stimulus generalization* (often called the *rub-off effect*). The basic principle is that whenever a response is learned in one stimulus situation, other stimuli similar to those in the initial situation acquire some tendency to produce that response. Stimulus generalization is the basis for the transfer of learning and is particularly relevant to marketing.

Consider the consumer learning problem that a marketer faces when trying to introduce a new brand into the marketplace to compete with already successful brands. If the new brand has no significant advantage, consumers must learn that it is at least as good as the existing choices. An important way to bring about this learning is to make the new brand similar to existing brands so consumers can generalize their previous learning. Similar brand names, product shapes, packaging, and advertising can all help this happen. Exhibit 9–4 illustrates how Yardley of London used this principle to launch Yardley Leather by placing it in the same category as English Leather.

The value of *family branding strategies* (often termed *umbrella* or *brand expansion* strategies) is derived from stimulus generalization. A family branding policy is when the same brand name, for example, General Electric or Campbell's is given to every product in the line. The reasons for doing so are obvious—the consumer can generalize from the successful use of one product in the line to others that have not yet been tried. In the case of Campbell's, the products are very similar (soups) and so the transfer is particularly easy. For General Electric, however, the differences between products are significantly larger (a jet engine versus a refrigerator), yet learning about quality and dependability can be transferred easily.

However, stimulus generalization does not occur just because two products have the same brand name. There must be a connection between the products. Gillette was unsuccessful with a facial moisturizer line under the *Silkience* brand name. Silkience's excellent reputation in haircare simply did not translate to face creams. Bacardi is particularly conservative in using its name for fear of adversely affecting sales of Bacardi rum, the world's largest-selling distilled spirit. However, they successfully launched Bacardi Tropical Fruit Mixers (frozen nonalcoholic drinks) based on the following rationale:

> Our research found that tropical drinks—piña coladas and frozen daiquiris—are highly associated with Bacardi rum. We already have credibility in that area, which made this new venture right. Bacardi has a lot of equity in its name; it means quality in areas related to rum. . . . But we feel the name wouldn't have that equity in another area. Bacardi wine, for example, wouldn't mean a lot because rum has nothing to do with wine.[34]

This ability to learn via generalization of the brand name means that the marketer can concentrate on a single stimulus in promotion campaigns instead of having to develop separate and expensive individual brand strategies. Black & Decker, Procter & Gamble, Lever Brothers, Minnetonka, and Colgate-Palmolive have recently had major new product launches using this approach. Nabisco Brands is moving to establish the Nabisco name on its Oreo cookies, Planters nuts, Life Savers candy, Fleichmann's margarine, and other products.

One must remember that if favorable brand attributes can be learned via generalization, so can unfavorable ones. Witness the case of Bon Vivant soups. The company had a line of soups, among which was a vichyssoise. Unfortunately, a number of food poisonings were traced to a shipment of Bon Vivant's vichyssoise. Naturally, the product was withdrawn from the market, but consumers

Exhibit 9–4 Yardley Leather Strategy Utilizes Stimulus Generalization

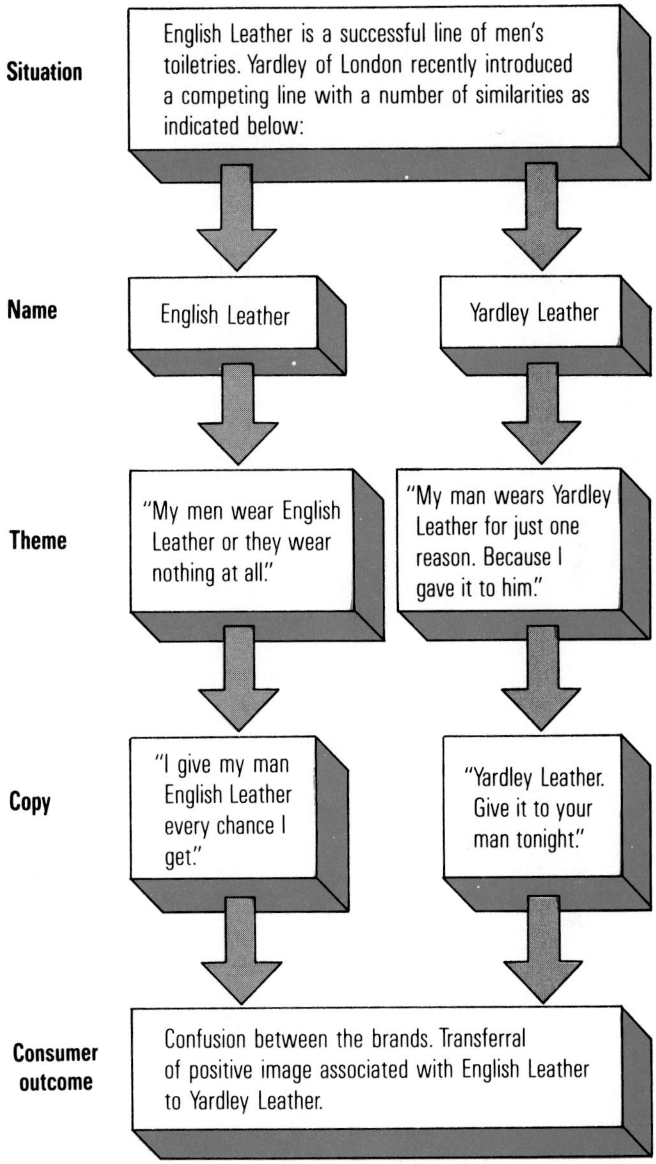

Situation
English Leather is a successful line of men's toiletries. Yardley of London recently introduced a competing line with a number of similarities as indicated below:
Name
English Leather
Yardley Leather
Theme
"My men wear English Leather or they wear nothing at all."
"My man wears Yardley Leather for just one reason. Because I gave it to him."
Copy
"I give my man English Leather every chance I get."
"Yardley Leather. Give it to your man tonight."
Consumer outcome
Confusion between the brands. Transferral of positive image associated with English Leather to Yardley Leather.

Source: "Men Note Similarities in Yardley Leather Ads," *Advertising Age*, January 21, 1980, p. 12.

also generalized to all of the other soups under the Bon Vivant brand, and sales for the entire line were drastically affected. As we saw earlier, quality problems in GE's appliance line caused sales problems for their jet engines because of stimulus generalization and a family brand policy.

Stimulus Discrimination

Stimulus discrimination refers to the process of learning to respond differently to somewhat similar stimuli. At some point, stimulus generalization becomes dysfunctional because less and less similar stimuli are still being grouped together. At this point consumers must begin to be able to differentiate among the stimuli. For example, the management of Bayer aspirin feels that consumers should not see their aspirin as being just like every other brand. In order to develop a brand-loyal market for Bayer, consumers had to be taught to differentiate among all the similar brands.

Marketers have a number of ways to do this, not the least obvious of which is advertising that specifically points out brand differences, real or symbolic. The product itself is frequently altered in shape or design to help increase product differentiation. For example, to serve different consumer needs in the detergent market, Procter & Gamble has created several brands of detergent that include Tide, Cheer, Bold, Gain, Dash, Oxydol, Duz, Bonus, Salvo, and Era. Each brand is distinctive in brand name, packaging, and primary consumer benefit in order to achieve stimulus discrimination.

Note that not all marketing managers want to bring stimulus discrimination about for their brands. There is a very definite "me-too" strategy that many companies follow. These marketers are willing to accept the market share (a sometimes significant one) gained by simply being as similar to the leading brand as possible. The costs of bringing about stimulus or brand differentiation are high and the me-too brands can sometimes be profitable by obtaining a smaller, but less expensive, market share.

Response Environment

As discussed in the section on long-term memory, it appears that consumers generally have learned more information than they can readily retrieve. That is, we frequently have relevant information stored in memory that we cannot access when needed. One factor that influences our ability to retrieve stored information is the strength of the original learning. The stronger the original learning, the more likely relevant information will be retrieved when required.

The second factor affecting retrieval is the similarity of the retrieval environment to the original learning environment.[35] Thus, the more the retrieval situation offers cues similar to the cues present during learning, the more likely effective retrieval is to occur. (This suggests that exam performance might be enhanced by studying at a desk in a quiet environment rather than on a sofa with music playing.) While we still have much to learn about this, it appears that marketers should do one of two things: (1) configure the learning environment to resemble the most likely retrieval environment, or (2) configure the retrieval environment to resemble the original learning environment.

Matching the retrieval and learning environments requires an understanding of when and where consumers make brand or store decisions. Decisions on brand or store made at home do not have the same set of cues that are available at a retail outlet or in a shopping mall. Suppose a firm teaches consumers to have a positive feeling toward its brand of gum by consistently pairing the pronouncement of its brand name with a very pleasant, fun scene in a television ad (classical conditioning). However, it does not show the package, and the name is presented visually only briefly. In the purchase situation, the consumer faces a shelf with many packages but no auditory presentation of brand name. Thus, the retrieval environment is not conducive to triggering the learned response.

Quaker Oats applied this concept in a very direct manner. It developed and ran an extremely popular advertising campaign for Life cereal. As the popularity of the campaign became evident, Quaker placed a photo of a scene from the commercial on the front of the Life cereal package. This enhanced the ability of consumers to recall both affect and information from the commercial and was very successful.[36]

Conclusions on Consumer Learning

Thus far, we have examined specific theories and approaches to learning. Knowledge of learning theories can be used to structure communications that will assist consumers in learning relevant facts, behaviors, and feelings about our products. The sum of what a group of consumers has learned about a brand or store relative to competing brands or stores is known as *product position*. A marketer's overall objective is to have consumers learn favorable positions for their brands.

PRODUCT POSITIONING STRATEGY

A *product position* refers to the schematic memory of a brand in relation to competing brands, products, or stores.[37] *Brand image*, a closely related concept, is the schematic memory of a brand without reference to competing brands. However, the terms are often used interchangeably.

Anheuser-Busch, Inc., has developed unique product positions for its Michelob, Budweiser, and Busch beers. Each beer is differentiated physically on the basis of price and taste. Busch ad copy stresses quality and price while using baseball as a theme. Budweiser ad copy stresses fun, fellowship, and quality while using football and hockey themes. Michelob ad copy emphasizes superior quality and uses country club sports.

The importance of a proper position is readily apparent in the following quote attributed to a former Schlitz marketing executive:

> Beer is not a drink; it's a symbol. When a guy goes into a bar and orders a Bud or a Miller, he's making a statement about himself. Schlitz's image is so bad that, regardless of taste, the consumer doesn't want to be seen drinking that product.[38]

The stimuli that marketing managers employ to influence a product's interpretation and thus its position can be quite subtle.[39] Sunkist Growers has a pectin-based (a carbohydrate obtained from orange and lemon peels) candy available in various fruit flavors. It contains no preservatives and less sugar than most fruit jelly candies. Until recently the candy was available in restaurants, hospitals, and, to a limited extent, supermarket candy sections.

Now, Sunkist Growers is actively promoting the candy, called Sunkist Fruit Gems, as a "healthful, natural" snack. The company hopes to attract adults as well as children. As part of the overall marketing strategy, Sunkist is attempting to distribute the candy through the produce departments of supermarkets.[40] Notice how the distribution plan supports the desired product position or image. A consumer receiving a message that this is a healthful, natural product may agree when the product is found near other healthful, natural products such as apples and oranges.

Exhibit 9–5 provides a description of an attempt to reposition an existing brand. Such endeavors are a major aspect of marketing.[41] The results of successful positioning can be seen in Calvin Klein jeans, Polo shirts, and Zales' stores.[42] Failures such as Seagram's Von Konig (an imported liquor) are less visible, as they tend to have short lives.[43]

Marketing managers frequently fail to achieve the type of product image or position they desire because they fail to anticipate or test for consumer reactions. Toro's initial light-weight snow thrower was not successful. Why? It was named the Snowpup, and consumers interpreted this to mean that it was a toy or lacked sufficient power. Sales success came only after a more macho, power-based name was utilized—first Snowmaster and later Toro.[44]

Perceptual mapping offers marketing managers a useful technique for measuring and developing a product's position.[45] Perceptual mapping takes consumers' perceptions of how similar various brands or products are to each other and relates these perceptions to product attributes. Figure 9–10 is a perceptual map for several automobile manufacturers. The marketing implications of the positions held by Olds and Buick are serious. Not only are they viewed as being rather unexciting, they also appear to compete primarily with each other rather than with the products of other manufacturers.

Successful product positioning requires careful attention to all aspects of information processing. Consumers must be exposed to the firm's messages through appropriate media and outlets. They must attend to the message using either low- or high-involvement processes. The total message sent must be structured in a manner that will lead to the desired interpretation. Thus, all aspects of the marketing mix—price, product design and quality, outlets, and advertising messages—must be consistent. Sufficient repetitions, rewards, and so forth must be offered to ensure that the desired interpretation (product position) is learned.

Exhibit 9–5

Repositioning a Consumer Product: B&B

Courtesy Benedictine Marketing Services, Inc.

B&B is a liqueur initially developed by Benedictine monks. It has historically stressed its exotic origin, the fact that it is imported from France, and its prestige. The firm's president described the advertising theme during this period as "once you get successful, come up and try it."

Sales had not increased for five years. A research study found that B&B had a low level of awareness, particularly among younger consumers. While the liqueur market is split evenly between males and females, the typical B&B consumer is a male over 40. The research also showed that there is not a strict B&B drinker or a Remy drinker or Amaretto drinker. Cordials offer a range of flavors to choose with different occasions and moods. The brand is chosen for a particular moment.

Based on the research, B&B is being repositioned as a drink appropriate for younger males and females. It is designed to show the product as appropriate for a range of special moments. All of the ads will show a closeup shot of two people using the product in a special moment. All the ads will contain a mnemonic headline such as "B&Beloved," "B&Begin," or "B&Bewitch." A copy of the first ad in the repositioning campaign is shown above.

Figure 9–10
Perceptual Map for Automobiles

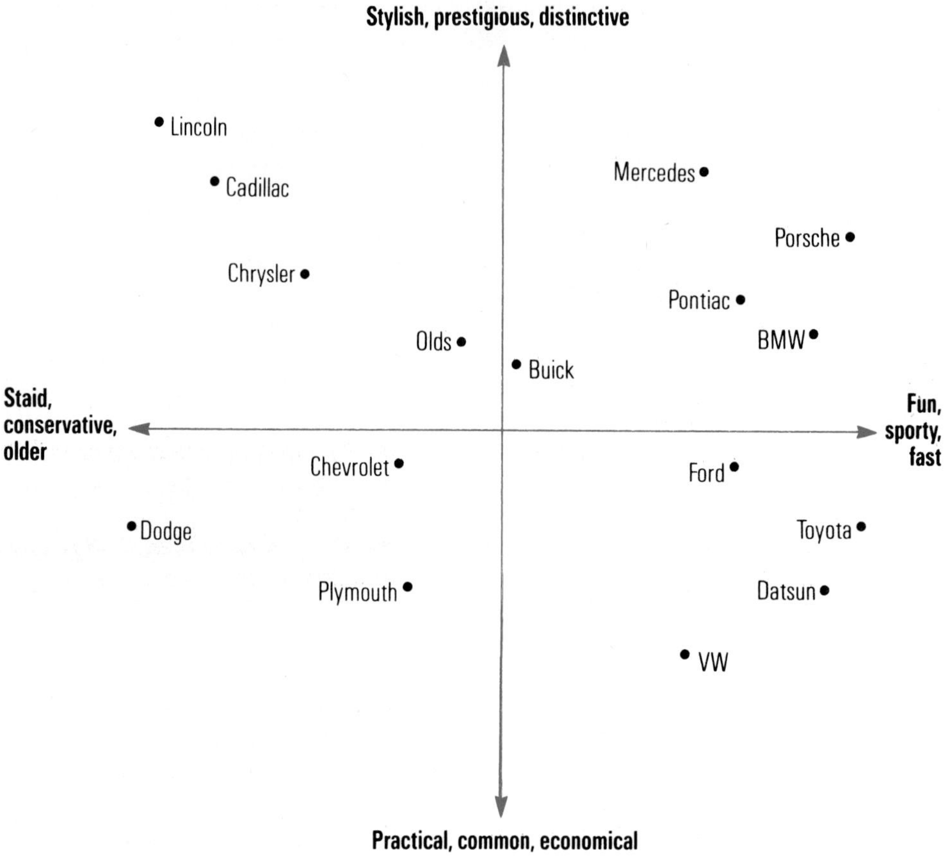

Finally, product positions are developed and evolve over time. Therefore, the messages consumers receive from the firm must be consistent, or change in a deliberate manner to reflect a desired change in a brand's position.[46] Unfortunately, many firms have a tendency to alter promotional themes, prices, and other aspects of the marketing mix in response to short-run sales objectives and competitor tactics. One survey of large firms found that 55 percent developed advertising campaigns focusing solely on achieving short-term results, 34 percent concentrated on long-term results, and 11 percent sought a balance.[47] Such overemphasis on immediate sales results can easily detract from a firm's ability to develop or maintain a sound product position.

SUMMARY

Consumers must learn almost everything related to being a consumer—product existence, performance, availability, values, preference, and so forth. Marketing managers, therefore, are very interested in the nature of consumer learning.

After perception has occurred, the meaningful information is stored. Most commonly, information goes directly into *short-term memory* for problem solving or elaboration where two basic activities occur—maintenance rehearsal and elaborative activities. *Maintenance rehearsal* is the continual repetition of a piece of information in order to hold it in current memory. *Elaborative activities* are the use of stored experiences, values, attitudes, and feelings to interpret and evaluate information in current memory.

Long-term memory is information from previous information processing that has been stored for future use. It undergoes continual restructuring as new information is acquired. Information is retrieved from retention for problem solving, and the success of the retrieval process depends on how well the material was learned and the match between the retrieval and learning environment.

Learning is defined as any change in the content or organization of long-term memory. Thus, it is an outcome of information processing.

Two basic types of learning, *conditioning* and *cognition,* are used by consumers. There are two forms of conditioned learning—classical and operant. *Classical conditioning* refers to the process of using an existing relationship between a stimulus and response to bring about the learning of the same response to a different stimulus.

Reinforcement plays a much larger role in *operant conditioning* than it does in classical conditioning. No automatic stimulus-response relationship is involved, so the subject must first be induced to engage in the desired behavior and then this behavior must be reinforced.

The *cognitive* approach to learning encompasses the mental activities of humans as they work to solve problems, cope with complex situations, or function effectively in their environment. It includes *iconic rote learning* (forming associations between unconditioned stimuli without rewards), *vicarious/modeling learning* (learning by observing others), and *reasoning*.

Low-involvement learning occurs when an individual is paying only limited or indirect attention to an advertisement or other message. Low-involvement learning tends to be limited due to a lack of elaborative activities. Nonetheless, it explains a substantial amount of consumer learning. While all of the learning theories may operate in a low-involvement situation, classical conditioning, iconic rote learning, and modeling are most common.

The strength of learning depends on four basic factors: importance, reinforcement, repetition, and imagery. *Importance* refers to the value that the consumer places on the information to be learned—the greater the importance, the greater the learning. *Reinforcement* is anything that increases the likelihood that a response will be repeated in the future—the greater the reinforcement, the greater the learning. *Repetition* or practice refers to the number of times that we are exposed to the information or that we practice a behavior. Repetition increases the strength and speed of learning. *Imagery* is the degree to which concepts evoke well-defined mental images. High-image concepts are easier to learn.

Stimulus generalization is one way of transferring learning by generalizing from one stimulus situation to other, similar ones. Family branding is an excellent example of the use of stimulus generalization by marketers. *Stimulus discrimination* refers to the opposite process of learning to respond differently to somewhat similar stimuli. Marketers interested in building brand-loyal customer segments must bring about the ability to discriminate between similar brands.

Extinction, or forgetting, is also of interest to marketing managers. Extinction is directly related to the strength of original learning, modified by continued repetition. *Corrective advertising* is designed to increase the rate of extinction for incorrect material that consumers have learned.

Product positioning, a brand's position in a consumer's schematic memory in relation to competing brands, is a major focus of marketing activity. It is the final outcome of the consumer's information processing activities for a product category.

REVIEW QUESTIONS

1. What is *learning*?
2. What is *memory*?
3. Define *short-term memory* and *long-term memory*.
4. What is *schematic memory*?
5. How does a *schema* differ from a *script*?
6. What is *echoic memory*?
7. What is an *evoked set*?
8. What is *maintenance rehearsal*?
9. What is meant by *elaborative activities*?
10. What is meant by *imagery* in working memory?
11. Describe *low-involvement learning*. How does it differ from *high-involvement learning*?
12. What do we mean by *cognitive learning,* and how does it differ from the *conditioning theory* approach to learning?
13. Distinguish between learning via classical conditioning and that which occurs via operant conditioning.
14. What is *iconic rote learning*? How does it differ from classical conditioning? Operant conditioning?
15. Define *modeling*.
16. What is meant by *learning by reasoning?*
17. What factors affect the strength of learning?
18. What is *imagery*?
19. What is meant by *stimulus generation*? When is it used by marketers?

20. Define *stimulus discrimination*. Why is it important?
21. Explain *extinction* and tell why marketing managers are interested in it.
22. What is *corrective advertising*? Is it effective?
23. Why is it useful to match the retrieval and learning environments?
24. What is *product positioning strategy*? What is it based on?

DISCUSSION QUESTIONS

1. How would you ensure that consumers learn a favorable product position for:
   a. BIC Sailboards?
   b. Soft Sense Skin Lotion with Vitamin E?
   c. M & F Department Stores?
   d. Orelda Frozen French Fried Potatoes?
2. Is low-involvement learning really widespread? Which products are most affected by low-involvement learning?
3. Almex and Company introduced a new coffee-flavored liqueur in direct competition with Hiram Walker's tremendously successful Kahlua brand. Almex named its new entry Kamora and packaged it in a bottle similar to that of Kahlua, using a pre-Columbian label design. The ad copy for Kamora reads: "If you like coffee—you'll love Kamora." Explain Almex's marketing strategy in terms of learning theory.
4. The FTC has required manufacturers to produce corrective advertisements in cases in which the manufacturer deceived the public with a particular claim or implied claim that was not true. The purpose of the corrective ad is to properly inform the public so they are not deceived in their perceptions of a particular brand. When this is accomplished, the firm may remove the corrective ad. This is based on the assumption that new learning has occurred. Some feel that after the corrective ad is removed, it is only a matter of time before consumer perceptions of the falsely advertised product will return to their prior level as shown below. Do you agree? Why?

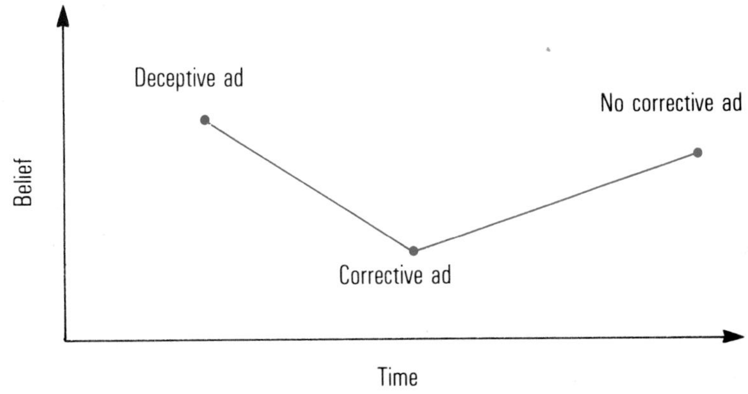

5. Discuss stimulus generalization and discrimination with respect to a firm's branding strategy. Identify five brand names that encourage learning by utilizing stimulus generalization, and five brand names that avoid this type of learning. Why would the marketers of these respective products either encourage or discourage stimulus generalization?
6. What information do you think the average student on your campus has memory about: (*a*) V8 juice, (*b*) Quaker rice cakes, (*c*) H&R Block, (*d*) Reebok shoes, and (*e*) the Salvation Army? List the information by the four information components. Are there any differences between males and females?
7. What product position do you think the brands listed in question 6 occupy among students on your campus? Do you think these product positions differ significantly among different target markets such as high school students, young blue-collar workers, or ethnic groups?
8. What is the relationship between imagery and schema?
9. Why do a majority of large advertisers design campaigns based exclusively on short-term goals?
10. Describe the two approaches to positioning shown in Exhibit 9–5. When is each approach most likely to be effective?

PROJECT QUESTIONS

1. Fulfill the requirements of Discussion Question 6 by interviewing five male and five female students.
2. Answer Discussion Question 7 based on a sample of students. How, if at all, do you think your results would change if you interviewed: (*a*) the students' parents and (*b*) individuals the same age who are not attending college?
3. Pick a consumer convenience product, perhaps a personal care product such as a deodorant or mouthwash, and create advertising copy stressing: (*a*) a positive reinforcement, (*b*) a negative reinforcement, and (*c*) a punishment.
4. Pick a small sample of friends and interview them to find out which type of reinforcement appeal (from question 3 above) would be most effective. To do this, you might present each friend with one of the appeals and then ask him/her to respond to the following questions:

   What is your overall reaction to this advertisement?

   Unfavorable ___:___:___:___:___:___:___ Favorable

   How likely would you be to try this product based on this advertising appeal?

   Very likely ___:___:___:___:___:___:___ Very unlikely
5. Identify three advertisements, one based on cognitive learning, another based on operant conditioning, and the third based on classical conditioning. Discuss the nature of each advertisement and how it utilizes a certain type of learning.
6. Identify three advertisements which you believe are based on low-involvement learning and three which are based on high-involvement learning. Justify your selection.

7. Identify an advertisement which you believe to be misleading. Develop a corrective advertising remedy.
8. Select a product and develop an advertisement based on low-involvement learning and one based on high-involvement learning. When should each be used (be specific)?
9. Measure 10 students' schema for the brands listed below. Also measure the imagery they have of the brands. How are they different? What explains this?
   a. Michelob.
   b. Coca-Cola.
   c. Quaker Oats.
   d. Del Monte.
   e. IRS.
   f. Democrats.
   g. Honda.
   h. Pontiac.

REFERENCES

[1] "PR Campaign Seeks to Improve Image of Sludge," *Marketing News,* October 23, 1987, p. 6.

[2] A. A. Mitchell, "Cognitive Processes Initiated by Exposure to Advertising," in *Information Processing Research in Advertising,* ed. R. Harris (Lawrence Erlbaum Associates, 1983), pp. 13–42.

[3] See J. R. Bettman, "Memory Factors in Consumer Choice: A Review," *Journal of Marketing,* Spring 1979, pp. 37–53.

[4] M. D. Posner, *Cognition: An Introduction* (Glenview, Ill.: Scott, Foresman, 1977), p. 16.

[5] R. A. Smith, M. J. Houston, and T. L. Childers, "The Effects of Schematic Memory on Imaginal Information Processing," *Psychology & Marketing,* Spring 1985, pp. 13–29.

[6] A. A. Mitchell, "An Information Processing View of Consumer Behavior," in *Research Frontiers in Marketing: Dialogues and Directions,* ed. S. C. Jain (Chicago: American Marketing Association, 1978), p. 189.

[7] Ibid., pp. 188–97.

[8] D. J. MacInnis and L. L. Price, "The Role of Imagery in Information Processing," *Journal of Consumer Research,* March 1987, pp. 473–91.

[9] See J. L. Zaichkowsky, "Measuring the Involvement Construct," *Journal of Consumer Research,* December 1985, pp. 341–52, and J. L. Zaichkowsky, "Conceptualizing Involvement," *Journal of Advertising,* 2, 1986, pp. 4–14.

[10] W. R. Nord and J. P. Peter, "A Behavior Modification Perspective on Marketing." *Journal of Marketing,* Spring 1980, pp. 36–47.

[11] See F. K. McSweeny and C. Bierley, "Recent Developments in Classical Conditioning," *Journal of Consumer Research,* September 1984, pp. 619–31; C. T. Allen and T. J. Madden, "A Closer Look at Classical Conditioning," and C. Bierley, F. K. McSweeney, and R. Vannieuwkerk, "Classical Conditioning of Preferences for Stimuli," both in *Journal of Consumer Research,* December 1985, pp. 301–15 and pp. 316–23; L. R. Kahle, S. E. Beatty, and P. Kennedy, "Comment on Classically Conditioning Human Consumers," and G. J. Gorn, W. J. Jacobs, and M. J. Mana,

"Observations on Awareness and Conditioning," both in *Advances in Consumer Research XIV* (Provo, Utah: Association for Consumer Research, 1987), pp. 441–14 and 415–16; and E. W. Stuart, T. A. Shimp, and R. W. Engle, "Classical Conditioning of Consumer Attitudes," *Journal of Consumer Research,* December 1987, pp. 334–49.

[12] See Nord and Peter, "A Behavior Modification."

[13] For details, see M. L. Rothschild and W. C. Gaidis, "Behavioral Learning Theory: Its Relevance to Marketing and Promotions," *Journal of Marketing,* Spring 1981, pp. 70–78; and J. P. Peter and W. R. Nord, "A Clarification and Extension of Operant Conditioning Principles in Marketing," *Journal of Marketing,* Summer 1982, pp. 102–7.

[14] B. J. Bergiel and C. Trosclair, "Instrumental Learning," *Journal of Consumer Marketing,* Fall 1985, pp. 23–28. See also W. Gaidis and J. Cross, "Behavior Modification as a Framework for Sales Promotion Management," *Journal of Consumer Marketing,* Spring 1987, pp. 65–74.

[15] See J. R. Rossiter and L. Percy, "Visual Communication in Advertising," in *Information Processing Research in Advertising,* ed. Harris, pp. 83–126.

[16] See Nord and Peter, "A Behavioral Modification," pp. 40–41.

[17] See R. Weijo and L. Lawton, "Message Repetition, Experience, and Motivation," *Psychology & Marketing,* Fall 1986, pp. 165–79.

[18] See Rothschild and Gaidis, "Behavioral Learning Theory," and B. C. Deslauriers and P. B. Everett, "The Effects of Intermittent and Continuous Token Reinforcement on Bus Ridership," *Journal of Applied Psychology,* August 1977, pp. 369–75.

[19] S. Widrick and E. Fram, "Identifying Negative Products," *Journal of Consumer Marketing,* no. 2, 1983, pp. 59–66.

[20] V. Mahajan and E. Muller, "Advertising Pulsing Policies for Generating Awareness for New Products," *Marketing Science,* Spring 1986, pp. 89–111.

[21] P. H. Chook, "A Continuing Study of Magazine Environment, Frequency, and Advertising Performance," *Journal of Advertising Research,* August/September 1985, pp. 23–33.

[22] J. O. Eastlack, Jr., "How to Get More Bang from Your Television Bucks," *Journal of Consumer Marketing,* Third Quarter 1984, pp. 25–34. Conflicting results are in G. F. Belch, "The Effects of Television Commercial Repetition on Cognitive Response and Message Acceptance," *Journal of Consumer Research,* June 1982, pp. 56–65.

[23] R. Hartley, *Marketing Mistakes* (Grid, 1976), p. 114.

[24] See J. N. Axelrod, "Advertising Wearout," *Journal of Advertising Research,* October 1980, pp. 13–20; and A. J. Rethans, J. L. Swasy, and L. J. Marks, "Effects of Television Commercial Repetition, Receiver Knowledge, and Commercial Length," *Journal of Marketing Research,* February 1986, pp. 50–61.

[25] G. M. Zinkhan and C. R. Martin, Jr., "New Brand Names and Inferential Beliefs," *Journal of Business Research,* April 1987, pp. 157–72.

[26] K. R. Robertson, "Recall and Recognition Effects of Brand Name Imagery," *Psychology & Marketing,* Spring 1987, pp. 3–15.

[27] T. L. Childers and M. J. Houston, "Conditions for a Picture-Superiority Effect on Consumer Memory," *Journal of Consumer Research,* September 1984, pp. 643–54; J. Kisielus and B. Sternthal, "Examining the Vividness Controversy," *Journal of*

Consumer Research, March 1986, pp. 418–31; M. P. Gardner and M. J. Houston, "The Effects of Verbal and Visual Components of Retail Communications," *Journal of Retailing,* Spring 1986, pp. 64–78; T. L. Childers, S. E. Heckler, and M. J. Houston, "Memory for the Visual and Verbal Components of Print Advertisements," *Psychology & Marketing,* Fall 1986, pp. 137–50; and MacInnis and Price, "The Role of Imagery."

[28] T. Clark, "Echoic Memory Explored and Applied," *Journal of Consumer Marketing,* Winter 1987, pp. 39–46.

[29] "L&M Lights Up Again," *Marketing & Media Decisions,* February 1984, p. 69.

[30] For an example of how to combat an unfavorable rumor, see A. M Tybout, B. J. Calder, and B. Sternthal, "Using Information Processing Theory to Design Marketing Strategies," *Journal of Marketing Research,* February 1981, pp. 73–79.

[31] "U.S. Car Makers Weak on Image," *Advertising Age,* September 14, 1987, p. 108.

[32] R. J. Semenik, "Corrective Advertisement: An Experimental Evaluation of Alternative Television Messages," *Journal of Advertising,* Summer 1980, pp. 21–31; J. Jacoby, M. C. Nelson, and D. W. Hayer, "Corrective Advertising and Affirmative Disclosure Statements," *Journal of Marketing,* Winter 1982, pp. 61–72; G. M. Armstrong, G. R. Franke, and F. A. Russ, "The Effects of Corrective Advertising on Company Image," *Journal of Advertising,* Fourth Quarter 1982, pp. 39–47; G. M. Armstrong, M. N. Gurol, and F. A. Russ, "A Longitudinal Evaluation of the Listerine Corrective Advertising Campaign"; M. B. Mazis, D. L. McNeill, and K. L. Bernhardt, "Day-After Recall of Listerine Corrective Commercials"; and T. C. Kinnear, J. R. Taylor, and O. Gur-Arie, "Affirmative Disclosure," all in *Journal of Public Policy & Marketing,* vol. 2, 1983, pp. 16–28, 29–37, and 38–45; and K. L. Bernhardt, T. C. Kinnear, and M. B. Mazis, "A Field Study of Corrective Advertising Effectiveness," *Journal of Public Policy and Marketing,* vol. 5, 1986, pp. 146–62.

[33] "General Electric: The Financial Wizard's Switch Back to Technology," Business Week, March 16, 1981, p. 113.

[34] L. Freeman and P. Winters, "Franchise Players," *Advertising Age,* August 18, 1986, pp. 3, 61.

[35] K. L. Keller, "Memory Factors in Advertising," *Journal of Consumer Research,* December 1987, pp. 316–33.

[36] Ibid., pp. 316–17; see also C. J. Cobb and W. D. Hoyer, "The Influence of Advertising at the Moment of Brand Choice," *Journal of Advertising,* no. 4, 1985, pp. 5–12.

[37] See D. A. Aaker and J. G. Shansby, "Positioning Your Product," *Business Horizons,* May/June 1982, pp. 56–62; T. J. Reynolds and J. Gutman, "Advertising As Image Management," *Journal of Advertising Research,* February/March 1984, pp. 27–38; and C. W. Park, B. J. Jaworski, and D. J. MacInnis, "Strategic Brand Concept-Image Management," *Journal of Marketing,* October 1986, pp. 135–45.

[38] J. Neher, "Schlitz to Taste-Test," *Advertising Age,* December 8, 1980, p. 90.

[39] D. Mazursky and J. Jacoby, "Exploring the Development of Store Images," *Journal of Retailing,* Summer 1986, pp. 145–65.

[40] J. Pendleton, "Sunkist Launching Candy via Store Produce Sections," *Advertising Age,* December 4, 1978, p. 17.

[41] See J. Alter, "Johnson Adds Lotion," *Advertising Age,* July 21, 1981, p. 2; "Mission to Position Tortillas against Bread," *Advertising Age,* July 21, 1980, p. 3;

"Visa Shifts Positioning," *Advertising Age,* October 13, 1980, p. 3; and J. Neiman, "Water Pik to Reposition from Gift Theme," *Advertising Age,* August 10, 1981, p. 31.

[42] R. H. Bloom, "Product Redefinition Begins with Consumer," *Advertising Age,* October 26, 1981, p. 51.

[43] "Seagram Von Konig Test Dies," *Advertising Age,* September 28, 1981, p. 41.

[44] J. Neher, "Toro Cutting a Wide Swath in Outdoor Appliance Marketing," *Advertising Age,* February 25, 1978, p. 21.

[45] See J. W. Keon, "Product Positioning," *Journal of Marketing Research,* November 1983, pp. 380–92; R. Friedmann, "Psychological Meaning of Products," *Psychology & Marketing,* Spring 1986, pp. 1–15; W. R. Dillon, T. Dormzal, and T. J. Madden, "Evaluating Alternative Product Positioning Strategies," *Journal of Advertising Research,* August/September 1986, pp. 29–35; and W. DeSarbo and V. R. Rao, "A Constrained Unfolding Methodology for Product Positioning," *Marketing Science,* Winter 1986, pp. 1–19.

[46] See Park, Jaworski, and MacInnis, "Strategic Brand."

[47] L. Freeman, "Short-term Focus Hurts Reputation of Brands," *Advertising Age,* December 14, 1987, p. 12.

CHAPTER

10 Motivation, Personality, and Emotion

One of the fastest selling new products today is a "food" product that has no calories, additives, or artificial coloring. In addition, it is essential to everyone's diet. This miracle product is water.

Water is virtually cost free from municipal agencies, yet millions of consumers now pay 1,000 times the price of municipal water to purchase bottled water. While heavily advertised brands such as Perrier are well known, bulk water, delivered to homes and offices in five-gallon containers, makes up half the market.

Why do consumers pay to purchase a virtually free item? There appear to be three major purchase motives. Health concerns focusing on nutrition and fitness motivate some users. These individuals want natural, untreated, "pure" water. Safety motivates other purchases. Many consumers are concerned with ground water contamination and reports of deteriorating water quality levels. The third motivating factor is "snob appeal" or status. Ordering or serving Perrier is more chic and higher status than plain water. The strategy implications of these differing motivations are shown on the facing page.

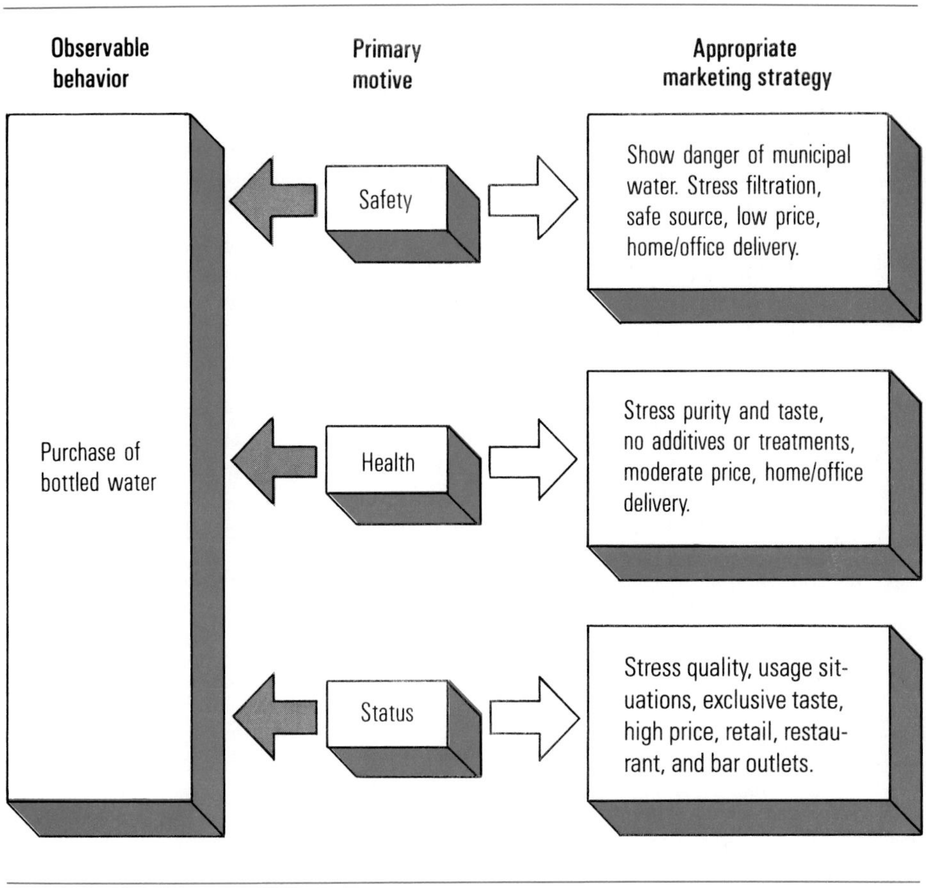
Observable behavior
Primary motive
Appropriate marketing strategy
Purchase of bottled water
Safety
Show danger of municipal water. Stress filtration, safe source, low price, home/office delivery.
Health
Stress purity and taste, no additives or treatments, moderate price, home/office delivery.
Status
Stress quality, usage situations, exclusive taste, high price, retail, restaurant, and bar outlets.

As this example indicates, a variety of motives may underlie the consumption of even a basic product like water. This chapter focuses on motivation and two closely related concepts: personality and emotion.

Consumer motivation is the energizing force that activates behavior and provides purpose and direction to that behavior. Personality reflects the common responses (behaviors) that individuals make to a variety of recurring situations. Emotions are strong, relatively uncontrollable feelings that affect our behavior. The three concepts are closely interrelated and are frequently difficult to separate. For example, consumers who are self-confident (a personality characteristic) are more likely to have a need for assertion (a characteristic of motivation) and to seek situations that allow them to feel powerful (an emotional response).

THE NATURE OF MOTIVATION

Motivation is the reason for behavior. A *motive* is a construct representing an unobservable inner force that stimulates and compels a behavioral response and provides specific direction to that response.[1] Thus, like most constructs in consumer behavior, we cannot see a motive. We can only infer the existence of motives from the behavior of individuals.

To illustrate the nature of consumer motivation and goal-directed behavior, consider consumer motives in the purchase of clothing. At one level, many clothing purchases are partially motivated by a physiological need (for shelter) or a safety need (avoidance of arrest/harassment). In addition, consumers may be motivated to purchase clothing that expresses or symbolizes status because they have a strong need to express that aspect of their identity (or desired identity) to others. On the other hand, consumers with a strong need for affiliation may purchase a certain wardrobe in order to feel more comfortable in their relationships with people they want to be liked by.

While these motivations may be strong, they are still dependent on the situation. For example, a consumer with a high need for affiliation may not be guided by that motivation in a purchase of underwear if the purchase or use of this product is unlikely to be observed by others. Likewise, individuals who have a strong need for achievement demonstrate achievement-related behavior in situations they perceive as ego-involving or evaluative, but not in situations they perceive as nonevaluative. Therefore, we need to keep in mind that motives directing behavior in one situation may not exist or may be quite different from motives shaping behavior in another situation.

THEORIES OF MOTIVATION

There are numerous theories of motivation and many of them offer potentially useful insights for the marketing manager. This section describes two particularly useful approaches to understanding consumer motivation. The first approach, Maslow's motive hierarchy, is a macro theory designed to account for most human behavior in general terms. The second approach, based on McGuire's psychological motives, uses a fairly detailed set of motives to account for a limited range of consumer behavior.

Hierarchy of Needs

Maslow's hierarchy of needs approach is based on four premises:

1. All humans acquire a similar set of motives through genetic endowment and social interaction.
2. Some motives are more basic or critical than others.
3. The more basic motives must be satisfied to a minimum level before other motives are activated.
4. As soon as the basic motives are satisfied, more advanced motives come into play.[2]

Thus, Maslow proposes a motive hierarchy shared by all. Table 10–1 illustrates this hierarchy and briefly describes each level.

Table 10–1
Maslow's Motive Hierarchy

Basic

1. **Physiological:** Food, water, sleep, and, to a limited extent, sex, are physiological motives. Unless they are minimally satisfied, other motives are not activated.
2. **Safety:** Seeking physical safety and security, stability, familiar surroundings, and so forth are manifestations of safety needs. They are aroused after physiological motives are minimally satisfied, and before other motives.
3. **Belongingness:** Belongingness motives are reflected in a desire for love, friendship, affiliation, and group acceptance.
4. **Esteem:** Desires for status, superiority, self-respect, and prestige are examples of esteem needs. These needs relate to the individual's feelings of usefulness and accomplishment.
5. **Self-actualization:** This involves the desire for self-fulfillment, to become all that one is capable of becoming.

Advanced

Exhibit 10–1 Marketing Strategies and Maslow's Motive Hierarchy

PHYSIOLOGICAL

Products: Limited in the United States. Generic foods, medicines, special drinks, and foods for athletes.

Specific themes:
- Campbell's Soup—"Soup is good food," with copy that stresses the nutritional benefits of soup.
- Raisins—"Thank goodness I found a snack kids will sit for. And mothers will stand for."
- Kellogg's All-Bran—"At last, some news about cancer you can live with," with copy that stresses the role of fiber in the diet.

SAFETY

Products: Smoke detectors, preventive medicines, insurance, social security, retirement investments, seat belts, burglar alarms, safes.

Specific themes:
- Sleep Safe—"We've designed a travel alarm that just might wake you in the middle of the night—because a fire is sending smoke into your room. You see, ours is a smoke alarm as well as an alarm clock."

(continued)

Exhibit 10–1 *(concluded)*

SAFETY *(continued)*

Specific themes:

- General Electric—"Taking a trip usually means leaving your troubles behind. But there are times when you just might need help or information on the road. And that's when you need HELP, the portable CB from GE."
- Alka-Seltzer—"Will it be there when you need it?"

BELONGINGNESS

Products: Personal grooming, foods, entertainment, clothing, and many others.

Specific themes:

- Atari—"Atari brings the computer age home," with a picture of a family using an Atari home computer.
- Oil of Olay—"When was the last time you and your husband met for lunch?"
- J.C. Penney—"Wherever teens gather, you'll hear it. It's the language of terrific fit and fashion. . . ."

ESTEEM

Products: Clothing, furniture, liquors, hobbies, stores, cars, and many others.

Specific themes:

- Sheaffer—"Your hand should look as contemporary as the rest of you."
- St. Pauli Girl—"People who know the difference in fine things know the difference between imported beer and St. Pauli Girl. . . ."
- Cadillac—". . . those long hours have paid off. In recognition, financial success, and in the way you reward yourself. Isn't it time you owned a Cadillac?"

SELF-ACTUALIZATION

Products: Education, hobbies, sports, some vacations, gourmet foods, museums.

Specific themes:

- U.S. Army—"Be all you can be."
- U.S. Home—"Make the rest of your life . . . the best of your life."
- Outward Bound School—"Challenges, adventure, growth."

Maslow's theory is a good guide to general behavior. It is not an ironclad rule, however. Numerous examples exist of individuals who sacrificed their lives for friends or ideas, or who gave up food and shelter to seek self-actualization. However, we do tend to regard such behavior as exceptional, which indicates the general validity of Maslow's overall approach. It is important to remember that any given consumption behavior can satisfy more than one need. Likewise, the same consumption behavior can satisfy different needs at different times. For example, the consumption of Perrier could satisfy both physiological and esteem needs, just physiological needs, or just esteem needs (or perhaps social needs or even safety needs). Exhibit 10–1 provides illustrations of marketing appeals associated with each of Maslow's motive levels.

Table 10–2
Psychological Motives Relevant to the Practice of Marketing

	Internal, nonsocial motives or needs
Consistency:	The need for internal equilibrium or balance.
Causation:	The need to determine who or what causes the things that happen to us.
Categorization:	The need to establish categories or mental partitions that provide frames of reference.
Cues:	The need for observable cues or symbols which enable us to infer what we feel and know.
Independence:	The need for feeling of self-governance or self-control.
Novelty:	The need for variety and difference.
	External, social motives or needs
Self-expression:	The need to express self-identity to others.
Ego-defense:	The need to defend or protect our identities or egos.
Assertion:	The need to increase self-esteem.
Reinforcement:	The need to act in such a way that others will reward us.
Affiliation:	The need to develop mutually satisfying relationships with others.
Modeling:	The need to base behaviors on those of others.

Source: Adapted from W. J. McGuire, "Psychological Motives and Communication Gratification," in *The Uses of Mass Communications: Current Perspectives on Gratifications Research*, eds. J. G. Blumler and C. Katz (Beverly Hills, Calif.: Sage Publications, 1974), pp. 167–96.

McGuire's Psychological Motives

McGuire has developed a motive classification system that is more specific than Maslow's.[3] McGuire's motives that are of most use to marketing are briefly described in Table 10–2. These motives are divided into two categories: internal, nonsocial motives, and external, social motives.

Internal, nonsocial motives reflect needs that individuals have with respect to themselves strictly as individuals, apart from others. External, social motives, on the other hand, deal with human needs directly related to interactions with others.

Internal, Nonsocial Motives

Need for Consistency. A basic desire is to have all facets or parts of oneself consistent with each other. These facets include attitudes, behaviors, opinions, self-images, views of others, and so forth. Following a major purchase, a consumer may have feelings of dissonance (feelings inconsistent with his or her purchase) and be motivated to seek additional information to reduce these feelings of inconsistency. This concern for "Did I make the right purchase?" must be reduced to establish a comfortable balance between feelings, attitudes, and behavior. The need for consistency, particularly with respect to purchase behavior, is discussed in depth in Chapter 18 in the section on postpurchase dissonance.

Need to Attribute Causation. This set of motives deals with our need to determine who or what causes the things that happen to us. Do we attribute the cause of a favorable or unfavorable outcome to ourselves or to some outside force?

The need to attribute cause has led to an area of research known as *attribution theory*. [4] This approach to understanding the reasons consumers assign particular meanings to the behaviors of others has been used primarily for analyzing consumer reactions to promotional messages (in terms of credibility).[5] Thus, when consumers attribute a sales motive to advice given by a salesperson or advertising message, they tend to discount the advice. This has lead some marketers to use highly believable spokespersons, such as O. J. Simpson, Robert Young, and Karl Malden in their campaigns (see Chapter 12 for a complete discussion).

Need to Categorize. We have a need to be able to categorize and organize information and experiences in some meaningful yet manageable way. So we establish categories or mental partitions which allow us to process large quantities of information. Prices are often categorized such that different prices connote different categories of goods. Automobiles over $15,000 and automobiles under $8,000 may elicit two different meanings because of information categorized on the basis of price level. Cowden Manufacturing prices its jeans at $9.86 at its 20 factory-outlet stores. They feel that "when people see $9.99 they say 'That's

$10.' " They believe that people group a different cluster of brands in the $10 and over category. They try to avoid this category by pricing at $9.86 which they feel produces a "less than $10" categorization.[6]

Need for Cues. These motives reflect needs for observable cues or symbols which enable us to infer what we feel and know. Impressions, feelings, and attitudes are subtly established by viewing our own behavior and that of others and drawing inferences as to what we feel and think. In many instances, clothing plays an important role in presenting the subtle meaning of a desired image and consumer lifestyle.[7] This is so critical at companies such as Anheuser-Busch that it uses a special clothing consulting firm to tailor clothes for its executives that are consistent with the firm's desired image.[8] Hart Schaffner and Marx capitalizes on this motive in their advertising in business magazines:

> **The right suit might not help you achieve success.**
> **But, the wrong suit could limit your chances.**

Need for Independence. An individual's need for independence or feeling of self-governance is derived from a need to establish a sense of self-worth and meaning by achieving self-actualization. Marketers have responded to this motive by providing products that suggest that you "do your own thing" and "be your own person." This, in essence, is the underlying theme of Camel's cigarette advertisements. Likewise, a recent Levis ad proclaims:

> **Don't mimic someone else's style.**
> **Set your own with**
> **Levi's Women's wear.**

The current MasterCard campaign, "Master the Possibilities," is based on this theme. Both the copy and the use of celebrity spokespersons known for their individualism reinforce the independence motive. As their CEO states: "Independence and the desire to exercise choice have always been an integral part of the American character."[9]

Need for Novelty. We often seek variety and difference simply out of a need for novelty. This may be a prime reason for brand switching and so-called impulse purchasing.[10] Underberg, a German after-dinner drink, has tried to capitalize on the novelty motive in its U.S. advertising with billboards that exclaim: "It cannot be explained. It must be experienced." Ronrico Rum's appeal to this motive is illustrated in Exhibit 10–2.

The need for novelty is curvilinear and changes over time. That is, individuals experiencing rapid change generally become satiated and desire stability while individuals in stable environments become "bored" and desire change. The travel industry segments the vacation market in part by promoting "adventure" vacations or "relaxing" vacations to groups, depending on their likely need for novelty.[11]

Exhibit 10–2 Appeal to Novelty Need

Courtesy General Wine & Spirits Co.

External, Social Motives

Need for Self-Expression. This motive is externally oriented and deals with the need to express one's identity to others. We feel the need to let others know by our actions (which include the purchase and display of goods) who we are and what we are. The purchase of many products, particularly clothing and automobiles, allows consumers to express an identity to others since these products have symbolic or expressive meanings. Thus, the purchase of the latest in ski wear may reflect much more than a desire to remain warm while skiing.

The following ad copy involves an appeal to individuals' desires to express their self-concept through the products they utilize:

Acme women.
They've got the world by the reins.

Confident. Self-assured. Dressed for success.
Complete with the boots to prove it.
Acme.
Western boots for every fashion.
Every ambition.
Acme.

Need for Ego-Defense. The need to defend our identities or egos is another important external, social motive. When our identity is threatened, we are motivated to protect our self-concept and utilize defensive behaviors and attitudes. Many products can provide ego-defense. A consumer who feels insecure may rely on well-known brands for all socially visible products to avoid any chance of making a socially incorrect purchase:

Every time you scratch your head
You could be telling someone
You have dandruff.
Now he knows . . . and you may never get the date.
'Cause even if you don't see flakes, or no one tells you,
that little itch could be telling a lot of your friends you
have some dandruff.

The Head & Shoulders ad partially reproduced above attempts to utilize our ego-defensive needs. It does not claim that dandruff is physically uncomfortable or unhealthy. Instead, it claims that others will know you have it and look down on you ("you may never get that date").

Need for Assertion. The need for assertion reflects a consumer's need for engaging in those types of activities that will bring about an increase in self-esteem, as well as esteem in the eyes of others.[12] Individuals with a strong need for assertion are more likely to complain when dissatisfied with a purchase. DeBeers exemplifies marketing strategies using this motive. In the ad, a male skier (possibly a racer) is shown wearing an attractive diamond ring. The copy is:

You've always had an edge on the competition.

The implication is that wearing a diamond will allow you to gain an advantage over others. Likewise, Jaguar ad copy claims:

> **Frankly created for the very few, this is the most luxurious Jaguar sedan you can buy. . . . Its pleasures are many and accessible only to a very few. Perhaps you can be one of them.**

Need for Reinforcement. We quite often are motivated to act in certain ways because we were rewarded for doing so. Products designed to be used in public situations (clothing, furniture, and artwork) are frequently sold on the basis of the amount and type of reinforcement that will be received. Keepsake diamonds uses this motive with an advertisement that states: *"Enter a room and you are immediately surrounded by friends sharing your excitement."* An ad claim by Dittos jeans also relies on this motive:

> **DITTOS. FOR BOY SCOUTING.**
> **You're liable to scout up**
> **a lot of attention in a new**
> **pair of Dittos jeans.**
> **If you wear them around**
> **a lot of boys, you're likely to**
> **become an instant troop leader.**

Need for Affiliation. Affiliation is the need to develop mutually helpful and satisfying relationships with others. The need here is to share and to be accepted by others. As we saw in Chapter 5, group membership is a critical part of most consumers' lives, and many consumer decisions are based on the need to maintain satisfying relationships with others. Marketers frequently use such affiliation-based themes as, "Your kids will love you for it," in advertisements. The following ad copy from Club Med exemplifies this approach:

> **And in addition to making all the activities accessible, Club Med does the same for people. Instead of the pomp and ceremony typical of resort hotels, the atmosphere of a Club Med village is comfortable and casual. An atmosphere in which meeting your fellow vacationers becomes effortless.**

Need for Modeling. The need for modeling reflects a tendency to base behavior on that of others. Modeling is a major means by which children learn to become consumers. The tendency to model explains some of the conformity that occurs within reference groups. Marketers utilize this motive by showing desirable types of individuals using their brands. For example, some Rolex ads devote most of their copy to a description of John Newcombe. They then state that he owns a Rolex. The following excerpt indicates how these ads encourage modeling:

> **He's leading the kind of life the rest of us would like to . . . affluent, active, and assured.**
>
> **And he wears the kind of watch that suits his lifestyle. The incomparable Rolex. Made for a man like Newk.**

MOTIVATION THEORY AND MARKETING STRATEGY

Consumers do not buy products. Instead they buy motive satisfaction or problem solutions. Thus, a consumer does not buy a perfume (or a chemical compound with certain odoriferous characteristics); she buys "atmosphere and hope and the feeling she is something special."[13] Thus, managers must discover the motives that their product and brand can satisfy and develop their marketing mix around these motives.

The preceding section provided a number of examples of firms appealing to specific consumer motives. We often find that multiple motives are involved in consumption behavior. In this section we examine: (1) how to discover which motives are likely to affect the purchase of a product category by a particular target market; (2) how to develop strategy based on the total array of motives that are operating; and (3) how to reduce conflict between motives.

Marketing Strategy Based on Multiple Motives

Suppose a marketing researcher interviewed you and asked why you wear designer jeans (or drink Heineken, or ski, or whatever). Odds are you would offer several reasons such as "They're in style," "My friends wear them," "I like the way they fit," and "They look good on me." However, there may be other reasons which you are reluctant to admit to or perhaps are not even aware of: "They show that I have money," "They make me sexually desirable," or "They show I'm still young." All or any combination of the above motives could influence the purchase of a pair of designer jeans.

The first group of motives described above were known to the consumer and admitted to the researcher. Motives that are known and freely admitted are called *manifest motives*. Any of the motives we have discussed can be manifest. However, motives that conform to a society's prevailing value system are more likely to be manifest than are those that are in conflict with such values.

The second group of motives described above were either unknown to the consumer or were such that the consumer was very reluctant to admit them. Such motives are *latent motives*. *Both* latent and manifest motives may influence a purchase or only manifest motives may be operating. Figure 10–1 illustrates how the two types of motives might influence a purchase.

Given that a variety of manifest and latent motives may be operative in a particular purchase such as that shown in Figure 10–1, the first task of the marketing manager is to determine the combination of motives influencing the target market. Manifest motives are relatively easy to determine. Direct questions (Why did you buy a Mercedes?) will generally produce reasonably accurate assessments of manifest motives.

Determining latent motives is substantially more complex. Sophisticated analytical techniques, such as multidimensional scaling, can sometimes provide insights into latent motives. "Motivation research" or projective techniques are designed to provide information on latent motives.[14] Projective techniques require consumers to make up a story or complete a sentence based on vague or incom-

Figure 10–1
Latent and Manifest Motives in a Purchase Situation

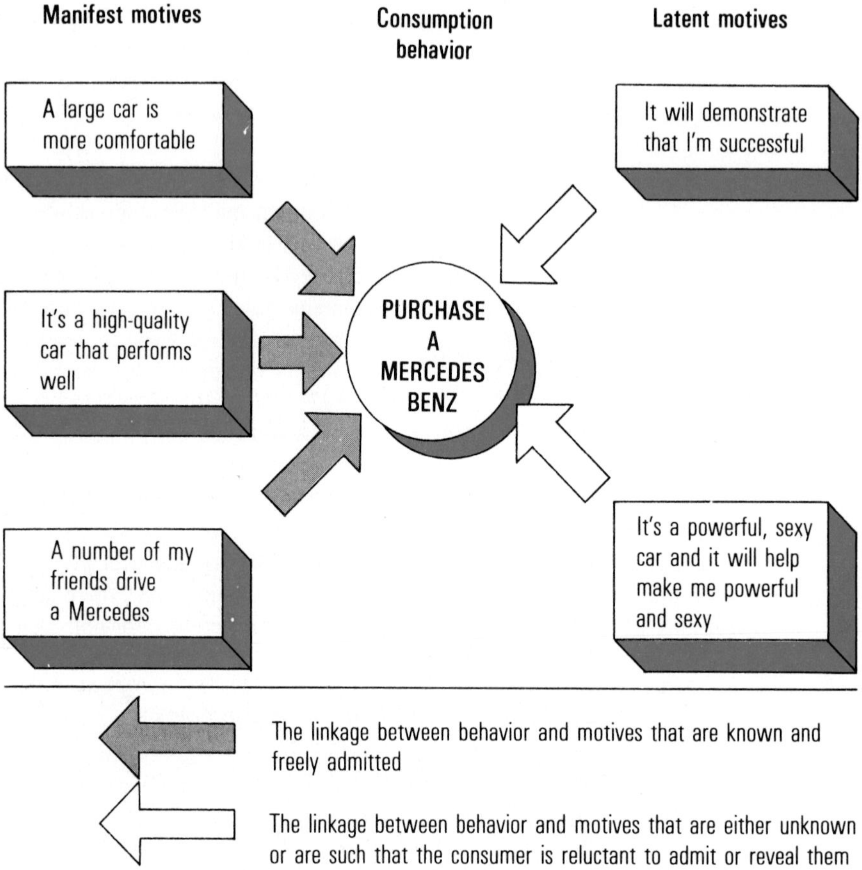
Manifest motives
Consumption behavior
Latent motives
A large car is more comfortable
It will demonstrate that I'm successful
It's a high-quality car that performs well
PURCHASE A MERCEDES BENZ
A number of my friends drive a Mercedes
It's a powerful, sexy car and it will help make me powerful and sexy
The linkage between behavior and motives that are known and freely admitted
The linkage between behavior and motives that are either unknown or are such that the consumer is reluctant to admit or reveal them

plete information. Presumably, such stories require consumers to project their own motives into the characters in the story. Exhibit 10–3 describes some of the more common projective techniques.

Once the marketing manager has isolated the combination(s) of motives influencing the target market, the next task is to design the marketing strategy around the appropriate set of motives. This task involves everything from product design to marketing communications. The nature of these decisions is most apparent in the communications area. Suppose that the motives shown in Figure 10–1 are an accurate reflection of a desired target market. What communications strategy should the manager use?

First, to the extent that more than one motive is important, the product must provide more than one benefit and the advertising for the product must communicate these multiple benefits. Communicating manifest benefits is relatively

Exhibit 10–3 Motivation Research Techniques

I. Association techniques:	
Word association	Consumers respond to a list of words with the first word that comes to mind.
Successive word association	Consumers give the series of words that come to mind after hearing each word on the list.
Analysis and use	Responses are analyzed to see if negative associations exist. When the time to respond (response latency) is also measured, the emotionality of the word can be estimated. These techniques tap semantic memory more than motives and are used for brand name and advertising copy tests.
II. Completion techniques:	
Sentence completion	Consumers complete a sentence such as "People who buy a Mercedes ______ ______."
Story completion	Consumers complete a partial story.
Analysis and use	Responses are analyzed to determine what themes are expressed. Content analysis—examining responses for themes and key concepts—is used.
III. Construction techniques:	
Cartoon techniques	Consumers fill in the words and/or thoughts of one of the characters in a cartoon drawing.
Third-person techniques	Consumers tell why "an average woman," "most doctors," or "people in general" purchase or use a certain product. Shopping lists (describe a person who would go shopping with this list) and lost wallets (describe a person with these items in their wallet) are also third-person techniques.
Picture response	Consumers tell a story about a person shown buying or using a product in a picture or line drawing.
Analysis and use	Same as for completion techniques.

Source: Adapted from D. S. Tull and D. I. Hawkins, *Marketing Research* (New York: Macmillan, 1987), pp. 318–25.

easy. For example, an advertisement for Cadillac states, "From the triple-sanded finish (once with water and twice with oil) to that superbly refined Cadillac ride, the quality comes standard on Cadillac." This is a direct appeal to a manifest motive for product quality. Direct appeals are generally effective for manifest motives since these are motives that consumers are aware of and will discuss.

Appeals to latent motives are more difficult to implement. On occasion, one can use direct appeals. For example, the Jaguar ad described in the earlier section on need for assertion is a very direct appeal to status, elitism, and snobbery. However, since latent motives often are less than completely socially desirable, indirect appeals frequently are used. The bulk of the copy of the Cadillac ad referred to above focused on the quality of the product. However, the artwork (about 60 percent of the ad) showed the car being driven by apparently wealthy individuals in front of a luxurious club. Thus, a dual appeal was used. The direct appeal in the copy focused on quality while the indirect appeal in the artwork focused on status.

While any given advertisement for a product may focus on only one or a few purchasing motives, the campaign needs to cover all the important purchase motives of the target market. In essence, the overall campaign attempts to position the product in the schematic memory of the target market in a manner that corresponds with the target market's manifest and latent motives for purchasing the product.

Marketing Strategies Based on Motivation Conflict

With the many motives we have and the many situations in which these motives are activated, there are frequent conflicts between motives. The resolution of a motivational conflict often affects consumption patterns. In many instances the marketer can analyze situations which are likely to result in a motivational conflict, provide a solution to the motivational conflict, and attract the patronage of those consumers facing the motivational conflict. There are three types of motivational conflict of importance to marketing managers: approach-approach conflict, approach-avoidance conflict, and avoidance-avoidance conflict.[15]

Approach-Approach Motivational Conflict. In an *approach-approach motivational conflict,* a consumer faces a choice between two attractive alternatives. The more equal this attraction, the greater the conflict. A consumer who recently received a large income tax refund (situational variable) may be torn between a vacation in Hawaii (perhaps powered by the novelty motive) and a compact disc player (perhaps powered by the need for self-expression). This conflict could be resolved by a timely advertisement designed to encourage one or the other action. Or, a price modification, such as "fly now, pay later," could result in a resolution whereby both alternatives are selected.

Aqua-Fresh is a product designed to reduce approach-approach conflict within an individual and within a family unit. Most individuals desire to have healthy teeth (a physiological or safety motive) and to have fresh breath (a belongingness motive). It is often assumed that parents are more concerned with the health of their children's teeth while children, particularly teenagers, are more concerned with the social desire for fresh breath. Initially, most toothpastes were positioned as cavity fighters (Crest) or breath fresheners (CloseUp). Therefore, there was ample opportunity for both individual and family conflict. Aqua-Fresh was po-

Exhibit 10–4 Product/Advertising Strategy Based on Approach-Approach Conflict

Used with permission from Beecham Inc.

sitioned to solve this conflict. Exhibit 10–4 illustrates the brand's characteristics and advertising strategy. The portion of the advertisement not shown stresses the dual attributes of the product.

Approach-Avoidance Motivational Conflict. In an *approach-avoidance motivational conflict,* the consumer faces both positive and negative consequences in the purchase of a particular product. A consumer who is concerned about gaining weight yet likes beer, faces this conflict. The development of lower-calorie beers reduces this conflict and allows the weight-sensitive beer consumer to drink beer and also control calorie intake. Nonalcoholic beers reduce the conflict between liking beer and being concerned about alcohol consumption. This is a common type of conflict in purchasing many consumer products, since acquiring the benefits represented by the product (approach) requires that we surrender purchasing power (avoidance). Instant retail credit through charge cards is a means of reducing this type of conflict.

Avoidance-Avoidance Motivational Conflict. An *avoidance-avoidance motivational conflict* is one in which the consumer faces two undesirable alternatives.

This occurs for some students the night before an exam: they neither want to study nor fail the exam. When a consumer's old washing machine finally fails, the same conflict occurs. The person may not want to spend money on a new washing machine or go without one. The availability of credit is one way of reducing this motivational conflict. Advertisements stressing the importance of regular maintenance, such as oil filter changes, also use this type of motive conflict: "Pay me now, or pay me (more) later."

PERSONALITY

While motivations are the energizing and directing force that makes consumer behavior purposeful and goal directed, the personality of the consumer guides and directs the behavior chosen to accomplish goals in different situations. Personality deals with those relatively long-lasting personal qualities that allow us to cope with and respond to the world around us.

We can easily (though perhaps not always accurately) describe our own personality or the personality of a friend. For example, you might say that one of your friends is "fairly aggressive, very opinionated, competitive, outgoing, and witty." What you have described are the behaviors your friend has exhibited over time across a variety of situations. These characteristic ways of responding to a wide range of situations should, of course, also include responses to marketing strategies. For example, the person described above is also likely to wear signature goods as described in Exhibit 10–5. It is for this reason that personality has been of interest to marketing managers for many years.

There is controversy in the field of psychology as to the exact nature of personality, the value of studying such a broad area, and the problems with

Exhibit 10–5 The Personality of the Signature-Goods Consumer

A study of 600 urban consumers found that the more aggressive the individual, the more prone they were to wear signature goods as an indicator of status.

"People who wear Gloria Vanderbilt, Gucci, LaCoste, St. Laurent, or other signature goods are outwardly ambitious, competitive, and motivated by self-interest. Typically, they include country club members, gourmet diners, photography buffs, and avid TV viewers and radio listeners. They are also more likely to be female than male, and blacks of both sexes are more prone than whites to consider signature purchases."

Source: "Signs of the Times," *Parade*, November 23, 1980, p. 28. See also M. A. Jolson, R. E. Anderson, and N. J. Leber, "Profiles of Signature Goods Consumers and Avoiders," *Journal of Retailing*, Winter 1981, pp. 19–25; and T. A. Swartz, "Brand Symbols and Message Differentiation," *Journal of Advertising Research*, October 1983, pp. 59–64.

measurement. Much of the same controversy exists in the marketing literature.[16] However, the concept is a very real and meaningful one to all of us on a daily basis. People do have personalities! Personality characteristics exist in those we know, and help us to describe and differentiate between individuals. Personality characteristics also can be used to help structure successful marketing strategies. Personality theories can be categorized as being either individual theories or social learning theories. Understanding these two general approaches to personality will provide an appreciation of the potential uses of personality in marketing decisions.

Individual Personality Theories

All individual personality theories have two common assumptions: (1) that all individuals have internal characteristics or traits, and (2) that there are consistent and measurable differences between individuals on those characteristics. The external environment or events around us (situations) are not considered in these theories and are assumed not to influence personality-based behaviors. Most of these theories state that the traits or characteristics are formed at a very early age and are relatively unchanging over the years. Differences between individual theories center around the definition of which traits or characteristics are the most important.

Cattell's theory is a representative example of the individual approach.[17] Cattell believes that traits are acquired at an early age through learning or are inherited. A unique aspect of his approach is the delineation of surface traits or observable behaviors that are similar and cluster together, and source traits that represent the causes of those behaviors. Cattell felt that if one could observe the surface traits that correlate highly with one another, they would identify an underlying source trait. For example, a source trait of assertiveness may account for the surface traits of aggressiveness, competitiveness, and stubbornness. Table 10–3 gives examples of some of Cattell's major source traits and corresponding surface traits.

While Cattell's theory is representative of multitrait personality theories (more than one trait influences behavior), there are a number of single-trait theories. Single-trait theories stress one trait as being of overwhelming importance. Some examples of single-trait theories are those that deal with dogmatism, authoritarianism, anxiety, locus of control, and social character (tradition-, inner-, other-directed).

Social Learning Theories

Social learning theories, as opposed to individual theories, emphasize the environment as the important determinant of behavior. Hence, there is a focus on external versus internal factors. Also, there is little concern with variation be-

Table 10–3
Cattell's Traits

Reserved: detached, critical, aloof, stiff	versus	***Outgoing:*** warmhearted, easygoing, participating
Affected by feeling: emotionally less stable	versus	***Emotionally stable:*** mature, faces reality, calm
Humble: stable, mild, easily led, docile, accommodating	versus	***Assertive:*** aggressive, competitive, stubborn
Sober: taciturn, serious	versus	***Happy-go-lucky:*** enthusiastic
Expedient: disregards rules	versus	***Conscientious:*** persistent, moralistic, staid
Shy: timid, threat-sensitive	versus	***Venturesome:*** uninhibited, socially bold
Tough-minded: self-reliant, realistic	versus	***Tender-minded:*** sensitive, clinging, overprotected
Practical: down-to-earth	versus	***Imaginative:*** bohemian, absent-minded
Forthright: unpretentious, genuine, but socially clumsy	versus	***Astute:*** polished, socially aware
Self-assured: placid, secure, complacent, serene	versus	***Apprehensive:*** self-reproaching, insecure, worrying, troubled
Conservative: respecting traditional ideas, conservatism of temperament	versus	***Experimenting:*** liberal, freethinking, radicalism
Group dependent: a joiner and sound follower	versus	***Self-sufficient:*** resourceful, prefers own decisions
Undisciplined: lax, follows own urges, careless of social rules	versus	***Controlled:*** exacting will-power, socially precise, compulsive, following self-image
Relaxed: tranquil, torpid, unfrustrated, composed	versus	***Tense:*** frustrated, driven, over-wrought

Source: Adapted from R. B. Cattell, H. W. Eber, and M. M. Tasuoka, *Handbook for the Sixteen Personality Factor Questionnaire* (Champaign, Ill.: Institute for Personality and Ability Testing, 1970), pp. 16–17. Reprinted by permission of the copyright owner.

tween individuals in terms of individual traits. Systematic differences in situations, in stimuli, or in social settings are the major interest of social theorists—not differences in traits, needs, or other properties of individuals. Rather than classifying individuals, the social theorists classify situations.

Social learning theories deal with how people learn to respond to the environment and the patterns of responses they learn. As situations change, individuals change their reactions. In the extreme case, every interpersonal interaction may be viewed as a different situation, with the result being a different response pattern. Some people may see you as an extrovert and others as an introvert. Each can be accurate in their assessment of your personality because individuals express different aspects of their personalities to each person.

Exhibit 10–6 An Advertisement Based on a Situational View of Personality

Wear Musk by English Leather when you're feeling bold. Or when you're feeling shy. Either way, Musk by English Leather will speak for you.
We know that the same guy can be outgoing sometimes, laid back other times.
So we created an easy way to communicate without saying a word.
Get the bold/shy scent of English Leather Musk.

Courtesy MEM Company, Inc.

The English Leather advertisement shown in Exhibit 10–6 is based on a recognition that personalities do indeed vary with the situation. Note how this theme is stressed in both the headlines and the copy.

A Combined Approach

In essence, the differences between individual and social theories of personality can be defined as state versus trait. Individual or trait theorists see behavior as largely determined by internal characteristics common to all persons but existing in differing amounts within individuals. Social or state theories claim just the opposite—situations that people face are the determinants of behavior, and different behaviors among people are the result of differing situations. We take the position that behavior is a result of some combination of individual traits or characteristics and situations that people face.

While research seems to indicate that individual traits are not good predictors of behavior, our basic intuitions disagree and we look for and expect to see some basic stability in individual behavior across situations. For example, a person who is assertive will probably tend to exhibit assertive behaviors in a variety of situations. Certainly some situations would result in less assertive behavior than others, but it seems reasonable to assume that the assertive person will generally act in a more assertive way than a shy person would in the same situation. Thus, the situation modifies the general trait and together they affect behavior.

Bem and Allen provide a potentially accurate and productive approach to using individual traits. They propose that some people are consistent across situations and some people are not.[18] It is a fact of life, they claim, that we will never be able to predict more than some of the people some of the time. The way one goes about doing this is to have individuals identify or classify themselves as to whether or not they are consistent on a particular trait across situations. Those who classify themselves as consistent would be much more predictable on behaviors that relate to that trait. This same reasoning could be applied to the predictive ability of situations: "In short, if some of the people can be predicted some of the time from personality traits, then some of the people can be predicted some of the time from situational variables."[19]

THE USE OF PERSONALITY IN MARKETING PRACTICE

While we each have a variety of personality traits and become involved in many situations which activate different aspects of our personality, some of these traits or characteristics are more desirable than others and some may even be undesirable. That is, in some situations we may be shy when we wish we were bold, or timid when we would like to be assertive. Thus, we all can find some areas of our personality that need bolstering or improvement.

Like individuals, many consumer products also have a "personality."[20] One brand of perfume may project youth, sensuality, and adventure, while another perfume may be viewed as modest, conservative, and aristocratic. In this example, each perfume has a distinct personality and is likely to be purchased by a different type of consumer or for a different situation. Consumers will tend to purchase the product with the personality that is most pleasing to them (not necessarily the one with a personality most like their own).

Brand Preference and Personality

Anheuser-Busch created four commercial advertisements for four new brands of beer. Each commercial represented one of the new brands and was created to portray the beer as appropriate for a specific "drinker personality." For example, one brand was featured in a commercial that portrayed the "reparative drinker," a self-sacrificing, middle-aged person who could have achieved more if he had not sacrificed personal objectives in the interest of others. For this consumer, drinking a beer serves as a reward for sacrifices. Other personality types—such as the "social drinker" who resembles the campus guzzler, and the "indulgent drinker" who sees himself as a total failure—were used to develop product personalities for the other new brands of beer in the study.

Then 250 beer consumers watched these commercials and tasted all four brands of beer. After given sufficient time to see each commercial and sample each beer, consumers were asked to state a brand preference and complete a questionnaire which measured their own "drinker personality." The results showed that most consumers preferred the brand of beer that matched their own drinker personality. Furthermore, the effect of personality on brand preferences was so strong that most consumers also felt that at least one brand of beer was not fit to drink. Unknown to these 250 consumers was the fact that all four brands were the same beer.[21] Thus, the product personalities created in these commercials attracted consumers with like personalities.

Advertising Preference and Personality

In another study, Kassarjian utilized measures of Reisman's inner- and other-directed social character as a basis for creating advertisements. *Inner-directed* people turn to and rely on their own inner values and standards for guiding their behavior, while *other-directed* persons depend on the people around them to give direction to their actions. For example, an inner-directed person may be more interested in individual sports, while an other-directed person may be more interested in group sports. Kassarjian hypothesized that inner-directed individuals would prefer advertisements that portrayed an inner-directed personality, and other-directed individuals would prefer ads that portrayed an other-directed personality.

Kassarjian created two versions of the same basic advertisement for 27 different products. For each product there was an inner-directed advertisement that

Exhibit 10–7 Inner- and Other-Directed Personality Appeals

	Inner-Directed Appeal		Other-Directed Appeal	
Product	**Slogan**	**Illustration**	**Slogan**	**Illustration**
Telephone company	Just dial. It's so easy, fast, and dependable.	Attractive girl holding telephone and staring into space.	The personal touch for every occasion.	Five pictures of young ladies in a variety of situations talking on the telephone.
Sea & Ski	For proper sun protection—Sea & Ski.	Beach scene with three unrelated couples.	For a desirable vacation glow—Sea & Ski.	Two men and three women water skiing from same boat.
Bayer aspirin	Don't spoil your leisure time—Bayer aspirin.	Man working in "do-it-yourself" workshop.	Don't spoil your leisure time—Bayer aspirin.	Two men holding drinks, talking at cocktail party.
Kodak	For a lasting record.	Man photographing London Bridge.	Share your experiences with friends at home.	Man photographing women in front of building. European posters in foreground.
Fairchild's restaurant	The height of sophistication.	Waiter in tuxedo.	Good food, reasonable price, festive atmosphere.	People being served in fancy restaurant.

Source: H. H. Kassarjian, "Social Character and Differential Preference for Mass Communication," *Journal of Marketing Research,* May 1965, pp. 146–53.

featured solitary, personal activities, and an other-directed advertisement that featured group or interaction appeals. Exhibit 10–7 provides brief descriptions of five of the advertisements used in the study. Consumers selected one of the two advertisements for each product based on the appeal the ad held for them. Inner-directed individuals tended to prefer the inner-directed advertisements, while other-directed individuals preferred the other-directed advertisements.[22] A similar study found extroverts preferring louder television commercials while introverts preferred lower-volume commercials.[23]

Problems in Utilizing Personality Theories

The examples just described demonstrate how personality can be used to influence brand and advertising preferences. Both were the result of carefully planned marketing studies. Each utilized appropriate measures of personality for the use intended as well as careful control of the situation and measurement of behavior. Other personality studies have been much less successful.

There are a number of reasons for the frequent failure of personality to predict consumer behavior.[24] In the first place, the social theorists are correct in their belief that no individual characteristics overpower all situational influences. Many of the studies showing limited or no personality influences did not account for, or control, situational variation and hence could be expected to provide less than completely predictive results.

Another reason why personality researchers seem to be unable to predict purchase preference could well be related to the methods of measuring personality characteristics. All too often researchers adopt, without change, a personality measurement instrument that was developed for a very different reason than to predict consumer behavior. As Kassarjian points out, "Instruments originally intended to measure gross personality characteristics such as sociability, emotional stability, introversion, or neuroticism have been used to make predictions of the chosen brand of toothpaste or cigarettes."[25]

Often, we should expect personality to correlate more with product type than with brand. For instance, personality is probably a better predictor of sports car ownership than brand of car, user versus nonuser of running shoes than brand of shoes, and so forth.

Finally, we must remember that consumers may purchase products to *reflect* or *enhance* aspects of their personality. Thus, both a timid and an aggressive individual may purchase a Corvette. One may buy because she is timid and thinks this brand may help offset her shyness; the other, because she is aggressive and feels the car matches her personality.

EMOTION

Earlier we defined emotion as strong, relatively uncontrollable feelings that affect our behavior.[26] All of us experience a wide array of emotions. Think for a moment about a recent emotional experience. What characterized this experience? All emotional experiences tend to have several elements in common.

Emotions are generally triggered by *environmental events*. Anger, joy, and sadness are most frequently a response of a set of external events. However, we can also initiate emotional reactions by internal processes such as imagery. Athletes frequently use imagery to "psyche" themselves into a desired emotional state.

Emotions are accompanied by *physiological changes*. Some characteristic changes are: (1) eye pupil dilation, (2) increased perspiration, (3) more rapid breathing, (4) increased heart rate and blood pressure, and (5) enhanced blood sugar level. The consistent presence of physiological changes during emotional experiences led to the James-Lange theory of emotion. This theory holds that physiological responses precede emotion. That is, we start to fall, the physiological changes described above occur, then we experience fear.

While very well known, the James-Lange theory is not an adequate explanation, primarily because all emotions, as subjectively experienced and identified, appear to be associated with similar physiological changes. That is, the emotions we would label as joy, fear, and anger occur in conjunction with very similar physiological patterns. Current thinking leans toward accepting the primacy of physiological changes, which are then interpreted based on environmental occurrences.[27] Thus, a sudden falling sensation will initiate physiological changes. We interpret these changes based on the situation in which they occur: exhilaration or excitement if jumping from a diving board; fear if falling from a ledge.

Another characteristic feature of an emotional experience is *cognitive thought*. Emotions generally, though not necessarily, are accompanied by thinking. The types of thoughts and our ability to think "rationally" vary with the type and degree of emotion. Extreme emotional responses are frequently used as an explanation for inappropriate thoughts or actions: "I was so mad I couldn't think straight."

Emotions also have associated *behaviors*. While the behaviors vary across individuals, and within individuals across time and situations, there are unique behaviors characteristically associated with different emotions: fear triggers fleeing responses; anger triggers striking-out; grief triggers crying, and so forth.

Finally, and most important, emotions involve *subjective feelings*. In fact, it is the feeling component we generally refer to when we think of emotions. Grief, joy, anger, jealousy, and fear *feel* very differently to us. These subjectively determined feelings are the essence of emotion.

These feelings have a specific component that we label as the emotion, such as sad or happy. In addition, emotions carry an evaluative or a like/dislike component. While the terms are used inconsistently in the literature, we use the term *emotion* to refer to the identifiable, specific feeling, and the term *affect* to refer to the liking/disliking aspect of the specific feeling.[28] While emotions are generally evaluated (liked and disliked) in a consistent manner across individuals, and within individuals over time, there is some individual and situational variation.

Figure 10–2 reflects current thinking on the nature of emotions.

Types of Emotions

If asked, you could doubtless name numerous emotions. A group of 20 or so people can generally name or describe several hundred emotions. Thus, it is not surprising that researchers have attempted to categorize or "type" emotions into more manageable clusters. Plutchik lists eight basic emotional categories: (1) fear, (2) anger, (3) joy, (4) sadness, (5) acceptance, (6) disgust, (7) expectancy, and (8) surprise. According to Plutchik, all other emotions are secondary emotions and represent combinations of these basic categories.[29] For example, delight is a combination of surprise and joy, and contempt is composed of disgust and anger.

Other authors have suggested that three basic dimensions—pleasure, arousal, and dominance (PAD)—underlie all emotions. Specific emotions reflect various

Figure 10–2
Nature of Emotions

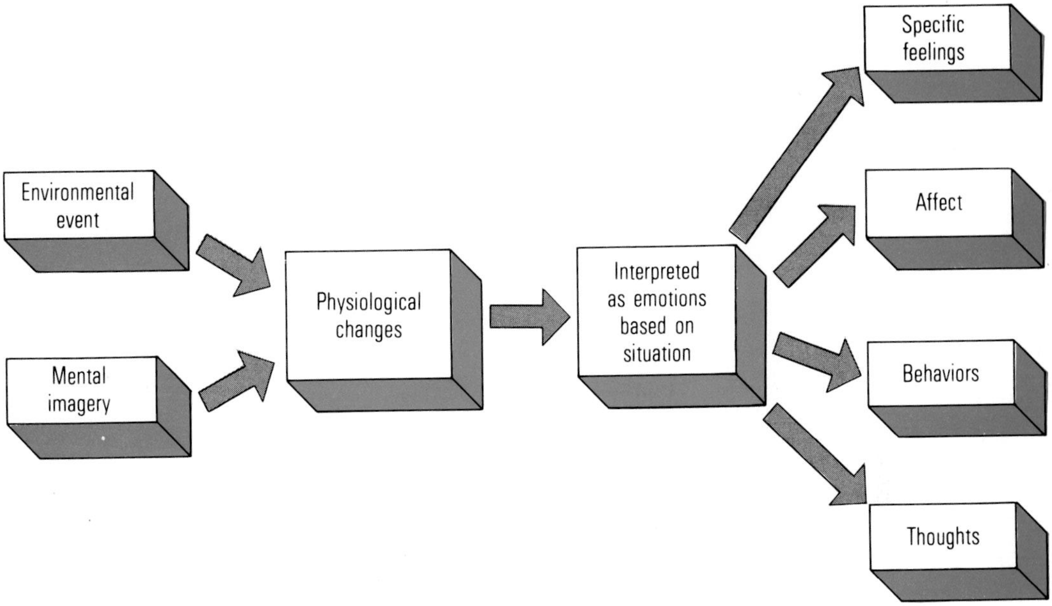

combinations and levels of these three dimensions.[30] While consumer researchers have used both typologies, the PAD approach appears superior.[31] Table 10–4 lists the three primary PAD dimensions, a variety of emotions or emotional categories associated with each dimension, and indicators or items that can be used to measure each emotion.[32]

EMOTIONS AND MARKETING STRATEGY

While marketers have always used emotions to guide product positioning, sales presentations, and advertising on an intuitive level, the deliberate, systematic study of the relevance of emotions in marketing strategy is new. In this section we will briefly describe strategies focused on emotion arousal as a product benefit, emotion reduction as a product benefit, and emotion arousal in the context of advertising.

Emotional Arousal as a Product Feature

Emotions are characterized by positive or negative evaluations. Consumers actively seek products whose primary or secondary benefit is emotion arousal.

Table 10–4
Emotional Dimensions, Emotions, and Emotional Indicators

Dimension	Emotion	Indicator/Feeling
Pleasure	Duty	Moral, virtuous, dutiful
	Faith	Reverent, worshipful, spiritual
	Pride	Proud, superior, worthy
	Affection	Loving, affectionate, friendly
	Innocence	Innocent, pure, blameless
	Gratitude	Grateful, thankful, appreciative
	Serenity	Restful, serene, comfortable, soothed
	Desire	Desirous, wishful, craving, hopeful
	Joy	Joyful, happy, delighted, pleased
	Competence	Confident, in control, competent
Arousal	Interest	Attentive, curious
	Hypoactivation	Bored, drowsy, sluggish
	Activation	Aroused, active, excited
	Surprise	Surprised, annoyed, astonished
	Déjà vu	Unimpressed, uninformed, unexcited
	Involvement	Involved, informed, enlightened, benefited
	Distraction	Distracted, preoccupied, inattentive
	Surgency	Playful, entertained, lighthearted
	Contempt	Scornful, contemptuous, disdainful
Dominance	Conflict	Tense, frustrated, conflictful
	Guilt	Guilty, remorseful, regretful
	Helplessness	Powerless, helpless, dominated
	Sadness	Sad, distressed, sorrowful, dejected
	Fear	Fearful, afraid, anxious
	Shame	Ashamed, embarrassed, humiliated
	Anger	Angry, initiated, enraged, mad
	Hyperactivation	Panicked, confused, overstimulated
	Disgust	Disgusted, revolted, annoyed, full of loathing
	Skepticism	Skeptical, suspicious, distrustful

Source: Adapted from M. B. Holbrook and R. Batra, "Assessing the Role of Emotions as Mediators of Consumer Responses to Advertising," *Journal of Consumer Research,* December 1987, pp. 404–20.

While positive emotions are sought the majority of the time, this is not always the case ("The movie was so sad, I cried and cried. I loved it. You should see it.").[33]

Many products feature emotion arousal as a primary benefit. Movies, books, and music are the most obvious examples. Las Vegas, Atlantic City, and Disney

World are positioned as emotion-arousing destinations, as are various types of adventure travel programs. Long-distance telephone calls have been positioned as emotion-arousing products ("Reach out and touch someone"). Several brands of soft drinks and beers stress excitement and fun as primary benefits. Even automobiles are sometimes positioned as emotion-arousing products: Toyota—"Oh What a Feeling"; and Pontiac—"We Build Excitement."

Emotion Reduction as a Product Benefit

As a glance at Table 10–4 indicates, many emotional states are unpleasant to most individuals most of the time. Few of us like to feel sad, powerless, humiliated, or digusted. Responding to this, marketers design and/or position many products to prevent or reduce the arousal of unpleasant emotions.

The most obvious of these products are the various over-the-counter medications designed to deal with anxiety or depression. Shopping malls, department stores, and other retail outlets are often visited to alleviate boredom.[34] Flowers are heavily promoted as an antidote to sadness. Weight-loss products and other self-improvement products are frequently positioned primarily in terms of guilt, helplessness, shame, or disgust reduction benefits. Personal grooming products often stress anxiety reduction as a major benefit. Exhibit 10–8 illustrates this approach.

Emotion in Advertising

Emotion arousal is often used in advertising even when emotion arousal or reduction is not a product benefit. We are just beginning to develop a sound understanding of how emotional responses to advertising influence consumer responses.[35] Therefore, the general conclusions discussed below must be regarded as tentative.

Emotional content in advertisements *enhances their attention attraction and maintenance capabilities*. Advertising messages that trigger emotional reactions of joy, warmth, or even disgust are more likely to be attended to than are more neutral ads. As we saw in Chapter 8, attention is a critical step in the perception process.

Emotions are characterized by a state of heightened physiological arousal. Individuals become more alert and active when aroused. Given this enhanced level of arousal, *emotional messages may be processed more thoroughly* than neutral messages. More effort and increased elaboration activities may occur in response to the emotional state.

Emotional advertisements that *trigger a positively evaluated emotion enhance liking of the ad itself*. For example, "warmth" is a positively valued emotion that is triggered by experiencing directly or vicariously a love, family, or friendship relationship. Ads high in warmth, such as the McDonald's ads showing father-daughter and father-son relationships, trigger the physiological changes

Exhibit 10–8 Anxiety-Reduction Advertising

Just because
your blouse is dry,
doesn't mean
you smell good.
SURE
Underarm odor
is invisible.
So why walk
around with a dry blouse
and a false sense of security?
Use Sure Roll-on.
And be just as sure about odor
as you are about wetness.
© 1987 Procter & Gamble

Courtesy Procter & Gamble. Reproduced with permission.

described previously. In addition, warm ads such as these are liked more than neutral ads.[36] Liking an ad has a positive impact on liking the product (see Chapter 12). Exhibit 10–9 shows an ad likely to arouse warmth.

Emotional ads *may be remembered better than neutral ads*.[37] As discussed in Chapter 9, recognition measures rather than recall measures may be required

Exhibit 10–9 Warmth Arousal Advertising

Courtesy Johnson & Johnson

to measure this enhanced memory. The improvement in memory may be due to the increased processing mentioned above, or it may reflect message structure elements, differing levels of message involvement, or other factors.

Repeated exposure to positive-emotion-eliciting ads may *increase brand preference through classical conditioning*. Repeated pairings of the unconditioned response (positive emotion) with the conditioned stimulus (brand name), may result in the positive affect occurring when the brand name is presented (see pages 322–23). *Brand liking may also occur in a direct, high-involvement manner*. A person having a single or few exposures to an emotional ad may simply "decide" that the product is a good, or likeable, product. This is a much more conscious process than implied by classical conditioning. For example, viewing warmth-arousing ads has been found to increase purchase intentions, an outcome of liking a product.

Advertising using emotion-based appeals is gaining popularity. For example, Warner-Lambert recently dropped its fact-based comparative ad campaign for its e.p.t. Stick Test home-pregnancy-test product in favor of a strong emotional campaign. Their 30-second TV spots capture the moment when a young husband learns his wife is pregnant. The wife playfully hints at the news of her pregnancy by chanting the lines from familiar songs that use the word "baby," such as "Baby Face," until her husband catches on.[38]

SUMMARY

Consumer motivations are energizing forces that activate behavior and provide purpose and direction to that behavior. In terms of specific product purchases, consumer motivations seem highly dependent on the situation at hand. It is necessary, therefore, to understand what motives stimulate what types of behavior and how these motives and behaviors are influenced by specific situations in which consumers engage in goal-directed behavior.

There are numerous motivation theories. *Maslow's need hierarchy* states that basic motives must be minimally satisfied before more advanced motives are activated. It proposes five levels of motivation: physiological, safety, belongingness, esteem, and self-actualization.

McGuire has developed a more detailed set of motives organized around nonsocial and social motives. *Internal, nonsocial motives* reflect needs that people have with respect to themselves as individuals, such as consistency, causation, categorization, cues, independence, and curiosity. *External, social motives*—self-expression, ego-defense, assertion, reinforcement, affiliation, and modeling—deal with human needs directly related to interactions with significant others.

Consumers are often aware of and will admit to the motives causing their behavior. These are *manifest motives*. They can be discovered by standard marketing research techniques such as direct questioning. Direct advertising appeals can be made to these motives. At other times, consumers are unable or are unwilling to admit to the motives that are influencing them. These are *latent motives*. They can be determined by *motivation research techniques* such as word association, sentence completion, and picture response. While direct advertising appeals can be used, indirect appeals are often necessary. Both manifest and latent motives are operative in many purchase situations.

Because of the large number of motives and the many different situations that consumers face, *motivational conflict* can occur. In an *approach-approach conflict,* the consumer faces a choice between two attractive alternatives. In an *approach-avoidance conflict,* the consumer faces both positive and negative consequences in the purchase of a particular product. And finally, in the *avoidance-avoidance conflict* the consumer faces two undesirable alternatives.

The *personality* of a consumer guides and directs the behavior chosen to accomplish goals in different situations. Personality is the relatively long-lasting personal quality that allows us to respond to the world around us. Though there are many controversies in the area of personality research, personalities do exist and are meaningful to consumers and, therefore, to marketing managers.

There are two basic approaches to understanding personality. *Individual theories* have two common assumptions: (1) all individuals have internal characteristics or traits, and (2) there are consistent differences between individuals on these characteristics or traits that can be measured. Most of the individual theories state that traits are formed at an early age and are relatively unchanging over the years. *Social learning theories* emphasize the environment as the important determinant of behavior. Therefore, the focus is on external (situational) versus internal factors.

Brands, like individuals, have personalities, and consumers tend to prefer products with personalities that are pleasing to them. It is also apparent that consumers prefer advertising messages that portray their own or a desired personality. However, for most product categories, personality plays only a limited role in brand selection.

Emotions are strong, relatively uncontrollable feelings that affect our behavior. Emotions occur when environmental events or our mental processes trigger physiological changes including increased perspiration, eye pupil dilation, increased heart and breath rate, and elevated blood sugar level. These changes are interpreted as specific emotions based on the situation. They affect consumers' thoughts and behaviors. Marketers design and position products to both arouse and reduce emotions. Advertisements include emotion-arousing material to increase attention, degree of processing, remembering, and brand preference through classical conditioning or direct evaluation.

REVIEW QUESTIONS

1. What is a *motive?*
2. What is meant by a *motive hierarchy?* How does Maslow's hierarchy of needs function?
3. Describe *internal, nonsocial motives,* and how knowledge of them would be useful to a marketing manager.
4. What are *external, social motives,* and how would knowledge of them be useful to a marketing manager?
5. What is meant by *motivational conflict,* and what relevance does it have for marketing managers?

6. What is a *manifest motive?* A *latent motive?*
7. How do you measure manifest motives? Latent motives?
8. How do you appeal to manifest motives? Latent motives?
9. What are *projective techniques?* How do they work?
10. Describe the following projective techniques:
    a. Association.
    b. Completion.
    c. Construction.
11. What is *personality?*
12. Describe the *individual* and the *social learning* approaches to personality.
13. What are major criticisms of the individual approach? How is this approach potentially useful to marketing managers?
14. What do we mean by *single-trait* and *multiple-trait individual theories*?
15. How can knowledge of personality be used to influence brand preferences?
16. How can a knowledge of personality be used to affect consumers' preferences for advertisements?
17. Describe some of the major problems marketing managers face when attempting to utilize personality theory.
18. What is an *emotion?*
19. What triggers an emotion?
20. What physiological changes accompany emotional arousal?
21. What is the relationship between emotions and physiological changes?
22. What factors characterize emotions?
23. How can we type or categorize emotions?
24. How do marketers use emotions in product design and positioning?
25. What is the role of emotional content in advertising?

DISCUSSION QUESTIONS

1. How could Maslow's motive hierarchy be used to develop marketing strategy for:
    a. Low-calorie frozen dinners?
    b. Recruiting women for the Navy?
    c. Fish and chips restaurant chain?
    d. Bottled water?
    e. Green beans (canned)?
    f. Sports cars?
2. Which *(a)* internal and *(b)* external motives would be useful in developing a promotional campaign for:
    a. Low-alcohol beer?
    b. Seat-belt use?
    c. Expensive men's watches?
    d. Natural foods store?
    e. Army recruiting?
    f. Attracting students to a university?

3. Describe how motivational conflict might arise in purchasing [or giving to]:
   a. United Fund.
   b. New carpeting.
   c. Lettuce.
   d. Low-alcohol beer.
   e. Personal computer.
4. Describe the manifest and latent motives that might arise in purchasing, shopping at, or giving to:
   a. Del Monte canned peas.
   b. IBM PC.
   c. Low-alcohol wine.
   d. University alumni fund.
   e. Jewelry store.
5. How might a knowledge of personality be used to develop an advertising campaign for:
   a. University alumni fund?
   b. Discount store?
   c. Sports car?
   d. Green beans (canned)?
   e. Disc player?
   f. Chewing gum?
6. For each of the external, social motives identify a brand that may be purchased because of this motive. For each brand and external motive, discuss how you would go about using this motive in promotion.
7. Using Table 10–3, discuss how you would use one of the personality source traits in developing a package design for a low-alcohol beer aimed at women.
8. Discuss the various problems that can be encountered in relating personality to brand purchase behavior. How can each of these problem areas be overcome? How would you suggest that personality be used in product positioning?
9. How would you use emotion to develop marketing strategy for the products listed in discussion question 2?
10. List all the emotions you can think of. Which ones are not explicitly mentioned in Table 10–4? Where would you place them in this table?
11. What products or brands, other than those described in the chapter, arouse or reduce emotions?

PROJECT QUESTIONS

1. Develop an advertisement for the following based on relevant internal and external motives:
   a. Compact disc player.
   b. "Adopt-a-Pet" program for a city pound.
   c. Eggs.
   d. U.S. Senate candidate.
   e. Tax service.
   f. Chain of women's clothing stores.

Explain which motives the ad reflects and why they are relevant to the purchase.

2. Repeat question 1 for Maslow's need hierarchy.
3. Repeat question 1 for emotions.
4. Find two advertisements that appeal to each level of Maslow's hierarchy. Explain why the ad appeals to this level and speculate on why the firm selected this level to appeal to.
5. Find two ads that contain direct appeals to manifest motives and indirect appeals to latent motives. Explain how the ads are using indirect appeals.
6. Select a product of interest and use motivation research techniques to determine the latent purchase motives for 10 consumers.
7. Find and cut out two newspaper or magazine advertisements, one that is based on an inner-directed personality and the other based on other-directed personality. Discuss how the ad copy and illustration each contributed to the personality of the advertisement. Also, discuss what you feel might have been the rationale in using each personality in positioning each product.
8. Have 10 students describe the personality of ____________. To what extent are the descriptions similar? Why are there differences?
   a. Corona beer.
   b. Macintosh computer.
   c. Corvette automobile.
   d. Your university.
   e. A major local retailer, restaurant, or tavern.
   f. Crest toothpaste.
9. Find and copy five ads with strong emotional appeals, and five ads from the same product categories with limited emotional appeals.
   a. Have 10 students rank or rate the ads in terms of their preferences and then explain their rankings or ratings.
   b. Have 10 different students talk about their reactions to each ad as they view it.

REFERENCES

[1] R. F. Thompson, *Introduction to Physiological Psychology* (New York: Harper & Row, 1975), p. 295.

[2] A. H. Maslow, *Motivation and Personality,* 2d ed. (New York: Harper & Row, 1970).

[3] W. J. McGuire, "Psychological Motives and Communication Gratification," in *The Uses of Mass Communications,* ed. J. G. Blumler and C. Katz (Beverly Hills, Calif.: Sage Publications, 1974), pp. 167–96; and W. J. McGuire, "Some Internal Psychological Factors Influencing Consumer Choice," *Journal of Consumer Research,* March 1976, pp. 302–19.

[4] See R. W. Mizerski, L. L. Golden, and J. B. Kernan, "The Attribution Process in Consumer Decision Making," *Journal of Consumer Research,* September 1979, pp. 123–40.

[5] See R. M. Sparkman, Jr., and W. B. Locander, "Attribution Theory and Advertising Effectiveness," *Journal of Consumer Research,* December 1980, pp. 219–24; and H. H. Kelley and J. L. Michela, "Attribution Theory and Research," *Annual Review of Psychology,* 1980, pp. 457–501.

[6] J. Birnbaum, "Pricing of Products Is Still an Art Often Having Little Link to Costs," *The Wall Street Journal,* November 25, 1981, p. 29.

[7] S. Dawson and J. Cavell, "Status Recognition in the 1980s," in *Advances in Consumer Research XIV,* ed. M. Wallendorf and P. Anderson (Provo, Utah: Association for Consumer Research, 1987) pp. 487–91; and R. Belk and R. Pollay, "Images of Ourselves," *Journal of Consumer Research,* March 1985, pp. 887–97.

[8] P. Sloan, "Tailoring Exec to Suit Company," *Advertising Age,* June 1, 1981, p. 30. See also R. Belk, K. D. Bahn, and R. N. Mayer, "Developmental Recognition of Consumption Symbolism," *Journal of Consumer Research,* June 1982, pp. 4–17.

[9] " 'Individualism' Stressed in Ads," *Marketing News,* June 6, 1986, p. 13.

[10] E. Pessemier and M. Handelsman, "Temporal Variety in Consumer Behavior," *Journal of Marketing Research,* November 1984, pp. 435–44; E. A. Joachimsthaler and J. L. Lastovicka, "Optimal Stimulation Level," *Journal of Consumer Research,* December 1984, pp. 830–35; J. M. Lattin and L. McAlister, "Using a Variety-Seeking Model," *Journal of Marketing Research,* August 1985, pp. 330–39; and B. E. Kahn, M. U. Kalwani, and D. G. Morrison, "Measuring Variety-Seeking and Reinforcement Behaviors," *Journal of Marketing Research,* May 1986, pp. 89–100.

[11] D. C. Bello and M. J. Etzel, "The Role of Novelty in the Pleasure Travel Experience," *Journal of Travel Research,* Summer 1985, pp. 20–26.

[12] See J. F. Durgee, "Self-Esteem Advertising," *Journal of Advertising,* no. 4, 1986, pp. 21–27.

[13] Birnbaum, "Pricing of Products."

[14] For details, see D. S. Tull and D. I. Hawkins, *Marketing Research* (New York: Macmillan, 1987), pp. 318–25.

[15] Based on K. Lewin, *A Dynamic Theory of Personality* (New York: McGraw-Hill, 1935), pp. 88–91.

[16] See H. H. Kassarjian and M. J. Sheffet, "Personality and Consumer Behavior: An Update," in *Perspectives in Consumer Behavior,* ed. H. H. Kassarjian and T. S. Robertson (Glenview, Ill.: Scott, Foresman, 1981), pp. 160–80.

[17] C. S. Hall and G. Lindzey, *Theories of Personality,* 2d ed. (New York: John Wiley & Sons, 1970), chap. 10.

[18] D. J. Bem and A. Allen, "On Predicting Some of the People Some of the Time: The Search for Cross-Situational Consistency in Behavior," *Psychological Review,* November 1974, pp. 506–20. See also D. J. Bem and D. C. Funder, "Predicting More of the People More of the Time: Assessing the Personality of Situations," *Psychological Review,* November 1978, pp. 485–501; and S. Epstein, "The Stability of Behavior: I. On Predicting Most of the People Much of the Time," *Journal of Personality and Social Psychology,* July 1979, pp. 1097–1126.

[19] Bem and Allen, "On Predicting," p. 17.

[20] J. J. Plummer, "How Personality Makes a Difference," *Journal of Advertising Research,* January 1985, pp. 27–31; and R. S. Duboff, "Brands, Like People, Have Personalities," *Marketing News,* January 3, 1986, p. 8.

[21] R. L. Ackoff and J. R. Emsoff, "Advertising at Anheuser-Busch, Inc.," *Sloan Management Review,* Spring 1975, pp. 1–15.

[22] H. H. Kassarjian, "Social Character and Differential Preference for Mass Communication," *Journal of Marketing Research,* May 1965, pp. 146–53. See also R. W. Mizerski and R. B. Settle, "The Influence of Social Character on Preference for Social versus Objective Information in Advertising," *Journal of Marketing Research,* November 1979, pp. 552–58; and G. M. Zinkhan and A. Shermohamad, "Is Other-Directed on the Increase?" *Journal of Consumer Research,* June 1986, pp. 127–30.

[23] H. Cetola and K. Prinkey, "Introversion-Extroversion and Loud Commercials," *Psychology & Marketing,* Summer 1986, pp. 123–32.

[24] S. Onkvisit and J. T. Shaw, "Personality as a Predictor Variable," in *Developments in Marketing Science Vol. VI,* ed. J. C. Rogers III (Academy of Marketing Science, 1983), pp. 104–9.

[25] H. H. Kassarjian, "Personality and Consumer Behavior: A Review," *Journal of Marketing Research,* November 1971, p. 41.

[26] J. P. Houston, *Motivation* (New York: Macmillan, 1985), p. 271. See also R. Peterson et al., *The Role of Affect in Consumer Behavior* (Lexington, Mass.: D.C. Heath, 1986).

[27] Ibid., p. 278.

[28] See M. B. Holbrook and J. O'Shaughnessy, "The Role of Emotion in Advertising," *Psychology & Marketing,* Summer 1984, pp. 45–63; and R. Batra and M. L. Ray, "Affective Responses Mediating Acceptance of Advertising," *Journal of Consumer Research,* September 1986, pp. 234–49.

[29] R. Plutchik, *Emotion: A Psychoevolutionary Synthesis* (New York: Harper & Row, 1980).

[30] A. Mehrabian and J. A. Russell, *An Approach to Environmental Psychology* (Cambridge, Mass.: MIT Press, 1974).

[31] W. J. Havlena and M. B. Holbrook, "The Varieties of Consumption Experience," *Journal of Consumer Research,* December 1986, pp. 394–404. A contradictory view is presented by D. M. Zeitlin and R. A. Westwood, "Measuring Emotional Response," *Journal of Advertising Research,* October/November 1986, pp. 34–44.

[32] See also M. B. Holbrook and R. Batra, "Toward a Standardized Emotional Profile (SEP) Useful in Measuring Responses to the Nonverbal Components of Advertising," in *Nonverbal Communication in Advertising,* ed. S. Hecker and D. W. Stewart (Lexington, Mass.: D. C. Heath, 1988).

[33] See C. Campbell, *The Romantic Ethic and the Spirit of Modern Consumerism* (Oxford: Blackwell, 1987).

[34] See R. A. Westbrook and W. C. Black, "A Motivation-Based Shopper Typology," *Journal of Retailing,* Spring 1985, pp. 78–103.

[35] Holbrook and O'Shaughnessy, "The Role of Emotion"; D. A. Aaker, D. M. Stagman, and M. R. Hagerty, "Warmth in Advertising," *Journal of Consumer Research,* March 1986, pp. 365–81; Batra and Ray, "Affective Responses"; Zeitlin and Westwood, "Measuring Emotional Response"; P. A. Stout and J. D. Leckenby, "Measuring Emotional Response to Advertising," *Journal of Advertising,* no. 4, 1986,

pp. 35–42; M. E. Goldberg and G. J. Gorn, "Happy and Sad TV Programs"; M. B. Holbrook and R. Batra, "Assessing the Role of Emotions as Mediators of Consumer Responses to Advertising"; and J. A. Edell and M. C. Burke, "The Power of Feelings in Understanding Advertising Effects," all in *Journal of Consumer Research,* December 1987, pp. 387–403, 404–20, and 421–33; and E. Thorson and T. J. Page, Jr., "Effects of Product Involvement and Emotional Commercials"; and A. A. Mitchell, "Current Perspectives and Issues concerning the Explanation of 'Feeling' Advertising Effects," both in *Nonverbal Communication in Advertising,* ed. S. Hecker and D. W. Stewart (Lexington, Mass.: D. C. Heath, 1988).

[36] Aaker, Stagman, and Hagerty, "Warmth in Advertising."

[37] M. Friestad and E. Thorson, "Emotion-Eliciting Advertising," in *Advances in Consumer Research XIII,* ed. R. J. Lutz (Provo, Utah: Association for Consumer Research, 1986), pp. 111–16.

[38] P. Winters, "W-L Touches Emotions in E.P.T. Ads," *Advertising Age,* October 19, 1987, p. 24.

CHAPTER

11 Lifestyle

Dr Pepper recently embarked on a new ad campaign with a new slogan:

> Hold out for the out-of-the-ordinary—hold out for Dr Pepper.

The new campaign comes out of an evaluation of SRI's Values and Lifestyles Study. According to David Millhesier, brand manager for Dr Pepper:

> As we see it, there is a new trend among the inner directed, and a whole new realm opening up. We currently see 30 percent of the young population as being inner directed; it's the most rapidly growing segment. Our projections indicate inner directs will make up 60 percent of the population by 1990.

The Dr Pepper appeal is targeted at the inner directed in an attempt to position itself appropriately for the 1990s.[1]

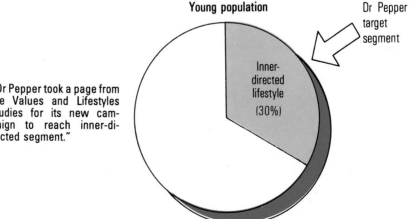

"Dr Pepper took a page from the Values and Lifestyles studies for its new campaign to reach inner-directed segment."

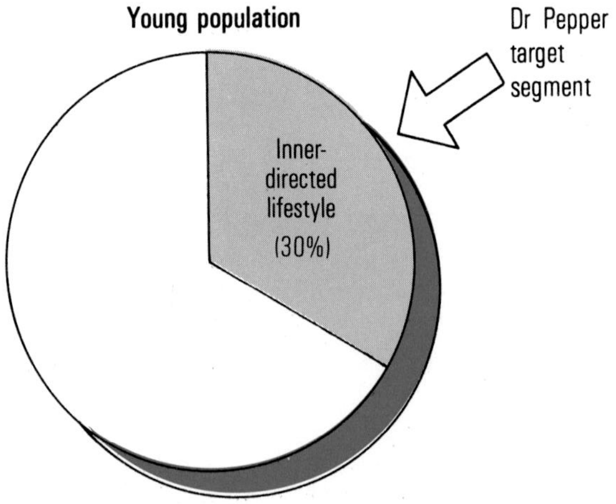

The lifestyle each of us leads is an expression of our situation, life experiences, values, attitudes, and expectations. In this chapter we will discuss the meaning of lifestyle and the role it plays in developing marketing strategies. We will also examine ways in which lifestyle is measured and examples of how lifestyle is being used to develop well-targeted marketing programs.

THE NATURE OF LIFESTYLE

Lifestyle is defined simply as *how one lives*.[2] One's lifestyle is a function of inherent individual characteristics that have been shaped and formed through social interaction as one moves through the life cycle. Thus, lifestyle is influenced by the factors discussed in the past 10 chapters—values, demographics, social class, reference groups, family, and individual characteristics such as motives, emotions, and personality. Figure 11–1 illustrates the variables that influence and make up consumer lifestyles and the relationship that lifestyle has to decision making and consumption.

Exhibit 11–1 contains brief profiles of five market segments that were found in an analysis of consumer lifestyles in relation to outdoor activities. While not included in the exhibit, other aspects of their lifestyles—such as media preferences—also differ. If you were marketing a line of canoes, which group or groups would you target? How would your advertising and product positioning

Figure 11–1
How We Live (Lifestyle) Impacts Our Consumer Behavior

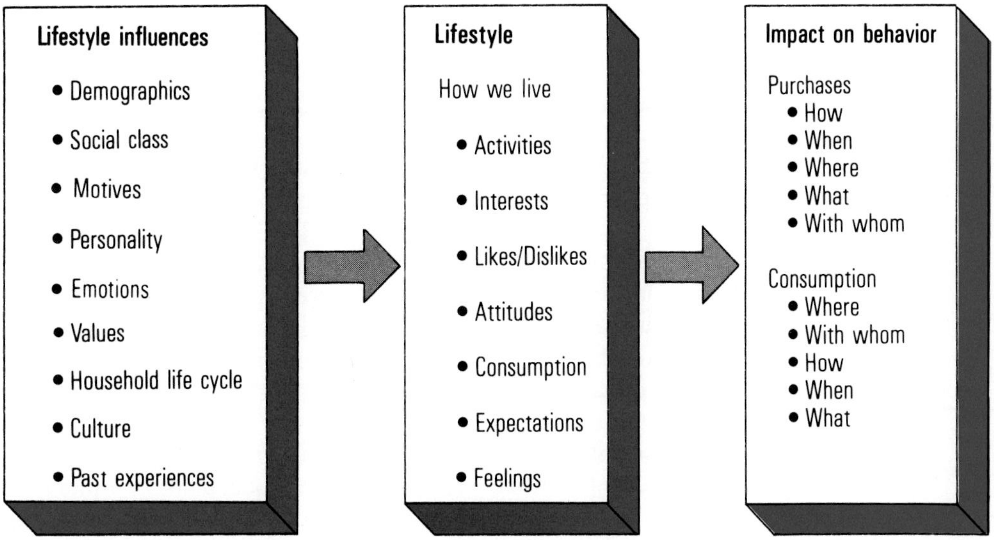

Exhibit 11–1 Lifestyle Analysis for Outdoor Activities

• **EXCITEMENT-SEEKING COMPETITIVES (16 PERCENT):** Like risk, some danger, and competition, though they also like social and fitness benefits. Participate in team and individual competitive sports. Half belong to a sports club or team. Median age of 32, two thirds are male. Upper-middle class, and about half are single.

• **GETAWAY ACTIVES (33 PERCENT):** Like the opportunity to be alone or experience nature. Active in camping, fishing, and birdwatching. Not loners; focus on families or close friends. Half use outdoor recreation to reduce stress. Median age of 35, equally divided between men and women.

• **FITNESS-DRIVEN (10 PERCENT):** Engage in outdoor activities strictly for fitness benefits. Walking, bicycling, and jogging are popular activities. Upscale economically. Median age of 46, over half of which are women.

• **HEALTH-CONSCIOUS SOCIABLES (33 PERCENT):** Relatively inactive despite stated health concerns. Most involved with spectator activities such as sightseeing, driving for pleasure, visiting zoos, and so forth. Median age of 49, two thirds are female.

• **UNSTRESSED AND UNMOTIVATED (8 PERCENT):** Not interested in outdoor recreation except as an opportunity for the family to be together. Median age of 49, equally divided between males and females.

Source: B. E. Bryant, "Built for Excitement," *American Demographics,* March 1987, pp. 39–42.

differ among the groups? Notice how much more insight even oversimplified lifestyle descriptions such as these provide, compared to solely demographic data.

Lifestyle is a basic motivator that influences many of our needs and attitudes. This in return influences many purchase and use activities. That is, the need to make certain purchases arises from who we are, what we are, and the problems and opportunities that we face in life. Thus, we have elected to make lifestyle central in the consumer behavior model we have used throughout the text (see Figure 11–2).

Consumers are seldom explicitly aware of the role lifestyle plays in their purchase decisions. For example, few consumers would think, "I will buy High Point instant coffee to maintain my lifestyle." However, individuals pursuing an active lifestyle might purchase High Point because of its convenience, since time is important in an active lifestyle. Thus, lifestyle frequently provides the basic

Figure 11–2
Lifestyle and the Consumption Process

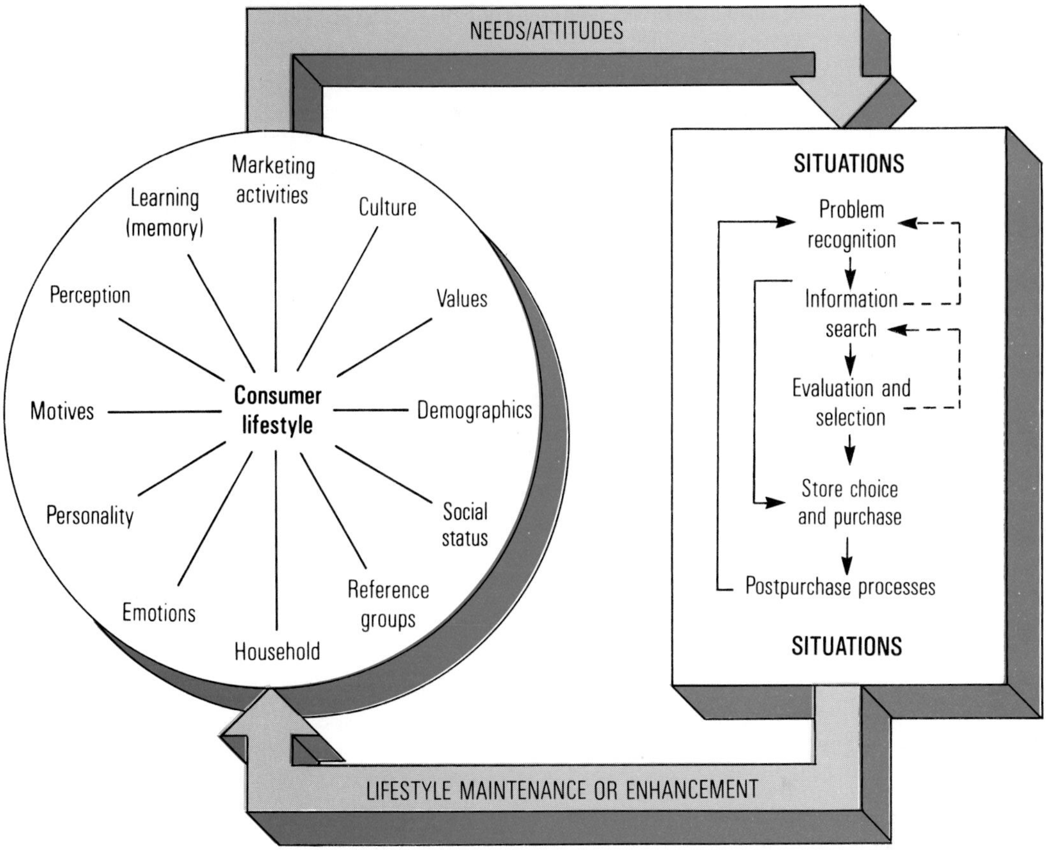

motivation and guidelines for purchases but generally does so in an indirect, subtle manner. Of course, some products and marketing strategies focus on an explicit recognition of a particular lifestyle.

Another aspect of lifestyle that interests marketing managers is its changing nature as a result of the consumer decision process. As Figure 11–2 indicates, the decisions consumers make about products provide experiences that can alter or reinforce lifestyles. For example, the purchase, use, and evaluation of a vacation may lead to a more travel-oriented lifestyle. Desired lifestyles also change due to changes in the individual, reference groups, family, and so forth. When lifestyle changes do occur, they usually bring to light new consumption-related problems and/or opportunities that in turn necessitate new consumer decisions. Therefore, the process is dynamic and constantly changing.

A final factor to emphasize is that individuals, families, and households all have lifestyles. Family and household lifestyles are in part determined by the lifestyles of the individual members. However, factors such as stage of household life cycle, demographics (such as age, income, race, and so on), and social class (the influence of occupation, education, and so forth) also shape the lifestyle of a family or household.

In this chapter we are going to examine two important aspects of lifestyle: self-concept and psychographics; and two commercial sources of data on lifestyles: SRI's VALS program and CLARITAS's PRIZM system.

SELF-CONCEPT

Self-concept can be defined as "the totality of the individual's thoughts and feelings having reference to himself as an object."[3] In other words, your self-concept is composed of the attitudes you hold toward yourself. Self-concept is a value around which life revolves, so the individual's evaluation of self greatly influences behavior. Furthermore, since the self-concept grows from interactions with parents, peers, teachers, and significant others, self-enhancement will depend on the reactions of these people. As a result, individuals strive for and direct behavior toward obtaining positive reactions from others they perceive as important.

The self-concept is, in fact, the personal or internal basis of the lifestyle of an individual, since the self-concept denotes the totality of one's attitudes, feelings, perceptions, and evaluations of oneself.

The self-concept is really divided into four basic parts, as shown in Table 11–1: actual versus ideal, and private versus social. The actual/ideal distinction refers to your perception of *who I am now* (actual) and *who I would like to be* (ideal). The private self refers to *how I am or would like to be to myself* (private self), while the social self is *how I am seen by others or how I would like to be seen by others* (social self).

The distinction between private and social self-concepts is an important one.[4] The private self-concept alone cannot explain all of the lifestyle behavior in which we see individuals engage. This is exemplified in the following quote:

Table 11–1
Dimensions of a Consumer's Self-Concept

Dimensions of self-concept	Actual self-image	Ideal self-image
Private self	How I actually see myself	How I would like to see myself
Social self	How others actually see me	How I would like others to see me

Figure 11–3
Our Goal Is to Move Closer to Our Ideal Self-Image

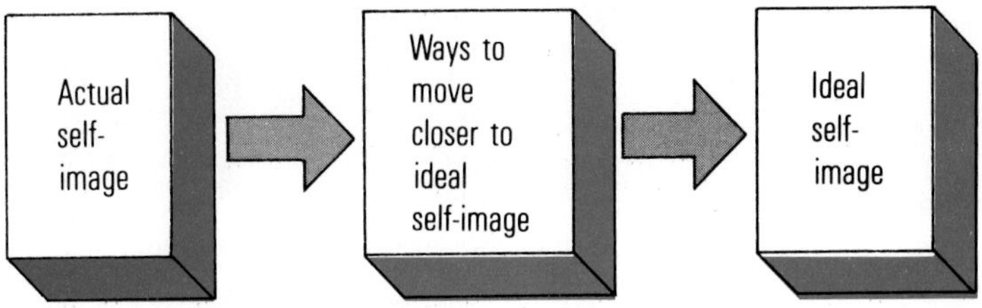

> Two systems have now developed, both of which determine behavior. The one, based on self-actualization, approaches or avoids depending on whether or not the resulting experience is seen as one which will enhance the person. The other, based on the need for positive regard, approaches or avoids depending on whether or not the resulting experience is seen as one which will meet with approval from significant others (or from the self, when the viewpoint of others has been internalized). Needless to say, the person often encounters situations in which one basic need says "approach" while the other says "avoid." Learning a new skill, for example, often means embarrassment in the early, awkward stages, but, when accomplished, adds to the competence of the individual.[5]

As Figure 11–3 indicates, there is a very definite relationship between the actual and ideal private self-concept and between the actual and ideal social self-concept. In both cases, we strive to move our real (actual) self-concept toward our ideal self-concept. A basic motivation then, according to self-concept theorists, is to achieve the ideal self-concept, or at least to move toward an ideal self-concept.

We frequently engage in behaviors such as product purchases when we think those purchases will enhance the attainment of our ideal self-concept—private and/or social.[6] The advertising copy presented in Exhibit 11–2 appears to be based on this approach. In other words, the Excalibur is appropriate for those desiring a private or social self-concept of a confident, self-assured, unique individual with refined taste.

Measuring Self-Concept

Utilizing self-concept requires that we be able to measure it. The most common measurement approach is the semantic differential (see Appendix A). While most studies use the semantic differential, the selection of adjectives has typically

Exhibit 11–2 Ideal Image-Oriented Advertisement

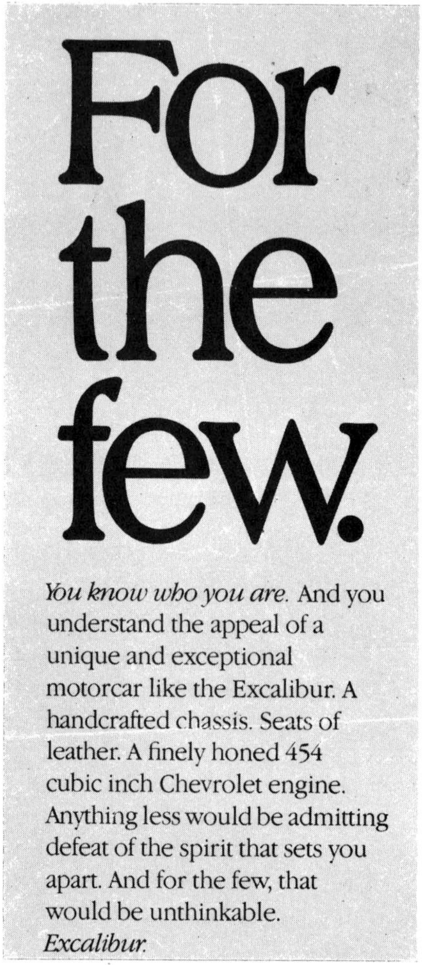
For the few.
You know who you are. And you understand the appeal of a unique and exceptional motorcar like the Excalibur. A handcrafted chassis. Seats of leather. A finely honed 454 cubic inch Chevrolet engine. Anything less would be admitting defeat of the spirit that sets you apart. And for the few, that would be unthinkable.
Excalibur.

Used with permission from Excalibur Automobile Corporation.

been done on an intuitive basis. That is, each researcher develops a unique list of components of self-concept.

Fortunately, Malhotra has developed a set of 15 pairs of adjectives that offer promise of being applicable across a variety of settings.[7] These terms, shown in Table 11–2, were found effective in describing ideal, actual, and social self-concepts, automobiles, and celebrities. Thus, they could be used to insure a match between the self-concept (actual or ideal) of a target market, the product concept, and the characteristics of an advertising spokesperson.

Table 11–2
Measurement Scales for Self-Concepts, Person Concepts and Product Concepts

1. Rugged	....	Delicate
2. Excitable	....	Calm
3. Uncomfortable	....	Comfortable
4. Dominating	....	Submissive
5. Thrifty	....	Indulgent
6. Pleasant	....	Unpleasant
7. Contemporary	....	Noncontemporary
8. Organized	....	Unorganized
9. Rational	....	Emotional
10. Youthful	....	Mature
11. Formal	....	Informal
12. Orthodox	....	Liberal
13. Complex	....	Simple
14. Colorless	....	Colorful
15. Modest	....	Vain

Source: N. K. Malhotra, "A Scale to Measure Self-Concepts, Person Concepts, and Product Concepts," *Journal of Marketing Research,* November 1981, p. 462.

Using Self-Concept to Position Products

The use of the self-concept by marketing managers is explained by the following logical sequence that leads to a relationship between the self-concept and product purchase:

- An individual has a self-concept. The self-concept is formed through interaction with parents, peers, teachers, and significant others.
- One's self-concept is of value to the individual.
- Because the self-concept is valued, individuals strive to enhance their self-concept.
- Certain products serve as social symbols and communicate social meaning about those who own or use such products.
- The use of products as symbols communicates meaning to one's self and to others, causing an impact on the individual's self-concept.
- As a result, the behavior of an individual may be directed toward the consumption of goods as symbols which maintain or enhance a desired self-concept.[8]

Figure 11–4
The Relationship between Self-Concept and Brand Image Influence

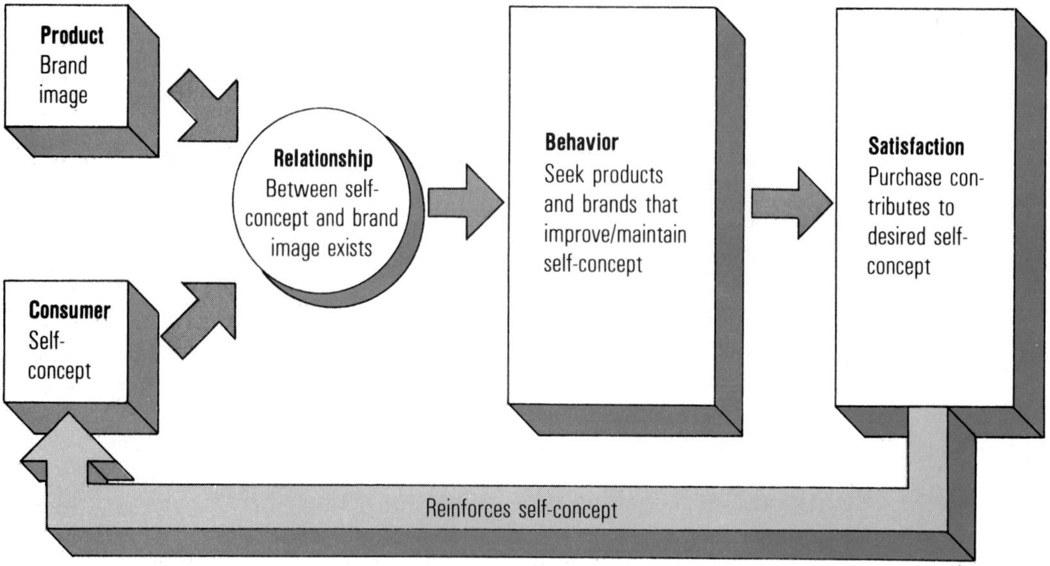

As shown in Figure 11–4, before self-concept is a relevant marketing tool there has to be a relationship between self-concept and brand image. Furthermore, for this to impact purchase and consumption there has to be both expected and actual satisfaction. That is, the brand purchased must help deliver the desired self-concept.

While it has been shown that consumers prefer brands that are similar to their self-concepts (actual or ideal, private or social), the degree to which they would be attracted to a product varies with the *symbolism* and *conspicuousness* of that product class. Furthermore, the interaction between self-concept and product image is situation specific.[9] That is, the situation may heighten or lessen the degree to which a product or store would enhance an individual's self-image.

In summary then, the self-concepts that individuals have of themselves—actual and ideal, private and social—serve as a guide for many product and brand choices.[10] As marketing managers strive to develop new products and new appeals for consumers, they need to keep in mind this important variable. Products seen as expressive of self-image will be judged by consumers on "how well they help make me what I want to be, and how I want others to see me."

Exhibit 11–3 illustrates the actual and ideal self-concepts of two types of female perfume buyers. Each type of consumer has meaningful differences between their actual and ideal self-concepts. To successfully market perfume to this group of consumers one would have to:

Exhibit 11–3 Actual and Ideal Self-Concepts of Perfume Buyers

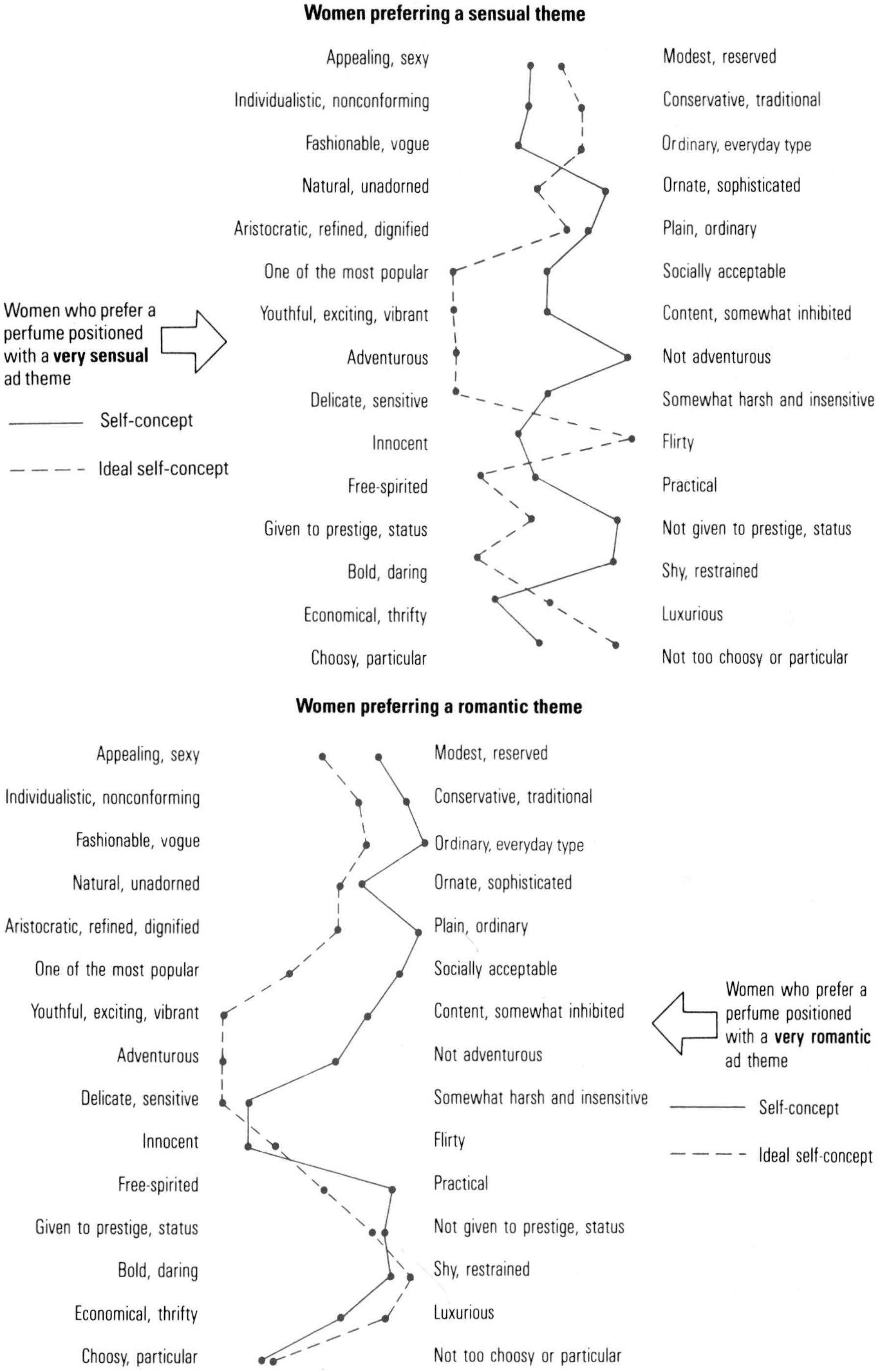

Source: Adapted from M. W. DeLozier, *Consumer Behavior Dynamics*, Puritan Cosmetics, Inc. (Merrill Publishing Co., 1977).

- Recognize the major differences in self-concept that differentiate the two segments of female perfume buyers.
- Build brand image positioning around the key components of ideal self-concept, including the characteristics of a spokeswoman if one is used.
- Measure brand image, and continue to develop strategy to move it closer to the target perfume consumers' ideal self-concept.

PSYCHOGRAPHICS

Lifestyles to a large degree reflect an individual's attempts to realize a desired self-concept. Operationalizing or measuring lifestyle has been and continues to be a major challenge.

Psychographics are the primary way that lifestyle has been made operationally useful to marketing managers. Psychographics are a way of describing (graphics) the psychological (psycho) makeup or lifestyle of a consumer or segment of consumers. Psychographic research is quantitative research intended to place consumers on psychological—as distinguished from solely demographic—dimensions.[11] As with all measurement tools in marketing, there are some problems with the psychographic technique. Managers need to be fully aware of both the advantages and disadvantages of psychographics before using the results.[12]

Psychographics in the strict sense of the term focus on individual's activities (behaviors), interests, and opinions (reflecting both attitudes and values). However, marketers generally add several additional dimensions when developing psychographic profiles. The most commonly used dimensions include:

- *Demographics:* age, education, income, occupation, family structure, ethnic background, gender, and geographic location.
- *Attitudes:* evaluative statements about other people, places, ideas, products, and so forth.
- *Values:* widely held beliefs about what is acceptable and/or desirable.
- *Personality traits:* That set of characteristics that are unique to the personal makeup of an individual.

Table 11–3
Several Components of AIO Questionnaires

Activities	Interests	Opinions
Work	Family	Themselves
Hobbies	Home	Social issues
Social events	Job	Politics
Vacation	Community	Business
Entertainment	Recreation	Economics
Club membership	Fashion	Education
Community	Food	Products
Shopping	Media	Future
Sports	Achievement	Culture

Figure 11–5
Psychographic Continuum for AIO Statements

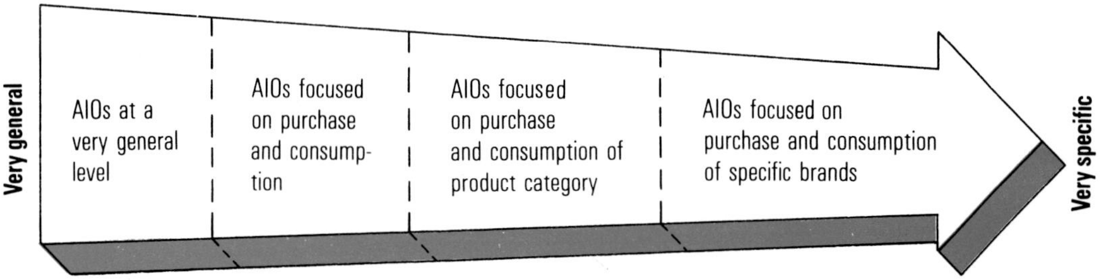

Source: F. A. Bushman, "Systematic Life Styles for New Product Segmentation," *Journal of the Academy of Marketing Science,* Fall 1982, pp. 377–94.

- *Activities and interests:* nonoccupational behaviors to which consumers devote time and effort, such as hobbies, sports, public service, and church.
- *Usage rates:* measurements of consumer consumption within a specified product category. Often consumers are categorized as heavy, medium, light, or nonusers.[13]

These variables are measured via standard demographic and product usage questionnaires in conjunction with AIO (activity, interest, and opinion) inventories. AIO inventories consist of a large number (often as many as 300) of statements with which respondents express a degree of agreement or disagreement. Table 11–3 lists some of the components of an AIO analysis. As illustrated in Figure 11–5, AIO inventories can be constructed with varying degrees of specificity. At one extreme are very general AIO statements dealing with general ways of living. At the other, AIO statements are product or activity specific.[14] (For an illustration, see Table 15–5, page 583). For example, a manufacturer of floor tiles might include items on home entertainment, the behavior and role of children in the home, pet ownership, usage of credit, interest in fashion, and so forth. The value of such lifestyle information on a particular target market is easy to understand. General or "product free" lifestyles can be used to discover new product opportunities, while brand-specific lifestyle analysis may help reposition existing products.

Exhibit 11–4 illustrates the result of a general lifestyle study of women in which AIO statements reflected the more general aspects of activities, interests, and opinions. When we add information on each segment's consumption behavior (Table 11–4) and media preference (Table 11–5), we are able to see how a marketer could use this information to develop product positioning and advertising strategies. For example, "Candice," "Cathy," and "Mildred" are all above-

Exhibit 11–4 Female Lifestyle Segments

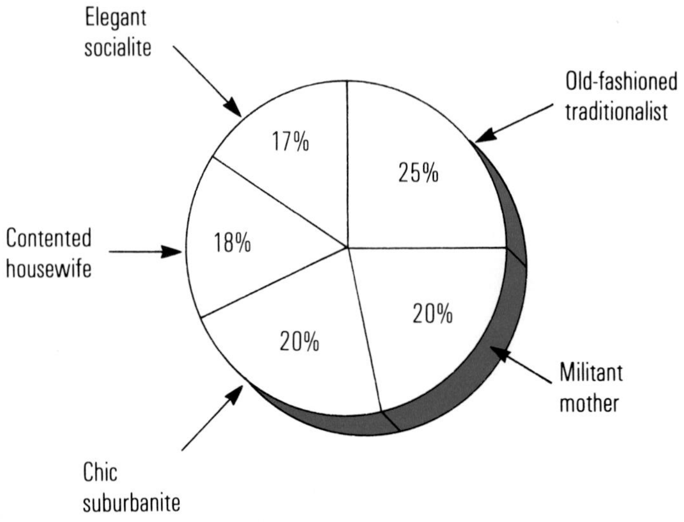

THELMA, THE OLD-FASHIONED TRADITIONALIST (25 PERCENT)

This lady has lived a "good" life—she has been a devoted wife, a doting mother, and a conscientious housewife. She has lived her life by these traditional values and she cherishes them to this day. She does not condone contemporary sexual activities or political liberalism, nor can she sympathize with the women's libbers. Even today, when most of her children have left home, her life is centered around the kitchen. Her one abiding interest outside the household is the church which she attends every week. She lacks higher education and hence has little appreciation for the arts or cultural activities. Her spare time is spent watching TV, which is her prime source of entertainment and information.

MILDRED, THE MILITANT MOTHER (20 PERCENT)

Mildred married young and had children before she was quite ready to raise a family. Now she is unhappy. She is having trouble making ends meet on her blue-collar husband's income. She is frustrated and she vents her frustrations by rebelling against the system. She finds escape from her unhappy world in soap operas and movies. Television provides an ideal medium for her to live out her fantasies. She watches TV all through the day and late into the night. She likes heavy rock and probably soul music, and she doesn't read much except escapist magazines such as *True Story*.

CANDICE, THE CHIC SUBURBANITE (20 PERCENT)

Candice is an urbane woman. She is well educated and genteel. She is a prime mover in her community, active in club affairs, and working on

Exhibit 11–4 *(concluded)*

community projects. Socializing is an important part of her life. She is a doer, interested in sports and the outdoors, politics and current affairs. Her life is hectic and lived at a fast clip. She is a voracious reader, and there are few magazines she doesn't read. However, TV does relatively poorly in competing for her attention—it is too inane for her.

CATHY, THE CONTENTED HOUSEWIFE (18 PERCENT)

Cathy epitomizes simplicity. Her life is untangled. She is married to a worker in the middle of the socioeconomic scale, and they, along with their several preteen children, live in a small town. She is devoted to her family and faithfully serves them as mother, housewife, and cook. There is a certain tranquility in her life. She enjoys a relaxed pace and avoids anything that might disturb her equilibrium. She doesn't like news or news-type programs on TV but enjoys wholesome family shows.

ELEANOR, THE ELEGANT SOCIALITE (17 PERCENT)

Eleanor is a woman with style. She lives in the city because that is where she wants to be. She likes the economic and social aspects of big city living and takes advantage of the city in terms of her career and leisure-time activities. She is a self-confident on-the-go woman, not a homebody. She is fashion-conscious and dresses well. She is a woman with panache. She is financially secure; as a result she is not a careful shopper. She shops for quality and style, not price. She is a cosmopolitan woman who has traveled or wants to travel abroad.

Source: Sunil Mehrota and William D. Wells, "Psychographics and Buyer Behavior: Theory and Recent Empirical Findings," in *Consumer and Industrial Buying Behavior,* ed. Arch G. Woodside et al. (New York: Elsevier, North-Holland, 1977), p. 54.

average users of shampoo. How would your product features, advertising theme, and advertising media differ if you were developing a separate product for each group? What problems would you have marketing one product to all three groups (the heavy-user segment)?

THE VALS LIFESTYLES

By far the most popular application of lifestyle and psychographic research by marketing managers is SRI International's Value and Lifestyles (VALS) program. VALS provides a systematic classification of American adults into nine distinct value and lifestyle patterns that are useful in developing marketing strategy.[15]

Table 11–4
An Index of Cosmetic Usage for Five Psychographic Segments*

I Often Wear	Thelma	Eleanor	Candice	Cathy	Mildred
Expensive cologne	79	175	111	80	82
Lipstick	100	156	111	100	81
Hairspray	114	150	92	100	72
Nail polish	76	142	100	88	142
Hair coloring	200	142	150	65	15
Eye makeup	31	135	115	104	127
Wig	80	124	100	106	103
Breath freshener	132	139	86	82	93
Medicated face makeup	70	106	94	106	140
Hand lotion	100	99	108	100	95
Shampoo	90	92	107	106	111

*An index of 100 represents average consumption.

Source: Sunil Mehrota and William D. Wells, "Psychographics and Buyer Behavior: Theory and Recent Empirical Findings," in *Consumer and Industrial Buying Behavior,* ed. Arch G. Woodside et al. (Elsevier, New York: North-Holland, 1977), p. 57.

Table 11–5
An Index of Media Habits for the Five Female Psychographic Segments*

	Thelma	Eleanor	Candice	Cathy	Mildred
Heavy rock	14	71	92	86	257
Popular music	65	92	98	112	143
Middle-of-the-road music	79	102	130	100	98
Country and western	112	89	81	115	102
Classical/semiclassical	90	97	162	67	79
Time	64	100	206	53	92
People	46	115	154	85	115
Cosmopolitan	43	150	121	64	136
Vogue	50	167	167	33	83
Glamour	40	130	130	80	120
Playboy	21	129	121	100	171
True Story	83	50	33	133	233
Redbook	83	93	113	103	113
TV Guide	76	103	84	108	137
Parents	60	70	130	120	180
Family Circle	93	100	115	171	85
Better Homes and Gardens	92	106	129	90	86
Good Housekeeping	86	104	120	104	88
Ladies Home Journal	95	115	117	102	80
McCall's	95	114	116	93	86
Reader's Digest	106	100	110	100	82
Morning newspaper	107	115	144	78	60

*An index of 100 represents average usage.

Source: Sunil Mehrota and William D. Wells, "Psychographics and Buyer Behavior: Theory and Recent Empirical Findings," in *Consumer and Industrial Buying Behavior,* ed. Arch G. Woodside et al. (Elsevier, New York: North-Holland, 1977), p. 58.

Figure 11–6
SRI's Hierarchy of Values and Lifestyle Categories

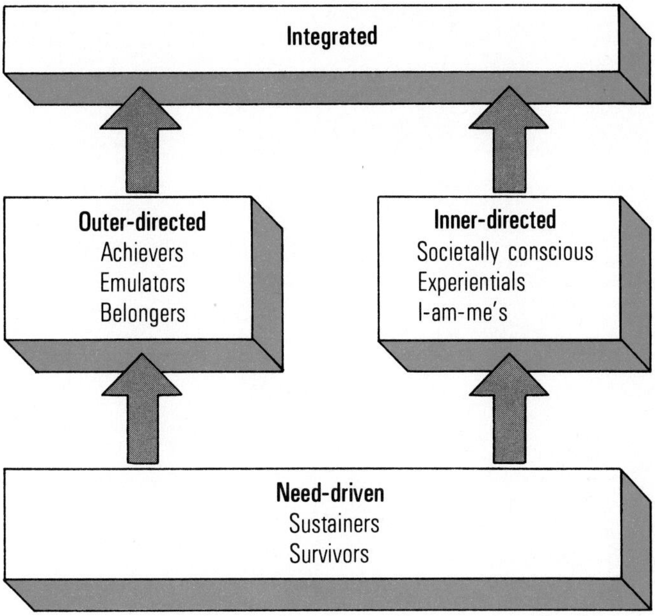

This program has been used by 60 of the largest retail firms in the country to better understand the attitudes and sentiments of the American consumer.[16] The program's aim is to give retailers insight into how to tailor their operations in terms of merchandise mix, product presentation, advertising, and point-of-purchase displays. Corporations such as AT&T, *New York Times, Penthouse,* Atlantic Richfield, and Ranier National Bank have also found VALS useful.

SRI's VALS classification scheme is developed from a variety of theory and empirical data.[17] As shown in Figure 11–6, the nine VALS profiles are grouped into a hierarchy of four major categories. Table 11–6 provides demographic and attitude data across the nine lifestyles; Table 11–7 contains consumption data; Table 11–8 has activity data; and Table 11–9 provides media usage information. The following paragraphs describe each category.

Need-Driven Lifestyles

This lifestyle category contains approximately 11 percent of the U.S. population but accounts for only 4 percent of total U.S. annual purchases. These consumers are concerned with security and prices and are struggling to survive in our consumption-driven culture.

Table 11–6
Demographics and Attitudes of SRI VALS Lifestyle Categories

Lifestyle Categories	Millions of Adults	Median Age	Median Household Income	Believe a Woman's Place Is in the Home	Believe People Are Honest	Are More Experimental than Conventional	Believe Industrial Growth Should Be Limited	Believe the United States Should Be Active in Foreign Affairs
Outer-directed:								
Achievers	32	42	$35,000	16%	50%	7%	8%	39%
Emulators	13	28	19,000	9	22	10	16	24
Belongers	63	54	17,500	34	51	6	16	23
Inner-directed:								
Societally conscious	18	38	30,000	2	37	25	18	36
Experiential	10	27	26,000	5	44	33	25	30
I-am-me	5	21	12,500	7	35	29	18	16
Need-driven:								
Sustainers	11	32	11,000	32	22	12	18	24
Survivors	6	66	Under $5,000	46	28	15	21	26

Source: T. C. Thomas and S. Crocker, *Values and Lifestyles—The New Psychographics* (Menlo Park, Calif.: Stanford Research Institute, 1981), pp. 16–18.

Table 11–7
Consumption Differences between VALS Categories

Lifestyle Categories	Breakfast Foods: Cold Cereal	Breakfast Foods: Hot Cereal	Breakfast Foods: Breakfast Bars	Camera Ownership: Instant	Camera Ownership: Movie	Camera Ownership: 35mm Reflex
Achievers	94	93	108	122	144	156
Emulators	71	64	100	100	62	89
Belongers	126	129	69	92	88	44
Societally conscious	85	57	100	97	112	200
Experiential	82	64	115	100	106	167
I-am-me	94	71	262	122	94	111
Sustainers	82	100	169	128	94	33
Survivors	106	229	131	31	25	0

Lifestyle Categories	Soft Drinks: Regular	Soft Drinks: Sugar-Free	Keep/Stay-Alert Aids	Contact Lenses
Need-driven	112	50	167	50
Belongers	82	80	67	50
Emulators	171	90	200	112
Achievers	94	110	100	112
I-am-me	176	120	500	213
Experiential	94	150	67	150
Societally conscious	59	170	33	162

Source: T. C. Thomas and S. Crocker, *Values and Lifestyles—The New Psychographics* (Menlo Park, Calif.: Stanford Research Institute, 1981).

Sustainers. Individuals in this group are struggling on the edge of poverty. They are relatively young and eager to get ahead. Many female, single heads of households fall into this lifestyle category. Sustainers make up 7 percent of the U.S. population and account for 3 percent of U.S. spending.

- Values: Somewhat optimistic, feel left out, feel things are changing too fast, agree with "am a bit of a swinger," feel social status is important.
- Activities: Football, basketball, baseball, bowling, fishing, listen to music, drink hard liquor, attend discos.
- Media: Game shows, comedies, outdoor shows, soap operas, reading tabloids.
- Buying style: Basic needs, localized outlets, erratic patterns, time payments.

Survivors. This group of need-driven consumers is typically older (median age of 66) and poor (median household income under $5,000). They are far removed from the cultural mainstream. Survivors represent 4 percent of the U.S. population and 1 percent of all spending.

- Values: Suspicious, discontented, pessimistic, home-focused, conservative, lack self-confidence, unsatisfied.
- Activities: Virtually none beyond mass media, family, and peer interaction.
- Media: Heavy television viewing, particularly game shows, and some tabloid readership.
- Buying style: Cautious, price, brand names, guarantees, reassurances.

Outer-Directed Lifestyles

This lifestyle category is outwardly directed in behavior. This group includes achievers, emulators, and belongers. It represents about 67 percent of the U.S. population and 80 percent of total purchases. They buy with an eye on appearance and in accord with established social norms.

Achievers. They are the leaders in business, professions, and government. Efficiency, fame, status, the good life, comfort, and materialism are the hallmarks of the achievers. They have a high median household income, and a median age of 42. This group makes up 20 percent of the U.S. population but accounts for 41 percent of the annual dollars spent.

Table 11–8
Activities Pursued by Different Lifestyles (Base = 100)

	Men's Activities*			Women's Activities†		
Lifestyle Categories	Golf	Tennis	Fishing	Tennis*	Attend Opera/ Ballet/Dance Performances	Attend Art Galleries/ Museums
Survivors	0	0	48	18	30	43
Sustainers	100	100	200	88	20	52
Belongers	54	38	126	47	40	79
Emulators	62	69	100	171	90	61
Achievers	162	100	87	88	150	165
I-am-me	162	223	91	347	100	74
Experiential	108	200	100	259	230	126
Societally conscious	85	115	74	88	270	191

*Once a month or more often.

†Two to nine times a year or more often.

Source: T. C. Thomas and S. Crocker, *Values and Lifestyles—The New Psychographics* (Menlo Park, Calif.: Stanford Research Institute, 1981), p. 29.

Table 11–9
Media Habits of SRI Lifestyle Categories (Base = 100)

	TV Programs Watched Regularly			
Lifestyle Categories	Comedies	Game Shows	Early Evening News (5–7 P.M.)	Late Evening News (10 P.M. or Later)
Survivors	67	233	126	93
Sustainers	195	225	87	115
Belongers	86	158	121	110
Emulators	152	108	79	88
Achievers	67	42	98	102
I-am-me	176	17	47	55
Experiential	138	42	72	90
Societally conscious	67	50	96	115

	Magazine Readership*				
Lifestyle Categories	Tabloids (*National Enquirer,* the *Star,* etc.)	Business Magazines (*Business Week, Fortune,* etc.)	News Magazines (*Time, Newsweek,* etc.)	General Sports (*Sports Illustrated,* etc.)	Literary (*New Yorker,* etc.)
Survivors	118	36	56	0	86
Sustainers	247	64	62	79	129
Belongers	129	100	74	68	57
Emulators	106	36	76	121	43
Achievers	53	186	129	100	100
I-am-me	100	100	132	195	71
Experiential	59	114	132	132	200
Societally conscious	47	157	147	110	200

*One or more of the last four issues.

Source: T. C. Thomas and S. Crocker, *Values and Lifestyles—The New Psychographics* (Menlo Park, Calif.: Stanford Research Institute, 1981), pp. 26–27.

- Values: Success/fame, puritan ethic, materialism, efficiency, dominant, comfort, contented, self-confident, deliberate.
- Activities: Golf, cultural events, adult education, drinks before dinner, spectator sports, pleasure travel.
- Media: Limited TV, heavy newspaper, news, and business magazine readership.
- Buying styles: Originators, luxury, top of life, technology.

Emulators. They strive to burst into the system and attain the lifestyle of the achiever. They are ambitious and competitive, with a median age of 28 and median household income of $19,000. Their attempts to imitate the achievers often fail because they lack the skills, background, training, and resources. Emulators represent 8 percent of the U.S. population and 10 percent of total U.S. spending.

- Values: Status, display, aspiring, manipulative, competitive, optimistic, conventional in most areas but liberal on sex and drugs, little self-confidence.
- Activities: Golf, spectator sports, drinks before dinner, pleasure travel.
- Media: Limited TV except comedies, reads newspapers and business magazines.
- Buying styles: Conspicuous, in vogue, extremes, overstatement.

Belongers. They are traditional, conservative, nostalgic, and unexperimental. The home is their domain. Belongers are the traditional mass market and often the silent majority who would rather fit in than stand out. Their median age is 54 and median household income is $17,500. Belongers make up 39 percent of the U.S. population and represent 27 percent of U.S. annual spending.

- Values: Fitting in, conventional, group membership, tradition, nostalgia, reliable, home focused, family oriented, contented though somewhat pessimistic.
- Activities: Limited activities—fishing, gardening, and collecting recipes are popular.
- Media: Watch game shows and the news, read tabloids.
- Buying style: Popularity, stable/mass market, brand names, made in America, convenience.

Inner-Directed Lifestyles

This lifestyle category is inward looking in much of their behavior. They buy to satisfy their self-expression and individual needs. This group represents about 20 percent of the U.S. population and about 15 percent of total purchases.

Societally Conscious. These individuals have a high sense of social responsibility that leads them to support such causes as conservation, environmentalism, and consumerism. They are attracted to simple living and smallness of scale. They want to pursue lives that conserve, protect, and heal. Their median age is 38 and median household income is $30,000. Societally conscious consumers make up 11 percent of the population and 8 percent of total spending.

- Values: Socially responsible, voluntary simplicity, inner growth, small scale, somewhat optimistic, liberal, very pro women's rights, experimental, individualistic, self-confident, not status conscious.
- Activities: Swimming, sailing, writing, attending cultural events, library, adult education, travel.
- Media: Educational TV and late news, magazines, particularly literary.
- Buying style: Conservation, authenticity, nonconsumption, health-conscious, not brand focused, complain when dissatisfied.

Experientials. These inner-directed individuals want direct experience and vigorous involvement. Experientials are artistic, experimental, and participative. To the experiential, life is a light show at one moment and introspection the next. They are typically in their mid-20s with a median household income of $26,000. Experientials make up 6 percent of the population and 5 percent of total spending.

- Values: Direct experience, participative, hedonistic, intuitive, believe in "inner self," optimistic, like to party, like change, liberal, support women's rights, happy.
- Activities: All active sports, camping, backpacking, chess, backgammon, writing, cultural events, concerts, dancing, meditation, poker, adult education, travel.
- Media: Read books, literary and news magazines, limited TV.
- Buying style: Making, doing, crafts, health conscious, no brand loyalty, quality concerned.

I-Am-Me. The I-am-me's are zippy, dramatic, impulsive, fiercely individualistic, and profoundly intuitive. In many instances they will be the fashion innovators and the ones most likely to set new trends. They are younger (median age is 21), high-energy people whose median household income is $12,500. They represent 3 percent of the population and 2 percent of total spending.

- Values: Experimental, self-expressive, impulsive, individualistic, optimistic, love to party, like change, low family focus, liberal, happy.
- Activities: All active sports, all outdoor activities, painting, writing, chess, billiards, concerts, discos, poker, eating out, second job, pleasure travel, movies.
- Media: Late night TV, comedies, sports magazines, radio.
- Buying style: Display, fad, clique, far-out, convenience.

Integrated

This lifestyle group combines the outwardness components of the outer-directed lifestyle and the sensitivity and introspectiveness of the inner-directed. They are focused on self-actualization as described in Chapter 10. They are concerned with both personal development and the world around them. They are highest in education and have a median age of 40. Their median income is $40,000. They make up 2 percent of the U.S. population and spend 3 percent of all dollars spent. They value maturity, individualism, tolerance, world view, compromise, self-confidence, and wisdom. Because they compose such a small percent of the population and are highly diverse, a meaningful portrayal of their activities and media preferences is not practical. Their buying styles focus on ecology, quality, esthetics, the unique, and high standards.

Exhibit 11–5 Marketing Applications of VALS

AVON*

Avon has used VALS to help recruit sales representatives. Historically, Avon representatives have been *belongers*. To reach a broader market, Avon explicitly recruits representatives from other typologies. This is because representatives tend to call on and be effective with people much like themselves.

TIMEX MEDICAL PRODUCTS GROUP†

Three digital products—scale, thermometer, and blood pressure monitor—are targeted at various VALS segments.

After matching the innovativeness of the products with the lifestyles of each VALS segment, Timex focused on *achievers* and *societally conscious,* since both groups had high levels of education, early adoption of new technology, and a concern for staying healthy. The matching process rules out *belongers,* who are tradition bound and not oriented toward high tech.

MERRILL LYNCH‡

While a popular and memorable ad, Merrill Lynch's "Bullish on America" was a technical error. Although their intended target market was *achievers,* the ad appealed more to *belongers*. The shift from "Bullish on America" to "A Breed Apart" was a repositioning to appeal more to the lifestyle of the *achievers*.

***READER'S DIGEST*§**

Clairol was reluctant to advertise in *Reader's Digest* because they were convinced its readers were stodgy, middle-aged housewives. However, *Reader's Digest* showed that its audience was definitely outer-directed, with a strong *belonger* component. With this and other VALS information, Clairol restructured their ad copy from inner-directed to a clear-cut, outer-directed theme.

*B. Townsend, "Psychographic Glitter and Gold," *American Demographics,* November 1985, p. 25.

†"Timex and VALS Engineer a Psychographic Product Launch," *Ad Forum,* September 1984, pp. 12–14.

‡J. Atlas, "Beyond Demographics," *The Atlantic Monthly,* October 1984, p. 49.

§Ibid., p. 56.

Using VALS

VALS can be used to segment markets, define appropriate product positions, and structure advertising. Exhibit 11–5 illustrates several of the thousands of applications of this methodology.[18] However, VALS must be used with caution and common sense.[19] A number of concerns and issues exist including:

- VALS are *individual* measures, but most consumption decisions are *household* decisions, or are heavily influenced by other household members.
- Few individuals are "pure." That is, most individuals have characteristics of several categories. This lack of "purity" is similar to the concept of status crystallization discussed in Chapter 4. In fact, VALS now provides information on "combination" individuals such as Achiever/Belonger and Achiever/Societally Conscious (the first group tends to be relatively conservative, older, female, and less well-educated, while the second is composed primarily of younger, socially liberal professionals).
- VALS categories are heavily demographic. That is, much of the variance between the groups can be explained by age, education, and income rather than values. This led ABC to develop its own segmentation scheme based primarily on psychological variables.
- The types of values and demographics measured by VALS may be inappropriate for particular products or situations. Product- or activity-specific lifestyles may provide more useful information.
- Other general value measurement systems may provide superior results. Evidence indicates that the List of Values (LOV), when coupled with the same demographic variables used in VALS, provides more accurate predictions of consumption.[20] LOV is composed of nine values (self-respect, security, warm relationships with others, sense of accomplishment, self-fulfillment, sense of belonging, being well respected, fun and enjoyment in life, and excitement). Individuals rate or rank these values in terms of importance to themselves.[21] This system is easy to administer, has a strong theoretical and empirical base, and relates closely to the daily activities and thoughts of individuals.

GEO-LIFESTYLE ANALYSIS

During the early 1970s several firms began to use the rapidly expanding power of the computer to classify geographic areas based on the demographic data available from the 1970 Census. CLARITAS, a leading firm in this industry describes the logic of the approach:

> People with similar cultural backgrounds, means, and perspectives naturally gravitate toward one another. They choose to live amongst their

> peers in neighborhoods offering affordable advantages and compatible lifestyles.
>
> Once settled in, people naturally emulate their neighbors. They adopt similar social values, tastes, and expectations. They exhibit shared patterns of consumer behavior toward products, services, media and promotions.[22]

Analyses of this type are known as *geo-demographic* analyses. They focus on the demographics of geographic areas based on the belief that lifestyle, and thus consumption, is largely driven by demographic factors, as described above. The geographic regions analyzed can be quite small, ranging from Standard Metropolitan Statistical Areas, through 5-digit ZIP Codes, Census Tracts, and down to Census Blocks (averaging only 340 households). Such data are used for target market selection, promotional emphasis, and so forth, by numerous consumer goods marketers.

CLARITAS has taken geo-demographic analysis one step further and incorporated extensive data on consumption patterns. The output is a set of 40 lifestyle clusters organized into 12 broad social groups, as briefly described in Exhibit 11–6 (at the end of this chapter). This is called the PRIZM system. Every neighborhood in the U.S. can be profiled in terms of these 40 lifestyle groups. For example, one of the authors lives outside of Eugene, Oregon, in a large ZIP code area that includes part of the city. Its profile is:

Towns and gowns	37.9%
Young influentials	26.3
Blue-blood estates	10.7
Bohemian mix	8.9
Smalltown downtown	6.5
Money and brains	5.3
Single-city blues	4.4

Unlike the VALS typology, PRIZM does not measure values or attitudes (though the distribution of VALS types within each geographic area covered by PRIZM is available). It is primarily driven by demographics with substantial support from consumption and media usage data. CLARITAS and its competitors are widely used by consumer marketing firms such as General Motors, Hertz, and Mountain Bell Telephone.[23] To illustrate how firms can use such data, we will describe an application for a hypothetical imported beer, Brinker.[24]

Brinker had stable sales in the U.S. for several years. Annual surveys indicated that 65 percent of the consumers were male, 80 percent were under 50 years of age, and 58 percent had above average household incomes. Thus, the firm defined its target market as males, age 18–49, with above-average incomes. This target market definition includes 30 percent of the brand's consumers ($.65 \times .80 \times .58 = .30$).

While this target definition was workable for media planning, it did not function well for market expansion, or for estimating and targeting potential Brinker consumers by geographic markets. Nearly *all* major markets show similar concentrations of males between 21 and 49. Should Brinker target solely by

Figure 11–7
Brinker Beer Drinker Index

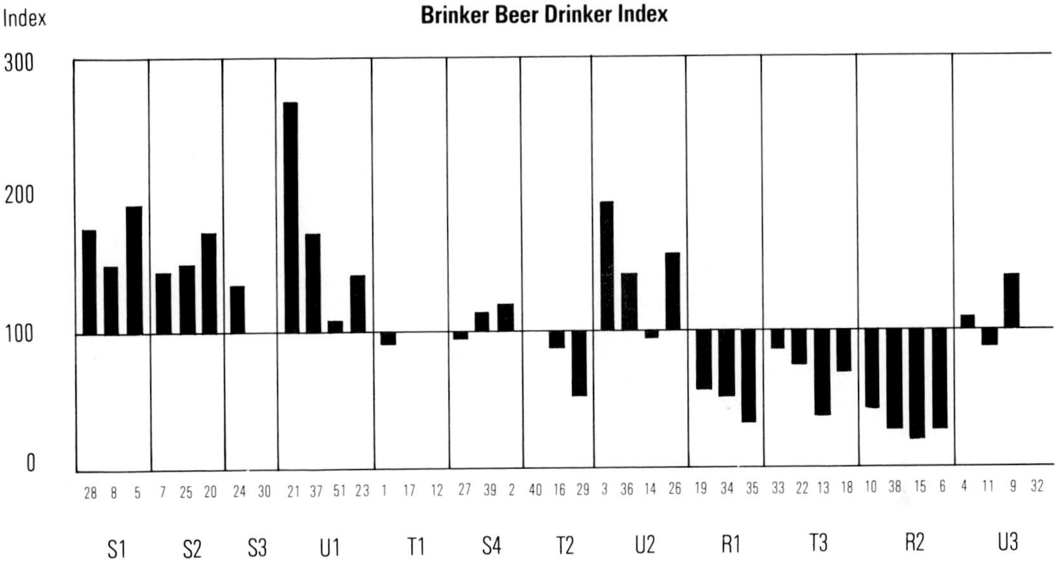

Used with permission from CLARITAS.

household income? And what of the remaining 70 percent of brand drinkers? In short, where was the real potential for growth?

Based on Brinker's survey data, its consumers were categorized by the PRIZM lifestyle clusters. Figure 11–7 shows the 40 clusters arrayed from left to right in descending social rank, and the height of each cluster bar shows its concentration of brand drinkers relative to the U.S. average (100).

Fourteen lifestyle clusters appeared to represent good target markets. Further analysis suggested three major targets. The seven upscale clusters in groups S1, S2, and S3 buy Brinker to drink and serve at home. These were labeled the "Suburban Entertainers." The six heavy-user clusters in U1 and U2 consume Brinker at home and in bars and taverns. The firm called these the "Singles Bar Trade." Finally, Cluster 9 in U3 was labeled "Urban Hispanics." They appear to have a strong taste preference for Brinker and other imports. The market segmentation strategy was as follows:

Selected PRIZM Target Groups	Percent Total Adults	Percent Brand Drinkers	Index Concentration
Primary (Main-thrust marketing)			
G1—Suburban entertainers	15.6%	24.2%	156
G2—Singles bar trade	12.4	19.4	155
Subtotal	28.0	43.6	155
Secondary (special market promos)			
Cluster 9—Urban Hispanics	1.6%	2.2%	135

Having selected these targets, the next question was, "*Where* are they located?" Table 11–10 contains the first part of a report showing the concentration of Brinker's target markets in each of 200 TV market areas.

In the report, all TV markets are ranked by column four, the Index of Concentration for Brinker's *primary* target of "Suburban Entertainers" and "Singles Bar Trade" clusters. Once ranked, the markets are grouped into "deciles" (tenths) of the total U.S. population. Note that the top three deciles (30 percent of total U.S.) include only 12 TV markets, but these markets contain 56 percent of Brinker's total national primary target. Note also that these same 12 markets deliver over 76 percent of the secondary target of "Urban Hispanics."

A comparison of actual sales to market potential across the 200 TV markets (or any other geographic measure of interest) allowed Brinker to effectively allocate advertising and sales efforts to areas with the greatest potential. Further, census block analyses within target cities allowed precise targeting of retail outlets and bars for special promotions. Data on the media habits of the 14 clusters provided guidance for effective media strategies.

As our ability to manage large-scale data bases continues to improve, demographic and lifestyle systems such as PRIZM will grow in both complexity and value.

Table 11–10
PRIZM Marketscan Report for Brinker Beer (TV markets ranked by concentration of primary target)

	Base	**Primary Target Groups**			**Urban Hispanics**		
TV Market	Market % of U.S.	% Target in Market	% of Market in Target	Index Concentration	% Target in Market	% of Market in Target	Index Concentration
San Francisco	2.45	6.08	70.42	248	.34	.21	14
New York	7.77	15.41	56.36	198	32.57	6.36	419
Decile 1	10.22	21.49		210	32.91		322
Los Angeles	5.41	10.56	55.52	195	20.73	5.81	383
Washington, D.C.	1.79	3.46	55.01	194	—	—	—
Houston	1.78	3.02	48.24	170	4.76	4.06	268
Denver	1.11	1.83	46.80	165	2.68	3.65	241
Decile 2	10.09	18.87		187	28.17		279
Top quintile	20.31	40.36		199	61.08		301
Boston	2.23	3.60	45.91	162	.21	.14	9
San Diego	.90	1.45	45.71	161	1.00	1.67	110
Chicago	3.50	5.46	44.31	156	9.30	4.03	266
Tucson	.32	.49	43.33	152	1.63	7.71	508
Mpls.-St. Paul	1.33	2.02	43.01	151	—	—	—
Dallas-Ft. Worth	1.79	2.60	41.27	145	3.26	2.77	182
Decile 3	10.07	15.62		155	15.40		153
Top 30% U.S.	30.38	55.98		184	76.48		252

Used with permission from CLARITAS.

Exhibit 11–6 PRIZM Lifestyle Clusters

S1	S2	S3
Educated, Affluent Executives and Professionals in Elite Metro Suburbs The three clusters in Group S1 are characterized by top socioeconomic status, college-plus educations, executive and professional occupations, expensive owner-occupied housing, and conspicuous consumption levels for many products. Representing 5 percent of U.S. households, Group S1 contains about 32 percent of the nation's $75K+ household incomes, and an estimated third of its personal net worth. **Blue-Blood Estates (28)** are America's wealthiest socioeconomic neighborhoods, populated by super-upper established managers, professionals, and heirs to "old money," accustomed to privilege and living in luxurious surroundings.	**Pre- and Post-Child Families and Singles in Upscale, White-Collar Suburbs** The three clusters of Group S2 typify a major U.S. trend toward pre- and post-child communities, with predominantly one- and two-person households surrounding closed and half-filled schools. While significantly below S1 in socioeconomic levels, S2s display all of the characteristics of success, including high-end educations, incomes, home values, and white-collar occupations, with consumption levels to match. **Pools and Patios (7)** once resembled Furs and Station Wagons, being upscale greenbelt suburbs in a late child-rearing mode. But today, most of these children have grown and departed, leaving aging couples in empty nests too costly for young homemakers. Good educations, high white-collar employment levels, and double incomes assure "the good life" in these neighborhoods.	**Upper-Middle, Child-Raising Families in Outlying, Owner-Occupied Suburbs** The two clusters of Group S3 represent our newest minority—the traditional family—Mom, Dad, and the kids. In this case, the families are upscale. Both clusters show high indices for married couples, school-age children, double incomes, two or more cars, and single-unit, owner-occupied, suburban housing. In short, S3 is the essence of the traditional American Dream. **Young Suburbia (24)** is one of our largest clusters, found coast to coast in most major markets. It runs to large, young families, and ranks second in incidence of married couples with children. These neighborhoods are distinguished by their relative affluence and high white-collar employment levels. As a result, they are strong consumers of most family products.

Exhibit 11–6 (*continued*)

S1	S2	S3
Money and Brains (8) have the nation's second highest socioeconomic rank. These neighborhoods are typified by swank, shipshape townhouses, apartments, and condos. This group has relatively few children and is dominated by childless couples and a mix of upscale singles. They are sophisticated consumers of adult luxuries—apparel, restaurants, travel, and the like. **Furs and Station Wagons (5)** is typified by "new money," living in expensive new neighborhoods in the greenbelt suburbs of the nation's major metros, coast to coast. These are well-educated, mobile professionals and managers with the nations's highest incidence of teenage children. They are winners—big producers and big spenders.	**Young Influentials (20)** could be imagined as tomorrow's Money & Brains. These are young, metropolitan sophisticates, with exceptional high-tech, white-collar employment levels. Double incomes afford high spending, and lifestyles are open, with singles, childless couples, and unrelated adults predominating in expensive one- and two-person homes, apartments, and condos. They are skewed to the new West. **Two More Rungs (25)** has a high concentration of foreign-born European ethnics and is somewhat older, with even fewer children. It is also more dense, with a higher incidence of renters in multiple-unit, high-rise housing, and has a northeastern geo-center. Two More Rungs neighborhoods show a high index for professionals, and somewhat conservative spending patterns.	**Blue-Chip Blues (30)** ranked fourth in married couples with children, is similar to Young Suburbia on most dimensions except social rank. Its predominant high school educations and blue-collar occupations are reflected in fewer high-end incomes and lower home values. However, high employment and double incomes yield similar discretionary spending patterns, and make this cluster an outstanding market.

U1	T2	S4
Educated, White-Collar Singles and Couples in Upscale, Urban Areas With minor exceptions for Black Enterprise, Group U1 is characterized by millions of young, white-collar couples and singles (many divorced and separated), dense mid- and high-rise housing, upscale socioeconomic status, cosmopolitan lifestyles, big-city universities and students, high concentrations of foreign born, and an undeniable panache and notoriety. **Urban Gold Coast (21)** is altogether unique. It is the most densely populated per square mile, with the highest concentration of one-person households in multi-unit, high-rise buildings, and the lowest incidence of auto ownership. Other mosts: most white collar, most childless, and most New York. Urban Gold Coast is the top in Urbania, a fit address for the 21 Club.	**Educated, Young, Mobile Families in Exurban Satellites and Boom Towns** The three clusters of Group T1 share a lot of American geography, most of it around our younger boom towns or in the satellite towns and exurbs far beyond the beltways of major metros. Other shared characteristics are young, white-collar adults, extremely high mobility rates, and new, low-density single-unit housing. Most evident is growth. T1s have been the chief recipients of a major urban exodus, and are among the nation's fastest-growing areas. **God's Country (1)** contains the highest socioeconomic, white-collar neighborhoods primarily located outside major metros. These are well-educated frontier types, who have opted to live away from the big metros in some of our most beautiful mountain and coastal areas. They are highly mobile, and are among the nation's fastest-growing neighborhoods. God's Country is an outstanding consumer of both products and media.	**Middle-Class, Post-Child Families in Aging Suburbs and Retirement Areas** The three clusters of Group S4, while each distinct, all represent a continuing U.S. trend toward post-child communities. As a group, S4s include many aging married couples, widows, and retirees on pensions and Social Security incomes. Except Gray Power, they are tightly geo-centered in the Northeast. **Levittown USA (27)** was formed when the post-WWII baby boom caused an explosion of tract housing in the late 40s and 50s—brand new suburbs for young white-collar and well-paid blue-collar families. The children are now largely grown and gone. Aging couples remain in comfortable, middle-class, suburban homes. Employment levels are still high, including double incomes, and living is comfortable.

Exhibit 11–6 (*continued*)

U1	T1	S4
Bohemian Mix (37) is America's Bohemia, a largely integrated, singles-dominated, high-rise hodge-podge of white collars, students, divorced persons, actors, writers, artists, aging hippies, and races. **Black Enterprise (31)** neighborhoods are nearly 70 percent black, with median black household incomes well above average and with consumption behavior to match. It is the most family-oriented of the U1 clusters. A few downscale pockets can be found, but the majority of blacks in these neighborhoods are educated, employed, and solidly set in the upper middle class. **New Beginnings (23)** is represented in nearly all markets, but shows its strongest concentrations in the West. It provides new homes to many victims of the divorce boom in search of new job opportunities and lifestyles. The predominant age is 18–34, and the mode is pre-child with employment concentrated in lower-level white-collar and clerical occupations.	**New Homesteaders (17)** is much like God's Country in its mobility, housing, and family characteristics. The big difference is that these neighborhoods are nine rungs down on the socioeconomic scale, with all measures of education and affluence being significantly lower. It shows peak concentrations of military personnel, and has a strong Western skew. It is one of our largest and fastest-growing clusters. **Towns and Gowns (12)** contains hundreds of mid-scale college and university towns in nonmetropolitan America. The population ratio is three quarters local ("towns") to one quarter students ("gowns"), giving this cluster its name and unique profile. It shows extreme concentrations of age 18–24 singles and students in group quarters, very high educational, professional, and technical levels, and a taste for prestige products in contrast with modest income and home values.	**Gray Power (39)** represents nearly two million senior citizens who have chosen to pull up their roots and retire amongst their peers. Primarily concentrated in sunbelt communities of the South Atlantic and Pacific regions, these are the nation's most affluent elderly, retired, and widowed neighborhoods, with the highest concentration of childless married couples, living in mixed multi-units, condos, and mobile homes on nonsalaried incomes. **Rank and File (2)** is a blue-collar version of Levittown, U.S.A., five rungs down on the socioeconomic scale. This cluster contains many traditional, blue-collar family neighborhoods where children have grown and departed, leaving an aging population. Rank and File shows high concentrations of protective-service and blue-collar workers living in aged duplex rows and multi-unit "railroad" flats. It leads the nation in durable manufacturing.

T2	U2	R1
Mid-Class, Child-Raising, Blue-Collar Families in Remote Suburbs and Towns The three clusters in Group T2 might be characterized as America's blue-collar baby factories (equivalent to white-collar Furs and Station Wagons and Young Suburbia). These neighborhoods are very middle class and married. They show high indices for large families, household incomes close to the U.S. mean, and owner-occupied single-unit houses in factory towns and remote suburbs of industrial metros. While anchored in the Midwest, T2s are broadly distributed across the nation. **Blue-Collar Nursery (40)** leads the nation in craftsmen, the elite of the blue-collar world. It is also No. 1 in married couples with children and households of three or more. These are low-density satellite towns and suburbs of smaller industrial cities. They are well paid and very stable.	**Mid-Scale Families, Singles and Elders in Dense, Urban Row and High-Rise Areas** The four clusters in Group U2 encompass densely urban, middle-class neighborhoods, mainly composed of duplex rows and multi-unit rented flats built more than thirty years ago in second-city centers and major-market fringes. U2s show high concentrations of foreign born, working women, clerical and service occupations, singles and widows in one-person households, continuing deterioration, and increasing minority presence. **New Melting Pot (3)** neighborhoods are situated in the major ports of entry on both coasts. The original European stock of many old urban neighborhoods has given way to new immigrant populations, often with Hispanic, Asian, and Middle-Eastern origins.	**Rural Towns and Villages amidst Farms and Ranches across Agrarian Mid-America** The three clusters of Group R1 are geo-centered in a broad swath across the Corn Belt, through the wheat fields of the Great Plains states, and on into ranch and mining country. R1 clusters share large numbers of sparsely populated communities, lower-middle to downscale socioeconomic levels, high concentrations of German and Scandinavian ancestries, negligible black presence, high incidence of large families headed by married parents, low incidence of college educations, and maximum stability. These people are well described as "rugged conservatives."

Exhibit 11–6 (*continued*)

S1	S2	S3
Middle America (16) is composed of mid-sized, middle-class satellite suburbs and towns. It is at center on the socioeconomic scale, and is close to the U.S. average on most measures of age, ethnicity, household composition and life cycle. It is also centered in the Great Lakes industrial region, near the population geo-center of the United States. **Coalburg and Corntown (29)** fits a popular image of the Midwest, being concentrated in small peaceful cities with names like Terre Haute, Indiana, and Lima, Ohio, surrounded by rich farmland, and populated by solid, blue-collar citizens raising sturdy, Tom Sawyer-ish children in decent, front-porch houses.	**Old Yankee Rows (36)** matches the New Melting Pot in age, housing mix, family composition, and income. However, it has a high concentration of high-school educated Catholics of European origin with very few minorities. These are well paid, mixed blue/white-collar areas, geo-centered in the older industrial cities of the Northeast. **Emergent Minorities (14)** is almost 80 percent black, the remainder largely Hispanics and other minorities. Unlike other U2s, Emergent Minorities shows above-average concentrations for children, almost half of them with single parents. It also shows below-average levels of education and white-collar employment. The struggle for emergence from poverty is still evident in these neighborhoods. **Single City Blues (26)** represents the nation's densely urban, downscale singles areas. Many are located near city colleges, and the cluster displays a bi-modal education profile. With very few children and its odd mixture of races, classes, transients, and night trades, Single City Blues could be aptly described as the poor man's Bohemia.	**Shotguns and Pickups (19)** aggregates hundreds of small, outlying townships and crossroad villages which serve the nation's breadbasket and other rural areas. It has a more easterly distribution than other R1s, and shows peak indices for large families with school-age children, headed by blue-collar craftsmen, equipment operators, and transport workers with high-school educations. These areas are home to many dedicated outdoorsmen. **Agri-Business (34)** is geo-centered in the Great Plains and mountain states. These are, in good part, prosperous ranching, farming, lumbering, and mining areas. However, the picture is marred by rural poverty where weather-worn old men and a continuing youth exodus testify to hard living. **Grain Belt (35)** is a close match to Agri-Business on most demographic measures. However, these areas show a far higher concentration of working farm owners and less affluent tenant farmers. Tightly geo-centered in the Great Plains and mountain states, these are the nation's most stable and sparsely populated rural communities.

T3	R2	U3
Mixed Gentry and Blue-Collar Labor in Low-Mid Rustic, Mill and Factory Towns	**Landowners, Migrants and Rustics in Poor Rural Towns, Farms and Uplands**	**Mixed, Unskilled Service and Labor in Aging, Urban Row and Hi-Rise Areas**
The four clusters in Group T3 cover a host of predominantly blue-collar neighborhoods in the nation's smaller industrial cities, factory, mining, and mill towns, and rustic coastal villages. The T3 clusters share broad characteristics such as lower-middle incomes, limited educations, and (except Smalltown Downtown) single units and mobile homes in medium- to low-density areas. However, it is the differences between clusters which make Group T3 interesting.	The four clusters in group R2 pepper rural America and blanket the rural South with thousands of small agrarian communities, towns, villages and hamlets. As a group, R2s have long shared such characteristics as very low population densities, low socioeconomic rankings, minimal educations, large, highly stable households with widowed elders, predominantly blue-collar/farm labor, and peak concentrations of mobile homes. Since 1970, they have also shared rapid short-term growth and economic gains.	The four clusters of Group U3 represent the least advantaged neighborhoods of urban America. They show peak indices for minorities, high indices for equipment operators, service workers and laborers, very low income and education levels, large families headed by solo parents, high concentrations of singles (widowed, divorced, separated, and never married), peak concentrations of renters in multi-unit housing, and chronic unemployment.
Golden Ponds (33) includes hundreds of small, rustic towns and villages in coastal resort, mountain, lake, and valley areas, where seniors in cottages choose to retire amongst country neighbors. While neither as affluent nor as elderly as Gray Power, Golden Ponds ranks high on all measures of retirement.	**Back-Country Folks (10)** abounds in remote rural towns, geo-centered in the Ozark and Appalachian uplands. It is strongly blue collar, with some farmers, and leads all clusters in concentration of mobile homes and trailers.	**Heavy Industry (4)** is much like Rank and File, nine rungs down on the socioeconomic scale and hard hit by unemployment. It is chiefly concentrated in the older industrial markets of northeastern United States and is very Catholic, with an above-average incidence of Hispanics. These neighborhoods have deteriorated rapidly during the past decade. There are fewer children, and many broken homes.

Exhibit 11–6 (*concluded*)

S1	S2	S3
Mines and Mills (22) gathers hundreds of mining and mill towns scattered throughout the Appalachian mountains, from New England to the Pennsylvania-Ohio industrial complex and points south. It ranks first in total manufacturing and blue-collar occupations. **Norma Rae-Ville (13)** is concentrated in the South, with its geo-center in the Appalachian and Piedmont regions. These neighborhoods include hundreds of industrial suburbs and mill towns, a great many in textiles and other light industries. They are country folk with minimal educations, unique amongst the T3s in having a high index for blacks, and lead the nation in nondurable manufacturing. **Smalltown Downtown (18)** is unique among the T3s in its relatively high population densities. A hundred-odd years ago, our nation was laced with railroads and booming with heavy industry. All along these tracks, factory towns sprang up to be filled with laborers, in working-class row-house neighborhoods. Many can be seen today in Smalltown Downtown, mixed with the aging, downtown portions of other minor cities and towns.	**Share Croppers (38)** is represented in 48 states but is deeply rooted in the heart of Dixie. Traditionally, these areas were devoted to such industries as tenant farming, chicken breeding, pulpwood, and paper milling, etc. But sunbelt migration and a ready labor pool have continued to attract light industry and some population growth. **Tobacco Roads (15)** is found throughout the South with its greatest concentrations in the river basins and coastal, scrub-pine flatlands of the Carolinas, Georgia, and the Gulf states. These areas are above average for children of all ages, nearly a third in single-parent households, and unique among the R2s with a large black population. Dependent upon agriculture, Tobacco Roads ranks at the bottom in white-collar occupations. **Hard Scrabble (6)** neighborhoods represent our poorest rural areas, from Appalachia to the Ozarks, Mexican border country, and the Dakota Bad Lands. Hard Scrabble leads all other clusters in concentration of adults with less than eight years of education, and trails all other clusters in concentration of working women.	**Downtown Dixie-Style (11)** has a southern geo-center. These middle-density urban neighborhoods are nearly 70 percent black and fall between Emergent Minorities and Public Assistance in relative affluence. Unemployment is high, with service occupations dominating amongst the employed. **Hispanic Mix (9)** represents the nation's Hispanic barrios and is, therefore, chiefly concentrated in the Mid-Atlantic and West. These neighborhoods feature dense, row-house areas containing large families with small children, many headed by solo parents. They rank second in percentage of foreign born, first in short-term immigration, and are essentially bilingual neighborhoods. **Public Assistance (32)** with 70 percent of its households black, represents the Harlems of America. These are the nation's poorest neighborhoods. These areas have been urban-renewal targets for three decades and show large, solo-parent families in rented or public high-rise buildings interspersed with aging tenement rows.

SUMMARY

Lifestyle, a major factor that influences the consumer decision-making process, can be defined simply as how one lives. Lifestyle is a function of one's inherent individual characteristics that have been shaped through social interaction as one moves through one's life cycle.

Lifestyle has two important characteristics for marketers. First, it is a basic motivation for many purchase and use activities. Second, because of changing environments and the results of decisions that consumers make about products, lifestyles are altered or reinforced. Therefore, over time and due to learning, lifestyles undergo change.

The self-concept can be defined as the attitudes one holds toward oneself and, as such, it serves as the basis for one's lifestyle. The self-concept is composed of four basic parts: the actual self, how I actually see myself now; the ideal self, how I would like to see myself; the actual social self, how I perceive others actually see me; and the ideal social self, how I would like to have others see me. Consumers strive to move the actual self-concept toward the ideal.

To the extent that marketers can tie products to the ideal concept, purchase of those products would be seen by consumers as a good way to help attain their ideal self-concept.

Psychographics are the primary way that lifestyle is made operationally useful to marketing managers. This is a way of describing the psychological makeup or lifestyle of consumers by assessing such lifestyle dimensions as activities, interests, and opinions. While there are operational problems with psychographic measurement, it is a widely used tool by consumer goods companies and advertising agencies.

The VALS system, developed by SRI, divides the United States into nine general lifestyle segments: survivors, sustainers, belongers, emulators, achievers, I-am-me's, experientials, societally conscious, and integrated. Each has unique demographics, consumption patterns, and media habits. VALS is widely used by consumer goods' firms to segment markets and develop strategies.

Geo-lifestyle analysis is based on the premise that individuals with similar lifestyles tend to live near each other. PRIZM is one system which has analyzed demographic and consumption data down to the Census Block. It has developed profiles of each block in terms of 40 lifestyle clusters. Like VALS, it is widely used in marketing applications.

REVIEW QUESTIONS

1. What do we mean by *consumer lifestyle?* What factors determine and influence that lifestyle?
2. What relationship exists between consumer lifestyle and consumer decision making?
3. What is the *self-concept?* How does it act as a motivating force for consumer behavior?

4. What are the components of the self-concept?
5. How do we measure self-concept?
6. How do we use self-concept in positioning products?
7. Define *psychographics,* and explain how it is potentially useful to marketing managers.
8. What types of variables do marketing managers use to construct a psychographic instrument?
9. When is a product or activity-specific psychographic instrument superior to a general one?
10. Describe *VALS*.
11. How do the outer-directed lifestyles of achievers, emulators, and belongers differ?
12. What differentiates the lifestyles of the societally conscious from the experientials and I-am-me's? What makes an inner-directed experiential different from an inner-directed I-am-me?
13. How can lifestyles such as the VALS lifestyle segments be used to develop marketing strategy?
14. What is *geo-demographic analysis?*
15. Describe the PRIZM system.

DISCUSSION QUESTIONS

1. How would you use a measure of ideal self-concept to develop a name for a new wine (or if you don't like wine, a new shampoo or car)?
2. How could you use measures of self-concept to determine if *Julie* is an appropriate brand name for a perfume?
3. How would you use measures of self-concept to determine if Clint Eastwood would be a good spokesperson for a new aftershave lotion?
4. Develop a marketing strategy of the following products based on Exhibit 11–1:
   a. Bicycle.
   b. Canoe.
   c. Health club.
   d. Golf clubs.
   e. Tennis racquets.
   f. Walking shoe.
5. The following quote is from Paul Casi, president of Glenmore distilleries:

   > Selling cordials is a lot different from selling liquor. Cordials are like the perfume of our industry. You're really talking high fashion and you're talking generally to a different audience—I don't mean male versus female—I'm talking about lifestyle.[25]

   a. In what ways do you think the lifestyle of cordial drinkers would differ from those who drink liquor, but not cordials?
   b. How would you determine the nature of any such differences?

c. Of what use would knowledge of such lifestyle differences be to a marketing manager introducing a new cordial?

6. How would you develop a psychographic questionnaire for the following purposes:
   a. Guiding the strategy of a presidential candidate?
   b. Developing strategy for a diversified firm such as Procter & Gamble?
   c. Developing strategy for a large grocery store chain such as Safeway?
   d. Developing strategy for Chrysler?
7. How would you use the SRI VALS segmentation profiles to market a 35mm camera? Be specific as to which segment or segments and how you would best reach them through television and print media.
8. Identify a male and a female TV personality or role played on television that fits for each of the nine SRI VALS profiles outlined.
9. Discuss how you would use the SRI values and lifestyle segmentation profiles to develop an advertising campaign for a men's shampoo. Be specific as to which segment you would target and what lifestyle characteristics you would like that target market to associate with this product.
10. Is the PRIZM system really a measure of lifestyle?
11. How would you use PRIZM for the purposes described in Question 6?
12. How is one likely to change one's lifestyle at different stages of one's household life cycle? Over one's life, is one likely to assume more than one of the VALS lifestyle profiles described? PRIZM's?
13. To which VALS category do you belong? To which do your parents belong? Which will you belong to when you are your parents age?
14. Repeat Question 13 for PRIZM.

PROJECT QUESTIONS

1. Using the self-concept items presented in Table 11–2, measure your actual self-concepts and your ideal self-concepts. Using the same items, evaluate your favorite car (regardless of price) and a car you dislike. Then compare the similarities and differences among the profiles.
2. Repeat Question 1 for a sample of 10 students.
3. Using the self-concept items in Table 11–2, identify appropriate spokespersons for:
   a. Honda.
   b. *The Wall Street Journal.*
   c. Marlboro.
   d. Apple computer.
   e. Levi jeans.
4. Develop an advertisement based on each of the four parts of the self-concept for a personal computer. Define the market segment the ad would be targeted at and explain how it reflects self-concept.

5. Develop your own psychographic instrument (set of relevant questions) that measures the outdoor activity consumption lifestyle of college students.
6. Using the psychographic instrument developed in Question 5 interview 10 students (using the questionnaire instrument). Based on their responses categorize them into one of the lifestyle segments shown in Exhibit 11–1.
7. Develop 15 statements related to the attitudes, interests, and opinions of students on your campus. Using a five-category agree-disagree scale, interview five other students not enrolled in the class. Then, using all the information collected by the entire class, divide up the individuals surveyed into groups based on similarity. For two groups of reasonable size that are dissimilar in agreement with AIO statements, discuss what campus activities would appeal most to each group. Are there new activities these groups would enjoy using if available?
8. Develop an ad for the products in Question 3 for each of the VALS categories that represent a potential target market.
9. Develop an ad for the products in Question 3 for each of the 10 most likely target clusters in the PRIZM system.

REFERENCES

[1] "Soft Drinks: Brand Report No. 95," *Marketing and Media Decisions,* February 1984, p. 140.

[2] For a review and different definition, see W. T. Anderson and L. L. Golden, "Lifestyle and Psychographics," in *Advances in Consumer Research XI,* ed. T. C. Kinnear (Provo, Utah: Association for Consumer Research, 1984), pp. 405–11.

[3] M. J. Sirgy, "Self-Concept in Consumer Behavior," *Journal of Consumer Research,* December 1982, pp. 287–300. For a differing conceptualization, see R. W. Belk, "Possessions and the Extended Self," *Journal of Consumer Research,* September 1988.

[4] R. Burnkrant and T. Page, Jr., "On the Management of Social Situations: The Role of Public Self-Consciousness," in *Advances in Consumer Research,* ed. A. Mitchell (Chicago: Association for Consumer Research, 1982), pp. 452–55.

[5] P. J. Gaiwtz, *Non-Freudian Personality Theories* (Monterey, Calif: Brooks/Cole Publishing, 1969), p. 87.

[6] M. Sirgy and J. Danes, "Self-Image/Product-Image Congruence Models: Testing Selected Models," in *Advances in Consumer Research,* ed. A. Mitchell (Chicago: Association for Consumer Research, 1982), pp. 556–61; M. J. Sirgy, "Using Self-Congruity and Ideal Congruity to Predict Purchase Motivation," *Journal of Business Research,* June 1985, pp. 195–206; and S. Onkvisit and J. Shaw, "Self-Concept and Image Congruence," *Journal of Consumer Marketing,* Winter 1987, pp. 13–23.

[7] See N. Malhotra, "A Scale to Measure Self-Concepts, Person Concepts, and Product Concepts," *Journal of Marketing Research,* November 1981, pp. 456–64.

[8] E. L. Grubb and H. L Grathwol, "Consumer Self-Concept, Symbolism and Market Behavior: A Theoretical Approach," *Journal of Marketing,* October 1967, pp. 22–27.

[9] J. M. Munson and W. A. Spivey, "Assessing Self-Concept," in *Advances in Consumer Research,* ed. J. Olson (Chicago: Association for Consumer Research, 1980), pp. 598–603; and C. Schenk and R. Holman, "A Sociological Approach to Brand Choice: The Concept of Situational Self-Image," in Olson, *Advances,* pp. 610–14.

[10] R. Belk, R. Mayer, and K. Bahn, "The Eye of the Beholder: Individual Differences in Perceptions of Consumption Symbolism," *Advances in Consumer Research,* ed. A. Mitchell (Chicago: Association for Consumer Research, 1982), pp. 523–30.

[11] W. D. Wells, "Psychographics: A Critical Review," *Journal of Marketing Research,* May 1975, pp. 196–213.

[12] A. Boste, "Interactions in Psychographics Segmentation: Implications for Advertising," *Journal of Advertising,* 1984, pp. 4–48; J. L. Lastovicka, "On the Validation of Lifestyle Traits: A Review and Illustration," *Journal of Marketing Research,* February 1982, pp. 126–38.

[13] L. Uusitalo, "Identification of Consumption Style Segments on the Basis of Household Budget Allocation," in *Advances in Consumer Research,* ed. J. Olson (Chicago: Association for Consumer Research, 1980), pp. 451–59.

[14] J. A. Lesser and M. A. Hughes, "The Generalizability of Psychographic Market Segments across Geographic Locations," *Journal of Marketing,* January 1986, pp. 18–27.

[15] T. C. Thomas and S. Crocker, *Values and Lifestyles—The New Psychographics* (Menlo Park, Calif.: Stanford Research Institute, 1981); A. Mitchell, *The Nine American Lifestyles* (New York: Warner Books, 1983); and B. Townsend, "Psychographic Glitter and Gold," *American Demographics,* November 1985, pp. 23–29.

[16] "Who'll Be the 80s Apparel Shoppers?" *Chain Store Age,* January 1980, pp. 65–69.

[17] L. R. Kahle, S. E. Beatty, and P. Homer, "Alternative Measurement Approaches to Consumer Values," *Journal of Consumer Research,* December 1986, pp. 405–9.

[18] See also ibid.; and J. Atlas, "Beyond Demographics," *The Atlantic,* October 1984, pp. 49–58.

[19] Townsend, "Psychographic Glitter," and E. Dichter, "Whose Lifestyle Is It Anyway?" *Psychology & Marketing,* Fall 1986, pp. 151–63.

[20] Kahle, Beatty, and Homer, "Alternative Measurement Approaches."

[21] See ibid.; S. E. Beatty et al., "Alternative Measurement Approaches to Consumer Values," *Psychology and Marketing,* Fall 1985, pp. 185–200; and L. R. Kahle, *Social Values and Social Change* (New York: Praeger, 1983).

[22] *How to Use PRIZM* (Alexandria, Va: CLARITAS, 1986), p. 1.

[23] B. Morris, "Marketing Firm Slices U.S. into 240,000 Parts to Spur Clients' Sales," *Wall Street Journal,* November 3, 1986, p. 1.

[24] Copyrighted by and used with permission of CLARITAS.

[25] N. F. Millman, "Glenmore Moves to Follow Up Amaretto Success," *Advertising Age,* June 25, 1979, p. 4.

CHAPTER

12 Attitudes and Influencing Attitudes

Cocaine can make you blind.

The above headline is designed to attract the readers' attention and motivate them to read the extensive copy underneath (see Exhibit 12–5). It and the ad copy are also designed to scare people. The copy describes how cocaine use leads to suspicion, health loss, addiction, paranoia, hallucinations, violent and/or suicidal tendencies, and psychosis. The sponsors, the Partnership for a Drug-Free America, hope that the combination of fear appeals and factual information will lead to a negative attitude toward cocaine use.

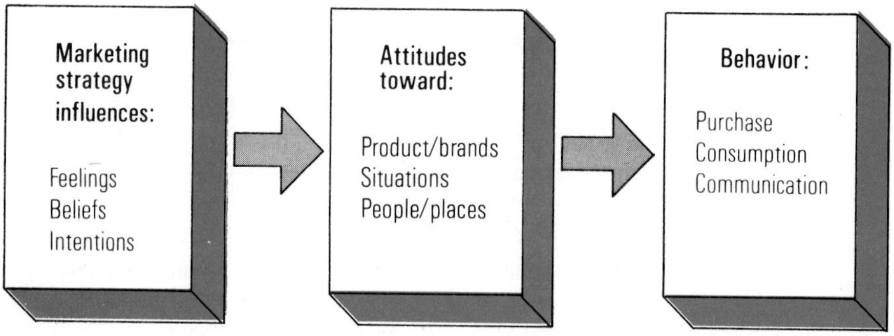

The goal of the advertising effort described above is to influence attitudes toward cocaine in the hope that these attitudes will in turn influence behavior. For many, these ads may reinforce their decision not to become cocaine users. For others who may have just started using, the ads may influence them to stop. And others more committed to use may avoid the ads or discredit them to retain a comfortable balance between their attitudes toward cocaine and their decision to continue as cocaine users.

An attitude is *an enduring organization of motivational, emotional, perceptual, and cognitive processes with respect to some aspect of our environment.*[1] It is "a learned predisposition to respond in a consistently favorable or unfavorable manner with respect to a given object."[2] Thus, an attitude is the way we think, feel, and act toward some aspect of our environment such as a retail store, television program, or product.

Attitudes are formed as the result of all the influences we have been describing in the previous chapters, and they represent an important influence on and reflection of an individual's lifestyle. Because of their importance, attitudes are the focal point for a substantial amount of marketing strategy.

In this chapter we will examine attitude components, the general strategies that can be used to change attitudes, and the effect of marketing communications on attitudes.

ATTITUDE COMPONENTS

As Figure 12–1 illustrates, it is useful to consider attitudes as having three components: cognitive, affective, and behavioral. Each of these attitude components is discussed in more detail below.

Cognitive Component

The cognitive component consists of a consumer's beliefs and knowledge about an object. For most attitude objects, we have a number of beliefs. For example, we may believe that Procter & Gamble's High Point coffee:

- Is an instant coffee.
- Is decaffeinated.
- Is competitively priced.
- Is made by a large company.

Each of these beliefs reflects knowledge about an attribute of this brand of coffee. The total configuration of beliefs about this brand of coffee represents the cognitive component of an attitude toward High Point. It is important to keep in mind that beliefs need not be correct or true; they only need to exist.

Many beliefs about attributes are evaluative in nature. That is, good gas

Figure 12–1
Attitude Components and Manifestations

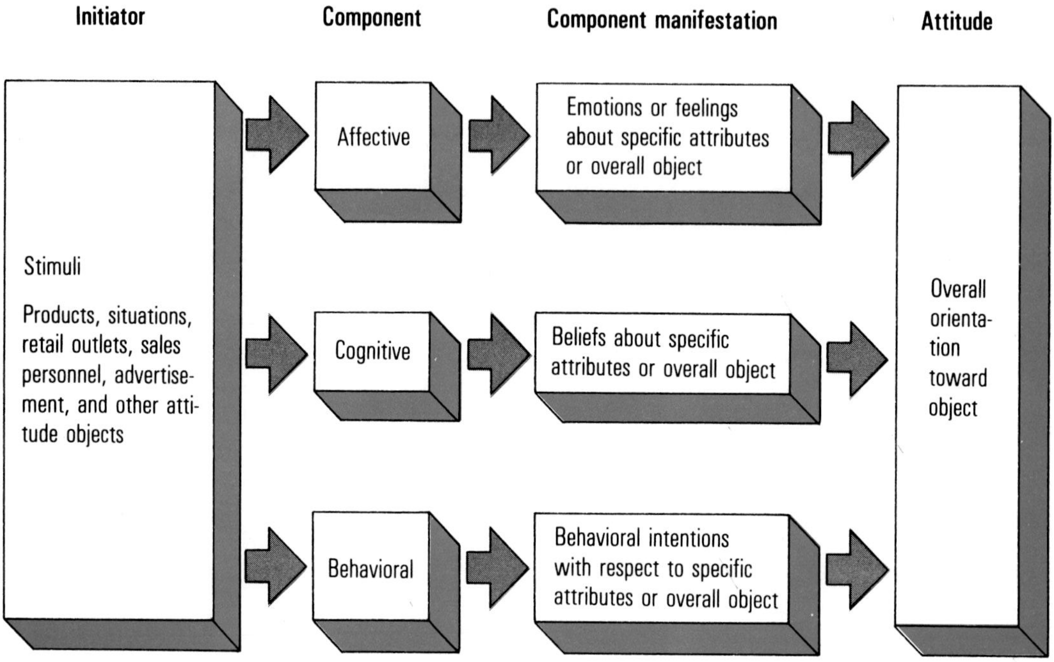

mileage, attractive styling, and reliable performance are generally viewed as positive beliefs. The more positive beliefs there are associated with a brand and the more positive each belief is, the more favorable the overall cognitive component is presumed to be. And, since all of the components of an attitude are generally consistent, the more favorable the overall attitude is. This logic underlies what is known as the *multiattribute attitude model.*

There are several versions of this model. The simplest is:

$$A_b = \sum_{i=1}^{n} X_{ib}$$

where:

A_b = The consumer's attitude toward a particular brand b.
X_{ib} = The consumer's belief about brand b's performance on attribute i.
n = The number of attributes considered.

This version assumes that all attributes are equally important in determining our overall evaluation. However, a moment's reflection suggests that for some products a few attributes such as price, quality, or style are more important than others. Thus, it is often desirable to add an importance weight to each attribute:

$$A_b = \sum_{i=1}^{n} W_i X_{ib}$$

where:

W_i = The importance the consumer attaches to attribute i.

This version of the model is useful in a variety of situations. However, it assumes that more (or less) is always better. This is frequently the case. More miles to the gallon is always better than fewer miles to the gallon, all other things equal. This version is completely adequate for such situations.

For some attributes, more (or less) is good up to a point but then further increases (decreases) become bad. For example, adding salt to a saltless pretzel will generally improve our attitude toward the pretzel up to a point. After that point, additional amounts of salt will decrease our attitude. In such situations, we need to introduce an "ideal point" into the multiattribute attitude model:

$$A_b = \sum_{i=1}^{n} W_i |I_i - X_{ib}|$$

where:

I_i = The consumer's ideal level of performance on attribute i.

Since multivariate attitude models are widely used by marketing researchers and managers, we will work through an example using the weighted, ideal point model. The simpler models would work in a similar manner.

Assume that a segment of beer consumers perceive Lowenbrau to have the following levels of performance on four attributes:

	(1)	(2)	(3)	(4)	(5)	(6)	(7)	
Low price	___	___	___	___	I	___	X	High price
Mild taste	___	___	I	___	___	X	___	Bitter taste
High status	I	X	___	___	___	___	___	Low status
Low calories	I	___	___	___	___	X	___	High calories

This segment of consumers believes (the X's) that Lowenbrau is extremely high priced, very bitter in taste, very high in status, and very high in calories. Their ideal beer (the I's) would be slightly high priced, slightly mild in taste, extremely high in status, and extremely low in calories. Since these attributes are not equally important to consumers, attributes are assigned weights based on the relative importance a consumer or segment of consumers attaches to each attribute. A popular way of measuring importance weights is with a 100-point constant sum scale. For example, the importance weights shown below express the relative importance of four beer attributes such that the total adds up to 100 points.

Attribute	Importance
Price	10
Taste	20
Status	40
Calories	30
	100 points

In this case, status is considered the most important beer attribute with calories slightly less important. The price of a beer is given little importance.

From this information we can index this consumer's or segment's attitude toward Lowenbrau as follows:

$$
\begin{aligned}
A_{\text{Lowenbrau}} &= (10)(|5 - 7|) + (20)(|3 - 6|) + (40)(|1 - 2|) \\
&\quad + (30)(|1 - 6|) \\
&= (10)(2) + (20)(3) + (40)(1) + (30)(5) \\
&= 270
\end{aligned}
$$

This involves taking the absolute difference between the consumer's ideal beer attributes and beliefs about Lowenbrau's attributes and multiplying these differences times the importance attached to each attribute. In this case, the attitude index is computed as 270. Is this good or bad? An attitude index is a relative measure, so in order to determine whether this index reflects a favorable or unfavorable attitude we must evaluate it relative to attitudes toward competing products or brands.

If Lowenbrau were perceived as their ideal beer, then all their beliefs and ideals would be equal and an attitude index of zero would be computed, since there would be no difference between what is desired and what the consumers believe to be provided. On the other hand, if beliefs and ideals are at extreme opposite ends of the scale for each attribute, there is a maximum difference possible between desired and perceived beliefs.

In this example, an index of 540 represents the worst possible evaluation and hence implies the least favorable attitude. The following diagram shows that an attitude index of 270 could be inferred as a neutral attitude since it is very near the center of this attitude index scale. It is possible that this score of 270 could be *relatively* favorable, if all other competing brands have larger (less favorable) scores.

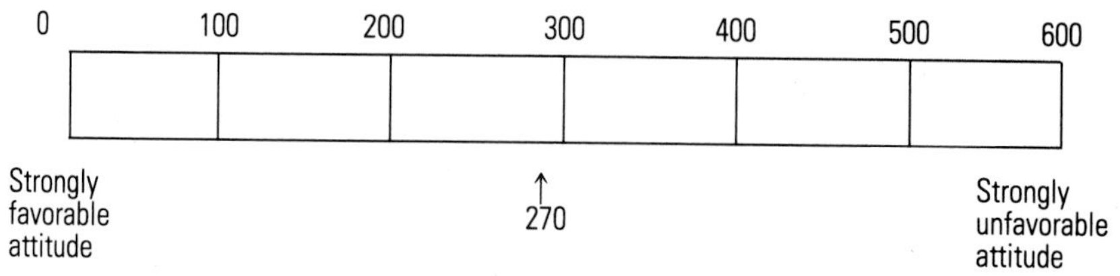

We have been discussing the multiattribute view of the cognitive component as though consumers explicitly and consciously went through a series of deliberate evaluations and summed them to form an overall impression. However, this level of effort would occur only in *very* high-involvement purchase situations. In general, the multiattribute attitude model merely *represents* a nonconscious process that is much less precise and structured than implied by the model.

Affective Component

Our feelings or emotional reactions to an object represent the *affective component* of an attitude. A consumer who states, "I like High Point," or, "High Point is a terrible coffee," is expressing the results of an emotional or affective evaluation of the product. This overall evaluation may be simply a vague, general feeling developed without cognitive information or beliefs about the product. Or, it may be the result of several evaluations of the product's performance on each of several attributes. Thus, the statements, "High Point tastes bad," and "High Point is overpriced," imply a negative affective reaction to specific aspects of the product which, in combination with feelings about other attributes, will determine the overall reaction to this brand of coffee.

Most beliefs about a product have associated affective reactions or evaluations. For example, the belief that High Point costs $5.35 a pound could produce a positive reaction (affective statement or feeling) of "this is a bargain," a negative reaction of "this is overpriced," or a neutral feeling of "this is an average price." The emotion or feeling attached to a given belief depends on the individual and the situation.

Since products, like other objects we react to, are evaluated in the context of a specific situation, a consumer's affective reaction to a product (as well as beliefs about the product) may change as the situation changes. For example, a consumer may believe that (1) High Point is decaffeinated, and (2) decaffeinated coffee will not help keep you awake. The belief that High Point is decaffeinated may cause a negative affective response when the consumer needs to stay awake to study for an exam, and a positive response when he wants to drink something hot late in the evening that won't keep him awake later.[3]

Due to unique motivations and personalities, past experiences, reference groups, and physical conditions, individuals may evaluate the same belief differently. Some individuals may have a positive feeling toward the belief that "High Point is a strong-tasting coffee," while others could respond with a negative reaction. Despite individual variations, most individuals within a given culture react in a similar manner to beliefs that are closely associated with cultural values. For example, beliefs and feelings about a restaurant with respect to cleanliness are likely to be very similar among individuals in the United States since this value is important in our culture. Thus, there often is a strong association between how a belief is evaluated and a related value that is of importance within a culture.[4]

While feelings are often the result of evaluating specific attributes of a product, they can precede and influence cognitions. As we discuss in depth in the next section, one may come to like a product through classical conditioning *without acquiring any cognitive beliefs about the product*. Indeed, our initial reaction to a product may be one of like or dislike without any cognitive basis for the feeling. This initial affect can then influence how we react to the product itself.[5]

Behavioral Component

A series of decisions to not purchase High Point or to recommend other brands to friends would reflect the behavioral component of an attitude. Since behavior is generally directed toward an entire object, it is less likely to be attribute-specific than either beliefs or affect. However, this is not always the case, particularly with respect to retail outlets. For example, many consumers buy canned goods at discount or warehouse-type grocery outlets but purchase meats and fresh vegetables at regular supermarkets. Thus, for retail outlets it is possible and common to react behaviorally to specific beliefs about the outlet. This is generally difficult to do with products because we have to either buy or not buy the complete product.

Component Consistency

Figure 12–2 illustrates a critical aspect of attitudes: all three components tend to be consistent. This means that a change in one attitude component tends to produce related changes in the other components. This tendency is the basis for a substantial amount of marketing strategy.

As marketing managers, we are ultimately concerned with influencing behavior. However, it is often difficult to influence behavior directly. That is, we are frequently unable to directly cause consumers to buy our products. However, consumers will often listen to our sales personnel, attend to our advertisements, or examine our packages. We can, therefore, indirectly influence behavior by providing information, music, or other stimuli that influence a belief or feeling about the product *if* the three components are indeed consistent with each other.

A number of research studies have found only a limited relationship among the three components, particularly between the cognitive and the behavioral components.[6] Let's examine the sources of this inconsistency by considering an example. Suppose an individual has a set of positive beliefs toward the Macintosh computer and also has a positive affective response to this brand and model. Further, suppose that these beliefs and affect are more favorable toward the Macintosh than any other computer. Our customer responds to a questionnaire and indicates these positive beliefs and feelings. However, the consumer does not own a Macintosh, or purchases another brand or model. Thus, a researcher might conclude that the three components are not consistent.

Figure 12–2
Attitude Component Consistency

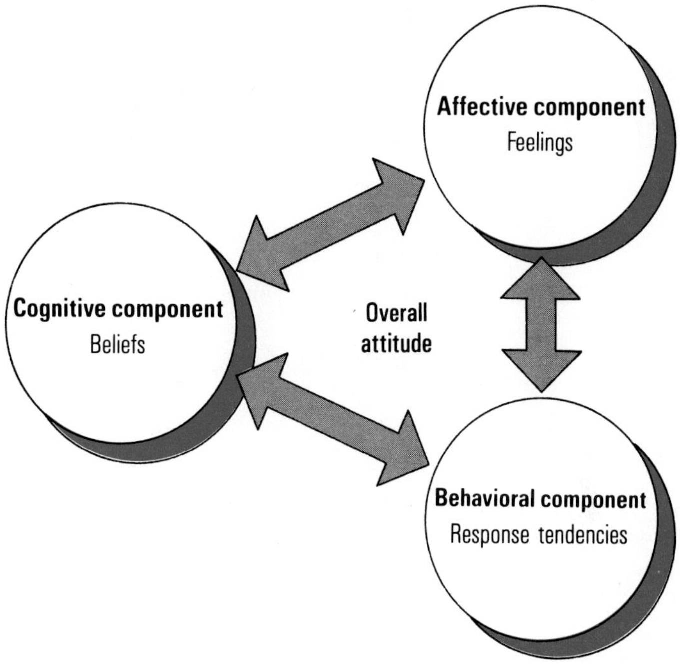

At least seven factors can operate to reduce the consistency between measures of beliefs and feelings and observations of behavior:

First, a favorable attitude requires a need or motive before it can be translated into action. Thus, our consumer may not feel a need for a computer or might already own an acceptable, though less preferred, brand.

Second, translating favorable beliefs and feelings into ownership requires ability. One might not own a computer or might purchase a less expensive model due to insufficient funds to purchase a Macintosh.

Third, we measured attitudes only toward computers. Purchases often involve trade-offs both within and between product categories. Thus our consumer might purchase a less expensive computer in order to save resources to buy new skis, a camera, or an automobile.

Fourth, if the cognitive and affective components are weakly held, when the consumer obtains additional information while shopping, the initial attitudes may give way to new ones.

Fifth, we measured an individual's attitudes. However, as we saw in Chapter 7, many purchase decisions involve other household members either directly or indirectly. Thus, our shopper may purchase a simpler computer so that other family members can operate it.

Sixth, we generally measure brand attitudes independent of the purchase situation. However, many items are purchased for, or in, specific situations.[7] A very inexpensive computer might be purchased if the consumer anticipates access to more sophisticated equipment in the near future.

Seventh, it is difficult to measure all of the relevant aspects of an attitude. Consumers may be unwilling or unable to articulate all of their feelings and beliefs about various products or brands. Therefore, attitude components are sometimes more consistent than our measures suggest them to be.

In summary, attitude components—cognitive, affective, and behavioral—tend

Figure 12–3
Measuring Attitude Components

Cognitive component (measuring beliefs about specific attributes)

High Point

Strong taste	___	___	___	___	___	___	___	Mild taste
Low priced	___	___	___	___	___	___	___	High priced
Caffeine free	___	___	___	___	___	___	___	High in caffeine
Distinctive in taste	___	___	___	___	___	___	___	Similar in taste to most

Affective component (measuring feeling about specific attributes or the overall brand)

	Strongly Agree	Agree	Neither Agree nor Disagree	Disagree	Strongly Disagree
I like the taste of High Point.	___	___	___	___	___
High Point is overpriced.	___	___	___	___	___
Caffeine is bad for your health.	___	___	___	___	___
I like High Point.	___	___	___	___	___

Behavioral component (measuring actions or intended actions)

Have you ever purchased High Point?

- ☐ Yes (how often? ___)
- ☐ No

What is the likelihood you will buy High Point the next time you purchase an instant coffee?

- ☐ Definitely will buy
- ☐ Probably will buy
- ☐ Might buy
- ☐ Probably will *not* buy
- ☐ Definitely will *not* buy

to be consistent. However, the degree of apparent consistency between measures of cognitions and affect and observations of behavior may be reduced by:

- Lack of need for the attitude object.
- Inability to acquire the attitude object.
- Failure to consider purchase alternatives outside of the measured product category.
- Weakly held affective and cognitive components that may be altered at the point of sale.
- Joint decision making (or "taking into account other's desires") that may produce compromise purchases.
- General measures of attitude that do not predict situation-specific purchases.
- Inaccurate or incomplete measures of cognition or affect.

Measurement of Attitude Components

Purchase and use behavior at the brand level is predicted most accurately by overall measures of brand liking or affect. However, since components of attitudes are often an integral part of a marketing strategy, it is important that we be able to measure each component. Approaches to measuring the components are shown in Figure 12–3, with details provided in Appendix A.

In Figure 12–3, the cognitive component is measured by the beliefs consumers have about High Point. Naturally, a lack of product knowledge as well as inaccurate knowledge could hinder the development of a positive overall attitude toward High Point. The affective or evaluative component is how consumers feel about the product. In this example, feelings about High Point are expressed in terms of taste, price, and caffeine as well as in overall terms. Finally, the behavioral component is often measured by the strength of intentions to buy on the next purchase occasion or by past purchases.

ATTITUDE CHANGE STRATEGIES

Examine Exhibit 12–1. The attitude change induced by manipulating the marketing mix for Marlboro is a classic in marketing history. As this example illustrates, managers can form and change attitudes toward products and brands. As we saw in Figure 12–2, changing any one attitude component is likely to produce related changes in the other components. Therefore, managers may focus on any one or more of the components, as they attempt to develop favorable attitudes toward their brands.

Exhibit 12–1 Changing Perceptions, Attitudes, and Behavior: The Marlboro Story

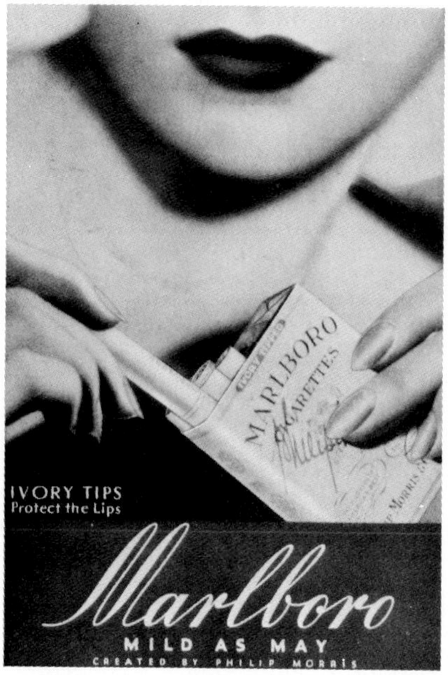

Close your eyes and think of Marlboro cigarettes. What comes to mind? Is it an effeminate, sissy cigarette with an ivory tip or a red beauty tip? Certainly not when one thinks of the Marlboro man!

Philip Morris began marketing Marlboro in 1924 as an extremely mild filter cigarette with either an ivory tip or a red beauty tip! It was advertised in a very plush atmosphere and was widely used by women. By the 1950s, the image described above was firmly established. In addition, all filter cigarettes were viewed as somewhat effeminate.

By the mid-1950s, it was becoming increasingly apparent that filter cigarettes would eventually take over the market. Philip Morris decided to make Marlboro acceptable to the heavy user market segment—males. To accomplish this, everything but the name was changed. A more flavorful blend of tobaccos was selected along with a new filter. The package design was changed to red and white with an angular design (more masculine than a curved or circular design). One version of the package was the crushproof box—again, a very rugged, masculine option.

The advertising used "regular guys," not professional models, who typified masculine confidence. The Marlboro cowboy (a real cowboy) was introduced as "the most generally accepted symbol of masculinity in America." To lend credence to the new brand it was tied to the well-known Philip Morris name with "new from Philip Morris" in the introductory advertising.

How successful was it? What did you think of a few minutes ago when asked to think about Marlboro? Think how drastically attitudes had to be changed to bring about such a dramatic product image shift. *Attitudes can be created, changed, and reinforced given an understanding of what attitudes do for consumers and how attitudes are structured.*

Used with permission from Philip Morris

Figure 12–4
Attitude Change Strategy Focusing on Affect

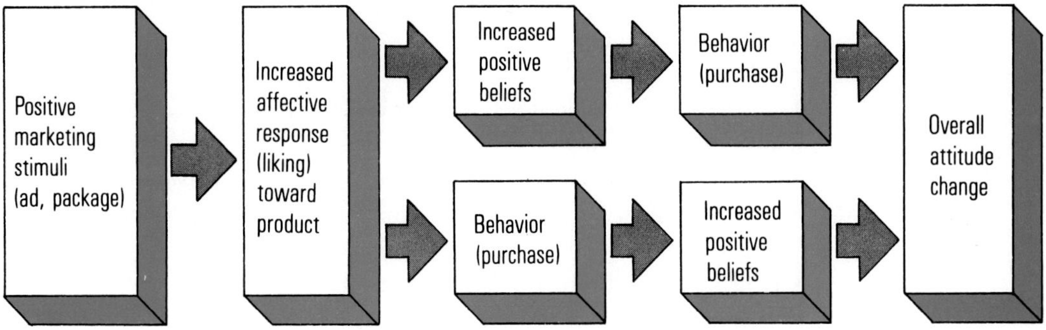

Change the Affective Component

It is increasingly common for a firm to attempt to influence consumers' liking of their brand without directly influencing either beliefs or behavior. If the firm is successful, increased liking will tend to lead to increase positive beliefs, which could lead to purchase behavior should a need for the product category arise. Or, perhaps more commonly, increased liking will lead to a tendency to purchase the brand should a need arise, with purchase and use leading to increased positive beliefs. Both of these outcomes are shown in Figure 12–4. Marketers use three basic approaches to directly increase affect: classical conditioning, affect toward the ad itself, and "mere" exposure.

Classical Conditioning. One way of directly influencing the affective component is through classical conditioning (Chapter 9, pp. 322–23). In this approach, a stimulus the audience likes such as music is consistently paired with the brand name. Over time some of the positive affect associated with the music will transfer to the brand. Other "liked" stimuli, such as pictures, are frequently used for this reason.[8]

Affect toward the Ad. Liking the advertisement increases the tendency to like the product.[9] Positive affect toward the ad may increase liking of the brand through classical conditioning, or it may be a more high-involvement, conscious process. Using humor, celebrities, or emotional appeals increases affect toward the ad. Each is discussed in the last section of this chapter.

Mere Exposure. While controversial, there is evidence that affect may also be increased by "mere exposure."[10] That is, simply presenting a brand to an individual on a large number of occasions might make the individual's attitude toward the brand more positive. Thus, the continued repetition of advertisements for low-involvement products may well increase liking and subsequent purchase of the advertised brands *without* altering the initial belief structure.

The fact that advertising may alter affect directly and, by altering affect, indirectly alter purchase behavior *without* first changing beliefs, has a number of important implications:

- Ads designed to alter affect need not contain any cognitive (factual or attribute) information.
- Classical conditioning principles should guide such campaigns.
- Attitudes (liking) toward the ad itself are critical for this type of campaign (unless "mere exposure" is being used).
- Repetition is critical for affect-based campaigns.
- Traditional measures of advertising effectiveness focus on the cognitive component and are inappropriate for affect-based campaigns.

Change the Behavior Component

Behavior, specifically purchase or consumption behavior, may precede the development of cognition and affect. Or, it may occur in contrast to the cognitive and affective components. For example, a consumer may dislike the taste of diet soft drinks and believe that artificial sweeteners are unhealthy. However, rather than appear rude, the same consumer may accept a diet drink when offered one by a friend. Drinking the beverage may alter her perceptions of its taste and lead to liking; this in turn may lead to increased learning, which changes the cognitive component. Evidence suggests that attitudes formed as a consequence of product trial are strongly held.[11]

Figure 12–5 illustrates this approach. Behavior can lead directly to affect, to cognitions, or to both simultaneously. Consumers frequently try new brands or

Figure 12–5
Attitude Change Strategy Focusing on Behavior

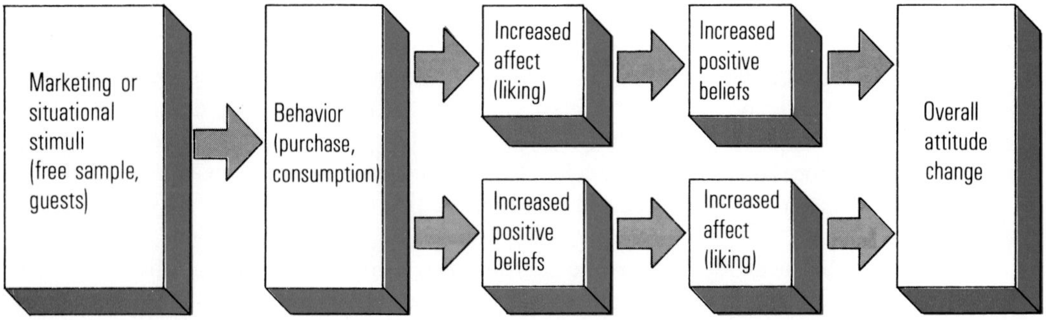

Figure 12–6
Attitude Change Strategy Focusing on Cognitions

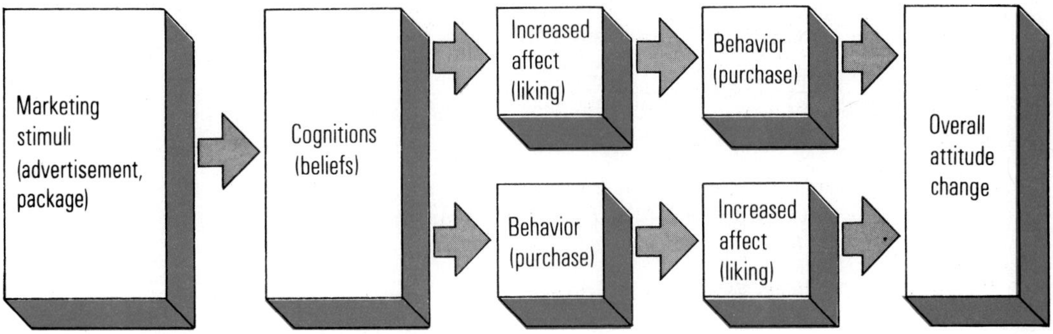

types of low-cost items in the absence of prior knowledge or affect. Such purchases are as much for information ("will I like this brand") as for satisfaction of some underlying need such as hunger.

Changing behavior prior to changing affect or cognition is based primarily on operant conditioning (Chapter 9, pp. 323–27). Thus, the key marketing task is to induce people to purchase or consume the product while ensuring that the purchase/consumption will indeed be rewarding. Coupons,[12] free samples, point-of-purchase displays, tie-in purchases, and price reductions are common techniques for inducing trial behavior. Since behavior often leads to strong positive attitudes toward the consumed brand, a sound distribution system (limited stock outs) is important to prevent current customers from trying competing brands.

Change the Cognitive Component

The most common approach to changing attitudes is to focus on the cognitive component. Thus, to change attitudes toward cigarette smoking, the American Cancer Society has presented information on the negative health consequences of smoking. The theory is that by influencing this belief, affect and behavior will then change. This sequence is shown in Figure 12–6. It is also possible for a changed cognition to lead directly to purchase which could then lead to increased liking. This is also shown in Figure 12–6.

Four basic marketing strategies are used for altering the cognitive structure of a consumer's attitude:

1. Change the beliefs about the attributes of the brand.
2. Change the relative importance of these beliefs.
3. Add new beliefs.
4. Change the beliefs about the attributes of the ideal brand.

Table 12–1
Alternative Cognitive Component Change Strategies

Attribute	Importance	Ideal	Belief
Initial belief structure and attitude (attitude = 300)			
Price	50	3	5
Taste	50	5	1
Social status	0	3	4
	100		
A. Strategy I: Change beliefs about brand (attitude = 200)			
Price	50	3	5
Taste	50	5	3
Social status	0	3	4
	100		
B. Strategy II: Shift attribute importance (attitude = 220)			
Price	30	3	5
Taste	30	5	1
Social status	40	3	4
	100		
C. Strategy III: Add beliefs (attitude = 220)			
Price	30	3	5
Taste	30	5	1
Social status	0	3	4
Fewer calories	40	5	4
	100		
D. Strategy IV: Change beliefs about ideal (attitude = 150)			
Price	50	3	5
Taste	50	2	1
Social status	0	3	4
	100		

Each of these strategies is illustrated in Table 12–1 and is described below.

Change Beliefs. The first strategy involves shifting beliefs about the performance of the brand on one or more attitudes. The attitude of a consumer who believes that Lowenbrau is overpriced and tastes bitter is shown in Table 12–1. Based on this structure of beliefs, ideal beliefs, and belief importance, an attitude index of 300 was computed. By shifting this consumer's perception of the taste of Lowenbrau (perhaps through advertising) to a middle position, the attitude index is improved to 200 (Table 12–1A).

Shift Importance. As shown in Table 12–1, this consumer considers some beliefs to be more important than others. Therefore, another way to change the attitude is to shift the relative importance away from poorly evaluated attributes to positively evaluated attributes. This strategy is illustrated in Table 12–1B, as importance was shifted from price and taste to the social status of the beer.

Add Beliefs. The third attitude change strategy involves adding new beliefs to the consumer's belief structure. Let us assume that Lowenbrau is able to offer one-third fewer calories in a beer without altering the taste. Let us also assume that our consumer views this as a very favorable new product feature. The addition of this positive feature contributes to a better overall attitude toward this brand, as illustrated in Table 12–1C.

Change Ideal. The final change strategy involves altering the perceptions of the ideal brand. For example, Lowenbrau might attempt to convince our consumer that good beer has a strong taste. The result of succeeding in this strategy can be seen in Table 12–1D.

MARKET SEGMENTATION AND PRODUCT DEVELOPMENT STRATEGIES BASED ON ATTITUDES

Market Segmentation

The identification of market segments is a key aspect of marketing. Properly designed marketing programs should be built around the unique needs of each market segment. The importance of various attributes is one way of defining customer needs for a given product. Segmenting consumers on the basis of their important attributes or attribute is called *benefit segmentation.*[13]

To define benefit segments, a marketer needs to know the importance attached to the respective attributes of a particular product or service. Then benefit segments can be formed by grouping consumers with similar attribute importance ratings into segments, such that within a segment consumers are seeking the same benefit(s).

Additional information about consumers within each segment is obtained to develop a more complete picture of each segment. Then, knowing the primary benefit sought by each segment and the descriptive characteristics of each segment, separate marketing programs can be developed for each of the segments to be served by a particular organization. Exhibit 12–2 shows benefit segments of relevance to the arts market.[14]

Product Development

While the importance consumers attach to key attributes provides a meaningful way to understand needs and form benefit segments, the ideal levels of performance indicate their desired level of performance in satisfying those needs. Thus, these ideal levels of performance can provide valuable guidelines in developing a new product or reformulating an existing one.

To illustrate how ideal levels can be used in product development, Figure 12–7 describes how Coca-Cola used this approach in developing a new soft drink.[15] The first step is to *construct a profile of a segment of consumers' ideal level of performance* with respect to key attributes of a soft drink. For a particular type of soft drink, four attributes were identified and the average ideal level of performance was obtained from consumer ratings. If there is a wide

Exhibit 12–2 Benefit Segments for the Arts Market

	CURRENT USERS		
	Cultural Aspirants	Temporary Diversion	Peak Aesthetic Experience
Benefits sought	Enlightenment; cultural exposure. Intellectual expansion. Identification with the "cognoscenti."	Passive entertainment; relaxation. Noncognitive diversion. A social medium. An evening out.	Emotional and intellectual involvement/ stimulation. Professional excellence; creativity and beauty.
Category beliefs	Arts attendance helps provide the intellectual sophistication of the "cognoscenti" with whom I identify.	Arts performances should offer entertainment and diversion; a relaxing atmosphere while enjoying the company of friends and family.	Arts performances should offer a high level of artistic excellence, and permit complete emotional and intellectual involvement.
Preferred leisure activities	Reading, crafts, antiquing. "Serious" arts performances.	Dining out, movies, skiing, biking, sightseeing. Lighter art performances.	Crafts, sailing, reading, skiing, etc. "Professional" arts performances of particular merit.
Participation	Frequent.	Infrequent to moderate.	Moderate to frequent.
Occasions of participation	Evening, weekends—whenever programs offered.	Predominantly weekends.	Evenings, weekends—performances and activities of special interest.
Media habits	Local/national newspapers. Posters, mailers, handbills.	Local newspapers, posters, and handbills. Moderate TV and radio.	Local/national newspapers. Posters, mailers, handbills. Light TV and radio.
Personality/ lifestyle	Other-directed. Impressionable.	Other-oriented and socially active.	Sophisticated and well educated; inner-directed. Socially active.
Demographics	Age: Younger, 21–35. College education. Beginning professional career.	Age: 25–49. High school or some college education. Income: $10,000–$15,000.	Sophisticates of all ages. College educated; professional. Income: $15,000 and over.

Reprinted from M. Steinberg, G. Miaoulis, and D. Lloyd, "Benefit Segmentations Strategies for the Performing Arts," in *1982 Educators Conference Proceedings*, ed. B. J. Walker (Chicago: American Marketing Association, 1982), pp. 289–93.

	NONUSER			
	Security Seeker	**Hedonist**	**Pragmatist**	**Children-Oriented**
Benefits sought	Relaxation, security of family and friends. Peer approval. To feel at ease.	Entertainment. Excitement. Action.	Convenience Diversion Feeling of productivity and involvement.	Upward mobility for children; well-rounded education for children.
Category beliefs	Arts are designed for more sophisticated group. Would feel insecure, uncomfortable, and out of place.	Arts are too formal, serious, and passive.	Arts are for snobbish, nonactive people. Don't understand or relate to arts. Find them boring, uninteresting.	Children should have the educational and social opportunities needed for a successful life.
Preferred leisure activities	Television, dining out, family outings. Peer and family-oriented activities.	Hunting, fishing, boating, sports, etc. Action-oriented activities.	Gardening, hunting, woodworking, sewing. Productive activities.	Family activities: outings, camping, sports, etc. Scouting, school, clubs encouraged.
Participation	Low to moderate.	High.	Moderate to high.	Moderate to high.
Occasions of participation	Weekends, holidays, vacations.	Evenings, weekends, whenever possible.	Evenings, weekends, vacations.	Encouraged to become involved frequently.
Media habits	Local newspapers. Heavy radio and TV.	Local/national newspapers. Moderate radio and TV. Special-interest magazines; posters.	Local newspapers. Low to moderate TV. Special-interest magazines, posters, mailers.	Local newspapers. Mailers. Moderate radio and TV.
Personality/ lifestyle	Reticent, insecure, conforming, Oriented toward family and friends.	Outgoing, active, fast-paced lifestyle.	Practical, organized. Family- and work-oriented.	Conservative, practical, hard-working. Family-oriented.
Demographics	Age: 25–64; unskilled or semiskilled. Education: High school or less. Income: Below average.	Age: 25–49; technician, white collar. Education: High school/college. Income: Above average.	Age: 35–64; tradesman. Education: High school or technical school. Income: Above average.	Age: 35–49; semiskilled or clerical. Education: High school. Income: Average.

range of ideal ratings for a particular attribute, further segmentation may be required.

A second step involves *creation of a product concept that closely matches the ideal profile*. The concept could be a written description, picture, or actual prototype of the product to be developed. As shown in section B of Figure 12–7, consumers evaluated the product concept developed by Coca-Cola as being fairly close to their ideal level of performance on each of the four attributes. It appears that only their concept of color was off target by being a little too dark.

The next step is to *translate the concept into an actual product*. When this was done by Coca-Cola and presented to the consumers, consumers did not perceive it to be similar to either the product concept or their ideal levels of performance (see section C of Figure 12–7). While the actual product achieved a reasonable attitude rating, the product concept scored higher (section D, Figure 12–7). Thus, the product could benefit from further improvement.

Based on this information, management would attempt to further improve the actual product to better align it with ideal levels of performance prior to market introduction. This same type of procedure can be used to help design appealing ads, packages, or retail outlets.

COMMUNICATION CHARACTERISTICS THAT INFLUENCE ATTITUDE FORMATION AND CHANGE

Exhibit 12–3 describes how Standard Oil pretests advertisements to ascertain their impact on attitudes. This method is employed *after* the ads are developed but *before* they are shown. In this section, we are going to discuss the various strategies that can be used to develop messages that will influence attitudes.

Source Characteristics

Source Credibility. Influencing attitudes is easier when the source of the message is viewed as highly credible by the target market. This is referred to as *source credibility*.[16]

Source credibility appears to be composed of two basic dimensions: *trustworthiness* and *expertise*.[17] A source that has no apparent reason to provide other than complete, objective, and accurate information would generally be considered as trustworthy. Most of us would consider our good friends trustworthy on most matters. However, our friends might not have the knowledge necessary to be credible in a certain area. While sales personnel and advertisers often have ample knowledge, many consumers doubt the trustworthiness of sales personnel and advertisements because it might be to their advantage to mislead the consumer. There is evidence that source credibility is enhanced if the source is physically attractive.[18]

Figure 12–7
Using the Multiattribute Attitude Model in the Product Development Process

A. Ideal soft drink*

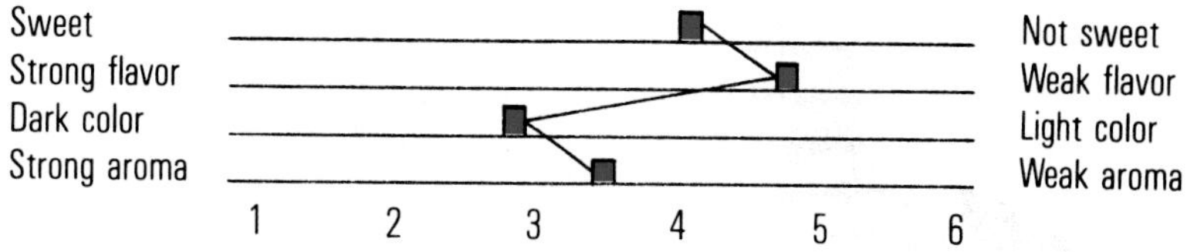

B. Product concept*

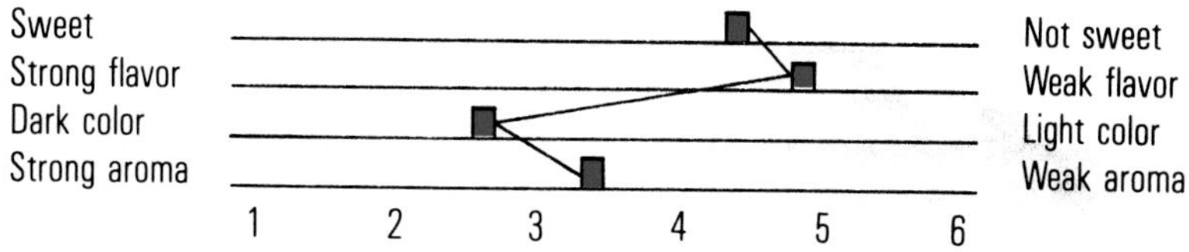

C. Actual product*

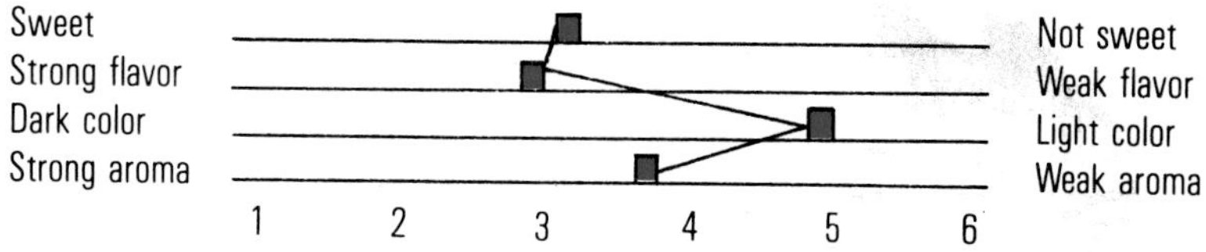

D. Attitude toward concept and product

$$A_{concept} = 25|4.17-4.43| + 25|4.63-4.90| + 25|3.16-2.60| + 25|3.64-3.62|$$
$$= 25(.15) + 25(.27) + 25(.56) + 25(.02)$$
$$= 25$$

$$A_{product} = 25|4.17-3.25| + 25|4.63-3.17| + 25|3.16-4.64| + 25|3.64-3.68|$$
$$= 25(.92) + 25(1.46) + 25(1.48) + 25(.04)$$
$$= 97.5$$

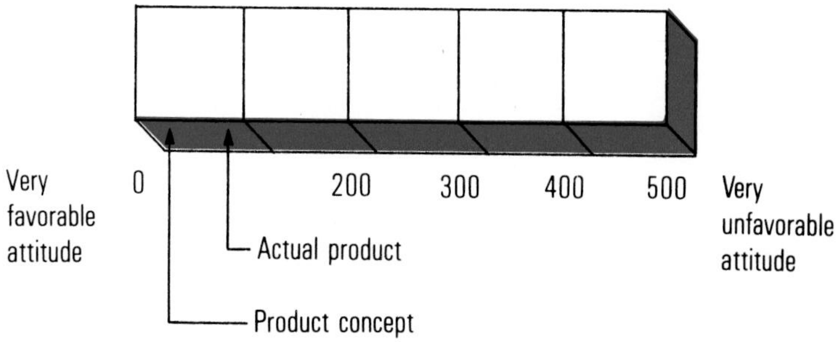

*Measured on a six-point schematic differential scale.

Source: Adapted from H. E. Bloom, "Match the Concept and the Product," *Journal of Advertising Research,* October 1977, pp. 25–27.

Exhibit 12–3

Pretesting for Attitude Change

Standard Oil of California does extensive testing of its ad campaigns to determine the impact that specific ads have on attitude change. Outlined below is an example of a method of pretesting that is done to determine if attitude change is likely to be achieved by a particular commercial.

- Two groups of target consumers are formed. One is an *experimental group* that will be shown the Standard Oil ad and the other a *control group* that will not see the Standard Oil ad.
- Each group is shown (separately) two short TV shows and two additional brief shows. The *experimental group* was exposed to the Standard Oil ad as part of the clutter between the television shows. And, after two more brief shows, the experimental group was asked to recall the commercials they saw. The percentage remembering the Standard Oil commercial is used as a measure of *recall* or *awareness*.
- Each group is separately shown another show with four commercial breaks. The *experimental group* is exposed to the Standard Oil ad again during one of the four commercial breaks, while the *control group* is not exposed to any Standard Oil commercials.
- After the final show people are asked attitude and other questions about Standard Oil as a company, its products, and the commercial.
- Attitude scores are computed for each group and compared. When there is a large difference between the attitudes of the experimental and control groups, attitude shift is inferred.

Source: "Pretests Improve Attitude-Altering Power of Chevron Ads," *Marketing News*, May 14, 1982, pp. 6–7.

Such organizations as the American Dental Association (ADA), which are widely viewed as both trustworthy and expert, can have a tremendous influence on attitudes. The remarkable success of Crest toothpaste is largely attributable to the ADA endorsement. Underwriters Laboratories, *Good Housekeeping,* and other trustworthy and expert sources are widely sought for their endorsements. Exhibit 12–4 illustrates an effective use of a credible source.

While highly credible sources have an immediate, positive impact on attitude change, low-credible sources tend to have the opposite effect. That is, a message that would induce attitude change if associated with a positive or neutral source, often will *not* do so if associated with a source of low credibility. However, under at least some conditions, the discounting of the message caused by the noncredible source dissipates over time and the message produces attitude changes similar to one delivered by a credible source. This is known as the *sleeper*

Exhibit 12–4

The Use of Source Credibility in Advertising

Courtesy Ford Motor Co.

effect.[19] Although the sleeper effect occurs given certain conditions, marketing managers would be foolish to rely on it. Neutral or credible sources should be used.

Celebrity Sources. The source of a communication can be an identifiable person, an unidentifiable person (a "typical" homemaker), a company or organization, an inanimate figure such as a cartoon character, or even the infamous "they."[20] Increasingly, firms are using celebrities as the source of their marketing communications. Ten percent of television advertising involves a celebrity.[21] Celebrities involved in advertising campaigns are most often television or movie stars (Bill Cosby, Alan Alda, Linda Evans), entertainers (Michael Jackson, Lionel Richie), or sports figures (O. J. Simpson, Larry Bird). However, politicians (Geraldine Ferraro) and business leaders (Lee Iacocca)[22] are also used.

Celebrity sources may enhance attitude change for a variety of reasons.[23] They may attract more attention to the advertisement than would noncelebrities.

Figure 12–8
Matching Up Endorser with Product and Target Audience

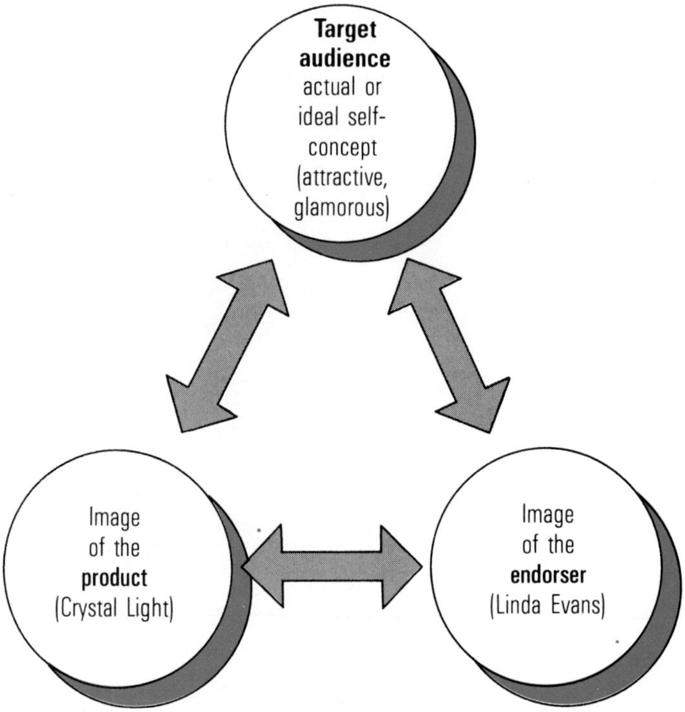

Or, in many cases, they may be viewed as more credible than noncelebrities. Third, consumers may identify with or desire to emulate the celebrity. Finally, consumers may associate known characteristics of the celebrity with attributes of the product which coincide with their own needs or desires.

The effectiveness of using a celebrity to endorse a firm's product can be improved by matching the image of the celebrity with the personality of the product and the actual or desired self-concept of the target market.[24] For example, Linda Evans ("Dynasty") scored higher than average in brand awareness and attitude shift with her endorsement of Crystal Light.[25] Her image of mature, sophisticated, sexy glamour matched the ideal self-concept of many members of the target audience and the benefits and product positioning of Crystal Light (a powdered, diet soft drink). When the three components shown in Figure 12–8 are well matched, effective attitude formation or change can result.

Failure to match properly can cause serious problems. Robert Young ("Marcus Welby, M.D." on television) was used extensively by Sanka decaffeinated coffee. Although liked and respected (many thought he was actually an M.D.), younger consumers (the fastest-growing segment) did not identify with him at all. Further, *his image as a doctor apparently gave Sanka a medicinal image as a product*. This was clearly an undesirable product positioning and Young was dropped as Sanka's spokesperson.[26]

Using a celebrity as a company spokesperson creates special risks for the sponsoring organization. Few well-known personalities are admired by everyone. Thus, it is important to be certain that most of the members of the relevant target markets will respond favorably to the spokesperson. An additional risk is that some behavior involving the spokesperson will affect the individual's credibility after he/she is associated with the firm. Ace Hardware Corporation temporarily stopped using Suzanne Sommers as their spokesperson after she appeared in a 10-page nude photo layout in *Playboy*. The president of Ace stated that the "photos could be potentially embarrassing" and therefore decided to cease advertising featuring Ms. Sommers.[27] American Greetings and Gillette Company faced a similar dilemma when nude photos of Miss America Vanessa Williams appeared in *Penthouse*.

Appeal Characteristics

Fear appeals. Fear appeals make use *of the threat of negative (unpleasant) consequences if attitudes or behaviors are not altered*. While fear appeals have been studied primarily in terms of physical fear (physical harm from smoking, unsafe driving, and so forth), social fears (disapproval of one's peers for incorrect clothing, bad breath, or inadequate coffee) are also frequently used in advertising.[28] For fear appeals to be successful, the level of fear induced must not be so high as to cause the consumer to distort or reject the message.[29] In addition, it is critical that the source of the fear-arousing message be viewed as highly credible.[30] Using a fear appeal as a way to gain attention and stress the dangers of cocaine use, the Partnership for a Drug-Free America sponsors the ad shown in Exhibit 12–5. While it may not always be appropriate and is often difficult to utilize, fear appeals can influence attitudes.[31]

Humorous Appeals. At almost the opposite end of the spectrum from fear appeals are message appeals built around humor.[32] These types of messages are particularly effective at gaining attention. Yet for humorous appeals to be effective in terms of influencing beliefs and behavioral intentions, the following performance criteria must be met:

- The brand must be identified within the opening 10 seconds, or there is danger of inhibiting recall of important selling points.
- The type of humor makes a difference. Subtlety is more effective than the bizarre.

Exhibit 12–5 Fear Appeals in Attitude Change Advertising

Cocaine can make you blind.

Cocaine fools your brain.

When you first use it, you may feel more alert, more confident, more sociable, more in control of your life.

In reality, of course, nothing has changed. But to your brain, the feeling seems real.

From euphoria...

You want to experience it again. So you do some more coke.

Once more, you like the effects. It's a very clean high. It doesn't really feel like you're drugged. Only this time, you notice you don't feel so good when you come down. You're confused, edgy, anxious, even depressed.

Fortunately, that's easy to fix. At least for the next 20 minutes or so. All it takes is another few lines, or a few more hits on the pipe.

You're discovering one of the things that makes cocaine so dangerous.

It compels you to keep on using it. (Given unlimited access, laboratory monkeys take cocaine until they have seizures and die.)

If you keep experimenting with cocaine, quite soon you may feel you need it just to function well. To perform better at work, to cope with stress, to escape depression, just to have a good time at a party or a concert.

Like speed, cocaine makes you talk a lot and sleep a little. You can't sit still. You have difficulty concentrating and remembering. You feel aggressive and suspicious towards people. You don't want to eat very much. You become uninterested in sex.

To paranoia...

Compulsion is now definitely addiction. And there's worse to come.

You stop caring how you look or how you feel. You become paranoid. You may feel people are persecuting you, and you may have an intense fear that the police are waiting to arrest you. (Not surprising, since cocaine is illegal.)

You may have hallucinations. Because coke heightens your senses, they may seem terrifyingly real.

As one woman overdosed, she heard laughter nearby and a voice that said, "I've got you now." So many people have been totally convinced that bugs were crawling on or out of their skin, that the hallucination has a nickname: the coke bugs.

Especially if you've been smoking cocaine, you may become violent, or feel suicidal.

When coke gets you really strung out, you may turn to other drugs to slow down. Particularly downers like alcohol, tranquilizers, marijuana and heroin. (A speedball—heroin and cocaine—is what killed John Belushi.)

If you saw your doctor now and he didn't know you were using coke, he'd probably diagnose you as a manic-depressive.

To psychosis...

Literally, you're crazy.

But you know what's truly frightening? Despite everything that's happening to you, even now, you may still feel totally in control.

That's the drug talking. Cocaine really does make you blind to reality. And with what's known about it today, you probably have to be something else to start using coke in the first place.

Dumb.

© 1987, DDB Needham Worldwide Inc.

Partnership for a Drug-Free America

Courtesy DDB Needham Inc.

- The humor must be relevant to the brand or key idea. Recall and persuasion are both decreased when the linkage is not made.
- Humorous commercials that entertain by belittling potential users do not perform well.

In addition to the guidelines above, one should only use humor if it is consistent with the desired brand image and theme of the message. With regard to image appropriateness we need to ask ourselves: Is the product one whose image will be enhanced by humor? Would humor get in the way of the image or help the image? Humor helped Volkswagen, but it would seem wrong for Rolls Royce. Humor could work in ads for frozen food, but not be right for fire insurance.

A second major consideration in using humor is—does humor enhance, underscore, or make more memorable a message or does it get in the way? Does humor overpower the ad? Obviously, a very delicate balance must be achieved between the effects of humor and the basic message. If the ad is too funny, the basic message may be obscured. However, when well done, humor can gain attention, influence attitudes, and increase sales. When appropriate and the humorous message remains focused on the brand or key selling point, humor offers an effective way to communicate a message. For example, the Sunsweet Prune's campaign, "Today the pits, tomorrow the wrinkles," achieved a 400 percent sales increase.[33]

Comparative Ads. In an effort to stimulate comparative shopping, the FTC has encouraged companies to use comparisons of their products against competitors in their advertisements, such as shown in Exhibit 12–6. The FTC's reasoning is that the consumer benefits when competition is strongest, and comparative advertising is intended to promote competition as companies strive to improve their products relative to competing products.

Comparative ads often produce no additional gain to the image of the sponsoring brand, and sometimes unfavorable impressions result. However, in other instances comparative ads produce positive results for advertisers as well as consumers. Available evidence suggests that comparative ads should follow these guidelines:

- Comparative advertising may be particularly effective for promoting *new* brands with strong product attributes.
- Comparative advertising is likely to be more effective if its claims are *substantiated* by *credible* sources.
- Comparative advertising may be used effectively to establish a brand's *position* or to upgrade its *image* by association.
- *Audience characteristics,* especially the extent of *brand loyalty* associated with the sponsoring brand, are important. Users or owners of the named competitor brands appear to be resistant to comparative claims.

Exhibit 12–6 Comparative Advertisement

Courtesy Texas Instruments.

- Since people consider comparative advertisements to be more *interesting* than noncomparative advertisements (as well as being more "offensive"), these commercials may be effective if the product category is relatively static and noncomparative advertising has ceased to be effective.
- Appropriate *theme* construction can significantly increase the overall effectiveness of comparative advertising.
- It is important to ascertain how many product *attributes to mention* in a comparative advertisement.
- *Print media* appear to be better vehicles for comparative advertisements since print lends itself to more thorough comparisons.[34]

Emotional Appeals. Emotional or feeling ads are being used with increasing frequency. Emotional ads are designed primarily to elicit a positive response rather than provide information or arguments.[35] As we saw in Chapter 10 (pages 377–84), emotional ads such as those that arouse feelings of warmth trigger a physiological reaction. They are also liked more than neutral ads and produce more positive attitudes toward the product.[36] Emotional advertisements may enhance attitude formation or change by (see pages 443–44):

- increasing the ad's ability to attract and maintain attention.
- increasing the level of mental processing given the ad.
- increasing ad memorability.
- increasing liking of the ad.
- increasing product liking through classical conditioning.
- increasing product liking through high-involvement processes.

Message Structure Characteristics

One-Sided versus Two-Sided Messages. In advertisements and sales presentations, marketers generally present only the benefits of their product without mentioning any negative characteristics it might possess or any advantages a competitor might have. These are *one-sided* messages since only one point of view is expressed. The idea of a *two-sided message,* presenting both good and bad points, is counterintuitive, and most marketers are reluctant to try such an approach. However, two-sided messages are generally more effective than one-sided messages in terms of changing a strongly held attitude. In addition, they are particularly effective with highly educated consumers.[37] One-sided messages are most effective at reinforcing existing attitudes.[38] However, product type, situational variables, and advertisement format influence the relative effectiveness of the two approaches.[39]

Distraction. Consumers frequently counterargue with advertisements and other messages that conflict with their existing attitudes.[40] That is, a consumer com-

Figure 12–9
Ad Message Recall as a Function of Order of Presentation

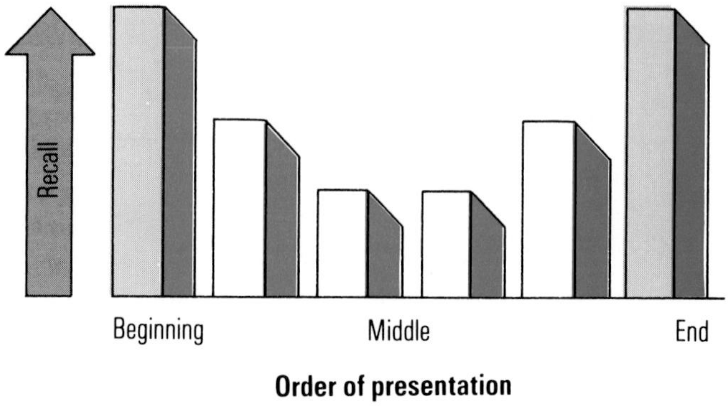

Source: H. E. Krugman, "On Application of Learning Theory to TV Copy Testing," *Public Opinion Quarterly*, 1962, pp. 626–39.

mitted to driving a private automobile may counterargue with a message promoting bus transportation something like this:

ADVERTISEMENT: Let us do the driving, it's less stressful!

CONSUMER: Yeah, and I can listen to some bore next to me chatter.

ADVERTISEMENT: And there are no parking problems.

CONSUMER: Of course not; you drop me off five blocks from my office.

The impact of counterargument is often to strengthen the consumer's initial attitude. Therefore, marketers are interested in reducing counterarguments. One way of achieving this goal is with distraction.[41] This can be done with the use of humor or the presentation of competing stimuli such as background music or noise. Coupons also appear to reduce counterarguing.[42] While distraction can reduce counterargumentation, it also can reduce attention and comprehension of the message.[43] Therefore, it is very important to thoroughly pretest messages using this approach.

Order of Presentation. Because the learning of many marketing messages, particularly advertisements, involves a low-involvement learning process, the order of presentation of information presented in the ad is critical to the message's success.[44] Important information, like the brand's name and/or key ideas, should be presented at the very beginning and/or end of the ad message, as information presented in the middle of the message is not recalled as well in a low-involvement learning process. This is illustrated in Figure 12–9, and demonstrates the effects of "primacy" (material presented first) and "recency" (material presented last) in low-involvement learning. That is, for much information presented in advertisements that consumers are not interested in, the highest level of recall is for information presented at the beginning and end of the message.

Nonverbal Components. In Chapter 9 (pages 334–35), we discussed how pictures enhance imagery and facilitate learning.[45] Pictures,[46] music,[47] surrealism,[48] and other nonverbal cues are also effective in attitude change.[49] Emotional ads, described earlier, often rely primarily or exclusively on nonverbal content to arouse an emotional response. Nonverbal ad content can also affect cognitions about a product. For example, an ad showing a person drinking a new drink product after exercise provides information about appropriate usage situations without stating "good after exercise."

While the impact of nonverbal ad elements is not yet completely understood, it is clear that they can have significant influence, both positive and negative. Therefore, the nonverbal portion of advertising messages should be designed and tested with as much care as the verbal portion.

SUMMARY

Attitudes can be defined as the way we think, feel, and act toward some aspect of our environment. A result of all the influences discussed so far in the text, attitudes influence, as well as reflect, the lifestyle individuals pursue. Attitudes, therefore, are the focal point of a great deal of marketing strategy.

The understanding and use of attitudes is clearer when they are perceived as having three component parts: cognitive, affective, and behavioral. The cognitive component consists of the individual's beliefs or knowledge about the object. The cognitive component is generally assessed by using a version of the multiattribute attitude model. Feelings or emotional reactions to an object represent the affective component of the attitude. The behavioral component reflects overt actions and statements of behavioral intentions with respect to specific attributes of the object or the overall object. In general, all three components of an attitude tend to be consistent with each other. Thus, if marketing managers can influence one component, the other components may also be influenced.

Attitude change strategies can focus on affect, behavior, cognition, or some combination. Attempts to change affect generally rely on classical conditioning. Change strategies focusing on behavior rely more on operant conditioning. Changing cognitions usually involves information processing and cognitive learning.

There are four basic strategies for influencing attitudes by altering the cognitive structure of a consumer's attitude: First, it is possible to change the beliefs about the attributes of the brand. Second, one might change the relative importance of these beliefs. Third, new beliefs could be added to the present attitude. And finally, the beliefs about the attributes of the ideal brand could be changed.

Attitudes, particularly the cognitive component, are the basis for market segmentation strategies, such as benefit segmentation, and for new product development strategies.

Source credibility influences attitudes. It appears to be composed of two basic dimensions: trustworthiness and expertise. Influencing attitudes is much easier when the source of the message is viewed as highly credible by the target market.

Celebrities are widely used as product or company spokespersons. They are most effective when their image matches the personality of the product and the actual or desired self-concept of the target market.

Fear appeals make use of the threat of negative consequences if attitudes or behaviors are not altered. They are useful in persuasive messages for certain types of products. While fear appeals have been studied primarily in terms of physical fear, social fears are also used in advertising. Humorous appeals can also be effective in influencing attitudes. However, the humorous message must remain focused on the brand or main selling point to be effective. It is not clear yet what causes comparative ads to succeed or fail. Thus, they require extensive pretesting. Emotional appeals have been found to have a strong effect on attitudes toward both the ad and the product.

The effectiveness of one- versus two-sided messages depends largely on the situation and characteristics of the target audience. The order of presentation also can affect attitudes. Generally, we remember the first and last parts of the message better than the middle. Nonverbal aspects of the ad, such as pictures, surrealism, and music can affect attitudes even more than the verbal content.

REVIEW QUESTIONS

1. What is an *attitude?*
2. What are the *components* of an attitude?
3. Are the components of an attitude consistent? What factors reduce the apparent consistency between attitude components?
4. What is a *multiattribute attitude model?*
5. What strategies can be used to change the ______ component of an attitude?
   a. Affective.
   b. Behavioral.
   c. Cognitive.
6. How can attitudes guide new product development?
7. What is a *benefit segment?*
8. What is *source credibility?* What causes it? What is the "sleeper" effect?
9. Why are *celebrity sources* sometimes effective? What risks are associated with using a celebrity source?
10. Are *fear appeals* always effective in changing attitudes? Why?
11. What characteristics should *humorous ads* have?
12. Are *emotional appeals* effective? Why?

13. Are *comparative appeals* effective? Why?
14. What are the *nonverbal* components of an ad? What impact do they have on attitudes?
15. When is a *two-sided message* likely to be more effective than a *one-sided message*?
16. Why is distraction sometimes used? What risks are associated with using distraction?
17. What is meant by order effects in message structure?

DISCUSSION QUESTIONS

1. Which version of the multiattribute attitude model and which attributes would you use to assess student attitudes toward ______? Justify your answer.
   a. Various careers?
   b. Various religions?
   c. Brands of running shoes?
   d. Brands of compact disc players?
   e. Brands of pens?
   f. Types of fruit?
2. Assume you wanted to improve or create favorable attitudes among college students toward a ______. Would you focus primarily on the affective, cognitive, or behavioral component? Why?
   a. Brand of compact disc player.
   b. Type of fruit.
   c. Charity.
   d. Brand of toothpaste.
   e. Brand of automobile.
3. Using the benefit segments shown in Exhibit 12–2, develop a marketing strategy to increase patronage among ______.
   a. Current users.
   b. Nonusers.
4. What benefit segments do you think exist for college football?
5. How would you use the multiattribute attitude model to develop a ______?
   a. Student union?
   b. College dorm?
   c. Shampoo targeted at college students?
   d. Clothing store targeted at college students?
6. Suppose you wanted to form highly negative attitudes toward drug use among high school students.
   a. Which attitude component would you focus on? Why?
   b. Which message characteristic would you use? Why?
   c. What type of appeal would you use? Why?

7. Which appeal type would you use in an attempt to improve college students' attitudes toward ______?
   a. Compact disc players?
   b. Bananas?
   c. Exercise?
   d. Levi jeans?
   e. U.S. Army?
   f. Del Monte ketchup?
8. Who would be a good celebrity spokesperson for the products in Question 7?

PROJECT QUESTIONS

1. Find and copy two magazine or newspaper advertisements, one based on the affective component and the other on the cognitive component. Discuss the motive of each ad in terms of its copy and illustration and what effect it creates in terms of attitude. Also, discuss why the marketer might have taken that approach in each advertisement.
2. Identify a television commercial that uses a humorous appeal and then interview five other individuals not enrolled in your class and measure their:
   a. Awareness of this commercial.
   b. Recall of brand advertised.
   c. Recall of relevant information.
   d. Liking of the commercial.
   e. Preference for the product advertised.

   Then evaluate your results and assess the level of communication that has taken place in terms of these five consumers' exposure, attention, comprehension, and preferences for this product and commercial.
3. Describe a magazine or television advertisement using ______. Evaluate the effectiveness of the ad.
   a. Source credibility.
   b. Celebrity source.
   c. Fear appeal.
   d. Humorous appeal.
   e. Emotional appeal.
   f. Comparative approach.
   g. Extensive nonverbal elements.
   h. A one-sided appeal.
   i. A two-sided appeal.
   j. Distraction.
4. Measure another student's ideal beliefs and belief importance for ______. Examine these ideal beliefs and importance weights and then develop a verbal description (i.e., concept) of a new brand of ______ that would satisfy this student's needs. Next, measure that student's attitude toward the concept you have developed in your verbal description.
   a. Candy bar.
   b. Slacks.
   c. Restaurant.
   d. Job.

5. Use the multiattribute attitude model to assess 10 students' attitudes toward various ______. Measure their behavior with respect to these objects. Are they consistent? Explain any inconsistencies.
   a. Fruits.
   b. Brands of cereal.
   c. Magazines.
   d. Deodorants.
   e. Pain relievers.
   f. Types of exercise.
6. Develop two advertisements for ______. One ad should focus on the cognitive component and the other on the affective component.
   a. A type of fruit.
   b. Breakfast cereal.
   c. Compact disc player.
   d. Aftershave lotion.
   e. Adopt-a-Pet (animal shelter).
   f. Personal computer.
7. Describe three instances when your purchase behavior was inconsistent with your attitude toward the brand you purchased. Explain why.
8. Repeat Project Question 1 for a primarily nonverbal ad and a primarily verbal ad.
9. Answer Discussion Question 8 using a sample of 10 students and the methodology suggested in this chapter (hint: see also Table 11–2).

REFERENCES

[1] D. Krech and R. S. Crutchfield, *Theory and Problems in Social Psychology* (New York: McGraw-Hill, 1984), p. 152.

[2] M. Fishbein and I. Aizen, *Belief, Attitude, Intention and Behavior: An Introduction to Theory and Research* (Reading, Mass.: Addison Wesley Publishing, 1975), p. 6.

[3] K. E. Miller and J. L. Ginter, "An Investigation of Situational Variation in Brand Choice Behavior and Attitude," *Journal of Marketing Research,* February 1979, pp. 111–23.

[4] See L. R. Kahle et al., "Social Values in the Eighties: A Special Issue," *Psychology and Marketing,* Winter 1985, pp. 231–306.

[5] R. B. Zajonc, "Feeling and Thinking: Preferences Need No Inferences," *American Psychologist,* February 1980, pp. 151–75. See also L. G. Gresham, A. J. Bush, and R. A. Davis, "Measures of Brand Attitude," *Journal of Business Research,* no. 3, 1984, pp. 353–61; R. B. Zajonc and H. Markus, "Affective and Cognitive Factors in Preferences," *Journal of Consumer Research,* September 1982, pp. 123–31; Y. Tsal, "On the Relationship between Cognitive and Affective Processes," and R. B. Zajonc and H. Markus, "Must All Affect Be Mediated by Cognition," both in *Journal of Consumer Research,* December 1985, pp. 358–62, 363–64; and J. A. Muncy, "Affect and Cognition," in *Advances in Consumer Research XIII,* ed. R. J. Lutz (Provo, Utah: Association for Consumer Research, 1986), pp. 226–30.

[6] G. S. Day and T. Deutscher, "Attitudinal Predictions of Choices of Major Appliance Brands," *Journal of Marketing Research,* May 1982, pp. 192–99; R. E. Smith and W. R. Swinyard, "Attitude-Behavior Consistency: The Impact of Product Trial versus Advertising," *Journal of Marketing Research,* August 1983, pp. 257–67;

W. D. Wells, "Attitudes and Behavior," *Journal of Advertising Research,* March 1985, pp. 40–44; and B. Loken and R. Hoverstad, "Relationships between Information Recall and Subsequent Attitudes," *Journal of Consumer Research,* September 1985, pp. 155–68.

[7] Miller and Ginter, "An Investigation"; P. R. Warshaw, "Predicting Purchase and Other Behaviors from General and Contextually Specific Intentions," *Journal of Marketing Research,* February 1980, pp. 26–33; and J. A. Cote, J. McCullough, and M. Reilly, "Effects of Unexpected Situations on Behavior-Intention Differences," *Journal of Consumer Research,* September 1985, pp. 188–94.

[8] See Chapter 9, footnote 11.

[9] M. P. Gardner, "Does Attitude toward the Ad Affect Brand Attitude under a Brand Evaluation Set?" *Journal of Marketing Research,* May 1985, pp. 192–98; S. B. Mackenzie, R. J. Lutz, and G. E. Belch, "The Role of Attitude toward the Ad as a Mediator of Advertising Effectiveness," *Journal of Marketing Research,* May 1986, pp. 130–4; A. A. Mitchell, "The Effect of Verbal and Visual Components," and M. C. Burke and J. A. Edell, "Ad Reactions Over Time," both in *Journal of Consumer Research,* June 1986, pp. 12–24, 114–18.

[10] C. Obermiller, "Varieties of Mere Exposure," *Journal of Consumer Research,* June 1985, pp. 17–30. For a critical view, see A. G. Sawyer, "Repetition, Cognitive Responses, and Persuasion," in *Cognitive Responses in Persuasion,* ed. R. E. Petty, T. M. Ostrum, and T. C. Brock (Hillsdale, N.J.: Lawrence Erlbaum, 1981).

[11] R. E. Smith and W. R. Swinyard, "Attitude-Behavior Consistency: The Impact of Product Trial versus Advertising," *Journal of Marketing Research,* August 1983, pp. 257–67; and Zajonc and Markus, "Affective and Cognitive."

[12] P. S. Raju and M. Hastak, "Pre-Trial Cognitive Effects of Cents-Off Coupons," *Journal of Advertising,* Second Quarter 1983, pp. 24–33.

[13] R. Haley, "Benefit Segmentation—20 Years Later," *Journal of Consumer Marketing,* no. 2, 1983, pp. 5–13; S. Van Auken and S. C. Lonial, "Assessing Mutual Association between Alternative Market Segmentation Bases," *Journal of Advertising,* March 1984, pp. 11–16; D. W. Eckrich, "Benefits or Problems as Market Segmentation Bases," *Journal of Advertising,* Second Quarter 1984, pp. 57–59; P. E. Green, A. M. Krieger, and C. M. Schaffer, "Quick and Simple Benefit Segmentation," *Journal of Advertising Research,* July 1985, pp. 9–15; and R. I. Haley and P. J. Weingarden, "Running Reliable Attitude Segmentation Studies," *Journal of Advertising Research,* January 1987, pp. 51–55.

[14] Other examples are K. D. Bahn and K. L. Granzin, "Benefit Segmentation in the Restaurant Industry," *Journal of the Academy of Marketing Science,* Summer 1985, pp. 226–47; A. G. Woodside and L. W. Jacobs, "Step Two in Benefit Segmentation," *Journal of Travel Research,* Summer 1985, pp. 7–13; and B. D. Davis and B. Sternquist, "Appealing to the Elusive Tourist," *Journal of Travel Research,* Spring 1987, pp. 25–31.

[15] H. E. Bloom, "Match the Concept and the Product," *Journal of Advertising Research,* October 1977, pp. 25–27.

[16] R. R. Harmon and K. A. Coney, "The Persuasive Effects of Source Credibility in Buy and Lease Situations," *Journal of Marketing Research,* May 1982, pp. 255–60; T. A. Swartz, "Relationship between Source Expertise and Source Similarity in an Advertising Context," *Journal of Advertising,* Second Quarter 1984, pp. 49–55; S. E. Moldovan, "Copy Factors Related to Persuasion Scores," *Journal of Advertising Research,* January 1985, pp. 16–22; and P. F. Bone and P. S. Ellen, "A Comment,"

and T. A. Swartz, "A Further Examination," both in *Journal of Advertising,* no. 1, 1986, pp. 47–48, 49–50.

[17] J. L. Wiener and J. C. Mowen, "Source Credibility," in *Advances in Consumer Research XIII,* ed. R. J. Lutz (Provo, Utah: Association for Consumer Research, 1986), pp. 306–10.

[18] W. B. Joseph, "The Credibility of Physically Attractive Communicators," *Journal of Advertising,* Third Quarter 1982, pp. 15–24; and G. L. Patzer, "Source Credibility as a Function of Communicator Physical Attractiveness," *Journal of Business Research,* Second Quarter 1983, pp. 229–41.

[19] D. B. Hannah and B. Sternthal, "Detecting and Explaining the Sleeper Effect," *Journal of Consumer Research,* September 1984, pp. 632–42.

[20] J. B. Freiden, "Advertising Spokesperson Effects," *Journal of Advertising Research,* November 1984, pp. 33–41.

[21] S. P. Sherman, "When You Wish Upon a Star," *Fortune,* August 19, 1985, p. 68.

[22] See R. E. Reidenbach and R. E. Pitts, "Not All CEO's Are Created Equal," *Journal of Advertising,* no. 1, 1986, pp. 30–36.

[23] C. Atkin and M. Block, "Effectiveness of Celebrity Endorsers," *Journal of Advertising Research,* March 1983, pp. 57–61; R. E. Petty, J. T. Cacioppo, and D. Schumann, "Central and Peripheral Routes to Advertising Effectiveness," *Journal of Consumer Research,* September 1983, pp. 135–46; L. Kahle and P. Homer, "Physical Attractiveness of the Celebrity Endorser," *Journal of Consumer Research,* March 1985, pp. 954–61; and K. Debevec and E. Iyer, "The Influence of Spokespersons in Altering a Product's Gender Image," *Journal of Advertising,* no. 4, 1986, pp. 12–20.

[24] Sherman, "When You Wish," p. 69.

[25] J. Forkan, "Product Matchup Key to Effective Star Presentations," *Advertising Age,* October 6, 1980, p. 42; and A. Howard, "More than Just a Passing Fancy," *Advertising Age,* July 20, 1979, p. S-2.

[26] Sherman, "When You Wish," p. 70.

[27] J. Neher, "Sommers' Photos Get Cold Shoulder at Ace," *Advertising Age,* December 31, 1979, p. 6.

[28] See B. Sternthal and C. S. Craig, "Fear Appeals: Revisited and Revised," *Journal of Consumer Research,* December 1974, pp. 22–34; M. Menasco and P. Baron, "Threats and Promises in Advertising Appeals," in *Advances in Consumer Research IX,* ed. A. Mitchell (Chicago: Association for Consumer Research, 1983), pp. 221–27; L. S. Unger and J. M. Stearns, "The Use of Fear and Guilt Messages in Television Advertising," in *1983 AMA Conference Proceedings,* ed. P. E. Murphy et al. (Chicago: American Marketing Association, 1983), pp. 16–20; and S. W. McDaniel and V. A. Zeithaul, *Psychology and Marketing,* Fall/Winter 1984, pp. 73–82.

[29] J. R. Stuteville, "Psychic Defenses against High Fear Appeals," *Journal of Marketing,* April 1970, pp. 39–45.

[30] Sternthal and Craig, "Fear Appeals."

[31] J. J. Burnett and R. L. Oliver, "Fear Appeal Effects in the Field: A Segmentation Approach," *Journal of Marketing Research,* May 1979, pp. 181–90; and J. Burnett, "Internal-External Locus of Control as a Moderator of Fear Appeals," *Journal of Applied Psychology,* 1981, pp. 390–93.

[32] See H. B. Lammers et al., "Humor and Cognitive Responses to Advertising Stimuli," *Journal of Business Research,* Second Quarter 1983, pp. 173–85; G. E. Belch and M. A. Belch, "The Effects of Repetition on Cognitive and Affective Reactions to Humorous and Serious Television Commercials," and C. P. Duncan, J. E. Nelson, and N. T. Frontczake, "The Effect of Humor on Advertising Comprehension," both in *Advances in Consumer Research XI,* ed. T. C. Kinnear (Chicago: Association for Consumer Research, 1984), pp. 4–10; T. J. Madden and M. G. Weinberger, "Humor in Advertising," *Journal of Advertising Research,* September 1984, pp. 23–29; J. S. Wagle, "Using Humor in the Industrial Selling Process," *Industrial Marketing Management,* vol. 14, 1985, pp. 221–26; B. D. Gelb and G. M. Zinkhan, "The Effect of Repetition on Humor in a Radio Advertising Study," *Journal of Advertising,* no. 4, 1985, pp. 13–20; B. D. Gelb and G. M. Zinkhan, "Humor and Advertising Effectiveness after Repeated Exposures to a Radio Commercial," *Journal of Advertising,* no. 2, 1986, pp. 15–20; and J. Nelson, "Comment," and G. M. Zinkhan and B. D. Gelb, "Humor and Advertising Effectiveness Reexamined," both in *Journal of Advertising,* no. 1, 1987, pp. 63–65, 66–67.

[33] "Funny Ads Provide Welcome Relief during These Gloom and Doom Days," *Marketing News,* April 17, 1981, p. 3.

[34] S. R. Cox, K. A. Coney, and P. F. Ruppe, "Impact of Comparative Product Ingredient Information," *Journal of Public Policy and Marketing,* vol. 2, 1983, pp. 57–69; G. J. Gorn and C. B. Weinberg, "The Impact of Comparative Advertising on Perception and Attitude," *Journal of Consumer Research,* September 1984, pp. 719–27; C. B. Schneider, "Problems of Comparative-Test Commercials," *Journal of Consumer Marketing,* no. 4, 1984, pp. 73–77; D. D. Muehling and N. Kangun, "The Multi-Dimensionality of Comparative Advertising," *Journal of Public Policy and Marketing,* no. 4, 1985, pp. 112–28; Byer and E. F. Cooke, "Comparative Advertising's Dilemma," *Journal of Consumer Marketing,* Summer 1985, pp. 67–71; and S. Grosshart, D. D. Muehling, and N. Kangun; "Verbal and Visual References to Competition in Comparative Advertising," *Journal of Advertising,* no. 1, 1986, pp. 10–23.

[35] See R. W. Mizerski and J. D. White, "Understanding and Using Emotions in Advertising," *Journal of Consumer Marketing,* Fall 1986, pp. 57–69; J. H. Holmes and K. E. Crocker, "Predispositions and the Comparative Effectiveness of Rational, Emotional, and Discrepant Appeals," *Journal of the Academy of Marketing Science,* Spring 1987, pp. 27–35, and chap. 10, pp. 28–32.

[36] D. A. Aaker, D. M. Stayman, and M. R. Hagerty, "Warmth in Advertising," *Journal of Consumer Research,* March 1986, pp. 365–81.

[37] M. J. Alpert and L. L. Golden, "The Impact of Education on the Relative Effectiveness of One-Sided and Two-Sided Communications," in *1982 Proceedings,* ed. Walker, pp. 30–33.

[38] See W. R. Swinyard, "Interaction between Comparative Advertising and Copy Claim Variation," *Journal of Marketing Research,* May 1981, pp. 175–86; G. E. Belch, "An Examination of Comparative and Noncomparative Television Commercials," *Journal of Marketing Research,* August 1981, pp. 339–49; and M. Etgar and S. A. Goodwin, "One-Sided versus Two-Sided Comparative Message Appeals for New Brand Introductions," *Journal of Consumer Research,* March 1982, pp. 460–64.

[39] M. A. Kamins and H. Assael, "Two-Sided versus One-Sided Appeals," *Journal of Marketing Research,* February 1987, pp. 29–39; J. M. Hunt and M. F. Smith, "The

Persuasive Impact of Two-Sided Selling Appeals for an Unknown Brand Name," *Journal of the Academy of Marketing Science,* Spring 1987, pp. 11–17; and L. L. Golden and M. I. Alpert, "Comparative Analysis of the Relative Effectiveness of One- and Two-Sided Communication for Contrasting Products," *Journal of Advertising,* no. 1, 1987, pp. 18–25.

[40] J. C. Olson, D. R. Toy, and P. A. Dover, "Do Cognitive Responses Mediate the Effects of Advertising Content on Cognitive Structure?" *Journal of Consumer Research,* December 1982, pp. 245–62; and L. Bozinoff and M. Ghingold, "Evaluating Guilt Arousing Marketing Communications," *Journal of Business Research,* Second Quarter 1983, pp. 243–55.

[41] D. Gardner, "The Distraction Hypothesis in Marketing," *Journal of Advertising Research,* 1970, pp. 25–30; and S. Bither, "Effects of Distraction and Commitment on the Persuasiveness of Television Advertising," *Journal of Marketing Research,* February 1972, pp. 1–5. For conflicting results, see J. E. Nelson, C. P. Duncan, and N. T. Frontczak, "The Distraction Hypothesis and Radio Advertising," *Journal of Marketing,* Winter 1985, pp. 60–71.

[42] Raju and Hostak, "Pre-Trial Cognitive Effects."

[43] See C. W. Park and S. M. Young, "Consumer Response to Television Commercials," *Journal of Marketing Research,* February 1986, pp. 11–24.

[44] H. E. Krugman, "The Impact of Television Advertising: Learning without Involvement," *Public Opinion Quarterly,* 1965, pp. 349–56; and H. E. Krugman, "Memory without Recall, Exposure without Perception," *Journal of Advertising Research,* August 1977, pp. 7–12.

[45] See Chapter 10, footnote 27.

[46] E. C. Hirschman, "The Effect of Verbal and Pictorial Advertising Stimuli," *Journal of Advertising,* no. 2, 1986, pp. 27–34; and M. P. Gardner and M. J. Houston, "The Effects of Verbal and Visual Components of Retail Communications," *Journal of Retailing,* Spring 1986, pp. 64–78.

[47] S. Hecker, "Music for Advertising Effect," *Psychology and Marketing,* Fall/Winter 1984, pp. 3–8.

[48] P. N. Homer and L. R. Kahle, "A Social Adaptation Explanation of the Effects of Surrealism on Advertising," *Journal of Advertising,* no. 2, 1986, pp. 50–54.

[49] See J. Kisielius and B. Sternthal, "Examining the Vividness Controversy," *Journal of Consumer Research,* March 1986, pp. 418–31.

C A S E S

CASE 3–1 FEDERATED STORES, INC.*

In an advertising experiment, a large department store tracks its target market's awareness, comprehension, intentions, and purchases to better understand the effectiveness of its advertising.

A large, well-known department store (a member of Federated Stores, Inc.) wanted to better understand the effectiveness of its retail promotions. The store, which had above-average quality and competitive prices, typically ran newspaper and radio advertisements during a retail promotion. Its television advertising was primarily institutional and did not address specific retail promotions. While the management team knew that they had to advertise their retail promotions, they never felt comfortable with the effectiveness of their advertising efforts. What they really wanted to know was how they could improve their advertising efforts in order to get a bigger response per dollar spent.

Advertising Study

Pre-Promotion Survey. To better understand the effectiveness of their advertising, a study of advertising exposure, comprehension, and purchases was conducted. A well-defined target market of 50,000 potential buyers was iden-

Figure A
Store Image among Target Consumers

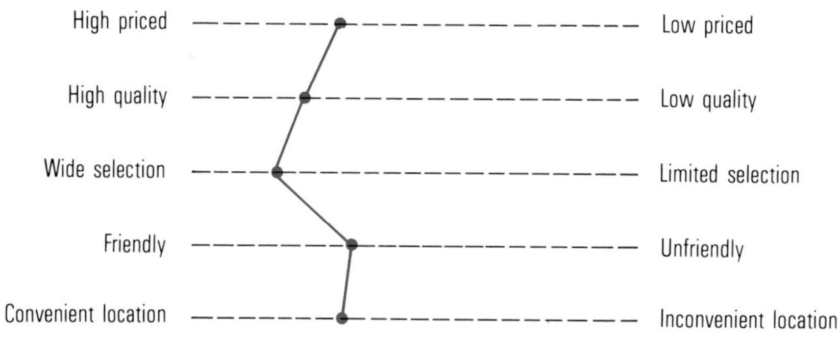

*Based on a consulting project by one of the authors.

Figure B
Advertising Awareness over Five Days of Advertising

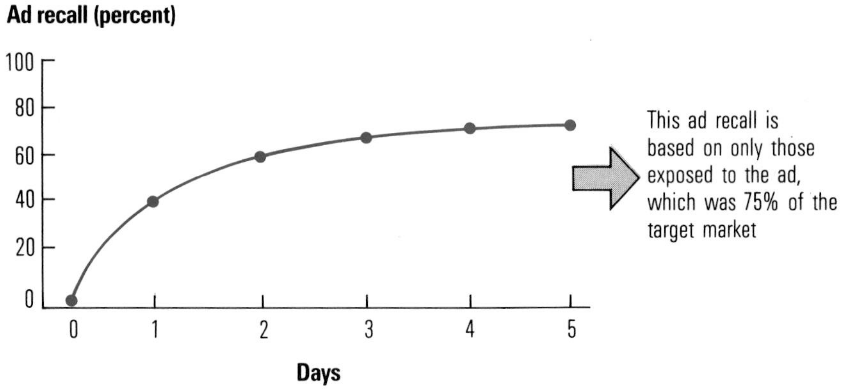

tified, and 50 in-depth interviews were conducted to best determine the appropriate merchandise, price, ad copy, and media for the test. In addition, the store's image and that of three competing stores were measured to better understand the store's position among the target consumers. A profile of the store's image among target consumers is shown in Figure A.

Based on this information, a line of merchandise that would appeal to consumers in this target market was selected. The merchandise was attractively priced and ad copy was carefully created to communicate and appeal to the demographics and lifestyles of the target consumers. The retail promotion was run for one week, and full-page newspaper ads promoting the retail merchandise were run each day of the five-day promotion in the two local newspapers. Radio advertisements also ran on two radio stations whose listener demographics matched the target market. Eight radio advertisements were aired each day of the promotion, two in each of four time slots: early morning, mid-day, early evening (7–10 P.M.), and late evening (after 10 P.M.).

In-Promotion Survey. Each evening a sample of 100 target market consumers was interviewed by telephone as follows:

1. Target consumers were asked if they had read the newspaper or listened to the radio that day. If so, how extensively? This would determine their exposure to the advertisement.
2. After a general description of the merchandise, they were asked to recall any related retail advertisements they had seen or heard.
3. If they recalled the ad, they were asked to describe the ad, the merchandise promoted, sale prices, and the sponsoring store.
4. If they were accurate in their ad comprehension, they were asked to express their intentions to purchase.

Figure C
Overall Ad Effectiveness and Market Penetration

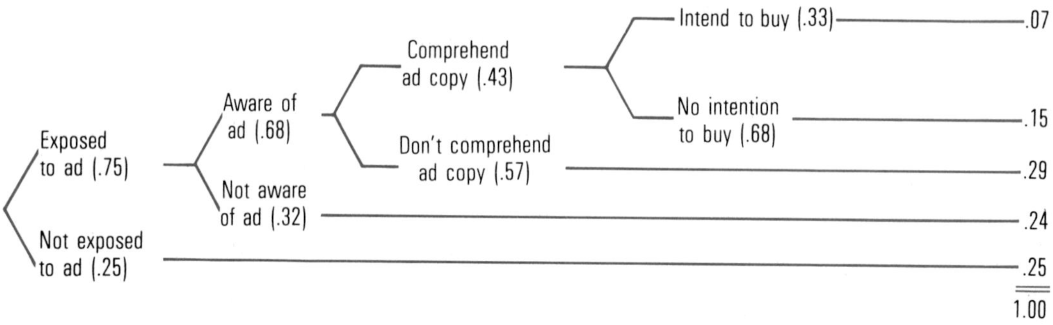

5. Additional questions that could be useful in future promotions targeted at this consumer segment were also asked.

Post-Promotion Survey. Immediately following the retail promotion, 500 target market consumers were surveyed to determine what percentage of the target market actually purchased the promoted merchandise. It was also important to determine which sources of information influenced them in their decision to purchase and the amount of their purchase.

Results of Study

The combination of targeted daily newspaper and radio advertising produced a cumulative recall of the advertisement among those exposed to the ad by either newspaper, radio, or both. As shown in Figure B, the largest gains in recall (awareness) were made in the first two days of advertising effort. After day two, only marginal gains in awareness occurred.

After five days of ad exposure, ad awareness reached a maximum of 68 percent. However, effectiveness of the advertising effort cannot be judged only on awareness of the promotion. Information collected on ad comprehension and intentions to buy is also important in evaluating the effectiveness of advertising. Using the information collected during the promotion, Figure C was constructed.

While ad exposure (75 percent) and ad awareness (68 percent) were high, correct comprehension of the ad was low. In this case only 43 percent of those exposed to *and* aware of the ad copy could accurately recall important details, such as which store was promoting the retail sale. Of those that did comprehend the ad copy, 33 percent intended to respond by purchasing the advertised merchandise. This yields an overall intention to buy based on the ad, of 7 percent. As shown in Figure C, the biggest area of lost opportunity was due to those who did not accurately comprehend the ad copy.

The post-promotion survey estimated that only 4.2 percent of the target market consumers made purchases of the promotional merchandise during the promotion period. However, the average total amount of purchase was $45, roughly double the average price of the promotion merchandise. In terms of how these buyers learned of the promotion, 46 percent mentioned newspaper A, 23 percent mentioned newspaper B, 15 percent learned of the sale through word-of-mouth communication, and 10 percent mentioned the radio as the source of information contributing to their awareness of this promotion.

Overall, the retail promotion yielded almost $100,000 in sales and was judged a success in many ways. However, management was concerned over the results presented in Figure C, since a significant sales opportunity was missed by not achieving a higher level of ad comprehension. They believe that a more effective ad would capture at least 75 percent ad comprehension among those aware of the ad. This in turn would almost double sales with no additional cost.

Questions

1. Discuss how their store image presented in Figure A may have enhanced the awareness achieved in Figure B. How might a poor store image hamper learning and hence result in lower levels of awareness?
2. Discuss the learning and retention of information in this case within the context of high- and low-involvement learning. Why might some target consumers have higher levels of involvement in learning of this retail promotion than others?
3. Discuss Figure C and why the overall estimated market penetration (7 percent) was higher than actual market penetration (4.2 percent). How might this model be improved to achieve a more accurate estimate of market penetration?
4. With respect to future retail advertising promotions, what recommendations would you make to improve the overall profitability of the advertising effort? Recall that their ultimate concern was to achieve a "bigger response per dollar spent."
5. Is management realistic in desiring 75 percent comprehension among those aware of the ad? What could be done to increase comprehension?

CASE 3–2 SPRITE*

In an effort to build market share through advertising, a controlled study of billboard advertising is conducted.

For many years the Coca-Cola Company has sought to develop a noncola soft drink to compete with 7UP. In blind taste tests, Sprite was often preferred over 7UP, but in the marketplace, 7UP has consistently outperformed Sprite in share of market. In part, 7UP's superior share performance is due to its larger advertising budget and well-established brand image. To better understand if and how billboard advertising could attract consumers to Sprite, a small-scale consumer study was conducted.

---

*Based on a private project by one of the authors.

Table A
Soft Drinks Used in the Consumption Study

	Cola Taste	
Sweetener	Cola	Noncola
Sugared	Coca-Cola Pepsi-Cola	7UP Sprite
Nonsugared	Tab Diet Pepsi	Fresca Diet 7UP

The Consumption Study

Eighty employees from a large commercial organization were recruited to participate in a soft drink consumption study. This group of employees included a wide mix of office workers, managers, and blue-collar workers. A refrigerator with eight soft drinks was set up in the employee lunchroom, and participants

Figure A
Perceptual Map of Competing Brands and Ideal Brands

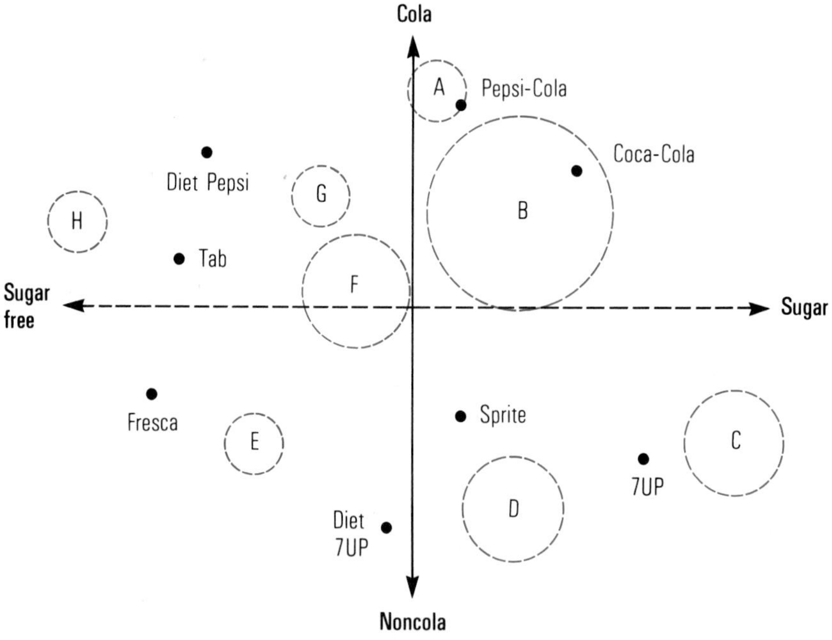

could take a soft drink at any time throughout the workday. They were instructed to put the cap of the soft drink they selected in a slotted bin adjacent to the refrigerator. Each participant was assigned a slot with his or her name below it. In this way, an individual history of brand choice could be recorded each day. Participants consumed an average of two soft drinks per day. The soft drinks used in the study are shown in Table A.

A one-week warm-up period enabled the participants to adjust to the novelty of the situation. Following this, their individual choice behavior was tracked for ten weeks. After the fourth week, a Sprite advertisement occupied the space on a large billboard that could be seen easily by all employees entering and exiting this commercial establishment. The Sprite billboard looked very much like Sprite magazine print ads. In this manner, the study was able to track consumption of the eight soft drinks for a four-week period prior to exposure to the billboard ad, and then measure how that behavior changed with the presence of a Sprite billboard advertisement.

The Results

The perceptual map shown in Figure A was created using consumer perceptions and brand preferences. It indicates the perceived similarity of competing brands and the location of ideal brands for different groups of consumers (indicated by the circles with the size of the circle representing the number of consumers with that ideal brand). The letters shown indicate the ideal soft drink based on consumer preferences. The larger the circle, the larger the proportion of consumers preferring that ideal brand. As can be seen, Sprite is perceived to be more similar to 7UP than to other soft drinks, and consumers with ideal brands near 7UP

Table B
Sprite's Weekly Market Share

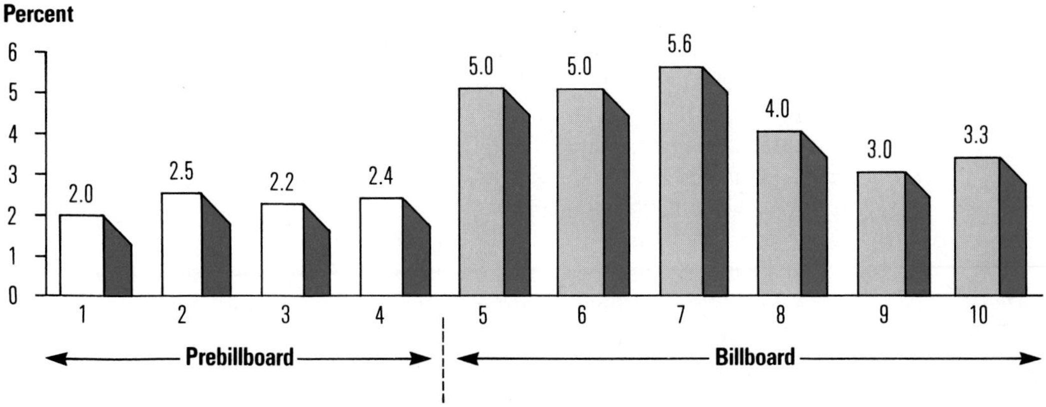

should be more attracted to Sprite if the Sprite advertisement has the desired effect.

As shown in Table B, Sprite's share in this study was very close to 2 percent through the four weeks leading up to the introduction of the Sprite billboard advertisement. Immediately following the introduction, Sprite's share more than doubled and stayed over 5 percent for three weeks. Sprite's share then dropped to 4 percent in week four of the billboard ad (week eight overall), and stabilized around 3 percent for the remainder of the study.

Analysis of competing brand shares showed that after introduction of the Sprite billboard, 7UP, Diet 7UP, and Fresca lost market share. By the end of the ten weeks (six weeks of billboard advertising) Fresca had recovered its lost share, but 7UP and Diet 7UP were still down in share although some of their lost share was gained back.

Questions

1. What factors would cause Sprite's market share to go up after introduction of a billboard advertisement? Be specific as to the perceptual and learning processes that had to take place.
2. What factors contributed to Sprite's share decline after three weeks of billboard exposure?
3. Describe the results of this experiment with respect to low-involvement learning.
4. What are the marketing strategy implications of this billboard advertising experiment?

CASE 3–3 GENERAL FOODS*

The dog food market is segmented on the basis of dog owners' attitudes and emotions toward their dogs. When combined with demographic differences, marketing strategies can be developed for each segment.

Over many years of consumer research, General Foods Pet Food Division uncovered several unique psychological differences among dog owners. As a major manufacturer and marketer of dog food, they have had a long tradition of trying to better understand the needs of this market. While several demographic studies of dog owners failed to uncover a meaningful basis for market segmentation, an attitude study yielded some very useful insights.

The attitude study focused on the attitudes dog owners held with respect to their dogs. These attitudes covered a wide range of topics such as nutrition, comfort, and owners' affection for their dogs. From the attitude components studied, a key difference among dog owners surfaced. Some dog owners expressed feelings or emotions toward their dogs that would be similar to feelings

*Based on materials supplied by General Foods.

held toward family members or close friends. Other dog owners did not express these emotions, but instead regarded their dogs as animals rather than persons. Based on this key difference, a variety of other behaviors, preferences, and demographics began to make more sense.

My Dog Is a Person

This segment of dog owners was more concerned about health, nutrition, and the general well-being of their dogs. These owners shopped carefully for the highest quality dog foods that provided both good taste and nutrition. Price was a secondary issue.

One might be tempted to assume that these were older people whose dogs took on a role that a child once provided. In fact, dog owners in this segment included a wide range of age groups, although absence of children was common. Thus, young singles and young married couples without children held the same attitudes as middle-aged and older dog owners without children living in the household. In all cases this segment tended to have personal and "humanistic" feelings about their dogs.

My Dog Is a Dog

In this segment, dog owners had feelings of affection but they were far less intense. Their attitudes suggested that the dog carried less importance in the owner's life, and affection was not a major concern when buying dog food. Where the dog slept, what it ate, and how it was thought of on a day-to-day basis were all less personalized than in the other segment.

The key demographic characteristic of this segment was household structure. The presence of children, and usually other pets, lessened the importance of the dog's role. In this household situation, a particular child is usually responsible for the dog's care and feeding. Parents often help a great deal, but the dog takes on a lower priority in the household. As a result, extensive search for the "right dog food" is not common. These dog owners prefer to buy in bulk quantities, where the price is lower and the frequency of purchase is reduced.

Questions

1. Would an attitude measure focusing on the cognitive component have uncovered these segments? Develop a measuring instrument that would capture both the cognitive and emotional aspects of dog ownership.
2. How would product positioning differ for each segment?
3. Given the predicted changes in America's demographics and household structure, which segment is likely to have greater growth in the future? Why?
4. Would this segmentation system work for cat owners?

5. What other business opportunities might exist based on this segmentation of the dog owner market?

CASE 3–4 BLITZ-WEINHARD BREWING CO.*

Changing needs, perceptions, and preferences among beer customers has lead to increased market segmentation and the need for multiple segment-based strategies.

Changes in beer preferences have been enormous over the past 25 years. In the sixties, there were five basic segments to the beer market, as shown in Figure A. The biggest segment was the quality segment. It was dominated by heavily advertised national brands such as Budweiser, Miller, and Schlitz. The second largest segment was dominated by regional beer producers which offered good value: a quality beer at a price lower than that of national beers such as Budweiser. This segment provided breweries such as the Blitz-Weinhard Brewing Company with most of their sales.

Comprising the third segment were lighter tasting regional beers such as Coors and Olympia, which achieved a higher status and gained national appeal throughout the sixties and seventies. A fourth market segment was the price segment of the beer market. In this segment, Blitz-Weinhard offered Bohemia Club and competed with other regional discount beers. Finally, a small segment of con-

Figure A
Beer Market Preferences and Segmentation in the Sixties

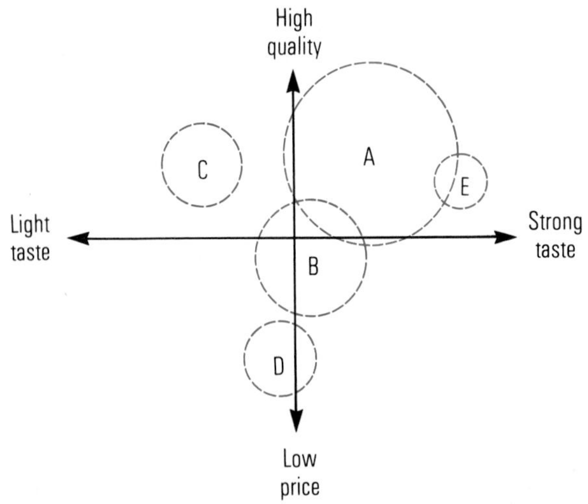

Beer segment	Primary attribute	Typical beer
A	Quality	Budweiser
B	Value	Blitz
C	Light taste	Coors
D	Price	Bohemia
E	Strong taste	Colt-45

*Based on materials supplied by Blitz-Weinhard Brewing Company.

Figure B
Beer Market Preferences and Segmentation in the Eighties

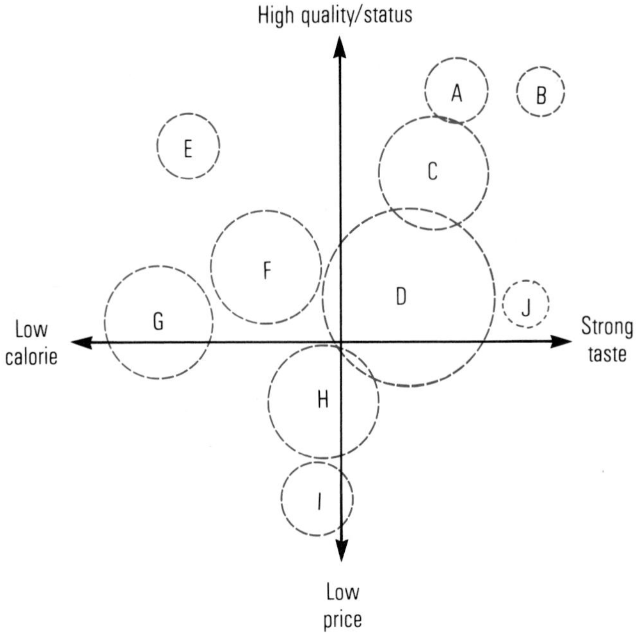

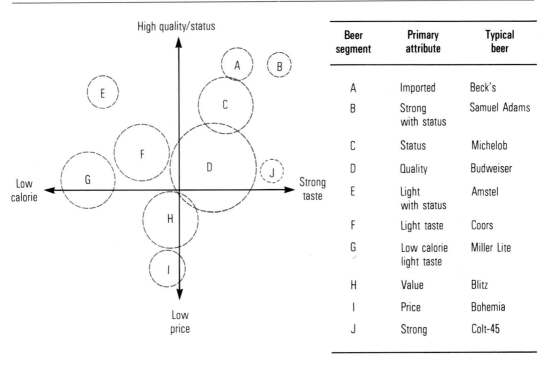

Beer segment	Primary attribute	Typical beer
A	Imported	Beck's
B	Strong with status	Samuel Adams
C	Status	Michelob
D	Quality	Budweiser
E	Light with status	Amstel
F	Light taste	Coors
G	Low calorie light taste	Miller Lite
H	Value	Blitz
I	Price	Bohemia
J	Strong	Colt-45

sumers preferred stronger tasting beers. These were typically ales or malt liquors and were marketed on both a national basis (Colt-45) and on a regional basis.

The perceptual map and segmentation shown in Figure A was useful for brand positioning in the sixties, but things began to change in the seventies and continued to change in the eighties. Social and economic changes—such as the women's movement, greater health consciousness, increasing income, and increasing concern with social status—created a new set of beer preferences that reshaped the beer market. These changes in consumer needs and preferences created a variety of new segments, shown in Figure B. This in turn opened the door to a host of new brands and new competition.

The Beer Market of the Eighties

As shown in Figure B, the beer market of the eighties presented a much more complex situation. The simplicity of the sixties had given way to a much more individualized set of market needs. In this transition, the tradition segments of the sixties lost ground and new segments emerged. For a regional brewer such as Blitz-Weinhard, this could have meant disaster as its served market shifted to other beer preferences. To survive, Blitz-Weinhard had to make a strategic move.

One option would have been to try to reposition its regional beer (Blitz) in a more lucrative, growing segment. To accomplish this would require time and a great many advertising dollars, and in the process would probably lose its present customer base. One alternative was to enter segment C with a new brand that would be positioned as a high quality, high status beer. Product positioning was critical because these consumers wanted a product that was clearly differentiated from regional and national beers such as Blitz and Budweiser, respectively.

Positioning Strategy

To capture the taste and psychological needs of segment C, Blitz-Weinhard introduced Henry's Private Reserve. The packaging, name, bottle, and ad copy provided no hint of a Blitz image. Although the name was taken from the first name of one of the founders of the brewery, Henry Weinhard, the positioning was geared to segment C. Early packaging included a description of the brewing process that went into making Henry's Private Reserve. Early production runs were numbered so as to further increase its air of speciality. And with a distinct taste and premium price, it took off. For the Blitz-Weinhard Brewing Company it has been a tremendous success.

Questions

1. Discuss the demographic and lifestyle changes that occurred in the seventies that would give rise to the segmentation of beer preferences we can observe in the eighties.
2. Why was the Blitz-Weinhard Brewing Co. successful in attracting consumers in segment C? What risks does it now face in this segment?
3. What attributes would you use to measure the image of different brands of beer? How could you use these attributes to measure consumer attitudes toward alternative beers that could be positioned in Figure B? Be sure to cover both the emotional and cognitive factors.
4. Develop a new version of Figures A and B based on your view of how the market will look in 1995. What should Blitz-Weinhard do next in order to continue its growth and insure its future in this continuously changing market?

CASE 3–5 LEVI STRAUSS*

Using lifestyle as a basis of segmenting the men's apparel market, Levi Strauss needs to develop a marketing strategy to gain entry into a new and attractive target market.

---

*Based on *Not By Jeans Alone* (Enterprise, undated).

Figure A
Segmentation of the Men's Apparel Market

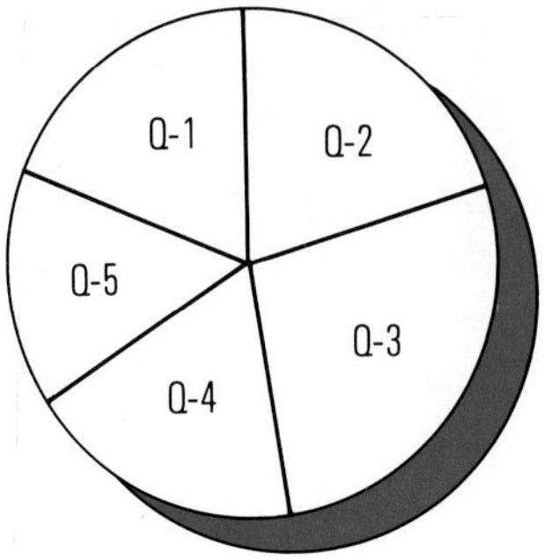

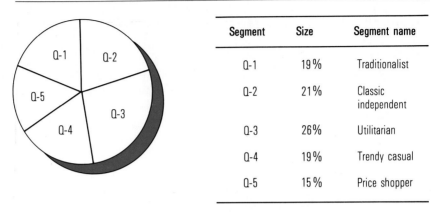

Segment	Size	Segment name
Q-1	19%	Traditionalist
Q-2	21%	Classic independent
Q-3	26%	Utilitarian
Q-4	19%	Trendy casual
Q-5	15%	Price shopper

By the early eighties, Levi Strauss had grown to a $2.8 billion a year company. Over half this revenue was derived from the sale of jeans, which grew at the rate of 23 percent per year in the seventies. However, by the eighties this market was becoming saturated. To continue to grow, Levi Strauss had to develop new products and penetrate new markets.

To better understand the clothing market, they invested in a large-scale consumer behavior study that examined the clothing preferences, buying habits, demographics, and lifestyles of some 2,000 males. From this very large base of information they hoped to discover new market opportunities for Levi Strauss & Co. They uncovered five distinct market segments for men's clothing, depicted in Figure A. Each segment has unique lifestyles and clothing preferences.

The Utilitarian

This segment of the men's apparel market represents about 26 percent of male consumers. These consumers wear jeans as a way of life, for work and play. Jeans are an important part of their lifestyle and communicate the casualness they desire to portray. This segment represents a very important part of Levi's present sales in the jeans market.

The Trendy Casual

This segment is more contemporary and conscious of the latest fashion trend. In the study they were characterized as your "John Travolta type." They represent 19 percent of the men's apparel market. These consumers like to be noticed, and having the right clothes is important to them. They are very active socially and are a large part of the urban night-life scene.

Table A
Levi's Marketing Mix Strategy for the Classic Independent

Marketing Mix	Description
Product	Tailored suits, pants, and sports coats
Price	$160 suits, $85–$100 coats, $30–$45 pants
Brand name	Levi's Tailored Classic
Distribution	Higher-quality department stores
Advertising	Heavy television advertising

Price Shopper

These men shop for the lowest price. They represent 15 percent of the men's apparel market. Because they are price shoppers, they are more inclined to shop discount stores and lower-priced department stores, and to respond to price-off sales.

The Traditionalist

A hard-core department store shopper, the traditionalist is very conservative. This conservativism is reflected in his political preferences as well as his clothing preferences. Traditionalists are the largest consumers of polyester clothing and are generally slow to adopt new clothing changes. They make up 19 percent of the market. They prefer to shop for clothes with their wives or girlfriends whose opinions they value in making clothing purchase decisions.

The Classic Independent

Clearly the most significant thing to come out of the men's apparel consumer research study was uncovering the Q–2 segment, the "Classic Independent." This segment makes up 21 percent of male shoppers, but it consumes 46 percent of men's natural fiber clothing. These men take a great deal of pride in how they look, and their clothes have to be right. Price is not a major consideration, and they prefer to shop at specialty stores. They purchase the best clothing and prestigious brands. They want the best fit, which they believe requires tailoring, and they are willing to pay for it. They prefer to shop alone and enjoy the process of picking out their clothing. The Levi Strauss team felt that this segment represented a significant opportunity.

Proposed Target Market Strategy

To attract the Classic Independent, Levi Strauss developed a line of tailored clothing that includes men's three-piece suits, slacks, and sports coats. The new line is called Levi's Tailored Classics. The clothing requires no tailoring. The consumer can select individual pants, vest, and jacket to assure a desired fit.

The pants will retail for $30 to $45, coats for $85 to $100, and three-piece suits for $160 (1982 prices). These prices are consistent with this segment's standard expenditures. Levi's Tailored Classics will be sold through department stores. A heavy television and print advertising campaign is planned to launch and properly position the Levi's Tailored Classic. Considerable effort will have to be made to inform and convince the Classic Independent that the Levi's line of suits fits their needs. Summarized in Table A is the marketing mix strategy Levi Strauss plans to implement in going after the Classic Independent.

Questions

1. How well does Levi Strauss understand the clothing preferences and lifestyles of consumers in the men's wear market? To what degree did they do a good job of segmenting the men's apparel market? Do they fully understand the emotional aspect of clothing purchase and use?
2. Construct a list of demographics, use behaviors, clothing preferences, general attitudes toward life, and specific attitudes toward clothes that would need to be measured to produce the market segmentation they obtained.
3. What problems do you see with their proposed target market strategy? Describe the information processing that a Classic Independent would go through in reacting to the Levi's market offering.
4. What changes would you recommend in their strategy? Describe these changes with respect to how they would better fit the clothing preferences and lifestyle of the target buyer.

CASE 3–6 WEYERHAEUSER BRANDING STRATEGIES*

How can Weyerhaeuser create brand name preference for its lumber products which do-it-yourselfers currently view as commodities?

Bill Wachtler recently found himself once again reviewing Weyerhaeuser's tentative plans to utilize a branding strategy for most of its lumber and building materials products (including dimension lumber such as 2×4s and plywood). The need for such an approach seemed obvious.

The repair and remodel (R&R) market accounted for 20 percent of lumber consumption and over $90 billion in expenditures (lumber and nonlumber) in 1987. Unlike housing, R&R consumption did not fluctuate widely with economic shifts. Further, this market is projected to continue growing in importance. R&R lumber consumption is divided approximately equally between do-it-yourselfers (DIYers) and contractors. Most of the contractors are relatively small.

*Used with permission from Weyerhaeuser Corporation.

Figure A
Demographic and Behavioral Profile of Do-It-Yourself Consumers

- 35–44 year olds are most active.
- 85 percent of projects involve homes over 10 years of age.
- 60 percent have lived in the home 10 years or more.
- 53 percent have incomes between $20,000 and $50,000.
- 43 percent are two-income families.
- Major projects generally involve both DIY and contractor activities.
- Renters do about one third of the projects.
- Store location is a key factor in outlet selection, though a third will drive 16–30 minutes to reach a preferred store.
- 90 percent of all purchases are planned in advance.
- 52 percent of all projects are initiated by females.
- A sense of accomplishment is a major motivation for DIY projects (both male and female).
- Financial necessity is also an important motivation, but cost-conscious shoppers are after value rather than lowest cost.
- 70 percent of DIYers say brand names are an important factor in buying nonlumber home-improvement products.
- Leading causes, in order, for brand switching between nonlumber home-improvement brands: quality/warranty, special prices, salesperson, brand availability, and package information.

Home centers and similar large chains and buying units have grown rapidly in importance and will soon dominate distribution to DIYers and many smaller contractors. These chains have sophisticated buying units and push hard to minimize prices paid to the lumber producers. With lumber viewed as a commodity, they can play one producer against another for price concessions. The target market DIY consumer has distinctive characteristics and behavior, as summarized in Figure A.

Bill felt that the above facts indicated both the need and opportunity to introduce branded lumber. He was also mindful of the price premium obtained by firms that had successfully branded "commodity" products, such as "Perdue" in chickens and "Sunkist" in oranges.

Despite what appeared to be obvious advantages to a branding strategy, several factors caused Bill to worry. First, if it was such an obvious strategy, why was no other lumber company pursuing it? Second, there was a widespread belief that, within lumber grades, "a 2 × 4 is a 2 × 4." Finally, there were the results of yet another company study indicating that brand name was not important to lumber buyers (see Figure B). Bill wondered how he could convince a very

Figure B
Do-It-Yourselfers' Ratings of the Importance of Attributes of Boards

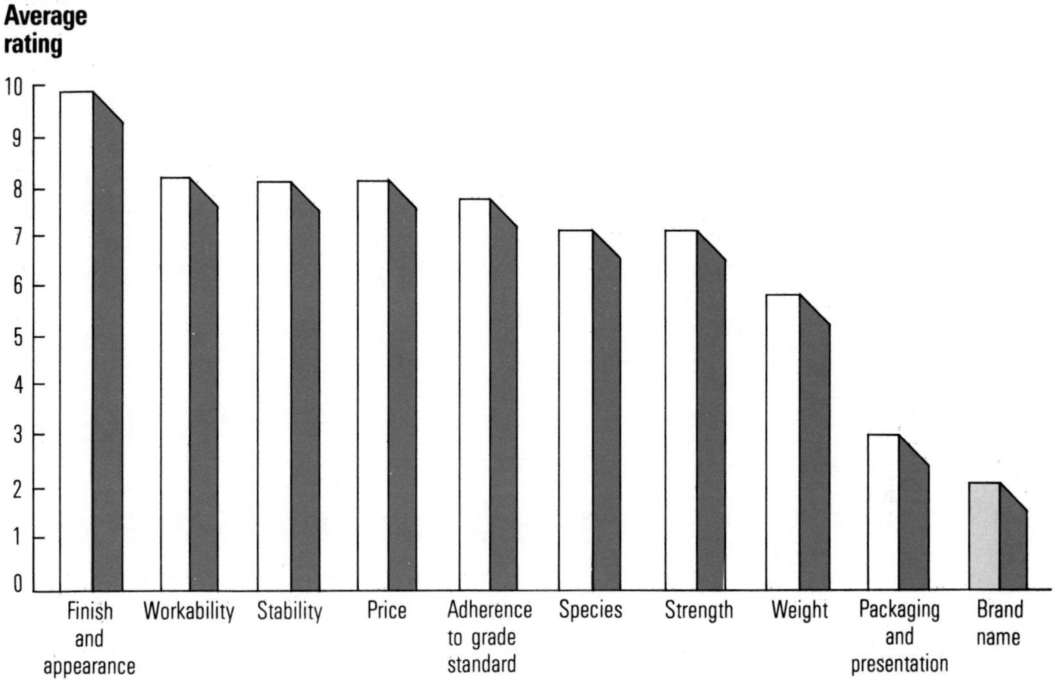

Source: C. Casson, "The Many Faces of Home Modernization," *Building Supply Home Center*, May 1986, pp. 52–64; and Weyerhaeuser internal reports.

customer-oriented management that branding was a good strategy when customers consistently said they did not consider brand name in their purchase decisions.

Questions

1. Why does brand name rate as unimportant in this market?
2. Can consumers learn (be taught) that brand name is an important product attribute?
3. If it decides to brand lumber, how should Weyerhaeuser position its brand?
4. Would lifestyle segmentation be an appropriate way to segment this market?
5. Develop a presentation for Wachtler to present to top management arguing for an aggressive branding strategy.

CASE 3–7 IRVINGTON GENERAL HOSPITAL*

How can a newly organized, private, nonprofit hospital create awareness in new target markets with a very limited marketing budget?

Irvington General Hospital was founded in 1923 as an acute-care municipal hospital owned and operated by the northern New Jersey township of Irvington. The majority of its patients came from Irvington township. Due to its limited facilities, however, the range of hospital health-care services was also limited. And as a city-run operation, it was perceived to be more bureaucratic and less efficient than necessary. Its image in the Irvington community, then, was not a source of strength.

In 1984, the hospital was restructured as a private, nonprofit organization, a

Figure A
Features of the Annual Report and Calendar

Features of Direct Mailer

- President's message describing growth and modernization of facilities.
- Each calender month offset by a picture highlighting Irvington Hospital's features.
- Financial statement and summary of operations and funding.
- A centerfold explanation of its nonprofit status and an invitation to send a contribution in the provided envelope.
- A chronological set of pictures showing Irvington Hospital's development.
- A list of of its medical staff, by area of specialization.
- Coupons for services and with their redemption, a free meal in the hospital café.

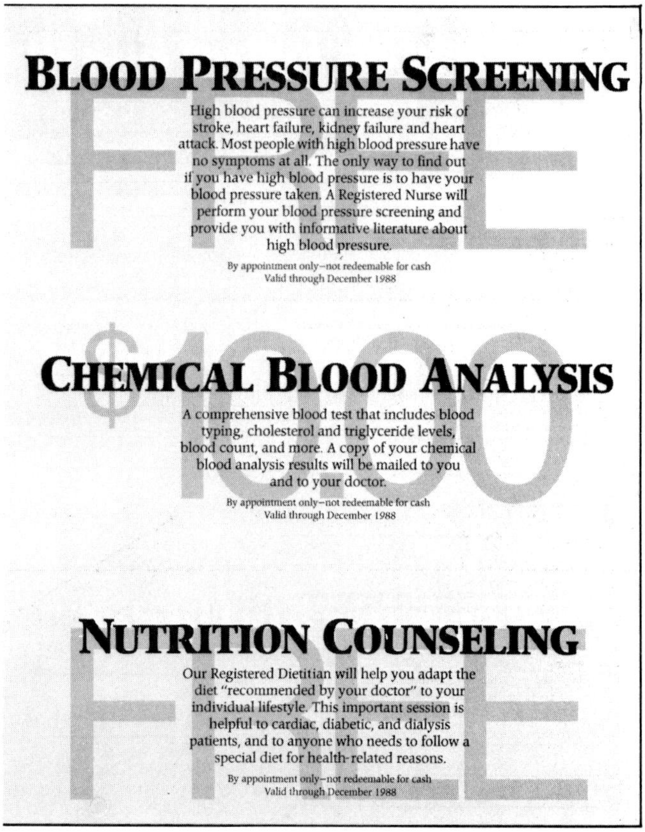

BLOOD PRESSURE SCREENING
High blood pressure can increase your risk of stroke, heart failure, kidney failure and heart attack. Most people with high blood pressure have no symptoms at all. The only way to find out if you have high blood pressure is to have your blood pressure taken. A Registered Nurse will perform your blood pressure screening and provide you with informative literature about high blood pressure.
By appointment only–not redeemable for cash
Valid through December 1988
CHEMICAL BLOOD ANALYSIS
A comprehensive blood test that includes blood typing, cholesterol and triglyceride levels, blood count, and more. A copy of your chemical blood analysis results will be mailed to you and to your doctor.
By appointment only–not redeemable for cash
Valid through December 1988
NUTRITION COUNSELING
Our Registered Dietitian will help you adapt the diet "recommended by your doctor" to your individual lifestyle. This important session is helpful to cardiac, diabetic, and dialysis patients, and to anyone who needs to follow a special diet for health-related reasons.
By appointment only–not redeemable for cash
Valid through December 1988

*Used with permission from Irvington General Hospital.

move that provided the independence needed to add facilities and grow. A $23 million modernization project was undertaken, which made Irvington General one of the most technologically advanced and aesthetically pleasing health care facilities in the area. By the late eighties, it also enjoyed the distinction of having the lowest cost per case in the region.

While Irvington General's capabilities had grown dramatically, many doctors and potential patients in surrounding communities were unaware of these changes. To fully utilize its capabilities, Irvington General had to increase awareness and communicate its improved capabilities.

Market Communications Program

Irvington General decided to focus its communications efforts on three upscale communities not far from Irvington township. These communities' doctors and potential patients were generally unaware of the changes that had taken place, and therefore represented a new market opportunity for Irvington General. However, a nonprofit organization with a very limited marketing budget can not afford traditional television or radio advertising. As a result, it had to find a very efficient way to reach its target market and communicate the services and quality now offered.

Direct mail seemed to offer the most economical means of reaching the target market. While a variety of direct-mail pieces were considered, the idea of combining an annual report and calendar gained the most votes. Figure A outlines the features of this unusual combination. The full-color mailer had the quality of a first-class annual report. However, in this instance the annual report was secondary to communicating the hospital's changed status and improved facilities.

Each calendar month features a high quality, glossy photograph of the hospital and staff at work. Accompanying copy explains various aspects of Irvington General Hospital, from cardiology to radiology and from social services to food services. The calendar's centerfold offers the hospital's financial statement, an explanation of how it derives funds as a private, nonprofit organization, and an invitation to donate money to the hospital. At the end of the calendar are three more features: a list of medical staff, pictures of Irvington Hospital's recent development, and the set of coupons shown in Figure A. The copy invites users of the coupons to enjoy a free meal in the hospital café.

A targeted mailing list was created and the calendar was mailed in late 1987 to 26,000 doctors and potential patients in the target communities. The hope was that recipients would read portions of the annual report and then hang the calendar on their walls. In this way the calendar and the message would be visible in the doctor's office and in the home twelve months of the year. Also, because calendars are often placed in the kitchen or family room, they would be seen frequently by women. This was important since women make most of the family health care decisions.

Finally, the free coupons for blood pressure screening, blood analysis, and nutrition counseling were intended to bring people in at a time when there was not an emergency or health care problem. A free meal at the hospital café would further solidify a pleasant experience.

Results of Communications Effort

The campaign was judged a success, but several directors wondered if they could have done better. Over the year following the mailing, the hospital received a number of donations. They also received many telephone calls from people who had not received a calendar and requesting that they be added to the hospital's mailing list. In the first quarter of the new year, 30 people came to Irvington General Hospital for the free coupon services. Because the free coupons are on the last page of the calendar, it is possible that many people will not discover them until the end of the year and the offer is only good for the year. While it is not known how many people actually have the Irvington Hospital calendar hanging in their homes or offices, a market research study is planned near year end to determine this.

Questions

1. Describe how different households would respond to this type of direct mailer. What factors would cause some households to hang this calendar in their kitchens or family room?
2. Discuss how the annual report/calendar would influence awareness of and attitudes toward Irvington General Hospital.
3. Design an attitude survey that would enable you to measure attitude change with respect to Irvington General caused by receipt of the calendar. When would you recommend doing the attitude survey?
4. Was placement of the free coupons effective? How could the response rate be increased? What are the benefits of getting more potential patients to use these free coupons?
5. What other type of mailers could Irvington General Hospital use to further enhance its image among target market doctors and potential patients?

CASE 3–8 SWATCH*

Swatch has been a tremendous success, but to sustain this success it needs to reach new markets and continue to introduce new Swatch designs to maintain sales to its existing base of Swatch customers.

The U.S. watch market in the mid-eighties was estimated to be between 90 and 95 million watch purchases per year. This is a 400 percent increase over the last 10 years. In 1985, Americans were buying a new watch once every two years, compared to once every 6 to 10 years a decade earlier. This rate of purchase has led to rate of ownership of 3.5 watches per owner.

---

*Used with permission from *Swatch* (Fontainebleau, France, INSEAD/CEDEP, 1987), prepared by Helen Chase Kimball under the supervision of Christian Pinson, Exhibit 16.

Figure A
Market Segmentation and Competition in U.S. Watch Market

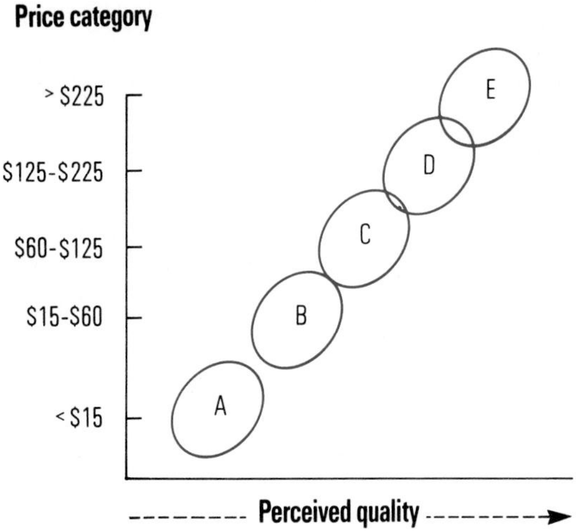

Competition	
Segment	Type of competitor
A	Hong Kong LCD and cheap mechanicals
B	Swatch, Timex, Casio, and Hamilton
C	Seiko, Citizen, Bulova, and Hamilton
D	Omega, Longines, Seiko, Citizen, and Bulova
E	Rolex, Piaget, and Cartier

While the U.S. market is large and growing, it is also segmented and served by a large number of world competitors. As shown in Figure A, there are five segments, differentiated on the basis of price and quality. At the high end of the market ($225 and over) are a few very prestigious competitors that offer the consumer much more than a device that keeps time. Consumers in this segment are also buying jewelry and high fashion along with a watch. At the other extreme are watches priced under $15 that are supplied primarily by Hong Kong manufacturers. These are either inexpensive electronic watches with a liquid crystal display (LCD) or cheap mechanical watches.

The three segments in between have much more overlap in terms of competition. Hamilton, for example, is in both segments B and C, while Seiko is positioned in segments C and D. Swatch, with a price of $15 to $50, is in segment B, the second lowest price-quality segment.

Consistent with this positioning, Swatch is sold primarily through department stores, sports shops, and by mass merchandisers. Their primary market is younger consumers between the ages of 11 and 22. This is reflected in their advertising, as shown in Figure B. The Swatch ads feature wild colors and exotic designs and their ad copy stresses excitement and having fun. Management wants Swatch to have symbolic meaning as well as provide accurate time. Its wild colors and many designs are intended to make Swatch a part of consumers' wardrobes. With certain clothes one should wear a certain Swatch. In this manner, Swatch is more than a watch, it is part of consumers' total dress.

Figure B
Swatch Advertisements

While this strategy works well with the target segment in the U.S. market, sales of Swatch to other potential market segments has been disappointing. To understand the needs and lifestyles of other segments, a psychographic study was conducted. A brief profile of each segment is provided below.

Children 6–10

These under-10 consumers think Swatch is "cool," something the big kids wear. Forty-two percent are aware of Swatch and 4 percent own a Swatch. They are dependent upon parents who buy watches for this group in department stores and from mass merchandisers. This target market is best reached through television, cartoon shows in particular.

Teeny Boppers

This particular group of 11 to 15 year olds is almost 100 percent female. They come from middle and upper-middle social classes. They are clique-oriented, very fashion conscious, and prefer outrageous, trendy styles. They like Madonna and can be reached through television (MTV), fashion magazines, and radio (top-40). They are heavy purchasers at department stores and record stores. They spend substantial time shopping. Swatch provides them with a sense of identity. It is a lifestyle enhancer, but they view it as becoming too commonplace. To them Swatch is not a line of clothing, but a rock 'n roll timepiece.

Young Teen Rockers

This group is also in the 11-to-15 age category but is 80 percent male. They are also from middle and upper-middle class households but avoid belonging to cliques and seek independence. They like Sylvester Stallone and Arnold Schwarzenegger but think Madonna is useless. They can be reached on album-oriented radio stations and are dedicated viewers of MTV. They are not shopping-oriented but do go to malls and record stores. Only 16 percent of this segment wear watches. They view Swatch as a product that represents a Teeny Bopper lifestyle.

Students

This group of 11 to 15 year olds is split evenly between males and females. They come from middle- and lower-middle-class households. They are more conservative and often participate in sports. They do not have a strong music preference. They can be reached with network TV and AM radio. They are not shopping-oriented and prefer to shop at Sears, K mart and chain drug stores. To them price and function outweigh fashion. Swatch is too wild for their lifestyle, yet they like to fit in.

Rockers

This group between 16 and 22 years of age is 60 percent male. They have long hair, are clique-oriented, committed to rock groups, and are very frequent concert-goers. They can be reached on album-oriented radio stations and MTV (77 percent regular viewers). They are not heavy shoppers but prefer American-made products. They are aware of Swatch and like its disposability and price, but dislike what it stands for—teeny boppers and male-model geeks. They consider multiple Swatch ownership too trendy.

Preppies

This group is also between the ages of 16 and 22. They are career-oriented and have more traditional views than rockers. They like designs more than colors and like songs more than the artists that sing them. They can be reached with cable TV, some fashion magazines, and album-oriented radio stations, although they have very low station loyalty. They are mainstream department store shoppers. Ninety-two percent are aware of Swatch but prefer traditional designs. While they like the Swatch price and durability, they dislike its young teen image. Seventy-three percent prefer dressier watches. They do not like digital watches.

Trendies

This 16-to-22-year-old group is similar to the hippies of the sixties but on a smaller scale. They have avant-garde tastes and are outspoken on issues they consider important. They are socially and politically left and are anti-rock 'n roll. They do not like popular groups. They can be reached through newspapers and artsy magazines. They are anti-MTV and do not like commercial radio. They consider fashion a vehicle of expression but reject anything too popular. Seventy-three percent do not wear a watch and most believe Swatch is a rip-off and equivalent to the fast-food of timepieces.

Transitionaries

This group is 22 to 32 years old. They are conservative social climbers who like to watch sports not participate in them. Females in this group can be reached with fashion magazines, and males with *Time, Newsweek,* and *Sports Illustrated.* They do not watch MTV and are pro-American in their purchases. Seventy-six percent are aware of Swatch. They are major users of department stores. They like Swatch's durability, disposability, price, and reliability.

Older Casuals

This group is 22 to 43 years old and ultra-conservative. They are the hidden mainstream, very family-oriented and heavy users of fast-food establishments. They are socially inactive and uninterested in fashion. Their music preferences are traditional, and they can be reached with network TV, local newspapers, and tabloids such as the *National Enquirer*. They prefer traditional watches made by Timex and Bulova and view watches as functional. As a group only 4 percent were aware of Swatch in unaided awareness tests.

Weekend Hippies

This 33-to-43-year-old group is characterized as mellowed former hippies. They look like, but hate to be called, Yuppies and still subscribe to the basic sixties principles. They can be reached with cable TV and with magazines such as *Time* and *Newsweek*. They are heavy shoppers and appreciate quality products. Females in this segment shop at upscale department stores such as Saks Fifth Avenue and I. Magnin, while men are department store shoppers. They have a high awareness of Swatch, but 43 percent of those aware of Swatch have never seen one. They like its light weight, functionality, and durability but dislike its cheap, teen-item image.

Questions

1. How do the different lifestyles described impact consumer preference for a certain style or type of watch?
2. Explain how psychographics might be an important addition to demographics in attempting to understand consumer needs for watches.
3. To which segments could Swatch market, given its present positioning?
4. What changes in positioning would Swatch have to make in order to succeed in each segment? Is it possible for Swatch to have a multi-segment strategy? Explain your point of view.

CASE 3–9 THE SUGAR ASSOCIATION, INC.*

How can the Sugar Association educate the public about the virtues of sugar, and counter the potentially negative impression caused by extensive promotion of sugar-free products?

Answer the following true/false questions:

1. A teaspoon of sugar contains less than 20 calories.
2. The Academy of General Dentistry recommends a low-sugar diet to minimize risks of tooth decay.
3. The American Dietetic Association does not recommend a reduced-sugar diet for Americans.
4. The FDA places sugar on its list of foods that are Generally Recognized as Safe (GRAS).
5. No artificial sweetener is on the FDA's GRAS list.

The answers are true (16 calories), false, true, true, and true. While evidence on the nutritional as well as taste benefits of sugar has been accumulating rapidly, many Americans remain unaware of these facts. To correct any misperceptions concerning sugar, as well as to counter aggressive marketing activities for artificial sweeteners, the Sugar Association recently launched a $4 million promotional campaign.

Prior to designing the campaign, the association conducted a major consumer survey to determine demographics, attitudes, and values associated with sugar consumption. Some of the key findings are as follows:

- Eighty-six percent "like" or "love" sweets
- Sugar and sugar-sweetened foods are associated with the happy, pleasurable moments in life
- Users of artificial sweetener like sugar and sugar-sweetened foods to the same extent as nonusers and they use about as much sugar

*Used with permission from The Sugar Association, Inc.

Figure A

PHENYLALANINE
ASPARTAME
SILICON DIOXIDE
TRIBASIC CALCIUM PHOSPHATE
BENZOSULFIMIDE
CALCIUM SILICATE
PURE 100% NATURAL
SUGAR
WHICH WOULD YOU RATHER PUT ON YOUR KIDS' CEREAL?
The decision is in your hands. But before you make it, here are some things to think about.
SUGAR IS SAFE
Unlike any artificial sweetener, sugar is on the government's FDA GRAS list (Generally Recognized As Safe).
100% NATURAL
Sugar is pure and 100% natural. It contains no mysterious, unnatural ingredients. No man-made chemicals. And no warning labels.
ONLY 16 CALORIES
Surprisingly, real sugar has only 16 calories per teaspoon—16 naturally satisfying calories.
SUGAR TASTES BEST
In a recent taste test, sugar was preferred nearly 3 to 1 over the leading artificial sweetener.
So if you want your kids to have a low calorie sweetener that's 100% natural and perfectly safe, give them real sugar. After all, don't they deserve to have it as good as you did?
100% NATURAL SUGAR.
THERE'S REALLY NO SUBSTITUTE.
The Sugar Association, Inc. 1511 K St. NW, Washington, D.C. 20005. (202) 628-0189

Courtesy The Sugar Association, Inc.

Figure B

The Sugar Association
"GOING STEADY"

1ST GIRL: Did you see the color of her dress?
MUSIC: UNDER THROUGHOUT

2ND GIRL: No, but I saw Rooster Magillicuddy kissing you on the lips.

3RD GIRL: Mary Beth,

does this mean you're going steady?

1ST GIRL (UNDER V/O): Well, maybe.
(V/O): Remember when the best things in life were sweet, pure and natural . . .

one still is, sugar.

Courtesy The Sugar Association, Inc.

- Heavy-user households (40+ pounds per year) constitute 30 percent of sugar users, but represent 77 percent of household sugar consumption. They bake more often and are more likely to eat sugar-sweetened snacks, desserts, and breakfasts. Seventy-five percent have children at home compared to 48 percent of light users (10 pounds or less per year). Heavy users say they "love" sweets, while light and moderate users "like" sweets.
- Over two thirds of the respondents agreed with these statements:

  "I feel I can enjoy snacks/desserts because my eating habits are generally healthy."

  "Enjoying sweets is a natural and normal part of a child's life."
- Over half the respondents felt they should limit their families' consumption of both sugar and artificial sweeteners.

While the results of the survey are generally very positive, officials of the Sugar Association are concerned about the continued existence of concern over the quantity of sugar consumed. They are also concerned that the continued extensive promotion of sugar-free products will cause consumers to presume that sugar is somehow bad.

To deal with these concerns as well as educate the general public on the virtues of sugar, the Sugar Association is using both a print and television campaign. One color print has the headline, "Nobody's Been Able To Duplicate Real Sugar, Either," under a photo that contrasts a hollow, plastic apple with a juicy, fresh, natural one. The copy is similar to that in the other print ad which is shown in Figure A. These ads were placed in *Reader's Digest, Good Housekeeping, Family Circle, McCall's, TV Guide, People, Weight Watchers,* and *Cooking Light.*

The network television campaign, which will run daytime and late night, is based on three 15-second commercials with a 1950s look (Figure B). The underlying theme of the commercials is the positive association of sugar and sweets with special moments in one's life, such as baking a first cake, the first box of candy from a beau, or sweet snacks after a party.

Questions

1. Explain how consumers might "learn" that sugar is bad, based on frequently seen promotions for sugar-free products.
2. What values are involved in the consumption of sugar versus artificial sweeteners?
3. The attitude survey produced strong positive attitudes toward sugar and yet over half the respondents felt they should limit their families' intake of sugar. How do you account for this?
4. Would you consider the ad in Figure A to be a fear appeal? How effective do you think it will be?

5. Do you consider the television commercial to be an emotional appeal? How effective do you think it will be?
6. Evaluate the overall campaign in terms of the product position it appears to be attempting to establish for sugar. Will it achieve that positioning?

SECTION FOUR

Consumer Decision Process

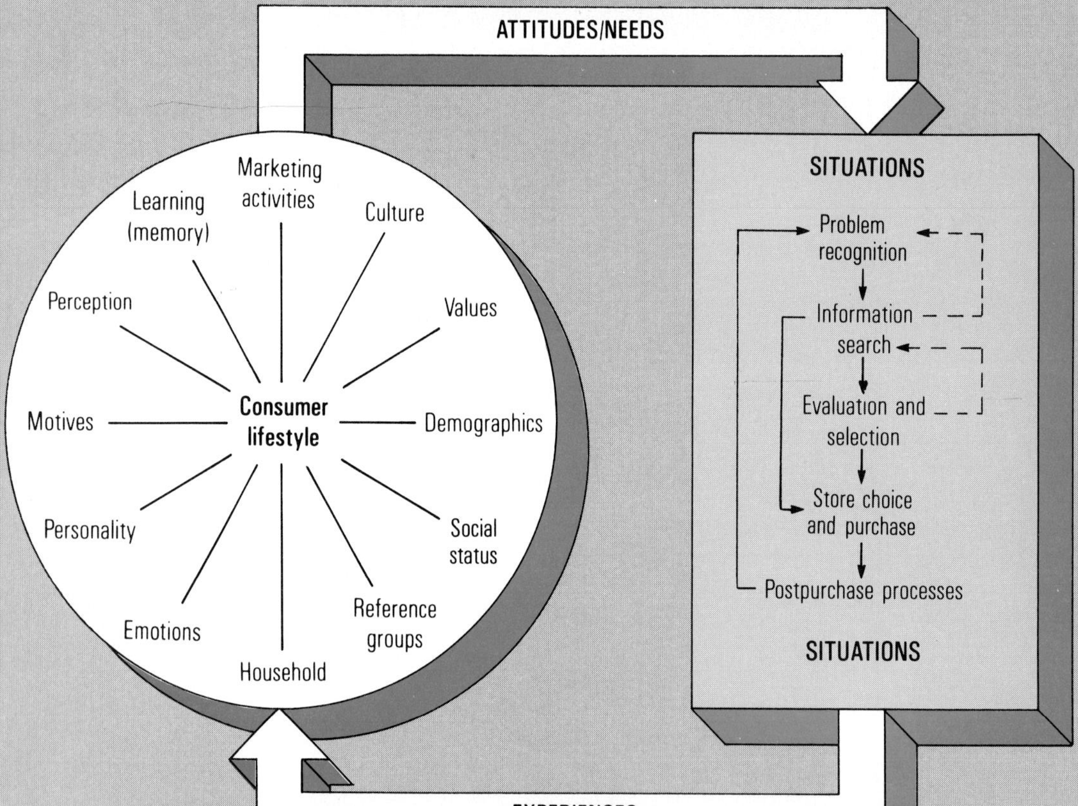

Up to now we have focused on various sociological and psychological factors that contribute to different patterns of consumer behavior. Though these various influences play a significant role in behavior, all behavior takes place within the context of a situation. Therefore, behavior may vary among consumers as well as for the same consumer from one situation to another. Chapter 13 provides a discussion of the impact situational variables have on consumer behavior.

Of particular importance to marketers is how situations and internal and external sources of influence affect the consumer purchase decision process. The extended consumer decision process, as shown in the figure at left, is composed of a sequential process: problem recognition; information search; brand evaluation; store choice and purchase; and use, satisfaction, disposition, and repurchase motivation. However, extended decision making occurs only in those relatively rare situations when the consumer is highly involved in the purchase. Lower levels of purchase involvement produce limited or habitual decision making. Chapter 14 describes those various types of decisions and their relationship to involvement. It also analyzes the first stage of the process—problem recognition.

Information search constitutes the second stage in the consumer decision process and it is discussed in Chapter 15. The nature of consumer information search and those factors that influence different levels of prepurchase information search are considered. Chapter 16 examines the brand evaluation and selection process. Chapter 17 deals with outlet selection and the in-store influences that often contribute to brand switching. The final stage of the consumer decision process, presented in Chapter 18 involves behavior after purchase, including postpurchase feelings, use behavior, satisfaction, disposition, and repurchase motivation. Throughout these six chapters we attempt to present what consumers do at different stages of the consumer decision process, what factors contribute to their behavior, and what actions can be taken by marketers to affect their behavior.

CHAPTER

13 Situational Influences

Information Professionals, Inc., a start-up firm, offers a new service called "advertiming." The service relies on an extensive computer data base that compares consumption patterns with the current weather. Based on observed relationships between weather and product category sales, the firm uses weather forecasts to advise its clients on spot advertising buys, sales, point-of-purchase displays, and related issues.

A number of firms have used simpler versions of this approach for some time. For example, Blistex, Inc., and Campbell Soup have based spot radio advertising on weather forecasts for several years. However, Information Professionals provides data on less obvious relationships and products. For example, does hot cocoa sell better on a warm but dark winter day or on a frigid but bright day? The answer is dark and warm. Therefore, cocoa advertisers would be better off timing spot buys and special promotions to coincide with dark, cloudy days as opposed to average days, or cold, clear days.[1]

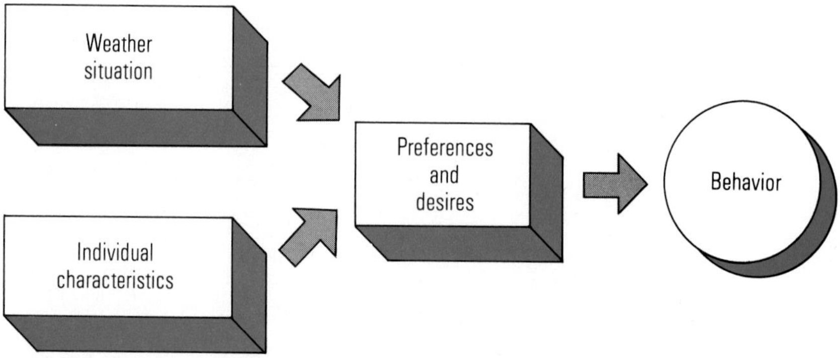

As the model we have used to organize this text stresses, the purchase decision and consumption process always occur in the context of a specific situation. Therefore, before examining the decision process, we must first develop an understanding of situations.

As marketers we need to understand which situations affect the purchase of our products and how we might best serve target market buyers when these situations arise. We should view the consumer and the marketing activities designed to influence that consumer in light of the situations the consumer faces. The relative effectiveness of an advertisement or personal sales presentation can vary tremendously as the situation changes.

To the extent possible, we want to be able to predict how various situations and marketing mix strategies interact. In this chapter we define *situation,* and then present a situation classification scheme that will be useful for judging when the situation is an active influence on behavior and how it affects the consumer. The final section of the chapter describes the managerial approach to situational analysis in making marketing decisions.

TYPES OF SITUATIONS

The consumption process occurs within three broad categories of situations: the communications situation, the purchase situation, and the usage situation. Each is described below.

The Communications Situation

The situation in which consumers receive information has an impact on their behavior. Whether we are alone or in a group, in a good mood or bad, in a hurry or not, influences the degree to which we see and listen to marketing communications. If we are interested in the product and in a receptive communications situation, a marketer is able to deliver an effective message to us. However, finding high-interest potential buyers in receptive communications situations is a difficult challenge. For example, consider the difficulty a marketer would have in communicating to you in the following communications situations:

- You just lost your part-time job.
- Final exams begin tomorrow.
- Your roommates only watch news programs.
- You have the flu.
- You are driving home on a cold night, and your car heater doesn't work.

The Purchase Situation

Situations can also affect product selection in a purchase situation. Mothers shopping with children are more apt to be influenced by the product preferences of their children than when shopping without them. A shortage of time, such as trying to make a purchase between classes, can affect the store chosen, the number of brands considered, and the price you are willing to pay.

Marketers must understand *how* purchase situations influence consumers in order to develop marketing strategies that enhance the purchase of their products. For example, how would you alter your decision to purchase a beverage in the following purchase situations?

- You are in a very bad mood.
- A good friend says, "That stuff is bad for you."
- You have an upset stomach.
- There is a long line at the checkout counter as you enter the store.
- You are with someone you want to impress.

The Usage Situation

A consumer may use a different brand of wine to serve dinner guests than for personal use in a nonsocial situation. A family may choose a different vacation depending on who is going. As Figure 13–1 illustrates, the product selected depends a great deal on the situation in which it will be consumed.

Marketers need to understand the consumption situations for which their products are, or may become, appropriate. Based on this knowledge, marketers can communicate how their products can create consumer satisfaction in each relevant consumption situation. For example, what beverage would you prefer to consume in each of the following consumption situations?

- Friday afternoon after your last final exam.
- With your parents for lunch.
- After dinner on a cold stormy evening.
- At a dinner with a friend you have not seen in several years.
- After working in the yard on a hot day.

To be effective in developing marketing strategy, a marketer must understand how the target market behaves in consumption situations, purchase situations, and communications situations.

CHARACTERISTICS OF SITUATIONAL INFLUENCE

While there are many formal definitions that could be used to define *situational influence,* we use one provided by Russell Belk:

Figure 13–1
Fruit Preferences for Different Consumption Situations

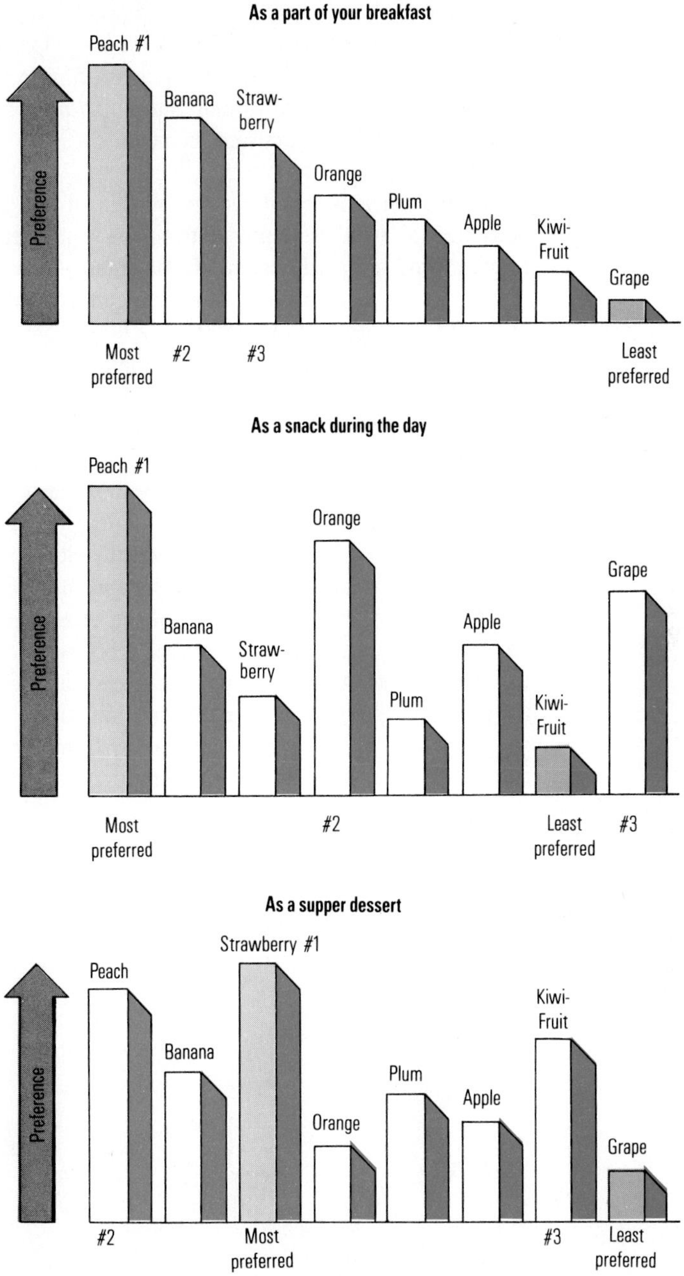

Based on the students surveyed in this study:

- Peaches were most preferred, particularly with breakfast and as a snack.
- Strawberries were most preferred as a supper dessert, and number three overall as a part of breakfast.
- Oranges and grapes were rated two and three, respectively, as a snack.

Source: Adapted from P. Dickson, "Person-Situation: Segmentation's Missing Link," *Journal of Marketing*, Fall 1982, pp. 56–64.

> All those factors particular to a time and place of observation which do not follow from a knowledge of personal (intra-individual) and stimulus (choice alternative) attributes and which have a demonstrable and systematic effect on current behavior.[2]

A situation is a set of factors outside of and removed from the individual consumer as well as removed from the characteristics of the stimulus object (e.g., a product, a television advertisement) to which the consumer is reacting (e.g., purchasing a product, viewing a commercial). We are also only interested in those situations that actually have a noticeable impact on consumer behavior. We can ignore situations when the characteristics of the buyer or the stimulus are so intense that they are influential across all relevant situations. An example of this would be a consumer so loyal to a particular brand that it is the only brand purchased.

Figure 13–2 illustrates the relationship that the situation has with the consumer, the object of the consumer's interest, and the consumer behavior that results. As we can see, the object and the situation (stimuli) influence the consumer (the organism), who in turn engages in some behavior (response).[3] While marketers have traditionally studied the effect an object such as a product or advertisement has on the consumer's behavior, they have often ignored the influence of the situation. Thus, marketers stand to gain a great deal by studying the roles their products play in different situations. For example, a wine marketer should be able to develop better strategy from knowing that wine is often given as a house gift, but seldom as a birthday gift.[4]

Figure 13–2
The Role of Situation in Consumer Behavior

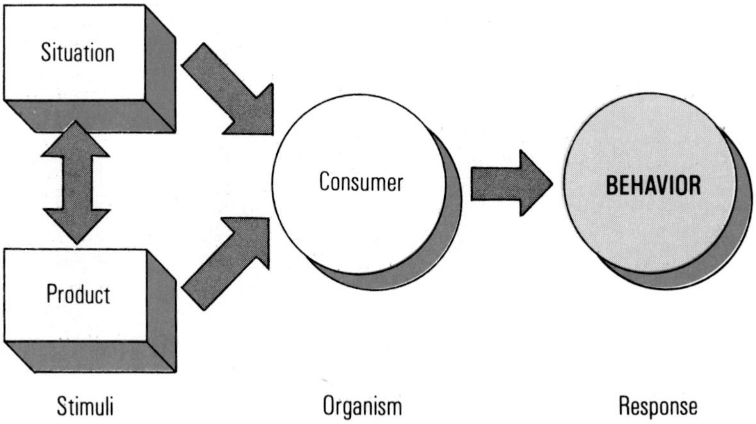

Source: Adapted from R. W. Belk, "Situational Variables and Consumer Behavior," *Journal of Consumer Research,* December 1975, p. 158.

In order to utilize situational influences, a marketer must understand three important aspects of this influence:

- When a particular situation affects consumer behavior.
- How strong the effect is likely to be.
- The way in which the situation influences behavior.

To integrate the influence of situation into marketing strategy, we must first give careful attention to the degree that the situation *interacts* with a given product and a given set of target consumers. Then we must evaluate the situation more

Exhibit 13–1

A Situational Positioning Strategy for Coffee

America's consumption of coffee has declined steadily over the past 20 years. This is particularly true for people in their 20s, where consumption has slipped from 3.4 cups a day to 1.3 cups.

General Foods is looking for new coffee products to counter this trend. General Foods® International Coffees are targeted at younger adults and are positioned as a substitute for a sweet snack. To accomplish this product positioning, General Foods® has developed a series of consumption situation advertisements such as the ones shown below.

Focus on a Summer Situation

Courtesy General Foods Corporation

Focus on a Winter Situation

Courtesy General Foods Corporation

Source: "Brand Report No. 91: Coffee and Tea Cup Runneth Under," *Marketing and Media Decisions,* October 1983, p. 18.

systematically in terms of *when it occurs,* the *strength of its influence,* and the *nature of its influence on behavior.* For example, time spent doing leisure activities is influenced by physical surroundings (e.g., temperature and weather), social influences, and a person's mood.[5] To be effective in marketing a particular leisure activity (e.g., sports event, movies), a marketer must understand how and when these situational influences will impact a consumer's decision to spend time on that activity.

SITUATION CLASSIFICATION

Exhibit 13–1 illustrates General Foods' use of the weather situation to position one of its coffee brands. Weather is but one of several important situation variables that influence consumer behavior. There have been a number of attempts to classify situations relevant to consumer behavior.[6] We use a classification scheme that is based on five types of objectively measured situations.[7] As outlined

Figure 13–3
Five Classes of Situational Influence

1. **Physical surroundings** include geographical and institutional location, decor, sounds, aromas, lighting, weather, and visible configurations of merchandise or other material surrounding the stimulus object.
2. **Social surroundings** provide additional depth to a description of a situation. Examples are other persons present, their characteristics, their apparent roles, and interpersonal interactions occurring.
3. **Temporal perspective** may be specified in units ranging from time of day to seasons of the year. Time may also be measured relative to some past or future event for the situational participant. This allows conceptions such as time constraints imposed by prior commitments.
4. **Task definition** includes an intent or requirement to select, shop for, or obtain information about a general or specific purchase. In addition, task may reflect different buyer and user roles anticipated by the individual. For instance, a person shopping for a small appliance as a wedding gift for a friend is in a different situation than he or she would be in shopping for a small appliance for personal use.
5. **Antecedent states** are momentary moods (such as anxiety, pleasantness, hostility, and excitation) or momentary conditions (such as cash on hand, fatigue, and illness), rather than chronic individual traits.

Source: R. W. Belk, "Situational Variables and Consumer Behavior," *Journal of Consumer Research,* December 1975, p. 161.

in Figure 13–3, this system includes situational influences created by physical surroundings, social influences, time perspectives, tasks to be accomplished, and antecedent states. This classification scheme provides a system that managers can use in determining if a situation has an effect on a consumer's purchase behavior. That is, it provides the manager with a series of appropriate questions to ask concerning the purchase and consumption of the manager's product.

Physical Surroundings

Physical surroundings comprise a widely recognized type of situational influence. For example, store interiors are often designed to create specific feelings in

Exhibit 13–2 Impact of Color on Physical Attraction in a Retail Store

PHYSICAL ATTRACTION TO A STORE'S EXTERIOR

To physically draw customers into a retail store, department, or display area, *warm colors* such as yellow and red are better than *cool colors* such as blue and green. Warm colors are particularly appropriate for store windows, entrances, and point of purchase displays.

Shown below is the physical attraction of a furniture store exterior when highlighted with five different colors.

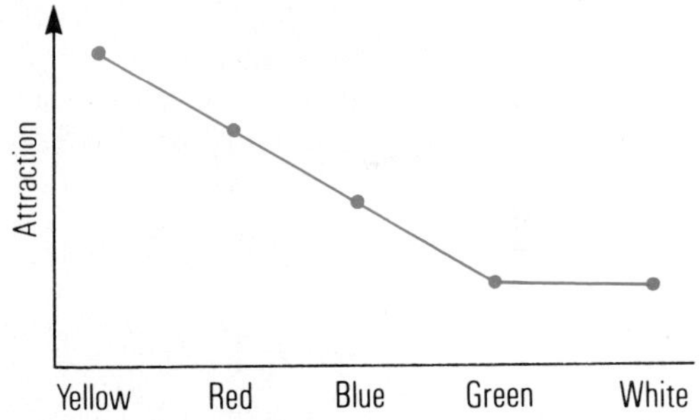

PHYSICAL ATTRACTION TO A STORE'S INTERIOR

Cool colors such as blue and green are viewed as relaxing, positive, and less threatening, and reflect favorably on the store's merchandise. Cool colors are more appropriate where customers face tough purchase decisions. Warm colors in such a situation are viewed as more tense and have the potential of making the decision task unpleasant, and perhaps postponing the decision and terminating the shopping trip.

Source: Adapted from J. Bellizzi, A. Crawley, and R. Hasty, "The Effects of Color in Store Design," *Journal of Retailing*, Spring 1983, pp. 21–45.

shoppers that can have an important cuing or reinforcing effect on purchase.[8] A retail clothing store specializing in extremely stylish, modern clothing would want to reflect this to customers in the physical characteristics of the purchase situation. The fixtures, furnishings, and colors should all reflect an overall mood of style, flair, and newness. In addition, the store personnel should appear to carry this theme in terms of their own appearance and apparel. These influences generate appropriate perceptions of the retail environment which in turn influence the purchase decision.[9]

Exhibit 13–2 illustrates the impact the use of color can have on attracting customers to a store. An even more impressive example of the influence of a physical situational variable's influence on consumer behavior is background music in restaurants. Is slow-tempo or fast-tempo background music better for a restaurant? Table 13–1 indicates that slow music increased gross margin for one restaurant by almost 15 percent per customer group compared to fast music! However, before concluding that all restaurants should play slow music, examine the table carefully. Slow music appears to have relaxed and slowed down the customers, resulting in more time in the restaurant and substantially more purchases from the bar. Restaurants without bars that rely on rapid customer turnover would be better off with fast-tempo music.

To illustrate the negative impact a physical situation can have on buyer behavior, consider the effect of crowding on shopper perceptions, strategies, and postpurchase responses.[10] As diagrammed in Figure 13–4, increased physical density of the store created perceptions of confinement and crowding. These perceptions in turn caused shoppers to modify their shopping strategies in that they reduced the time spent shopping, purchased fewer items, and altered their use of in-store information. The net outcome of this physical situation was dissatisfaction with the store, an unpleasant shopping experience, and reduced confidence in the shopping that took place.

In many instances, marketers have limited control over the physical situation.

Table 13–1
The Impact of Background Music on Restaurant Patrons

Variables	Slow Music	Fast Music
Service time	29 min.	27 min.
Customer time at table	56 min.	45 min.
Customer groups leaving before seated	10.5%	12.0%
Amount of food purchased	$55.81	$55.12
Amount of bar purchases	$30.47	$21.62
Estimated gross margin	$55.82	$48.62

Source: R. E. Milliman, "The Influence of Background Music on the Behavior of Restaurant Patrons," *Journal of Consumer Research,* September 1986, p. 289.

Figure 13–4
The Impact of Physical Density on Shopper Perceptions, Shopping Strategies, and Postpurchase Processes

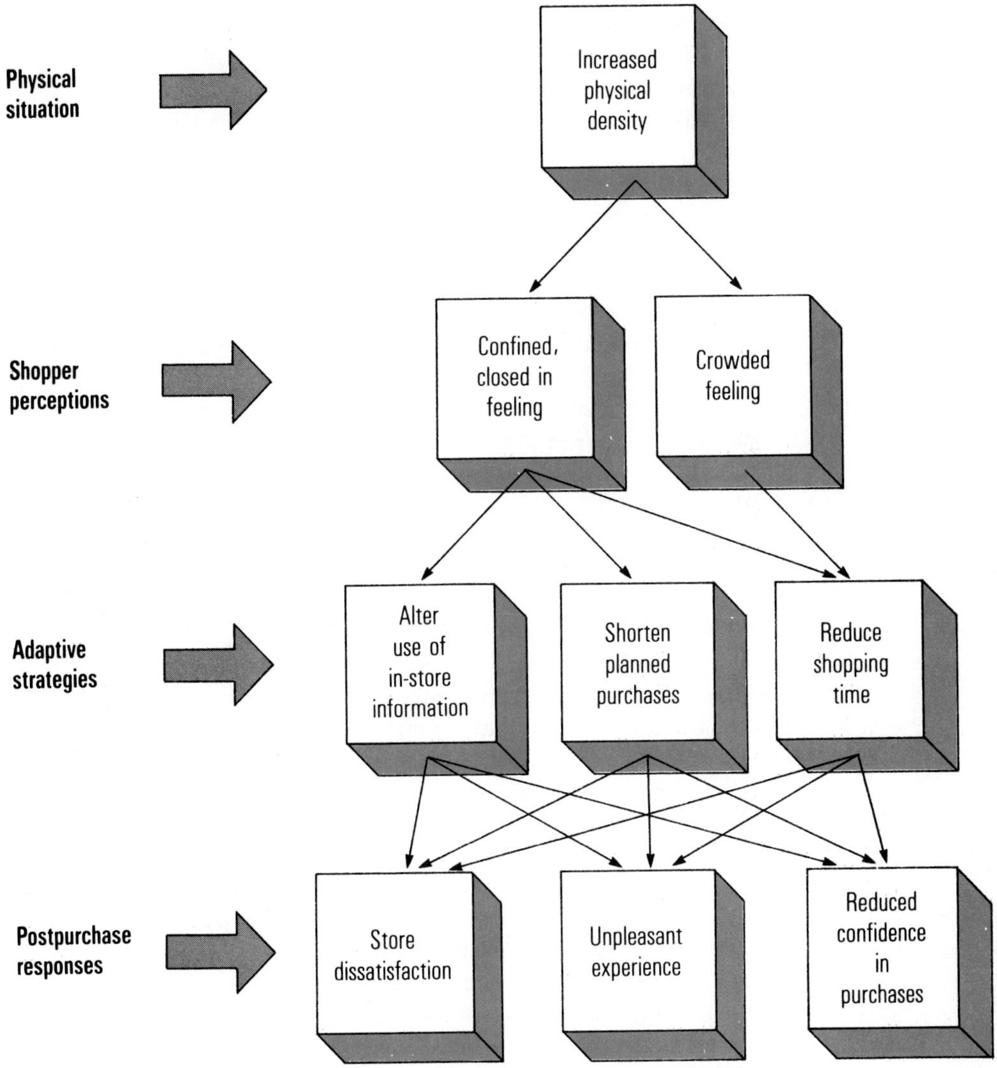

Source: Adapted from G. Harrell, M. Hutt, and J. Anderson, "Path Analysis of Buyer Behavior under Conditions of Crowding," *Journal of Marketing Research,* February 1980, pp. 45–51.

For example, there are many forms of retailing, such as mail order, door-to-door, and vending machines, where control is minimal. Still, the marketer tries to account for the physical situation by carefully selecting appropriate outlets and product mixes for vending machines,[11] and instructing door-to-door sales personnel to "control the situation" by rearranging furniture, turning off televisions or radios, and bringing in point-of-purchase displays.

As a marketing manager you should ask yourself if the physical surroundings could possibly affect the behavior you are interested in and, if so, in what ways. Note that there are many possible behaviors that a marketer could be interested in: actual purchase, shopping (looking), receiving information (such as watching TV advertisements), and so forth. Tauber, in an analysis of nonpurchase motivations for shopping, found physical activity and sensory stimulation to be two important motives.[12] Enclosed shopping malls offer clear advantages in providing a safe, comfortable area for leisurely strolls. The sights and sounds of a variety of stores and individuals also provide a high degree of sensory stimulation. Both these factors may play an important role in the overall success of shopping centers and other shopping areas. If there are physical aspects of the situation that you can influence and/or control, then you should do so in a manner that will make the physical situation compatible with the lifestyle of your target market.

Often you can neither control nor influence the physical situation the consumer will encounter, such as winter versus summer for beverage consumption. In these cases, it is appropriate to alter the various elements of the marketing mix to match the needs and expectations of the target market. Both Dr Pepper and Lipton's tea have varied their advertising, in terms of product usage, between summer and winter based on physical changes in the environment and consumers' reactions to these changes. General Foods® International Coffees' advertisements shown in Exhibit 13–1 reflect a similar strategy.

Social Surroundings

Social surroundings deal primarily with the presence of other persons who could have an impact on the individual consumer's behavior. Our actions are frequently influenced, if not altogether determined, by those around us. For example, one study found variation in behavior due to social situations (20–45 percent) to be slightly greater than the variation due to individual characteristics (15–30 percent). However, the interaction between individual characteristics and social situations accounts for an additional 30 to 50 percent of variation in behavior.[13] Figure 13–5 illustrates the impact of the social situation on the attributes desired in a dessert. Notice that economy and taste are critical for personal and family consumption, while general acceptance is the key for the party situation. What does this suggest in terms of advertising strategy? In Exhibit 13–3, Philip Morris is positioning Players cigarettes in an active social situation ("Players Go Places").

Social influence is a significant force acting on our behavior since individuals tend to comply with group expectations, particularly when the behavior is visible.

Figure 13–5
Impact of Social Situations on Desired Dessert Attributes

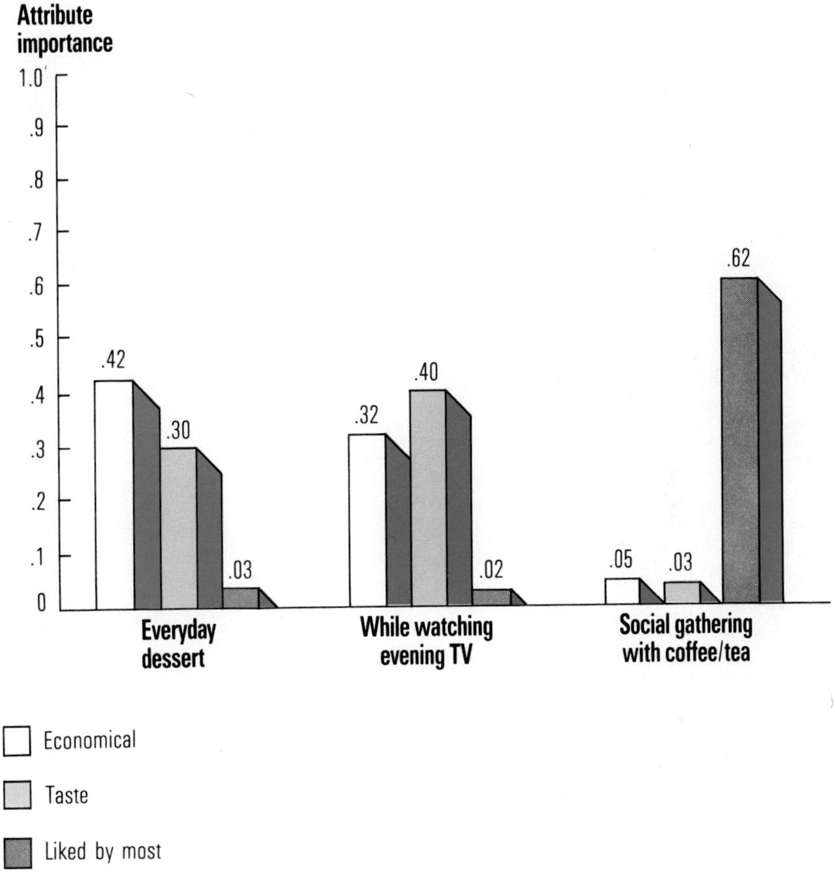

Source: J. B. Palmer and R. H. Cropnick, "New Dimension Added to Conjoint Analysis," *Marketing News*, January 3, 1986, p. 62.

Thus shopping, a highly visible activity, and the use of many publicly consumed brands are subject to social influences. The behavior of others, even strangers, can affect an individual's perceptions. For example, the presence and role of another person (i.e., immediate family, close friend, young children, or church minister) has been shown to affect our perceptions of various television programs.[14] Shopping with others has been found to influence the purchase of such standard products as meat, chicken, and cereal, while beer consumption changes with the presence of guests, at parties, and during holidays.[15]

Tauber found social motives to be an important reason for visiting retail outlets.[16] Shopping can provide a social experience outside the home for making

Exhibit 13–3 Product Positioning within a Social Situation

Formal Social Consumption Situation

Informal Social Consumption Situation

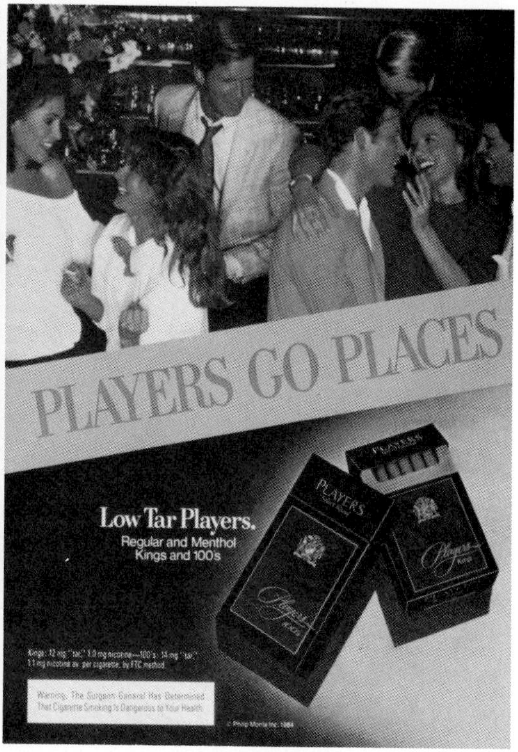

Used with permission from Philip Morris, Inc.

Philip Morris, Inc., utilizes social situations in which to position its Players cigarettes. One situation is a formal social situation while the other is informal. However, both ads project Players in a social situation in which people are having fun. To the degree these social situations appeal to target-market consumers, Philip Morris will succeed in positioning Players in the situations shown.

new acquaintances, meeting existing friends, or just being near other people. It allows one to communicate with others having similar interests. For example, music lovers often gather at record stores, while avid fishermen migrate to sporting goods stores. Sales personnel are often sought out because they share an interest with the shopper in a product-related activity.

Some people seek status and authority in shopping since the salesperson's job is to wait on the customer. This allows these individuals a measure of respect or prestige that may otherwise be lacking in their lives. Thus, consumers, on occasion, shop *for* social situations rather than, or in addition to, products.

Frequently, as a marketing manager, you will not have any control over the social characteristics of a situation. For example, when a television advertisement is sent into the home, the advertising manager cannot control who the viewer is with at the time of the reception or their relative status relationship. However, the manager can utilize the knowledge that some programs are generally viewed alone (weekday, daytime programs), some are viewed by the entire family (Walt Disney), and others by groups of friends (Super Bowl). The message presented can be structured to these viewing situations. For example, a message presented on a program frequently viewed by family groups might stress a family decision to purchase a given product, while an advertisement for the same product presented on daytime television might have a "surprise your family" theme.

There are a number of occasions where marketing managers can influence the social aspects of a situation. For instance, the advertiser can encourage you to "ask a friend" or, better yet, "bring a friend along." Some firms, such as Tupperware, have been ingenious in structuring social situations that encourage sales. Salespersons know that frequently they can use the shopper's companion as an effective sales aid by soliciting his or her opinion and advice. Alluding to the positive social implications of product purchase ("Won't your friends think you look good?") has long been a utilization of social situational effects by advertisers.

Temporal Perspectives

Temporal perspectives are situational characteristics that deal with the effect of time on consumer behavior. We must be careful to note at this point that we are not considering time as a product. Time, of course, is a purchasable commodity and an increasingly important one.[17]

Time as a situational factor can manifest itself in a number of different ways.[18] It has been determined, for instance, that the length of time between your last meal and your grocery shopping trip will probably affect the amount of impulse purchasing you do.

> For most people who shop on an empty stomach, supermarket aisles are lined with temptations. Imagination readily places potatoes and onions around roasts and transforms pancake mix into a steaming, buttered stack. An egg-and-milk run can turn out to cost considerable money and time. When one has recently eaten, on the other hand, roasts are examined with an efficient, dispassionate eye and pancake mix is just pancake mix. The trip may be less enjoyable, but escape with budget and schedule intact is more likely.[19]

It is interesting to note that in the study from which the above quote was taken, the effect of time on impulse purchase behavior was significantly affected by an individual characteristic—weight. Overweight people were not affected by the amount of time between eating and shopping. With regard to a different time-related effect on grocery shopping, the "after-5 P.M." shopper has been shown

Exhibit 13–4 Time-Directed Product Use Situation

Courtesy Hunt-Wesson Foods, Inc.

to be different from the "before-5 P.M." shopper. The "after-5" shopper (who is generally employed full time) spends less time in the store and is less likely to use coupons, read ads, or use a shopping list.[20]

The amount of time available for the purchase has a substantial impact on the consumer decision process. As a generalization, we can say that the less time there is available (i.e., increased time pressure), the shorter will be the information search or even the utilization of available information.[21]

Time as a situational influence affects our choice of stores. For example, consumers are less likely to visit department stores when they are time-pressured than when not time-pressured.[22] A number of retail firms have taken advantage of the temporal perspective factor. Perhaps the most successful of these is the 7-Eleven chain, which caters almost exclusively to individuals who either are in a hurry or who want to make a purchase after regular shopping hours.

Limited purchase time can also result in a smaller number of product alternatives being considered. The increased time pressure experienced by many

Figure 13–6
Interactive Effect of Task and Personality

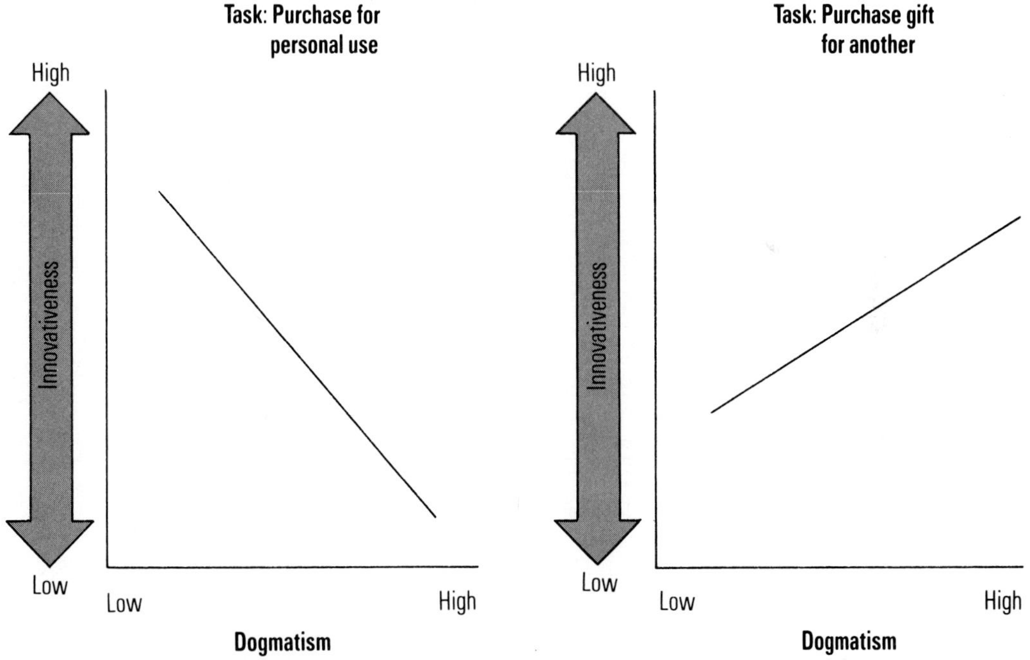

Source: K. A. Coney, "Dogmatism and Innovation: A Replication," *Journal of Marketing Research,* November 1972, pp. 453–55; and K. A. Coney and R. R. Harmon, "Dogmatism and Innovation: A Situational Perspective," in *Advances in Consumer Research VI,* ed. W. L. Wilkie (Chicago: Association for Consumer Research, 1979), pp. 118–21.

working wives tends to increase the incidence of brand loyalty, particularly for nationally branded products. The obvious implication is that working wives feel safer with nationally branded or "known" products, particularly when they do not have the time to engage in extensive comparison shopping. Exhibit 13–4 illustrates how Hunt's Manwich is positioned to capitalize on time pressure at mealtime.

Task Definition

To illustrate the impact of a task-influenced situation as it interacts with a personal characteristic, we can examine the dogmatism-innovation proneness relationship.[23] *Dogmatism* is defined as the personality characteristic of closed mindedness, and *innovation proneness* as the tendency to choose new and different items. It would seem logical that highly dogmatic individuals would not be highly innovative in product choice (i.e., they would not choose new or different brands over established ones), and indeed this relationship was found to be true

Table 13–2
Buying Factors in Gift-Giving Purchase Situations

Buying factors "sought" by purchaser	
Birthday	Wedding
Enjoyability	Durability
Uniqueness	Usefulness
Durability	Receiver's need for product
High performance	High performance
Usefulness	Enjoyability
Innovativeness	Uniqueness
Imaginativeness	Presence of warranty
Receiver's need for product	Tangibility
Novelty	Innovativeness
Allows receiver creativity	Prettiness
Buying factors "avoided" by purchaser	
Birthday	Wedding
Low quality	Low quality
Unreliability	Lack of receiver desire for product
Lack of receiver desire for product	Lack of thoughtfulness
Lack of thoughtfulness	Gaudiness
Gaudiness	Lack of style
No reflection on receiver's personality	Unreliability
Lack of tastefulness	Lack of tastefulness
Disliked by friends and family	Disliked by friends and family
Lack of style	Inconvenience
Inconvenience	Inappropriate for occasion

Source: S. DeVere, C. Scott, and W. Shulby, "Consumer Perceptions of Gift-Giving Occasions: Attribute Sales and Structure," in *Advances in Consumer Research X,* ed. R. P. Bagozzi and A. M. Tybout (Chicago: Association for Consumer Research, 1983), pp. 185–90.

for college females. This finding was later replicated for college males.[24] Both studies posed a *personal-purchase situation*. In order to see the effects of task, a study was conducted which presented a *gift-giving situation* to subjects. The original studies were repeated exactly except there were two task situations—*gift giving* and *personal use*.[25] As shown in Figure 13–6, the inverse relationship (higher dogmatism/lower innovativeness) was found again for the self-purchase situation, but a direct relationship that was slightly positive (higher dogmatism/higher innovativeness) was found for persons in the gift-purchase situation. Thus, purchase intent or task definition reversed the normally predicted relationship between dogmatism and innovativeness.

Shown on Table 13–2 are the buying factors "sought" and "avoided" when buying a gift for a birthday and wedding. In the buying factors "sought," 7 of the 10 listed are the same for a birthday or wedding. Likewise, nine of the buying factors "avoided" are the same for birthday and wedding gifts. However, closer examination reveals that wedding gifts tend to be *utilitarian* (the top four attributes are durability, usefulness, receiver's need, and high performance), while birthday gifts tend to be *fun* (the top four attributes are enjoyability, uniqueness, durability, and high performance). Thus, both the general task definition (gift giving) and the specific task definition (gift-giving occasion) influence purchase behavior.[26]

Exhibit 13–5 illustrates how the flower industry is combating a decline in the purchase of flowers by promoting gift-giving purchase situations.

Antecedent States

Antecedent states are features of the individual person that are not lasting characteristics. Rather, they are momentary moods or conditions. For example, we all experience states of depression or high excitement from time to time that are not normally part of our individual makeup.

Moods are transient feeling states that are generally not tied to a specific event or object.[27] They tend to be less intense than emotions and may operate without the individual's awareness. While moods may affect all aspects of a person's behavior, they generally do not completely interrupt ongoing behavior as an emotion might. Individuals use such terms as happy, cheerful, peaceful, sad, blue, and depressed to describe their moods.

Moods both affect and are affected by the consumption process.[28] Moods influence our ability to process and retrieve information,[29] as well as the purchase, consumption, and evaluation of products. Tauber's description of the influence of moods on the shopping process is worth repeating:

> Different emotional states or moods may be relevant for explaining why and when someone goes shopping. For example, a person may go to a store in search of social contact when he feels lonely. Likewise, he may go to a store to buy "something nice" for himself when he is depressed. Several subjects in this study reported that often they alleviate depression

Exhibit 13–5 Flower Gift-Giving

Flowers are frequently purchased as gifts, yet they account for only a small percentage of gift purchases. With economic pressures, as well as decline in the number of people who purchase flowers, the industry is attempting to encourage the purchase of flowers for oneself, and expand the range of gift situations for which flowers are appropriate.

Courtesy Florists' Transworld Delivery Association

Source: D. Seammon, R. Shaw, and G. Barmossy, "Is a Gift Always a Gift? An Investigation of Flower Purchasing Behavior across Situations," in *Advances in Consumer Research IX*, ed. A. Mitchell (Chicago: Association for Consumer Research, 1982), pp. 531–36.

by simply spending money on themselves. In this case, the shopping trip is motivated not by the expected utility of consuming, but by the utility of the buying process itself.[30]

Exhibit 13–6 illustrates two products positioned to satisfy different moods. In addition to responding to consumer needs induced by moods, marketers attempt to influence moods and to time marketing activities with positive mood-inducing events.[31] Restaurants, bars, shopping malls, and many other retail outlets are designed to induce positive moods in patrons. Music is often played for this reason. Many companies prefer to advertise during "light" television programs because viewers tend to be in a good mood while watching these shows.

Momentary conditions differ somewhat from moods. Whereas moods reflect states of mind, momentary conditions reflect states of being or conditions, such as being tired, being ill, having a great deal of money, being broke, and so forth. However, for conditions, as for moods, to fit under the definition of antecedent states, they must be momentary and not constantly with the individual. Hence, an individual who is short of cash only momentarily will probably act differently than someone who is always short of cash (i.e., poor).

In Table 13–3, situations 9 and 10 represent antecedent conditions. In situation 9, a tougher than normal day at the office leaves you very fatigued and too tired to cook dinner; situation 10 depicts a time to celebrate and reward oneself for all the hard work endured in the last semester. Each situation may motivate the

Exhibit 13–6 Product Positioning that Focuses on How You Feel

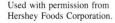

Used with permission from Hershey Foods Corporation.

Used with permission from General Foods®.

Table 13-3
Ten Examples of How Situation Might Influence the Decision to Eat Out and Choice of Restaurant

Situational Influence	Description of the Situation	Type of Restaurant Used
1. **Physical**	It is very hot and your air conditioning isn't working.	Full/limited service
2. **Physical**	You're downtown Christmas shopping and the stores and streets are very crowded.	Full service
3. **Social**	Your fiancee's parents are going to take you out for dinner and ask you to pick the restaurant.	Full service
4. **Social**	Your neighbor comes over to visit, you are having a pleasant chat, and you discover it is time for lunch.	Fast food
5. **Temporal**	You plan to go to a show at 7:30 P.M. It is 6:30 P.M. now.	Fast food
6. **Temporal**	You want to have an evening meal with the family when not rushed for time.	Limited service
7. **Task**	It's your parents' 25th wedding anniversary and you want to take them out to dinner.	Full service
8. **Task**	Your spouse won't be home for dinner and you are wondering what to feed the children.	Fast food
9. **Antecedent**	You are too tired to cook dinner because you have had a very fatiguing day at the office.	Limited/full service
10. **Antecedent**	You have just finished a tough semester and you're in the mood to really reward yourself.	Full service

use of a restaurant for dinner but, depending on time and money, the type of restaurant selected may be different.

SITUATIONAL INFLUENCES AND MARKETING STRATEGY

We have presented a basic classification system of situational characteristics and provided a number of examples of how managers could respond to specific situations in ways that are likely to increase the probability of purchase. Given that situations do have an impact, how do we as marketing managers respond to them? What actions do we take to influence the situation? Unfortunately, there is no magical formula that will allow you to recognize the potential influence of the situation other than simply being aware of situational characteristics and on the lookout for their impacts.

As we have indicated previously, situational variables not only have direct influences, they also interact with product and individual characteristics to influence behavior.

It should also be stressed that individuals do not encounter situations ran-

Figure 13–7
Use Situations and Product Positioning

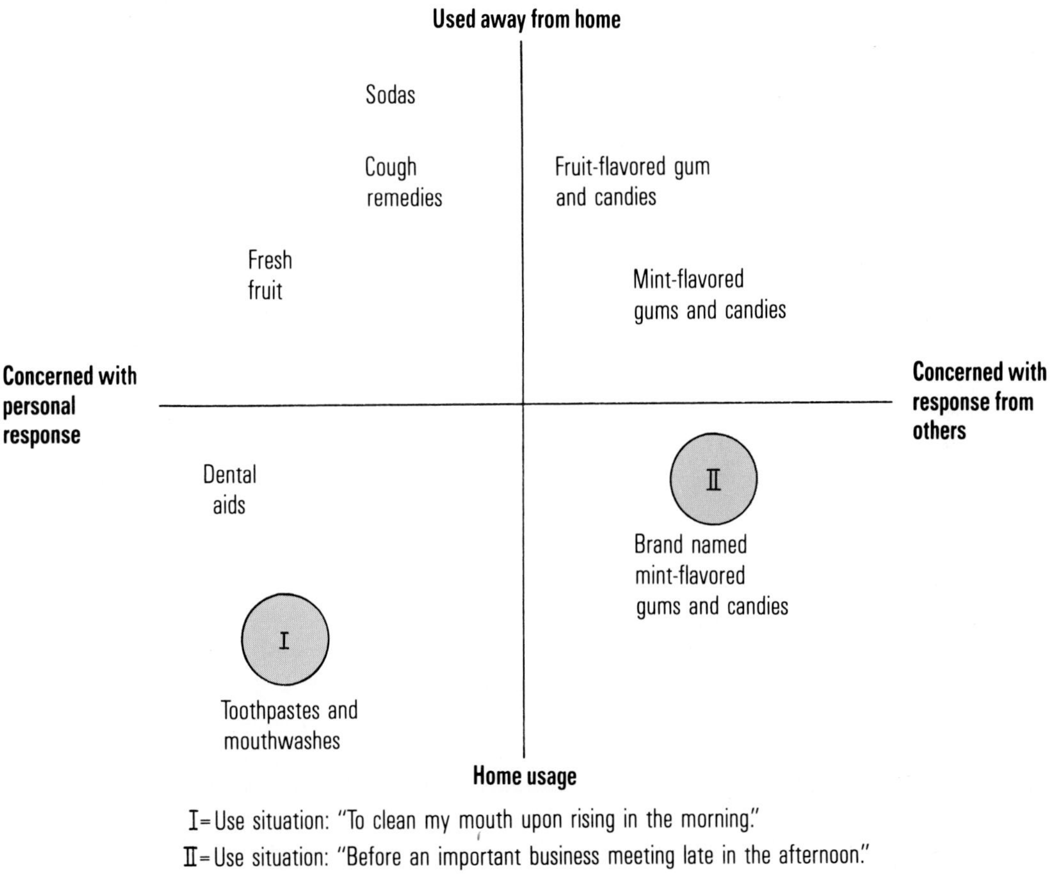

Source: Adapted from R. Srivastava, A. Shocker, and G. Day, "An Exploratory Study of the Influences of Usage Situation on Perceptions of Product Markets," in *Advances in Consumer Research V*, ed. K. Hunt (Chicago: Association for Consumer Research, 1978), p. 36.

domly. Instead, most people "create" many of the situations they face. Thus, individuals who choose to engage in physically demanding sports such as jogging, tennis, or racquetball are indirectly choosing to expose themselves to the situation of "being tired" or "being thirsty." This allows marketers to consider advertising and segmentation strategies based on the situations that individuals selecting given lifestyles are likely to encounter.

Market Segmentation

After determining the influence of different situations on purchase behavior for a product category, a marketer must determine which products or brands are

Exhibit 13–7 Person-Situation Segmentation Procedure

SEGMENTATION PROCEDURE

Step 1: Use observational studies, focus group discussions, and secondary data to discover whether different usage situations exist and whether they are determinant, in the sense that they appear to affect the importance of various product characteristics.

Step 2: If step 1 produces promising results, survey consumers to better understand benefits, product perceptions, and product use. Measure benefits and perceptions by usage situation, as well as by individual difference characteristics. Assess situation-usage frequency by recall estimates or usage situation diaries.

Step 3: Construct a person-situation segmentation matrix. The rows are the major usage situations and the columns are groups of users identified by a single characteristic or combination of characteristics.

Step 4: Rank the cells in the matrix in terms of their submarket sales volume. The situation-person combination that results in the greatest consumption of the product would be ranked first.

Step 5: State the major benefits sought, important product dimensions, and unique market behavior for each nonempty cell of the matrix.

Step 6: Position your competitor's offerings within the matrix. The person-situation segments they currently serve can be determined by the product features they promote and other marketing strategies.

Step 7: Position your offering within the matrix on the same criteria.

Step 8: Assess how well your current offering and marketing strategy meet the needs of the submarkets compared to the competition.

Step 9: Identify market opportunities based on submarket size, needs, and competitive advantage in each person-situation segment.

Exhibit 13–7 *(concluded)*

ILLUSTRATIVE EXAMPLE FOR SUNTAN LOTION

SUNTAN LOTION USE SITUATIONS	POTENTIAL USERS OF SUNTAN LOTION				SITUATION BENEFITS
	Young Children	Teenagers	Adult Women	Adult Men	
Beach/Boat Activities	Prevent sunburn	Prevent sunburn while tanning	Prevent sunburn	Prevent sunburn	Container floats
Home/Pools Sunbathing	Prevent sunburn	Tanning	Tanning with summer perfume scent	Tanning	Lotion won't stain clothes or furniture
Sunlamp/ Sunbathing		Tanning	Tanning with moisturizer		Designed for sunlamps
Snow Skiing		Prevent sunburn while tanning	Prevent sunburn with winter perfume scent	Prevent sunburn	Anti-freeze formula
PERSON BENEFITS	Protection	Tanning	Protection and tanning with perfume scent	Protection and tanning	

Source: Adapted from P. Dickson, "Person-Situation: Segmentation's Missing Link," *Journal of Marketing,* Fall 1982, pp. 56–64.

most likely to be purchased when that situation arises. A common method of dealing with this question is to jointly scale situations and products.[32] An example is shown in Figure 13–7. Here, *use situations* that ranged from "private consumption at home" to "consumption away from home where there is a concern for other people's reaction to you" were scaled in terms of their similarity and relationship to products appropriate for that situation. For a use situation described as "to clean my mouth upon rising in the morning," toothpastes and mouthwashes are viewed as most appropriate. However, a use situation described as "before an important business meeting late in the afternoon," involves both consumption away from home and a concern for the response others have to you. As a result, mint-flavored gums or candies would best serve this use situation.

Product Positioning

As more marketers have recognized the importance of situational influences on purchase and consumption, a greater effort has been made to incorporate use situations in marketing strategy. Exhibit 13–7 outlines the steps a firm can take in studying the use situation to better segment markets, position products, and create advertisements designed to communicate this positioning. As discussed in Exhibit 13–7, more effective market segmentation and product positioning can be accomplished when use situations can be grouped together with needs (created by the situation) and products perceived to be appropriate.

SUMMARY

Marketing managers should view the consumer and marketing activities designed to affect and influence that consumer in light of the situations that the consumer faces. A consumer situation is a set of factors outside of and removed from the individual consumer, as well as removed from the characteristics or attributes of the product.

Situations, for the purpose of helping to explain consumer behavior, have been classified into a scheme of five objectively measured variables. Physical surroundings are the most obvious and readily apparent features of a situation. Physical surroundings include geographical and institutional location, decor, sound, aromas, lighting, weather, and displays of merchandise or other material surrounding the product. Retailers are particularly concerned with the effects of physical surroundings.

Social surroundings deal primarily with other persons present that could have an impact on the individual consumer's behavior. The characteristics of the other persons present, their roles, and interpersonal interactions are potentially important social situational influences.

Temporal perspectives deal with the effect of time on consumer behavior. This dimension of a situation may be specified in units ranging from time of day to seasons of the year. Time may also be measured relative to some past or future event. This allows concepts such as time since last purchase, time since or until meals or payday, and time constraints imposed by commitments. Convenience stores have evolved and been successful by taking advantage of the temporal perspective factor.

Task definition reflects the purpose or reason for engaging in the consumption behavior. The task may reflect different buyer and user roles anticipated by the individual. For example, a person shopping for dishes to be given as a wedding present is in a different situation than if the dishes were for personal use.

Antecedent states are features of the individual person that are not lasting or relatively enduring characteristics. They are momentary moods or conditions. Momentary moods are such things as temporary states of depression or high excitement, which all people experience. Momentary conditions are such things as being tired, ill, having a great deal of money (or none at all), and so forth.

Situational influences may have very direct influences, but they also interact with product and individual characteristics to influence behavior. In some cases, the situation will have no influence whatsoever, because the individual's characteristics or choices are so intense that they override everything else. But the situation is always potentially important and therefore is of concern to marketing managers.

REVIEW QUESTIONS

1. What is meant by the term *situation*? Why is it important for a marketing manager to understand situational influences on purchasing behavior?
2. What are *physical surroundings* (as a situational variable)? Give an example of how they can influence the consumption process.
3. What are *social surroundings* (as a situational variable)? Give an example of how they can influence the consumption process.
4. What is *temporal perspective* (as a situational variable)? Give an example of how it can influence the consumption process.
5. What is *task definition* (as a situational variable)? Give an example of how it can influence the consumption process.
6. What are *antecedent conditions* (as a situational variable)? Give an example of how they can influence the consumption process.
7. What is a *mood*? How does it differ from an *emotion?* How do moods influence behavior?
8. What is meant by the statement, "Situational variables may interact with object or personal characteristics"?
9. Are individuals randomly exposed to situational influences? Why?
10. How can use situations be used in market segmentation?
11. How does crowding affect shopping behavior?
12. How do the desired attributes in a wedding gift differ from those in a birthday gift?

DISCUSSION QUESTIONS

1. Discuss the potential importance of each situational influence in developing a marketing strategy to promote the purchase of:
   a. Women's hats.
   b. Aftershave lotion.
   c. Breath freshener.
   d. Yogurt.
   e. Compact disc player.
2. What product categories seem most susceptible to situational influences? Why?
3. In those instances where marketers have little control over the consumption situation, why is it important for them to understand how the situation relates to the consumption of their product?
4. How would you change the situational classification scheme presented in the chapter?
5. What marketing strategies are suggested by Figure 13–1 for a trade association focused on:
   a. Kiwi-fruit?
   b. Strawberries?
   c. Bananas?
   d. Grapes?
6. Flowers are "appropriate" gifts for women over many situations but seem to be appropriate for men only when they are ill. Why is this so? Could FTD change this?
7. Utilizing Exhibit 13–7 as a model, construct a matrix for:
   a. Wine.
   b. Restaurant.
   c. Bicycle.
   d. Breath freshener.
8. Discuss the strategy implications of Table 13–1 for:
   a. Fast-food restaurants.
   b. Supermarkets.
   c. Department stores.
   d. Shopping malls.
9. What are the marketing strategy implications of Figure 13–5?

PROJECT QUESTIONS

1. Interview 10 people who have recently purchased a ______. Determine the role, if any, played by situational factors.
   a. Magazine.
   b. Dog.
   c. Soft drink.
   d. Bottle of wine.
   e. Video rental.
2. Interview a ______ salesperson. Determine the role, if any, this individual feels situational variables play in his/her sales.
   a. Men's suit.
   b. Furniture.
   c. Compact disc player.
   d. Women's shoes.

3. Conduct a study using a small (10 or so) sample of your friends in which you attempt to isolate the situational factors that influence the type or brand of ______ purchased or used.
   a. Beer.
   b. Toothpaste.
   c. Movie.
   d. Breakfast food.
4. Create a list of 10 to 20 use situations relevant to campus area restaurants. Then interview 10 students and have them indicate which of these situations they have encountered and ask them to rank order these situations in terms of how likely they are to occur. Discuss how a restaurant could use this information in trying to appeal to the student market.
5. Select a product and develop three distinct marketing strategies based on situational influences that affect the consumption of that product.
6. Copy three advertisements that are clearly based on a situational appeal. For each advertisement, indicate:
   a. Which situational variable is involved.
   b. Why the company would use this variable.
   c. Your evaluation of the effectiveness of this approach.
7. Based on Table 13–2, create a "wedding gift" and a "birthday gift" ad for the same brand of each of the following products:
   a. Microwave oven.
   b. Wine.
   c. Toaster.
   d. Tool kit.

REFERENCES

[1] D. A. Michals, "Pitching Products by the Barometer," *Business Week,* July 8, 1985, p. 45.

[2] R. W. Belk, "Situational Variables and Consumer Behavior," *Journal of Consumer Research,* December 1975, p. 158.

[3] For a discussion of situational influence paradigms, see J. Leigh and C. Martin, "A Review of Situational Influence Paradigms and Research," in *1981 Review of Marketing,* ed. B. M. Enis and K. J. Roering (Chicago: American Marketing Association, 1981), pp. 57–74.

[4] *The Wine Marketing Handbook* (Gavin-Johnson Publication, 1980), p. 18.

[5] J. Hornik, "Situational Effects on the Consumption of Time," *Journal of Marketing,* Fall 1982, pp. 44–55.

[6] See P. G. Bonner, "Considerations for Situational Research," in *Advances in Consumer Research XII,* ed. E. C. Hirschman and M. B. Holbrook (Provo, Utah: Association for Consumer Research, 1985), pp. 368–73; and J. A. Cote, "The Person by Situation Myth," in *Advances in Consumer Research XIII,* ed. R. J. Lutz (Provo, Utah: Association for Consumer Research, 1986), pp. 37–41.

[7] Belk, "Situational Variables," p. 161.

[8] Philip Kotler, "Atmospherics as a Marketing Tool," *Journal of Retailing,* Winter 1973–74, pp. 48–64.

[9] R. Markin, C. Lillis, and C. Narayana, "Social-Psychological Significance of Store Space," *Journal of Retailing,* Spring 1976, pp. 43–54; B. Wysock, "Sight, Smell, Sound: They're All Arms in Retailer's Arsenal," *The Wall Street Journal,* April 17, 1979, p. 1; R. J. Donovan and J. R. Rossiter, "Store Atmosphere: An Environmental Psychology Approach," *Journal of Retailing,* Spring 1982, pp. 34–57; and M. P. Gardner and G. J. Siomkas, "Toward a Methodology for Assessing Effects of In-Store Atmospherics," in Lutz, *Advances XIII,* pp. 27–31.

[10] G. Harrell, M. Hutt, and J. Anderson, "Path Analysis of Buyer Behavior under Conditions of Crowding," *Journal of Marketing Research,* February 1980, pp. 45–51; and S. Eroglu and G. D. Harrell, "Retail Crowding," *Journal of Retailing,* Winter 1986, pp. 346–63.

[11] J. Huber, M. B. Holbrook, and S. Schiffman, "Situational Psychophysics and the Vending Machine Problem," *Journal of Retailing,* Spring 1982, pp. 82–94.

[12] E. M. Tauber, "Why Do People Shop?" *Journal of Marketing,* October 1972, p. 47. See also R. A. Westbrook and W. C. Black, "A Motivation-Based Shopper Typology," *Journal of Retailing,* Spring 1985, pp. 78–103.

[13] A. Branthwaite, "Situations and Social Actions," *Journal of the Market Research Society,* First Quarter 1983, pp. 19–38.

[14] E. Dupnick, "The Effect of Context on Cognitive Structure," (Ph.D. dissertation, University of Arizona, 1979). For contradictory results, see T. C. Brock and S. Shavitt, "Consumer Research Validity," in *Advances in Consumer Research XI,* ed. T. C. Kinnear (Chicago: Association for Consumer Research, 1984), pp. 16–23.

[15] J. A. Cote, J. McCullough, and M. Reilly, "Effects of Unexpected Situations on Behavior-Intention Differences," *Journal of Consumer Research,* September 1985, p. 193.

[16] Tauber, "Why Do People Shop?" p. 48.

[17] See special issue devoted to the consumption of time, *Journal of Consumer Research,* March 1981, and "Despite Ad Media Explosion, It's Still Difficult to Reach Short-on-Time Consumers," *Marketing News,* February 19, 1982, p. 19.

[18] R. Holman and R. D. Wilson, "The Availability of Discretionary Time: Influences on Interactive Patterns of Consumer Shopping Behavior," *Advances in Consumer Research VII,* ed. J. Olson (Chicago: Association for Consumer Research, 1980), pp. 431–36.

[19] R. E. Nisbett and D. E. Kanouse, "Obesity, Food Deprivation, and Supermarket Shopping Behavior," *Journal of Personality and Social Psychology,* August 1969, p. 290.

[20] J. Zbytniewski, "The After-Five Shopper," *Progressive Grower's Shopper Behavior Kit,* September 1979.

[21] B. E. Mattson and A. J. Dobinsky, "Shopping Patterns," *Psychology & Marketing,* Spring 1987, pp. 42–62.

[22] B. E. Mattson, "Situational Influences on Store Choice," *Journal of Retailing,* Fall 1982, pp. 46–58. See ibid. for different results.

[23] J. Jacoby, "Personality and Innovation Proneness," *Journal of Marketing Research,* May 1971, pp. 244–47.

[24] K. A. Coney, "Dogmatism and Innovation: A Replication," *Journal of Marketing Research,* November 1972, pp. 453–55.

[25] K. A. Coney and R. R. Harmon, "Dogmatism and Innovation: A Situational Perspective," in *Advances in Consumer Research VI,* ed. W. L. Wilkie (Chicago: Association for Consumer Research, 1979), pp. 118–21.

[26] See Mattson and Dubinsky, "Shopping Patterns"; S. M. Smith and S. E. Beatty, "An Examination of Gift Purchasing Behavior," in *1985 Marketing Educators Conference,* ed. R. F. Lusch et al. (Chicago: American Marketing Association, 1985), pp. 69–74; and D. M. Andrus, E. Silver, and D. E. Johnson, "Status Brand Management and Gift Purchase," *Journal of Consumer Marketing,* Winter 1986, pp. 5–13.

[27] M. P. Gardner, "Mood States and Consumer Behavior," *Journal of Consumer Research,* December 1985, pp. 281–300.

[28] R. P. Hill and M. P. Gardner, "The Buying Process," in *Advances in Consumer Research XIV,* ed. M. Wallendorf and P. Anderson (Provo, Utah: Association for Consumer Research, 1987), pp. 408–10.

[29] T. K. Srull, "The Effects of Subjective Affective States on Memory and Judgment," and A. M. Isen, "The Influence of Positive Affect," both in *Advances in Consumer Research XI,* ed. T. C. Kinnear (Chicago: Association for Consumer Research, 1984), pp. 530–33, 534–37; R. Lawson, "The Effects of Mood on Retrieving Consumer Product Information," in *Advances XII,* ed. Hirschman and Holbrook, pp. 399–403; and T. K. Srull, "Memory, Mood, and Consumer Judgment," in *Advances XIV,* ed. Wallendorf and Anderson, pp. 404–7.

[30] Tauber, "Why Do People Shop?" p. 47.

[31] See M. Gardner and M. Vandersteel, "The Consumer's Mood," and R. Belk, "Applications of Mood Inducement in Buyer Behavior," both in *Advances XI,* ed. Kinnear, pp. 525–29, 544–47; and Gardner, "Mood States."

[32] R. Srivastava, "Usage-Situational Influences on Perceptions of Product Markets: Response Homogeneity and Its Implications for Consumer Research," in *Advances VII,* ed. Olson, pp. 644–49.

CHAPTER

14 Consumer Decision Process and Problem Recognition

Polaroid recently introduced its new 600 instant camera and film system. The new system is generally regarded as an important technological breakthrough. However, its ultimate success in the marketplace is still in doubt. As one industry analyst expressed: "The company is marketing the 600 as the answer to a question most people who take snapshots haven't even asked: How do you get rid of minor shadows in photographs?"

Since few people are concerned about the shadows, one can ask: "Is the 600 then a solution looking for problems?" Not according to W. J. McCune, Jr., Polaroid's chief executive officer: "Things like that can be taught so the process becomes meaningful." To "teach" the market that such a problem exists, Polaroid will spend twice as much on advertising for this introduction than for any previous new product introduction.[1]

The success of Polaroid's new camera hinges on the firm's ability to convince consumers that a problem exists with other photographic systems which the 600 will solve. Since consumers are not aware of this problem, Polaroid must devote substantial resources to convincing them that a problem exists, that it is worth resolving, and that this new product is the best solution.

In contrast, the original Polaroid camera solved a problem (long wait for film development) that many photographers were acutely aware of. Thus, their initial promotional efforts did not have to generate problem recognition. These two situations are shown on the facing page.

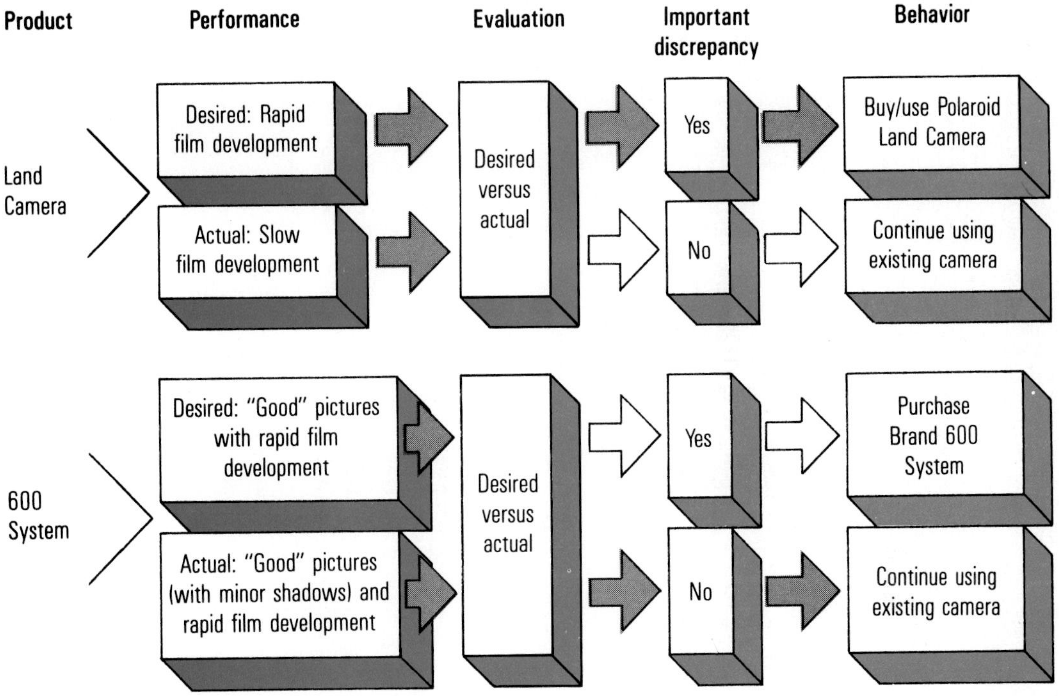

Problem recognition is the first stage of the consumer decision process. This chapter examines the nature of the consumer decision process and analyzes the first step in that process, problem recognition, in some detail. Within problem recognition, we focus on: (1) the process of problem recognition, (2) the uncontrollable determinants of problem recognition, and (3) marketing strategies based on the problem recognition process.

TYPES OF CONSUMER DECISIONS

As Figure 14-1 indicates, there are various types of consumer decision processes. As the consumer moves from a very low level of involvement *with the purchase* to a high level of involvement, decision making becomes increasingly complex. While purchase involvement is a continuum, it is useful to consider habitual, limited, and extended decision making as general descriptions of the types of processes that occur along various points on the continuum. You should keep in mind that the types of decision processes are not distinct but blend into each other.

Before describing each type of decision process, the concept of purchase involvement must be clarified. We define *purchase involvement* as the *level of*

Figure 14–1
Involvement and Types of Decision Making

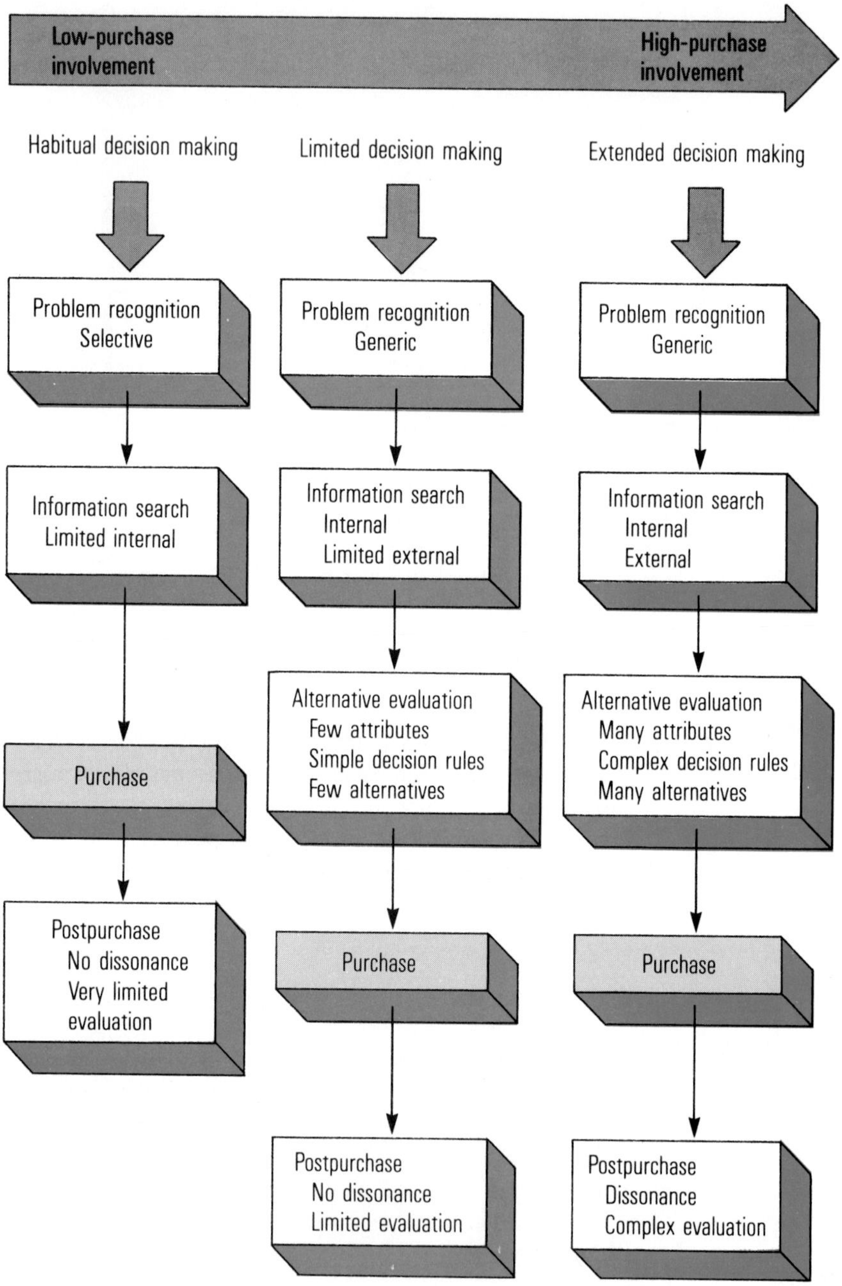

concern for, or interest in, the purchase process triggered by the need to consider a particular purchase.[2] Thus, purchase involvement is a temporary state of an individual, family, or household unit. It is influenced by the interaction of individual, product, and situational characteristics.[3]

Note that purchase involvement is *not* the same as product involvement. You may be very involved with a brand (Budweiser or Crest or Volvo) or a product category (beer or toothpaste or cars) and yet have a very low level of involvement with the purchase process because of brand loyalty. Or, you may have a rather low level of involvement with a product (school supplies or automobile tires) but have high level of purchase involvement because you desire to set an example for a child, impress a friend who is on the shopping trip, or save money. Of course, there are individual differences in general involvement level and in the involvement response to particular situations.

The following sections provide a brief description of how the purchasing process changes as purchase involvement increases.

Habitual Decision Making

Habitual decision making in effect involves *no* decision per se. As Figure 14-1 indicates, a problem is recognized, internal search (long-term memory) provides a single preferred solution (brand), that brand is purchased, and an evaluation occurs only if the brand fails to perform as expected. Habitual decisions occur when there is very low involvement with the purchase and result in repeat purchasing behavior.

A completely habitual decision does not even include consideration of the "do not purchase" alternative. For example, you might notice that you are nearly out of Aim toothpaste and resolve to purchase some the next time you are at the store. You don't even consider not replacing the toothpaste or purchasing another brand. At the store, you scan the shelf for Aim and pick it up without considering alternative brands.

Habitual decisions can be broken into two distinct categories: brand loyal decisions and repeat purchase decisions. These two categories are described briefly below and examined in detail in Chapter 18.

Brand Loyalty. At one time you may have been highly involved in selecting a toothpaste and, in response, used an extensive decision-making process. Having selected Aim as a result of this process, you may now purchase it without further consideration, even though using the best available toothpaste is still important to you. Thus, you are committed to Aim because you believe it best meets your overall needs. You are brand loyal.[4] It will be very difficult for a competitor to gain your patronage.

Repeat Purchases. In contrast, you may believe that all catsups are about the same and you may not attach much importance to the product category or purchase. Having tried Del Monte and found it satisfactory, you now purchase it using habitual decision making. Thus, you are a repeat purchaser of Del Monte catsup, but you are not committed to it. A competitor could gain your patronage rather easily.

Limited Decision Making

Limited decision making covers the middle ground between habitual decision making and extensive decision making. In its simplest form (lowest level of purchase involvement), limited decision making is very similar to habitual decision making.[5] For example, while in a store you may notice a point-of-purchase display for Jell-O and pick up two boxes without seeking information beyond your memory that "Jell-O tastes good," or "Gee, I haven't had Jell-O in a long time." In addition, you may have considered no other alternative except possibly a very limited examination of a "do not buy" option. Or, you may have a decision rule that you buy the cheapest brand of instant coffee available. When you run low on coffee (problem recognition), you simply examine coffee prices the next time you are in the store and select the cheapest brand.

Limited decision making is very common in daily purchases and presents the marketer with a different set of challenges than does habitual decision making.[6]

Extended Decision Making

As Figure 14-1 indicates, extended decision making is the response to a very high level of purchase involvement. Extensive internal and external information search is followed by a complex evaluation of multiple alternatives. After the purchase, doubt about its correctness is likely and a thorough evaluation of the purchase takes place. Relatively few consumer decisions reach this extreme level of complexity. However, products such as homes, personal computers, and complex recreational items such as backpacks and tents are frequently purchased via extended decision making.

Marketing Strategy and Types of Consumer Decisions

The brief descriptions of the various types of consumer decisions provided above should be ample to indicate that marketing strategies appropriate for extended decision making would be less than optimal for limited or habitual decisions. As Figure 14-1 illustrates, most stages of the consumption process are affected by purchase involvement. We devote a chapter to each of these stages. Within each chapter we will describe the impact of purchase involvement on that stage of the decision process and indicate how marketing strategy is affected.

THE PROCESS OF PROBLEM RECOGNITION

A day rarely passes in which we do not face several consumption problems. Routine problems of depletion, such as the need to get gasoline as the gauge approaches empty, or the need to replace a frequently used food item, are readily

Figure 14–2
The Process of Problem Recognition

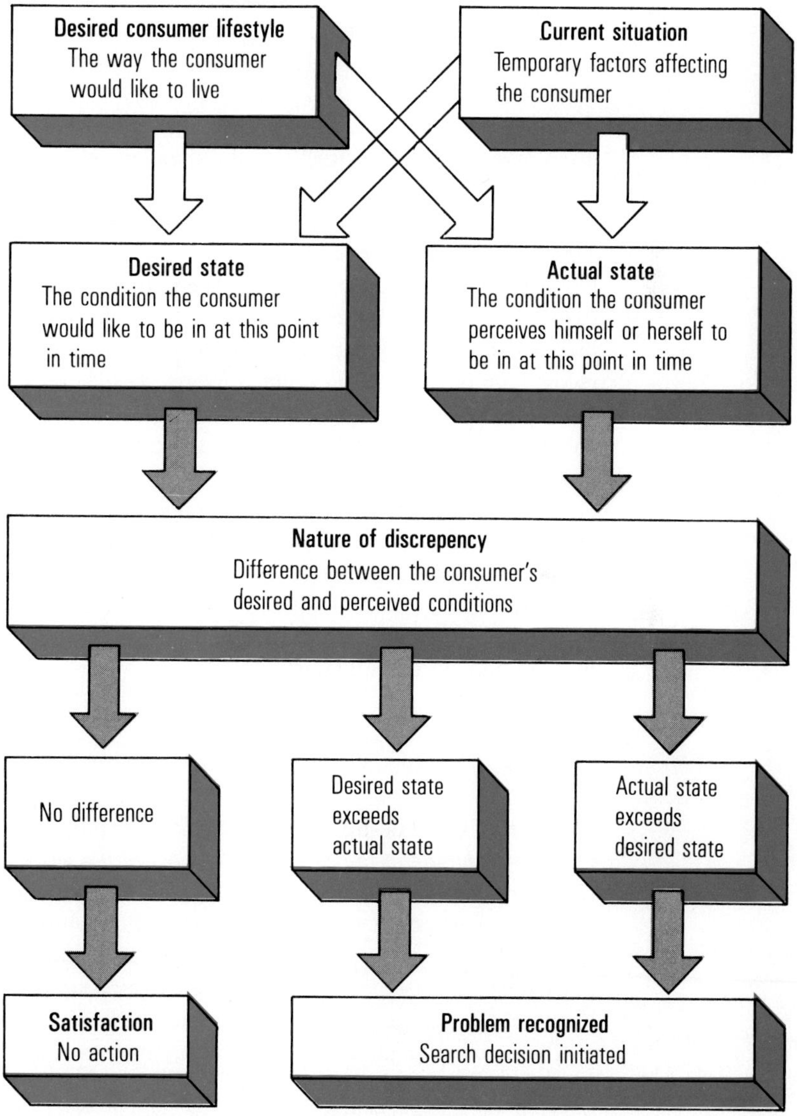

recognized, defined, and resolved. The unexpected breakdown of a major appliance such as a refrigerator or stove creates an unplanned problem which is also easily recognized but is often more difficult to resolve. Recognition of other problems, such as the need for a personal computer, may take longer as they may be subtle and evolve slowly over time.

The Nature of Problem Recognition

Problem recognition is the first stage in the consumer decision process, and it must occur before decision making can begin. In each of the situations described above, *the recognition of a problem is the result of a discrepancy between a desired state and an actual state that is sufficient to arouse and activate the decision process.* The kind of action taken by consumers in response to recognized problems relates directly to the situation, its importance to the consumer, and the dissatisfaction or inconvenience created by the problem.

Without recognition of a problem, there is no need for a consumer decision. This condition is illustrated in Figure 14–2 when there is no discrepancy between the consumer's desired state (what the consumer would like) and the actual state (what the consumer perceives as already existing). On the other hand, when there is a discrepancy between a consumer desire and the perceived actual state, recognition of a problem occurs.[7] Figure 14–2 shows that any time the desired state is perceived as being greater than or less than the actual state, a problem has been recognized. Any time the desired state is equal to the actual state, no problem exists.

At the heart of the problem recognition process is the *degree* to which a desired condition is out of alignment with an actual condition. In Figure 14–2, consumer desires are represented as the result of the desired lifestyle of the consumer and the current situation (time pressures, physical surroundings, and so forth). Perceptions of the actual state also vary in relation to a consumer's lifestyle and current situation.

The Desire to Resolve Recognized Problems

The level of one's desire to resolve a particular problem depends on two factors: (1) *the magnitude of the discrepancy between the desired and actual states* and (2) *the relative importance of the problem.* An individual could desire to have a car that averages at least 25 miles per gallon while still meeting certain size and power desires. If the current car obtains an average of 24.5 miles per gallon, a discrepancy exists, but it may not be large enough to motivate the consumer to proceed to the next step in the decision process.

On the other hand, a large discrepancy may exist and the consumer may not proceed to information search because the *relative importance* of the problem is small. A consumer may desire a new Honda Accord and own a 10-year-old Ford Pinto. The discrepancy is large. However, the relative importance of this particular discrepancy may be small compared to other consumption problems such as those related to housing, utilities, and food. Relative importance is a critical concept because all consumers have budget constraints, time constraints, or both.Only the relatively more important problems are likely to be solved. In general, importance is determined by how critical the problem is to the maintenance of the desired lifestyle.

The role of relative importance can be seen in a package decision made by General Foods. Consumers indicated that cereal packages did not fit well on their pantry and cabinet shelves. In response, General Foods introduced compact cereal boxes, which eventually failed. The problem, although recognizable, was of relatively little importance to customers.

Exhibit 14–1

Marketing Strategy for Active and Inactive Consumer Problems

Timberlane Lumber Co., acquired a source of supply of Honduran Pitch Pine. This natural product lights at the touch of a match, even when damp, and burns for 15 to 20 minutes. It will not flare up and is therefore relatively safe. It can be procured in sticks 15 to 18 inches long and 1 inch in diameter. These sticks can be used to ignite fireplace fires, or they can be shredded and used to ignite charcoal in charcoal grills.

Prior to marketing the product, Timberlane commissioned a marketing study to estimate demand and guide in developing marketing strategy. Two large samples of potential consumers were interviewed. The first sample was asked how they lit their fireplace fires and what problems they had with this procedure. Almost all of the respondents used newspaper, kindling, or both, and almost none experienced any problems. The new product was then described, and the respondents were asked to express the likelihood that they would purchase such a product. Only a small percentage expressed any interest. However, a sample of consumers that actually used the new product for several weeks felt it was a substantial improvement over existing methods and expressed a desire to continue using the product. Thus, the problem was there (because the new product was strongly preferred over the old by those who tried it), but most consumers were not aware of it. This is an *inactive problem*. Before the product can be successfully sold, the firm must activate problem recognition.

In contrast, a substantial percentage of those interviewed about lighting charcoal fires expressed a strong concern about the safety of liquid charcoal lighter. These individuals expressed great interest in purchasing a safer product. This is an *active problem*. Timberlane need not worry about problem recognition in this case. Instead, it can concentrate on illustrating how its product solves the problem that the consumers already know exists.

Types of Consumer Problems

Consumer problems may be either active or inactive. An *active problem* is one the consumer is aware of or will become aware of in the normal course of events. An *inactive problem* is one of which the consumer is not yet aware. This concept is very similar to the concept of felt need discussed in the Diffusion of Innovation section of Chapter 6. The example in Exhibit 14–1 should clarify the distinction between active and inactive problems. As the exhibit indicates, active and inactive problems require vastly different marketing strategies. The problem addressed by Polaroid's 600 instant camera described at the beginning of the chapter appears to be an inactive problem.

UNCONTROLLABLE DETERMINANTS OF PROBLEM RECOGNITION

A discrepancy between what is desired by a consumer and what the consumer has is the necessary condition for problem recognition. A discrepancy can be the result of a variety of factors that influence consumer desires, perceptions of the existing state, or both. These factors are often beyond the direct influence of the marketing manager—for example, a change in family composition.

Marketing efforts such as advertising can also influence problem recognition. This section of the chapter reviews some of the uncontrollable factors that affect problem recognition. These factors are illustrated in Figure 14–3. Most have been described in detail in earlier chapters of the book. Here we relate them more directly to the problem recognition process.

Figure 14–3
Nonmarketing Factors Affecting Problem Recognition

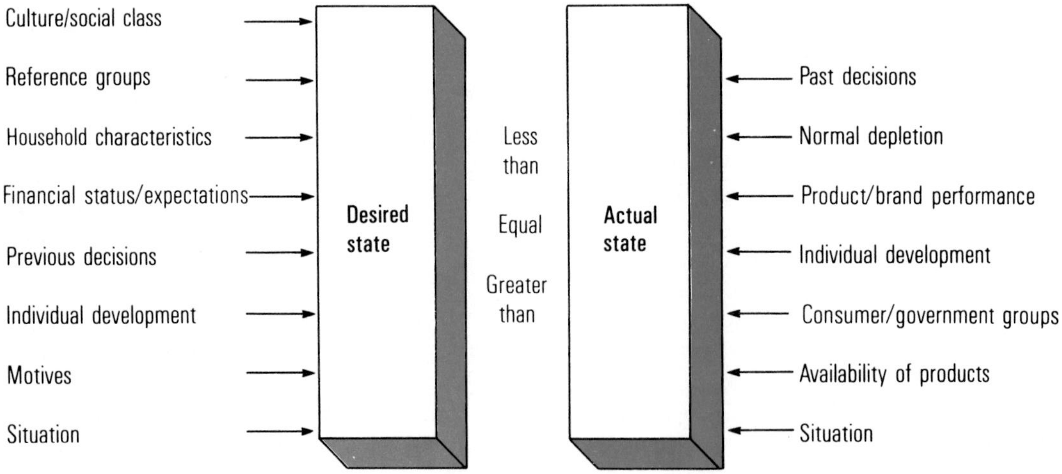

Factors Influencing the Desired State

There are many factors that can affect a consumer's lifestyle and desires. The most important of these factors are:

- Culture/social class.
- Reference groups.
- Household characteristics.
- Financial status/expectations.
- Previous decisions.
- Individual development.
- Motives.
- The situation.

Culture and *social class* provide broad parameters for lifestyle and thus indicate appropriate desired states. Desired clothing, housing, food, transportation, and many other aspects of lifestyle are heavily influenced by culture. In the United States, social class exerts a similar but much less powerful influence.

Reference groups exert a major influence on a consumer's lifestyle, and a *change in reference groups* is likely to alter a consumer's lifestyle which in turn can affect desires. This happens to many college students following graduation. In just a matter of days, a student's environment and major point of reference changes from the campus to the corporate environment. The conspicuous differences in clothing and behavior quickly influence new employees as they discover many discrepancies between their previous lifestyle and reference groups and the lifestyle exhibited by their new reference groups. These discrepancies create problems that new employees resolve in order to adjust to the explicit and implicit standards of their new reference groups.

Household characteristics such as the number and age of children determine many consumer desires. *Changes in household characteristics* produce changes in lifestyle and dramatic changes in consumer desires. As shown in Chapter 7, marriage or divorce creates substantial changes in the desired state for housing, home furnishings, leisure activities, and numerous other products. The birth of a child also alters needs, attitudes, and consumer lifestyles. For example, the addition of a first child often results in recognizing a need for greater financial security and subsequently purchasing life insurance to reduce a discrepancy between desired financial security and an existing lack of such security.

Changes in financial status and/or *changes in financial expectations* can also affect a consumer's desired state. A salary increase, large tax return, inheritance, or anticipation of any of these can cause the consumer to change desires and decide that an existing state is less satisfying. For example, anticipated income has been found to have an impact on the timing of automobile purchases.[8] Some automobile retailers take advantage of income tax refunds by advancing a down payment to individuals who have filed a return but have yet to receive the refund.

A financial loss or a change in economy[9] also can change consumer expectations and lead to problem recognition. In periods of rapid inflation or declining earnings, many households are forced to cut back on extras, such as entertainment, and to purchase lower quality levels of other products, such as food. For example, one survey found that 11 percent of the respondents were postponing their regular dental checkups, and 16 percent were postponing needed dental work because of tight finances.[10]

Previous decisions affect problem recognition. The purchase of a car or home may trigger a recognition of a need for financing or insurance. The purchase of a plant may lead to a desire for plant food. The decision to participate in a sport such as cycling, skiing, or sailing generally creates a need for a host of supporting products. Exhibit 14–2 is an advertisement based on this fact.

Individual development can influence the desired state. It is difficult to separate individual development from associated changes in reference groups, household life cycle, and income. However, it appears to influence the desired state independently of these other factors. For example, with increasing maturity, excitement and adventure appear to become less desirable. Thus, an advertisement by the Old West Regional Commission aimed at older vacationers stresses that "the pace is strictly relaxed."

Motives such as those suggested by Maslow and McGuire (Chapter 10) have a major impact on the desired state. For example, Maslow holds that as a person becomes increasingly hungry, the desired state focuses primarily on being "not hungry." Once hunger is satisfied, higher order motives come to dominate the desired state.

An individual's *current situation* strongly influences the desired condition. An individual with limited time may desire fast service, while the same individual with more time may desire friendly service. During cold weather many people prefer hot drinks, while hot weather makes cold drinks more desirable. During normal weather you may desire the flexibility of private transportation. A shift to snow and ice may change your desired transportation state to one of reliability and safety.

Factors Influencing the Actual State

Factors beyond the control of marketers which influence perceptions of the existing state include:

- Past decisions.
- Normal depletion.
- Product/brand performance.
- Individual development.
- The efforts of consumer groups and governmental agencies.
- Availability of products.
- The current situation.

Exhibit 14–2 Advertisement Based on Problem Recognition Triggered by Previous Decisions

SIERRA DESIGNS KEEPS YOU DRY, NO SWEAT.
DESIGNED FOR COMFORT, GEARED FOR THE CHALLENGE.
Dripping, soggy, steamy, wind-whipped and chilled. Think of the times you've been caught in less than perfect weather.
Now imagine active gear that keeps you dry whether you're cycling in the rain, sailing in a high wind or cross-country skiing.
Sierra Designs Liquid Asset pants and Anorak windbreaker. Laminated with Gore-Tex,® the Liquid Asset system won't let wet or windy weather in, yet allows your hard-earned sweat to efficiently steam out.
Combine Gore-Tex® with the velcroed, snapped, flapped, billed, draw-stringed, double-needle lap-stitched, factory-sealed seam quality of Sierra Designs and the result is added comfort that lets you perform at the peak of your ability.
We've been outfitting serious expeditioners for 18 years. So when you choose your next challenge, choose Sierra Designs. We guarantee that our collection of 14 Gore-Tex® garments and our extensive line of tents, sleeping bags and outdoorwear will last through a lifetime of challenges.
See your Sierra Designs dealer or write for a list of dealers nearest you. 247 Fourth Street, Oakland, California 94607.
GORE-TEX® fabrics
SIERRA DESIGNS

Courtesy Sierra Designs

Past decisions determine one's existing set of problem solutions. A decision to rent rather than purchase a home or car has obvious ramifications for one's existing state with respect to home or car ownership. The sum of one's past consumption decisions (both purchases and nonpurchases) provides the framework for the existing state.

Normal depletion is the cause of most routine problems as frequently used foods and household items are used up and need to be replaced. Depletion can also be subtle, such as the need for an oil change or the replacement of a tire that is beginning to show wear. With most problems of this type, the condition of depletion is easily recognized and resolved with a consumer purchase.

The *performance* of existing problem solutions (products and brands) has an obvious impact on the actual state. Many products must perform on two levels—instrumental and expressive. *Instrumental performance* relates to the physical or functional performance of the product. If your car or bicycle brakes fail, its instrumental performance is inadequate. *Expressive performance* relates to the symbolic performance of the product. If your car or bicycle does not reflect your desired self-concept, its expressive performance is inadequate. These concepts are discussed in depth in Chapter 18.

The normal processes of *individual development* may alter our perceptions of our existing states. This is particularly true with respect to physical attributes. As we age, many of us experience complexion problems, weight problems, heart and/or stomach problems, and hearing problems. Likewise, our mental development may lead to dissatisfaction with our existing reading material or music collection. Development of skills such as raquetball or guitar may lead to dissatisfaction with our current equipment.

With increasing concern for consumer welfare, *consumer groups and many governmental agencies* attempt to cause a particular type of problem recognition among consumers. The goal is to produce dissatisfaction with current solutions that are unhealthy, dangerous, or ecologically unsound. For example, the American Cancer Society spends a substantial amount of effort in attempting to create dissatisfaction with the current state of affairs among cigarette smokers. Exhibit 14–3 contains an example of the society's attempt to generate problem recognition concerning the risk to children when parents smoke.

The *availability of products* also affects the actual state. The absence of particular products, lack of awareness of products or brands, or inability to afford certain products affect the existing state. For example, the relative lack of sodium-free food products in the United States has a major impact on the existing state of health of many consumers.

Finally, the *current situation* has a major impact on perceptions of the actual state. The presence of others, physical conditions, temporal perspective, and antecedent states are, in fact, key elements of the actual state. Situational influences can operate in both obvious and subtle ways. Unusually hot weather may trigger problem recognition related to air conditioning and home insulation. Less obviously, a mood such as depression may initiate a clothing purchase.[11] The problem in this case is an unpleasant emotional state (actual state) which the consumer attempts to resolve by doing something nice for himself or herself (purchasing a personal item).

Exhibit 14–3 An Attempt to Generate Dissatisfaction with the Current Situation

Courtesy American Cancer Society

MARKETING STRATEGY AND PROBLEM RECOGNITION

Marketing managers have four concerns related to problem recognition. First, they need to know what problems consumers are facing. Second, managers must know how to develop the marketing mix to solve consumer problems. Third, they occasionally want to cause consumers to recognize problems. Finally, there are times when managers desire to suppress problem recognition among consumers. The remainder of this chapter discusses these issues.

Measuring Problem Recognition

A wide variety of approaches are used to determine the problems consumers face. The most common approach undoubtedly is *intuition*. That is, a manager can analyze a given product category and logically determine where improvements could be made. Thus, soundless vacuum cleaners or dishwashers are logical solutions to potential consumer problems. The difficulty with this approach is that the problem identified may be of low importance to most consumers.

A common research technique is the *survey,* which asks relatively large numbers of individuals about the problems they are facing. This was the technique used by Timberlane (see Exhibit 14–1). A second common technique is *focus groups*. Focus groups are composed of 8 to 12 similar individuals—such as male college students, female lawyers, or teenage girls—brought together to discuss a particular topic. A moderator is present to keep the discussion moving and focused on the topic, but otherwise the sessions are free flowing. Focus group research played a major role in the development of L'Eggs panty hose and the marketing strategy used to position it.[12] Both surveys and focus groups tend to take one of three approaches to problem identification: activity analysis, product analysis, or problem analysis. A fourth approach, human factors research, does not rely on surveys or focus groups.

Activity Analysis. *Activity analysis* focuses on a particular activity such as preparing dinner, maintaining the lawn, or (as in Exhibit 14–1) lighting the fireplace fire. The survey or focus group attempts to determine what problems the consumers feel occur during the performance of the activity. For example, Johnson Wax had a national panel of women report on how they cared for their hair and the problems they encountered. Their responses revealed a perceived problem with oiliness that existing brands could not resolve. As a result, Johnson Wax developed Agree Shampoo and Agree Creme Rinse, both of which became very successful.[13]

Product Analysis. *Product analysis* is similar to activity analysis, but examines the purchase and/or use of a particular product or brand. Thus, consumers may be asked about problems associated with using their lawn mower or their popcorn popper. Curlee Clothing used focus groups to analyze the purchase and

Exhibit 14–4 Results of a Problem Inventory Analysis about Food Products

1. The package of ____ doesn't fit well on the shelf.

Cereal	49%
Flour	6

2. My husband/children refuse to eat ____.

Liver	18%
Vegetables	5
Spinach	4

3. ____ doesn't quench my thirst.

Soft drinks	58%
Milk	9
Coffee	6

4. Packaged ____ doesn't dissolve fast enough.

Jello/gelatin	32%
Bouillon cubes	8
Pudding	5

5. Everyone always wants different ____.

Vegetables	23%
Cereal	11
Meat	10
Desserts	9

6. ____ makes a mess in the oven.

Broiling steaks	19%
Pie	17
Roast/pork/rib	8

7. Packaged ____ tastes artificial.

Instant potatoes	12%
Macaroni and cheese	4

8. It's difficult to get ____ to pour easily.

Catsup	16%
Syrup	13
Gallon of milk	11

9. Packaged ____ looks unappetizing.

Hamburger Helper	6%
Lunch meat	3
Liver	3

10. I wish my husband/children could take ____ in a carried lunch.

Hot meal	11%
Soup	9
Ice cream	4

Source: E. Tauber, "Discovering New Product Opportunities with Problem Inventory Analysis," *Journal of Marketing* (Chicago: American Marketing Association, January 1975), p. 70.

use of men's fashion clothing. The results indicated a high level of insecurity in purchasing men's clothing. This insecurity was combined with a distrust of both the motivations and competence of retail sales personnel. As a result, Curlee initiated a major effort to train retail sales personnel through specially prepared films and training sessions.

Problem Analysis. *Problem analysis* takes the opposite approach from the previous techniques. It starts with a list of problems and asks the respondent to indicate which activities, products, or brands are associated with those problems. Exhibit 14–4 illustrates the results of one study using this approach.

Exhibit 14–5 Defining Consumer Needs with Human Factors Research Findings

An example of problem identification and solution using human factors information concerns the physical capabilities of infants to feed themselves. To better understand this problem, an anthropometric survey was conducted on a sample of infants in a defined age-group to determine the maximum container diameter which could be easily grasped and the most desirable lip design. To confirm this information, slow-motion pictures were made of infants feeding themselves with prototype products (such as the one shown below) while mothers were preparing and serving baby food in their homes. The product that resulted and the benefits it provides in solving this problem are outlined below.

Adjusta-Flo Training Tumbler

- Locking cap won't come off when dropped.
- Prevents spills because the Tumbler is designed to roll when dropped so holes are at the top when it stops.
- Metered flow control adjusts to baby's drinking capabilities.
- Specially designed lip aids baby's natural transition from sucking to drinking, and allows baby to drink without tilting head back.

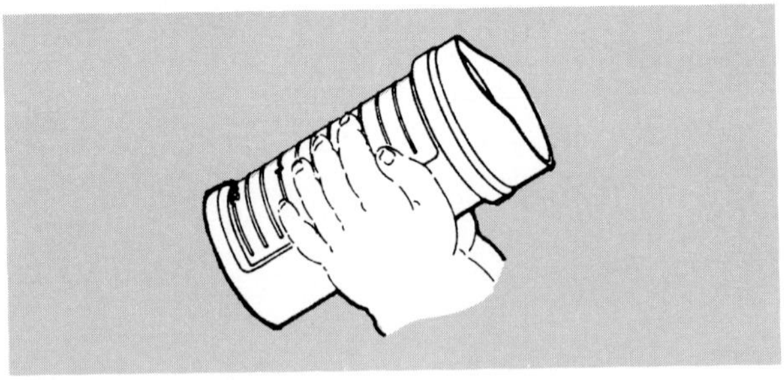

Source: T. Cannon and R. Hasty, "Identifying Consumer Needs Using Human Factors and Market Research Techniques," *Advances in Consumer Research V,* ed. E. K. Hunt (Chicago: Association for Consumer Research, 1978), pp. 494–98.

Human Factors Research. While many methods can be employed in human factors research, observational techniques such as slow-motion and time-lapse photography, video recording, and event recorders are particularly useful to marketers. Human factors research attempts to determine human capabilities in areas such as vision, strength, response time, flexibility, and fatigue and the effect on these capabilities of lighting, temperature, and sound. Exhibit 14–5 illustrates how this type of research was used to develop an improved beverage container for infants.

Reacting to Problem Recognition

Once a consumer problem is identified, the manager may structure the marketing mix to solve the problem. This can involve product development or alteration, modifying channels of distribution, changing pricing policy, or revising advertising strategy. For example, many people must minimize their salt intake. Most of these individuals are aware of the problem (minimizing salt intake) but are not aware of the products that can assist with this process. Tums utilizes the following advertising copy to show how its product can help:

> **GET A LOT OF RELIEF FROM HEARTBURN WITHOUT A LOT OF SODIUM**
>
> When you get a touch of heartburn and you've got to watch your salt (sodium) intake, get relief with Tums.
>
> Tums has only a trace of sodium—less than 3 milligrams per tablet. A lot less than many other antacids. (You should always read the labels.)

As you approach graduation, you will be presented with opportunities to purchase insurance, acquire credit cards, and solve other problems associated with the onset of financial independence and a major change in lifestyle. These opportunities, which will be presented through both personal sales contacts and advertising media, reflect various firms' knowledge that many individuals in your situation face problems that their products will help solve.

Weekend and night store hours are a response of retailers to the consumer problem of limited weekday shopping opportunities. Solving this problem has become particularly important to families with both spouses employed.

The examples described above represent only a small sample of the ways in which marketers react to consumer problem recognition. Basically, each firm must be aware of the consumer problems it can solve, which consumers have these problems, and the situations in which the problems arise.

Activating Problem Recognition

There are occasions when the manager will want to influence problem recognition rather than react to it. In the earlier example (Exhibit 14–1) involving the fire starters, Timberlane faced having to activate problem recognition in order to sell its product as a fireplace starter. Toy marketers are attempting to reduce their

Exhibit 14–6 An Attempt to Influence Generic Problem Recognition

BETA CAROTENE. JUST ANOTHER HEALTH FAD? OR DOES IT HELP REDUCE CANCER RISK?
You have probably been reading or hearing about a natural food substance called Beta Carotene. Newspapers, such as The New York Times and U.S.A. Today have been reporting on research findings published in leading professional publications on the association between Beta Carotene in the diet and lower incidence of certain cancers.
For example, The New England Journal of Medicine* recently published a study done at Johns Hopkins University which showed a significantly lower occurrence of lung cancer in a group of people who had high blood levels of Beta Carotene. Based on these findings, it makes sense to eat foods rich in Beta Carotene. In fact, that is one of the recommendations made by the National Cancer Institute and the American Cancer Society.
Where can you find Beta Carotene? In dark green leafy vegetables like broccoli, spinach, kale, Swiss chard and greens from beets, collards and turnips. Also in yellow-orange vegetables like carrots, pumpkins, sweet potatoes. And fruits like apricots, peaches, papayas, cantaloupe and similar melons.
Including these foods in your diet isn't just another fad, it's a sound idea for anyone who is looking for ways to help reduce cancer risk. Remember, in addition to including plenty of fruits and vegetables in your diet, don't smoke and get regular medical check-ups.
*"Serum Beta-Carotene, Vitamins A and E, Selenium and the Risk of Lung Cancer" New England Journal of Medicine, Nov. 13, 1986.
A health message from Hoffmann-LaRoche Inc.
ROCHE

Courtesy Hoffman-LaRoche Inc.

dependence on the Christmas season by activating problem recognition at other times of the year. For example, Fisher-Price has had "rainy day" and "sunny day" promotions in the spring and summer months.[14]

Generic versus Selective Problem Recognition. Two basic approaches to causing problem recognition are *generic problem recognition* and *selective problem recognition*. These are analogous to the economic concepts of generic and selective demand. Generic problem recognition involves a *discrepancy that a variety of brands within a product category can reduce*.

Generally, a firm will attempt to influence generic problem recognition when the problem is latent or of low importance and:

1. It is early in the product life cycle.
2. The firm has a very high percentage of the market.
3. External search after problem recognition is apt to be limited.
4. It is an industrywide cooperative effort.

Consider the advertising copy in Exhibit 14–6. This ad by Hoffman-LaRoche, Inc., attempts to generate generic problem recognition by increasing consumer recognition of the value of beta carotene as a color and nutrient in food products. As a major supplier of beta carotene supplement, Hoffman-LaRoche will benefit from increased demand for this product category.

Door-to-door sales for such products as encyclopedias and vacuum cleaners attempt to arouse problem recognition, in part because the salesperson can then limit external search to one brand. Cooperative advertising ("I heard it through the grapevine") frequently focuses on generic problem recognition. Likewise, virtual monopolies such as U.S. Tobacco in the moist snuff industry (Skoal, Copenhagen, Happy Days) can focus on generic problem recognition since any sales increase will probably come to their brands. However, a smaller firm that generates generic problem recognition for its product category may be generating more sales for its competitors than for itself.

Exhibit 14–7 illustrates an attempt to influence selective problem recognition. Notice that the advertisement focuses heavily on Allstate and how Allstate may cost less for the same coverage (desired state) than your existing insurance (actual state). Firms attempt to cause selective problem recognition to gain or maintain market share, while generic problem recognition generally results in an expansion of the total market.

Approaches to Activating Problem Recognition. How can a firm influence problem recognition? Recall that problem recognition is a function of the (1) *importance* and (2) *magnitude* of a discrepancy between a desired state and an existing state. Thus, the firm can attempt to influence the size of the discrepancy by altering the desired state or the perceptions of the existing state. Or, the firm can attempt to influence the perception of the importance of an existing discrepancy.

Exhibit 14–7 An Attempt to Influence Selective Problem Recognition

Allstate challenges you to compare.

Bring in your homeowners policy and compare with Allstate. We just might save you some money.

① Just bring in your present homeowners policy to any Allstate office or Allstate booth in Sears.

② Give it to the Allstate agent who will compare your homeowners policy with Allstate's.

③ Chances are, we just might save you some money. For home protection, you're in good hands with Allstate.

Allstate®
You're in good hands.

Used with permission from Allstate Insurance Company.

There is evidence that both individuals and product categories differ in their responsiveness to attempts to change desired or perceived existing states.[15] Thus, marketers must be sure that the selected approach is appropriate for their product category and target market.

Influence desired state. Most marketing efforts attempt to influence the desired state. Many new consumer products are developed in response to changes in consumers' desired states. In recent years, clinical evidence has convinced many people that protection from the damaging aspects of the sun's rays is important. However, most sunscreen products contain oils which are harmful to some skin types. Exhibit 14–8 illustrates Eclipse Laboratories' solution to this problem.

Influence perceptions of existing state. It is also possible to influence perceptions of the existing state through advertisements. Many personal care and

Exhibit 14–8 An Attempt to Indicate that a Brand Will Provide a Desired State

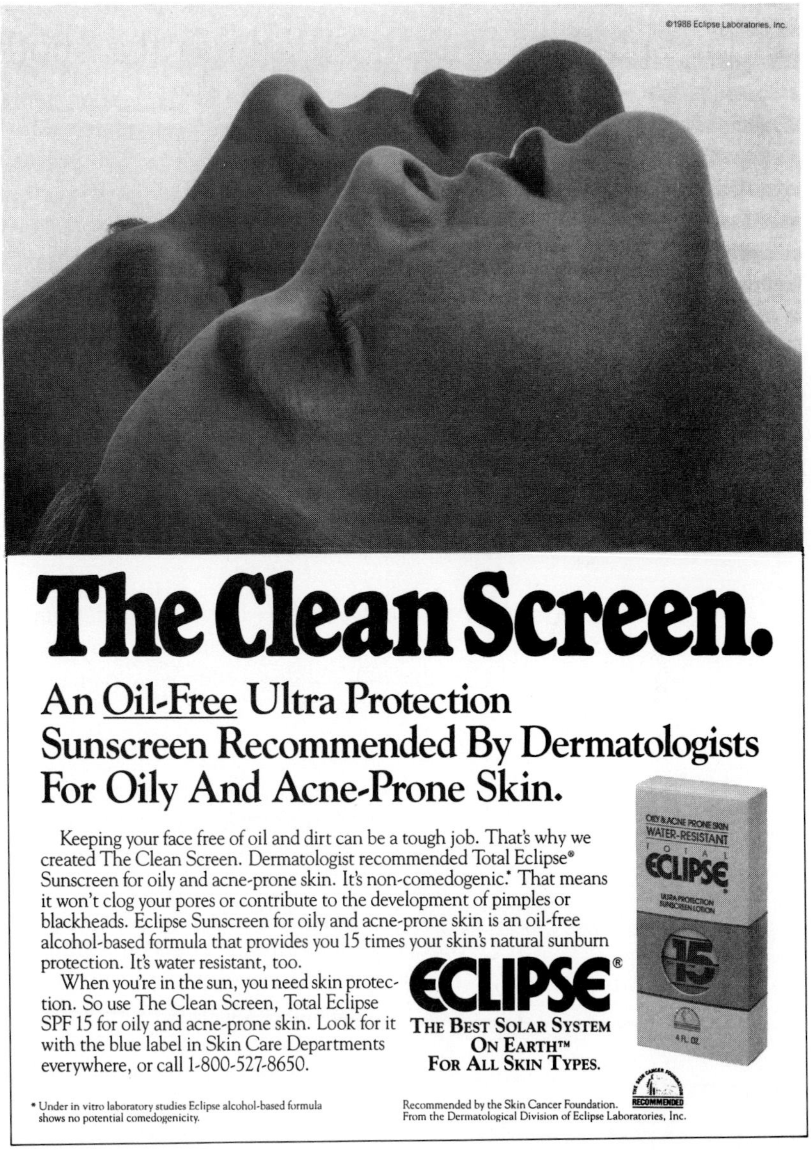

Courtesy Eclipse Laboratories, Inc.

social products take this approach. "Even your best friend won't tell you . . ." or "Mary is a great worker but her coffee . . ." are examples of messages designed to generate concern about an existing state. The desired state is assumed to be fresh breath and good coffee. These messages are designed to cause individuals to question if their existing state coincides with this desired state.

Attempts by firms to "break into" habitual or limited decision making when their brand is not currently used generally focus on the existing state. For example, the annual renewal of homeowner's insurance is a habitual decision for most consumers. Notice how the Allstate ad directly challenges the homeowner to engage in more extensive decision making. It suggests that the existing state for most individuals not insured by Allstate is excessive cost.

Influence importance of discrepancy. The final approach to influencing problem recognition is to change the importance associated with an existing discrepancy. The American Cancer Society devotes considerable effort toward persuading smokers (most of whom express a desire to quit—problem recognition) that it is important to quit immediately. Likewise, many Americans express a desire to conserve energy. Yet, in many cases, this desire is not strong enough to influence important consumption decisions such as the use of public transportation versus a private automobile. Exhibit 14–9 illustrates how the American Dental Association is attempting to increase the importance associated with preventive dentistry.

Exhibit 14–9

American Dental Association's Attempt to Generate Problem Recognition

SITUATION

Surveys have shown that many Americans are delaying regular dental checkups or needed dental work because of tight finances. Many dentists, particularly young ones, are dissatisfied with their low patient load.

ACTION

The American Dental Association will spend over $2 million in a magazine effort to increase the perceived importance of preventive dentistry. One print ad will feature a beaming woman's face with this copy:

> It doesn't come in a jar or tube. And it lasts more than a few hours, in fact, for a lifetime. It's the special confident feeling you have only with regular dental checkups and cleanings. If you've let it slip for a while, even for years, you can still get it back by resuming regular visits. Remember, it takes just a few hours of your time and it probably costs less than what you paid for the cosmetics in your bag right now.

Source: "Dental Drive Drills Early Care," *Advertising Age*, December 31, 1979, p. 3.

The Timing of Problem Recognition. Consumers often recognize problems at times when purchasing a solution is difficult or impossible:

- We decide we need snow chains when caught in a blizzard.
- We become aware of a need for insurance *after* an accident.
- We desire a flower bed full of tulips in the spring but forgot to plant bulbs in the fall.
- We want cold medicine when we are sick and don't feel like driving to the store.

In some instances, marketers attempt to help consumers solve such problems after they arise. For example, some pharmacies will make home deliveries. However, the more common strategy is to trigger problem recognition in advance of the actual problem. That is, it is often to the consumer's and the marketer's advantage for the consumer to recognize and solve potential problems *before* they become actual problems.

While some companies, particularly insurance companies, attempt to initiate potential problem recognition through mass media advertising, others rely more on point-of-purchase displays and other in-store influences (see Chapter 17). Retailers, as well as manufacturers, are involved in this activity. For example, prior to snow season, the following sign was placed on a large rack of snow shovels in the main aisle of a large hardware store:

> **REMEMBER LAST WINTER**
> **WHEN YOU *NEEDED***
> **A SNOW SHOVEL?**
> **THIS YEAR**
> **BE PREPARED!**

Suppressing Problem Recognition

As we have seen, competition, consumer organizations, and governmental agencies occasionally introduce information in the marketplace that triggers problem recognition that particular marketers would prefer to avoid.[16] The American tobacco industry has made strenuous attempts to minimize consumer recognition of the health problem associated with cigarette smoking. For example, a Newport cigarette advertisement shows a happy, laughing couple under the headline, "Alive with pleasure." This could easily be interpreted as an attempt to minimize any problem recognition caused by the mandatory warning at the bottom of the advertisement, "Warning: The Surgeon General has determined that cigarette smoking is dangerous to your health." Exhibit 14–10 contains an advertisement

Exhibit 14–10 An Advertisement Designed To Suppress a Perceived Problem

Courtesy Oregon Beef Council

designed to minimize problem recognition associated with beef consumption (similar ads are being run for pork).

Makers of brands with substantial habitual or limited decision purchases do not want their current customers to recognize problems with their brands. Effective quality control and distribution (limited out-of-stock situations) are important in these circumstances. Packages and package inserts that assure the consumer of the wisdom of the purchase are also common.

SUMMARY

Consumer decision making becomes more extensive and complex as purchase involvement increases. The lowest level of purchase involvement is represented by habitual decisions: a problem is recognized, long-term memory provides a single preferred brand, that brand is purchased, and only limited postpurchase evaluation occurs. As one moves from limited decision making toward extended decision making, information search increases, alternative evaluation becomes more extensive and complex, and postpurchase evaluation becomes more thorough.

Problem recognition involves the existence of a discrepancy between the consumer's desired state (what the consumer would like) and the actual state (what the consumer perceives as already existing). Both the desired state and the actual state are influenced by the consumer's lifestyle and current situation. If the discrepancy between these two states is sufficiently large and important, the consumer will begin to search for a solution to the problem.

A number of factors beyond the control of the marketing manager can affect problem recognition. The desired state is commonly influenced by:

1. Culture/social class.
2. Reference groups.
3. Family characteristics.
4. Financial status/expectations.
5. Previous decisions.
6. Individual development.
7. Motives
8. Current situations.

The actual state is influenced by:

1. Normal depletion.
2. Product/brand performance.
3. Individual development.
4. The efforts of consumer groups.
5. Past decisions.
6. Availability of products.
7. The situation.

Before marketing managers can respond to problem recognition generated by outside factors, they must be able to *measure* problem recognition. Surveys and focus groups using *activity, product,* or *problem analysis* are commonly used to measure problem recognition. *Human factors research* approaches the same task from an observational perspective.

Once managers are aware of problem recognition patterns among their target market, they can react by designing the marketing mix to solve the recognized problem. This may involve product development or repositioning, a change in store hours, a different price, or a host of other marketing strategies.

Marketing managers often want to influence problem recognition rather than react to it. They may desire to generate generic problem recognition, a discrepancy which a variety of brands within a product category can reduce; or to induce selective problem recognition, a discrepancy which only one brand in the product category can solve.

Attempts to activate problem recognition generally do so by focusing on the desired state. However, attempts to make consumers aware of negative aspects of the existing state are also common. In addition, marketers attempt to influence the timing of problem recognition by making consumers aware of potential problems before they arise.

Finally, managers attempt to minimize or suppress problem recognition by current users of their brands.

REVIEW QUESTIONS

1. What is meant by *purchase involvement?* How does it differ from product involvement?
2. What factors influence purchase involvement?
3. How does consumer decision making change as purchase involvement increases?
4. How do *habitual, limited,* and *extended decision making* differ? How do the two types of habitual decision making differ?
5. What is *problem recognition?*
6. What influences the motivation to resolve a recognized problem?
7. What is the difference between an *active* and an *inactive problem?* Why is this distinction important?
8. How does lifestyle relate to problem recognition?
9. What are the main uncontrollable factors that influence the *desired* state? Give an example of each.
10. What are the main uncontrollable factors that influence the *existing* state? Give an example of each.
11. How can you measure problem recognition?
12. In what ways can marketers react to problem recognition? Give several examples.
13. How does *generic problem recognition* differ from *selective problem recognition*? Under what conditions would a firm attempt to influence generic problem recognition? Why?
14. How can a firm influence problem recognition? Give examples.
15. How can a firm suppress problem recognition?

DISCUSSION QUESTIONS

1. What products do you think *generally* are associated with habitual, limited, and extended decision making? Under what conditions, if any, would these products be associated with a different form of decision making?

2. What products do you think *generally* are associated with brand loyal habitual decision making, and which with repeat purchase habitual decision making? Justify your response.
3. How would you measure problem recognition among:
   a. Aerobics participants?
   b. Newly married couples?
   c. New college graduates?
   d. Preschool children?
   e. Farmers?
4. What factors will contribute to problem recognition for you following graduation? How would each of these factors affect your lifestyle and cause changes in your desired state for products and services? Which products and services might you now view as less satisfactory, causing you to seek better solutions in the form of more personally satisfying products and services?
5. Discuss the types of products that resolve specific problems, which occur for most consumers at different stages of their household life cycle.
6. How would you activate problem recognition for:
   a. Compact disc players?
   b. Donations to United Way?
   c. Calvin Klein jeans?
   d. Scope mouthwash?
   e. Nonalcoholic beer?
7. How would you influence the timing of problem recognition for:
   a. Life insurance?
   b. Home insulation?
   c. Car tune-up?
   d. Toothbrush?
   e. Suntan lotion?

PROJECT QUESTIONS

1. Interview five other students and identify three consumer problems they have recognized. For each problem, determine:
   a. The relative importance of the problem.
   b. How the problem occurred.
   c. What caused the problem (i.e., change in desired or actual states).
   d. What action they have taken.
   e. What action is planned in order to resolve each problem.
2. Find and describe a newspaper or magazine advertisement that is attempting to activate problem recognition. Analyze the advertisement in terms of the type of problem and the action the ad is suggesting. Also, discuss any changes you would recommend to improve the effectiveness of the ad in terms of activating problem recognition.
3. Interview five other students and identify three recent instances when they engaged in habitual, limited, and extended decision making (a total of nine decisions). What specific factors appear to be associated with each type of decision?

4. Interview five other students and identify six products that each buys using a habitual decision process. Also, identify those that are based on brand loyalty and those that are merely repeat purchases. What characteristics, if any, distinguish the brand loyal products from the repeat purchase products.
5. Find and describe two advertisements or point-of-purchase displays that attempt to influence the timing of problem recognition. Evaluate their likely effectiveness.
6. Using a sample from a relevant market segment, conduct an activity analysis for an activity that interests you. Prepare a report on the marketing opportunities suggested by your analysis.
7. Using a sample from a relevant market segment, conduct a product analysis for a product that interests you. Prepare a report on the marketing opportunities suggested by your analysis.
8. Conduct a problem analysis using a sample of college freshmen. Prepare a report on the marketing opportunities suggested by your analysis.
9. Interview five smokers and ascertain what problems they see associated with smoking.
10. Interview someone from the local office of the American Cancer Society concerning their attempts to generate problem recognition among smokers.

REFERENCES

[1] L. A. Fanelli, "Polaroid Shows, but Can It Tell (and Sell)?" *Advertising Age,* June 6, 1981, pp. 3, 86; and M. C. Lynch, "Selling New Polaroid 600 Line May Require Teaching Camera Users Why They Need It," *The Wall Street Journal,* June 29, 1981.

[2] Based on A. A. Mitchell, "Involvement: A Potentially Important Mediator of Consumer Behavior," in *Advances in Consumer Research VI,* ed. W. L. Wilkie (Chicago: Association for Consumer Research, 1979), pp. 191–96. See also M. L. Ray, "Involvement and Other Variables Mediating Communication Effects as Opposed to Explaining All Consumer Behavior," in *Advances,* ed. Wilkie, pp. 197–99; J. A. Muney and S. D. Hunt, "Consumer Involvement"; P. H. Bloch and G. D. Bruce, "Product Involvement as Leisure Behavior"; J. H. Antil, "Conceptualization and Operationalization of Involvement"; and R. N. Stone, "The Marketing Characteristics of Involvement," all in *Advances in Consumer Research XIV,* ed. T. C. Kinnear (Chicago: Association for Consumer Research, 1984), pp. 193–96, 197–202, 203–9, and 210–15; and G. Laurent and J. Kapferer, "Measuring Consumer Involvement Profiles," *Journal of Marketing Research,* February 1985, pp. 41–53.

[3] Based on H. H. Kassarjian, "Low Involvement: A Second Look," in *Advances in Consumer Research VIII,* ed. K. B. Monroe (Chicago: Association for Consumer Research, 1981), pp. 31–33; Antil, ibid; and M. E. Slama and A. Tashchian, "Selected Socioeconomic and Demographic Characteristics Associated with Purchasing Involvement," *Journal of Marketing,* Winter 1985, pp. 72–82.

[4] J. Jacoby and D. B. Kyner, "Brand Loyalty versus Repeat Purchasing Behavior," *Journal of Marketing Research,* February 1973, pp. 1–9.

[5] R. W. Olshavsky and D. H. Granbois, "Consumer Decision Making—Fact or Fiction," *Journal of Consumer Research,* September 1979, pp. 93–100; and M. Ursic, "Consumer Decision Making—Fact or Fiction? Comment," and R. W. Olshavsky and D. H. Granbois, "Rejoinder," *Journal of Consumer Research,* December 1980, pp. 331–34.

[6] W. D. Hoger, "An Examination of Consumer Decision Making for a Common Repeat Purchase Product," *Journal of Consumer Research,* December 1984, pp. 822–29.

[7] For a more thorough treatment, see G. C. Bruner II, "Recent Contributions to the Theory of Problem Recognition," in *1985 AMA Educator's Proceedings,* ed. R. F. Lusch et al. (Chicago: American Marketing Association, 1985), pp. 11–15; and G. C. Bruner II and R. J. Pomazal, "Problem Recognition: The Crucial First Stage of the Consumer Decision Process," *Journal of Consumer Marketing,* forthcoming.

[8] J. W. Levedahl, "The Impact of Permanent and Transitory Income on Household and Automobile Expenditure," *Journal of Consumer Research,* June 1980, pp. 55–66.

[9] S. W. McDaniel, C. P. Rao, and R. W. Jackson, "Inflation-Induced Adaptive Behavior," *Psychology & Marketing,* Summer 1986, pp. 113–22.

[10] "Dental Drive Drills Early Care," *Advertising Age,* December 31, 1979, p. 3.

[11] G. C. Brunner II, *Problem Recognition in the Homeostatic Process of Consumer Decision Making* (North Texas State, unpublished doctoral dissertation, 1984).

[12] "L'Eggs Success Grows from Rumpled Bit of Cloth," *Marketing News,* December 29, 1978, p. 9.

[13] "Key Role of Research in Agree's Success Is Told," *Marketing News,* January 17, 1979, p. 14.

[14] J. P. Forkan, "Toy Marketers Eye More than One Season," *Advertising Age,* March 31, 1980, p. 71.

[15] Bruner and Pomazal, "Problem Recognition"; and G. C. Bruner II, "The Effect of Problem Recognition Style on Information Seeking," *Journal of the Academy of Marketing Science,* Winter 1987, pp. 33–41.

[16] See M. G. Weinberger and W. R. Dillon, "The Effects of Unfavorable Product Rating Information," in *Advances in Consumer Research VII,* ed. J. C. Olson (Chicago: Association for Consumer Research, 1980), pp. 528–32; M. Weinberger, C. T. Allen, and W. R. Dillon, "Negative Information: Perspectives and Research Directions," and C. A. Scott and A. M. Tybout, "Theoretical Perspectives on Corrective Advertising Effects," both in *Advances in Consumer Research VIII,* ed. Monroe, pp. 398–404 and 408–9; and A. M. Tybout, B. J. Calder, and B. Sternthal, "Using Information Processing Theory to Design Marketing Strategies," *Journal of Marketing Research,* February 1981, pp. 73–79.

CHAPTER

15 Information Search

In 1986 Burroughs Wellcome had a superior prescription drug treatment for herpes. However, it faced two major problems. First, most consumers knew that there was no cure for the disease and therefore believed that there was no treatment which would control or minimize the symptoms. Thus, individuals suffering from this affliction often did not seek treatment or information about potential treatments. Second, any advertisement using a specific drug name or the word *medication* would result in the FDA requiring full disclosure of all side effects, risks, and benefits in each ad. Most industry participants are convinced that the lengthy information required by the FDA would frighten and/or confuse consumers, as well as substantially increase the cost of the campaign.

To overcome these problems, Burroughs Wellcome ran an advertising campaign in 12 national magazines, such as *Cosmopolitan, Rolling Stone, Time,* and *TV Guide,* in which neither the product, the brand name, nor the word *medication* is mentioned. The ad shows a couple in their early thirties on the beach, a scene situated under a headline that says, "The hardest thing she ever had to do was tell Roger she had herpes. But thanks to her doctor, she could also tell him it's controllable." The copy goes on to explain that within the past year the medical community has gained "more information than ever before about the treatment of herpes." The campaign is tagged "See your doctor . . . there is help for herpes."

Thus, the purpose of the campaign was not to provide product or brand information. Rather, it sought to initiate and guide the search process. Given the nature of its product, the firm was confident that doctors would prescribe its brand if patients sought their advice.[1]

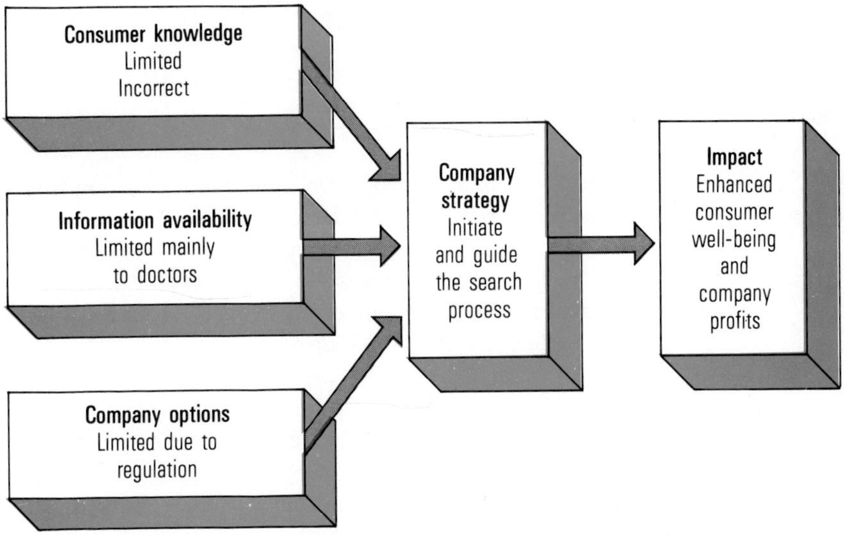

Through the marketing efforts described, the public's understanding of herpes increased, as did sales of Burroughs Wellcome's herpes treatment drug. The underlying reason for this success was recognition that many consumers would not seek out information from doctors about herpes. Once this was understood, the management was able to develop a promotional campaign based on the target market's pattern of information search.

Consumers continually recognize problems and opportunities, so internal and external searches for information to solve these problems are ongoing processes. Searching for information is not free. Information search involves mental as well as physical activities that consumers must perform. It takes time, energy, money, and can often require giving up more desirable activities.

The benefits of information search, however, often outweigh the cost of search. For example, search may produce a lower price, a preferred style of merchandise, a higher quality product, a reduction in perceived risk, or greater confidence in the choice. In addition, the physical and mental processes involved in information search are, on occasion, rewarding in themselves. Finally, we must keep in mind that consumers acquire a substantial amount of relevant information without deliberate search through low-involvement learning (Chapter 9).

This chapter examines seven questions related to information search:

1. What is the nature of information search?
2. What types of information are sought?
3. What sources of information are used?
4. How extensive is external information search?
5. Why do consumers engage in external search?

6. What conditions affect the level of external information search?
7. What marketing strategies can be developed based on patterns of search behavior?

NATURE OF INFORMATION SEARCH

Once a problem is recognized, relevant information from long-term memory is used to determine if a satisfactory solution is known, what the characteristics of potential solutions are, what are appropriate ways to compare solutions, and so forth. This is *internal search.* If a resolution is not reached through internal search, then the search process is focused on external stimuli relevant to solving the problem. This is *external search.*

A great many problems are resolved by the consumer using only previously stored information. If, in response to a problem, a consumer recalls a single, satisfactory solution (brand or store), no further information search or evaluation may occur. The consumer purchases the recalled brand and *habitual decision making* has occurred. For example, a consumer who catches a cold may recall that Dristan nasal spray provided relief in the past. Dristan then is purchased at the nearest store without further information search or evaluation.

Likewise, a consumer may notice a new product in a store because of the attention-attracting power of a point-of-purchase display. He or she reads about the attributes of the product and recalls an unresolved problem that these attributes would resolve. The purchase is made without seeking additional information. This represents *limited decision making* involving mainly internal information.

Had the consumer in the example above looked for other brands that would perform the same task or looked at another store for a lower price, we would have an example of limited decision making using both internal and external information. As we move into more *extended decision making,* the relative importance of external information search tends to increase. However, even in extended decision making, internal information often provides some or all of the appropriate alternatives, evaluative criteria, and characteristics of various alternatives. The nature of this shift from internal to external search is shown in Figure 15–1.

External information can include:

- The opinions, attitudes, and feelings of friends, neighbors, and relatives.
- Professional information provided in pamphlets, articles, and books.
- Direct experiences with the product through inspection or trial.
- Marketer-generated information presented in advertisements and displays and by sales personnel.

Deliberate external search (as opposed to low-involvement learning) also occurs in the absence of problem recognition.[2] Ongoing or exploratory search is done both to acquire information for later use and because the process itself is pleasurable. For example, individuals highly involved with a product category such as tennis equipment are apt to seek information about tennis-related products

Figure 15–1
Type of Decision and Nature of Information Search

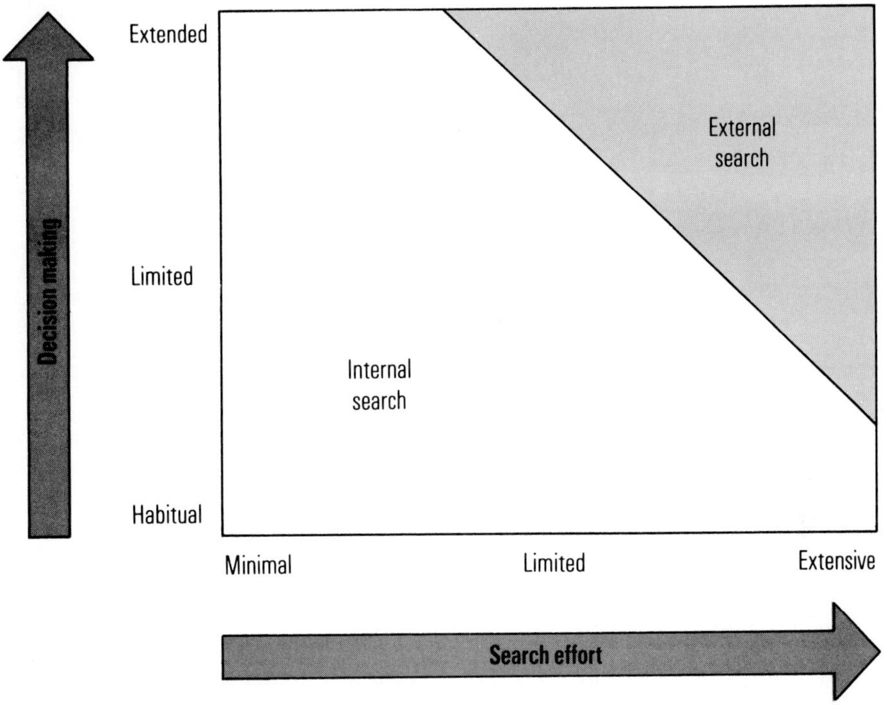

on an ongoing basis without a recognized problem with his or her existing tennis equipment. This search could involve reading ads in tennis magazines, visiting tennis equipment shops, observing professionals on television, and/or talking with and observing fellow players and local professionals. These activities would provide the individual both pleasure and information for future use.

Like search triggered by problem recognition, ongoing search is a function of individual, product, market, and situational factors. The outcome of search includes increased product and market knowledge leading to future buying efficiencies and enhanced personal influence, increased unplanned purchases, and personal satisfaction or pleasure.[3]

TYPES OF INFORMATION SOUGHT

A consumer decision requires information on the following:

- The appropriate evaluative criteria for the solution of a problem.
- The existence of various alternative solutions.
- The performance level or characteristic of each alternative solution on each evaluative criterion.

Figure 15–2
Information Search in Consumer Decisions

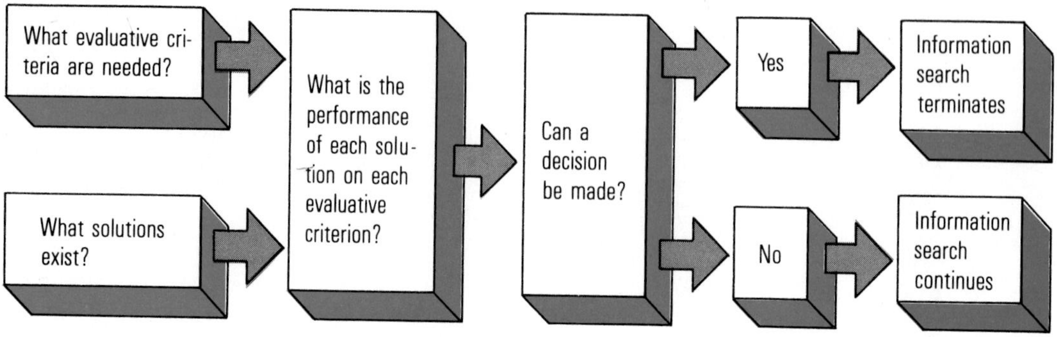

Information search, then, seeks each of these three types of information, as shown in Figure 15–2.

Evaluative Criteria

Suppose you are provided with money to purchase a personal computer, perhaps as a graduation present. Assuming you have not been in the market for a computer recently, your first thought would probably be: "What features do I want in a computer?" You would then engage in internal search to determine the features or characteristics required to meet your needs. These desired characteristics are your *evaluative criteria.* If you have had limited experience with home computers, you might also engage in external search to learn which characteristics a good computer should have. You could check with friends, read *Consumer Reports,* talk with sales personnel, or personally inspect several computers. Thus, one potential objective of both internal and external search is *the determination of appropriate evaluative criteria.*[4] A detailed discussion of evaluative criteria appears in the next chapter.

Appropriate Alternatives

After (and while) searching for appropriate evaluative criteria, you would probably seek *appropriate alternatives*—in this case brands or, possibly, stores. Again, you would start with an internal search. You might say to yourself:

> IBM, Compaq, Leading Edge, Apple, Commodore, Radio Shack, AST, and HP all make personal computers. After my brother's experience, I'd never buy Radio Shack. I've heard good things about IBM, Apple, and Compaq. I think I'll check them out.

The eight brands that you thought of are known as the *awareness set*. The awareness set is composed of three subcategories of considerable importance to marketers. The three brands that you have decided to investigate are known as the *evoked set*. An evoked set is those brands one will consider for the solution of a particular consumer problem. If you do not have an evoked set for home computers, or lack confidence that your evoked set is adequate, you would probably engage in external search to learn about additional alternatives. You may also learn about additional acceptable brands as an incidental aspect of moving through the decision process. Thus, an important outcome of information search is the development of a complete evoked set.

If you are initially satisfied with the evoked set, information search will be focused on the performance of the brands in the evoked set on the evaluative criteria. Thus, the evoked set is of particular importance in structuring subsequent information search.[5] This is illustrated by a study showing that a brand of paper towel not mentioned as one of the three a person would consider buying (one measure of evoked set) had a purchase probability of less than 1 percent![6]

The brand you found completely unworthy of further consideration is a member of what is called the *inept set*. Brands in the inept set are actively disliked by the consumer. Positive information about these brands is not likely to be processed even if it is readily available.

In our example, AST, Leading Edge, Commodore, and HP were brands of which you were aware but were basically indifferent toward. They compose what is known as an *inert set*. Consumers will generally accept favorable information about brands in the inert set, although they do not seek out such information. Brands in this set are generally acceptable when preferred brands are not available. Thus, the eight brands in the initial awareness set can be subdivided as follows:

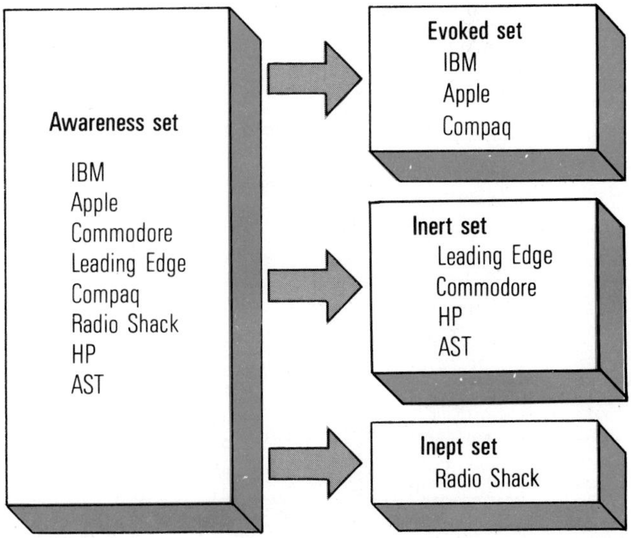

Figure 15–3 illustrates the general relationships among these classes of alternatives.[7]

Figure 15–4 illustrates the size of the awareness, evoked, inert, and inept sets of one group of consumers for three product categories. Notice that in all cases the evoked set is substantially smaller than the awareness set.[8] Since the evoked set generally is the one from which consumers make final evaluations and decisions, marketing strategy that focuses only on creating awareness may be inadequate.

Figure 15–3
Categories of Decision Alternatives

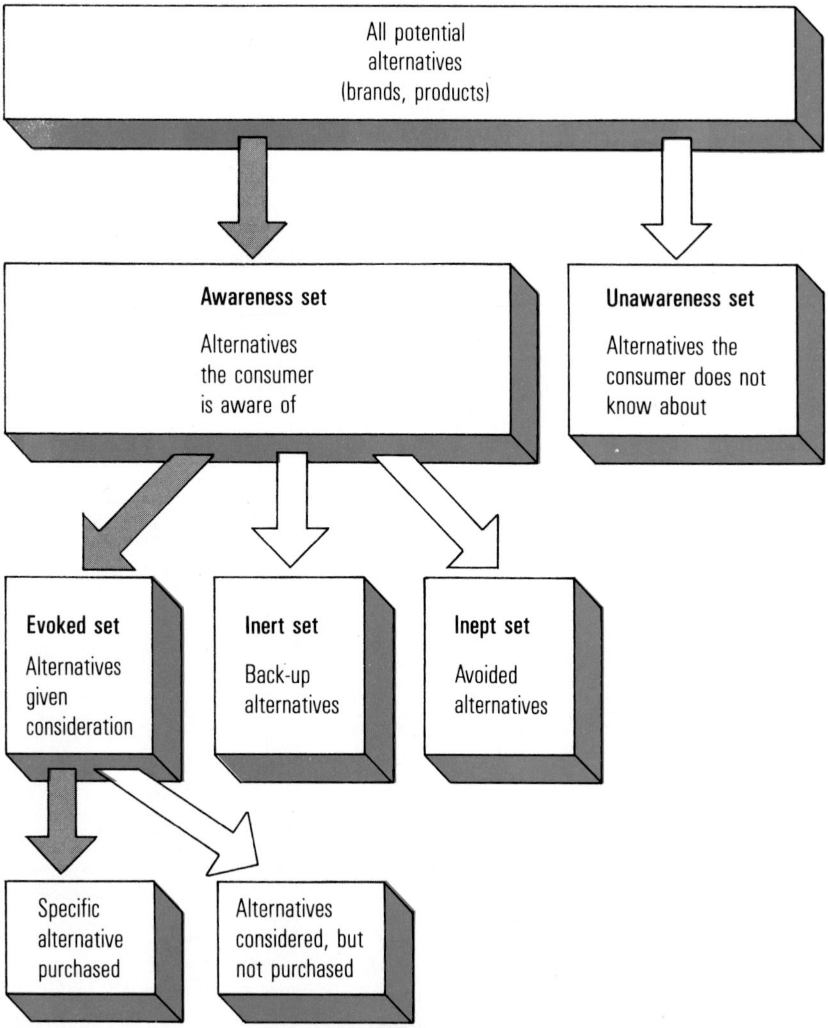

Figure 15–4
Awareness, Evoked, Inert, and Inept Brand Sets for Three Products

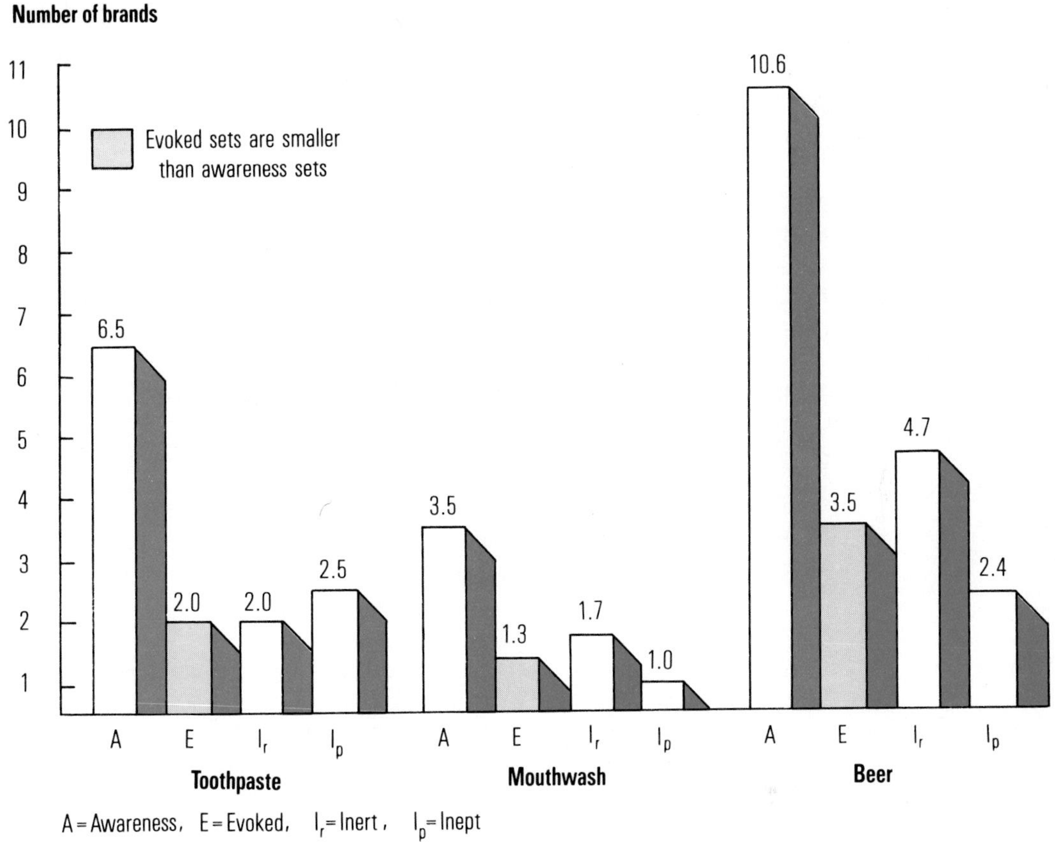

Source: C. Narayana and R. Markin, "Consumer Behavior and Product Performance: An Alternative Conceptualization," *Journal of Marketing*, October 1975, p. 4.

Alternative Characteristics

To choose among the brands in the evoked set, the consumer compares them on the relevant evaluative criteria. This process requires the consumer to gather information about *each brand on each pertinent evaluative criterion*. In our example of a computer purchase, you might collect information on the price, memory, availability of software, ease of programming, and ability to expand memory for each brand you are considering.

In summary, consumers engage in internal and external search for (1) appropriate evaluative criteria, (2) the existence of potential solutions, and (3) the characteristics of potential solutions. However, extensive search generally occurs for only a few consumption decisions. Habitual and limited decision making which involve little or no active external search are the rule. In addition, consumers acquire substantial information without deliberate search through low-involvement learning.

SOURCES OF INFORMATION

Refer again to our rather pleasant example of receiving cash with which to purchase a personal computer. We suggested that you might recall what you know about computers, check with friends, consult *Consumer Reports,* talk with sales personnel, or personally inspect several computers to collect relevant information. These represent the five primary sources of information available to consumers:

1. *Memory* of past searches, personal experiences, and low-involvement learning.
2. *Personal sources,* such as friends and family.
3. *Independent sources,* such as consumer groups and government agencies.
4. *Marketing sources,* such as sales personnel and advertising.
5. *Experiential sources,* such as inspection or product trial.

These sources are shown in Figure 15–5.

Internal information is the primary source used by most consumers most of the time (habitual and limited decision making).[9] However, note that information in long-term memory was *initially* obtained from external sources. That is, you may resolve a consumption problem using only or mainly stored information. At some point, however, you acquired that information from an external source, such as direct product experience, friends, or low-involvement learning.

Marketing-originated messages are only one of five potential information sources and they are frequently found to be of limited direct value in consumer decisions (see Figure 6–1).[10] However, marketing activities influence all five sources. Thus, the characteristics of the product, the distribution of the product, and the promotional messages about the product provide the underlying or basic information available in the market. An independent source such as *Consumer Reports* bases its report on the functional characteristics of the product. Personal sources such as friends also must base their information on experience with the product or its promotion (or on other sources that have had contact with the product or its promotion).

A substantial amount of marketing activity is designed to influence the information consumers will receive from nonmarketing sources. For example, when Johnson & Johnson introduced a new formula baby bath:

> Product information, demonstrations, monographs, journal ads, and direct-mail programs were targeted at pediatricians and nurses to capitalize on health-care professionals' direct contact with new mothers. Print ads and

Figure 15–5
Information Sources for a Purchase Decision

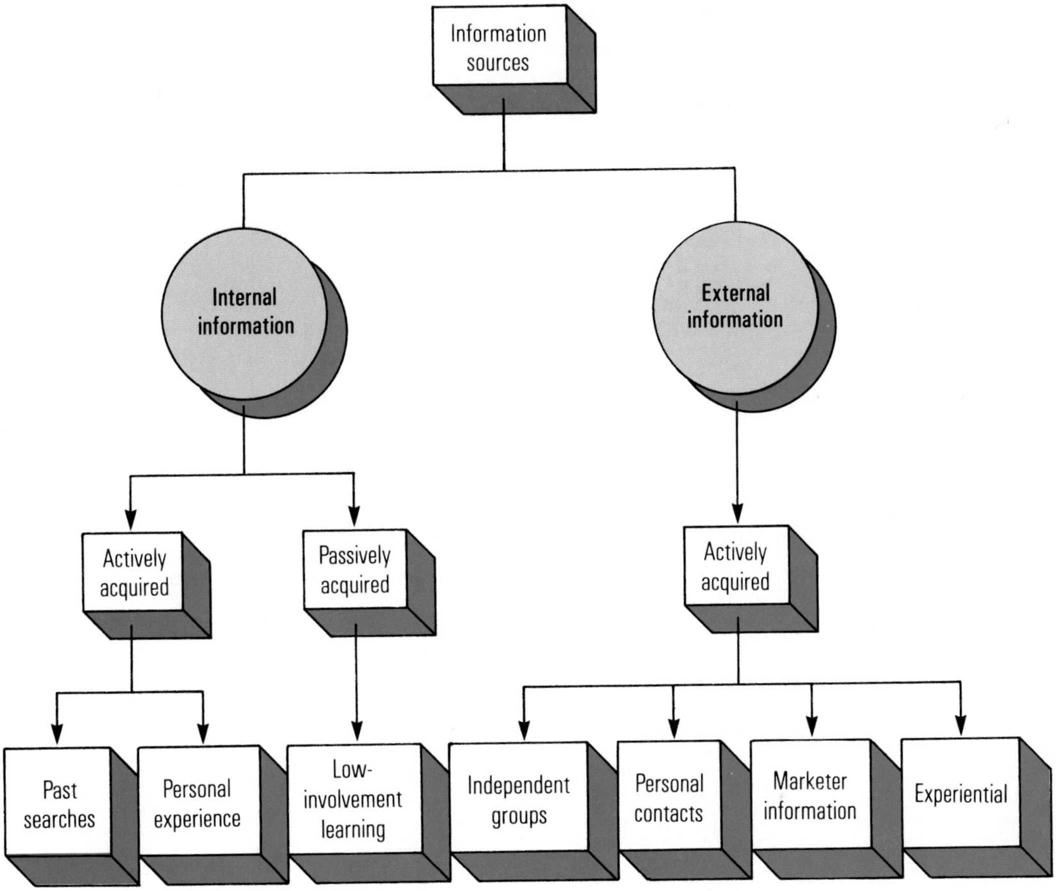

Source: Adapted from H. Beales, M. B. Jagis, S. C. Salop, and R. Staelin, "Consumer Search and Public Policy," *Journal Consumer Research*, June 1981, p. 12.

coupons appeared in baby care publications, and a film exploring the parent-infant bonding process was distributed to teaching centers, hospitals, and medical schools.

AMOUNT OF EXTERNAL INFORMATION SEARCH

Marketing managers are particularly interested in external information search, as this provides them with direct access to the consumer. How much external information search do consumers actually undertake? Most purchases are a result of habitual or limited decision making and therefore involve little or no external search immediately prior to purchase. This is particularly true for relatively low-priced convenience goods such as soft drinks, canned foods, and detergents. Therefore, the discussion in this section focuses on major purchases such as appliances, professional services, and automobiles. Intuitively, we would expect substantial amounts of direct external search prior to such purchases.

Three different measures of external information search have been used:

1. Number of stores visited.
2. Number of alternatives considered.
3. Overall or combination measures.

Each of these measures of search effort assesses a different aspect of behavior, yet each measure supports one observation: *external information search is skewed toward limited search, with the greatest proportion of consumers performing little external search immediately prior to purchase.*

Number of Stores Visited

The number of stores visited is a frequently used measure of external search. Surveys of shopping behavior have shown a significant percent of all durable

Figure 15–6
Number of Stores Visited prior to Purchase of a Major Appliance

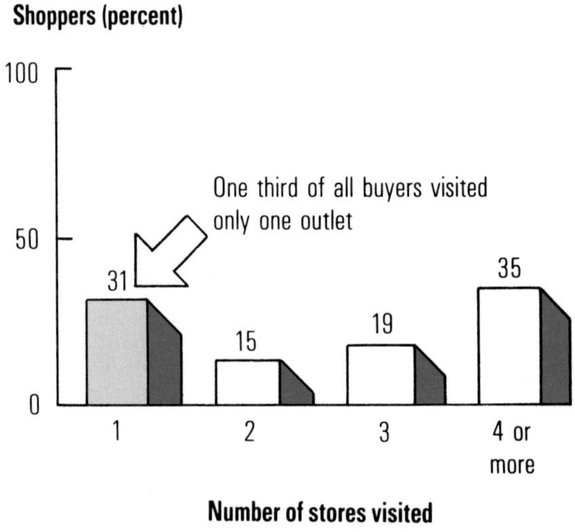

Source: R. A. Westbrook and C. Farnell, "Patterns of Information Source Usage among Durable Goods Buyers," *Journal of Marketing Research,* August 1979, pp. 303–12.

purchases are made after visiting only one store. For example, one-stop shoppers account for approximately 60 percent of the purchases of new automobiles; 60 to 80 percent of the purchases of various items of apparel and small appliances; and 85 to 90 percent of the purchases of cookware, towels, sheets, and toys.[11] Figure 15–6 illustrates the retail store shopping pattern used by purchasers of major appliances (refrigerators, freezers, washing machines, clothes dryers, range/ovens, and dishwashers).

Number of Alternatives Considered

Another approach to evaluating information search is to examine the number of alternatives considered prior to purchase. Like the previous measure of search behavior, the number of alternatives considered also shows a limited amount of

Figure 15–7
Percent of Purchasers Who Compare Brands or Models before Buying

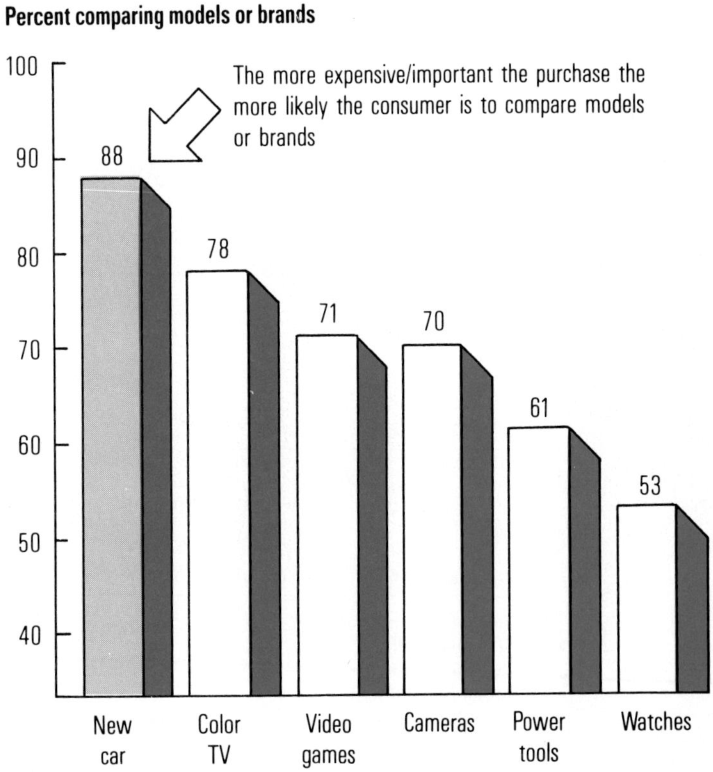

Source: *Warranties Rule Consumer Follow-Up* (Washington: D.C.: Federal Trade Commission, 1984), p. 26.

prepurchase search. For example, one study found that almost half of the purchasers of a new automobile considered only one brand.[12] Figure 15–7 indicates that for some product categories such as watches, almost half of the purchasers considered only one brand *and* one model.

Combination Measures

Because each of these measures of external search deals with a different aspect of search behavior, it is also useful to examine the total search effort. Based on four separate studies that span more than 30 years, two product categories, and two countries, we can classify consumers in terms of their total external information search as (1) nonsearchers, (2) limited information searchers, and (3) extended information searchers.[13] This classification system is shown in Table 15–1. Approximately half of the purchases are preceded by virtually no external information search; about a third are associated with limited information search; and only 12 percent involve extensive information seeking prior to the purchase.

A given individual might exhibit extended search for one purchase, limited for one, and be a nonsearcher for yet another. However, extended information seeking has been found to be characteristic of some individuals. Furthermore, these individuals exist in most high-consumption cultures and have similar demographic characteristics and attitudes. They tend to be above average in income and education, heavy users of a variety of media, opinion leaders, and to have high-performance standards for products, favorable overall attitudes toward business, and critical attitudes toward specific business practices.

These extensive information searchers are important to both marketing managers and public policy officials because:[14]

Table 15–1
Total Information-Seeking Behavior

Search Behavior	Katona and Mueller (1955)*	Newman and Staelin (1972)*	Claxton, Fry, and Portis (1974)*	Kiel and Layton (1981)†	Approximate Average
Nonsearchers	65%	49%	65%	24%	50%
Limited information seekers	25	38	27	58	38
Extended information seekers	10	13	8	18	12

*American consumers, major appliance.

†Australian consumers, automobiles.

- There is much to *learn* from them. They are expert buyers who know their way through the complexities of the marketplace in a mass-consumption economy.
- They are *leaders,* both in the sense of being opinion leaders for other consumers in their actual purchases and in the sense that they seem to be bellwethers for trends in general attitudes and behavior regarding consumption.
- They are *vigilantes* in the marketplace. They search diligently, complain vigorously, join organizations, pinpoint fraud and deception, and generally police the market.
- Their *purchasing power* is disproportionate to their numbers. They are both affluent and consumption-oriented, so that they account for a large number of total purchases and a large dollar volume in Western countries.

Conclusions on Degree of External Information Search. Most consumers engage in minimal external information search *immediately* prior to the purchase of consumer durables. The level of search for less important items is even lower. As you will see in the next section, limited information search does not *necessarily* mean that the consumer is not following a sound purchasing strategy.[15] Nor does it mean that substantial amounts of internal information are not being used.[16]

COSTS VERSUS BENEFITS OF EXTERNAL SEARCH

Why do 50 percent of the buyers of major appliances described above do little or no external search, while 12 percent engage in extensive external search? Part of the answer lies in the differences between the buyers in terms of their perceptions of the benefits and costs of search associated with a particular purchase situation as shown in Figure 15–8.

The benefits of external information search can be tangible, such as a lower price,[17] a preferred style, or higher quality product. Or the benefits can be intangible in terms of reduced risk, greater confidence in the purchase, or even providing enjoyment.[18] Perceptions of these benefits are likely to vary with the consumer's experience in the market, media habits, and the extent to which the consumer interacts with others or belongs to differing reference groups. Therefore, one reason 50 percent of major appliance buyers do little or no external search is that they do not perceive discernible benefits resulting from such an effort.

Furthermore, external acquisition of information is not free, and consumers may engage in limited search because the costs of search exceed the perceived benefits. For example, assume you are considering buying a fairly expensive toy as a Christmas present for a younger brother or sister at a nearby department store. The toy you would like to purchase is priced $3 or $4 more than expected,

Figure 15–8
Perceived Costs and Benefits of Consumer Search Guide Search Effort

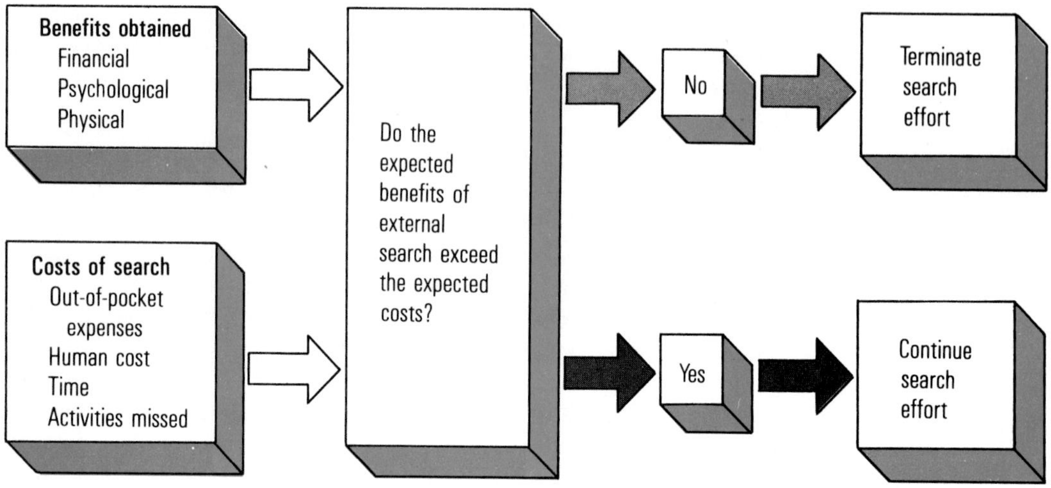

and you think you can buy it at another store five miles away at a lower price. Whether you buy the toy at the first store or go to the second store depends on the costs you attach to the extra search effort in that particular situation. For some, the benefit (a possible $3 or $4 savings) would exceed the cost (monetary, time, and psychological) of traveling five miles to visit another store, and they would make the required effort. Others might attach greater costs to this additional search effort, and because these costs exceed the potential or expected benefits, they would not engage in additional search.

The costs of search can be both monetary and nonmonetary. Monetary costs include out-of-pocket expenses related to the search effort, such as the cost of transportation, parking, and time-related costs which include lost wages, lost opportunities, charges for child care, and so forth. Nonmonetary costs of search are less obvious but may have an even greater impact than monetary costs. Almost every external search effort involves some physical and psychological strain. Frustration and conflict between the search task and other more desirable activities, as well as fatigue, may shorten the search effort.

FACTORS INFLUENCING THE LEVEL OF EXTERNAL SEARCH

External information search occurs when the expected benefits of the search are greater than the perceived costs of the search. In this section, we are going to examine four basic types of factors that influence the expected benefits and perceived costs of search: *market characteristics, product characteristics, con-*

Table 15–2
Factors Affecting External Search

Influencing Factor	Increasing the Influencing Factor Causes Search to:
I. Market characteristics	
A. Number of alternatives	Increase
B. Price range	Increase
C. Store concentration	Increase
D. Information availability	Increase
1. Advertising	
2. Point-of-purchase	
3. Sales personnel	
4. Packaging	
5. Experienced consumers	
6. Independent sources	
II. Product characteristics	
A. Price	Increase
B. Differentiation	Increase
C. Positive products	Increase
III. Consumer characteristics	
A. Learning and experience	Decrease
B. Shopping orientation	Mixed
C. Social status	Increase
D. Age, gender, and household life cycle	Mixed
E. Perceived risk	Increase
IV. Situational characteristics	
A. Time availability	Increase
B. Purchase for self	Decrease
C. Pleasant surroundings	Increase
D. Social surroundings	Mixed
E. Physical/mental energy	Increase

sumer characteristics, and *situational characteristics*. These four factors and their components are shown in Table 15–2.

Market Characteristics

Market characteristics include the *number of alternatives, price range, store distribution*, and *information availability*. It is important to keep in mind that it is the consumer's perception of, or beliefs about, the market characteristics that influence shopping behavior, *not* the actual characteristics.[19] While beliefs and reality are usually related, they often are not identical.

Number of Alternatives. Obviously, the greater the number of alternatives (products, stores, brands) available to resolve a particular problem, the more external search there is likely to be.[20] At the extreme, there is no need to search for information in the face of a complete monopoly such as utilities or driver's licenses. As the number of alternatives increases, the likelihood of external search also increases.

Price Range. The range of prices among equivalent brands in a product class is a major factor in stimulating external search. Consider the prices of five popular toys available in some 36 retail stores in Tucson, Arizona, approximately six weeks before Christmas. The total costs of the five toys shown in Table 15–3 varied from $51.27 to $105.95. Clearly, a consumer could gain from shopping for toys in this market. However, a simulation study of this toy market indicated that an extended search effort was warranted only when the costs of search were fairly low.[21]

Store Distribution. The number, location, and distances between retail stores in the market affect the number of store visits a consumer will make before purchase. Because store visits take time, energy, and in many cases money, a close proximity of stores will increase this aspect of external search. Shopping malls greatly reduce the cost of search among the stores in a mall.

Information Availability. Ready availability increases the utilization of external information. This rather obvious conclusion is not a complete statement, however, for two reasons. First, as we saw in Chapter 8, too much information at once can produce information overload. Consumers faced with information overload tend to withdraw from the task or use only very limited amounts of the available information.

The second qualification is that readily available information tends to produce learning over time. Thus, when confronted with a consumption problem, a consumer in an environment with ample information may not engage in extensive external search because of prior learning.

Table 15–2 indicated that external information relevant for consumer decisions can come from advertising, sales personnel, point-of-purchase displays, packaging and labeling, other consumers and independent sources. We will briefly examine each of these sources.

Table 15–3
Price Range of Five Toys

	Market Prices	
Product	Low	High
Play Family Sesame Street	$12.97	$ 27.50
Magic Jewel	10.44	26.50
Weeble Treasure Island	12.99	24.00
Monopoly	3.88	9.00
The Six-Million-Dollar Man	10.99	18.95
Total	$51.27	$105.95

Figure 15–9
Impact of Newspaper Advertising on Items Sold at Regular Prices

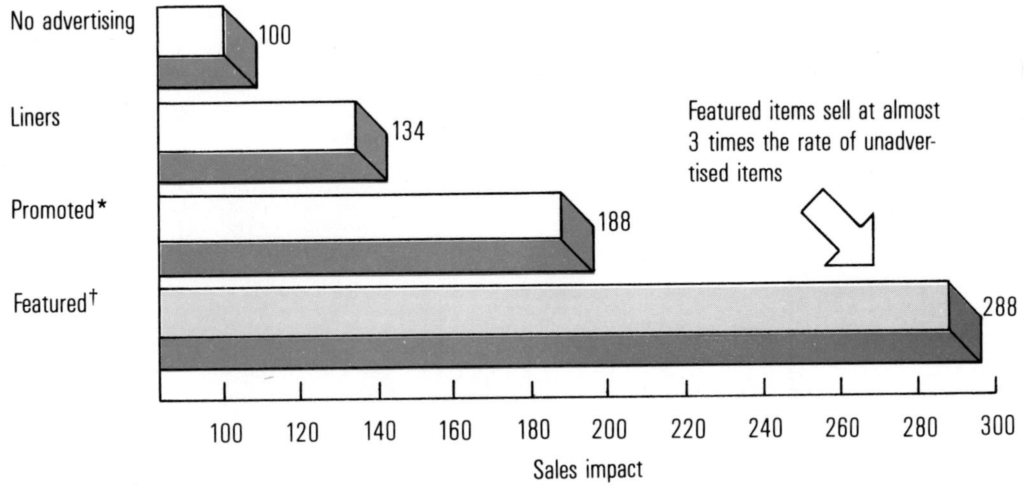

*Larger than a liner but less than four square inches.
†Four square inches or more.
Source: *Key Facts about Newspapers and Advertising 1984* (Newspaper Advertising Bureau, Inc., 1984).

Advertising is a potential source of information about product availability, features, prices, and places of purchase. It is a frequently used source when making relatively routine purchases. For example, one study found that about half the respondents used advertising as an information source for their last retail shopping trip.[22] Figure 15–9 shows the sales impact that newspaper advertising had on a group of items sold at regular prices. However, for advertisements to affect consumer choices, they must contain information relevant to the target market's evaluative criteria.[23]

Point-of-purchase displays offer another potential source of information. Figure 15–10 illustrates the sales impact of newspaper ads, point-of-purchase displays, and the combination of both on the purchase of snack foods. Similar results were obtained for numerous other product categories. Thus, advertising and point-of-purchase displays appear to attract attention and provide information that is used by many consumers in their purchase decisions.

Product categories vary considerably in the *availability of sales personnel.* Sales personnel serve as an important information source in those product categories where they are available. Another source of information that varies across product categories is the *label* of a packaged good. Labels provide information on a product's name, features, uses, ingredients, price, and so forth.

Labeling of ingredients in descending order based on volume has been required

Figure 15–10
Impact of Advertising and POP Displays on Purchase Incidence of Snack Foods

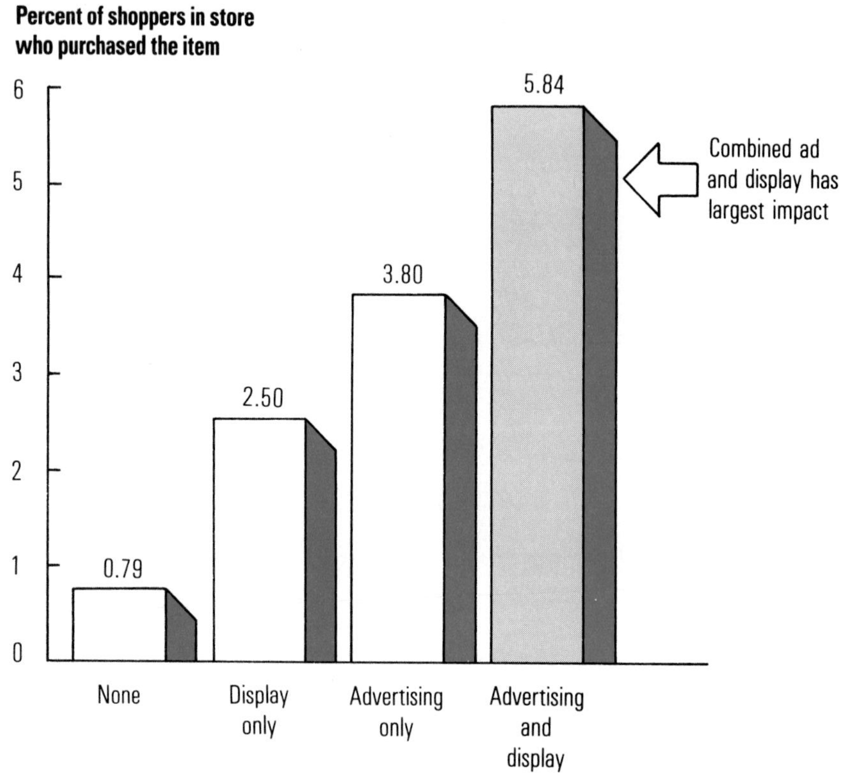

Source: *POPAI/DuPont Consumer Buying Habits Study* (Point-of-Purchase Advertising Institute, 1978).

for most food products for over 50 years. If a product has been fortified with nutrients or makes a nutritional claim, the manufacturer is now required to provide nutritional labeling. The addition of nutritional information to many food products was heralded as a major accomplishment and important move toward the full and complete disclosure of useful product information. However, a number of studies have indicated that while consumers want nutrition labeling and claim they would use it, they seldom actually use it or understand it correctly.[24] However, use and understanding are affected by the presentation format.[25]

Other consumers who have experience with the product are an important information source. Innovators and early adapters (see Chapter 6) are limited in their ability to use this information source. However, for the majority of consumers the experience and opinions of others are extremely useful, particularly for symbolic items such as clothing.[26] The final source of information generally available to consumers is *independent groups* such as testing associations, consumer groups, and government agencies. While used by relatively few consumers, there is evidence that those who do use independent sources are opinion leaders and influence others.[27]

Product Characteristics

Product characteristics such as price level and differentiation tend to influence external search.[28] It is often difficult to separate the effects of these two factors since expensive products tend to be more differentiated than inexpensive products.

Price Level. If the price of a product is trivial to the individuals involved, there is no economic incentive to carry out an external search. Thus, the higher the price level of the product category, the greater the amount of external information search. For external search to be justified on economic grounds, prices for the product category must be high enough so that a reasonable price savings can be obtained.

Product Differentiation. When consumers perceive a considerable and important difference among brands in features, style, or appearance, external information search is increased. Highly differentiated products for which consumers engage in relatively extensive external search include clothing, new furniture, and automobiles.

Positive Products. Consumers appear to enjoy shopping for products whose acquisition results in positive reinforcement.[29] Thus, shopping for flowers and plants, dress clothing, sports equipment, stereo equipment, and cameras is viewed as a positive experience by most consumers. In contrast, shopping for products whose primary benefit is negative reinforcement (removal of an unpleasant condition) is viewed as less pleasant. Thus, shopping for groceries, extermination services, and auto repairs is not enjoyed by most individuals. Other things being equal, consumers are more likely to engage in external search for positive products.

Consumer Characteristics

A variety of consumer characteristics affect perceptions of expected benefits, search costs, and thus the need to carry out a particular level of external information search.[30]

Learning and Experience. A satisfying experience with a particular brand is a positively reinforcing process. It increases the probability of a repeat purchase of that brand and decreases the likelihood of external search. As a result, external search is greater for consumers having a limited purchase experience with brands in a particular product category.

However, there is evidence that at least some familiarity[31] with a product class is necessary for external search to occur.[32] For example, external search prior to purchasing a new automobile is high for consumers who have a high level of *general knowledge about cars,* and low for consumers who have a substantial level of *knowledge about existing brands.*[33] Thus, consumers facing a completely unfamiliar product category may feel threatened by the amount of new information or may simply lack sufficient knowledge to conduct an external search.

Social Status. Education, occupation, and income are the major social status dimensions in our society. External search has been found to increase with increases in each of these categories, though middle-income individuals search more than those at either higher or lower levels.[34]

The FDA conducted a study to determine the amount of information used by food shoppers. It gave a shopper one point for each shopping aid used: making a shopping list, reading for specials, checking lists of ingredients, using unit pricing, looking for open dates, and using nutritional labeling. In Table 15–4 the results of this survey show that among college-educated shoppers, only 14 percent were classified as limited information users, while 45 percent of those not finishing high school were so classified. The reverse is also true as only 11 percent of the shoppers who did not finish high school were classified as high in amount of information used, while 34 percent of the college-educated shoppers were classified as high. The socioeconomic status category provides similar results.

Age, Gender, and Stage in the Household Life Cycle. Age of the shopper is inversely related to information search. That is, external search appears to decrease as the age of the shopper increases.[35] This is reflected in Table 15–4. The greatest percentage of shoppers who were classified as high in amount of information used were in the 18 to 34 age-group, and the smallest percentage of these shoppers were 50 or older. This may be explained in part by increased learning and product familiarity with age. New households and individuals moving into new stages of the household life cycle have a greater need for external information than established households.[36] Females tend to engage in more external search than males.[37]

Perceived Risk. Perceptions of risk associated with unsatisfactory product performance, either instrumental or symbolic, increase information search prior to purchase.[38] For example, high-fashion clothing items have greater perceived risk associated with them and, as a result, more information is sought prior to purchase. Perceived risk is a major cause of purchase involvement.

However, risk is unique to the individual. It may vary from one consumer

Table 15–4
Demographic Characteristics of Three Classifications of Shoppers in Terms of Their Use of Information prior to Purchase of Food Products

Demographic Characteristics	**Amount of Information Used** Very Little	Moderate	A Great Deal
All food shoppers	22%	50%	28%
Sex			
Female	20	50	30
Male	32	48	20
Education			
Less than high school	45	44	11
High school	20	51	30
College	14	52	34
Age			
18–34	20	50	31
35–49	19	52	29
50 and over	26	48	26
Race			
Nonblack	20	51	29
Black	35	42	23
Socioeconomic status			
Low	34	46	19
Medium	16	53	31
High	14	50	36

Source: J. Pearce, "Are Americans Careful Food Shoppers?" *FDA Consumer*, September 1976.

to another and vary for the same consumer from one situation to another. For example, the purchase of a bottle of wine may not involve much risk when buying for one's own consumption. However, the choice of wine may involve considerable risk when buying wine for a dinner party for one's boss. To deal with risk in this particular situation, the consumer may buy the most advertised brand, the brand used before and found to be satisfactory, a well-known brand, a brand recommended by a friend whose opinion is respected, or an expensive brand. In this situation, the risk of buying an inappropriate wine for an important occasion could greatly influence the information search and brand choice decision.

Shopping Orientation. Consumers tend to form general approaches or patterns to external search. These general approaches are termed shopping orientations.[39] While individuals will exhibit substantial variation from the general pattern across situations and product categories, many do take a stable shopping approach to most products across a wide range of situations.

Tables 15–5 and 15–6 provide a description of seven shopping orientations

Table 15–5
Seven Basic Shopper Orientations

Inactive Shoppers (15% of all shoppers) have extremely restricted lifestyles and shopping interests. Best characterized by their inactivity, Inactive Shoppers do not engage in outdoor or do-it-yourself activities except for working in the yard or garden. They do not express strong enjoyment or interest in shopping, nor are they particularly concerned about such shopping attributes as price, employee service, or product selection.

Active Shoppers (12.8%) have demanding lifestyles and are "tough" shoppers. They engage in all forms of outdoor activities and are usually do-it-yourselfers. Actives enjoy "shopping around," and price is a major consideration in their search. However, given their full range of interests outside of shopping, Actives appear to shop more as an expression of their intense lifestyles rather than being interested in finding bargains. Therefore, these shoppers balance price with quality, fashion, and selection in their search for value.

Service Shoppers (10%) demand a high level of in-store service when shopping. They usually seek convenient stores with friendly, helpful employees. Conversely, they quickly become impatient if they have to wait for a clerk to help them.

Traditional Shoppers (14.1%) share Active Shoppers' preoccupation with outdoor activities, but not their enthusiasm for shopping. They actively hike, camp, hunt, and fish, and are do-it-yourselfers who often work on their cars. In general, though, Traditional Shoppers are not price sensitive nor do they have other strong shopper requirements.

Dedicated Fringe Shoppers (8.8%) present clear motives for being heavy catalog shoppers. They are do-it-yourselfers and are more likely than average to try new products. They have almost a compulsion for being different. Dedicated Fringe Shoppers are disinterested in extreme socializing. They have little interest in television and radio advertisements and exhibit limited brand and store loyalty. Therefore, the catalog presents a medium for obtaining an expanded selection of do-it-yourself and other products, and this reflects their individualism.

Price Shoppers (10.4%), as the name implies, are most identifiable by their extreme price consciousness. Price Shoppers are willing to undertake an extended search to meet their price requirements, and they rely heavily on all forms of advertising to find the lowest prices.

Transitional Shoppers (6.9%) seem to be consumers in earlier stages of the family life cycle who have not yet formalized their lifestyle patterns and shopping values. They take an active interest in repairing and personalizing cars. Most participate in a variety of outdoor activities. They are more likely than average to try new products. Transitional Shoppers exhibit little interest in shopping around for low prices. They are probably "eclectic shoppers" because they appear to make up their minds quickly to buy products once they become interested.

Source: J. A. Lesser and M. A. Hughes, "The Generalizability of Psychographic Market Segments across Geographic Locations," *Journal of Marketing*, January 1986, p. 23.

Table 15-6
Selected Demographic Characteristics of Shopper Types (percentage distributions)

	Shopper Types						
Characteristics	Inactive	Active	Service	Traditional	Dedicated Fringe	Price	Transitional
Age							
18–34	35.5	54.6	40.9	52.3	46.3	36.9	63.8
35–44	20.4	21.3	23.7	21.3	21.7	22.4	12.6
45–64	31.5	19.7	28.3	22.9	25.2	29.0	19.1
65 or older	12.6	4.4	7.1	3.5	6.7	11.7	4.5
Sex							
Male	36.1	46.6	48.6	62.3	50.0	25.6	45.0
Female	63.9	53.4	51.4	37.7	50.0	74.4	55.0
Social Class							
Lower	49.9	51.5	43.4	43.7	48.8	45.4	55.9
Middle	46.3	46.0	52.6	53.2	47.5	50.0	40.5
Upper	3.8	2.5	4.0	3.1	3.7	4.6	3.6
Stage of Family Life Cycle (condensed)							
Young singles not living at home	7.7	5.0	6.8	8.0	5.9	2.5	8.5
Young married couples	21.4	38.6	26.4	34.7	33.9	26.5	46.9
Older married couples with dependent children	32.5	34.8	38.8	37.2	29.6	33.5	23.8
Older married couples without dependent children	27.9	20.0	23.1	18.8	27.2	29.3	17.8
Solitary survivors	10.6	1.6	4.9	1.3	3.4	8.2	3.0

Source: J. A. Lesser and M. A. Hughes, "The Generalizability of Psychographic Market Segments across Geographic Locations," *Journal of Marketing*, January 1986, p. 24.

and the characteristics of individuals with each orientation. These profiles were found to be consistent across seventeen different cities.[40]

Situational Characteristics

As was indicated in Chapter 13, situational variables can have a major impact on search behavior. For example, recall that one of the primary reactions of consumers to crowded store conditions is to minimize external information search. Temporal perspective is probably the most important situational variable with respect to search behavior. As the time available to solve a particular consumer problem decreases, so does the amount of external information search.[41] Gift-giving situations (task definition) tend to increase perceived risk which, as we have seen, increases external search.[42] Shoppers with limited physical or emotional energy (antecedent state) will search for less information than others. Pleasant physical surroundings increase the tendency to search for information (at least *within* that outlet). Social surroundings can increase or decrease search depending on the nature of the social setting.

MARKETING STRATEGIES BASED ON INFORMATION SEARCH PATTERNS

Sound marketing strategies take into account the nature of information search engaged in by the target market prior to purchase. Two dimensions of search are particularly appropriate: the type of decision making that influences the level of search, and the nature of the evoked set that influences the direction of the search. Figure 15–11 illustrates a strategy matrix based on these two dimensions. This matrix suggests the six distinct marketing strategies discussed in the following sections.

Maintenance Strategy

If our brand is purchased habitually by the target market, our strategy is to maintain that behavior. This requires consistent attention to product quality, distribution (avoiding out-of-stock situations), and a reinforcement advertising strategy. In addition, we must defend against the disruptive tactics of competitors. Thus, we need to maintain product development and improvements and to counter short-term competitive strategies such as coupons, point-of-purchase displays, or rebates.

Morton Salt and Del Monte canned vegetables have large habitual repeat purchaser segments which they have successfully maintained. Budweiser, Marlboro, and Crest have large brand-loyal habitual purchaser segments. They have successfully defended their market positions against assaults by major competitors in recent years. In contrast, Liggett & Myers lost 80 percent of its market share when it failed to engage in maintenance advertising.[43] Quality control problems caused Schlitz to lose substantial market share.

Figure 15–11
Marketing Strategies Based on Information Search Patterns

Target Market Decision-Making Pattern

Brand Position	Habitual Decision Making (no search)	Limited Decision Making (limited search)	Extended Decision Making (extensive search)
Brand in evoked set	Maintenance strategy	Capture strategy	Preference strategy
Brand not in evoked set	Disrupt strategy	Intercept strategy	Acceptance strategy

Disrupt Strategy

If our brand is not part of the evoked set and our target market engages in habitual decision making, our first task is to *disrupt* the existing decision pattern. This is a difficult task since the consumer does not seek external information or even consider alternative brands before a purchase. Low-involvement learning over time could generate a positive product position for our brand, but this alone would be unlikely to shift behavior.

In the long run, a major product improvement accompanied by attention-attracting advertising could shift the target market into a more extensive form of decision making. In the short run, attention-attracting advertising aimed specifically at breaking habitual decision making can be successful. Schlitz's campaign, which featured habitual consumers of other brands preferring Schlitz in blind taste tests, is an example of this approach. Free samples, coupons, rebates, and tie-in sales are common approaches to disrupting habitual decision making.

Exhibit 15–1 illustrates a disrupt-based advertisement. Notice that the headline focuses on the contest rather than on the product or brand. Because of the contest, some consumers are likely to read the advertisement even if they are habitual purchasers of a competing brand. Completing the contest entry blank requires the consumer to learn about the brand, Erace. To the extent that the contest is attractive to the target market, Max Factor will have succeeded in disrupting the habitual decision process of its competitor's customers.

Capture Strategy

Limited decision making generally involves a few brands that are evaluated on only a few criteria such as price or availability. Much of the information search occurs at the point-of-purchase or in readily available media prior to purchase. If our brand is one of the brands given this type of consideration by our target market, our objective is to capture as large a share of their purchases as practical.

Since these consumers engage in limited search, we need to know where they search and what information they are looking for. In general, we will want to supply information, often on price and availability, in local media through cooperative advertising and at the point-of-purchase through displays and adequate shelf space. Exhibit 15–2 shows how Nature's Family uses an added inducement (a free skin freshener) at the point-of-purchase to help capture purchases by consumers looking for a facial scrub. We will also be concerned with maintaining consistent product quality and adequate distribution.

Intercept Strategy

If our target market engages in limited decision making and our brand is not part of their evoked set, our objective will be to intercept the consumer during the search for information on the brands in the evoked set. Again, our emphasis

Exhibit 15–1 Max Factor Using a Disrupt Strategy

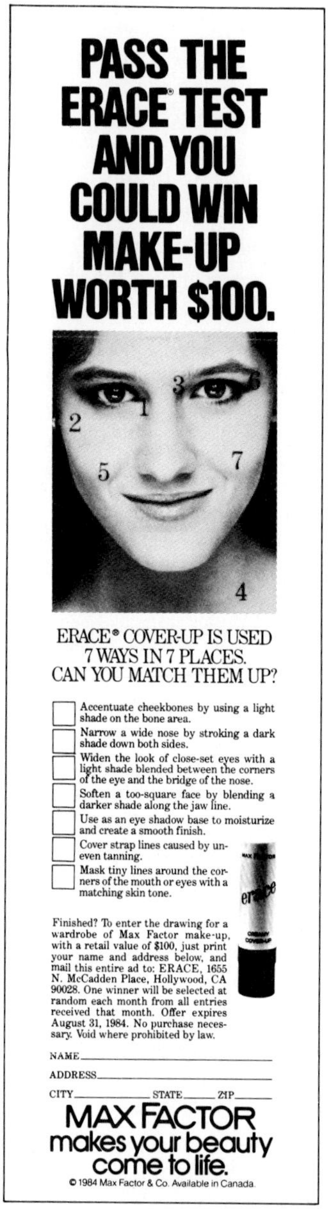

Courtesy Max Factor & Co.

Exhibit 15–2 Capture Strategy Based on an Extra Purchase Inducement

YOU GET THIS 8 OZ. SIZE ($4.50 value)
SKIN FRESHENER
FREE!
Nature's Family
70% Aloe Vera
FACIAL SCRUB
with Apricot Kernels
70% Aloe Vera
SKIN FRESHENER
WITH PURCHASE OF
THIS 4 OZ. SIZE ($4.50 value)
FACIAL SCRUB
Next to Nature's Family, the other facial scrubs haven't much to offer.
GET A FREE SKIN FRESHENER WHEN YOU BUY NEW 70% ALOE VERA FACIAL SCRUB.
Deep cleanse your skin with Nature's Family Aloe Vera facial scrub. Specially milled apricot kernals and walnut shells provide a mild abrasiveness to remove dead skin and stimulate circulation.
The invigorating Aloe Vera skin freshener tones, conditions and refreshes your skin, leaving it revitalized.
Only Nature's Family products contain 70% Aloe Vera gel which has natural astringent and freshening properties.
For skin you'll love at a price you'll love even more.
Nature's Family®
The Leader in Natural Skin and Hair Care for over 15 Years.

Courtesy Nature's Family, Inc.

will be on local media with cooperative advertising and at the point-of-purchase with displays, shelf space, package design, and so forth. Coupons can also be effective. We will have to place considerable emphasis on attracting the consumers' attention as they will not be seeking information on our brand. B. F. Goodrich engages in heavy advertising of its January battery sale. Since many batteries fail during the cold weather of January, this sale is likely to intercept many consumers as they look for a battery.

In addition to the short-run strategies mentioned above, low-involvement learning, product improvements, and free samples can be used to move the brand into the target market's evoked set.

Preference Strategy

Extended decision making with our brand in the evoked set requires a preference strategy. Since extended decision making generally involves several brands, many attributes, and a number of information sources, a simple capture strategy may not be adequate. Instead, we need to structure an information campaign that will result in our brand being preferred by members of the target market.

The first step is a strong position on those attributes important to the target market. This is discussed in considerable detail in the next chapter. Next, information must be provided in all the appropriate sources. This may require extensive advertising to groups that do not purchase the item but recommend it to others (i.e., druggists for over-the-counter drugs, veterinarians and county agents for agricultural products). Independent groups should be encouraged to test the brand, and sales personnel should be provided detailed information on the brand's attributes. In addition, it may be wise to provide the sales personnel with extra motivation (e.g., extra commissions paid by the manufacturer) to recommend the product. Point-of-purchase displays and pamphlets should also be available. These strategies are used by well-known manufacturers of microwave ovens (Amana, Litton), personal computers (Apple, IBM), and VCR equipment (Sanyo, RCA, Sharp).

Acceptance Strategy

Acceptance strategy is very similar to preference strategy. However, it is complicated by the fact that the target is not seeking information about our brand. Therefore, in addition to the activities involved in the preference strategy described above, we must attract their attention or otherwise motivate them to learn about our brand.

Consider the following quote by Lee Iacocca, head of Chrysler:

> Our biggest long-term job is to get people in [the showroom] to see how great these cars are—to get some traffic—and let them compare, so we're going head to head on price and value.[44]

Because of this situation, Chrysler implemented an acceptance strategy. In addition to product improvements and heavy advertising, Chrysler literally paid consumers to seek information about their cars! They did this by offering cash to individuals who would test drive a Chrysler product prior to purchasing a new car.

Long-term advertising designed to enhance low-involvement learning is another useful technique for gaining acceptance. Extensive advertising with strong emphasis on attracting attention can also be effective. The primary objective of these two approaches is not to "sell" the brand. Rather, they seek to move the brand into the evoked set. Then, when a purchase situation arises, the consumer will seek additional information on this brand.

SUMMARY

Following problem recognition, consumers may engage in extensive internal and external search, limited internal and external search, or only internal search. Information may be sought on (1) the appropriate evaluative criteria for the solution of the problem, (2) the existence of various alternative solutions, and (3) the performance of each alternative solution on each evaluative criterion.

Most consumers, when faced with a problem, can recall a limited number of brands that they feel are probably acceptable solutions. These acceptable brands, the evoked set, are the initial ones that the consumer seeks additional information on during the remaining internal and external search process. Therefore, marketers are very concerned that their brands fall within the evoked set of most members of their target market. A substantial amount of advertising has this as its primary objective.

Consumer internal information (information stored in memory) may have been actively acquired in previous searches and personal experiences or it may have been passively acquired through low-involvement learning. In addition to their own memory, consumers can seek information from four major types of external sources: (1) personal sources, such as friends and family; (2) independent sources, such as consumer groups, paid professionals, and government agencies; (3) marketing sources, such as sales personnel and advertising; and (4) experiential sources, such as direct product inspection or trial. The fact that only one of these four information sources is under the direct control of the firm suggests the need to pay close attention to product performance and customer satisfaction after the purchase.

Explicit external information search *after* problem recognition is limited. This emphasizes the need to communicate effectively with consumers prior to problem recognition. Characteristics of the market, the product, the consumer, and the situation interact to influence the level of search.

It is often suggested that consumers generally should engage in relatively extensive external search prior to purchasing an item. However, this view ignores the fact that information search is not free. It takes time, energy, money, and can often require giving up more desirable activities. Therefore, consumers should engage in external search only to the extent that the expected benefits such as a lower price or a more satisfactory purchase outweigh the expected costs.

Sound marketing strategy takes into account the nature of information search engaged in by the target market. The level of search and the brand's position in or out of the evoked set are two key dimensions. Based on these two dimensions, six potential information strategies are suggested: (1) maintenance, (2) disrupt, (3) capture, (4) intercept, (5) preference, and (6) acceptance.

REVIEW QUESTIONS

1. When does *information search* occur? What is the difference between internal and external information search?
2. What kind of information is sought in an external search for information?
3. What are *evaluative criteria* and how do they relate to information search?
4. How does a consumer's *awareness set* influence information search?
5. What roles do the *evoked set, inert set,* and *inept set* play in a consumer's information search? Why are some brands in a consumer's evoked set and others in the inert or inept sets?
6. Of the products shown in Figure 15–4, which product class is most likely to exhibit the most brand switching? Explain your answer in terms of the information provided in Figure 15–4.
7. What are the primary sources of information available to consumers, and what effect does each have on information search?
8. Discuss the different ways in which the amount of external information search can be evaluated.
9. Using the information presented in Figure 15–7, discuss the differences in comparison shopping between product categories. What factors might contribute to these differences?
10. How do *nonsearchers, information searchers,* and *extended information searchers* differ in their search for information? Which category of consumers appears most rational to you and why?
11. What factors might contribute to the search effort of consumers who are essentially one-stop shoppers? How do these factors differ in terms of how they influence information searchers and extended information searchers?
12. What factors have to be considered in the total cost of a purchase? How might these factors be different for different consumers?
13. Explain how different *market characteristics* affect information search.
14. How do different *consumer characteristics* influence a consumer's information search effort?
15. How do *product characteristics* influence a consumer's information search effort?
16. How do *situational characteristics* influence a consumer's information search effort?
17. How do individuals with differing shopping orientations differ in (a) shopping patterns, and (b) demographics?
18. Describe the information search characteristics that should lead to each of the following strategies:
    a. Maintenance.
    b. Disrupt.
    c. Capture.
    d. Intercept.
    e. Preference.
    f. Acceptance.
19. Describe each of the strategies listed in question 18.

DISCUSSION QUESTIONS

1. Pick two brands that you believe would fit in each cell in Figure 15–11 (12 brands in total). Justify your selection. Describe a specific marketing strategy for one of the brands in each cell.
2. How would you utilize Figure 15–5 to develop a marketing communications strategy for a particular brand?
3. What information sources do students on your campus use when purchasing:
   a. Movie?
   b. Perfume?
   c. Life insurance?
   d. Bicycle?
   e. Car insurance?
   f. Personal computer?
   g. Snack food?
   h. Toothpaste?

   Answer by assigning weights to each cell in Figure 15–5 to represent the relative use (the sum must equal 100). Do you think there will be individual differences? Why?
4. What factors contribute to the size of an awareness set, evoked set, inert set, and inept set? How can these factors be used to explain differences in the size of these respective sets for toothpaste and beer (Figure 15–4)?
5. Discuss factors that may contribute to external information search and factors that act to reduce external search for information before purchase of a novel and a tennis racket.
6. Is it ever in the best interest of a marketer to encourage potential customers to carry out an extended prepurchase search? Why or why not?
7. What implications for marketing strategy does Figure 15–3 suggest?
8. What implications for marketing strategy are suggested by Figure 15–5?
9. What role, if any, should the government play in ensuring that consumers have easy access to relevant product information? How should it accomplish this?

PROJECT QUESTIONS

1. Complete Discussion Question 3 using a questionnaire and information from 10 students not in your class. Prepare a report discussing the marketing implications of your findings.
2. For the same three products listed in Figure 15–4, ask 10 students to list all the brands they are aware of in each product category. Then have them indicate which ones they might buy (evoked set), which ones they are indifferent toward (inert set), and which brands of those they listed they strongly dislike and would not purchase (inept set). Arrange your results as shown in Figure 15–4, and evaluate the similarities and differences between your results and those shown in Figure 15–4.
3. Answer Project Question 2, but use soft drinks, deodorant, and fast-food outlets as product categories.

4. Develop a short questionnaire designed to measure the information search consumers engage in prior to purchasing (1) a personal computer and (2) a moped or bicycle. Your questionnaire should include measures of types of information sought, as well as sources that provide this information. Also include measures of the relevant consumer characteristics that might influence information search, as well as some measure of past experience with the products. Then interview two recent purchasers of each product, using the questionnaire you have developed. Analyze each consumer's response and classify each consumer in terms of information search as a nonsearcher, information searcher, or extended information searcher. Finally, class members should pool their classifications to get a more accurate picture of the search effort exhibited by consumers interviewed by the class.
5. For each of the cells in Figure 15–11, find one brand that appears to be following that strategy. Describe in detail how it is implementing the strategy.
6. Develop a questionnaire to measure shopping orientations among college students. Arrange for 50 students to complete the questionnaire. Classify the students into relevant orientations. Why do these differing orientations exist?
7. Develop a questionnaire to determine which products college students view as positive and which they view as negative. Measure the shopping effort associated with each type. Explain your overall results and any individual differences you find.

REFERENCES

[1] P. Winters, "Herpes Ads Put BW in Select Company," *Advertising Age,* July 14, 1986, p. 57.

[2] J. A. Lesser and S. Jain, "A Preliminary Investigation of the Relationship between Exploratory and Epistemic Shopping Behavior," in *1985 AMA Educators' Proceedings,* ed. R. F. Lusch et al. (Chicago: American Marketing Association, 1985), pp. 75–81; J. A. Lesser and S. S. Marine, "An Exploratory Investigation of the Relationship between Consumer Arousal and Shopping Behavior," in *Advances in Consumer Research XIII,* ed. R. J. Lutz (Provo, Utah: Association for Consumer Research, 1986), pp. 17–21; and P. H. Bloch, D. L. Sherrell, and N. M. Ridgway, "Consumer Search," *Journal of Consumer Research,* June 1986, pp. 119–26.

[3] Ibid., and L. F. Feick and L. L. Price, "The Market Maven," *Journal of Marketing,* January 1987, pp. 83–97.

[4] P. Wright and P. D. Rip, "Product Class Advertising Effects on First-Time Buyers' Decision Strategies," *Journal of Consumer Research,* September 1980, p. 176.

[5] D. W. Stewart and G. Punj, "Factors Associated with Changes in Evoked Set among Purchases of New Automobiles," in *1982 Educators Conference Proceedings* (Chicago: American Marketing Association, 1982), pp. 61–65; S. A. Erogh, G. S. Omura, and K. A. Machleit, "Evoked Set Size and Temporal Proximity to Purchase," in *1983 Educators Conference Proceedings* (Chicago: American Marketing Association, 1983), pp. 97–101; T. A. Swartz and N. Stephens, "Information Search

for Services," in *Advances in Consumer Research XI,* ed. T. C. Kinnear (Chicago: Association for Consumer Research, 1984), pp. 244–49; and J. W. Alba and A. Chattopadhyay, "Salience Effects in Brand Recall," *Journal of Marketing Research,* November 1986, pp. 363–69.

[6] C. E. Wilson, "A Procedure for the Analysis of Consumer Decision Making," *Journal of Advertising Research,* April 1981, p. 31.

[7] K. Gronhaug and S. V. Troye, "Exploring the Content of Evoked Set in Car Buying," in *Marketing in the 80s,* ed. R. P. Bagozzi et al. (Chicago: American Marketing Association, 1980); J. E. Brisoux and M. Laroche, "Evoked Set Formation and Composition," in *Advances in Consumer Research VIII,* ed. K. B. Monroe (Chicago: Association for Consumer Research, 1981), pp. 357–61.

[8] S. V. Troye, "Evoked Set Formation as a Categorization Process," in *Advances in Consumer Research XI,* ed. T. C. Kinnear (Chicago: Association for Consumer Research, 1984), pp. 180–86; M. Reilly and T. L. Parkinson, "Individual and Product Correlates of Evoked Set Size for Consumer Package Goods," in *Advances in Consumer Research XII,* ed. E. C. Hirschman and M. B. Holbrook (Provo, Utah: Association for Consumer Research, 1985), pp. 492–97; and W. Baker et al., "Brand Familiarity and Advertising," in *Advances XIII,* ed. Lutz, pp. 637–42.

[9] For example, see E. C. Hirschman and M. K. Mills, "Sources Shoppers Use to Pick Stores," *Journal of Advertising Research,* February 1980, pp. 47–51.

[10] See D. F. Midgley, "Patterns of Interpersonal Information Seeking for the Purchase of a Symbolic Product," *Journal of Marketing Research,* February 1983, pp. 74–83; Swartz and Stephens, *Information Search;* D. H. Furse, G. N. Punj, and D. W. Stewart, "A Typology of Individual Search Strategies among Purchasers of New Automobiles," *Journal of Consumer Research,* March 1984, pp. 417–31; and L. L. Price and L. F. Feick, "The Role of Interpersonal Sources in External Search," in *Advances XI,* ed. Kinnear, pp. 250–55.

[11] W. Newman, "Consumer External Search: Amount and Determinants," in *Consumer and Industrial Buying Behavior,* ed. A. Woodside, J. Sheth, and P. Bennett (New York: Elsevier North-Holland, 1977), pp. 79–94.

[12] Gronhaug and Troye, "Exploring the Content," p. 144.

[13] G. Katona and E. Mueller, "A Study of Purchase Decisions," in *Consumer Behavior: The Dynamics of Consumer Reaction,* ed. L. Clark (University Press, 1955), pp. 30–87; and J. Newman and R. Staelin, "Prepurchase Information Seeking for New Cars and Major Household Appliances," *Journal of Marketing Research,* August 1972, pp. 249–57; J. Claxton, J. Fry, and B. Portis, "A Taxonomy of Prepurchase Information Gathering Patterns," *Journal of Consumer Research,* December 1974, pp. 35–42; and G. C. Kiel and R. A. Layton, "Dimensions of Consumer Information Seeking Behavior," *Journal of Marketing Research,* May 1981, pp. 233–39.

[14] H. B. Thorelli and J. L. Engledow, "Information Seekers and Information Systems: A Policy Perspective," *Journal of Marketing,* Spring 1980, pp. 9–27. See also Feick and Price, "The Market Maven."

[15] See B. T. Ratchford, "The Value of Information for Selected Appliances," *Journal of Marketing Research,* February 1980, pp. 14–25; and R. M. Swagler, "Information as Human Capital: Toward a Time-Use Approach," in *Advances in Consumer Research VII,* ed. J. C. Olson (Chicago: Association for Consumer Research, 1980), pp. 195–97.

[16] G. Punj, "Presearch Decision Making in Consumer Durable Purchases," *Journal of Consumer Marketing,* Winter 1987, pp. 71–82.

[17] J. A. Carlson and R. J. Gieseke, "Price Search in a Product Market," *Journal of Consumer Research,* March 1983, pp. 357–65.

[18] R. A. Westbrook and W. C. Black, "A Motivation-Based Shopper Typology," *Journal of Retailing,* Spring 1985, pp. 78–103; T. Williams, M. Slama, and J. Rogers, "Behavioral Characteristics of the Recreational Shopper," *Journal of the Academy of Marketing Science,* Summer 1985, pp. 307–16; and B. Morris, "As a Favored Pastime, Shopping Ranks High," *The Wall Street Journal,* July 30, 1987, p. 1.

[19] C. P. Duncan and R. W. Olshavsky, "External Search: The Role of Consumer Beliefs," *Journal of Market Research,* February 1982, pp. 32–43.

[20] See D. R. Lehmann and W. L. Moore, "Validity of Information Display Boards: An Assessment Using Longitudinal Data," *Journal of Marketing Research,* November 1980, pp. 450–59.

[21] R. Best, J. Cady, and G. Hozier, Jr., "Searching for the Lowest Price," *Arizona Review,* January 1978, pp. 1–7.

[22] Hirschman and Mills, "Sources Shoppers Use."

[23] See S. R. Cox, K. A. Coney, and P. F. Ruppe, "The Impact of Comparative Product Information," *Journal of Public Policy and Marketing,* vol. 2, 1983, pp. 57–69; and A. S. Levy et al., "The Impact of a Nutrition Information Program on Food Purchases," *Journal of Public Policy and Marketing,* vol. 4, 1985, pp. 1–13.

[24] See T. E. Muller, "Structural Information Factors Which Stimulate the Use of Nutrition Information," *Journal of Marketing Research,* May 1985, pp. 143–57.

[25] See ibid.; Levy et al., "The Impact"; R. A. Winett and J. H. Kagel, "Effects of Information Presentation Format," *Journal of Consumer Research,* September 1984, pp. 655–67; M. Venkatesan, W. Lancaster, and K. W. Kendall, "An Empirical Study of Alternative Formats for Nutritional Information Disclosure," *Journal of Public Policy and Marketing,* vol. 5, 1986, pp. 29–43; and J. E. Russo et al., "Nutrition Information in the Supermarket," *Journal of Consumer Research,* June 1986, pp. 48–70.

[26] D. F. Midgley, "Patterns of Interpersonal Information."

[27] Thorelli and Engledow, "Information Seekers."

[28] C. M. Schaninger and D. Sciglimpaglia, "The Influence of Cognitive Personality Traits and Demographics on Consumer Information Acquisition," *Journal of Consumer Research,* September 1981, pp. 208–16.

[29] S. Widrick and E. Fram, "Identifying Negative Products," *Journal of Consumer Marketing,* no. 2, 1983, pp. 59–66.

[30] N. K. Malhotra, "On Individual Differences in Search Behavior for a Nondurable," *Journal of Consumer Research,* June 1983, pp. 125–31; Furse et al., "A Typology"; Swartz and Stephens, "Information Search"; and M. E. Slama and A. Taschian, "Selected Socioeconomic and Demographic Characteristics Associated with Purchasing Involvement," *Journal of Marketing,* Winter 1985, pp. 72–82.

[31] J. E. Russo and E. J. Johnson, "What Do Consumers Know about Familiar Products?" in *Advances VII,* ed. Olson, pp. 417–23.

[32] J. R. Bettman and C. W. Park, "Effects of Prior Knowledge and Experience and Phase of the Choice Process on Consumer Decision Processes: A Protocol Analysis,"

Journal of Consumer Research, December 1980, pp. 234–47; C. W. Park and V. P. Lessig, "Familiarity and Its Impact on Consumer Decision Biases and Heuristics," *Journal of Consumer Research,* September 1981, pp. 223–30; E. J. Johnson and J. E. Russo, "Product Familiarity and Learning New Information," in *Advances VIII,* ed. Monroe, pp. 151–55; M. Brucks, "The Effects of Product Class Knowledge on Information Search Behavior," *Journal of Consumer Research,* June 1985, pp. 1–16; and S. E. Beatty and S. M. Smith, "External Search Effort," *Journal of Consumer Research,* June 1987, pp. 83–95.

[33] G. N. Punj and R. Staelin, "A Model of Consumer Information Search Behavior for New Automobiles," *Journal of Consumer Research,* March 1983, pp. 368–80.

[34] N. Capon and M. Burke, "Individual, Product Class, and Task-Related Factors in Consumer Information Processing," *Journal of Consumer Research,* December 1980, pp. 314–26; Swagler, "Information"; and G. R. Foxall, "Social Factors in Consumer Choice: Replication and Extension," *Journal of Marketing Research,* June 1975, p. 62.

[35] Schaninger and Sciglimpaglia, "Influence of Cognitive."

[36] See J. Rudd and F. J. Kohout, "Individual and Group Consumer Information Acquisitions in Brand Choice Situations," *Journal of Consumer Research,* December 1983, pp. 303–9.

[37] Slama and Tashchian, "Selected Socioeconomic."

[38] See G. P. Lantas, "The Influences of Inherent Risk and Information Acquisitions on Consumer Risk Reduction Strategies," *Journal of the Academy of Marketing Science,* Fall 1983, pp. 358–81; G. Brooker, "An Assessment of an Expanded Measure of Perceived Risk," in *Advances XI,* ed. Kinnear, pp. 439–41; and G. R. Dowling, "Perceived Risk," *Psychology & Marketing,* Fall 1986, pp. 193–210.

[39] Westbrook and Black, "A Motivation-Based"; J. R. Lumpkin, "Shopping Orientation Segmentation of the Elderly Consumer," *Journal of the Academy of Marketing Science,* Spring 1985, pp. 271–89; T. Williams, M. Slama, and J. Rogers, "Behavioral Characteristics of the Recreational Shopper," *Journal of Academy of Marketing Science,* Summer 1985, pp. 307–16; and J. R. Lumpkin, J. M. Hawes, and W. R. Darden, "Shopping Patterns of the Rural Consumer," *Journal of Business Research,* February 1986, pp. 63–81.

[40] J. A. Lesser and M. A. Hughes, "The Generalizability of Psychographic Market Segments across Geographic Locations," *Journal of Marketing,* January 1986, pp. 18–27.

[41] Beatty and Smith, "External Search"; and B. E. Mattson and A. J. Dubinsky, "Shopping Patterns," *Psychology & Marketing,* Spring 1987, pp. 47–62.

[42] C. J. Cobb and W. D. Hoyer, "Direct Observation of Search Behavior," *Psychology & Marketing,* Fall 1985, pp. 161–79; and Mattson and Dubinsky, "Shopping Patterns."

[43] "L&M Lights Up Again," *Marketing and Media Decisions,* February 1984, p. 69.

[44] R. Gray, "Chrysler Hinges Price on Popularity," *Advertising Age,* October 5, 1981, p. 7.

CHAPTER

16 Alternative Evaluation and Selection

Sunbeam Appliance Company recently completed a very successful redesign of its many lines of small kitchen appliances. The redesign of their food processor line illustrates the four-stage process used:

1. *A Consumer Usage and Attitude Survey* to determine how and for what purpose products in the product category are used, frequency of use, brand ownership, brand awareness, and attitudes toward the product.
2. *A Consumer Attribute and Benefit Survey* to provide importance ratings of product attributes and benefits desired from the product category, along with perceptions of the degree to which each brand provides the various attributes and benefits.
3. *A Conjoint Analysis Study* (a technique described in this chapter) to provide data on the structure of consumers' preferences for product features and their willingness to trade one feature for more of another feature. Conjoint analysis provides the relative importance *each* consumer attaches to various levels of each potential product feature. This allows individuals with similar preference structures to be grouped into market segments.
4. *Product Line Sales and Market Share Simulations* to determine the best set of food processors to bring to the market. Based on the preference structures and sizes of the market segments discovered in step 3 above and the perceived characteristics of competing brands, the market share of various Sunbeam product sets was estimated using computer simulations.[1]

The above process involved interviewing hundreds of product category users. Twelve different product attributes were tested and four distinct market segments were uncovered. The existing product line was replaced with four new models (down from six) targeted at three of the four segments. The results were increased market share, reduced costs, and increased profitability.

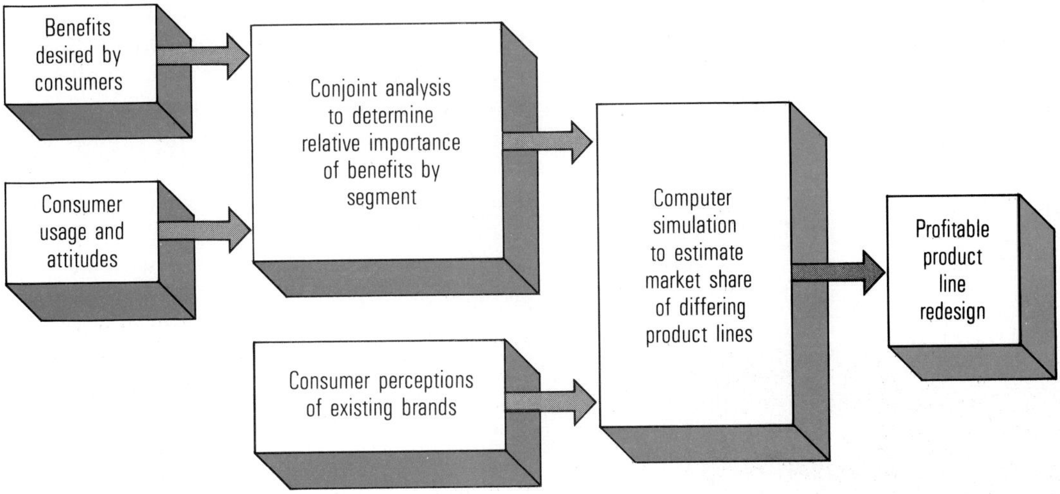

The example above describes Sunbeam's successful analysis of consumers' desired product benefits (evaluative criteria) and the manner in which they choose between products with differing combinations of benefits. The process by which consumers evaluate and choose among alternatives is illustrated in Figure 16–1, and is the focus of this chapter.

We concentrate on three main areas. First, the nature and characteristics of evaluative criteria (the features the product should have) will be described.

Figure 16–1
Alternative Evaluation and Selection Process

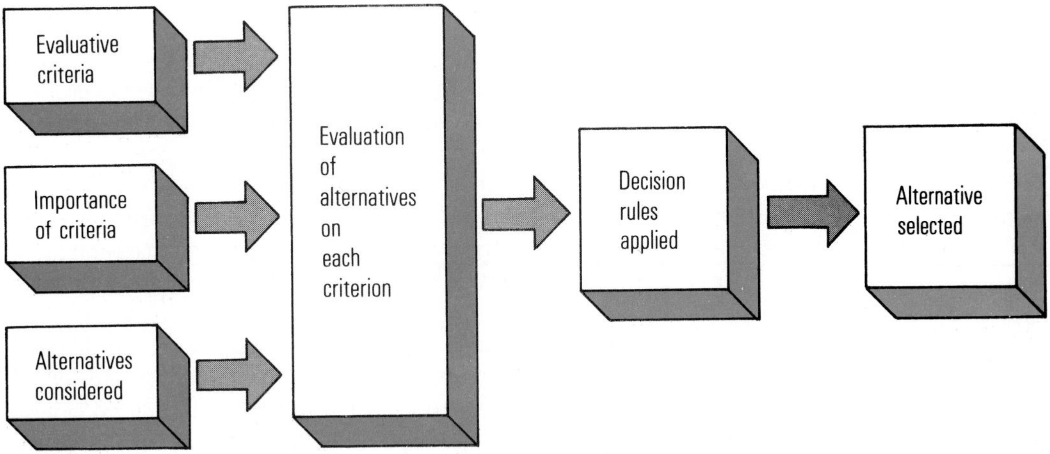

Evaluative criteria are particularly important since consumers select alternatives based on relative performance of the appropriate evaluative criteria.

After examining evaluative criteria, we focus on the ability of consumers to judge the performance of products. Finally, we examine the decision rules that consumers use in selecting one alternative from those considered.

Before delving into the evaluation and selection of alternatives, you should remember that many purchases involve little or no evaluation of alternatives. Habitual decisions do not require the evaluation of any alternatives. The last purchase is repeated without considering other information. Limited decisions may involve comparing a few brands (small evoked set) on one or two dimensions (I'll buy Heinz or Del Monte catsup depending on which is cheaper at Safeway). In contrast, extended decision making generally requires evaluating multiple brands on several attributes.

EVALUATIVE CRITERIA

Evaluative criteria are *the various features a consumer looks for in response to a particular type of problem*. Before purchasing a calculator, you might be concerned with cost, size, power source, capabilities, display, and warranty. These would be your evaluative criteria. Someone else could approach the same purchase with an entirely different set of evaluative criteria. This section of the chapter examines:

- The nature of evaluative criteria.
- The measurement of evaluative criteria.
- The role of evaluative criteria in marketing strategy.

Nature of Evaluative Criteria

Evaluative criteria can differ in type, number, and importance. The type of evaluative criteria a consumer uses in a decision varies from *tangible* cost and performance features to *intangible* factors such as style, taste, prestige, and brand image.[2] Equally important in many purchase decisions is the way we *feel* about a brand. Feelings or emotions surrounding a brand are difficult for consumers to articulate and for marketing managers to measure or manipulate. Yet the strong negative consumer reaction to Coca-Cola's change in the formula for Coke clearly illustrates the powerful, though subtle, role of feelings in purchase decisions.

Exhibit 16–1 illustrates the range of evaluative criteria marketers have assumed to be important. Such benefits as a reduced sex drive, stronger bones, cartoon character identification, low price, high quality, and reduced calories are or were promised by the products in the exhibit. Of course, this represents only a small fraction of the evaluative criteria consumers might consider.

Exhibit 16–1 Evaluative Criteria Stressed in Marketing Campaigns

1. **Breakfast cereal.** Cold breakfast cereals originally were marketed as a means of reducing sexual desires! Kellogg's cereals were among the brands initially promoted for this purpose.*
2. **Bubble gum.** Wrigley introduced Hubba Bubba, a soft bubble gum, and promoted its "amazing no-stick bubbles." Within a year it captured 10 percent of the $400 million bubble gum market.†
3. **Juice.** Procter & Gamble recently launched Citrus Hill Plus Calcium orange and grapefruit beverages containing 60 percent fruit juices with added calcium. A key selling feature is the product's endorsement by the American Medical Women's Association.‡
4. **Cartoon characters.** Bugs Bunny, Little Orphan Annie, Fred Flintstone, and many other cartoon characters (as well as actual movie and television personalities) have been licensed by manufacturers to represent their products. The marketer of Silly Putty states: "Licensing has taken over the world. Kids don't really care about our putty, they care about their favorite characters."§
5. **Paper products.** Paper products seem to be involved with what is called the "scrimp and splurge" theory of purchase. This theory is that consumers are very price sensitive in product areas in which they have low involvement and are very quality sensitive in product areas in which they have high involvement. The recent market-share gainers have been generic and private brands (presumably purchased by those with low involvement in housework, the kitchen, and so on) and the premium-priced, high-quality brands (presumably bought by those highly involved in this area).||
6. **Food.** Nestle Co. recently withdrew its New Cookery line from the marketplace. The foods were low in fats, starches, and sugars. Retailers complained that pricing was often higher than competitive products and listed that as a distinct disadvantage. Another problem was that many of the New Cookery items lacked "a clear-cut reason for being." For example, calories in New Cookery catsup were only slightly lower than Heinz or Del Monte, but the Nestle product generally was priced higher.#

*"No-Sex Cereals," *Parade Magazine,* November 29, 1981, p. 27.

†L. Edwards, "Wrigley Throws New Items into Battle for Market Lead," *Advertising Age,* April 2, 1979, p. 3; and "Bubble Gum Not about to Gum Up Works," *Advertising Age,* July 28, 1980, p. 10.

‡L. Freeman, "P&G Rolls Calcium-Enriched Citrus Hill," *Advertising Age,* June 1, 1987, p. 6.

§D. Rotbart, "Licensing Boom Envelops U.S. Industry," *The Wall Street Journal,* June 1, 1981, p. 1.

||N. Giges, "Scott a Paper Tiger," *Advertising Age,* November 3, 1980, p. 96.

#N. Giges, "Nestle Pulls Cookery," *Advertising Age,* June 22, 1981, p. 1.

Exhibit 16–2 Focusing Consumers' Attention on a New Evaluative Criterion

20 MINUTES EVERY OTHER DAY TO TOTAL FITNESS
ONLY THE SCHWINN AIR-DYNE EXERCISES BOTH UPPER AND LOWER BODY SIMULTANEOUSLY OR SEPARATELY
Ordinary stationary bicycles can't do what the Schwinn Air-Dyne does so well: provide upper as well as lower body exercise. You can use the unique moving hand levers to tone and build arm, shoulder, back and stomach muscles. Use just the pedals to exercise your legs, thighs and hips. Or use both together to enjoy the benefits of a total workout unmatched for efficiency.
TOTAL BODY INVOLVEMENT ADDS TO CARDIOVASCULAR BENEFITS
Research proves that the cardiovascular benefits of exercise are enhanced when the entire body is involved. The Schwinn Air-Dyne is designed to provide total body exercise. Even a moderate effort, performed on a consistent basis, can help you achieve the sense of well-being associated with cardiovascular fitness.
THE EFFICIENT WAY TO TOTAL FITNESS
Because the Schwinn Air-Dyne is so efficient, virtually anyone can spare the time it takes to achieve and maintain total fitness. Twenty minutes of actual workout time every other day is all it takes. You can work out as much as you like, in the convenience of your own home, whatever the weather.
MEASURE YOUR WORKLOAD, MONITOR YOUR PROGRESS
Schwinn's Air-Dyne is a precision ergometer. A built-in digital timer and workload indicator enable you to measure your performance in a given time. These instruments can help you avoid overexertion at the start, and measure your improvement on a continuing basis.
BACKED BY SCHWINN'S "NO-TIME-LIMIT" WARRANTY
The Air-Dyne is backed by the famous Schwinn "No-Time-Limit" warranty. Details available at your Schwinn dealer.
FULLY ASSEMBLED, READY TO RIDE AT YOUR AUTHORIZED SCHWINN FULL-SERVICE DEALER.
CALL TOLL-FREE 1-800-228-2230
SCHWINN® Air-Dyne®
The ultimate fitness machine
For free brochure, write Excelsior Fitness Equipment Co., 615 Landwehr Rd., Northbrook, IL 60062 · A Schwinn Company

Courtesy Excelsior Fitness Equipment Co.

The number of evaluative criteria used depends on the product, the consumer, and the situation.[3] Naturally, for fairly simple products such as toothpaste, soap, or facial tissue, the number of evaluative criteria used are few.[4] On the other hand, the purchase of an automobile, stereo system, or house may involve numerous criteria.[5] Characteristics of the individual (such as product familiarity and age) and characteristics of the purchase situation (such as time pressure) also influence the number of evaluative criteria considered.[6]

Table 16–1
Perceived Performance of Six Personal Computers

Evaluative Criteria	Consumer Perceptions*					
	AST	Compaq 286	Hewlett-Packard†	Macintosh	IBM AT	Leading Edge DZ
Price	4	3	3	4	2	5
Quality	3	4	5	4	3	3
Software	5	5	5	4	5	5
Portability	1	3	1	3	1	1
After-sale support	3	3	4	3	5	3

1: Very poor
2: Below average, poor
3: Average
4: Above average, good
5: Very good

*Consumer perceptions of how each computer performs on each evaluative criteria.

†Vectra.

Exhibit 16–2 illustrates Schwinn's use of evaluative criteria in promoting their Air-Dyne[R] machine. Notice that the ad copy stresses total body involvement as a key to total fitness. It goes on to emphasize that Air-Dyne's features allow one to exercise one's upper and lower body either simultaneously or separately. If the advertising campaign convinces the target market that this evaluative criterion is relevant and important, it will have a major advantage over competitors who lack this feature.

To illustrate the role of evaluative criteria in consumer decision making, six personal computers are evaluated on five criteria in Table 16–1. Table 16–2 shows how three consumers rank ordered the importance of these evaluative criteria. The three consumers are distinctly different from each other in what they think is important, even though they share the same set of evaluative criteria.

Table 16–2
Importance of Buyer Evaluative Criteria

Evaluative Criteria	Buyer A	Buyer B	Buyer C
Price	1	4	3
Quality	3	3	1
Software	4	2	2
Portability	5	1	5
After-sale support	2	5	4

Buyer A is more concerned with economic value in *price* and *after-sale support.*

Buyer B is focusing on *portability* and *software.*

Buyer C is buying *quality* and *software capability.*

If there were a substantial number of consumers like each of the three shown, we would have three distinct market segments. Each segment would be unique in the importance it attaches to the evaluative criteria used in evaluating a personal computer.

Notice the critical importance of properly determining the evaluative criteria used by consumers. In Table 16–1, the Macintosh rates reasonably well. However, if two additional criteria were added to the list—each of use and emotional response to the brand image—the Macintosh might be rated much higher. The next section describes how we determine which evaluative criteria are relevant.

Measurement of Evaluative Criteria

Before a marketing manager or a public policy decision maker can develop a sound strategy to affect consumer decisions, he or she must determine:

- Which evaluative criteria are used by the consumer.
- How the consumer perceives the various alternatives on each criterion.
- The relative importance of each criterion.

Because consumers sometimes will not or cannot verbalize their evaluative criteria for a product, it often is difficult to determine which criteria they are using in a particular brand-choice decision. This is even more of a problem when trying to determine the relative importance they attach to each evaluative criteria.

Determination of Which Evaluative Criteria Are Used. To determine which criteria are used by consumers in a specific product decision, the marketing researcher can utilize either *direct* or *indirect* methods of measurement. *Direct* methods include asking consumers what information they use in a particular purchase or, in a focus group setting, observing what consumers say about products and their attributes. Of course, direct measurement techniques assume that consumers can and will provide data on the desired attributes.

In the research that led to the development of Sunbeam's new food processor line, consumers readily described their desired product features and benefits. However, direct questioning is not always so successful. For example, Hanes Corporation suffered substantial losses ($30 million) on its *L'erin* cosmetics line when, *in response to consumer interviews,* it positioned it as a functional rather than a romantic or emotional product. Eventually the brand was successfully repositioned as glamorous and exotic, although consumers did not *express* these as desired attributes.[7]

Indirect measurement techniques differ from direct in that they assume consumers will not or cannot state their evaluative criteria. Hence, frequent use is made of indirect methods such as *projective techniques* (see Exhibit 10–3), which allow the person to indicate what criteria someone else might use. The "someone else" is very probably the person being asked of course, and we have indirectly determined the evaluative criteria used.

Perceptual mapping is another useful indirect technique for determining eval-

Figure 16–2
Perceptual Mapping of Beer Brand Perceptions

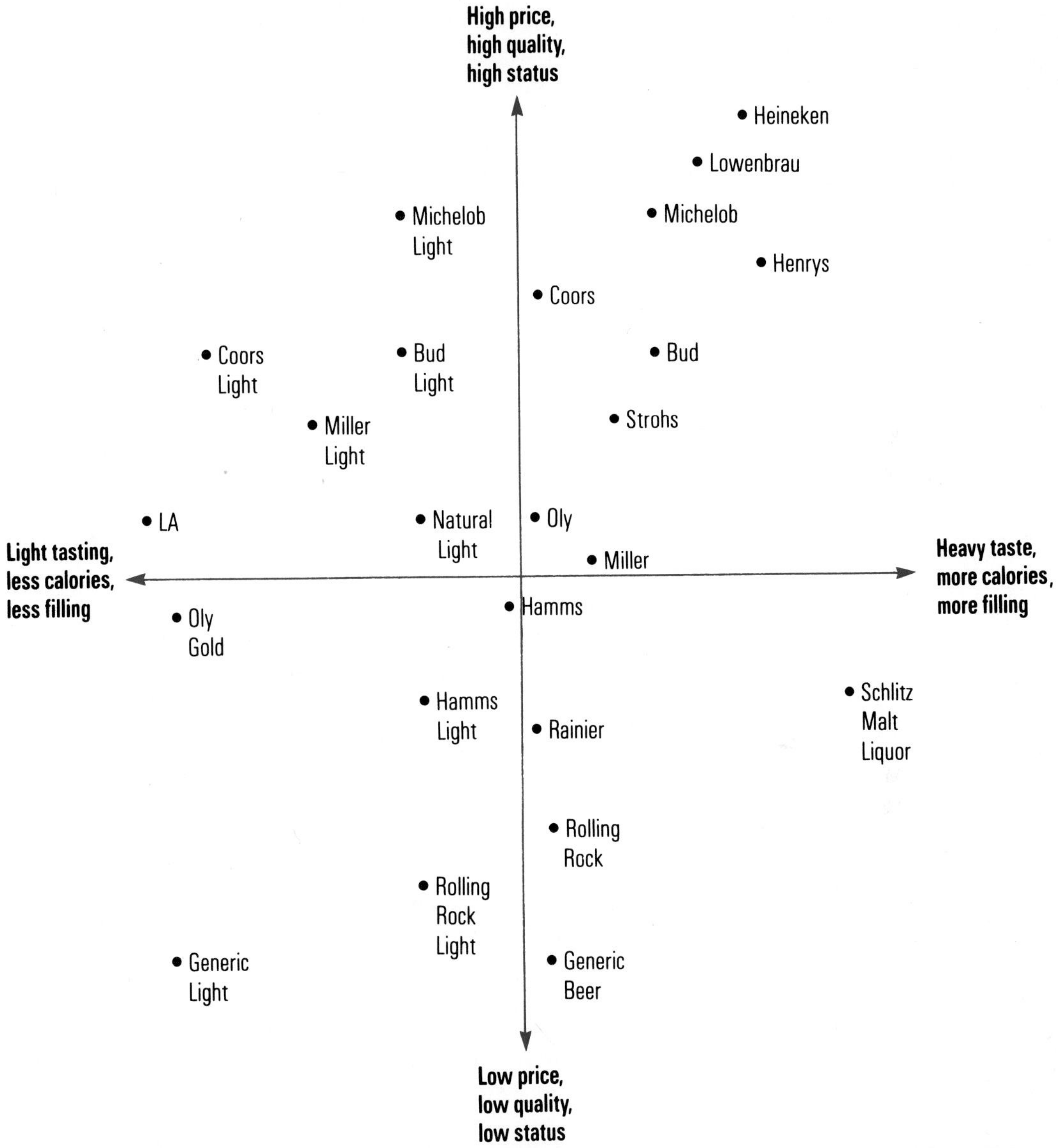

uative criteria. Consumers judge the similarity of alternative brands, then these judgments are processed via a computer to derive a spatial configuration or perceptual map of the brands. No evaluative criteria are specified. The consumer simply ranks the similarity between all pairs of alternatives, and a perceptual configuration is derived in which the consumer's evaluative criteria are the dimensions of the configuration.

For example, consider the perceptual map of beers shown in Figure 16–2. This configuration was derived from a consumer's evaluation of the relative similarity of these brands of beer. Examining this perceptual map, we can identify the horizontal axis on the basis of physical characteristics such as taste, calories, and fullness. The vertical axis is characterized by price, quality, and status that varies from low to high. This procedure allows us to understand consumer perceptions and the evaluative criteria they use to differentiate brands. With this type of information we can determine:

- How different brands are positioned according to evaluative criteria.
- How the position of brands changes in response to marketing efforts.
- How to position new products using evaluative criteria.

Determination of Consumers' Judgments of Brand Performance on Specific Evaluative Criteria. A variety of methods are available for measuring consumers' judgments of brand performance on specific attributes. These include *rank ordering scales, semantic differential scales, Stapel scales,* and *Likert scales* (see Appendix A). The semantic differential scale is probably the most widely used technique.

The semantic differential lists each evaluative criterion in terms of opposite levels of performance, such as fast-slow, expensive-inexpensive, and so forth. These opposites are separated by five to seven intervals and placed below the brand being considered, as shown below:

Macintosh Computer

Expensive	___	X	___	___	___	___	___	Inexpensive
High quality	X	___	___	___	___	___	___	Low quality
Software available	___	___	___	___	X	___	___	No software available
Easy to use	X	___	___	___	___	___	___	Hard to use

Consumers are asked to indicate their judgments of the performance of the brand by marking the blank that best indicates how accurately one or the other term describes or fits the brand. The end positions indicate *extremely,* the next pair *very,* the middle-most pair *somewhat,* and the middle position *neither-nor.* Thus, the respondent in the example above evaluated the Macintosh computer as very expensive, extremely high quality, somewhat short on software, and extremely easy to use.

Exhibit 16–3

Relative Importance of Evaluative Criteria and Marketing Strategy for a Fast-Food Restaurant

Jack in the Box, a fast-food chain, used a clown for its corporate symbol. The clown literally was exploded in a television campaign run in 1980 and now no longer represents the chain. Until 1980, advertising using the clown had stressed the fact that Jack in the Box had substantially more variety on its menu than other fast-food outlets. Robert Pasqualina of the firm's advertising agency explained the rationale for blowing up the clown:

> This campaign [the clown stressing menu variety] was a success in every traditional way: excellent viewer recall and favorable consumer reaction. Only thing was, sales were poor. It didn't work.
>
> We conducted new research which showed that consumers didn't care about menu variety. They cared about taste, convenient location of restaurants, and speed of service.
>
> We couldn't take on all three preferences, so we went with taste and set the new position as a quick-service restaurant that serves adult food which is better tasting than food at other fast-food restaurants. In February of 1980, we exploded the clown.

Tracking tests showed the highest brand and ad awareness in the restaurant's history. More important, sales increased dramatically. Clearly, focusing on the criteria consumers consider important is essential.

Source: "Jack in the Box Clown Explodes in TV Ads," *Marketing News*, December 11, 1981, p. 14.

Determination of the Relative Importance of Evaluative Criteria. Exhibit 16–3 illustrates the necessity of knowing the importance consumers attach to specific evaluative criteria. The importance assigned to evaluative criteria also can be measured by either direct or indirect methods. The *constant sum scale* is the most common method of direct measurement. This method requires the consumer to allocate 100 points to his or her evaluative criteria depending on how important each one is. For example, in evaluating the importance of computer criteria, a 100-point constant sum scale might produce the following results:

Evaluative Criteria	Importance (in points)
Price	20
Quality	15
Software	15
Portability	05
After-sale support	10
Ease of use	35
Total	100

This consumer has weighted ease of use most important, price second, quality and software tied for third, support fifth, and portability least in importance. Other evaluative criteria that could have been considered, such as input mode and screen size, presumably are not important to this consumer and therefore have implicit importance weights of zero.

One problem with the direct approach is that individuals tend to overweigh criteria of lesser importance while giving less weight than appropriate to important criteria.[8] One psychologist offered the following explanation for this problem:

> Possibly our feeling that we can take into account a host of different factors comes about because, although we remember that at some time or other we have attended to each of the different factors, we fail to notice that it is seldom more than one or two we consider at any one time.[9]

The most popular indirect measurement approach is *conjoint analysis*. In conjoint analysis, the consumer is presented with a set of products or product descriptions in which the potential evaluative criteria vary. For example, in Exhibit 16–4, a consumer was asked to rank in terms of overall preference 24 different computer designs featuring different levels of four key evaluative criteria. The preferences were then analyzed in light of the variations in the attributes. The result is a preference curve for each evaluative criterion, which reflects the importance of that attribute. For example, input mode and screen size are shown to be particularly important evaluative criteria for this consumer.

Conjoint analysis was used in the Sunbeam example that opened this chapter. Sunbeam tested 12 different attributes, such as price, motor power, number of blades, bowl shape, and so forth. As stated earlier, four segments emerged based on the relative importance of these attributes. In order of importance, the important attributes for two segments were:

Cheap/Large Segment	Multispeed/Multiuse Segment
$49.99 price	$99.99 price
4-quart bowl	2-quart bowl
Two speeds	Seven speeds
Seven blades	Functions as blender and mixer
Heavy-duty motor	Cylindrical bowl
Cylindrical bowl	
Pouring spout	

It should be noted that conjoint analysis is limited to the attributes listed by the researcher. Thus, a conjoint analysis of soft-drink attributes would not indicate anything about calorie content unless the researcher listed it as a feature. The Sunbeam study did not test such attributes as brand name, color, weight, or safety features. If an important attribute is omitted, incorrect market share predictions are likely to result.

Exhibit 16–4 Using Conjoint Analysis to Determine the Importance of Evaluative Criteria

Design features

Input mode
- Keyboard
- Mouse

Display monitor
- Black and white
- Color

Screen size
- 13 inch
- 9 inch

Price level
- $1,000
- $1,500
- $2,000

Design options

These design attributes produce 24 alternative computer design configurations

One design possibility

Input mode: Mouse
Display monitor: Color
Screen size: 13″
Price level: $1,500

Consumer preferences

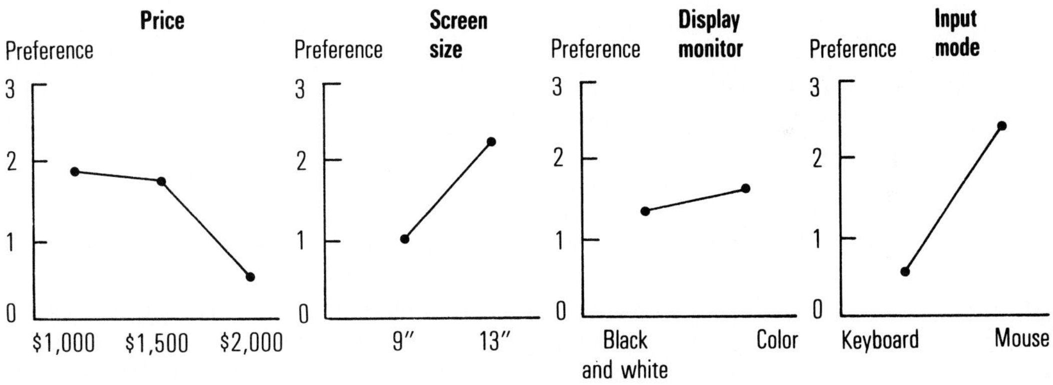

Relative importance

Evaluative criteria	Importance
Input mode	45%
Display monitor	5%
Screen size	25%
Price level	25%

- Input mode is the most important feature in this example, and the mouse is the preferred option.
- While price and screen size are also important, price becomes a factor between $1,500 and $2,000.

INDIVIDUAL JUDGMENT AND EVALUATIVE CRITERIA

Suppose quality of a personal computer was one of your evaluative criteria. How would you evaluate the quality of various brands? The simplest approach would be to apply a direct judgment based on a knowledge of technology, engineering, and craftsmanship. Such direct judgments commonly are applied to many evaluative criteria such as price, color, taste, and so forth. However, few of us possess the skills necessary to make a direct assessment of the quality of a computer. Therefore, many of us would make an indirect judgment by utilizing the reputation of the brand or the price level to *infer* quality. An attribute, such as price, used to estimate the level of a different attribute, such as quality, is known as a *surrogate indicator*. Marketing managers must be aware of the conditions in which consumers use surrogate indicators and the accuracy of those indicators.

Accuracy of Individual Judgments

The average consumer is not adequately trained to judge the performance of competing brands on complex evaluative criteria such as quality or durability. For more straightforward criteria, however, most consumers can and do make such judgments. Prices generally can be judged and compared directly. However, even this can be complex. Is a liter of Coca-Cola selling for 95 cents a better buy than a quart selling for 89 cents? Consumer groups have pushed for unit pricing to make such comparisons simpler. The federal truth-in-lending law was passed to facilitate direct price comparisons among alternative lenders.

The ability of an individual to distinguish between similar stimuli is called *sensory discrimination*. This involves such variables as the sound of stereo systems, the taste of food products, or the clarity of photos. The minimum amount that one brand can differ from another with the difference still being noticed is referred to as the *just noticeable difference* (j.n.d.). Marketers seeking to find a promotable difference between their brand and a competitor's must surpass the j.n.d. in order for the improvement or change to be noticed by consumers. On the other hand, a marketer sometimes may want to change a product feature but not have the consumer perceive any change and hence not surpass the j.n.d.

The higher the initial level of the attribute, the greater the amount that attribute must be changed before the change will be noticed. Thus, a small addition of salt to a pretzel would not distinguish the product from a competitor's unless the competitor's pretzel contained only a very limited amount of salt. This relationship is expressed formally as:

$$\text{j.n.d.} = \frac{\Delta I}{I} = K$$

where

$$\begin{aligned} \text{j.n.d.} &= \text{Just noticeable difference} \\ I &= \text{Initial level of the attribute} \\ \Delta I &= \text{Change in the attribute} \\ K &= \text{Constant that varies with each sense mode} \end{aligned}$$

Example: Lifting weights

$$\begin{aligned} I &= 100 \text{ lbs.} \\ K &= .02 \text{ for weight} \\ \text{j.n.d.} &= \frac{\Delta I}{100} = .02 \\ \Delta I &= 100 \text{ lbs.} \times .02 \\ \Delta I &= 2 \text{ lbs. for j.n.d.} \end{aligned}$$

For one to detect a weight change, more than 2 pounds would have to be added or taken away from the original 100 pounds. This formula is known as Weber's law. Values for K have been established for several senses and can be utilized in the development of functional aspects of products.[10] More useful than the formula itself is the general principle behind it—*individuals typically do not notice relatively small differences between brands or changes in brand attributes.* Makers of candy bars have utilized this principle for years. Since the price of cocoa fluctuates widely, they simply make small adjustments in the size of the candy bar rather than altering price. Marketers want some product changes, such as reductions in the size of the candy bars, to go unnoticed. These changes must be below the j.n.d. Positive changes, such as going from a quart to a liter, must be above the j.n.d. or it may not be worthwhile to make them, unless advertising can convince people that meaningful differences exist.

Packaging changes also can be determined by the j.n.d. Many times marketers want to redesign the package and improve it, but they must be careful that the consumer does not interpret a change in the package as a change (unless it is positive) in the product's quality and performance. Kendall Oil with its Pennsylvania motor oil, Helene Curtis with Everynight shampoo, United Vintners with Italian Swiss Colony wine, and White Rock Corporation with White Rock club soda all have recently modified packages while maintaining the favorable image associated with the original package.[11] As shown in Exhibit 16–5, Chix altered its name to Dundee in a series of small changes over a five-year period without losing customers.

Use of Surrogate Indicators

Consumers frequently use an observable attribute of a product to indicate the performance of the product on a less observable attribute. For example, most

Exhibit 16–5 A Brand Name Change Designed to Retain Loyalty

Original **Step 1** **Step 2** **Step 3**

When Dundee Mills acquired the Chix line of baby bedding and diapering accessories from Johnson & Johnson in 1977, a proviso was included that the Chix name revert to its original owners within five years.

The firm hired Gerstman & Meyers Inc. to effect the change from the Chix brand to the Dundee brand while retaining a loyal audience of retailers and consumers, and to update the package structure and graphics to reflect current marketing trends.

The result was a transition program that provided a virtually unnoticed changeover from a 50-year-old brand name to an unfamiliar one with no adverse market reaction.

The first step was the creation of a new, memorable Dundee logo and a bold, bright packaging format for the entire product line.

Graphics and colors provided continuity while the brand name gradually switched over the five-year period via a three-step process:

1. A new package design was introduced with a "**Chix** by Dundee" logo, with the old brand name much larger than the new one.
2. The size emphasis was reversed to the new name—"Chix by **Dundee**"—without changing any other graphic or packaging element.
3. The "Chix by" was deleted, and Dundee became the line's new brand name.

Courtesy Gerstman & Meyers, Inc. and Dundee Mills, Inc.

of us use price as a guide to the quality of at least some products. As stated earlier, an attribute used to stand for or indicate another attribute is known as a *surrogate indicator*.

Consumers' reliance on an attribute as a surrogate indicator of another attribute is a function of its *predictive value* and *confidence value*.[12] Predictive value refers to the consumer's perception that one attribute is an accurate predictor of the other. Thus, we saw in Exhibit 16–1 that Proctor & Gamble is hoping that consumers will believe that an endorsement by the American Medical Women's Association does indeed indicate health benefits from consuming Citrus Hill Plus Calcium.

The second component, confidence value, refers to the consumer's ability to distinguish between brands on the surrogate indicator. Thus, a consumer might believe that ingredients accurately (high predictive value) indicate the nutritional value of foods but not use them as indicators due to an inability to make the complex between-brand comparisons.

Perhaps the most widely used surrogate indicator, due in part to its high confidence value, is price. Price has been found to influence the perceived quality of shirts, radios, and after-shave lotion,[13] appliances,[14] carpeting,[15] automobiles,[16] and numerous other product categories.[17] These influences have been large, but, as might be expected, they decline as visible product differences, prior product use, and additional product information increase. Unfortunately, for many products the relationship between price and functional measures of quality is low.[18] Thus, consumers using price as a surrogate for quality frequently make suboptimal purchases.

Brand name often is used as a surrogate indicator of quality. It has been found to be very important when it is the only information the consumer has available and to interact with or, on occasion, replace the impact of relative price.[19] Store image,[20] packaging,[21] color,[22] country of manufacture,[23] and warranties[24] have also been found to affect perceptions of quality.

Evaluative Criteria, Individual Judgments, and Marketing Strategy

Marketers recognize and react to the ability of individuals to judge evaluative criteria, as well as to their tendency to use surrogate indicators. For example, most new consumer products are initially tested against competitors in *blind tests*. A blind test is one in which the consumer is not aware of the product's brand name. For example, Agree shampoo was not introduced until blind tests indicated it was preferred over a target competitor. Such tests enable the marketer to evaluate the functional characteristics of the product and to determine if a j.n.d. over a particular competitor has been obtained without the contaminating or "halo" effects of the brand name or the firm's reputation.

Marketers also make direct use of surrogate indicators. For example, Andecker is advertised as "the most expensive taste in beer." This is an obvious attempt to utilize the price-quality relationship that many consumers believe exists for beer. On occasion, prices are raised to increase sales because of the presumed price-quality relationship. For example, a new mustard packaged in a crockery jar did not achieve significant sales priced at 49 cents, but it did at one dollar.[25]

Marketers utilize brand names as indicators of quality in a number of ways. Elmer's glue stressed the well-established reputation of its brand in promoting a new super glue (ads for Elmer's Wonder Bond said, "Stick with a name you can trust"). And Texaco ("We're working to keep your trust") focuses almost entirely on the firm's image rather than on product attributes. Other types of surrogate indicators can be used. A marketer stressing the rich taste of a milk product, for example, would want to make it cream colored rather than white, and a hot, spicy sauce would be colored red.

How can a lesser-known brand convince a target market that it is equal or superior to a more prestigious competitor? Carnation has sought to convince consumers that its Coffee-Mate nondairy creamer tastes as good in coffee as cream does by advertising the results of a well-controlled blind taste test which confirmed this. Sylvania has followed a similar strategy by advertising the results of blind tests involving one of its models of television sets and similar models by General Electric, RCA, Sears, Sony, and Zenith. The Pepsi versus Coca-

Exhibit 16–6 GE's Product Quality Assurance Program

Courtesy GE Appliances

Cola comparisons touched off a national advertising war, with Pepsi claiming a two-to-one preference over Coca-Cola in blind taste tests. Coke countered with commercials claiming "one sip isn't enough" and generally tried to discredit the taste test process, before introducing New Coke. Similarly, Perrier came under attack from Canada Dry, which claimed that in a blind test connoisseurs preferred club soda over Perrier. Lipton, meanwhile, contended that consumers prefer Lipton's dry soup over Campbell's canned soup.

Exhibit 16–6 illustrates one of the most aggressive quality-assurance programs ever launched. In this campaign, GE guarantees absolute satisfaction with their major appliances for 90 days or a refund or exchange. This strategy not only greatly reduces any perceived risk associated with purchasing a GE major appliance, it serves as a strong surrogate indicator of product quality.

DECISION RULES

Suppose you have evaluated a particular model of each of the six computer brands in your evoked set on six evaluative criteria: price, quality, ease of use, software, portability, and after-sale support. Further, suppose that each brand excels on one attribute but falls short of one or more of the remaining attributes, as shown below:

	Consumer Perceptions*					
Evaluative Criteria	AST	Compaq 286	Hewlett-Packard†	Macintosh	IBM AT	Leading Edge DZ
Price	4	3	3	4	2	5
Quality	3	4	5	4	3	3
Software	5	5	5	4	5	5
Portability	1	3	1	3	1	1
After-sale support	3	3	4	3	5	3
Ease of use	3	3	3	5	3	3

*Rated from 1 (very poor) to 5 (very good).
†Vectra.

Which brand would you select? The answer would depend upon the decision rule you utilize.[26] Consumers frequently use five decision rules, either singularly or in combination: conjunctive, disjunctive, lexicographic, elimination-by-aspects, and compensatory. Table 16–3 provides a brief overview of each rule. Note that the conjunctive and disjunctive decision rules may produce a set of acceptable alternatives, while the remaining rules generally produce a single "best" alternative.

Conjunctive Decision Rule

The conjunctive decision rule *establishes minimum required performance standards for each evaluative criterion and selects all brands that surpass these minimum standards*. In essence, you would say: "I'll consider all (or I'll buy

Table 16–3
Decision Rules Used by Consumers

Conjunctive:	Select *all* (or any or first) brands that surpass a minimum level on *each* relevant evaluative criterion.
Disjunctive:	Select *all* (or any or first) brands that surpass a satisfactory level on *any* relevant evaluative criterion.
Elimination-by-aspects:	Rank the evaluative criteria in terms of importance and establish satisfactory levels for each. Start with the most important attribute and eliminate all brands that do not meet the satisfactory level. Continue through the attributes in order of importance until only *one* brand is left.
Lexicographic:	Rank the evaluative criteria in terms of importance. Start with the most important criterion and select *the* brand that scores highest on that dimension. If two or more brands tie, continue through the attributes in order of importance until *one* of the remaining brands outperforms the others.
Compensatory:	Select *the* brand that provides the highest total score when the performance ratings for all the relevant attributes are added (with or without importance weights) together for each brand.

the first) brands that are all right on the attributes I think are important." For example, assume the following represent your minimum standards:

Price	3
Quality	4
Software	3
Portability	1
After-sale support	2
Ease of use	3

Any brand of computer falling below *any* of these minimum standards (cutoff points) would be eliminated from further consideration. In this example, three computers are eliminated—IBM, AST, and Leading Edge. These are the computers that failed to exceed *all* the minimum standards. Under these circumstances, the remaining brands may be equally satisfying. Or, the consumer may choose to use another decision rule to select a single brand from these three alternatives.

Because individuals have limited ability to process information, the conjunctive rule is very useful in reducing the size of the information processing task to some manageable level. It first eliminates those alternatives which do not meet minimum standards. This is often done in the purchase of such products as homes or in the rental of apartments. A conjunctive rule is used to eliminate alternatives that are out of a consumer's price range, outside the location preferred, or that do not offer other desired features. Once alternatives not providing these features are eliminated, another choice rule may be used to make a brand choice among those alternatives that satisfy these minimum standards.

The conjunctive decision rule is commonly used in many low-involvement purchases as well. In such a purchase, the consumer evaluates a set of brands one at a time and selects the first brand that meets all the minimum requirements.

Disjunctive Decision Rule

The disjunctive decision rule establishes a minimum level of performance for each important attribute (often a fairly high level). All brands that surpass the performance level for *any* key attribute are considered acceptable.[27] Using this rule, you would say: "I'll consider all (or buy the first) brands that perform really well on any attribute I consider to be important." Assume that you are using a disjunctive decision rule and the attribute cutoff points shown below:

Price	5
Quality	5
Software	Not critical
Portability	Not critical
After-sale support	Not critical
Ease of use	5

You would find Leading Edge (price), Hewlett-Packard (quality), and Macintosh (ease of use) to warrant further consideration. As with the conjunctive decision rule you might purchase the first brand you find acceptable, use another decision rule to choose among the three, or add additional criteria to your list.

Elimination-by-Aspects Decision Rule

The elimination-by-aspects rule requires the consumer to rank the evaluative criteria in terms of their importance and to establish a cutoff point for each criterion. All brands are first considered on the most important criterion. Those that do not surpass the cutoff point are dropped from consideration. If more than one brand passes the cutoff point, the process is repeated on those brands for the second most important criterion. This continues until only one brand remains.[28] Thus, the consumer's logic is: "I want to buy the brand that has an important attribute that other brands do not have."

Consider the rank-order and cutoff points shown below. What would you choose using the elimination-by-aspects rule?

	Rank	Cutoff Point
Price	1	4
Quality	2	4
Ease of use	3	3
Software	4	3
After-sale support	5	3
Portability	6	3

Price would eliminate all but AST, Macintosh, and Leading Edge. Of these three, only Macintosh surpasses the quality hurdle. Notice that Compaq and Hewlett-Packard also exceeded the minimum quality requirement but were not considered because they had been eliminated in the initial consideration of price.

Using the elimination-by-aspects rule, we end up with a choice that has all the desired features of all the other alternatives, plus one more. In this case, Macintosh would be selected. The following narrative illustrates how this decision rule was used in the design of a television commercial:

> "There are more than two dozen companies in the San Francisco area which offer training in computer programming." The announcer puts some two dozen eggs and one walnut on the table to represent the alternatives and continues: "Let us examine the facts. How many of these schools have on-line computer facilities for training?" The announcer removes several eggs. "How many of these schools have placement services that would help find you a job?" The announcer removes some more eggs. "How many of these schools are approved for veteran's benefits?" This continues until the walnut alone remains. The announcer cracks the nutshell and concludes: "This is all you need to know in a nutshell."[29]

Lexicographic Decision Rule

The lexicographic decision rule requires the consumer to rank the criteria in order of importance. The consumer then selects the brand that performs *best* on the most important attribute. If two or more brands tie on this attribute, they are evaluated on the second most important attribute. This continues through the attributes until one brand outperforms the others. The consumer's thinking is something like this: "I want to get the brand that does best on the attribute of most importance to me. If there is a tie, I'll break it by choosing the one that does best on my second most important criterion."

The lexicographic decision rule is very similar to the elimination-by-aspects rule. The difference is that the lexicographic rule seeks maximum performance at each stage while the elimination-by-aspects seeks satisfactory performance at each stage. Thus, using the lexicographic rule and the data from the elimination-by-aspects example above would result in the selection of Leading Edge, because it has the best performance on the most important attribute. Had Leading Edge been rated a 4 on price, it would be tied with Macintosh and AST. Then, Macintosh would be chosen based on its superior quality rating.

When this rule is being used by a target market, it is essential that your product equal or exceed the performance of all other competitors on the most important criteria. Outstanding performance on lesser criteria will not matter if we are not competitive on the most important ones.

Compensatory Decision Rule

The four previous rules are *noncompensatory* decision rules, since very good performance on one evaluative criterion cannot compensate for poor performance on another evaluative criterion. On occasion, consumers may wish to average out some very good features with some less attractive features of a product in determining overall brand preference. Therefore, the compensatory decision rule states that *the brand that rates highest on the sum of the consumer's judgments of the relevant evaluative criteria will be chosen*. This can be illustrated as:

$$R_b = \sum_{i=1}^{n} W_i B_{ib}$$

where

R_b = Overall rating of brand b
W_i = Importance or weight attached to evaluative criterion i
B_{ib} = Evaluation of brand b on evaluative criterion i
n = Number of evaluative criteria considered relevant

If you used the relative importance scores shown below, which brand would you choose?

	Importance Score
Price	30
Quality	25
Software	10
Portability	05
After-sale support	10
Ease of use	20
	100

Using this rule, Macintosh has the highest preference. The calculations for Macintosh are as follows:

$$R_{\text{Macintosh}} = 30(4) + 25(4) + 10(4) + 5(3) + 10(3) + 20(5)$$
$$= 120 + 100 + 40 + 15 + 30 + 100$$
$$= 405$$

Table 16–4
Alternative Decision Rules and Selection of a Personal Computer

Decision Rule	Brand Choice
Conjunctive	Macintosh, Hewlett-Packard, Compaq
Disjunctive	Macintosh, Hewlett-Packard, Leading Edge
Elimination-by-aspects	Macintosh
Lexicographic	Leading Edge
Compensatory	Macintosh

As Table 16–4 indicates, each decision rule yields a somewhat different choice. Therefore, you must understand which decision rules are being used by target buyers in order to position a product within this decision framework.

Which Decision Rules Are Used by Consumers?

Consumers do not assign explicit numerical weights to the importance of attributes, nor do they assign numerical scores to the performance levels of various brands. These choice models are merely representations of the vague decision rules commonly used by consumers in brand selections.

To date, we cannot answer the question as to which rules are used by consumers in which situations. However, research done in specific situations indicates that people do *use* the rules.[30] A marketing manager then must determine, for the market segment under consideration, which is the most likely rule or combination of rules and then develop appropriate marketing strategy.

Research has shown that consumers are fairly consistent in their use of decision

Figure 16–3
Product Positioning Must Be Done with an Understanding of Target Buyers' Decision Rules

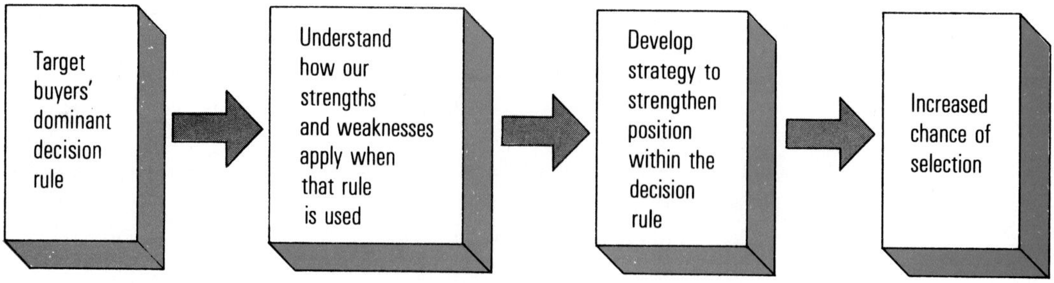

rules, as identical or very similar rules were used in the selection of different products and stores.[31] However, the time horizon involved,[32] as well as product complexity and product familiarity, have been found to influence the decision rules used.[33]

Low-involvement purchases probably involve relatively simple decision rules (conjunctive, disjunctive, elimination-by-aspects, or lexicographic), since consumers will attempt to minimize the mental "cost" of such decisions.[34] High-involvement decisions often may involve not only more complex rules (compensatory) but may involve stages of decision making with different attributes being evaluated using different rules at each stage.[35]

Marketing Applications of Decision Rules

As indicated in Figure 16–3 and Table 16–4, marketing managers should be aware of which decision rules are being used by their target market. Suppose that a target market for personal computers uses the six evaluative criteria shown below:

1. Price
2. Quality/Image
3. Software
4. Portability
5. After-sale support
6. Ease of use

What marketing strategy should IBM use to reach this market? Clearly, the answer depends in part on the decision rule or combination of rules being used. We will suggest some of the strategies that may be appropriate for each rule in the following paragraphs.

Conjunctive. IBM must meet the consumer's minimum requirements on *each* of the six criteria. The firm's promotional messages, either singularly or in combination, must inform the market of its performance on all six criteria. In our earlier example, they were outside the acceptable level on price and quality for this target buyer. This would have to be corrected to be successful if a conjunctive rule was being used. Since some consumers will buy the first acceptable brand, widespread distribution is desirable *if* other brands also meet the minimum criteria. Considerable effort should be directed toward retail sales personnel since they may help the consumer choose from among the several acceptable brands.

Disjunctive. The IBM AT must score above a (generally) high minimum on *at least one* of the key criteria. This means that product development and advertising can focus on a specific attribute such as quality. However, since this decision rule often produces a set of acceptable alternatives, the other attributes cannot be ignored.

Elimination-by-Aspects. In this case, IBM must determine the relative importance the target market assigns to each criterion, as well as the acceptable level of each attribute. Then it must make certain that its computer meets the acceptable level on each of the important criteria the competitors meet, plus one they do not meet. If the order of importance is price, quality, ease of use, software, after-sale support, and portability, IBM AT would have to be price competitive to make the first cut. Once price competitive, IBM would then have to focus on the remaining evaluative criteria, ensure it was in the acceptable range on each, and offer one feature that the other alternatives do not have.

Lexicographic. Again, IBM must determine the relative importance the target market assigns to each criterion. However, if the market uses this rule, IBM should attempt to beat the competition on the most important attribute. If it cannot beat the competition, it must at least tie them on this attribute. If it ties on the most important criterion, effort should shift to the second most important criterion. Assuming price is the most important attribute, with software next, promotional messages might be "IBM has the best software on the market, with a price competitive to other brands."

Compensatory. Once more, the importance of each of the criterion needs to be determined. However, IBM strategy now shifts to developing and promoting the best overall package of benefits. Although performance on the relatively important criteria must be fairly high, it is the total combination of performance that counts. Thus, price may be increased if necessary to allow for product improvements which will enhance attractiveness of the overall IBM product offering. Likewise, price reductions can be used to offset competitors' advantages in product features. Advertising should stress the strong features as well as the overall value of the IBM AT.

SUMMARY

During and after the time consumers gather information about various alternative solutions to a recognized problem, they evaluate the alternatives and select the course of action that seems most likely to solve the problem.

Evaluative criteria are the various features a consumer looks for in response to a particular problem. They are the performance levels or characteristics consumers use to compare different brands in light of their particular consumption problem. The number, type, and importance of evaluative criteria used differ from consumer to consumer and across product categories. Evaluative criteria are the factors the consumer considers in a purchase decision, so it is important for the marketing manager to know which criteria are used by the relevant target market.

The measurement of (1) which evaluative criteria are used by the consumer, (2) how the consumer perceives the various alternatives on each criterion, and (3) the relative importance of each criterion is a critical first step in utilizing evaluative criteria to develop marketing strategy. While the measurement task is not easy, a number of techniques ranging from direct questioning to projective techniques and multidimensional scaling are available.

Evaluative criteria such as price, size, and color can be judged easily and accurately by consumers. Other criteria, such as quality, durability, and health benefits, are much more difficult to judge. In such cases, consumers often use price, brand name, or some other variable as a surrogate indicator of quality. To overcome such surrogate indicators, many lesser-known or lower-priced brands advertise the results of (or encourage participation in) blind brand comparisons.

When consumers judge alternative brands on several evaluative criteria, they must have some method to select one brand from the various choices. Decision rules serve this function. A decision rule specifies how a consumer compares two or more brands. Five commonly used decision rules are disjunctive, conjunctive, lexicographic, elimination-by-aspects, and compensatory. Marketing managers must be aware of the decision rule(s) used by the target market, since different decision rules require different marketing strategies.

REVIEW QUESTIONS

1. What are *evaluative criteria* and on what characteristics can they vary?
2. How can you determine which evaluative criteria consumers use?
3. What methods are available for measuring consumers' judgments of brand performance on specific attributes?
4. How can the importance assigned to evaluative criteria be assessed?
5. What is *sensory discrimination,* and what role does it play in the evaluation of products? What is meant by a *just noticeable difference*? How have marketers used this concept in marketing products?
6. What are *surrogate indicators?* How are they used in the consumer evaluation process? How have marketers used surrogate indicators in positioning various products?
7. What is the *disjunctive decision rule?*
8. What is the *conjunctive decision rule?*
9. What is the *lexicographic decision rule?*
10. What is the *elimination-by-aspects decision rule?*
11. What is the *compensatory decision rule?*
12. How can knowledge of consumers' evaluative criteria and criteria importance be used in developing marketing strategy?
13. How can knowledge of the decision rule consumers might use in a certain purchase assist a firm in marketing products selected by use of this decision rule?

DISCUSSION QUESTIONS

1. List the evaluative criteria and the importance of each that you would use in purchasing ________. Would situational factors change the criteria? The importance weights? Why?
   a. Automobile.
   b. Mouthwash.
   c. Movie.
   d. Compact disc player.
   e. Car insurance.
   f. Haircut.

2. Repeat Question 1, but speculate on how your instructor would answer. In what ways might his or her answer differ from yours? Why?
3. Identify five products in which surrogate indicators may be used as evaluative criteria in a brand choice decision. Why are the indicators used, and how might a firm enhance their use (i.e., strengthen their importance)?
4. The table below represents a particular consumer's evaluative criteria, criteria importance, acceptable level of performance, and judgments of performance with respect to several brands of mopeds. Discuss the brand choice this consumer would make when using the lexicographic, compensatory, and conjunctive decision rules.

Evaluative Criteria	Criteria Importance	Minimum Acceptable Performance	Alternative Brands					
			Motobecane	Motron	Vespa	Cimatti	Garelli	Puch
Price	30	4	4	2	4	2	4	2
Horsepower	15	3	5	4	4	4	2	5
Weight	5	2	3	3	3	3	3	3
Gas economy	35	3	2	4	5	4	4	3
Color selection	10	3	2	5	2	4	4	3
Frame	5	2	3	3	3	4	2	3

Note: 1 = Very poor; 2 = Poor; 3 = Fair; 4 = Good; and 5 = Very good.

5. Describe the decision rule(s) you used or would use in the following situations:
   a. Choosing a bank.
   b. Choosing a restaurant.
   c. Choosing a career.
   d. Choosing a pencil.
   e. Choosing a toothpaste.
   f. Choosing a dentist.
   g. Choosing a Christmas gift for a friend.
   h. Selecting a television program.
   i. Deciding to donate blood.
   j. Selecting a pet.
6. Discuss surrogate indicators that could be used to evaluate the perceived quality of a television program, lawyer, or bicycle.
7. For what products would emotion or feeling be an important attribute? Why?

PROJECT QUESTIONS

1. Develop a list of evaluative criteria that students might use in evaluating alternative apartments they might rent. After listing these criteria, go to the local newspaper or student newspaper, select several apartments, and list them in a table similar to the one in Discussion Question 4. Then have five other students evaluate this information and have each indicate the apartment they would rent if given only those alternatives. Next, ask them to express the importance they attach to each evaluative criteria, using a 100-point constant sum scale. Finally, provide them with a series of statements which describe different decision rules and ask them to indicate the one that best describes the way they made their choice. Calculate the choice they should have made given their importance ratings and stated decision rules. Have them explain any inconsistent choices.
2. Develop a short questionnaire to elicit the evaluative criteria consumers might use in purchasing a __________. Also, have each respondent indicate the relative importance he/she attaches to each of the evaluative criteria. Then, working with several other students, combine your information and develop a segmentation strategy based on consumer evaluative criteria and criteria importance. Finally, develop an advertisement for each market segment to indicate that their needs would be served by your brand.
   a. VCR.
   b. Frozen pizza.
   c. Restaurant meal.
   d. "Spring break" vacation.
3. Set up a taste test experiment to determine if volunteer taste testers can perceive a just noticeable difference between three different brands of cola. To set up the experiment, store each cola in a separate but identical container and label the containers *L, M,* and *N*. Provide volunteer taste testers with an adequate opportunity to evaluate each brand before asking them to state their identification of the actual brands represented as *L, M,* and *N*. Evaluate the results and discuss the marketing implications of these results.
4. For a product considered high in social status, develop a questionnaire that measures the evaluative criteria of that product, using both a *direct* and an *indirect* method of measurement. Compare the results and discuss their similarities and differences and which evaluative criteria are most likely to be utilized in brand choice.
5. Find and copy three ads that encourage consumers to use a surrogate indicator.
6. Find and copy two ads that attempt to change the importance consumers assign to product class evaluative criteria.

REFERENCES

[1] A. L. Page and H. F. Rosenbaum, "Redesigning Product Lines with Conjoint Analysis," *Journal of Product Innovation Management,* no. 4, 1987, pp. 120–37.

[2] J. Hallaq and K. Pettit, "The Relationship of Product Type, Perceived Evaluative Criteria, and the Order of Consumption to the Evaluation of Consumer Products," in *Advances in Consumer Research,* ed. R. Bagozzi and A. Tybout (Chicago: Association for Consumer Research, 1983), pp. 600–604.

[3] Ibid.

[4] R. Wahlers, "Number of Choice Alternatives and Number of Product Characteristics as Determinants of the Consumer's Choice of an Evaluation Process Strategy," in *Advances in Consumer Research,* ed. A. Mitchell (Chicago: Association for Consumer Research, 1982), pp. 544–49.

[5] J. Freidenard and D. Bible, "The Home Purchase Process: Measurement of Evaluative Criteria through Purchase Measures," *Journal of the Academy of Marketing Science,* Fall 1982, pp. 359–76.

[6] D. Schellinch, "Cue Choice as a Function of Time Pressure and Perceived Risk," in *Advances in Consumer Research,* ed. R. Bagozzi and A. Tybout (Chicago: Association for Consumer Research, 1983), pp. 470–75.

[7] B. Abrams, "Hanes Finds L'eggs Methods Don't Work with Cosmetics," *The Wall Street Journal,* February 3, 1983, p. 33.

[8] P. Slovic and S. Lichtenstein, "Comparison of Bayesian and Regression Approaches to the Study of Information Processing in Judgment," *Organizational Behavior and Human Performance,* November 1971, p. 684.

[9] R. Shepard, "On Subjectively Optimum Selection among Multiattribute Alternatives," in *Human Judgments and Optimality,* ed. M. Shelly II and G. Bryan (New York: John Wiley & Sons, 1964), p. 266.

[10] R. L. Miller, "Dr. Weber and the Consumer," *Journal of Marketing,* January 1962, pp. 57–61; J. J. Wheatley, J. S. Y. Chiu, and A. Goldman, "Physical Quality, Price, and Perceptions of Product Quality: Implications for Retailers," *Journal of Retailing,* Summer 1981, pp. 100–116.

[11] W. P. Margulies, "Don't Shock Buyers—Subtle Package Updates Are Best," *Advertising Age,* February 19, 1979, pp. 53–54.

[12] G. L. Sullivan and K. J. Burger, "An Investigation of the Determinants of Cue Utilization," *Psychology & Marketing,* Spring 1987, pp. 63–74.

[13] B. Render and T. S. O'Connor, "The Influence of Price, Store Name, and Brand Name on Perception of Product Quality," *Journal of the Academy of Marketing Science,* Fall 1976, pp. 722–30.

[14] V. K. Venkataraman, "The Price-Quality Relationship in an Experimental Setting," *Journal of Advertising Research,* August 1981, pp. 49–52.

[15] J. J. Wheatley and J. S. Y. Chiu, "The Effects of Price, Store Image and Product and Respondent Characteristics on Perceptions of Quality," *Journal of Marketing Research,* May 1977, pp. 181–86; and Wheatley et al., "Physical Quality."

[16] G. M. Erickson and J. K. Johansson, "The Role of Price in Multi-Attribute Product Evaluations," *Journal of Consumer Research,* September 1985, pp. 195–99.

[17] K. Monroe, "The Influence of Price Differences and Brand Familiarity in Brand Preferences," *Journal of Consumer Research,* June 1976, pp. 42–49; D. R. Lambert, "Price as a Quality Cue in Industrial Buying," *Journal of the Academy of Marketing Science,* Summer 1981, pp. 227–38; M. Etgar and N. K. Malhotra, "Determinants of Price Dependency: Personal and Perceptual Factors," *Journal of Consumer Research,* September 1981, pp. 217–22; and Wheatley et al., "Physical Quality."

[18] E. Gerstner, "Do Higher Prices Signal Higher Quality?" *Journal of Marketing Research,* May 1985, pp. 209–15; and D. J. Curry and P. C. Riesz, "Prices and Price/Quality Relationships," *Journal of Marketing,* January 1988, pp. 36–49.

[19] Render and O'Connor, "Influence of Price"; J. Jacoby, J. Olson, and R. Haddock, "Price, Brand Name, and Product Composition Characteristics as Determinants of Perceived Quality," *Journal of Applied Psychology,* December 1971, pp. 470–79.

[20] Wheatley and Chiu, "Effects of Price"; Render and O'Connor, "Influence of Price"; Stafford and Enis, "Price Quality."

[21] Wheatley and Chiu, "Effects of Price"; C. McDaniel and R. C. Baker, "Convenience Food Packaging and the Perception of Product Quality," *Journal of Marketing,* October 1977, pp. 57–58; "Quality of House Brands Communicated via Packaging," *Marketing News,* January 30, 1987, p. 6.

[22] D. M. Gardner, "An Experimental Investigation on the Price Quality Relationship," *Journal of Retailing,* Fall 1970, pp. 39–40; and Wheatley and Chiu, "Effects of Price."

[23] C. K. Wang and C. W. Lamb, Jr., "Foreign Environmental Factors Influencing American Consumers' Predispositions toward European Products," *Journal of the Academy of Marketing Science,* Fall 1980, pp. 345–56; and P. Niffenegger, J. White, and G. Marmet, "How British Retail Managers View French and American Products," *European Journal of Marketing 14,* no. 8 (1980), pp. 493–98.

[24] J. L. Wiener, "Are Warranties Accurate Signals of Product Reliability?" *Journal of Consumer Research,* September 1985, pp. 245–50.

[25] K. B. Monroe, *Pricing* (New York: McGraw-Hill, 1979), p. 38.

[26] For an excellent technical discussion of decision theory, see J. J. Einhorn and R. M. Hogarth, "Behavioral Decision Theory: Processes of Judgment and Choice," in *Annual Review of Psychology,* ed. M. R. Rosenzweig and L. W. Porter (Palo Alto, Calif.: Annual Reviews, 1981), pp. 53–88. A marketing-oriented overview is J. R. Bettman, *An Information Processing Theory of Consumer Choice* (Reading, Mass.: Addison-Wesley Publishing, 1979), pp. 174–85.

[27] P. Wright, "Consumer Choice Strategies: Simplifying Versus Optimizing," *Journal of Marketing Research,* February 1975, pp. 60–67.

[28] A. Tversky, "Elimination by Aspects: A Theory of Choice," *Psychological Review,* July 1972, pp. 281–99.

[29] Ibid.

[30] C. W. Park, "The Effect of Individual and Situation-Related Factors on Consumer Selection of Judgmental Models," *Journal of Marketing Research,* May 1976, pp. 144–51; J. R. Bettman and C. W. Park, "Effects of Prior Knowledge and Experience and Phase of the Choice Process on Consumer Decision Processes: A Protocol Analysis," *Journal of Consumer Research,* December 1980, pp. 234–48.

[31] R. Blattberg, P. Peacock, and S. Sen, "Purchasing Strategies across Product Categories," *Journal of Consumer Research,* December 1976, pp. 143–54.

[32] P. Wright and B. Weitz, "Time Horizon Effects on Product Evaluation Strategies," *Journal of Marketing Research,* November 1977, pp. 429–43.

[33] C. W. Park, "The Effect of Individual and Situation-Related Factors on Consumer Selection of Judgment Models," *Journal of Marketing Research,* May 1976, pp. 144–51.

[34] See S. M. Shugan, "The Cost of Thinking," *Journal of Consumer Research,* September 1980, pp. 99–111; and W. D. Hoyer, "An Examination of Consumer Decision Making for a Common Repeat Purchase Product," *Journal of Consumer Research,* December 1984, pp. 822–29.

[35] See N. K. Malhotra, "Multi-Stage Information Processing Behavior," *Journal of the Academy of Marketing Science,* Winter 1982, pp. 54–71; and C. W. Park and R. J. Lutz, "Decision Plans and Consumer Chores Dynamics," *Journal of Marketing Research,* February 1982, pp. 180–215.

CHAPTER

17 Outlet Selection and Purchase

K mart is America's second largest retail chain. It achieved this position through aggressively positioning itself as a no-frills discount store offering mid- and lower-quality brands at rock-bottom prices. Martha Stewart is a syndicated columnist, author, and authority on food and entertaining. Her books on entertaining retail for around $50 and attract affluent, professional audiences. K mart and Ms. Stewart appear to have very little in common.

K mart recently signed Ms. Stewart as consultant and ad spokeswoman for its home fashions division. Ms. Stewart will make personal appearances in K mart stores and help create new kitchen, bed, and bath products, some of which will bear her name. She will also prepare a series of "Kitchen Kornerstone" brochures offering tips on cooking, decor, and entertaining which will be distributed by the Kitchen Korner boutiques located in K mart stores. Finally, she will represent K mart in both television and print media ads. Why is a discount image store using such an upscale strategy?

The answer is quite simple. Ms. Stewart represents a continuation of an attempt begun several years ago to give K mart an enhanced image. The Jaclyn Smith Signature collection, the use of Jaclyn Smith in ads, inclusion of more top national brands, and store redesigns began the process. The Jaclyn Smith strategy, bringing relatively upscale fashions into K mart, was seen as very risky when initiated in 1985 but has proven very successful.

K mart has examined the changes occurring in America's demographics and values and has concluded that the major growth opportunities are in the quality, style, and service areas, not the low-quality, low-price area. It is attempting to serve the mass market that increasingly values quality and style but retains a need for value as well.

To the extent K mart succeeds, top line manufacturers will face competition from K mart's private labels, as well as a need to secure distribution through its over 2,000 outlets.[1]

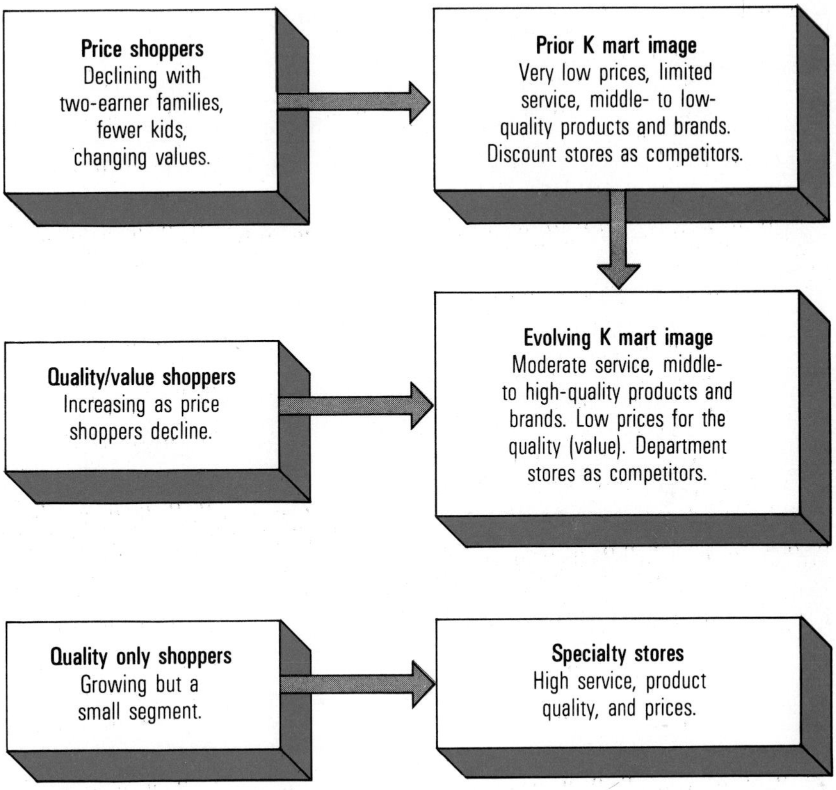

Outlet selection is obviously important to managers of retail firms such as K mart and L. L. Bean. However, it is equally important to consumer goods marketers. There are three basic sequences a consumer can follow when making a purchase decision: (1) brand (or item) first, outlet second; (2) outlet first, brand second; or (3) brand and outlet simultaneously.

Our model and discussion in the previous two chapters suggests that brands are selected first and outlets second. This situation may arise frequently. For example, in our computer example in the previous chapter, you may read about computers in relevant consumer publications and talk with knowledgeable individuals. Based on this information you select a brand and purchase it from the store with the lowest price (or best location, image, service, or other relevant attributes).

For many individuals and product categories, stores rather than brands form the evoked set.[2] One study found that two thirds of brand decisions for supermarket items were made in the store.[3] In our computer example, you might be familiar with one store—Campus Computers—that sells personal computers. You decide to visit that store and select a computer from the brands available there.

Table 17–1
Marketing Strategy Based on the Consumer Decision Sequence

Decision Sequence	Level in the Channel: Retailer	Level in the Channel: Manufacturer
(1) Outlet first, Brand second	• Image advertising. • Margin management on shelf space, displays. • Location analysis. • Appropriate pricing.	• Distribution in key outlets. • Point-of-purchase, shelf space, and position. • Programs to strengthen existing outlets.
(2) Brand first, Outlet second	• Many brands and/or key brands. • Co-op ads featuring brands. • Price specials on brands. • Yellow Pages listings under brands.	• More exclusive distribution. • Brand availability advertising (Yellow Pages). • Brand image management.
(3) Simultaneous	• Margin training for sales personnel. • Multiple brands/key brands. • High service or low price structure.	• Programs targeted at retail sales personnel. • Distribution in key outlets. • Co-op advertising.

A third strategy is to compare the brands in your evoked set at the stores in your evoked set. The decision would involve a simultaneous evaluation of both store and product attributes. Thus, you might choose between your second preferred computer at a store with friendly personnel and excellent service facilities versus your favorite computer at an impersonal outlet with no service facilities.

The appropriate marketing strategies for both retailers and manufacturers differ depending on the decision sequence generally used by the target market. Table 17–1 highlights some of the key strategic implications.

THE NATURE OF RETAIL OUTLET SELECTION

Selecting a retail outlet involves the same process as selecting a brand, as described in the previous chapters. That is, the consumer recognizes a problem which requires an outlet to be selected, engages in internal and possibly external search, evaluates the relevant alternatives, and applies a decision rule to make a selection.[4] We are not going to repeat our discussion of these steps. However,

Table 17–2
Advantages and Disadvantages of In-Home Shopping

Advantages
- Time savings: may reduce shopping and travel time.
- Time flexibility: can generally be done at any time of the day.
- Effort savings: less physical effort of travel, driving, and so forth.
- Psychological convenience: no frustrations with clerks, crowds, parking.
- Social risk reduction: no embarrassment when buying personal items or appearing "dumb" or "vain" to salespeople and others.
- Wide assortment: catalogs often have a much wider assortment than many stores.
- Entertainment: television shopping and, to a lesser extent, catalog shopping may be viewed as entertaining or fun.

Disadvantages
- Gratification delay: delivery takes time.
- Reduced social contacts: store shopping provides social contacts that many enjoy.
- Reduced personal attention: in-home shopping can seldom provide one-on-one advice.
- Increased product risk: one cannot physically examine items.
- Difficulty in comparing brands.

we will describe the evaluative criteria that consumers frequently use in choosing retail outlets, consumer characteristics that influence the criteria used, and in-store characteristics that affect the amounts and brands purchased.

Before turning to the above topics, we need to clarify the meaning of the term *retail outlet*. It refers to any source of products or services for consumers. In earlier editions of this text we used the term *store*. However, increasingly consumers see or hear descriptions of products in catalogs, direct-mail pieces, various print media, or on television or radio and acquire them through mail or telephone orders.[5] Generally referred to as in-home shopping, it represents a small but rapidly growing percent of total retail sales. In-home shopping offers the advantages and disadvantages shown in Table 17–2.[6] Given the advantages associated with in-home shopping, it is not surprising that most major retailers are becoming involved in this activity (just as many previously in-home only outlets are establishing retail stores).[7] Thus, the retail shopping environment is increasingly complex, challenging, and exciting for both consumers and marketers.

ATTRIBUTES AFFECTING RETAIL OUTLET SELECTION

The selection of a specific retail outlet, whether before or after a brand decision, involves a comparison of the alternative outlets on the consumer's evaluative criteria. This section considers a number of evaluative criteria commonly used by consumers.

Outlet Image

A given consumer's or target market's perception of all of the attributes associated with a retail outlet is generally referred to as the outlet's image.[8] Table 17–3 lists nine dimensions and some 23 components of these nine dimensions of store image.[9] The merchandise dimension, for example, takes into account such components as quality, selection, style, and price, while the service dimension includes components related to credit, financing, delivery, and sales personnel. Notice that the store atmosphere component is primarily emotional or feeling in nature.

Since the components in Table 17–3 were developed for stores, they require some adjustments for use with in-home outlets. For example, 800 numbers, 24-hour operations, and ample in-bound phone lines (no busy signals) are more relevant to the convenience of a catalog merchant such as L. L. Bean than are location and parking, as listed in the table.

Marketers make extensive use of image data in formulating retail strategies.[10] First, as Table 17–3 implies, marketers control most of the elements that determine an outlet's image.[11] Second, differing groups of consumers desire different things from various types of retail outlets.[12] Thus, a focused, managed image is essential for most retailers.

Table 17–3
The Dimensions and Components of Store Image

Dimension	Component(s)
Merchandise	Quality, selection, style, and price
Service	Layaway plan, sales personnel, easy return, credit, and delivery
Clientele	Customers
Physical facilities	Cleanliness, store layout, shopping ease, and attractiveness
Convenience	Location and parking
Promotion	Advertising
Store atmosphere	Congeniality, fun, excitement, comfort
Institutional	Store reputation
Posttransaction	Satisfaction

Source: R. Hansen and T. Deutscher, "An Empirical Investigation of Attribute Importance in Retail Store Selection," *Journal of Retailing*, Winter 1977–1978, pp. 59–73. Used with permission.

Department stores traditionally attempted to "be all things to all people." As a result, they suffered serious losses to more specialized competitors as markets became increasingly segmented during the 1980s. Their images were too diffuse to attract customers. In response they have sought to evolve into collections of distinctive specialty stores or stores-within-stores, each with a sharply focused image keyed to a well-defined target market.[13]

Other outlets concentrate on one or more attributes that are important to a segment of consumers or that are important to most consumers in certain situations. Catalog showroom merchants have successfully followed the first approach. They appeal to a segment that wants low prices on well-known brands but does not care about in-store sales help or pleasant decor.[14] Southland Corporation's 7-Eleven Food Stores have followed the second approach, which is to provide customers "what they want, when they want it, where they want it."[15] Thus, they focus on providing convenience for consumers in those situations where convenience is an important attribute.

Both individual stores and shopping areas (downtown, malls, neighborhoods) have images.[16] Thus, retailers should be concerned not only with their own image but also with the image of their shopping area. The ability to aggressively portray a consistent, integrated image is a significant advantage for shopping malls.

Retail Advertising

Retailers use advertising to communicate their attributes, particularly sale prices, to consumers. One study found that almost 55 percent of more than 500 adults surveyed checked newspaper advertisements before purchasing drugstore-type items.[17] Another study reported that approximately 40 percent used newspaper ads to help plan retail shopping trips.[18] Thus, a substantial percentage of consumers do seek store and product information from newspaper advertisements prior to purchase. A major study on the impact of retail grocery advertising concluded:

> In summary, a substantial number of consumers rely on newspaper grocery store advertising in making their choices about where to shop, what to buy, and when to do their shopping. They are apparently willing to modify their choice of products and stores or to shop at one time rather than another in the expectation of increasing their overall satisfaction.[19]

Of particular importance is the role of price advertising. It is clear that price advertising can attract people to stores. Revealing results were obtained in a major study involving newspaper ads in seven cities for a range of product categories (motor oil, sheets, digital watches, pants, suits, coffee makers, dresses, and mattresses). The impact of the retail advertisements varied widely by product category. For example, 88 percent of those who came to the store in response to the advertisement for motor oil purchased the advertised item, compared to

Figure 17–1
Expenditures of Individuals Drawn to a Store by an Advertised Item

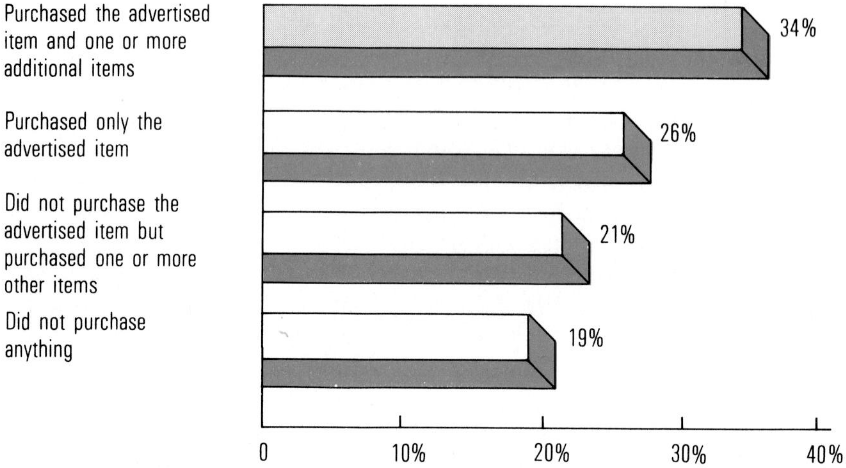

Source: Adapted from *The Double Dividend* (New York: Newspaper Advertising Bureau Inc., February 1977).

only 16 percent of those responding to the dress ad. Approximately 50 percent of the shoppers overall purchased the advertised item that attracted them to the store.

As Figure 17–1 illustrates, purchases of the advertised item understate the total impact of the ad. Sales of additional items to customers who came to purchase an advertised item are referred to as *spillover* sales. Spillover sales in this study equaled sales of the advertised items. That is, for every $1 spent on the sale item by people who came to the store in response to the advertising, another $1 was spent on some other item(s) in the store. The nature of these unplanned additional purchases is explored in the section of this chapter dealing with in-store influences.

Price Advertising Decisions. Retailers face three decisions when they consider using price advertising:

1. How large a price discount should be used?
2. Should comparison or reference prices be used?
3. What verbal statements should accompany the price information?

Unfortunately, only limited information is available to guide the manager in these decisions. Differences in the price discount of less than 10 percent, however, apparently have very little effect on consumer response.[20]

Exhibit 17–1 Sale Price Advertising

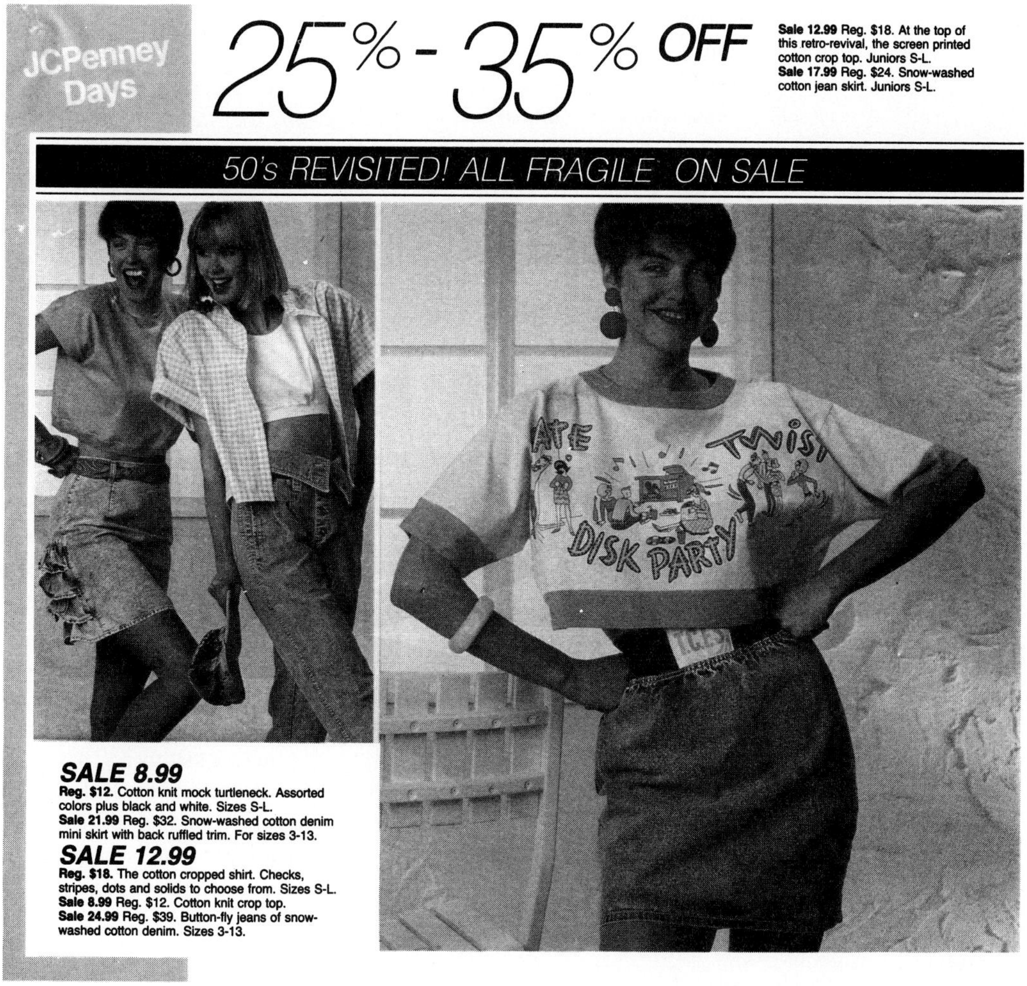
JCPenney Days
25% - 35% OFF
Sale 12.99 Reg. $18. At the top of this retro-revival, the screen printed cotton crop top. Juniors S-L.
Sale 17.99 Reg. $24. Snow-washed cotton jean skirt. Juniors S-L.
50's REVISITED! ALL FRAGILE ON SALE
SALE 8.99
Reg. $12. Cotton knit mock turtleneck. Assorted colors plus black and white. Sizes S-L.
Sale 21.99 Reg. $32. Snow-washed cotton denim mini skirt with back ruffled trim. For sizes 3-13.
SALE 12.99
Reg. $18. The cotton cropped shirt. Checks, stripes, dots and solids to choose from. Sizes S-L.
Sale 8.99 Reg. $12. Cotton knit crop top.
Sale 24.99 Reg. $39. Button-fly jeans of snow-washed cotton denim. Sizes 3-13.
DISK PARTY
TWIST

Courtesy J. C. Penney, Inc.

Consumers tend to assume that any advertised price represents a price reduction or sale price.[21] Showing a comparison price increases the perceived savings significantly.[22] However, the strength of the perception varies with the manner in which the comparison or reference price is presented. The best approach seems to be to present the sale price, the regular price, and the dollar amount saved. Most consumers understand reference prices and are influenced by them but do not completely believe them.[23] Since price and sale advertising have a strong impact on consumer purchases, the FTC and many states have special guidelines and regulations controlling their use.

The impact of such words or phrases as "now only," "compare at," or "special" is not clear. It does appear that such terms enhance the perceived value of a sale under at least some circumstances.[24] Unfortunately, the findings we have been discussing vary by product category, brand, initial price level, consumer group, and retail outlet. Thus, a retail manager must confirm these generalizations for his or her store and product line.

Exhibit 17–1 illustrates J. C. Penney's approach to reduced price advertising. In this ad, the sale price and the percentage reduction are emphasized, with the regular price presented for comparison purposes.

Outlet Location and Size

The location of a retail outlet such as a supermarket, bank, or restaurant plays an important role in consumer store choice. If all other things are approximately equal in a store selection decision, the consumer generally will select the closest store. This provides the store closest to a particular market a substantial advantage in attracting customers. Likewise, the size of an outlet is an important factor in store choice. Unless a customer is particularly interested in fast service or convenience, larger outlets are preferred over smaller outlets, all other things being equal. The increased selection of product lines, brands, and models associated with larger outlets appears to be highly desired by many customers.

These two factors have long been recognized by retailers, and several methods for calculating the level of store attraction based on store size and distance have been developed which predict retail trade fairly accurately. One such model is called the *retail attraction model* (also called the *retail gravitation model*). A popular version of this model, is

$$MS_i = \frac{\dfrac{S_i}{T_i^{\lambda}}}{\displaystyle\sum_{i=1}^{n} \frac{S_i}{T_i^{\lambda}}}$$

where:

MS_i = Market share of store i
S_i = Size of store i
T_i = Travel time to store i
λ = Attraction factor for a particular product category.[25]

In the retail gravitation model, store size generally is measured in square footage and assumed to be a measure of breadth of merchandise. Likewise, the distance or travel time to a store is assumed to be a measure of the effort, both physical and psychological, to reach a given retail area.[26] Because willingness to travel to shop varies by product class, the travel time is raised to the λ power.[27] This allows the effect of distance or travel time to vary by product.

For a convenience item or minor shopping good, the attraction coefficient is quite large since shoppers are unwilling to travel very far for such items.[28] However, major high-involvement purchases such as automobiles, or specialty items such as wedding dresses generate greater willingness to travel to distant trading areas.[29] When this is the case, the attraction coefficient is small and the effect of travel time as a deterrent is reduced.

Shown in Table 17–4 are the percentages of shoppers in Flagstaff, Arizona, who shop for various product lines *outside* of Flagstaff, a fairly small and isolated city in northern Arizona. As you can see, high-involvement purchases such as automobiles, furniture, and fashion clothing are associated with high levels of shopping outside the local community. In contrast, low-involvement purchases such as groceries are almost all made locally. These results are exactly what you would predict using the retail attraction model.

Table 17–4
Average Percentage of Various Product Categories Purchased Outside of Local Shopping Area

Product Type	Average Percentage of Purchases Outside the Area
Furniture	34%
Automobiles	33
Women's formal wear	28
Men's dress wear	27
Home furnishings	26
Home entertainment	25
Photo equipment	23
Women's everyday wear	22
Jewelry	21
Family footwear	21
Major appliances	20
Men's everyday wear	18
Sporting goods	18
Small appliances	17
Food and groceries	4

Source: R. Williams, "Outshopping: Problem or Opportunity?" *Arizona Business,* October/November 1981, p. 9.

Additional work in this area has shown that the availability of different transportation modes to retail centers affects consumer patronage.[30] Other attraction models include many of the economic and social aspects of time, money, and the value of shopping at a particular retail store.[31] Likewise, the situation is an important determinant of store choice.[32]

CONSUMER CHARACTERISTICS AND STORE CHOICE

The preceding discussion by and large has focused on store attributes independently of the specific characteristics of the consumers in the target market. However, different consumers have vastly differing desires and reasons for shopping, as Exhibit 17–2 illustrates.

This section of the chapter examines two consumer characteristics that are particularly relevant to store choice: perceived risk and shopper orientation.[33]

Perceived Risk

The purchase of products involves a certain amount of risk that may include both economic and social consequences. Certain products, because of their expense or technical complexity, represent high levels of *economic risk*. Products closely related to a consumer's public image present high levels of *social risk*. Table 17–5 shows that cookware and undergarments are low in economic and

Table 17–5
The Economic and Social Risk of Various Types of Products

Social Risk	**Economic Risk**	
	Low	High
Low	Sleepwear Ironing tables Undergarments Toys Cookware Hosiery	Vacuum cleaners Electric blenders Automobile tires Power tools Men's electric shavers Typewriters
High	Men's dress shirts Costume jewelry Women's blouses and sweaters Handbags Wall decorations Men's dress slacks	Draperies Ladies' coats Stereo hi-fi's Men's sports coats Ladies' dresses

Source: V. Prasad, "Socioeconomic Product Risk and Patronage Preferences of Retail Shoppers," *Journal of Marketing* (American Marketing Association, July 1975), p. 44.

Exhibit 17–2 Shopping Orientations of Clothing Shoppers

	PRICE SENSITIVE		**NOT PRICE SENSITIVE**	
	Conservative Taste	**Novelty Taste**	**Conservative Taste**	**Novelty Taste**
INVESTMENT BUYER	**Sensibles** Primarily women over age 35 with incomes under $35,000, they are likely to be homemakers or clericals, but their apparel spending is very low.	**Savvy shoppers** Primarily women age 25 and older with incomes of $20,000+, they are likely to be homemakers or clerical workers. Apparel spending is moderately high, and they are the most frequent shoppers.	**Executives** More likely to be men than women, they have high incomes, tend to be in management, professional, or technical occupations, and spend a lot on apparel.	**Clotheshorses** Men and women of all ages and occupations can belong to this group, but they are especially likely to be in sales. Apparel spending is very high.
UTILITY BUYER	**Make-do shoppers** Middle-aged and middle-income people, they are likely to have family responsibilities. All occupations are represented, but especially the skilled trades. Apparel spending is very low.	**Trendy savers** Primarily women age 18–45, they are in all income groups and are likely to be clericals, homemakers, or students. Their apparel spending is low.	**Reluctants** Primarily men, they are all ages and income ranges, although they tend to be blue-collar workers or retirees. They are infrequent shoppers and are low apparel spenders.	**Daddy's dollars** People under age 25 of all income ranges, most likely students, belong to this group. Apparel spending is moderate.

Source: Reprinted from R. C. Quarles, "Shopping Centers Use Fashion Lifestyle Research to Make Marketing Decisions," *Marketing News* (Chicago: American Marketing Association, January 22, 1982), p. 18.

Exhibit 17–3 L. L. Bean's Customer Service Policies

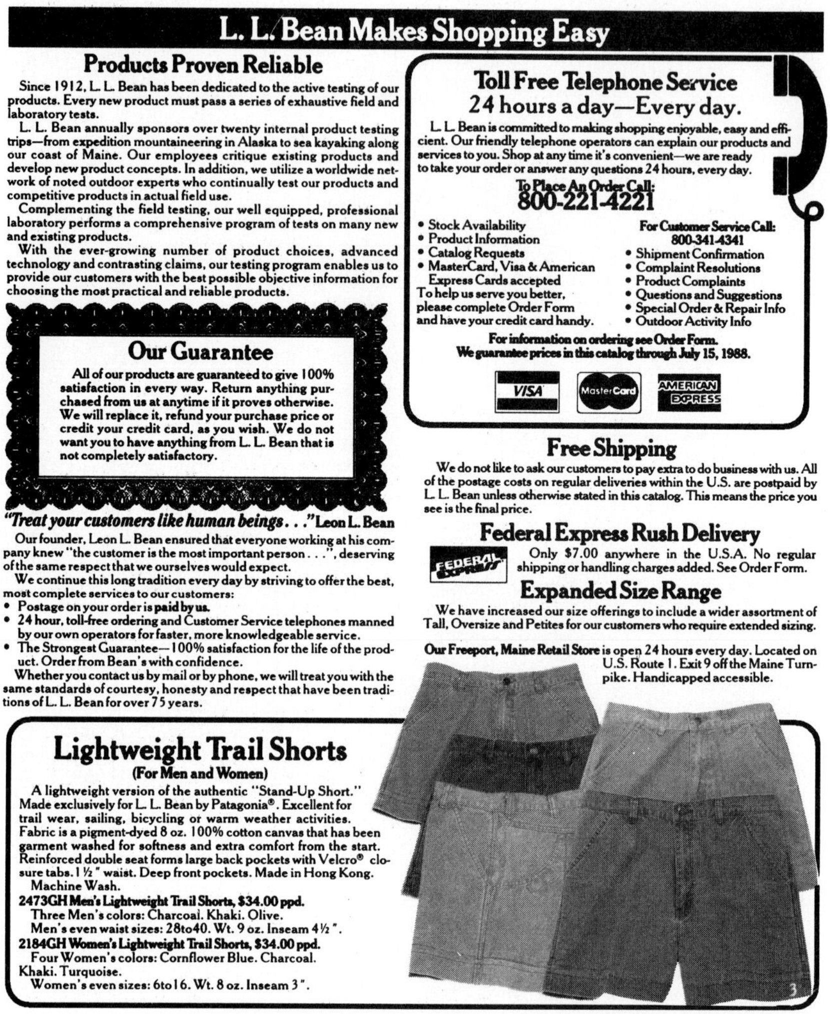

L. L. Bean Makes Shopping Easy

Products Proven Reliable

Since 1912, L. L. Bean has been dedicated to the active testing of our products. Every new product must pass a series of exhaustive field and laboratory tests.

L. L. Bean annually sponsors over twenty internal product testing trips—from expedition mountaineering in Alaska to sea kayaking along our coast of Maine. Our employees critique existing products and develop new product concepts. In addition, we utilize a worldwide network of noted outdoor experts who continually test our products and competitive products in actual field use.

Complementing the field testing, our well equipped, professional laboratory performs a comprehensive program of tests on many new and existing products.

With the ever-growing number of product choices, advanced technology and contrasting claims, our testing program enables us to provide our customers with the best possible objective information for choosing the most practical and reliable products.

Our Guarantee

All of our products are guaranteed to give 100% satisfaction in every way. Return anything purchased from us at anytime if it proves otherwise. We will replace it, refund your purchase price or credit your credit card, as you wish. We do not want you to have anything from L. L. Bean that is not completely satisfactory.

"Treat your customers like human beings. . ." **Leon L. Bean**

Our founder, Leon L. Bean ensured that everyone working at his company knew "the customer is the most important person . . .", deserving of the same respect that we ourselves would expect.

We continue this long tradition every day by striving to offer the best, most complete services to our customers:

- Postage on your order is **paid by us.**
- 24 hour, toll-free ordering and Customer Service telephones manned by our own operators for faster, more knowledgeable service.
- The Strongest Guarantee—100% satisfaction for the life of the product. Order from Bean's with confidence.

Whether you contact us by mail or by phone, we will treat you with the same standards of courtesy, honesty and respect that have been traditions of L. L. Bean for over 75 years.

Toll Free Telephone Service
24 hours a day—Every day.

L. L. Bean is committed to making shopping enjoyable, easy and efficient. Our friendly telephone operators can explain our products and services to you. Shop at any time it's convenient—we are ready to take your order or answer any questions 24 hours, every day.

To Place An Order Call:
800-221-4221

- Stock Availability
- Product Information
- Catalog Requests
- MasterCard, Visa & American Express Cards accepted

To help us serve you better, please complete Order Form and have your credit card handy.

For Customer Service Call:
800-341-4341

- Shipment Confirmation
- Complaint Resolutions
- Product Complaints
- Questions and Suggestions
- Special Order & Repair Info
- Outdoor Activity Info

For information on ordering see Order Form.
We guarantee prices in this catalog through July 15, 1988.

VISA MasterCard AMERICAN EXPRESS

Free Shipping

We do not like to ask our customers to pay extra to do business with us. All of the postage costs on regular deliveries within the U.S. are postpaid by L. L. Bean unless otherwise stated in this catalog. This means the price you see is the final price.

Federal Express Rush Delivery

FEDERAL EXPRESS

Only $7.00 anywhere in the U.S.A. No regular shipping or handling charges added. See Order Form.

Expanded Size Range

We have increased our size offerings to include a wider assortment of Tall, Oversize and Petites for our customers who require extended sizing.

Our Freeport, Maine Retail Store is open 24 hours every day. Located on U.S. Route 1. Exit 9 off the Maine Turnpike. Handicapped accessible.

Lightweight Trail Shorts
(For Men and Women)

A lightweight version of the authentic "Stand-Up Short." Made exclusively for L. L. Bean by Patagonia®. Excellent for trail wear, sailing, bicycling or warm weather activities. Fabric is a pigment-dyed 8 oz. 100% cotton canvas that has been garment washed for softness and extra comfort from the start. Reinforced double seat forms large back pockets with Velcro® closure tabs. 1 ½" waist. Deep front pockets. Made in Hong Kong. Machine Wash.

2473GH Men's Lightweight Trail Shorts, $34.00 ppd.
Three Men's colors: Charcoal. Khaki. Olive.
Men's even waist sizes: 28to40. Wt. 9 oz. Inseam 4½".

2184GH Women's Lightweight Trail Shorts, $34.00 ppd.
Four Women's colors: Cornflower Blue. Charcoal. Khaki. Turquoise.
Women's even sizes: 6to16. Wt. 8 oz. Inseam 3".

3

Reproduced courtesy of L. L. Bean, Inc.

social risk, while costume jewelry and men's dress shirts are low in economic risk but high in social risk. Other products, such as power tools and typewriters, are low in social risk but high in economic risk. Finally, men's sport coats and women's dresses are high in both economic and social risk.

The perception of these risks *differs* among consumers, based in part on their past experiences and lifestyles. For this reason, perceived risk is considered a consumer characteristic as well as a product characteristic.

Like product categories, retail outlets are perceived as having varying degrees of risk. Traditional outlets are perceived as low in risk, while more innovative outlets such as direct mail and television are viewed as higher risk.[34] And, as with products, consumers differ in how they assign and react to risk in retail outlets.[35]

A key aspect of consumer response to potential risk is self-confidence. Consumers who are more self-confident in an important purchase are more likely to purchase from a new store or specialty store than consumers who are less self-confident.[36] Under these conditions, less confident consumers tend to make their purchases at a well-established department store which, in their minds, reduces the risk of an unsatisfactory purchase.[37]

Based on the above, nontraditional retailers should attempt to minimize any perceived risk associated with this type of shopping if they hope to attract customers with relatively low levels of self-confidence. In response to this need, many catalog retailers have set up toll-free complaint lines, as well as automatic and rapid refunds for unsatisfactory orders.

Exhibit 17–3 shows how L. L. Bean attempts to reduce perceived risk by stressing product quality and testing, free shipment, 24-hour customer service telephones with trained assistants, and a 100 percent satisfaction guarantee for the life of the product. Word of mouth from satisfied customers reinforces these advertised policies.

Shopping Orientation

As we saw in the previous chapter, individuals go shopping for more complex reasons than simply acquiring a product or set of products. Diversion from routine activities, exercise, sensory stimulation, social interactions, learning about new trends, and even acquiring interpersonal power ("bossing" clerks) have been reported as nonpurchase reasons for shopping.[38] Of course, the relative importance of these motives varies both across individuals and within individuals over time as the situation changes. A shopping style that puts particular emphasis on certain activities is called a *shopping orientation.*

Shopping orientations are closely related to general lifestyle and are subject to similar influences. For example, one study found retail work experience, stage in the household life cycle, and income help to predict shopping orientation.[39]

A number of studies have described commonly held shopping orientations.[40] Exhibit 17–4 illustrates six distinct shopping orientations for grocery products. The opportunities for developing segmented marketing strategies for grocery shoppers is clearly reflected in this exhibit. Likewise, the diverse strategies required to appeal to broad market areas are easy to see (all of the groups shown in the exhibit were found in one market area).

Shopping orientation influences both the specific retail outlet selected and the general type of outlet. For example, shoppers who derive little or no pleasure from the shopping process itself are prime markets for convenience stores, at-

Exhibit 17–4 Shopping Orientations of Grocery Shoppers

Name/Characteristics	Description
1. In-store economy (19%) Price-oriented but not heavily involved in pretrip search or planning.	Compare prices, use unit prices, redeem coupons; shop for bargains and believe a person can save by shopping in different stores; do not believe grocery shopping is an important task, nor an opportunity to exercise or break out of the normal routine; do not plan menus; relatively young with a large family; well educated; desire store with many price specials and quality store brands.
2. Apathetic/mechanistic (9%) Little enthusiasm for shopping, perceive little utility in planning or search activities.	Negative attitudes toward shopping; negative feelings about value or enjoyment of shopping, menu planning, or cooking; small family size and relatively low concern for all attributes except trading stamps.
3. Involved traditional (24%) Enjoy shopping for economic and recreational reasons, heavy planners and researchers.	Positive attitudes toward trying new brands, planning, comparing prices, and redeeming coupons; positive feelings about value or enjoyment of shopping, use of recipes, and menu planning; older group.
4. Economy planners (25%) Price-oriented, heavily involved in budgeting and planning.	Positive attitudes toward using unit prices, coupons, and newspaper advertisements; compare prices; do not like to try new brands; like to plan menus and recipes; do not like to change stores; below average in age, largest family size; ideal attributes show emphasis on convenience, quality of store brands.
5. Homemakers (12%) Quality and brand oriented, they plan but do not engage in search or innovative activities.	Believe brand name implies quality; plan menus, believe grocery shopping is an important task; negative attitudes toward shopping in more than one store; average on all demographic variables; relatively less concerned about ideal attributes related to advertising, deals, friends that shop there.
6. Convenience (12%) Brand oriented, little planning, very convenience oriented.	Positive attitudes toward redeeming coupons, but do not use unit pricing; do not like to visit other stores because they know where things are in the present store, but are willing to visit other stores to see what is new; believe brand name implies quality; lowest educated group; very strong concern with ideal attributes related to convenience in reaching or in moving through store, low concern for store brands.

Source: Adapted from J. P. Guiltinan and K. B. Monroe, "Identifying and Analyzing Consumer Shopping Strategies," in *Advances in Consumer Research*, ed. J. Olson (Chicago: Association for Consumer Research, 1980), pp. 745–48.

home shopping (catalogs, telephone), and minimum in-store service outlets, such as catalog showroom merchants. Given the valuable strategic insights provided by thorough shopping orientation studies, this tool will play an increasingly important role in retail management.

IN-STORE INFLUENCES THAT ALTER BRAND CHOICES

As Figure 17–2 indicates, it is not uncommon to enter a retail outlet with the intention of purchasing a particular brand and to leave with a different brand or additional items. Influences operating within the store induce additional information processing and subsequently affect the final purchase decision. This portion of the chapter examines five variables that singularly and in combination influence brand decisions inside a retail store: *point-of-purchase displays, price reductions, store layout, stockout situations,* and *sales personnel.* As illustrated in Figure 17–3, each of these influences has the potential of altering a consumer's evaluation and purchase behavior.

The Nature of Unplanned Purchases

The fact that consumers often purchase brands different from or in addition to those planned has led to an interest in *impulse purchases*. Impulse purchases are

Figure 17–2
Supermarket Decisions: Two Thirds Are Made In-Store

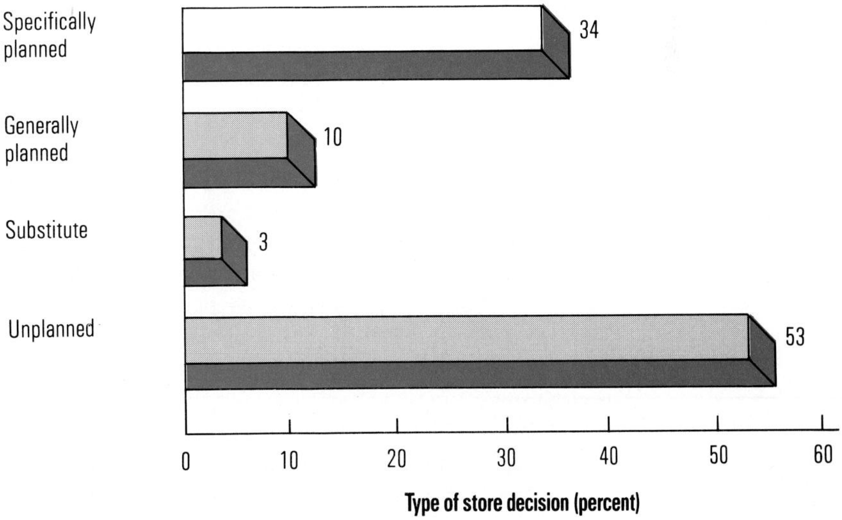

Source: J. Dagnoli, "Impulse Governs Shoppers," *Advertising Age,* October 5, 1987, p. 93.

Figure 17–3
In-Store Influences That Impact Alternative Evaluation and Purchase

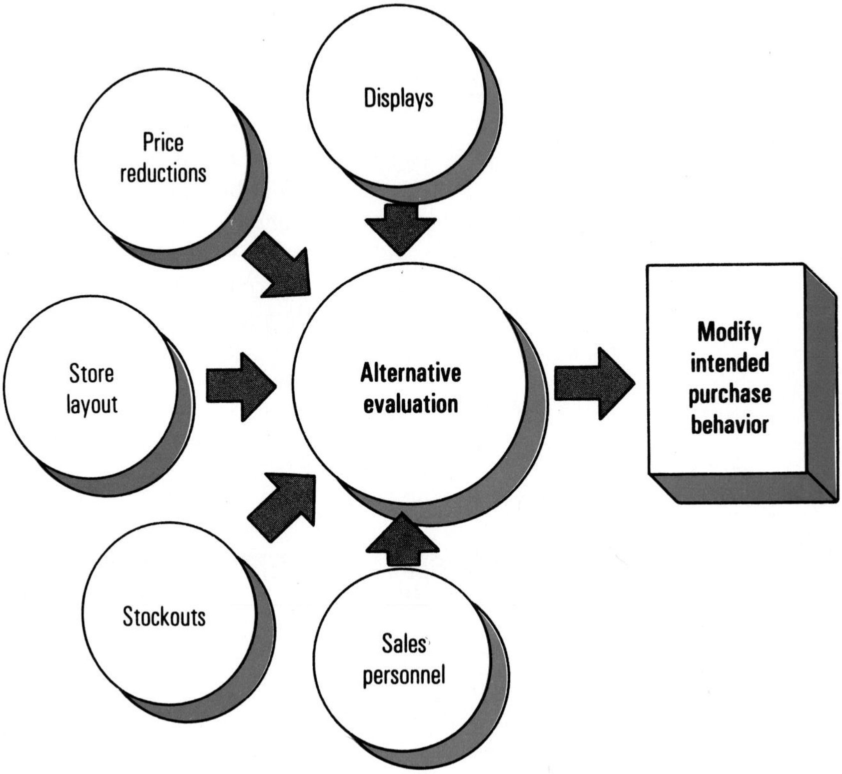

defined generally as *purchases made in a store that are different from those the consumer planned to make prior to entering the store*. Unfortunately, the term *impulse purchase,* and even its more accurate substitute, *unplanned purchase,* implies a lack of rationality or alternative evaluation. However, this is not necessarily true.[41] The decision to purchase Del Monte rather than Green Giant peas because Del Monte is on sale is certainly not illogical. Nor is an unplanned decision to take advantage of the unexpected availability of fresh strawberries.

Considering in-store purchase decisions as the result of additional information processing within the store leads to much more useful marketing strategies than considering these purchases to be random or illogical. This approach allows the marketer to utilize knowledge of the target market, its motives, and the perception process to increase sales of specific items.[42]

A major study of purchasing decisions in supermarkets, sponsored by Du Pont and the Point-of-Purchase Advertising Institute,[43] used the following definitions:

- *Specifically planned.* A specific brand or item decided on before visiting the store and purchased as planned.
- *Generally planned.* A pre-store decision to purchase a product category such as vegetables but not the specific item.
- *Substitute.* A change from a specifically or generally planned item to a functional substitute.
- *Unplanned.* An item bought that the shopper did not have in mind upon entering the store.
- *In-store decisions.* The sum of generally planned, substitute, and unplanned purchases.

Table 17–6 illustrates the extent of purchasing that is not specifically planned. It reveals that consumers make a great many brand decisions *after* entering the store. Thus, marketing managers not only must strive to position their brand in

Table 17–6
Shopper Purchase Behavior

Product	Specifically Planned	Generally Planned	+	Substituted	+	Unplanned	=	In-Store Decisions
Total study average	41.0%	22.5%		4.0%		33.5%		60.0%
Personal care	35.3	24.7		9.4		30.6		64.7
Magazines/newspapers/ books/stationery	41.6	28.6		1.3		28.6		58.4
Snack foods	22.2	23.8		4.8		49.2		77.8
Drugs/medicine	51.1	12.8		6.4		29.8		48.9
Tobacco products	66.7	8.9		—		24.4		33.3
Hardware/housewares	16.7	40.5		2.4		40.5		83.3
Prescriptions	100.0	—		—		—		—
Cosmetics	30.8	23.1		15.4		30.8		69.2
Soft goods/personal accessories	13.0	39.1		—		47.8		87.0
Nonalcoholic beverages	33.3	11.1		—		56.6		66.7
Alcoholic beverages	80.0	—		—		20.0		20.0
Photographic equipment	70.0	—		—		30.0		30.0
Garden supplies	50.0	50.0		—		—		50.0
Jewelry	—	20.0		—		80.0		100.0
Automotive supplies	20.0	20.0		—		60.0		80.0

Source: "Pilot Study Finds Final Product Choice Usually Made in Store," *Marketing News,* August 6, 1982, p. 5.

the target market's evoked set, they also must attempt to influence the in-store decisions of their potential consumers. Retailers must not only attract consumers to their outlets, they should structure the purchasing environment in a manner that provides maximum encouragement for unplanned purchases.

In-store marketing strategies are particularly important for product categories characterized by very high rates of in-store purchase decisions. For example, automotive supplies (80 percent in-store decisions) and books and magazines (58 percent in-store decisions) represent major opportunities. In contrast, tobacco products, alcoholic beverages, and photographic equipment represent less opportunity for in-store marketing strategies. More than 65 percent of these purchases are specifically planned prior to entering the store.

We now turn our attention to some of the variables that manufacturers and retailers can alter to influence in-store decisions.

Figure 17–4
Impact of Advertising and Point-of-Purchase Displays on Sales of Coffee

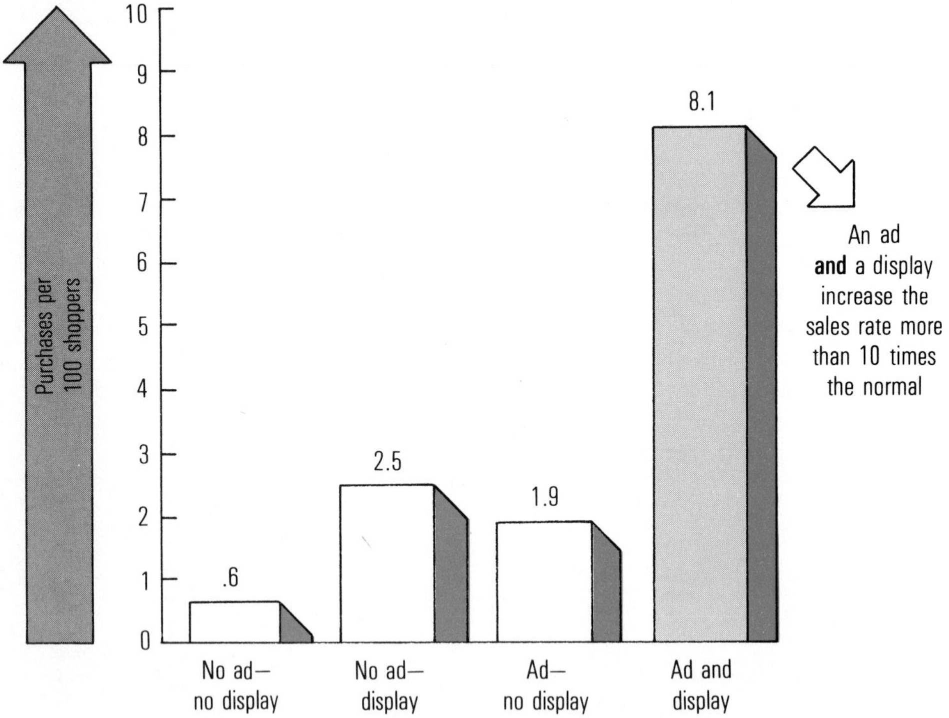

Source: POPAI/DuPont Consumer Buying Habits Study, 1978. Reprinted by permission of the Point-of-Purchase Advertising Institute.

Point-of-Purchase Displays

Point-of-purchase displays are common in the retailing of many products, and the impact these displays have on brand sales is often tremendous. Figure 17–4 provides a visual representation of this impact for coffee, and Exhibit 17–5 describes how several major marketers use point-of-purchase displays. Although the sales impact of displays (and ads) varies widely between product classes and between brands within a product category, there is a consistent and strong increase in sales.[44]

Though point-of-purchase displays vary greatly in size, shape, quality of construction, and appeal, one study found that even the addition of a simple mobile-type display was sufficient to increase purchases of cheese.[45] However,

Exhibit 17–5

Point-of-Purchase Marketing Efforts

- **Atari's Electronic Retail Information Center** (ERIC) is a computerized display installed in more than 500 stores. It is designed to help sell computers. An Atari 800 home computer linked to a video-disc player asks a series of questions to help the retailer determine a customer's level of computer ability and product needs. ERIC then switches on a video disc that plays the most appropriate of 13 messages based on the customer's inputs.*
- **Kodak's Disc Camera** was launched with a rotating display unit that presented the disc story to the consumer without the need for salesperson assistance. In addition to the display unit, the POP program included merchandising aids, sales training and meetings for retail store personnel, film display and dispenser units, giant film cartoons, window streamers, lapel buttons, and cash register display cards.†
- **Clarion** has developed an interactive computer as a POP device for its cosmetics line. Consumers interact with the unit by answering a series of multiple-choice questions on hair color, skin tone, and so forth. The computer then provides information which helps the consumer select the correct cosmetic.‡
- **Procter & Gamble** is considering using Sniff-Teasers to release a lemon aroma when consumers come within four feet of its "lemon fresh" Dash laundry detergent display.§

*"Firms Start Using Computers to Take the Place of Salesmen," *The Wall Street Journal,* July 15, 1982.
†"Kodak's Dazzling Disc Introduction," *Marketing Communications,* July 1982, p. 21.
‡J. Agnes, "P-O-P Displays Are Becoming a Matter of Consumer Convenience," *Marketing News,* October 9, 1987, p. 14.
§J. Freeman and J. Dagnoli, "Point-of-Purchase Rush is On," *Advertising Age,* February 8, 1988, p. 47.

the height and placement of the mobile display was critical. If the mobile was too high (10 feet off the ground) sales were unaffected; when the mobile was too low (7 feet off the ground) sales increased $13^1/_3$ percent; and when the mobile was at an intermediate height ($8^1/_2$ feet), sales increased 30 percent.

Time also had an impact on the sales effect of the mobile-type display. Most of the sales increase occurred in the first two weeks the display was utilized. When *new* materials were used each week:

- The percentage of shoppers buying cheese increased from 20 percent above normal the first week to 30 percent in the fifth week.
- The percentage buying milk increased from 40 to 60 percent.

In both cases, the average amount purchased by each shopper also was greater. When effective in-store display is combined with advertising, the results can be greater than the sum of the two individually. For example, in Exhibit 17–6, all

Exhibit 17–6 Impact of Display and Advertising on Peanut Butter Sales (percent sales gains)

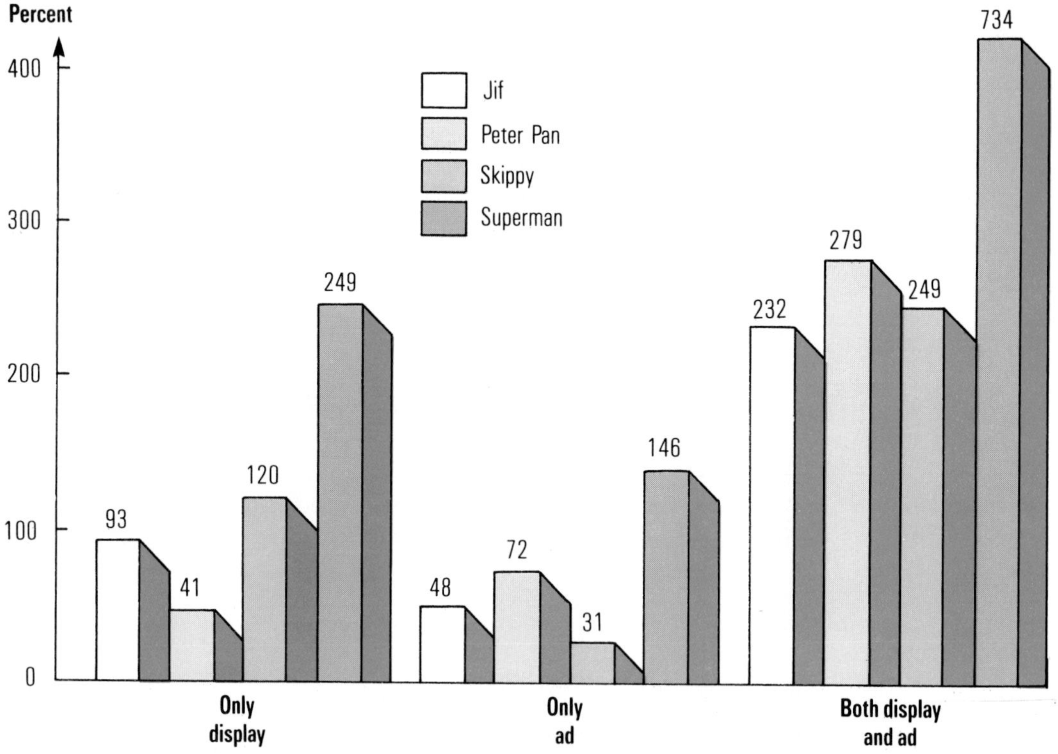

Source: "Display Effectiveness: An Evaluation, Part II," *The Nielsen Researcher*, 1983, p. 7.

four brands of peanut butter experienced percentage sales gains that were far greater when both the display and advertisements were utilized.

Price Reductions and Promotional Deals

Price reductions and promotional deals (coupons, multiple-item discounts, and gifts) almost always are accompanied by the use of some point-of-purchase materials. Therefore, the relative impact of each is sometimes not clear. Nonetheless, there is ample evidence that in-store price reductions affect brand decisions. Figure 17–5 illustrates the impact of promotion deals and in-store price reductions for a variety of dairy products. As can be seen, the impact is strong

Figure 17–5
Sales Impact of Promotional Deal

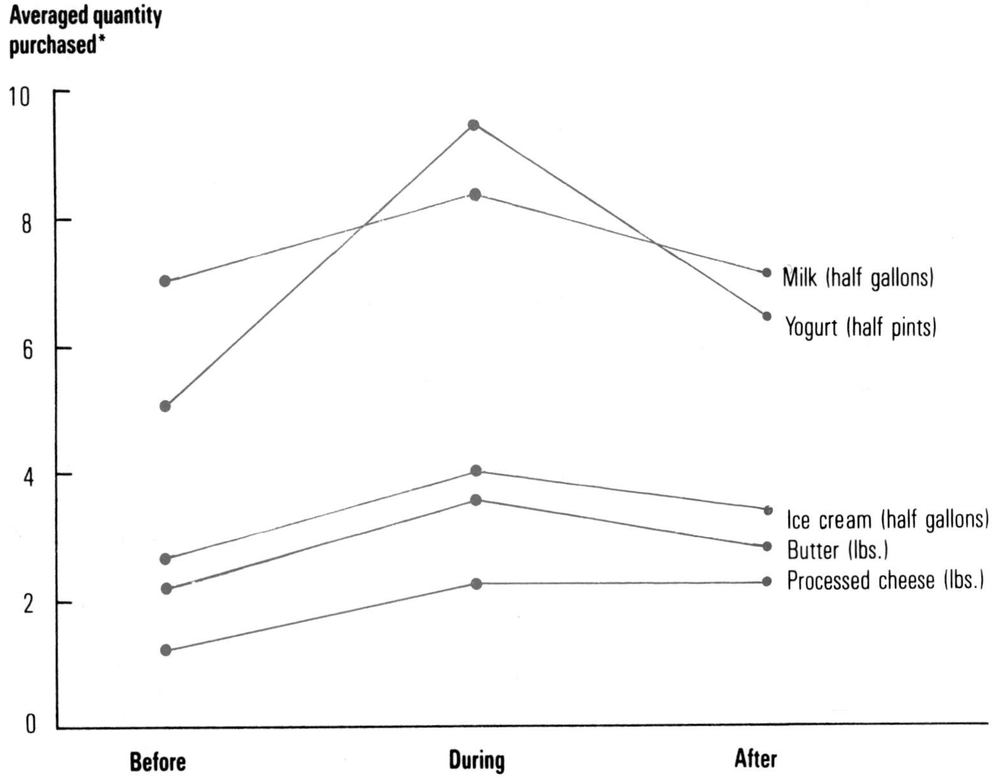

*Households that purchased in all three time periods.

Source: Adapted from B. C. Cotton and E. M. Babb, "Consumer Response to Promotional Deals," *Journal of Marketing*, July 1978, p. 111.

but short run in nature. That is, sales return to near normal after the special is removed.[46]

Sales increases in response to price reductions come from four sources.[47] First, current brand users may buy ahead of their anticipated needs (stockpiling). Stockpiling often leads to increased consumption of the brand since it is readily available. Second, users of competing brands may switch to the reduced price brand. These new brand buyers may or may not become repeat buyers of the brand. Third, nonproduct category buyers may buy the brand because it is now a superior value to the substitute product or "doing without." Finally, consumers who do not normally shop at the store may come to the store to buy the brand. Thus, consumer response to price reductions is complicated. Further, it offers differing advantages to the retailers and the manufacturer.

Not all households respond to price reductions and deals similarly. Available evidence suggests that households with ample resources (a strong financial base rather than a high income) are more likely to take advantage of deals than are other households.[48] Thus, stores oriented toward financially established consumers can anticipate a strong response to price reductions and other promotional deals. Similarly, products subject to stockpiling by consumers (nonperishables) exhibit more price elasticity than do perishable products.[49]

Store Layout

The location of items within a store has an important influence on the purchase of both product categories and brands. Typically, the more visibility a product receives, the greater the chance it will be purchased.[50] ShopRite grocery stores were forced to alter their standard store layout format when they acquired an odd-shaped lot. The major change involved moving the appetizer-deli section normally located adjacent to the meat section in the rear of the store to a heavy traffic area near the front of the store. The impact was unexpected:

- The appetizer-deli section accounts for 7 percent of this store's sales rather than the normal 2 percent.
- This increased profits, as these items average 35 percent gross margin compared to 10 percent gross margin for most items.

ShopRite began using the new layout for all future stores because of its dramatic effect on consumer purchase patterns and store profits.[51]

Store Atmosphere

While a store's layout has an influence on the traffic flow through the store, the store's *atmosphere* or internal environment affects the shopper's mood and willingness to visit and linger. The atmosphere is influenced by such attributes as lighting, layout, presentation of merchandise, fixtures, floor coverings, colors, sounds, odors, dress and behavior of sales personnel, and the number, characteristics, and behavior of other customers.

An example of the impact of the store atmosphere was presented in Chapter 13 (see Table 13–1). There we described how fast-tempo music decreased, and slow-tempo music increased, the amount of time restaurant patrons spent in the restaurant, the per table consumption of bar beverages, and the gross margin of the restaurant.

Most of the factors that influence store atmosphere are under the control of management. With this in mind, Montgomery Ward began a major remodeling of many of its stores, as described in Exhibit 17–7.

Techniques used by a successful "remodeling" specialist to create an appropriate store atmosphere include:

- Paint bright-colored interior walls beige and install neutral-colored carpet. Rainbow hues and patterns may look terrific as a backdrop, but they detract from the merchandise.

Exhibit 17–7 Ward's Effort to Improve Store Shopping Atmosphere

Special emphasis is on upgrading the apparel presentation, while keeping the actual merchandise at the same price level as before. Carpeting surrounds the redone apparel sections, and merchandise is individually highlighted with small, freestanding racks holding only a few items. The walls also are used for display, giving visual interest as well as squeezing more offerings into the same space. "The thrust of remodeling is to improve traffic patterns and attract more attention to the merchandise."

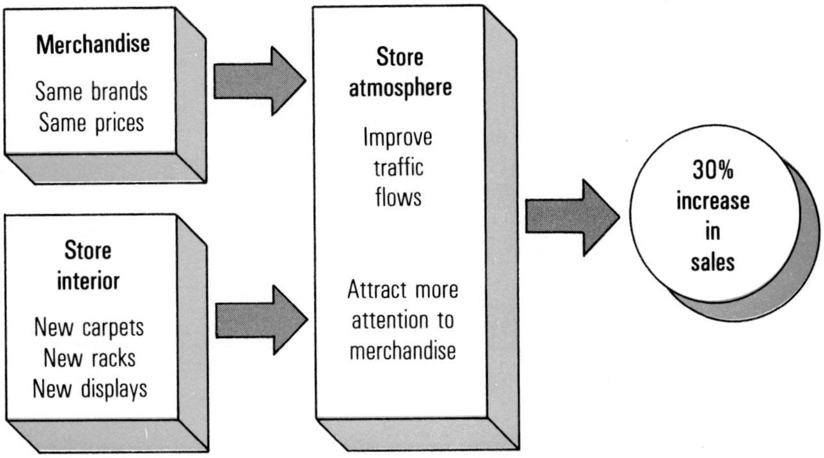

Source: Adapted from "Ward's Remodeling Its Image," *Advertising Age*, July 28, 1980, p. 40.

- Scrap long, supermarket-style aisles in favor of short aisles in a honeycomb-maze arrangement. This way, shoppers keep encountering aisle-ends, or "windows" in retail jargon, that are eye-catching places to display products.
- Install more interior walls. This helps organize products by category while boosting available display space as much as 25 percent.[52]

Stockouts

Stockouts, the store being temporarily out of a particular brand, obviously affects a consumer purchase decision. He or she then must decide whether to buy the same brand but at another store, switch brands, delay the purchase and buy the desired brand later at the same store, or forgo the purchase altogether. In addition, the consumer's verbal behaviors and attitudes may change. Table 17–7 sum-

Table 17–7
Impact of Stockout Situation

I. Purchase behavior

A. Purchase a substitute brand or product at the original store. The substitute brand/product may or may not replace the regular brand in future purchases.
B. Delay the purchase until the brand is available at the original store.
C. Forgo the purchase entirely.
D. Purchase the desired brand at a second store. All of the items initially desired may be purchased at the second store or only the stockout items. The second store may or may not replace the original store on future shopping trips.

II. Verbal behavior

A. The consumer may make negative comments to peers about the substitute store.
B. The consumer may make positive comments to peers about the substitute store.
C. The consumer may make positive comments to peers about the substitute brand/product.

III. Attitude shifts

A. The consumer may develop a less favorable attitude toward the original store.
B. The consumer may develop a more favorable attitude toward the second store.
C. The consumer may develop a more favorable attitude toward the second brand/product.

Figure 17–6
Shopper Behavior in Response to Frequent Stockouts

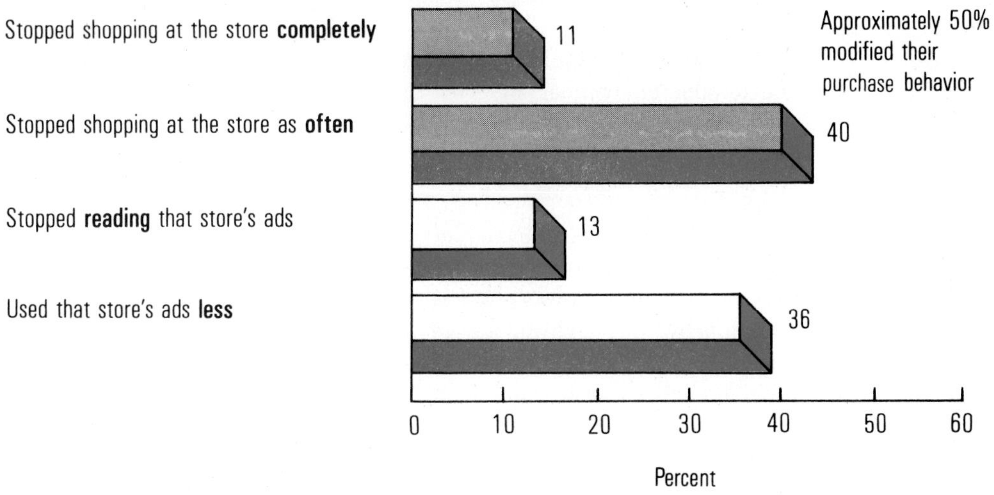

Source: Adapted from A Study of *Consumer Response to the Availability of Specials,* National Technical Information Service, U.S. Department of Commerce (B80–128507).

marizes the impacts that a stockout situation may have.[53] None of the likely outcomes is particularly favorable for the original store or brand. Thus, effective distribution and inventory management are critical for both manufacturers and retailers.

Which behavior a shopper engages in depends on his or her loyalty to the out-of-stock brand, the store, and the shopping situation. Figure 17–6 outlines common negative responses to stores that are frequently out of advertised specials.

Sales Personnel

Sales personnel can have a major impact on consumer purchases. In fact, many department stores are placing increased emphasis on effectively training their sales force. However, high cost and turnover are causing other outlets to move as close to total self-service as possible.[54]

For most low-involvement decisions, self-service is predominant. As purchase involvement increases, the likelihood of interaction with a salesperson also increases. Thus, most studies of effectiveness in sales interactions have focused on high-involvement purchases such as insurance, automobiles, or industrial products. There is no simple explanation for effective sales interactions. Instead, the effectiveness of sales efforts is influenced by the interactions of:

- The salesperson's resources.
- The nature of the customer's buying task.
- The customer-salesperson relationship.[55]

Thus, specific research is required for each target market and product category to determine the optimal personnel selling strategy.

PURCHASE

Once the brand and store have been selected, the consumer must complete the transaction. This involves what is normally called "purchasing" the product. Traditionally, this involved giving cash to acquire the rights to the product. However, credit plays a major role in consumer purchases in today's society. Without credit, a great many purchases simply could not be made.

The use of bank credit cards such as Visa, MasterCard, Diner's Club, and American Express, and store charge cards such as Sears, Ward's, and Penney's provides an increasingly popular way of financing a purchase decision.[56] For example, it is estimated that half of America's households have had Sears credit cards.[57]

Of course, credit not only is a means to purchase a product; it is a product itself. Thus, the decision to purchase a relatively expensive item may trigger problem recognition for credit. Since a variety of forms of credit are available, the decision process then may be repeated for this problem.[58]

SUMMARY

Most consumer products are acquired through some form of a retail outlet. Thus consumers must select outlets as well as products. There are three general ways these decisions can be made: (1) simultaneously; (2) item first, outlet second; or (3) outlet first, item second. Both the manufacturer and the retailer must be aware of the decision sequence used by their target market. It will have a major impact on their marketing strategy.

The decision process used by consumers to select a retail outlet is the same as the process described in Chapters 14 through 16 for selecting a brand. The only difference is in the nature of the evaluative criteria used. The store's image and the type and amount of retail advertising exert important influences as evaluative criteria. The major dimensions of store image are merchandise, service, clientele, physical facilities, convenience, promotion, store atmosphere, institutional, and posttransaction factors. Outlet location is an important attribute for many consumers, with closer outlets being preferred over more distant ones. Larger outlets generally are preferred over smaller outlets. These variables have been used to develop "retail gravitation" models. These models can predict the market share of competing shopping areas with reasonable accuracy.

Shopping orientation refers to the general approach one takes to acquiring both brands and nonpurchase satisfactions from various types of retail outlets. A knowledge of a target market's shopping orientations for a product category is extremely useful in structuring retailing strategy.

While in a store, consumers often purchase a brand or product that differs from their plans before entering the store. Such purchases are referred to as impulse or unplanned purchases. Unfortunately, both of these terms imply a lack of rationality or decision processes. It is more useful to consider such decisions as being the result of additional information processing induced by in-store stimuli. Such variables as point-of-purchase displays, price reductions, store layout, sales personnel, and brand or product stockouts can have a major impact on sales patterns.

Once the outlet and brand have been selected, the consumer must acquire the rights to the item. Increasingly this involves the use of credit—particularly the use of credit cards. However, major purchases often require the consumer to make a second purchase decision: "What type of credit shall I buy to finance this purchase?" Financial institutions increasingly recognize the opportunities in the consumer credit field and are beginning to utilize standard consumer goods marketing techniques.

REVIEW QUESTIONS

1. The consumer faces both the problem of what to buy and where to buy it. How do these two types of decisions differ?
2. How does the sequence in which the brand/outlet decision is made affect the brand strategy? The retailer strategy?
3. What are the advantages and disadvantages of *in-home shopping?*
4. What is a *store image* and what are its dimensions and components?
5. Describe the impact of retail advertising on retail sales.
6. What is meant by the term *spillover sales?* Why is it important?
7. What are the primary price advertising decisions confronting a retailer?
8. How does the size and distance to a retail outlet affect store selection and purchase behavior?
9. Describe the model of *retail gravitation* presented in the chapter.
10. How is store choice affected by the *perceived risk* of a purchase?
11. What is mean by *social risk?* How does it differ from *economic risk?*
12. What role does consumer confidence play in store choice?
13. What is a *shopping orientation?*
14. Describe the shopping orientations of (*a*) grocery shoppers, and (*b*) clothes shoppers.
15. What is meant by *in-store purchase decision?* Why is it important?
16. Once in a particular store, what in-store characteristics can influence brand choice? Give an example of each.

17. What can happen in response to a *stockout?*
18. What factors determine the effectiveness of a salesperson?
19. What is meant by *store atmosphere?*
20. What role does the method of payment play in the final implementation of a purchase decision?

DISCUSSION QUESTIONS

1. How would you measure the image of a retail outlet?
2. Does the image of a retail outlet affect the image of the brands it carries?
3. How are social and economic risks likely to affect different prospective buyers of ______? Will either type of risk affect store choice? If so, in what way?
   a. Compact disc player.
   b. Restaurant meal.
   c. Christmas present.
   d. Mouthwash.
   e. Suit.
   f. Tennis racket.
4. What in-store characteristics could retailers use to enhance the probability of purchase among individuals who visit a store? Describe each factor in terms of how it should be used, and describe its intended effect on the consumer for the following products:
   a. Mouthwash.
   b. Tennis racket.
   c. Tomatoes.
   d. Personal computer.
5. What type of store atmosphere is most appropriate for each of the store types listed in Question 4?
6. How would a retailer's and a manufacturer's interest differ in a price reduction on a brand?
7. Retailers often engage in "loss leader" advertising, in which a popular item is advertised at or below cost. Does this make sense? Why?
8. How do you respond to a stockout of your preferred brand of ______? What factors other than product category influence your response?
   a. Soft drink.
   b. Toothpaste.
   c. Perfume/after-shave lotion.
   d. Deodorant.
   e. Beer.
   f. Headache remedy.
9. What percent of your purchases are "unplanned"? Do you consider your unplanned purchases to be "irrational"?
10. What are the marketing strategy implications of:
    a. Table 17–2?
    b. Table 17–3?
    c. Figure 17–1?
    d. Exhibit 17–2?
    e. Table 17–5?
    f. Exhibit 17–4?
    g. Figure 17–2?
    h. Table 17–6?
    i. Figure 17–4?
    j. Figure 17–5?

PROJECT QUESTIONS

1. Pick a new residential area in your town and develop a gravitational model for (*a*) nearby supermarkets and (*b*) shopping malls. Conduct telephone surveys to test the accuracy of your model.
2. Develop a questionnaire to measure the image of ______. Have other students complete these questionnaires for three or four competing outlets. Discuss the marketing implications of your results.
   a. Grocery stores.
   b. Department stores.
   c. Specialty stores.
   d. Bookstores.
   e. Computer stores.
3. For several of the products listed in Table 17–6, interview several students not enrolled in your class and ask them to classify their last purchase as specially planned, generally planned, substitute, or unplanned. Then combine your results with your classmates' to obtain an estimate of student behavior. Compare student behavior with the behavior shown in Table 17–6, and discuss any similarities or differences.
4. Arrange with a local retailer (convenience store, drugstore, and so on) to temporarily install a point-of-purchase display. Then set up a procedure to unobtrusively observe the frequency of evaluation and selection at the display.
5. Visit three retail stores selling the same type of merchandise and prepare a report on their use of P-O-P displays.
6. Interview the manager of a drug, department or grocery store on their views of P-O-P displays and price advertising.
7. Find and copy two price advertisements you feel are effective and two you feel are ineffective. Justify your choices.
8. Develop an appropriate questionnaire and construct a new version of Table 17–5 using products relevant to college students.
9. Determine through interviews the general shopping orientations of students on your campus. What are the marketing implications of your findings?

REFERENCES

[1] P. Stenrad, "K mart Dangles Lure for Affluent Shoppers," *Advertising Age,* August 24, 1987, p. 12.

[2] S. Spiggle and M. A. Sewall, "A Choice Sets Model of Retail Selection," *Journal of Marketing,* April 1987, pp. 97–111.

[3] J. Agnew, "P-O-P Displays Are Becoming a Matter of Consumer Convenience," *Marketing News,* October 9, 1987, p. 14.

[4] See Spiggle and Sewall, "A Choice."

[5] J. Agnew, "Home Shopping: TV's Hit of the Season," *Marketing News,* March 13, 1987, pp. 1, 20; J. Dagnoli, "Home Shopping Net Expands Its Game Plan," *Advertising Age,* June 22, 1987, p. 44; J. Meyers, "Levi Gets Computer Blues,"

Advertising Age, June 29, 1987, p. 28; S. Hume, "Sears Tests Video Catalog," *Advertising Age,* November 1, 1987; and E. Norris, "Databased Marketing Sets Enticing Bait," *Advertising Age,* January 18, 1988, pp. S10–S12.

[6] See J. R. Lumpkin and J. M. Hawes, "Retailing without Stores," *Journal of Business Research,* April 1985, pp. 139–51; J. M. Hawes and J. R. Lumpkin, "Perceived Risk and the Selection of a Retail Patronage Mode," *Journal of the Academy of Marketing Science,* Winter 1986, pp. 37–42; and J. C. Darian, "In-Home Shopping," *Journal of Retailing,* Summer 1987, pp. 163–86.

[7] J. Y. Cleaver, "TV Shopping Intrigues Major Players," *Advertising Age,* October 26, 1987, p. S11; G. S. Trager, "Retailers, Catalogers Cross Channels," *Advertising Age,* October 26, 1987; and J. Cleaver, "Consumers at Home with Shopping," *Advertising Age,* January 18, 1988, pp. S15–S19.

[8] For a discussion of the validity of this concept, see J. J. Kasulis and R. F. Lusch, "Validating the Retail Store Image Concept," *Journal of the Academy of Marketing Science,* Fall 1981, pp. 419–35.

[9] For a conflicting view, see R. Arora, "Consumer Involvement in Retail Store Positioning," *Journal of the Academy of Marketing Science,* Spring 1981.

[10] See E. A. Pessemier, "Store Image and Positioning," *Journal of Retailing,* Spring 1980, pp. 94–106.

[11] D. Mazursky and J. Jacoby, "Exploring the Development of Store Images," *Journal of Retailing,* Summer 1986, pp. 145–65.

[12] For examples see J. R. Lumpkin, B. A. Greenberg, and J. L. Goldstucker, "Marketplace Needs of the Elderly," *Journal of Retailing,* Summer 1985, pp. 75–103; and J. E. G. Bateson, "Self-Service Consumer," *Journal of Retailing,* Fall 1985, pp. 49–76.

[13] "Department Stores 'Specialize,' " *Marketing News,* February 15, 1988, p. 14.

[14] P. K. Korgaonkar, "Shopping Orientation of Catalog Showroom Patrons," *Journal of Retailing,* Spring 1981, p. 87.

[15] T. Bayer, "7-Eleven Takes Steps to Move beyond Image," *Advertising Age,* December 7, 1981, p. 4.

[16] D. I. Hawkins and M. O'Neill, "Managerial Bias in Anticipated Images of Competing Shopping Areas," *Journal of Business Research,* December 1980, pp. 419–28; and M. J. Houston and J. R. Nevin, "Retail Shopping Area Image: Structure and Congruency between Downtown Areas and Shopping Centers," in *Advances in Consumer Research,* ed. K. B. Monroe (Chicago: Association for Consumer Research, 1981), pp. 677–81.

[17] D. I. Hawkins and J. H. Barnes, Jr., "Comparison of Shopping Behaviors and Attitudes between Employed Females, Unemployed Females, and Employed Males," *1979 Proceedings of the Southwestern Marketing Association Conference* (Secaucus, N.J.: Citadel Press, 1979).

[18] E. C. Hirschman and M. K. Mills, "Sources Shoppers Use to Pick Stores," *Journal of Advertising Research,* February 1980, p. 49.

[19] *A Study of Consumer Response to the Availability of Advertised Specials,* National Technical Information Service, U.S. Department of Commerce (PB80–128507).

[20] A. J. Della Bitta, K. B. Monroe, and J. M. McGinnis, "Consumer Perceptions of Comparative Price Advertisements," *Journal of Marketing Research,* November

1981, pp. 416–27. See also A. J. Della Bitta and K. B. Monroe, "A Multivariate Analysis of the Perception of Value from Retail Price Advertisements," in *Advances in Consumer Research,* ed. K. B. Monroe (Chicago: Association for Consumer Research, 1981), pp. 161–65.

[21] E. A. Blair and E. L. Landon, Jr., "The Effects of Reference Prices in Retail Advertisements," *Journal of Marketing Research,* Spring 1981, pp. 61–69; and W. O. Bearden, D. R. Lichtenstein, and J. E. Teel, "Comparison Price, Coupon, and Brand Effects on Consumer Reactions to Retail Newspaper Advertisements," *Journal of Retailing,* Summer 1984, pp. 11–34.

[22] E. N. Berkowitz and J. R. Walton, "Contextual Influences on Consumer Price Responses: An Experimental Analysis," *Journal of Marketing Research,* August 1980, pp. 349–58; and Della Bitta et al., "Consumer Perceptions."

[23] Blair and Landon, "The Effects"; and M. A. Sewall and M. E. Goldstein, "The Comparative Advertising Controversy; Consumer Perceptions of Catalog Showroom Reference Prices," *Journal of Marketing,* Summer 1979, pp. 85–92.

[24] Berkowitz and Walton, "Contextual Influences."

[25] D. Huff, "A Probabilistic Analysis of Consumer Spatial Behavior," in *Emerging Concepts of Marketing,* ed. W. S. Decker (Chicago: American Marketing Association, 1962), pp. 443–61.

[26] C. S. Craig, A. Ghosh, and S. McLafferty, "Models of the Retail Location Process: A Review," *Journal of Retailing,* Spring 1984, pp. 5–33.

[27] R. Ellinger and J. Lindquist, "The Gravity Model: A Study of Retail Goods Classification and Multiple Goods Shopping Effect," in *Advances in Consumer Research,* ed. T. Kinnear (Chicago: Association for Consumer Research, 1984), pp. 391–95.

[28] N. Papadopoulas, "Consumer Outshopping Research: Review and Extension," *Journal of Retailing,* Winter 1980, pp. 41–58; R. Williams, "Outshopping: Problem or Opportunity?" *Arizona Business,* October/November 1981, pp. 8–11.

[29] Ibid.

[30] D. Gautschi, "Specification of Patronage Models for Retail Center Choice," *Journal of Marketing Research,* May 1981, pp. 162–74.

[31] R. Lusch, "Integration of Economic Geography and Social Psychology Models of Patronage Behavior," in *Advances in Consumer Research,* ed. K. B. Monroe (Chicago: Association for Consumer Research, 1981), pp. 644–54.

[32] R. Howell and J. Rogers, "Research into Shopping Mall Choice Behavior," in *Advances,* ed. K. B. Monroe, pp. 671–76.

[33] For a comprehensive model, see W. R. Darden, D. K. Darden, R. Howell, and S. J. Miller, "Consumer Socialization in a Patronage Model of Consumer Behavior," in *Advances,* ed. K. B. Monroe, pp. 655–61.

[34] Hawes and Lumpkin, "Perceived Risk."

[35] Lumpkin and Hawes, "Retailing"; T. A. Festervand, D. R. Snyder, and J. D. Tsalikis, "Influence of Catalog vs. Store Shopping and Prior Satisfaction on Perceived Risk," *Journal of the Academy of Marketing Science,* Winter 1986, pp. 28–36; and Darian, "In-Home Shopping."

[36] J. Dash, L. Schiffman, and C. Berenson, "Risk and Personality-Related Dimensions of Store Choice," *Journal of Marketing,* January 1976, pp. 32–39; J. M. DeKorte, "Mail and Telephone Shopping as a Function of Consumer Self-Confidence,"

Journal of the Academy of Marketing Science, Fall 1977, pp. 295–306; and P. L. Gillett, "In-Home Shoppers—An Overview," *Journal of Marketing,* October 1976, pp. 81–83.

[37] Ibid.

[38] E. M. Tauber, "Why Do People Shop?" *Journal of Marketing,* October 1972, pp. 46–49. See also D. N. Bellenger and P. K. Korgaonkar, "Profiling the Recreational Shopper," *Journal of Retailing,* Fall 1980, pp. 77–82; and R. A. Westbrook and W. C. Black, "A Motivation-Based Shopper Typology," *Journal of Retailing,* Spring 1985, pp. 78–103.

[39] W. R. Darden and R. D. Howell, "Socialization Effects of Retail Work Experience on Shopping Orientations," *Journal of the Academy of Marketing Science,* Fall 1987, pp. 52–63.

[40] J. P. Guiltinan and K. B. Monroe, "Identifying and Analyzing Shopping Strategies," in *Advances in Consumer Research VII,* ed. J. Olson (Chicago: Association for Consumer Research, 1980), pp. 745–48; R. C. Quarles, "Shopping Centers Use Fashion Lifestyle Research," *Marketing News,* January 22, 1982, p. 18; Korgaonkar, "Shopping Orientations"; and footnotes 39 and 40, in Chapter 15.

[41] See S. Spiggle, "Grocery Shopping Lists," in *Advances in Consumer Research XIV,* ed. M. Wallendorf and P. Anderson (Provo, Utah: Association for Consumer Research, 1987), pp. 241–45.

[42] See C. J. Cobb and W. D. Hoger, "Planned Versus Impulse Purchase Behavior," *Journal of Retailing,* Winter 1986, pp. 384–409.

[43] *POPAI/DuPont Consumer Buying Habits Study* (New York: Point-of-Purchase Advertising Institute, 1978). A 1987 version of the study is now available from the POPAI.

[44] J. Quelch and K. Cannon-Bonventure, "Better Marketing at the Point of Purchase," *Harvard Business Review,* November–December, 1983, pp. 162–69; and J. P. Gagnon and J. T. Osterhaus, "Effectiveness of Floor Displays on the Sales of Retail Products," *Journal of Retailing,* Spring 1985, pp. 104–17; D. D. Achabal et al., "The Effect of Nutrition P-O-P Signs on Consumer Attitudes and Behavior," *Journal of Retailing,* Spring 1987, pp. 9–24, presents contrasting results.

[45] "How to Turn P-O-P into Sales Dollars," *Progressive Grocer,* June 1977, pp. 83–100. For a discussion of the appropriate content of point-of-purchase signs, see G. F. McKinnon, J. P. Kelly, and E. D. Robison, "Sales Effects of Point-of-Purchase In-Store Signing," *Journal of Retailing,* Summer 1981, pp. 49–63.

[46] B. C. Cotton and E. M. Babb, "Consumer Response to Promotional Deals," *Journal of Marketing,* July 1978, pp. 109–13. See also J. A. Dodson, A. M. Tybout, and B. Sternthal, "Impact of Deals and Deal Retraction on Brand Switching," *Journal of Marketing Research,* February 1978, pp. 72–81.

[47] M. M. Moriarity, "Retail Promotional Effects on Intra- and Interbrand Sales Performance," *Journal of Retailing,* Fall 1985, pp. 27–47.

[48] R. Blattberg, T. Buesing, P. Peacock, and S. Sen, "Identifying the Deal Prone Segment," *Journal of Marketing Research,* August 1978, pp. 369–77.

[49] D. S. Litvack, R. J. Calantone, and P. R. Warshaw, "An Examination of Short-Term Retail Grocery Price Effects," *Journal of Retailing,* Fall 1985, pp. 9–25.

[50] Gagnon and Osterhaus, "Effectiveness"; and S. MacZinko, "Increasing Retail Shelf Space Allocation," *The Nielsen Researcher,* no. 2, 1985, pp. 13–16.

[51] "Store of the Month," *Progressive Grocer,* October 1976, pp. 104–10.

[52] D. Robert, "Store Designer Raises Profits for Retailers," *The Wall Street Journal,* December 1980, pp. 9–10.

[53] C. E. Ferguson, Jr., J. B. Mason, and J. W. Wilkinson, "Simulating Food Shoppers' Economic Losses as a Result of Supermarket Unavailability," *Decision Sciences,* June 1980, pp. 535–55; P. H. Zinszer and J. A. Lesser, "An Empirical Evaluation of the Role of Stockout on Shopper Patronage Processes," in *Marketing in the 1980s,* ed. R. P. Bagozzi et al. (Chicago: American Marketing Association, 1980), pp. 221–24; and W. H. Motes and S. B. Castleberry, "A Longitudinal Field Test of Stockout Effects on Multi-Brand Inventories," *Journal of the Academy of Marketing Science,* Fall 1985, pp. 54–68.

[54] "Retail Trends to Affect Quality of Goods, In-Store Service," *Marketing News,* February 15, 1988, p. 18.

[55] See G. A. Churchill, Jr., et al., "The Determinants of Salesperson Performance," *Journal of Marketing Research,* May 1985, pp. 103–18; B. A. Weitz, H. Sujan, and M. Sujan, "Knowledge, Motivation, and Adaptive Behavior," *Journal of Marketing,* October 1986, pp. 174–91; N. M. Ford et al., "Psychological Tests and the Selection of Successful Salespeople," *Review of Marketing 1987,* ed. M. Houston (Chicago: American Marketing Association, 1987); and D. M. Szymanski, "Determinants of Selling Effectiveness," *Journal of Marketing,* January 1988, pp. 64–77.

[56] R. D. Blackwell and M. Hanke, "The Credit Card and the Aging Baby Boomers," *Journal of Retail Banking,* Spring 1987, pp. 17–25.

[57] "More than Half of U.S. Households Had Sears Credit Cards," *Marketing News,* August 10, 1979, p. 2.

[58] See O. C. Walker, Jr., and R. F. Sauter, "Consumer Preferences for Alternative Retail Credit Plans: A Concept Test of the Effects of Consumer Legislation," *Journal of Marketing Research,* February 1974, pp. 70–78; N. R. Burnstein, "A Comment on Consumer Preferences for Alternative Retail Credit Plans," *Journal of Marketing Research,* November 1978, pp. 639–43; and G. Albaum, "Consumer Reactions to Variable Rate Mortgages," *Journal of Consumer Affairs,* Winter 1979.

CHAPTER

18 Postpurchase Processes

For many years American consumers have evaluated American-made cars negatively. Further, they have viewed the purchasing process even more negatively. And, after-sale services have been consistently rated as completely unsatisfactory. As a result, foreign competitors have captured significant market share.

Indicative of American manufacturers' attitudes is the fact that Ford Motor Company did not begin to systematically monitor customer satisfaction until 1986. Fortunately, customer-satisfaction measures are now a key part of Ford's performance-measurement system. The logic is simple: satisfied customers are twice as likely as unhappy ones to stick with their current make, and three times as likely to return to the same dealer.

Ford now spends over $10 million annually to survey all its customers, once about a month after purchase and again a year later. Each dealership receives a monthly QCP (quality, commitment, performance) report covering sales, vehicle preparation, service, and overall performance. Customers also rate the automobile itself. These QCP ratings not only provide dealers feedback but also serve as the basis for contests, bonuses, new franchise awards, and so forth.

Many dealerships are adopting customer-satisfaction measures locally to monitor and reward their own sales and service personnel. For example, Tasca Lincoln-Mercury in Massachusetts has divided its service department into six teams, each of which wears a different-colored uniform. The teams compete for monthly bonuses of $500–$800 based on customer-satisfaction measures.[1]

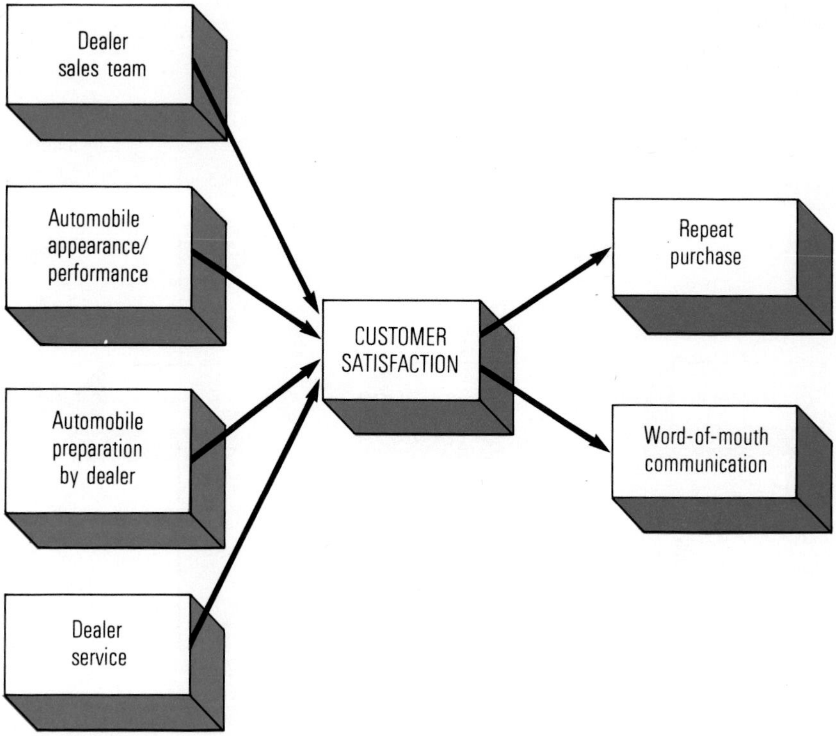

The above example illustrates the critical importance of postpurchase processes. American automobile manufacturers suffered huge losses due to insufficient attention to customer satisfaction, which is the result of the customer's evaluation of both the product and the purchasing process. This chapter focuses on those critical activities, outlined in Figure 18–1 that occur after a consumer makes a purchase.

POSTPURCHASE DISSONANCE

Try to recall the last time you made an important purchase in which you had to consider a variety of alternatives that differed in terms of the attributes they offered. Perhaps it was a decision such as selecting a college close to home where you would have many friends or one further away but better academically. Immediately after you committed yourself to one alternative or the other, you likely wondered:

- Did I make the right decision?
- Should I have done something else?

Figure 18–1
Postpurchase Consumer Behavior

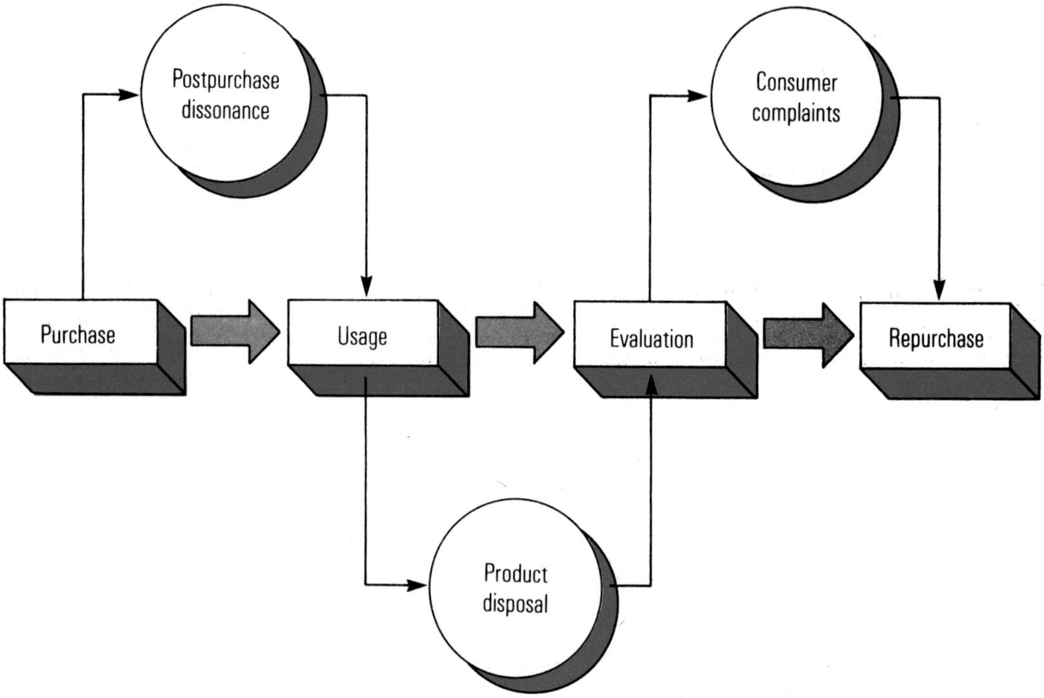

This is a very common reaction after making a difficult, relatively permanent decision. Doubt or anxiety of this type is referred to as *postpurchase dissonance*.[2]

Figure 18–1 indicates that some, but not all, consumer purchase decisions are followed by postpurchase dissonance. The probability of a consumer experiencing postpurchase dissonance, as well as the magnitude of such dissonance, is a function of:

- *The degree of commitment or irrevocability of the decision*. The easier it is to alter the decision, the less likely the consumer is to experience dissonance.
- *The importance of the decision to the consumer*. The more important the decision, the more likely dissonance will result.
- *The difficulty of choosing among the alternatives*. The more difficult it is to select from among the alternatives, the more likely the experience and magnitude of dissonance.[3] Decision difficulty is a function of the number of alternatives considered, the number of relevant attributes associated with each alternative, and the extent to which each alternative offers attributes not available with the other alternatives.

- *The individual's tendency to experience anxiety*. Some individuals have a higher tendency to experience anxiety than do others. The higher the tendency to experience anxiety, the more likely the individual will experience postpurchase dissonance.[4]

Dissonance occurs because making a relatively permanent commitment to a chosen alternative requires one to give up the attractive features of the unchosen alternatives. This is inconsistent with the desire for those features. Thus, habitual and most limited decision making will not produce postpurchase dissonance, since one does not consider any attractive features in an unchosen brand that do not also exist in the chosen brand. For example, a consumer who has an evoked set of four brands of coffee could consider them to be equivalent on all relevant attributes except price and, therefore, always purchases the least expensive brand. Such a purchase would not produce postpurchase dissonance.

Because most high-involvement purchase decisions involve one or more of the factors which lead to postpurchase dissonance, these decisions often are accompanied by dissonance. And, since dissonance is unpleasant, consumers generally attempt to reduce it.

The consumer may utilize one or more of the following approaches to reduce dissonance:

- Increase the desirability of the brand purchased.
- Decrease the desirability of rejected alternatives.
- Decrease the importance of the purchase decision.[5]

While postpurchase dissonance may be reduced by internal reevaluations, searching for additional external information that serves to confirm the wisdom of a particular choice is also a common strategy. Naturally, information that supports the consumer's choice acts to bolster confidence in the correctness of the purchase decision.

The consumer's search for information *after* purchase greatly enhances the role that advertising and follow-up sales efforts can have. To build customer confidence in their brand choice, many manufacturers design advertisements for recent purchasers, in hopes of helping reduce postpurchase dissonance.

PRODUCT USE

Most consumer purchases involve habitual or limited decision making and therefore arouse little or no postpurchase dissonance. Instead, the purchaser or some other member of the purchasing unit uses the product without first worrying about the wisdom of the purchase. And, as Figure 18–1 shows, even when postpurchase dissonance occurs, it is still generally followed by product use.

Observing consumers as they utilize products can be an important source of new product ideas. For example, observations of consumer modifications of existing bicycles led to the commercial development of the immensely popular "stingray" style of children's bicycle. However, almost all consumer-observation research is conducted in an artificial setting or is conducted with the consumer's permission. As a result, few "nonstandard" product uses are observed.

Many firms attempt to obtain relevant information on product usage via surveys using standard questionnaires or focus groups. Such surveys can lead to new product development or indicate new uses or markets for existing products. For example, consumers were using baking soda as a personal deodorant long before Arm & Hammer developed a baking soda-based deodorant. Likewise, consumers were using baking soda as a freshener in their refrigerators before such usage was encouraged by Arm & Hammer.

Understanding how products are used also can lead to more effective advertising, personal sales presentations, and packaging. For example, Table 18–1 summarizes the level of dissatisfaction with the packaging of various products. Because this type of dissatisfaction occurs at the time of use, it is difficult for marketers to monitor. To solve such problems, the marketer has to understand how the product and package are used.

Use behavior can vary regionally. For example, there are major regional variations in how coffee is consumed—with or without cream, with or without sugar, in a mug or a cup, and so forth. Thus, a coffee marketer may find it worthwhile to prepare regional versions of the major advertising theme to reflect regional usage patterns.

Retailers can frequently take advantage of the fact that the use of one product may require or suggest the use of other products. Consider the following product "sets": houseplants and fertilizer, canoes and life vests, cameras and carrying cases, sport coats and ties, and dresses and shoes. In each case, the use of the first product is made easier, more enjoyable, or safer by the use of the related product. Retailers can promote such items jointly or train their sales personnel

Table 18–1
Product Use Problems Due to Packaging*

Product	Percent Dissatisfied	Product	Percent Dissatisfied
Lunch meat	77	Noodles	49
Bacon	76	Lipstick	47
Flour	65	Nail polish	46
Sugar	63	Honey	44
Ice cream	57	Crackers	44
Snack chips	53	Frozen seafood	40
Cookies	51	Nuts	39
Detergents	50	Cooking oil	37
Fresh meat	50	Ketchup	34

*Percentage of respondents who indicated dissatisfaction with the packaging of these products.

Source: Bill Abrahms, "Packaging Often Irks Buyers, but Firms Are Slow to Change," *The Wall Street Journal*, January 29, 1982, p. 23.

to make relevant complementary sales. However, to do so requires a sound knowledge of how the products actually are utilized.

Increasingly stringent product liability laws are forcing marketing managers to examine how consumers use their products.[6] These laws have made firms responsible for harm caused by product failure *not only when the product is used as specified by the manufacturer but in any reasonably foreseeable use of the product*. For example, Parker Brothers voluntarily recalled its very successful plastic riveting tool, Riviton, at a cost approaching $10 million. The reason was the deaths of two children who choked after swallowing one of the tool's rubber rivets. Both Wham-O Manufacturing and Mattel have been involved in similar recalls in recent years.[7] Thus, the manufacturer must design products with both the primary purpose *and* other potential uses in mind. This requires substantial research into how consumers actually use the products.

Unfortunately, there are few published accounts of how products are actually used. Marketing managers generally must develop usage data for their own specific product categories.

DISPOSITION

Disposition of the product or the product's container may occur before, during, or after product use. Or, for products which are completely consumed, such as an ice cream cone, no disposition may be involved.

The United States produced 200 million tons of household and commercial refuse in 1987, over 1,500 pounds per person, and this figure does not include industrial waste. Landfills are rapidly being filled. Connecticut is projected to fill all its dump sites by 1990. New Jersey must truck half its household waste to out-of-state landfills up to 500 miles away. Collection and dumping costs for a household in suburban Union County near New York City increased to over $400 per year in 1987. Environmental concerns involving dioxins, lead, and mercury are growing.[8] Clearly, disposition is a major concern for marketers.

Both product and package design affect the disposition decision. Some packages are not efficient in terms of consumption behavior, since it is difficult to maintain the product's quality once the package has been opened. When this is the case, much more of the product will be wasted. Bread is a good example. Little waste is associated with white bread, which comes in a standard, resealable bread wrapper. However, specialty breads, often in packages that cannot be efficiently resealed, are a major source of waste. As a result, specialty breads account for only 16 percent of the total bread sales but more than 32 percent of all bread waste.[9] Clearly, marketing mix decisions can have a major impact on consumption efficiency.

Package Disposition

Millions of pounds of product packages are disposed of every day. These containers are thrown away as garbage or litter, used in some capacity by the

Exhibit 18–1 Reynolds Aluminum Advertisement Keyed to Recycling

Used with permission from Reynolds Aluminum.

consumer, or recycled. Creating packages that utilize a minimal amount of resources is important for economic reasons as well as being a matter of social responsibility. Producing containers that are easily recyclable or that can be reused also has important consequences beyond social responsibility. Certain market segments consider the recyclable nature of the product container to be an important product attribute. These consumers anticipate disposition of the package as an attribute of the brand during the alternative evaluation stage. Thus, ease of disposition can be used as a marketing mix variable in an attempt to capture certain market segments. Reynolds Aluminum has conducted a very successful corporate campaign focusing on the ease and benefits of recycling aluminum products, particularly aluminum cans. Exhibit 18–1 is one ad from this campaign.

Studies of individuals using recycling centers reveal two basic sets of motives.[10] One group of consumers recycles containers for the financial remuneration. These individuals tend to have lower socioeconomic standing. The second major motive for using recycling centers is a strong concern for ecology. Individuals who recycle packages for this reason generally are relatively young, from upper socioeconomic categories, somewhat liberal, and feel they can control their environment. These consumers share many characteristics with what is called the socially conscious consumer.[11]

Socially conscious consumers consider the impact of their purchase decisions on the social or physical environment as an important attribute in the decision process. Socially conscious consumers, including those concerned with recycling, are important for a variety of reasons. First, they represent a sizable, affluent market segment. Second, they tend to be influential and have the potential to influence other segments. Finally, they tend to be politically active and may influence the legal environment in which a firm operates. Their impact can be seen in the increasing number of states banning throw-away bottles and pull-tab cans.

Product Disposition

For many product categories, a physical product continues to exist even though it may no longer meet a consumer's needs. A product may no longer function physically (instrumental function) in a manner desired by a consumer. Or, it may no longer provide the symbolic meaning desired by the consumer. An automobile that no longer runs is an example of a product ceasing to function instrumentally. An automobile whose owner decides it is out of style no longer functions symbolically (for that particular consumer). In either case, once a replacement purchase is made (or even before the purchase), a disposition decision must be made.[12]

Figure 18–2 illustrates the various alternatives for disposing of a product. The three basic decisions are to keep the product, get rid of it temporarily, or get rid of it permanently. As Table 18–2 indicates, the method of disposition varies dramatically across product categories. For example, in almost 80 percent of the cases, a used toothbrush was thrown away, but less than 12 percent of the stereo amplifiers were disposed of in this manner.

Unfortunately, very little is known about the demographic or psychological characteristics of individuals who tend to select particular disposal methods. It appears that situational variables such as the availability of storage space, the current needs of friends, the availability of recycling or charitable organizations, and so forth *may* be the primary determinants of disposition behavior.

Figure 18–2
Product Disposition Alternatives

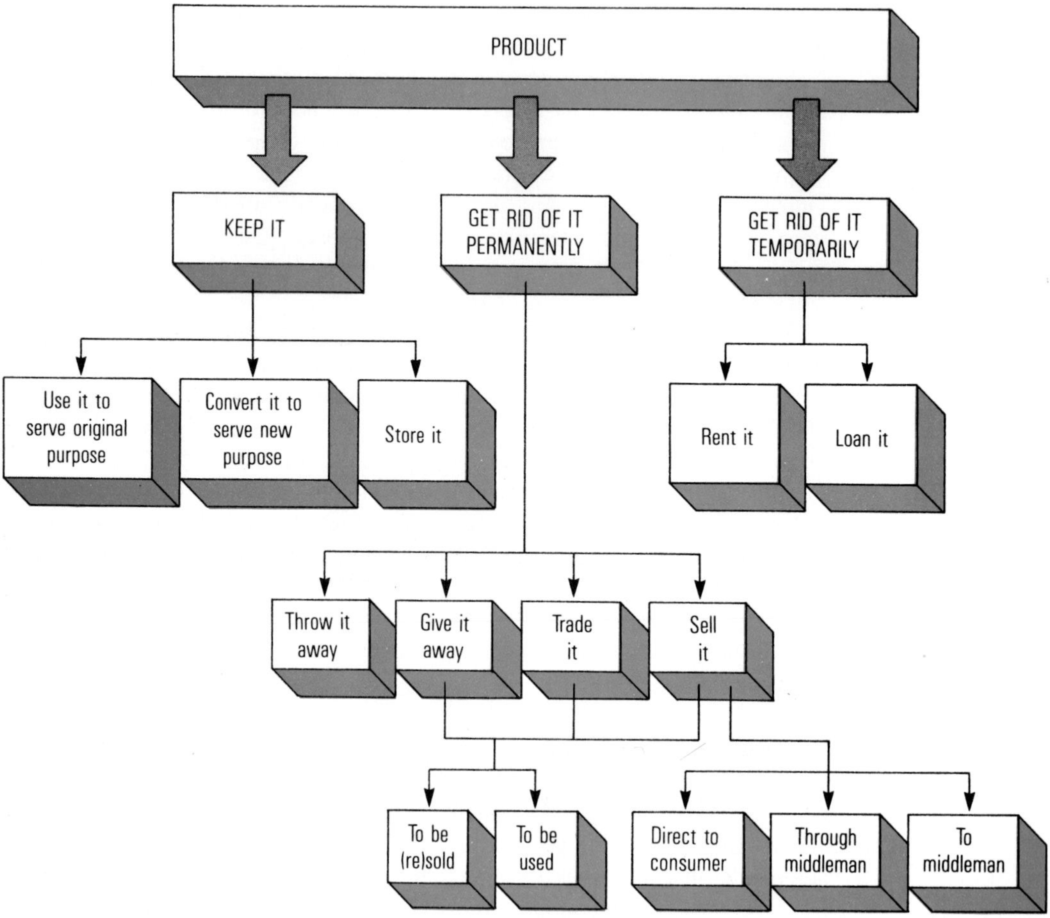

Source: J. Jacoby, C. K. Berning, and T. F. Dietvorst, "What about Disposition?" *Journal of Marketing*, April 1977, p. 23.

Product Disposition and Marketing Strategy. Why should a marketing manager be concerned about the disposition of a used product? The primary reason is that disposition decisions affect the purchase decisions of both the individual making the disposition and other individuals in the market for that product category.

There are three major ways in which disposition decisions can affect a firm's marketing strategy. *First,* disposition sometimes must occur before acquisition of a replacement because of physical space or financial limitations. For example, because of a lack of storage space, a family living in an apartment may find it necessary to dispose of an existing bedroom set before acquiring a new one. Or,

Table 18–2
Disposition Decisions for Six Products (Percent)

Disposition Alternatives	Stereo Amplifier	Wrist-watch	Tooth-brush	Phono-graph Record	Bicycle	Refrig-erator
Converted	1.6%	1.8%	17.2%	9.6%	1.5%	7.5%
Stored	—	28.7	—	32.8	3.1	—
Thrown away	11.5	30.6	79.7	43.2	17.3	22.6
Given away	31.1	23.1	—	9.6	40.2	19.3
Traded	4.9	5.6	—	0.8	3.2	20.4
Sold	42.6	5.6	—	—	17.3	25.8
Rented	—	0.9	—	—	—	3.2
Loaned	—	—	—	—	1.5	1.0
Other	8.3	3.7	3.1	4.0	15.9	—
	100.0%	100.0%	100.0%	100.0%	100.0%	100.0%

Source: J. Jacoby, C. K. Berning, and T. F. Dietvorst, "What about Disposition?" *Journal of Marketing,* April 1977, p. 26.

someone may need to sell his current bicycle to raise supplemental funds to pay for a new bicycle. If consumers experience difficulty in disposing of the existing product, they may become discouraged and withdraw from the purchasing process. Thus, it is to the manufacturer's and retailer's advantage to assist the consumer in the disposition process.

Second, frequent decisions by consumers to sell, trade, or give away used products may result in a large used product market which can reduce the market for new products. A manufacturer may want to enter such a market by buying used products or taking trade-ins and repairing them for the rebuilt market. This is common for automobile parts such as generators and, to a lesser extent, for vacuum cleaners.

A *third* reason for concern with product disposition is the fact that the United States is not completely a throwaway society. Many Americans continue to be very concerned with waste and how their purchase decisions affect waste. Such individuals might be willing to purchase, for example, a new vacuum cleaner if they were confident that the old one would be rebuilt and resold. However, they might be reluctant to throw their old vacuums away or to go to the effort of reselling the machines themselves. Thus, manufacturers and retailers could take steps to ensure that products are reused. Such steps could increase the demand for new products, while meeting the needs of consumers for less-expensive versions of the product.

PURCHASE EVALUATION

As we saw in Figure 18–1, a consumer's evaluation of a purchase is influenced by postpurchase dissonance, product use, and product disposition. Not all purchase evaluations are influenced by each of these three processes. Rather, these processes are potential influencing factors that may affect the evaluation of a particular purchase. You should also note that the outlet or the product or both may be involved in the evaluation.[13] Finally, keep in mind that habitual decisions and many limited decisions are actively evaluated only if some factor, such as an obvious product malfunction, directs attention to the purchase.[14]

The Evaluation Process

A particular alternative such as a product, brand, or retail outlet is selected because it is thought to be a better overall choice than other alternatives that

Figure 18–3
Expectations and Perceived Performance for a High- and Low-Involvement Purchase

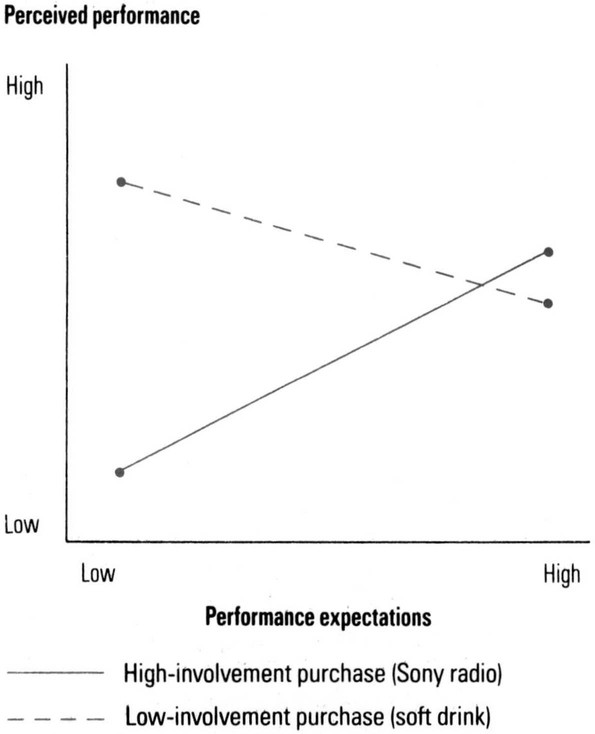

Source: Adapted from P. Korgaonkar and G. Moschis, "An Experimental Study of Cognitive Dissonance, Product Involvement, Expectations, Performance, and Consumer Judgment of Product Performance," *Journal of Advertising,* 1982, p. 40.

were considered in the purchase process. Whether that particular item was selected because of its presumed superior functional performance or because of some other feature, such as lower price or more appealing style, consumers have some level of expected performance that the brand should provide. The expected level of performance can range from quite low (this brand isn't very good but it's the only one available and I'm in a hurry) to quite high. Figure 18–3 shows the relationship that performance expectations can have with perceived product performance. Also important in the figure is how the relationship differs for low- and high-involvement products.

After using the product, the consumer will perceive some level of performance. This perceived performance level can be noticeably above the expected level, noticeably below the expected level, or at the expected level. As Table 18–3 indicates, satisfaction with the purchase is primarily a function of the initial performance expectations and perceived performance relative to those expectations. In addition, individuals differ somewhat in their tendency to be satisfied or dissatisfied with purchases.[15] As stated earlier, habitual and many limited decisions are actively evaluated *only* if there is a noticeable product failure.

In Table 18–3, you can see that a store or brand whose performance confirms a low-performance expectation generally will result in neither satisfaction nor dissatisfaction but rather with what can be termed *nonsatisfaction*. That is, you are not likely to feel disappointment or engage in complaint behavior. However, the use of the product will not reduce the likelihood of a search for a better alternative the next time the problem arises.

A brand whose perceived performance fails to confirm expectations generally produces dissatisfaction.[16] If the discrepancy between performance and expectation is sufficiently large or if initial expectations were low, the consumer may restart the entire decision process. The item causing the problem recognition most likely will be placed in the inept set (see Chapter 15) and no longer be considered. In addition, complaint behavior and negative word-of-mouth communications may be initiated.

Table 18–3
Expectations, Performance, and Satisfaction

Perceived Performance Relative to Expectation	**Expectation Level**	
	Below Minimum Desired Performance	Above Minimum Desired Performance
Better	Satisfaction*	Satisfaction
Same	Nonsatisfaction	Satisfaction
Worse	Dissatisfaction	Dissatisfaction

*Assuming the perceived performance surpasses the minimum desired level.

Source: Derived from R. L. Oliver, "Measurement and Evaluation of Satisfaction Processes in Retail Settings," *Journal of Retailing*, Fall 1981, pp. 25–48.

When perceptions of product performance match or exceed expectations that are at or above the minimum desired performance level, satisfaction generally results. Likewise, performance above the minimum desired level that exceeds a lower expectation tends to produce satisfaction. Satisfaction reduces the level of decision making the next time the problem is recognized. That is, a satisfactory purchase is rewarding and encourages one to repeat the same behavior in the future (habitual decision making).[17] Satisfied customers are also likely to engage in positive word-of-mouth communications about the brand. And, as Exhibit 18–2 illustrates, firms can use measures of customer satisfaction in their promotional activities.

The need to produce satisfied consumers has important implications in terms of positioning the level of promotional claims. Since dissatisfaction is, in part, a function of the disparity between expectations and perceived product performance, unrealistic consumer expectations created by excessive promotional exaggeration can contribute to consumer dissatisfaction.

The need to develop realistic consumer expectations poses a difficult problem for the marketing manager. For a brand or store to be selected by a consumer, it must be viewed as superior on the relevant combination of attributes. Therefore, the marketing manager naturally wants to emphasize the positive aspects of the brand or outlet. If such an emphasis creates expectations in the consumer that the product cannot fulfill, a negative evaluation may occur. Negative evaluations can produce brand switching, unfavorable word-of-mouth advertising, and complaint behavior. Thus, the marketing manager must balance enthusiasm for the product with a realistic view of the product's attributes.

Dimensions of Performance. Since performance expectations and actual performance are major factors in the evaluation process, we need to understand the dimensions of product performance.[18] For many products there are two dimensions to performance: instrumental, and expressive or symbolic. *Instrumental performance* relates to the physical functioning of the product. That the product operates properly is vital to the evaluation of a dishwasher, sewing machine, or other major appliance. *Symbolic performance* relates to aesthetic or image-enhancement performance. For example, the durability of a sport coat is an aspect of instrumental performance, while styling represents symbolic performance.

Is symbolic or instrumental performance more important to consumers as they evaluate product performance? The answer to this question undoubtedly varies by product category and across consumer groups. However, a number of studies focusing on clothing provide some insights into how these two types of performance are related.

Clothing appears to perform five major functions: protection from the environment; enhancement of sexual attraction; aesthetic and sensuous satisfaction; an indicator of status; and an extension of self-image. Except for protection from the environment, these functions are all dimensions of symbolic performance. Yet studies of clothing returns, complaints about clothing purchases, and discarded clothing indicate that physical product failures are the primary cause of dissatisfaction. One study on the relationship between performance expectations,

Exhibit 18–2 Customer Satisfaction as an Advertised Feature

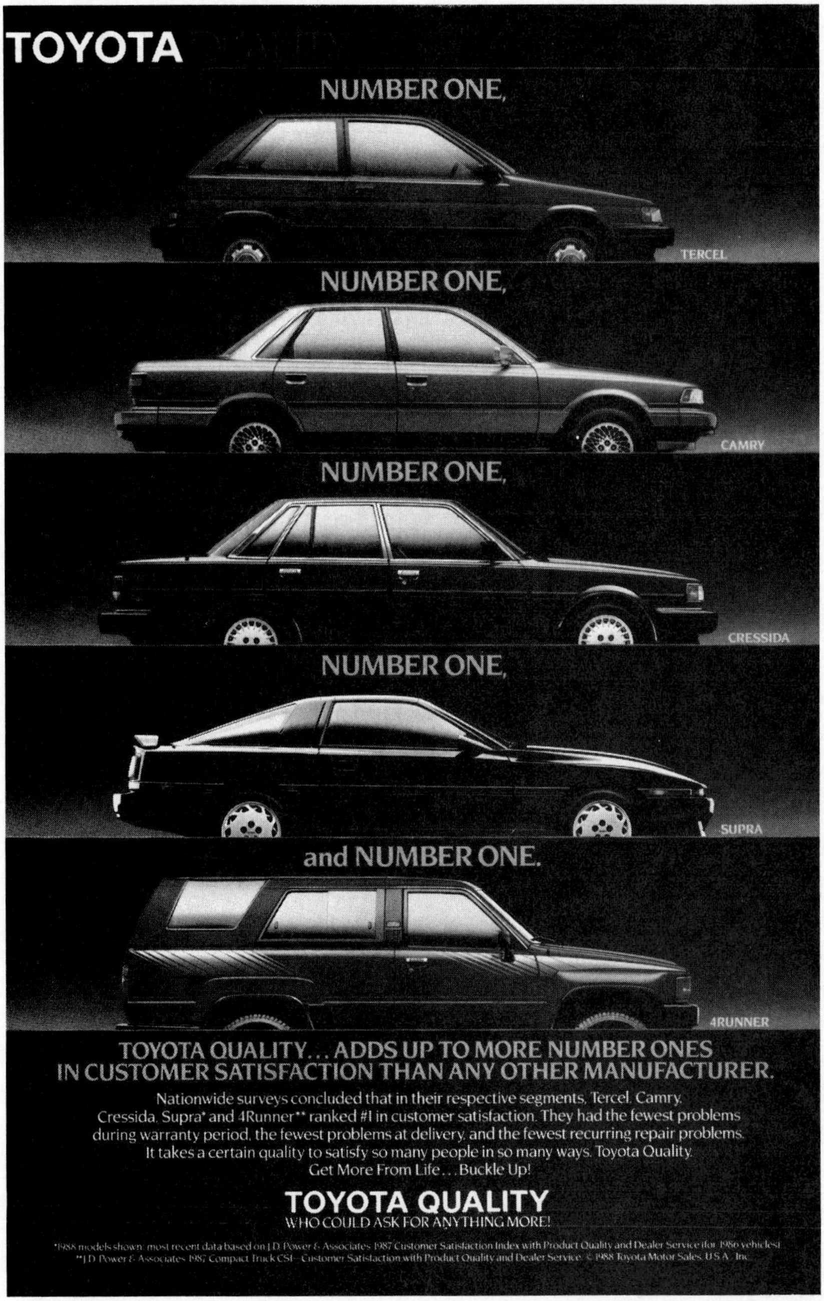

Courtesy Toyota Motor Sales U.S.A., Inc.

actual performance, and satisfaction with clothing purchases reached the following general conclusion:

> "Dissatisfaction is caused by a failure of instrumental performance, while complete satisfaction also requires the symbolic functions to perform at or above the expected levels."[19]

These findings certainly cannot be generalized to other product categories without additional research. However, they suggest that the marketing manager should maintain performance at the minimum expected level on those attributes that lead to dissatisfaction, while attempting to maximize performance on those attributes that lead to increased satisfaction.

Like all other aspects of the consumption process, evaluation involves an affective or emotional component as well as cognitive activities. While the affective aspects of postpurchase processes have received only limited attention, several tentative conclusions seem justified.[20] First, product purchase, ownership, and use give rise to a variety of emotional experiences. Second, positive and negative affective responses are relatively independent dimensions. That is, use of a product may be connected with both positive and negative feelings (joy, excitement, and anger).

A third finding is that positive and negative emotional responses relate directly to product satisfaction judgments, complaint behavior, and word-of-mouth communications. These are not merely the results of confirmation/disconfirmation of expectations but represent additional evaluative processes. Thus, marketers need to ensure that products (and the purchasing process) meet consumer expectations *and* are fun, exciting, or otherwise pleasurable to acquire and use.[21]

Dissatisfaction Responses

Figure 18–4 illustrates the major options available to consumers who are dissatisfied with a purchase.[22] The primary decision is whether or not to take some form of action. By taking no action, the consumer, in effect, decides to tolerate the dissatisfaction or to rationalize it.[23] A primary reason for taking no action is that action requires time and effort that may exceed the perceived value of any likely result.

Action in response to a state of dissatisfaction can be private in nature, such as warning friends or switching stores, brands, or products. There is also some evidence that dissatisfied consumers may engage in vandalism or other deviant acts.[24] Instead of, or in addition to, private actions, consumers may take public actions such as demanding redress from the firm involved, complaining to the firm or some other organization, or taking legal action against the firm. Obviously, dissatisfied customers may engage in various combinations of these actions.[25]

In general, consumers are satisfied with the vast majority of their purchases. Still, because of the large number of purchases individuals make each year, most

Figure 18–4
Actions Taken by Consumers in Response to Product Dissatisfaction

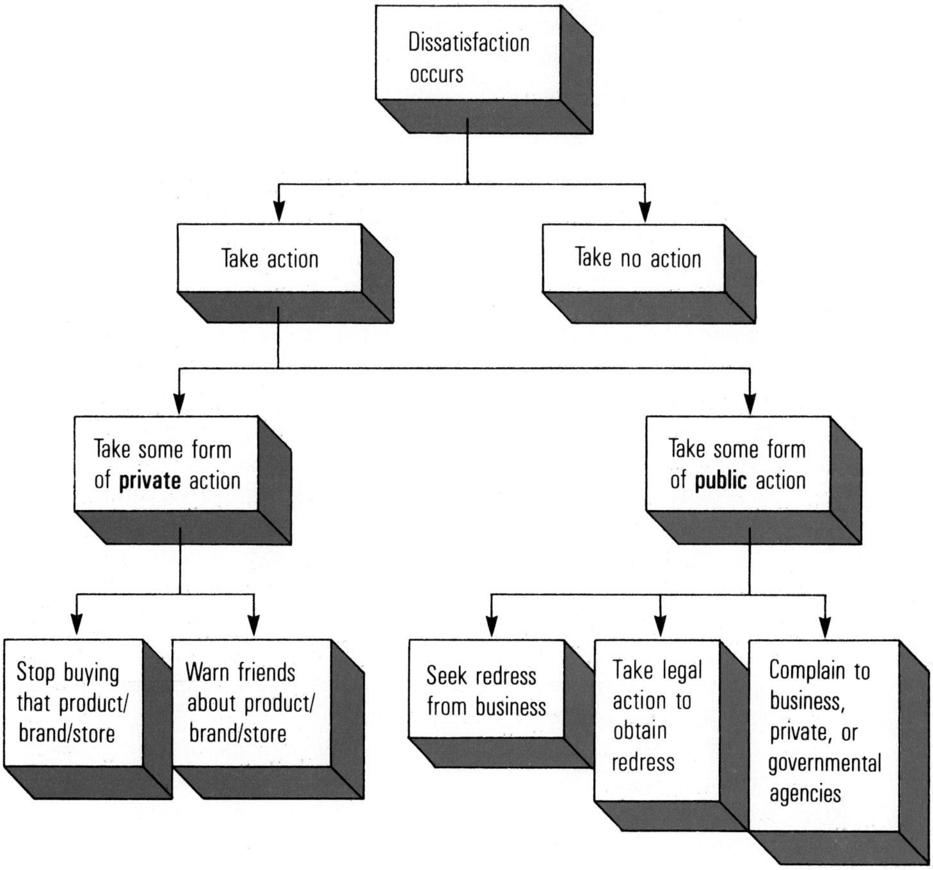

Source: R. Day, "Extending the Concept of Consumer Satisfaction," in *Advances in Consumer Research,* ed. W. D. Perreault, Jr. (Chicago: Association for Consumer Research, 1977), p. 153. Used with permission.

individuals experience dissatisfaction with some of their purchases.[26] For example, one study asked 540 consumers if they could recall a case in which one or more of the grocery products they normally purchase were defective. They recalled 1,307 separate unsatisfactory purchases. In terms of private actions:

- 25 percent of these unsatisfactory purchases resulted in brand switching.
- 19 percent caused the shopper to stop buying the products.
- 13 percent led to an in-store inspection of future purchases.
- 43 percent produced no private action.

These same defects caused the following public actions:

- 3 percent produced complaints to the manufacturer.
- 5 percent produced complaints to the retailer.
- 35 percent resulted in the item being returned.
- 58 percent produced no public action.

In a similar study of durable goods, 54 percent of the dissatisfied customers said they would not purchase the brand again, and 45 percent warned their friends about the product.

Marketing Strategy and Dissatisfied Consumers. Marketers need to satisfy consumer expectations by (1) creating reasonable expectations through promotional efforts and (2) maintaining consistent quality so the reasonable expectations are fulfilled. Since dissatisfied consumers tend to express their dissatisfaction to their friends, dissatisfaction may cause the firm to lose future sales to the unhappy consumer and current sales to that consumer's friends.[27]

The evidence presented in this chapter suggests that it is virtually impossible to "please all the people all the time." When a consumer is dissatisfied, the most favorable consequence is for the consumer to communicate this dissatisfaction to the firm but to no one else. This alerts the firm to problems, enables it to make amends where necessary, and minimizes negative word-of-mouth communications. In addition, complaints generally work to the consumer's advantage. Evidence indicates that about two thirds of all expressed complaints are resolved to the consumer's satisfaction.[28]

Unfortunately, many individuals do not communicate their dissatisfaction to the firm involved. Those who do complain tend to have more education, income, self-confidence, and independence, and are more confident in the business system than those who do not complain.[29] Thus, a firm that relies on complaints for feedback on problems will miss the concerns of key market segments.

Complaints about products frequently go to retailers and are not passed on to manufacturers. One study found that more than 80 percent of the complaints were presented to retailers, while less than 10 percent went directly to the manufacturer.[30] Many firms attempt to overcome this by establishing and promoting "consumer hot lines"—toll-free numbers that consumers can use to contact a representative of the firm when they have a complaint.[31] Whirlpool, for example, installed what was termed a *cool* line for customers having complaints. The idea was that the customer had direct access to the firm and could register complaints and problems immediately, thereby "cooling" down "hot" customers. Such activities can neutralize negative feelings and create a positive reaction among a vocal and influential population segment. Exhibit 18–3 provides details on some of the corporate benefits Procter & Gamble has obtained from having a toll-free complaint number on all of its product packages.

Automobile purchases and repairs are a common source of consumer problems. To encourage equitable resolutions of consumer grievances and to increase consumer confidence in their products, Ford has initiated the "Ford Consum-

Exhibit 18–3 Benefits Derived from Procter & Gamble's Consumer Hot Line

"If people have a problem with one of our products, we'd rather they tell us about it than switch to a competitor's product or say bad things about ours over the backyard fence," says Dorothy Puccini, head of P&G's consumer services department. Therefore, P&G has placed toll-free numbers on all of its product packages for consumers to use when they have a problem or suggestion. The results have included:

- Duncan Hines brownie mix: "We learned that people in high-altitude areas need special instructions for baking, and these soon were added to the packages. We also found that one of the recipes on a box label was confusing, so we changed it."
- Toothpaste: "We spotted a pattern of people complaining that they couldn't get the last bit of toothpaste out of the tube without it breaking, so the tubes were strengthened."
- A sudden group of calls indicated that the plastic tops on Downy fabric softener bottles were splintering when twisted on and off, creating the danger of cut fingers. P&G identified the supplier of the fragile caps and learned that it had recently changed its formula. The new formula caps were becoming brittle as they aged. Most of the bad caps had not left the factory, and P&G simply replaced them. Thus, a costly (financially and image-wise) product recall was avoided.
- P&G often receives calls with positive testimonials. These are forwarded to the appropriate advertising agency, where they are analyzed for insights into why people like the product. Several P&G campaigns have been based on these unsolicited consumer comments.

Source: J. A. Prestbo, "At Procter & Gamble, Success Is Largely Due to Heeding Consumer," *The Wall Street Journal,* April 29, 1980, p. 23.

er Appeals Board." The majority of its members are independent (not Ford employees). Its decisions are binding on Ford but not on the consumer. Chrysler has a similar program called the "Customer Satisfaction Arbitration Board Program."

Unfortunately, most corporations are not organized to effectively resolve and learn from consumer complaints, although individual managers strive to respond positively to complaints.[32]

This area represents a major opportunity for many businesses.[33] In fact, for many firms, retaining dissatisfied customers by encouraging and responding effectively to complaints is more economical than attracting new customers through advertising or other promotional activities.[34] The FTC has prepared a guideline to assist firms with this activity.[35]

REPEAT PURCHASE BEHAVIOR

Figure 18–1 indicates that the evaluation of the purchase decision and the outcome of any complaint behavior affect the consumer's repurchase motivation. As you might expect, when purchase expectations are fulfilled, there is a tendency to repurchase the brand or product that provided satisfaction. This is because such an experience is rewarding and therefore reinforcing.[36] Dissatisfaction with the purchase still may be followed by repeat purchases. The reason for this is that the expected benefits of renewed search and evaluation are less than the expected costs of such activities. However, the most likely outcome of dissatisfaction is discontinued brand or product use.

Nature of Repeat Purchasing Behavior

Repeat purchasing behavior is referred to frequently as *brand loyalty*. Brand loyalty implies a psychological commitment to the brand (much like friendship), whereas repeat purchasing behavior simply involves the frequent repurchase of the same brand (perhaps because it is the only one available, is generally the least expensive, and so forth). Brand loyalty is defined as:

1. A biased (i.e., nonrandom),
2. Behavioral response (i.e., purchase),
3. Expressed over time,
4. By some decision-making unit,
5. With respect to one or more alternative brands out of a set of such brands, and
6. Is a function of psychological (decision-making, evaluative) processes.[37]

Note that there is a great deal of difference between brand loyalty as defined above and repeat purchase behavior. This difference, and a marketing strategy based on it, has been explained by Seagram's president, Frank Berger:

> The goal of liquor advertising is more than getting a trial and repeat purchase of a product. . . . The consumer must *adopt* the brand. Until that time, he's always vulnerable to competing brands. . . . At Seagram's we raise prices on all brands continually, reinvesting the profits in advertising to obtain the reach and frequency needed to capture the consumer's brand loyalty.[38]

Figure 18–5 illustrates the potential makeup of the market share for a given brand at one point in time. There are three general categories of purchasers for any given brand:

Figure 18–5
Alternative Purchase Patterns

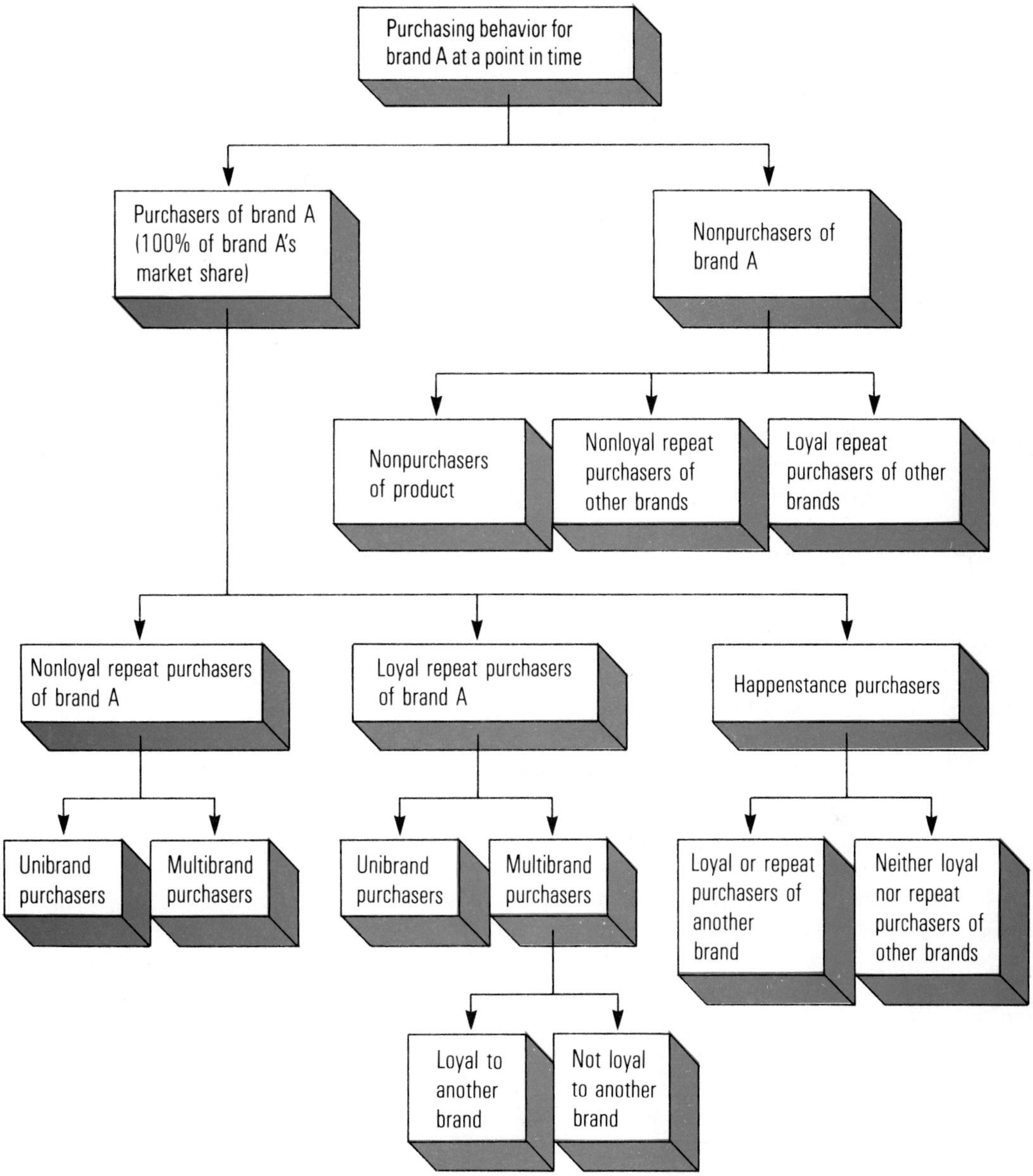

Source: J. Jacoby and R. W. Chestnut, *Brand Loyalty: Measurement and Management* (New York: John Wiley & Sons, 1978), p. 103. Used with permission.

1. Nonloyal repeat purchasers.
2. Loyal repeat purchasers.
3. Happenstance purchasers (purchase based on situational factors).

Each of these groups can be further subdivided based on their reactions to competing brands. Since each of these three categories of purchasers may require a unique marketing strategy, a substantial amount of research has been devoted to determining the characteristics of each group (although most studies have treated loyal and nonloyal repeat purchasers as a single group).

Research studies to date have produced two major conclusions. One is that *brand loyalty is a product specific phenomenon* and there is no such thing as a loyalty-prone consumer. That is, a consumer loyal to one brand in a given product category may not display similar loyalties to brands in other product classes. Loyal consumers do not differ significantly from nonloyal consumers in terms of demographics or personality measures. A second conclusion is that *brand-loyal consumers express greater levels of satisfaction than less loyal and nonloyal consumers.*[39]

Repeat Purchasing Behavior and Marketing Strategy

While consumer satisfaction contributes to repeat purchase behavior, it can also be affected by marketing efforts. In markets where there are many alternative brands, where there is greater price activity, and where products are easily substitutable, brand loyalty tends to decrease.[40]

There is widespread concern among marketers of consumer nondurables that the allocation of marketing dollars from product advertising to promotional deals (coupons and other forms of short-term price reductions) has eroded brand loyalty among consumers.[41] However, empirical studies suggest no real changes in the percentage of loyal (or at least repeat) purchasers over the past 10 years.[42] When satisfied consumers switch brands to take advantage of a promotional deal on a competing brand, they are likely to return to their original brand in future purchases.[43] However, nonloyal consumers often switch for deals, loyal consumers sometimes do, and loyal consumers may "stock up" when their brand is being promoted. In product categories characterized by frequent promotions, virtually all sales may occur on "deal."

A market analysis drawn from Figure 18–5 is the starting point for developing a marketing strategy based on repeat purchase patterns.[44] The firm must estimate the percentage of potential customers that fall into each of the cells in the figure. Then it should develop specific objectives. For example, your firm might want to convert nonloyal repeat multibrand purchasers to nonloyal repeat unibrand purchasers. This objective would require a different marketing strategy than attempting to convert happenstance purchasers to loyal repeat purchasers. Once the objective(s) are defined, you can develop and implement marketing strategies and evaluate their results.

Both Kodak and Maytag use versions of this approach.[45] Kodak monitors six groups: (1) current customers, (2) new customers, (3) brand switchers, (4) trial users, (5) customers who upgrade, and (6) trade-in customers. Maytag divides its current buyers into three categories: (1) new purchasers, (2) repeat purchasers, and (3) those who switched from Maytag to a competitor and back to Maytag. Clearly, sophisticated firms are moving beyond treating customers simply as buyers or nonbuyers.

SUMMARY

Following some purchases, consumers experience doubts or anxiety about the wisdom of the purchase. This is known as postpurchase dissonance. It is most likely to occur (1) among individuals with a tendency to experience anxiety, (2) after an irrevocable purchase, (3) when the purchase was important to the consumer, and (4) when it involved a difficult choice between two or more alternatives. Postpurchase dissonance is important to the marketing manager because, if not resolved, it can result in a returned product or a negative evaluation of the purchase.

Whether or not the consumer experiences dissonance, most purchases are followed by product use. This use may be by the purchaser or by some other member of the purchasing unit. Marketing managers are interested in product use for a variety of reasons. The major reason is that consumers use a product to fulfill certain needs. If the product does not fulfill these needs, a negative evaluation may result. Therefore, managers must be aware of how products perform in use. Monitoring product usage can indicate new uses for existing products, needed product modifications, appropriate advertising themes, and opportunities for new products. Product liability laws have made it increasingly important for marketing managers to be aware of all potential uses of their products.

Disposition of the product or its package may occur before, during, or after product use. Understanding disposition behavior has become increasingly important to marketing managers because of the ecological concerns of many consumers, the costs and scarcity of raw materials, and the activities of federal and state legislatures and regulatory agencies. The ease of recycling or reusing a product's container is a key product attribute for many consumers. These consumers, sometimes referred to as socially conscious consumers, are an important market segment not only because of their purchases but because of their social and political influence. Product disposition is a major consideration in marketing strategy because: (1) disposition sometimes must precede the purchase due to financial or space limitations; (2) certain disposition strategies may give rise to a used or rebuilt market; and (3) difficult or unsatisfactory disposition alternatives may cause some consumers to withdraw from the market for a particular item.

Postpurchase dissonance, product usage, and disposition are potential influences on the purchase evaluation process. Basically, consumers develop certain expectations about the ability of the product to fulfill instrumental and symbolic needs. To the extent that the product meets these needs, satisfaction is likely to result. When expectations are not met, dissatisfaction is the likely result.

Taking no action, switching brands, products, or stores, and warning friends are all common reactions to a negative purchase evaluation. A marketing manager generally should encourage dissatisfied consumers to complain directly to the firm and to no one else. This alerts the firm to problems and provides it with an opportunity to make amends. Unfortunately, only a fairly small, unique set of consumers tends to complain. Developing such strategies as consumer hot lines can increase the percentage of dissatisfied consumers who complain to the firm.

After the evaluation process and, where applicable, the complaint process, consumers have some degree of repurchase motivation. There may be a strong motive to avoid the brand, a willingness to repurchase it some of the time, a willingness to repurchase it all of the time, or some level of brand loyalty, which is a willingness to repurchase coupled with a psychological commitment to the brand.

Marketing strategy does not always have the creation of brand loyalty as its objective. Rather, the manager must examine the makeup of the brand's current and potential consumers and select the specific objectives most likely to maximize the overall organizational goals. For example, there may be a greater net payoff associated with converting nonpurchasers to happenstance purchasers than there is with converting repeat purchasers to loyal purchasers. The manager must select the appropriate objective and then develop marketing strategies to accomplish the objective.

REVIEW QUESTIONS

1. What are the major *postpurchase processes* engaged in by consumers?
2. How does the *type of decision process* affect the postpurchase processes?
3. What is *postpurchase dissonance?* What characteristics of a purchase situation are likely to contribute to postpurchase dissonance?
4. In what ways can a consumer reduce postpurchase dissonance?
5. In what ways can a marketer help reduce postpurchase dissonance?
6. What is meant by the *disposition of products and product packaging,* and why does it interest governmental regulatory agencies?
7. Why are marketers interested in disposition?
8. How does the disposition of products vary in Table 18–2? What factors influence the different patterns of disposition shown in Table 18–2?
9. What factors influence *consumer satisfaction?* In what way do they influence consumer satisfaction?
10. What is the difference between *instrumental* and *symbolic performance,* and how does each contribute to consumer satisfaction?

11. What role does *emotion* or *affect* play in consumer satisfaction?
12. What courses of action can a consumer take in response to dissatisfaction?
13. How do consumers typically respond when dissatisfied?
14. What would marketers like consumers to do when dissatisfied? How can marketers encourage this?
15. What is the relationship between *product satisfaction* and *repurchase behavior?* What is the difference between *repeat purchase* and *brand loyalty?*
16. What characteristics have been found to distinguish brand loyal consumers from nonbrand loyal consumers?
17. What are the effects of promotional deals on brand loyalty and brand switching?

DISCUSSION QUESTIONS

1. How should retailers deal with consumers immediately after purchase to reduce postpurchase dissonance? What specific action would you recommend, and what effect would you intend it to have on the recent purchaser of:

   a. Sports car?
   b. Compact disc player?
   c. Suit?
   d. Expensive watch?
   e. Mouthwash?

2. Answer Question 1 from a manufacturer's perspective.
3. Discuss how you could determine how consumers actually use their ___. How could this information be used to develop marketing strategy?

   a. Mouthwash.
   b. Soft drink.
   c. Radio.
   d. VCR.
   e. Calculator.
   f. Chain saw.

4. How would you go about measuring consumer satisfaction among purchasers of _________? What questions would you ask, and what additional information would you collect and why? How could this information be used for evaluating and planning marketing programs?

   a. Toothpaste.
   b. VCR.
   c. Restaurants.
   d. Automobile.
   e. Health insurance.

5. An A. C. Nielsen study found that 61 percent of the unsatisfactory purchases of health and beauty aids, such as deodorants, shampoos, or vitamins, were followed by continued purchase of the brand. Only 27 percent of the unsatisfactory purchases of paper products were followed by repeat purchases of the same brand. Why is there such a large difference?
6. Examine Figure 18–5 and pick three distinct conversion objectives (e.g., converting nonloyal repeat multibrand purchases to nonloyal repeat single-

brand purchases). Describe the marketing strategies required by each. Use mouthwash as a product category for your discussion.

7. Based on those characteristics that contribute to postpurchase dissonance, discuss several product purchases that are most likely to result in dissonance and several that will not create this effect.
8. Examine Table 18–2 and discuss the results in terms of the disposition alternatives used for the products evaluated. What consumer and product characteristics contribute to these differences in disposition behavior?
9. What level of product dissatisfaction should a marketer be content with in attempting to serve a particular target market? What characteristics contribute to dissatisfaction, regardless of the marketer's efforts?
10. What are the marketing implications of Table 18–1?
11. Will the increasing use of promotional deals "teach" most consumers to buy primarily brands "on deal"?
12. Describe the last time you were dissatisfied with a purchase. What action did you take? Why?

PROJECT QUESTIONS

1. Develop a questionnaire designed to measure consumer satisfaction of a nonclothing purchase of $25 or more. Include in your questionnaire items that measure the product's instrumental and expressive dimensions of performance, as well as what the consumer wanted in terms of instrumental and expressive performance. Then interview several consumers to obtain information on actual performance, expected performance, and satisfaction. Using this information, determine if the consumer received (i.e., evaluation of performance) what they expected, and relate this difference to consumer expressions of satisfaction.
2. Develop a survey to measure student dissatisfaction with retail purchases. For purchases they were dissatisfied with, determine what action they took to resolve this dissatisfaction and what was the end result of their efforts.
3. Develop a method of measuring brand loyalty, then measure the brand loyalty of several students with respect to soft drinks, restaurants, and mouthwash.
4. With the cooperation of a major durables retailer, assist the retailer in sending a postpurchase letter of thanks to every other customer immediately after purchase. Then approximately two weeks after purchase, contact the same customers (both those who received the letter and those who did not) and measure their purchase satisfaction. Evaluate the results.
5. For the products and disposition alternatives listed in Table 18–2, develop a questionnaire designed to collect this same information in either a student or nonstudent population. Create a similar table and evaluate the results with respect to those shown in Table 18–2.

6. Conduct a focus group interview (see appendix A) with a group of students to determine how they evaluate the purchase and use of a product of interest to you.

REFERENCES

[1] T. Moore, "Would You Buy a Car from This Man?" *Fortune,* April 11, 1988, pp. 72–74. See also R. Serafin, "Auto Makers Stress Consumer Satisfaction," *Advertising Age,* February 23, 1987, p. S-12.

[2] The basic theory of cognitive dissonance of which postpurchase dissonance is a subset is presented in L. Festinger, *A Theory of Cognitive Dissonance* (Stanford, Calif.: Stanford University Press, 1957). An overview is available in W. H. Cummings and M. Venkatesan, "Cognitive Dissonance and Consumer Behavior: A Review of the Evidence," *Journal of Marketing Research,* August 1976, pp. 303–8.

[3] M. Menasco and D. Hawkins, "A Field Test of the Relationship between Cognitive Dissonance and State Anxiety," *Journal of Marketing Research,* November 1978, pp. 650–55.

[4] S. Oshikawa, "The Measurement of Cognitive Dissonance: Some Experimental Findings," *Journal of Marketing,* January 1972, pp. 64–67; and D. I. Hawkins, "Reported Cognitive Dissonance and Anxiety: Some Additional Findings," *Journal of Marketing,* July 1972, pp. 63–66.

[5] Festinger, *Theory of Cognitive Dissonance.*

[6] "The Devils in the Product Liability Laws," *Business Week,* February 12, 1979, pp. 72–78.

[7] C. W. Stevens, "One Producer Finds Recall Is Best Policy for a Hazardous Toy," *The Wall Street Journal,* March 2, 1979, p. 1.

[8] F. Rice, "Where Will We Put All That Garbage?" *Fortune,* April 11, 1988, pp. 96–100.

[9] W. Rathje, W. Hughes, and S. Jernigan, "The Science of Garbage: Following the Consumer through His Garbage Can," *Business Proceedings* (Chicago: American Marketing Association, 1976), pp. 56–64.

[10] F. E. Webster, Jr., "Determining the Characteristics of the Socially Conscious Consumer," *Journal of Consumer Research,* December 1975, pp. 188–96; and J. Arbuthnot, "The Roles of Attitudinal and Personality Variables in the Prediction of Environmental Behavior and Change," *Environment and Behavior,* June 1977, pp. 217–33.

[11] See G. Brooker, "The Self-Actualizing Socially Conscious Consumer," *Journal of Consumer Research,* September 1978, pp. 107–12; L. R. Tucker, Jr., "The Environmentally Concerned Citizen," *Environment and Behavior,* September 1978, pp. 389–418; and P. E. Murphy, N. Kangun, and W. Locander, "Environmentally Concerned Consumers: Racial Variations," *Journal of Marketing,* October 1978, pp. 61–66.

[12] J. Hansen, "A Proposed Paradigm for Consumer Disposition Processes," *Journal of Consumer Affairs,* Summer 1980, pp. 49–67.

[13] See R. L. Oliver, "Measurement and Evaluation of Satisfaction Processes in Retail Settings," *Journal of Retailing,* Fall 1981, pp. 25–48; J. E. Swan and I. F.

Trawick, "Disconfirmation of Expectations and Satisfaction with a Retail Service," *Journal of Retailing,* Fall 1981, pp. 49–67; and R. A. Westbrook, "Sources of Consumer Satisfaction with Retail Outlets," *Journal of Retailing,* Fall 1981, pp. 68–85.

[14] See R. L. Day, "Extending the Concept of Consumer Satisfaction," in *Advances in Consumer Research,* ed. W. D. Perreault, Jr. (Chicago: Association for Consumer Research, 1977), pp. 149–54; and J. E. Swan and I. F. Trawick, "Triggering Cues and the Evaluation of Products as Satisfactory or Dissatisfactory," in *1979 Educator's Conference Proceedings,* ed. N. Beckwith et al. (Chicago: American Marketing Association, 1979), pp. 231–34.

[15] R. A. Westbrook and J. A. Cote, Jr., "An Exploratory Study of Nonproduct-Related Influences upon Consumer Satisfaction," in *Advances in Consumer Research,* ed. J. C. Olson (Chicago: Association for Consumer Research, 1980), pp. 577–81; R. A. Westbrook, "Intrapersonal Affective Influences on Consumer Satisfaction with Products," *Journal of Consumer Research,* June 1980, pp. 49–54; and A. R. Andreasen, "Life Status Changes and Changes in Consumer Preferences and Satisfaction," *Journal of Consumer Research,* December 1984, pp. 784–94.

[16] R. L. Oliver, "A Cognitive Model of the Antecedents and Consequences of Satisfaction Decisions," *Journal of Marketing Research,* November 1980, pp. 460–69; R. L. Oliver and W. O. Bearden, "Disconfirmation and Consumer Evaluations in Product Usage," *Journal of Business Research,* June 1985, pp. 235–46; and E. R. Cadotte, R. B. Woodruff, and R. L. Jenkins, "Expectations and Norms in Models of Consumer Satisfaction," *Journal of Marketing Research,* August 1987, pp. 305–14.

[17] See Oliver, "A Cognitive Model"; and R. L. Oliver and G. Linda, "Effect of Satisfaction and Its Antecedents on Consumer Preference and Intentions," in *Advances in Consumer Research,* ed. K. B. Monroe (Chicago: Association for Consumer Research, 1981), pp. 88–93.

[18] R. N. Maddox, "The Structure of Consumers' Satisfaction: Cross-product Comparisons," *Journal of the Academy of Marketing Science,* Winter 1982, pp. 37–53.

[19] J. E. Swan and L. J. Combs, "Product Performance and Consumer Satisfaction: A New Concept," *Journal of Marketing,* April 1976, pp. 25–33; see also B. D. Gelb, "How Marketers of Intangibles Can Raise the Odds for Consumer Satisfaction," *Journal of Consumer Marketing,* Spring 1985, pp. 55–61; and R. A. Westbrook, "Product/Consumption-Based Affective Responses and Postpurchase Processes," *Journal of Marketing Research,* August 1987, pp. 258–70.

[20] Westbrook, ibid.

[21] See also S. Widrick and E. Fram, "Identifying Negative Products," *Journal of Consumer Marketing,* Fall 1983, pp. 59–66.

[22] A different model is J. Singh, "Consumer Complaint Intentions and Behavior," *Journal of Marketing,* January 1988, pp. 93–107.

[23] See E. H. Demby, "Don't Count on Dissatisfied Customers to Make the Switch," *Marketing News,* January 18, 1988, pp. 4, 15.

[24] M. K. Mills, "Deviance and Dissatisfaction: An Exploratory Study," in *Advances,* ed. K. B. Monroe, pp. 682–86.

[25] See M. L. Richins, "A Multivariate Analysis of Responses to Dissatisfaction," *Journal of the Academy of Marketing Science,* Fall 1987, pp. 24–31.

[26] F. K. Shuptrine and G. Wenglorz, "Comprehensive Identification of Consumers' Marketplace Problems and What They Do about Them," in *Advances,* ed. K. B. Monroe, pp. 687–92.

[27] M. L. Richins, "Negative Word-of-Mouth by Dissatisfied Consumers," *Journal of Marketing,* Winter 1983, pp. 68–78; M. L. Richins, "Word-of-Mouth as Negative Information," in *Advances in Consumer Research XI,* ed. T. C. Kinnear (Provo, Utah: Association for Consumer Research, 1984), pp. 697–702; and M. T. Curren and V. S. Folkes, "Attributional Influences on Consumers' Desires to Communicate about Products," *Psychology & Marketing,* Spring 1987, pp. 31–45.

[28] *Better Business Bureau's Inquiries and Complaints, 1979 Statistical Summary* (New York: Council of Better Business Bureaus, Inc., undated), p. 7; and Shuptrine and Wenglorz, "Comprehensive Identification," p. 690.

[29] K. L. Bernhardt, "Consumer Problems and Complaint Actions of Older Americans: A National View," *Journal of Retailing,* Fall 1981, pp. 107–23; W. O. Bearden and J. E. Teel, "An Investigation of Personal Influences on Consumer Complaining," *Journal of Retailing,* Fall 1981, pp. 2–20; M. S. Moyer, "Characteristics of Consumer Complainants," *Journal of Public Policy & Marketing,* vol. 3, 1984, pp. 67–84; and M. A. Morganosky and H. M. Buckley, "Complaint Behavior," in *Advances in Consumer Research XIV,* ed. M. Wallendorf and P. Anderson (Provo, Utah: Association for Consumer Research, 1987), pp. 223–26.

[30] Shuptrine and Wenglorz, "Comprehensive Identification," p. 690.

[31] See P. A. LaBarbera and L. J. Rosenberg, "How Marketers Can Better Understand Consumers," *MSU Business Topics,* Winter 1980, pp. 29–36; and "Campbell Soup Uses Toll-Free Line to Solicit Opinions of Commercials," *Marketing News,* December 25, 1981, p. 1.

[32] C. Fornell and R. A. Westbrook, "Internal Processing of Consumer Complaints by Large Corporations," *Arizona Review 3,* 1980, pp. 10–15; "New FTC Manual Can Help Business Establish Systems for Handling Consumer Complaints," *FTC News Summary,* December 19, 1980, p. 2; A. J. Resnik and R. R. Harmon, "Consumer Complaints and Managerial Response," *Journal of Marketing,* Winter 1983, pp. 86–97; C. J. Cobb, G. C. Walgren, and M. Hollowed, "Differences in Organizational Responses to Consumer Letters of Satisfaction and Dissatisfaction," in *Advances in Consumer Research,* ed. M. Wallendorf and P. Anderson (Provo, Utah: Association for Consumer Research, 1987), pp. 227–31; and C. Fornell and R. Westbrook, "The Vicious Circle of Consumer Complaints," *Journal of Marketing,* Summer 1984, p. 68.

[33] M. J. Etzel and B. I. Silverman, "A Managerial Perspective on Directions for Retail Customer Dissatisfaction Research," *Journal of Retailing,* Fall 1981, 124–31; and M. C. Gilly and R. W. Hansen, "Consumer Complaint Handling as a Strategic Marketing Tool," *Journal of Consumer Marketing,* Fall 1985, pp. 5–16.

[34] C. Fornell and B. Wernerfelt, "Defensive Marketing Strategy by Customer Complaint Management," *Journal of Marketing Research,* November 1987, pp. 337–46.

[35] *Handling Consumer Complaints: In-House and Third-Party Strategies, no. 018-000-00284-1* (Washington, D.C.: U.S. Government Printing Office), p. 19.

[36] See S. B. Knouse, "Brand Loyalty and Sequential Learning Theory," *Psychology & Marketing,* Summer 1986, pp. 87–98.

[37] J. Jacoby and D. B. Kyner, "Brand Loyalty versus Repeat Purchasing Behavior," *Journal of Marketing Research,* February 1973, pp. 1–9.

[38] "Instill 'Brand Loyalty,' Seagram Exec Tells Marketers," *Advertising Age,* April 30, 1979, p. 26.

[39] See T. Exter, "Looking for Brand Loyalty," *American Demographics,* April 1986, pp. 32–33, 52–56. For a different view see G. P. Moschis, R. L. Moore, and T. J. Stanley, "An Exploratory Study of Brand Loyalty Development," in *Advances in Consumer Research XI,* ed. T. C. Kinnear (Provo, Utah: Association for Consumer Research, 1984), pp. 412–17.

[40] See S. P. Raj, "Striking a Balance between Brand 'Popularity' and Brand Loyalty," *Journal of Marketing,* Winter 1985, pp. 53–59.

[41] T. Johnson and A. M. Tarshis, "What Changes in Promotion Strategy Mean for Brand Franchise Loyalty," paper presented at the 1986 Annual Fall Conference, Advertising Research Foundation.

[42] Ibid; and T. Johnson, "The Myth of Declining Brand Loyalty," *Journal of Advertising Research,* March 1984, pp. 9–18. A conflicting view is M. L. Rothschild, "A Behavioral View of Promotion's Effects on Brand Loyalty," in *Advances in Consumer Research XIV,* ed. M. Wallendorf and P. Anderson (Provo, Utah: Association for Consumer Research, 1987), pp. 119–20.

[43] D. Mazursky, P. LaBarbera, and A. Aiello, "When Consumers Switch Brands," *Psychology and Marketing,* Spring 1987, pp. 17–30.

[44] See L. J. Rosenberg and J. A. Czepiel, "A Marketing Approach for Customer Retention," *Journal of Consumer Marketing,* Fall 1983, pp. 45–51.

[45] Ibid.

C A S E S

CASE 4–1 RSI/COMPU-PAK*

Using package design, a small manufacturer seeks to create an identity that will differentiate it from much larger competitors.

The computer diskette market is approaching $1 billion in annual sales. While this market is large and growing, it is dominated by large suppliers such as 3M, Memorex, Maxwell (a subsidiary of Hitachi), and Verbatim (a subsidiary of Eastman-Kodak). With annual sales of $1 million, RSI/Compu-pak is barely noticeable in this market. It specializes in custom-package diskettes and other computer supplies for private label marketers.

The problem facing RSI/Compu-pak is how to hold share and price in a market that doesn't offer much opportunity for product differentiation. "Diskettes are diskettes, pretty much. There are only two kinds, good and bad quality," according to President Barry Kukes. "If we branded them 'RSI Diskettes,' we wouldn't stand a chance in hell against the big firms."

To create a position in this billion dollar market, RSI/Compu-pak will spend $250,000 in 1988 on a combination of creative marketing approaches. This is a small amount of money when compared with the advertising budgets of well-established competitors. For example, Memorex will spend $1.6 million on advertising their diskettes while Verbatim will spend $750,000 and Maxwell, $435,000. With essentially no brand or corporate awareness, RSI/Compu-pak plans to capture attention and interest through the packaging of their diskettes.

The Swimsuit Diskette

Using packaging as a primary means of drawing attention and interest, RSI/Compu-pak diskettes will be called "Swimsuit Diskettes," featuring 24-year-old model Lori Quint in a variety of swimsuits. On the front of a box of ten diskettes shown in Figure A, Ms. Quint is featured in a tasteful one-piece bathing suit. Inside, each of the protective envelopes holding a diskette features her in a more revealing bikini. Each box of diskettes also includes a mail offer for a 20- by 30-inch color poster of Ms. Quint. The Swimsuit Diskette is the first of a planned series that may include Chevrolet Corvettes, landscapes, male swimsuit diskettes, puppies, and other themes.

*Used with permission from RSI/Compu-pak.

Figure A
Advertising Copy Promoting Swimsuit Diskettes

Because nearly 90 percent of computer diskettes are purchased by men, RSI/Compu-pak feels its packaging will be eye-catching and different enough to attract buyers even at a price premium over competing diskettes. RSI/Compu-pak feels that the Swimsuit Diskette with Lori Quint allows them to enter the diskette market without having to spend a fortune on advertising to establish their name. According to Mr. Kukes:

> Half the product introduction is getting customers to remember your name and pull your product off the shelf; the other half, initial and repeat sales, only can be won by the product itself.

RSI/Compu-pak believes it supplies a quality diskette and offers a very good warranty. Their warranty states on the box, "If for any reason one of our Swimsuit Diskettes fails, we will replace it with any diskette of your choice."

While direct sales to Fortune 500 companies has met resistance, reaction from dealers and distributors has been enthusiastic. Mr. Kukes believes that "we're not going to knock 3M or Maxwell out of this market; but you capture 1 or 2 percent of the market and you're in good shape."

Questions

1. Why would RSI/Compu-pak expect to capture high levels of awareness with this approach?
2. Why would a diskette buyer pay a premium price for the Swimsuit Diskette when there is no quality difference with well-known lower-priced diskettes?
3. What demographic and lifestyle characteristics would characterize potential buyers of the Swimsuit Diskette? Recognizing these characteristics, which print media would best reach these target consumers?
4. What actions will RSI/Compu-pak have to take to achieve more than one-time purchase on the basis of novelty? How can they build repeat purchase of this product?
5. What evaluative criteria do diskette buyers use? What decision rules? How does RSI/Compu-pak's strategy mesh with these factors?
6. What risks are associated with diskette failure? Does the firm's warranty adequately address these risks?

CASE 4–2 JACOBSON BOAT*

In an antitrust case, attorneys for Jacobson Boat want to estimate what Jacobson Boat's market share would have been if it had not been illegally restrained from competing.

The market demand for outboard motors grew steadily throughout the seventies and eighties, during which period Jacobson Boat enjoyed steady growth. While located a considerable distance from its major buying population, Jacobson maintained an active presence with heavy advertising and price promotions. These were supplemented with a larger-than-average inventory which provided buyers a wide variety of boat styles and colors from which to choose. With all this, Jacobson was able to attract a considerable market share despite being almost four times farther from the major market than other boat retailers serving this market.

In the mid-eighties, Jacobson's competitors became frustrated with Jacobson's aggressive promotion and pricing tactics. They felt they were unnecessarily losing market share and were being forced to price at lower margins than desirable. Therefore, the major retailers in Jacobson's market met and agreed to lessen competition by coercing a major boat manufacturer into not selling the most popular brand of boat to Jacobson. Several tactics were employed, the net effect being that Jacobson could not get access to the boat model that was in greatest demand by consumers.

This practice went on for two years, during which time Jacobson's sales volume was adversely affected. During this period, Jacobson initiated a lawsuit,

---

*Based on a proprietary project by one of the authors.

Table A
Marketing Mix for Popular Models for Competing Boat Retailers

	Relative Indices			
Firm	Distance	Price	Advertising	Square Footage
States Boat Supply	1.00	1.00	2.00	2.00
Western Marina and Boat	1.00	1.00	2.00	1.50
Capital Boat and Supply	2.00	.90	1.00	1.00
Jacobson Boat	4.00	.70	4.00	4.00

and the illegal activities of its competitors were uncovered. Subsequent legal action revealed that the law had unquestionably been broken and Jacobson had been damaged. The question was how much the court should award Jacobson in damages due to lost sales.

Jacobson hired a marketing consultant to help determine its lost sales due to this illegal activity. Jacobson's attorney subpoenaed the competitors for information relating to their activities over the past several years. This information included, by model of boat: prices, advertising expenditures, and inventory levels (measured by square foot allocated to the model). Adding to this information the distance from the market to each competitor, the consultant developed Table A.

Table A provides relative measures of the level of each marketing variable used by each retailer. A relative index used to facilitate comparisons between variables showed that Jacobson was four times farther from the market center, but advertised twice as much as States Boat Supply and Western Marina & Boat. Jacobson's prices were 30 percent lower than States Boat Supply and Western Marina & Boat, and 20 percent lower than Capital Boat & Supply. Also, for popular models, they carried twice the inventory of States Boat Supply and four times the inventory of Capital.

Using this information, the consultant constructed the following retail gravitation model:

$$MS_i = \frac{\left[\frac{1}{\text{Distance }(i)}\right] \times \left[\frac{1}{\text{Price}(i)}\right]^2 \times \left[\text{Advertising}(i)\right]^{.5} \times \left[\text{Square footage}(i)\right]}{\sum_{i=1}^{N}\left(\left[\frac{1}{\text{Distance }(i)}\right] \times \left[\frac{1}{\text{Price }(i)}\right]^2 \times \left[\text{Advertising }(i)\right]^{.5} \times \left[\text{Square footage }(i)\right]\right)}$$

In the above model, the market share of each competitor, *MS*, for any brand could be estimated as a function of its distance from the market, model price, model advertising, and square footage devoted to that model relative to these same influences for all *N* competitors in the market, which would include Jacobson Boat. To estimate the market share Jacobson would have had without the illegal restraints, the data in Table A were used.

Questions

1. Using the retail attraction model, estimate the expected market shares of each competitor, assuming Jacobson had access to this popular model of boat.
2. What would the expected market shares be without Jacobson in the market (i.e., three competitors without Jacobson)?
3. How could you use this information to determine the damages that should be awarded to Jacobson?
4. What other factors could alter estimates of market share?

CASE 4–3 K MART*

A marketing strategy is developed to reposition K mart as a higher quality/higher priced store.

Each month 52.5 million Americans shop at K mart. In 1986, sales across its 4,000 stores totaled $24.2 billion. In 1962, S.S. Kresge Company made the shift from the five-and-dime stores to discount department stores. By 1966, sales had reached $1 billion. By 1972 there were 485 K mart stores, and sales exceeded $2.5 billion. However, shoppers' needs in the eighties are far different from those in the sixties and seventies.

In the early eighties, K mart began to lose its middle-class customers to specialty stores and other department stores. The eighties' shopper wanted high-quality merchandise, better service, and a more pleasant atmosphere in which to shop. K mart, in the early eighties, clearly did not fit this need. Because the market was moving to higher-quality preferences, K mart had to move with it or lose sales. As shown in Figure A, its positioning in 1980 did not match the market and the desired position for 1990.

To initiate this move, a $2 billion program was launched in the early eighties to improve the appearance of K mart stores and stock them with higher-quality goods. K mart has done this through a stronger representation of national brands such as Samsonite luggage, Black & Decker power tools, Lee jeans, and MacGregor sporting goods. It has also targeted several other departments for significant upgrading, including auto, garden, and kitchen supplies.

Probably the best example of K mart's progress is in its family apparel operations. In 1980 the company was missing out on the apparel expenditures of many of its customers. Based on consumer research that showed consumers wanted better-quality apparel and were willing to pay a reasonable amount for it, K mart launched an aggressive strategy to upgrade its apparel operations. Included in that strategy was obtaining Jaclyn Smith as a spokesperson for the new line in 1986, and placing ads in Vogue and Mademoiselle magazines in the summer of the same year.

---

*Based on material supplied by K mart.

Figure A
Progressive Repositioning of K mart

Attributes Contributing Relative Quality

- Quality of merchandise
- Type of merchandise
- Store atmosphere
- Customer service
- Personnel
- Store location
- Advertising
- Prices
- Displays
- Customers

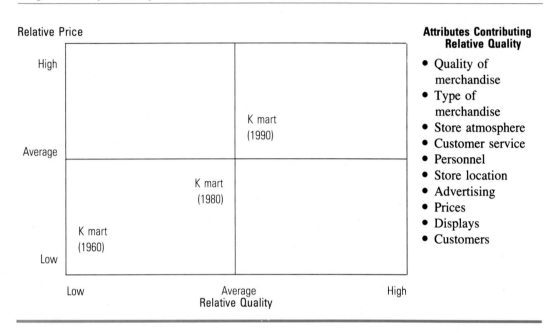

The response by the K mart shopper has been tremendous. To take advantage of the momentum, K mart plans, by 1992, to allocate an additional 4,000 square feet to apparel in 1,000 of its full-size stores in metropolitan markets.

And it is not stopping there. In 1987, K mart moved into retail banking. A pilot program launched in 1984 in 10 K mart stores in San Diego was expanded to 43 additional locations in California. More recently, another 21 K mart stores were added in Florida. In 1987 the company announced plans to go nationwide with 150 more convenience banks in K mart stores.

Questions

1. Using the factors listed in Figure A, as well as any others you feel are relevant, develop a store image rating scale as shown below for each of the factors. Then rate your perception of K mart as it existed prior to its current repositioning. Also indicate on each of the 10 scales where it will have to locate in the future in order to meet its new store image positioning.

Very High-Quality Merchandise	— — — — — — —	Very Low-Quality Merchandise

   In what order should K mart attempt to change these perceptions (which should it focus on first)? Why?

2. How does a celebrity spokesperson such as Jaclyn Smith influence K mart's store image? What are the advantages and potential problems in using her as a spokesperson?
3. What actions have to take place in order to achieve the desired repositioning? What factors beyond the direct control of K mart management will affect their success?
4. Is it necessary that K mart fully modify its image for all of its 4,000 stores? Explain.

CASE 4–4 LE JARDIN*

Le Jardin, a health oriented restaurant, undertakes marketing research to help expand its customer base and increase its sales without hurting its image or appeal among its current base of customers.

Throughout the eighties there has been an increasing awareness of the relationship between food consumption and health. This has led to an increased consumption of fish and white meats, and a general decline in the consumption of red meats. Along with this trend has been increased interest in meatless dishes, and the emergence of restaurants such as Le Jardin that specialize in meatless meals. Le Jardin ("the garden," in French) is a full-service, fashionably decorated restaurant. It is open for breakfast, lunch, and dinner seven days a week. While it serves eggs, alcoholic beverages, and other "nonhealth" foods, it avoids the use of meats, red or white, in its menu offerings.

To increase business, Le Jardin management needed to know more about their current and potential customer base. To do this, they commissioned a consumer research study which used a telephone interview of over 250 households in the served market. While a variety of general questions were asked, the real interest was in differentiating current customers from potential customers and noncustomers. They felt there was some portion of the population that would never eat at Le Jardin, given its nonmeat menu. Thus, with good consumer behavior data they hoped to properly target potential new customers, reinforce their image to existing customers, and avoid wasting marketing communications dollars on noncustomers.

Results of Consumer Survey

Figure A summarizes the restaurant selection criteria rated "very important" or "important" by the households interviewed. As one can see, of the top five selection criteria rated as important, only one has anything to do with food. Also noteworthy is the fact that price was rated sixth in importance. When asked to

*Based on a proprietary project by one of the authors.

Figure A
Restaurant Selection Criteria

Selection Criteria	Percent Rating Important
Quality of food	95%
Cleanliness of restaurant	95
Quality of service	95
Overall atmosphere	85
Waiting time under 30 minutes	82
Price of meal	70
Variety in menu	68
Access to parking	65
Quantity of food	50
Convenience of location	45
Take reservations	27
Honor credit cards	27
Open after 11 P.M.	20

name their favorite restaurant, Le Jardin came in 22nd out of the top 25 restaurants identified as favorites.

The top five restaurants identified as favorites had awareness scores that ranged from 76 to 92 percent. Sixty-two percent of those surveyed were aware of Le Jardin. The Black Angus, a steak house, had the highest awareness with 92 percent, and had been patronized by 45 percent of those interviewed. Of those who had gone to the Black Angus, 66 percent had gone back in the last year.

Figure B
Restaurant Awareness, Penetration, and Repeat Business among the Top 5 Restaurants Mentioned as Favorites and Le Jardin

Restaurants Rated as "Favorites"		Restaurant Awareness	Market Penetration	Repeat Customers
Black Angus	1	92%	45%	66%
	2	89	40	71
	3	83	38	60
	4	78	25	54
	5	76	18	47
	.	.	.	.
	.	.	.	.
	.	.	.	.
Le Jardin	22	62	18	58

Figure C
Segmentation of Le Jardin Customers

Segment	Size	Classification Criteria
Current customers	18%	Aware of Le Jardin and had been there over last year
Potential customers	21	Aware of Le Jardin and interested, but had not been there
Noncustomers	61	Aware of Le Jardin, but not interested, or unaware

Le Jardin had a lower awareness score but a higher repeat business than two of the top restaurants. Of those aware of Le Jardin (62 percent), only 18 percent had actually gone to the restaurant. Of those 18 percent, 58 percent had returned at least once over the preceding twelve months (see Figure B).

Customer Segmentation

To better utilize this information, the sample was divided as outlined in Figure C. Since Le Jardin was already reaching current customers, it was most interested in what distinguished those labeled "potential customers." These were individuals who had heard of Le Jardin and had interest in it but had not yet eaten there.

Figure D
Factors Differentiating Customer Segments

Important Differences	Current	Potential	Noncustomers
Behavior			
Eating out (once a week or more)	58%	51%	38%
Selection Criteria			
Price of meal (important)	47	68	74
Quantity of food (important)	37	48	63
Honor credit cards (important)	13	37	20
Demographics			
Age (26 to 45)	51	44	24
College graduate	54	35	21
Income (over $30,000)	42	45	24
Occupation (managerial, professional, or white collar)	64	51	21

Using this segmentation scheme, the next step was to determine what factors differentiated individuals categorized into the three groups. Figure D summarizes those factors which were found to differ among the groups. As one can see, there are several meaningful differences between "current customer" and "potential customer," based on what they want (selection criteria) and who they are (demographics). Likewise, there are important differences between each of these customer groups and the noncustomer group. While these differences are critical in designing a marketing strategy to attract more customers, it is equally important to point out the factors that did not differ among groups. None of the remaining selection criteria differed among groups, nor did other demographics such as home ownership, household size, or age of youngest child living at home. Taking into account these important differences and nondifferences, Le Jardin should be able to construct a marketing strategy to attract more customers. And because it obtains a good repeat business among current customers, it should be able to increase its sales volume significantly.

Questions

1. Based on the restaurant selection criteria and their importance in Figure A, and those selection criteria that differentiate customer segments in Figure D, describe the consumer decision process in terms of selecting one restaurant over another.
2. Should Le Jardin concentrate its resources on building awareness, or on converting "potential customers" to "current customers"?
3. In what other ways could Le Jardin segment its market?
4. Develop a marketing mix strategy designed to attract "potential customers" to Le Jardin.

CASE 4–5 MARIELLE*

A direct-mail campaign targeting two major competitors' customers is tracked over a two-year period to determine the total impact of the direct-mail effort.

Marielle is a relatively expensive brand of liquor that sells for $20 a bottle. Leading competing brands sell for $12 a bottle (see Figure A). Traditionally, Marielle has been viewed as the best money can buy in this line of liquor, and it has maintained a high price to enhance its perceived status. Marielle's two leading competitors have a good image for quality, and both support their positions through advertising and sales promotions. Private label and less advertised brands carry a lower image for quality and are sold below $10 per bottle.

---

*Adapted from: S. Rapt and T. Collins, Maximarketing (New York: McGraw-Hill, 1987), pp. 41–44.

Figure A
Price-Image for Quality Position for Marielle and Competitors

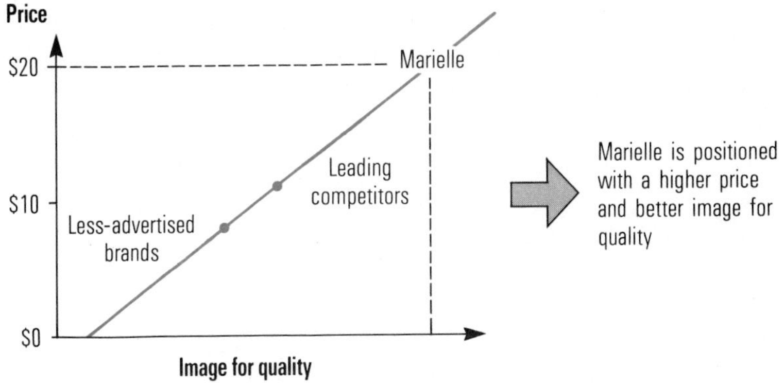

Marielle wanted to increase its sales without diluting its image. With its present positioning, Marielle appeals primarily to a demographically upscale market. Print media such as *The New Yorker, Smithsonian Magazine,* and *Town & Country* are used to reach target customers. However, the brand manager reasoned that Marielle could win over some of its leading competitors' customers if it could find a way to reach them without hurting its image among current customers.

Although advertising was discussed, Marielle felt it was too risky, since there would be some media overlap between current customers and the potential customers it wished to attract. Furthermore, because Marielle is higher priced, management felt they would have to use a price incentive to convince the new target customers to try it. This tactic also presented a problem, since Marielle did not want to damage its image among current customers with a price discount, nor give up margin in the form of a lower price to customers who would gladly pay full price. This discussion led the Marielle brand management team to develop a direct-mail program that would target the customers of their two leading competitors.

Direct-Mail Campaign

The Marielle brand management team secured the names and mailing addresses of 100,000 known consumers of their leading competitors' brands of liquor. An attractive direct-mail advertisement was created inviting these consumers to try Marielle and experience the difference in quality. Enclosed with the direct mailer was an $8 gift certificate to pay for the difference between the price of the competing brand they normally consumed at $12 a bottle and Marielle at $20 a bottle. They reasoned that the opportunity to try Marielle at the same price would be sufficient incentive to attract a trial purchase of Marielle. Because they had not used direct mail in this manner before, the team decided to carefully track consumer purchase and use behavior over a two-year period.

Consumer Purchase and Use Behavior

Utilizing a combination of returned gift certificates and telephone interviewing, the Marielle brand management team was able to track the impact of their direct-mail campaign. The tracking was divided into two parts: those "responding" to the direct mail offer and those "not responding." Nine percent responded to the direct mailer by using the gift certificate in a purchase of Marielle.

While the direct mailer produced immediate sales of 9,000 bottles of Marielle, the total additional first-year sales was 25,000 bottles as shown in Figure B. A third of the responders became regular users at the rate of five bottles per year, which contributed 15,000 bottles to the first-year total. Equally as important, each of these new regular consumers of Marielle influenced friends, such that for every three converts, one friend became an occasional consumer. This effect produced sales of 2,000 bottles. Two percent responding to the mailer became occasional consumers at the rate of two purchases per year, and four percent made purchases with the gift certificate but did not repurchase. Overall, the mailer produced new sales of 25,000 bottles the first year and 21,000 the second year. Thus, over a two-year period Marielle was able to attract 46,000 purchases away from its leading competitors while having to discount the sales of only 9,000 bottles.

Consumer research also tracked the behavior of the 91 percent who did not use the gift certificate. This research, as shown in Figure C, revealed that 53 percent read the direct mail advertisement and were favorably impressed with

Figure B
Purchase and Use Behavior of "Responders"

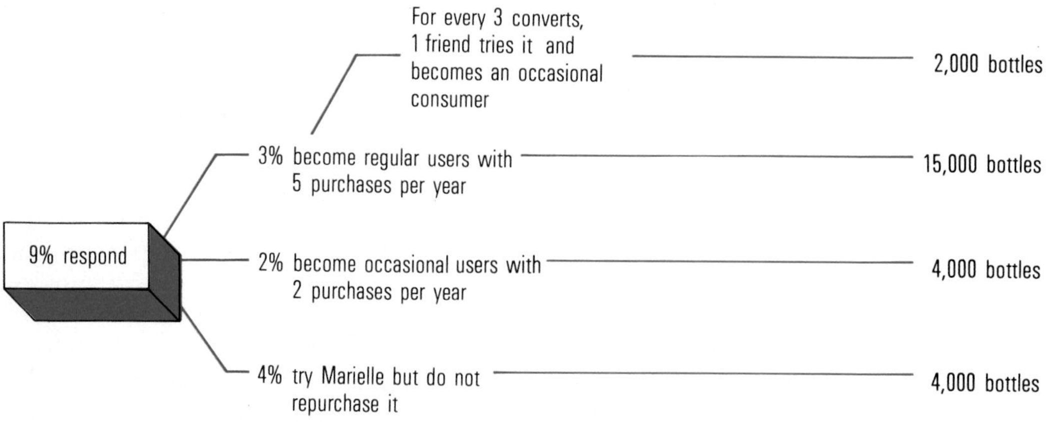
For every 3 converts, 1 friend tries it and becomes an occasional consumer
2,000 bottles
3% become regular users with 5 purchases per year
15,000 bottles
9% respond
2% become occasional users with 2 purchases per year
4,000 bottles
4% try Marielle but do not repurchase it
4,000 bottles

Figure C
Consumer Behavior of "Nonresponders"

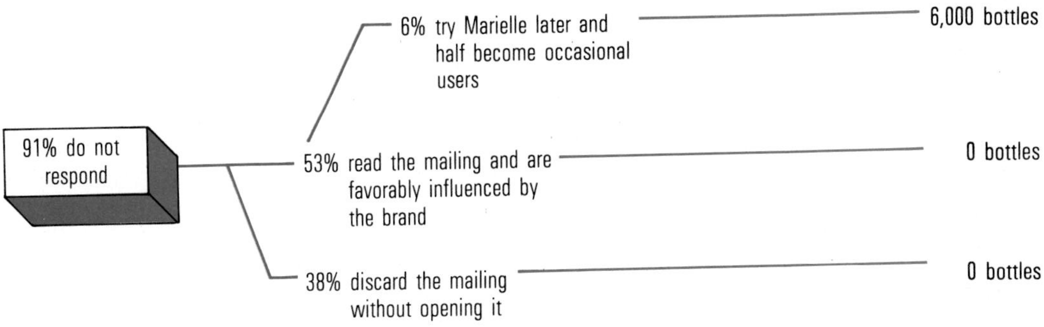
6% try Marielle later and half become occasional users
6,000 bottles
91% do not respond
53% read the mailing and are favorably influenced by the brand
0 bottles
38% discard the mailing without opening it
0 bottles

Marielle. More important, at a later date 6 percent purchased Marielle. Of those that made a "later trial purchase," half became occasional consumers. This produced first-year sales of 6,000 bottles from the delayed purchase of 6,000 customers, and second-year sales of another 6,000 bottles from the 3 percent that became occasional consumers of Marielle. Finally, 38 percent of the recipients of the direct mailer simply discarded it without opening it.

Overall, the direct-mail campaign was judged a tremendous success. The direct-mail effort was able to generate 31,000 first-year sales and sales of 27,000 bottles the second year. In the total the Marielle direct-mail campaign was able to attract sales of 58,000 bottles away from its leading competitors, with discount sales on only 9,000 bottles. As important, this was accomplished without damaging Marielle's reputation for quality.

Questions

1. Discuss the results with respect to low- and high-involvement information processing.
2. Discuss how the results might have been different for a direct mailer sent by a lower-priced brand of liquor.
3. While the direct mailer only produced a 9 percent response, the total sales over two years was 58,000 bottles. Discuss how subsequent consumer behavior should be included to evaluate the total impact of a direct-mail effort such as this.
4. What advantages did Marielle's direct-mail campaign have over a similar effort using television or magazine advertising?
5. What role does group communications appear to play in this product/market? How would you go about learning more about this process?

CASE 4–6 CITY RECYCLING*

A city develops a research-based strategy to encourage its citizens to recycle their newspapers instead of disposing them with their garbage?

Disposal of newspapers with garbage has three important implications for cities. One, they cannot be sold and hence generate money for the city. Two, it costs the city more in terms of refuse-site utilization. And three, in some instances it damages the environment. These are three good reasons to promote newspaper recycling.

To make recycling easier, the city introduced a system whereby households could set their newspapers beside their garbage cans and the city would pick them up with their garbage. Collection personnel would toss newspapers in one bin and garbage in another. After several years of operation, most households persisted in putting their newspapers in their garbage cans. Several city officials felt an advertising program was needed, but others doubted advertising's ability to change this behavior. To find out the answer to this question, a consumer research study was conducted in conjunction with a controlled advertising effort.

Household Research Study

An advertisement was created and run for three months. Prior to the ad campaign, 200 households were surveyed to determine a wide variety of stated behavior, attitudes, advertising awareness, and demographics. For purposes of the study, the city was divided into seven demographically distinct geographical regions. This division allowed the city to compare what people said they did to what they actually did in terms of disposing newspapers by demographic characteristics.

Actual disposal behavior was tracked before, during, and after the advertising campaign. Approximately 10 weeks after the advertising effort, a second survey of households was conducted. The intent of the postcampaign survey was to determine how behavior might change after the advertising was removed.

Results

Telephone surveys conducted before and after the advertising campaign indicated that 80 percent of households interviewed were receiving a daily newspaper. Of those receiving a newspaper, 36 percent stated they disposed of their newspapers in their garbage, as shown in Figure A. However, actual behavior observed by geographic area showed 56 percent of the households disposing of their newspapers in their garbage. This varied by geographical region as shown in Figure A.

The advertising effort corresponded with a reduction of from 56 percent to

*Based on as proprietary project by one of the authors.

Figure A
Stated and Actual Disposal of Newspapers with Garbage

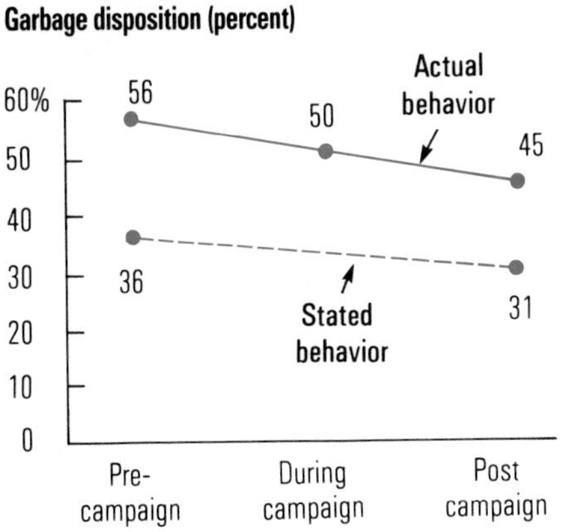

Geographic region	Behavior: Actual	Behavior: Stated
Upper class	57%	40%
White collar/older	65	33
White collar/family	59	37
Working class/family	47	42
Hispanic/family	55	37
University area	46	37
Poverty	56	36
Overall	56%	36%

50 percent of the households disposing of their newspapers in their garbage. This trend continued 10 weeks after the ad effort was stopped. Overall, 11 percent fewer households disposed of their newspapers in the garbage, although there was still a considerable gap between stated and actual behavior.

The postcampaign survey produced an ad awareness of 41 percent, as shown in Figure B. Of those aware of the ad, 63 percent could recall the content of the ad. However, only 53 percent could recall the content correctly in terms of the behavior the ad was promoting. Thus, approximately 14 percent of the

Figure B
Effectiveness of Advertising Effort

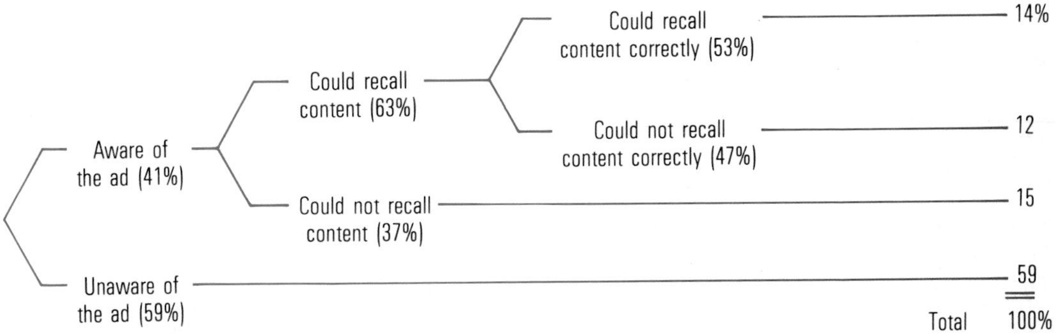

Figure C
Demographics That Differentiate the Geographic Regions

Geographic Region	College Graduate	Children at Home	Household 3 or More	Aware of City Program
Upper class	68%	42%	23%	73%
White collar/older	42	23	24	45
White collar/family	40	54	46	48
Working class/family	21	45	41	43
Hispanic/family	21	51	38	52
University area	41	23	21	42
Poverty area	7	27	28	30

population could correctly recall that the ad stressed the need to recycle newspapers along with garbage pickup.

Shown in Figure C are the demographics that differentiated each of the seven geographical regions used in the study. Overall awareness of the city's recycling program was 47 percent, although this varied from 30 percent for those living in a poverty area to 73 percent for those living in an upper-class neighborhood. Other demographic differences in terms of education and household structure are also shown by geographic location.

Questions

1. Discuss how differences in social status might contribute to differences in actual and stated behavior.
2. With respect to the advertising campaign, discuss the learning process that had to be operating in order for the results shown in Figure A to occur.
3. What will happen to behavior if further advertising efforts are not made? Explain your answer within the context of learning theory.
4. How might the city improve its advertising so as to further increase the tonnage of newspapers recycled?
5. How does the newspaper disposition decision differ from other types of disposition decisions?

CASE 4–7 SMALL CLAIMS COURT*

How can states create better access and utilization of small claims courts in consumer disputes?

*Based on "The Consumer Decision to Seek Legal Redress: A Path Analytic Theory and Imperical Test," by Michael L. Ursic, Ph.D. dissertation, 1981, University of Oregon.

As consumers, we are rarely satisfied with all of our purchases. When dissatisfied, a consumer can simply stop buying a product or shopping at a store. However, in some instances the consequences of consumer dissatisfaction are more enduring and a complaint is made with the manufacturer or retailer. If the complaint cannot be resolved, the consumer may have access to small claims courts where a legal judgment can be rendered. These consumer disputes are limited to a maximum dollar amount which varies by state.

Though the small claims courts exist for this purpose, many consumers do not pursue this option when they cannot resolve a dispute. To provide better access and utilization of small claims courts, it is first necessary to understand the factors that contribute to a consumer's decision to seek legal redress in a consumer dispute. To accomplish this, a model of the consumer decision to take legal action was developed.

Consumer Research

The model presented in Figure A represents a set of conditions that were believed to influence a consumer's decision to utilize a small claims court. As shown, these conditions were divided into four categories. The condition variables represent background variables that were believed to affect this decision process. The nature of prior court experience, amount of court experience, availability of a small claims court, social class, and amount of claim were each believed to be conditions which could influence a consumer to take legal action. Each of these condition variables in turn influenced process or inference variables.

Process variables involved some aspect of behavior, emotions, or attitudes. Anxiety about going to court, perceived effectiveness in court, utility for money, and extent of search for evidence were considered relevant in this area. While

Figure A
Conditions, Processes, and Inferences Impacting the Decision to Go to Court in a Consumer Dispute

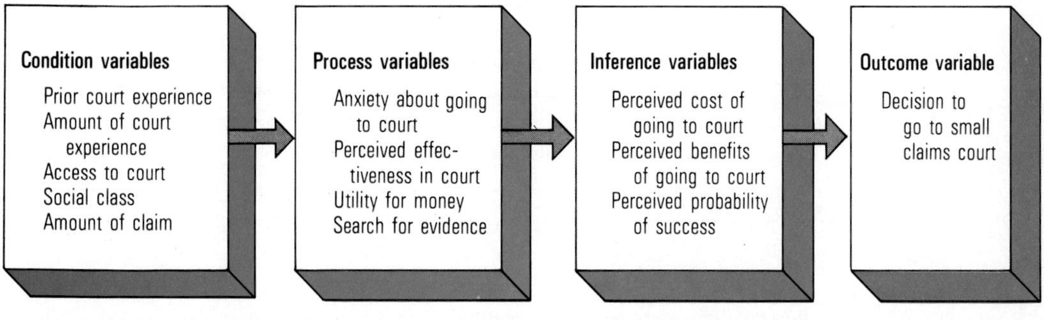

conditions influence process, process variables in turn influence inference variables. The three inference variables capture consumer thinking with respect to the benefits and costs of going to court in conjunction with their perceived probability of winning in court. These three inferences influence the decision to take legal action in a consumer dispute.

Figure B
Consumer Complaint Form

Mail To:
Consumer Services Division
Labor & Industries Building
Salem, Oregon 97310

CONSUMER COMPLAINT REPORT
(Please print in ink or type, if possible)

NAME ______________________ DATE ____________

Address ______________________

____

Telephone: Home ____________ Business ____________

Dealer Name and Address:

Manufacturer Name and Address:

Have you complained to the company? Yes ____ No ____ Name ________ Title ________

Amount Involved $________ Action you wish to be taken? ______________

DATE OF PURCHASE DATE DEFECT BECAME KNOWN

Explain below your specific complaints against the company or person. Please provide copies of all pertinent documents in your possession, such as: contract warranty, receipts and cancelled checks (both sides), etc. . . .If you wish, you may send originals for us to copy and return.

For office use only
Opened: ________
Code: ________
Closed: ________
Follow-up: ________
Status: ________
Certified: ________

Signed by:

COMPANY REPLY CAN BE MADE ON BACK

814-060-1 (Rev. 6/79)

Figure C
Consumer Decision to Take Legal Action

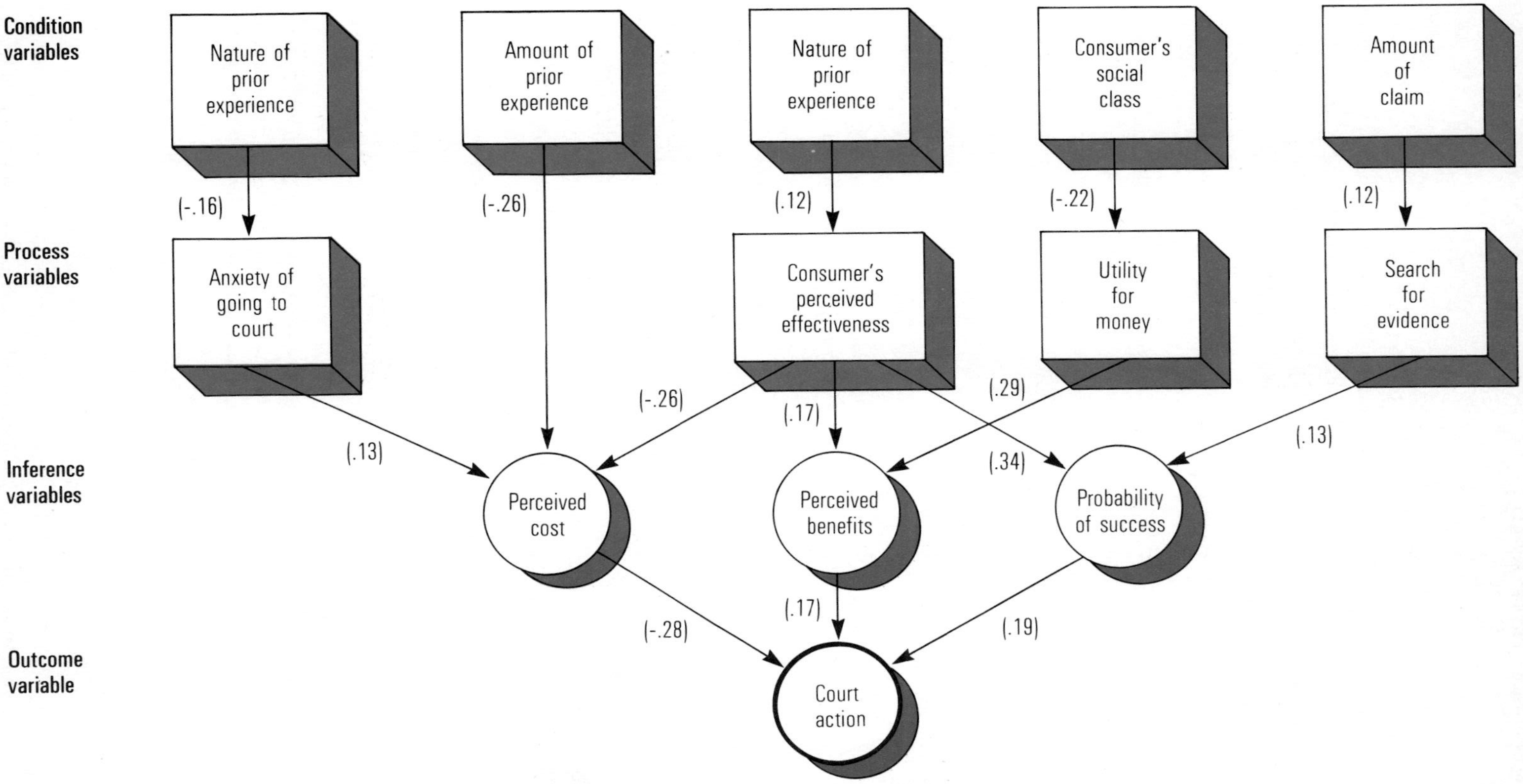

Note: All relationships significant at p = .05.

Sample

The state of Oregon maintains a Consumer Services Division to assist consumers in disputes with retailers or manufacturers. When a consumer contacts the division, they are instructed to complete the complaint form shown in Figure B. After reviewing returned complaint forms, the division seeks to negotiate a settlement. Eighty-five percent of the cases are resolved in this process. The remaining 15 percent are unresolved; these consumers are referred to the relevant small claims court.

Five hundred of those who were referred to seek legal action through the small claims court were sent a mail questionnaire. Of the 500, 41 were able to resolve their dissatisfaction without going to court, and 22 could not be reached. This left 437, of which 223 completed the questionnaire (a 51 percent response rate).

Results

As shown in Figure C, a variety of linkages were found between condition variables and process variables, which in turn were linked to inference variables and the decision to go to court. The decision to take legal action was influenced by all three inference variables. The higher the benefits and perceived probability of success and the lower the perceived costs of going to court, the more likely the consumer took legal action.

Each of the inference variables were influenced by process variables, and in one instance a condition variable. Perceived costs went up as anxiety about going to court went up, but went down as perceived effectiveness in court went up (inverse or negative relationship). Perceived costs decreased with easy access to small claims courts. Perceived benefits were positively affected by perceived effectiveness in court and consumer utility for money. And perceived probability of success went up as perceived effectiveness and search for evidence went up.

Anxiety about going to court was less when prior court experiences were not negative. Perceived effectiveness was higher for those who had greater amounts of prior court experience. The higher a consumer's social class, the lower their utility for money, and the larger the claim in dollars, the greater the consumer search for evidence.

With this model of the consumer decision to take legal action, one can better understand why some people would be inclined not to use the small claims court in resolving a consumer dispute.

Questions

1. Discuss the linkages between condition variables and process variables. Why are both sets of variables needed to understand the consumer decision to use or not use the small claims court in a consumer dispute?

2. Discuss how the process linkages impact the inferences a consumer may make regarding a decision to take legal action.
3. Develop a scenario for two consumers, one who takes legal action and one who does not. How do the inference conditions differ and why?
4. What could the Consumer Services Division do to increase the number of consumers using the small claims court in a consumer dispute? Which consumers would most benefit from their efforts?

SECTION FIVE

Organizational Buying Behavior

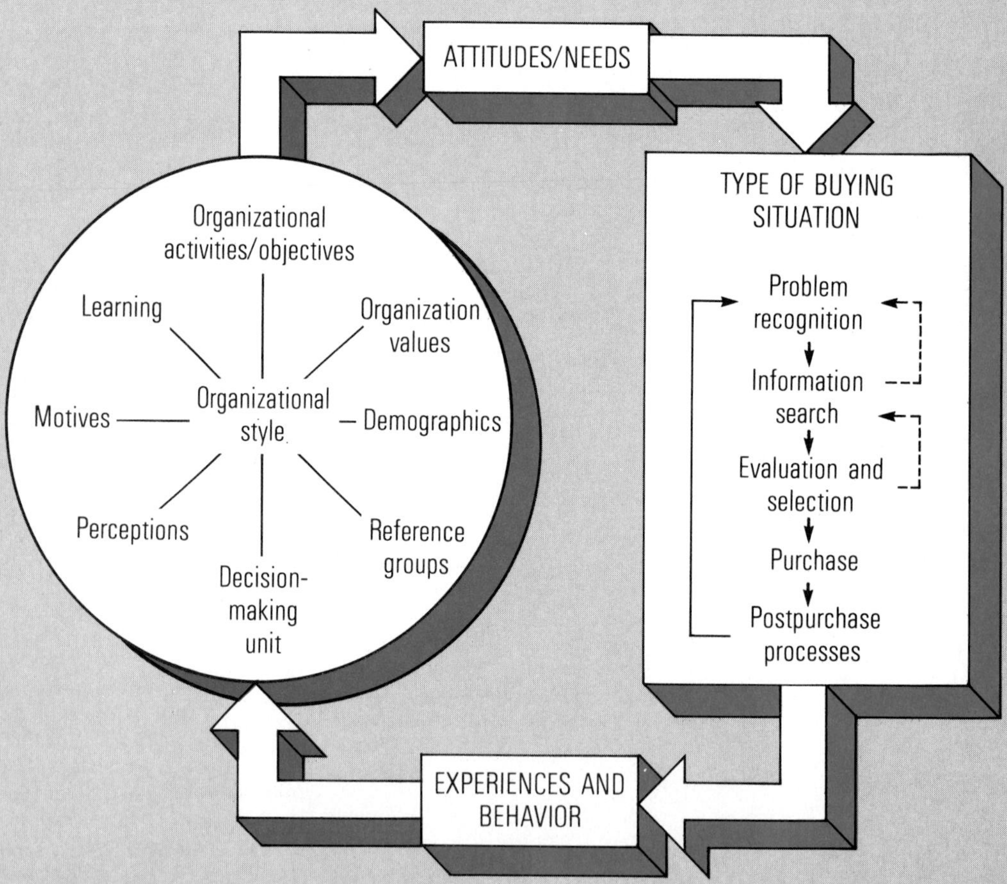

The stereotype of organizational buying behavior is one of a cold, efficient, economically rational process. Computers rather than humans could easily, and perhaps preferrably, fulfill this function. Fortunately, nothing could be further from the truth. In fact, organizational buying behavior is at least as "human" as individual or household buying behavior.

Organizations pay price premiums for well-known brands and for prestige brands. They avoid risk and fail to properly evaluate products and brands both before and after purchase. Individual members of organizations use the purchasing process as a political arena and attempt to increase their personal, departmental, or functional power through purchasing. Marketing communications are perceived and misperceived by individual organization members. Likewise, organizations and individual members of organizations learn correct and incorrect information about the world in which they operate.

Organizational decisions take place in situations with varying degrees of time pressure, importance, and newness. They typically involve more people and criteria than do individual or household decisions. Thus, the study of organizational buying behavior is a rich and fun-filled activity.

On the facing page, we present our model of consumer buying behavior as modified for organizational buying. This section of the text explains the required modifications.

CHAPTER

19 Organizational Buyer Behavior

Organizations such as Du Pont Corporation market products to other organizations such as boat manufacturers who in turn market finished boats to a variety of customers. Du Pont markets similar products to aircraft and automobile manufacturers who benefit from the application of Du Pont products in their vehicles. In each case, Du Pont has to possess considerable knowledge in order to understand their customers' needs and their customers' customers' needs. The process of understanding these needs is further complicated by the size, diversity, and complexity of the organizations involved in evaluating, purchasing, and using Du Pont products.

Exhibit 19–1 illustrates Du Pont's efforts to communicate the benefits users can derive from using Du Pont's Kevlar.[1] In both cases, Du Pont is communicating not only to purchasing organizations but also to specific decision influencers within the organization. While Kevlar has many unique technical properties and characteristics, Du Pont's success with this product depends on how well they communicate its customer benefits. For boat manufacturers, this means advantages in fuel savings, boat speed, and larger boat size. For the aircraft design engineer it means a lighter plane, which translates to fuel savings. In both examples, Du Pont had to analyze each organizational customer from top to bottom and deliver a solution that has meaning within the organizational context. To do otherwise would simply be a wasted effort.

Exhibit 19–1 Du Pont's Efforts to Communicate Product Benefits to Different Organizational Customers

Commercial Fishing **Aircraft Design**

Understanding the needs of organizations, large or small, profit or nonprofit, governmental or commercial requires many of the same skills and concepts used to understand individual consumer or household needs. While larger and often more complex, organizations—like consumers—develop preferences, attitudes, and behaviors through perceptions, information processing, and experience.[2] Likewise, organizations have an organizational style that creates a relatively stable pattern of organizational behavior.

Like households, organizations make many buying decisions. In some instances these buying decisions are routine replacement decisions for a frequently purchased, commodity-like product or service. At the other end of the continuum, organizations face new, complex purchase decisions which require careful problem definition, extensive information search, a long and often very technical evaluation process, perhaps a negotiated purchase, and a long period of use and postpurchase evaluation.[3] In many instances, each stage of this decision process is very formal, and prescribed guidelines are followed.

Because there are so many similarities between analyzing consumer behavior and organizational buyer behavior, our basic conceptual model of buyer behavior still holds. Of course, some aspects of the model such as social status do not apply, but most others apply with some modification. The purpose of this chapter is to discuss how this model of consumer behavior should be modified for application to organizational buyer behavior, and how the concepts of this model operate when marketing to organizations rather than to individual consumers or households.

OVERALL MODEL OF ORGANIZATIONAL BUYER BEHAVIOR

At the hub of our consumer model of buyer behavior is consumer lifestyle. Organizations also have a style or manner of operating that we characterize as organizational style (see Figure 19–1). Organizational style is much like lifestyle in that organizations vary dramatically in terms of how they make decisions and how they approach problems involving risk, innovation, and change.

Organizational Style

Organizational style reflects and shapes organizational needs and attitudes, which in turn influence how organizations make decisions (see Figure 19–2). For ex-

Figure 19–1
Overall Model of Organizational Buyer Behavior

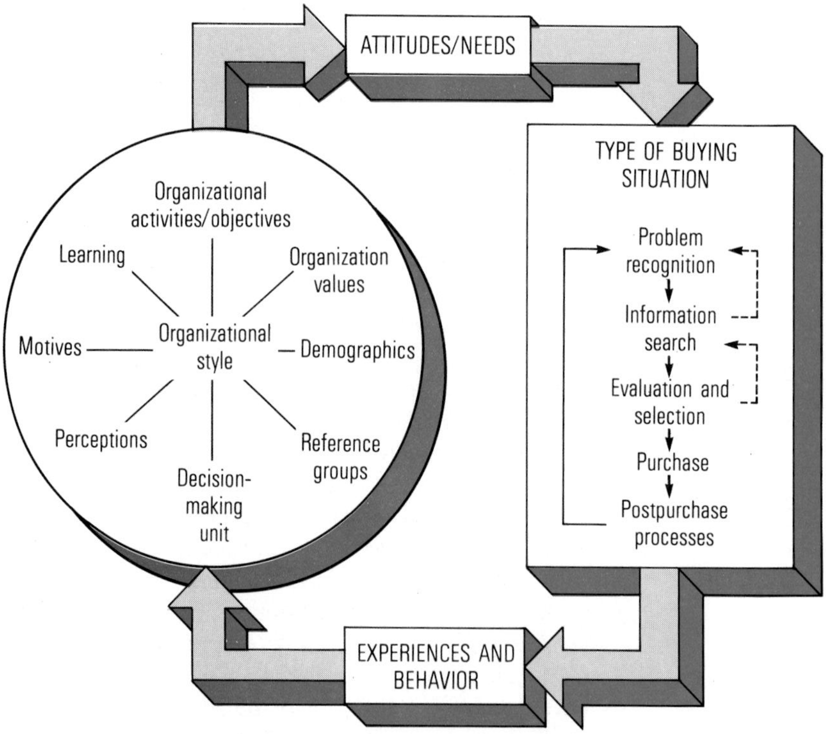

Figure 19–2
Organizational Style and Organizational Decisions

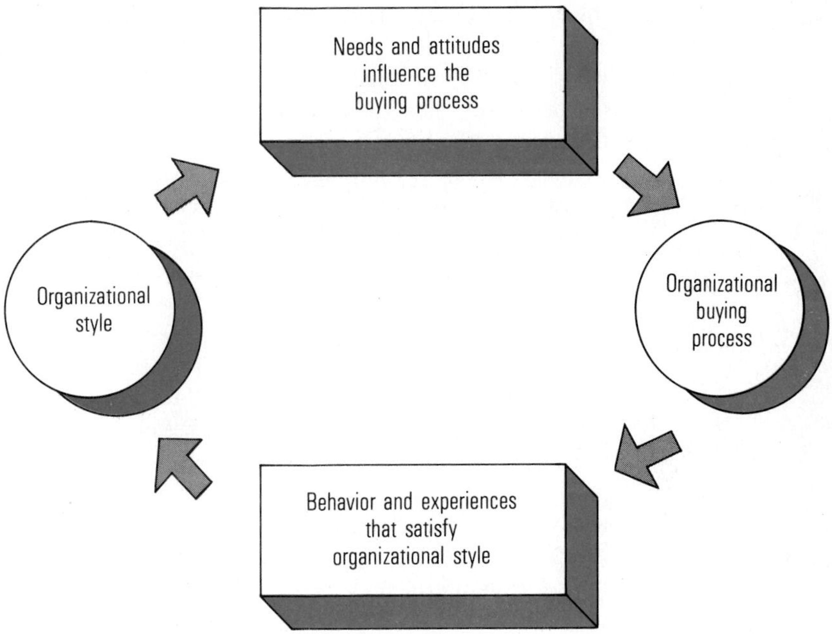

ample, the Environmental Protection Agency, the Red Cross, and IBM are three large organizations. Each has a different organization style with respect to how they gather information, process information, and make decisions. Because they each have different needs, objectives, and styles, they in turn have different experiences and attitudes. These differences influence how each organization solves purchase problems.

Organizations occasionally seek to change their organizational style. Jack Welch, the CEO of the General Electric Company, has sought to make GE more aggressive and entrepreneurial. To accomplish this, he has changed many values and organizational behaviors with respect to taking risk and challenging conventional thinking. It is his hope that this change in organizational style will create a more responsive, faster growing General Electric Company.

Another example is Apple Computer. Imagine how they have changed from a garage-type operation to small innovative company to a worldwide supplier of computers and computer software. At each stage of organizational evolution, the style of the Apple organization changed, as did its needs and attitudes which, in turn, altered how it purchased products and services. Xerox markets to both General Electric and Apple Computer. These are two very different kinds of organizations, and both are undergoing change. As a result, Xerox and others must analyze and understand the buyer behavior of each organization in order to develop marketing strategies that best serve the collective needs of each organizational customer.[4]

Interaction of Buyer-Seller Organizational Styles. Whenever two organizations engage in a marketing exchange, there is the possibility of different interorganizational relationships based on differences in organizational style. Under perfect market conditions, buyers and sellers operate *independently*, as there is a sufficient number of like buyers and sellers such that a fair market exchange is easily achieved. The relationship can also create a *dependence* of either buyer on seller or seller on buyer. In either case one organization holds more power and the relationship will reach a stable but less equitable market exchange. *Interdependence* between organizations can occur when it is in the best interests of both organizations to operate in a cooperative manner. IBM, who could dominate a small component supplier, may choose to seek a cooperative relationship with that vendor if it hopes to develop that vendor as a long-term, second supply source for a critical component.

External market conditions and internal organizational characteristics create three major styles of operation for both buying and selling organizations: Competitive, Cooperative, and Command.[5] When both organizations are operating with competitive organizational styles, they are likely to operate independently and a fair market exchange is most likely to occur (see Figure 19–3). However, if the buying organization is pursuing a cooperative style and the selling organization a competitive style, a mismatch occurs and a stable relationship cannot be achieved. When one organization possesses a dominant position, a command

Figure 19–3
Organizational Styles and Buyer-Seller Interactions

Seller Organizational Style	**Buyer Organizational Style**		
	Competitive	Cooperative	Command
Competitive	Perfect market (independent)	Mismatch	Buyer's market (independent)
Cooperative	Mismatch	Domesticated market (interdependent)	Subcontract market (dependent)
Command	Seller's market (independent)	Captive market (dependent)	Mismatch

Source: Adapted from N. C. G. Campbell, "An Interaction Approach to Organizational Buying Behavior," *Journal of Business Research,* no. 13, 1985, pp. 35–48.

style results. When the buying firm is a command style and the seller a competitive style, a buyer's market results, as shown in Figure 19–3. A seller's market occurs when the seller is in a command position and the buyer organization has a competitive style. When either buyer or seller organization is operating with a cooperative style and seek a relationship with a firm in a command position, a mismatch occurs.

If the selling organization is in a command position and the buying organization in a cooperative style, a dependent relationship results. In Figure 19–3 this is characterized as a captive market. When the opposite occurs, a subcontract market results. This is quite common among small vendors selling to the government or to large organizations such as General Motors.

There are also instances where both buyer and seller organizations seek a cooperative style. This may happen in normally competitive markets for strategic reasons, in government buyer markets, and in relationships between nonprofit and profit organizations. The whole idea of strategic partnerships is one of cooperation to the mutual benefit of both organizations. This interdependence creates a domesticated market condition. A balanced, equitable relationship is achievable as each organization works in a cooperative style with the other.

FACTORS INFLUENCING ORGANIZATIONAL STYLE

While we can imagine that the organizational style of the IRS and IBM would be quite different, we should also recognize that the behavior and style of IBM and DEC could be quite different, even though they compete for many of the same customers. As shown earlier in Figure 19–1, an organization's style is at the hub of our organizational buyer behavior model. The remainder of the chapter is devoted to how these factors help shape organizational style and influence purchase decision making.

Organizational Activities/Objectives

The activities and objectives of organizations influence their style and behavior. For example the Navy, in procuring an avionics system for a new fighter plane, operates differently than Boeing purchasing a very similar system for a commercial aircraft. The government is a nonprofit organization carrying out a public objective, while Boeing seeks a commercial objective at a profit. The objectives of the two organizations differ, as do their organizational style and buyer behavior.

However, we cannot assume two organizations have the same organizational style just because they share common objectives or activities. Scandinavian Airlines and Singapore Airlines are both government owned and operated, and both are noted internationally for offering the highest quality service. Few private airlines have been able to match their excellence in service, yet several other government-run airlines are renowned for poor service. Thus, an assumption

Table 19–1
Organizational Activities Based upon Type of Organization and Nature of Activity

Type of Organization	Nature of Organizational Activity		
	Routine	Complex	Technical
Commercial	Office management	Human resource management	New product development
Governmental	Highway maintenance	Tax collection	Space exploration
Nonprofit	Fund raising	Increase number of national parks	Organ donor program
Cooperative	Compile industry statistics	Establish industry standards	Applied research

that government organizations mean less (or more) service is not accurate. The activities an organization engages in and the objectives it pursues are only two of many influences that shape organizational style and behavior.

Table 19–1 is a matrix that provides examples of the interface between broad organizational objectives and activities. Organizational objectives are represented by the basic types of organization: commercial, governmental, nonprofit, and cooperative. The general nature of organizational activity is described as routine, complex, or technical. For example, a government organization purchasing highway maintenance services would operate differently from a government organization procuring missiles. Likewise, a cooperative wholesale organization set up as a buying cooperative for several retailers would have a different organizational style from a cooperative research institute set up by firms in the semiconductor industry. And a nonprofit organization involved in organ donations is likely to differ from one organized to gather industry statistics.

Organizational Values

IBM and Apple Computer both manufacture and market microcomputers. However, each organization has a distinct organizational style. IBM is corporate, formal, and takes itself seriously. Apple is less formal, creative, and promotes a more open organizational style. Both are successful, though each has a unique set of values which creates vastly different corporate cultures. Marketing managers must understand these differences in order to best serve their respective organizational needs.[6]

Table 19–2
Organizational Values Influence Organizational Style

1. Risk taking is admired and rewarded.
2. Competition is more important than cooperation.
3. Hard work comes first, leisure second.
4. Individual efforts take precedence over collective efforts.
5. Any problem can be solved.
6. Active decision making, passive decision makers will not survive.
7. Change is encouraged and actively sought.
8. Performance is more important than rank or status.

As you look across the eight values listed in Table 19–2, think of how IBM might differ from Apple or how Federal Express might differ from the United States Post Office. Each is a large organization, but each brings to mind a different set of values that underlies its organizational style. To the degree that organizations differ on these values, a firm marketing to them will have to adapt its marketing approach.

The values as presented in Table 19–2 are representative of an innovative organization that seeks change, views problems as opportunities, and rewards individual efforts. It is hard to imagine the U.S. Post Office or many other bureaucratic organizations in this way. On the other hand, these values underlie many high technology start-up organizations.

Shared Values and Value Conflicts. Both individuals and organizations have values. Unfortunately, these value sets are not always consistent. As a result, two different value systems can be operating within an organization. To the degree that these value systems are consistent, decision making and implementation of decisions will move smoothly.[7]

For example, Figure 19–4 lists the personal values for a software engineer in a small hi-tech firm along with the organization's values. The similarity between the individual's values and the organization's values creates a moderate degree of shared values. The greater the number of positive linkages between personal and organizational values, the less conflict and the easier it will be for this individual to make decisions that are consistent with his and the organization's values. In this example, six out of the ten values listed are shared.

The interaction between personal values and organizational values within a firm can be further extended to the interaction with the values of the selling organization and personal values of its representatives. Once again, the greater the number of shared values, the better the match and the more likely a good

Figure 19–4
Personal, Organizational, and Shared Values

Personal Values	Shared Value Linkages	Organizational Values
Individual	←————→	Individualistic
Youth oriented		Mature in orientation
Cooperative		Competitive
Performance driven	←————→	Performance driven
Likes change	←————→	Change is good
Risk taking	←————→	Risk taking is rewarded
Problem solver	←————→	Problem solving is good
Passive decision maker		Active decision making
Nonmaterialistic		Materialistic
Hard worker	←————→	Hard work is rewarded

———Positive linkages (shared values)

working relationship will result. In Figure 19–5 the overlap between these four sources of values represents the degree to which these value perspectives are shared. Exhibit 19–2 illustrates how a semiconductor manufacturer modified its advertising approach to accommodate the values of Japanese semiconductor engineers and businessmen.

Figure 19–5
Interaction between Personal and Organizational Values within Buying Organizations and with Selling Organizations

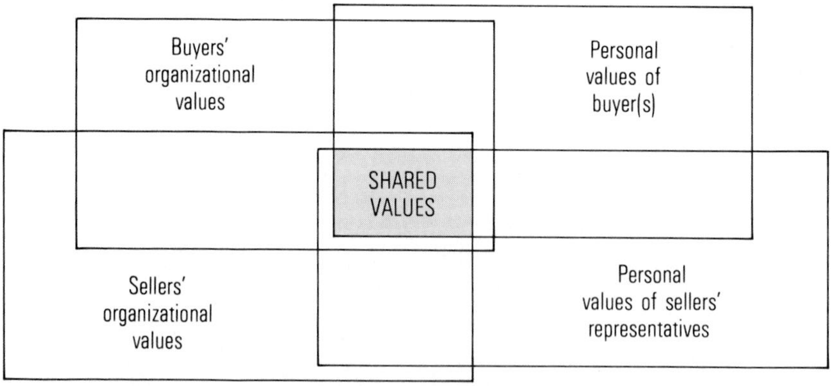

Exhibit 19–2

Adapting Advertising Copy to Cultural Values

Used with permission of Advanced Micro Devices, Inc.

In the United States, Advanced Micro Devices (AMD) is a well-known manufacturer of semiconductors. They advertise their products in the U.S. to target organizations by describing product features and emphasizing customer benefits. The ad copy is technical and full of detail.

Translations of this ad copy into Japanese for the Japanese semiconductor buyer did not work. To a Japanese person, an advertisement is supposed to create a feeling, emotion, or a mood. This is true for both consumer and industrial products. The ad shown above was adapted to the needs of the Japanese semiconductor customer. The AMD product and musical instrument are carefully integrated to create a warm feeling. The technical detail is of secondary importance.

Organizational Demographics

We discussed earlier the important role of consumer demographics in understanding consumer behavior. Organizational demographics are equally important. Organizational demographics involves both organization characteristics—such as size, location, industry category, and type of ownership—and characteristics of the composition of the organization, such as the gender, age, education, and income distribution of employees.[8]

Large organizations are more likely to have a variety of specialists who attend

Exhibit 19–3 Organizational Segmentation Strategy to Better Meet Customer Needs

Served Market. Several thousand firms that purchase electrical equipment for conversion and regulation of electricity.

Demographics. These electric utilities differ on the basis of:

Size:	Large, medium, and small.
Location:	Four geographical regions.
Organization:	Public utilities, rural electric co-ops, investor-owned utilities, and industrial firms.

Customer Needs. Based on these organizational demographics, meaningful differences were found for 12 distinct segments on the basis of the following purchase criteria:

1. Price
2. Quality
3. Warranty
4. Availability of spare parts
5. Reliability
6. Ease of installation
7. Maintenance requirements
8. Energy losses
9. Appearance of product

Customer Loyalty. Each of the 7,000 potential customers were classified on the basis of customer loyalty as:

Firm loyal:	Very loyal and not likely to switch.
Competitive:	Preferred vendor, but number two is very close.
Switchable:	A competitor is the preferred vendor, but we are a close second.
Competitor loyal:	Very loyal to a competitor.

Marketing Strategy

1. For each segment, focus on specific needs important to that segment.
2. Increase customer-need specific market communications to *each* of the 12 segments.
3. Increase sales coverage to customers classified as "competitive" and "switchable," while decreasing coverage of those classified as "firm loyal" and "competitor loyal."

Results. The year the marketing strategy was implemented, total market demand *decreased* by 15 percent. In addition, one of the three sales regions did not implement the strategy. Shown below are the percent changes in sales by sales region and customer loyalty. Which sales region do you think did not participate in the needs-based organizational marketing strategy? You're right!

	SALES REGION		
Customer Loyalty	**1**	**2**	**3**
Loyal	+2%	+3%	+3%
Competitive	+26	+18	−9
Switchable	+16	+8	−18
Competitor loyal	−4	−3	−4
Total	+18%	+12%	−10%

Source: Adapted from Dennis Gensch, "Targeting the Switchable Industrial Customer," *Marketing Science*, Winter 1984, pp. 41–54.

to purchasing, finance, marketing, and general management, while in smaller organizations one or two individuals may have these same responsibilities. Larger organizations are generally more complex since more individuals participate in managing the organization's operations. This creates a different style of organization and often requires a different marketing approach.

Exhibit 19–3 illustrates how one firm developed a successful marketing strategy using differences in organizational demographics and customer loyalty. Along with differences in type of ownership and location, firm size was one of the key differences that enabled them to meaningfully segment this large market.

Macrosegmentation. Organizations with like needs and distinguishing but similar demographics can be grouped into market segments. These segments, based on differences in needs due to organizational demographics, are called macrosegments. As we will discuss shortly, this is quite different from microsegmentation of the decision-making unit. Thus, organizational markets can have a two-tiered segmentation scheme referred to as macro- and microsegmentation.[9] In Exhibit 19–3, the 7,000 electricity-producing utilities were first grouped into macrosegments based on size, location, and type of ownership. Important differences on how decisions are made within these utilities could lead to a microsegmentation, which would further aid a firm's marketing efforts directed at these utilities.

Figure 19–6
Reference Group Infrastructure for Personal Computers and Microprocessors

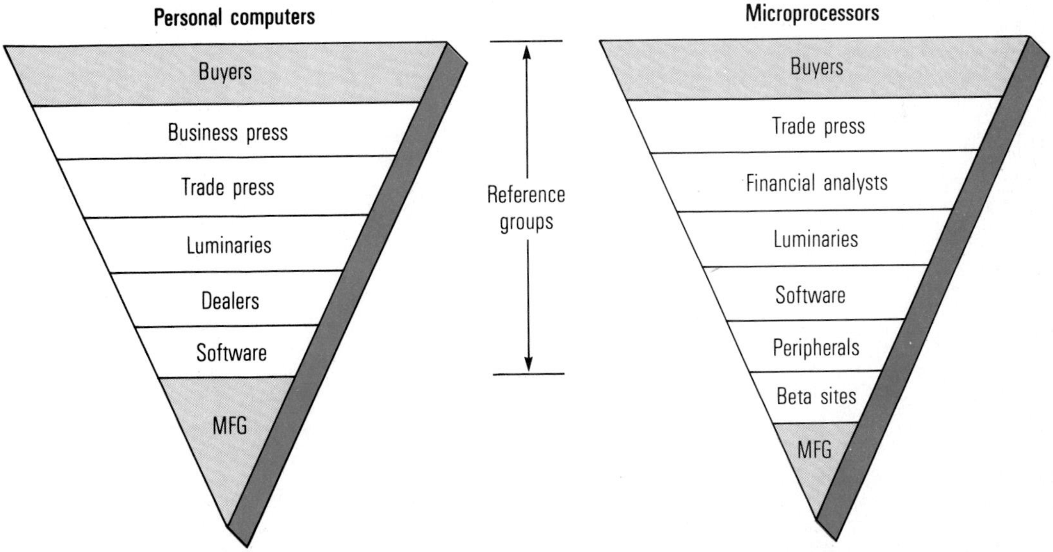

Source: Adapted from Regis McKenna, *The Regis Touch: The New Marketing Strategies for Uncertain Times* (Menlo Park, Calif.: Addison-Wesley, 1985).

Reference Groups

As in consumer behavior, organizational behavior and purchasing decisions are influenced by reference groups. Perhaps the most powerful type of reference group in industrial markets is that of lead users.[10] Lead users are innovative organizations that derive a great deal of their success from leading change. As a result, their adoption of a new product, service, technology, or manufacturing process is watched and emulated by the majority.[11]

Other reference groups such as trade associations, financial analysts, and dealer organizations also influence an organization's decision to buy or not buy a given product, or even to buy or not buy from a given supplier. To manage the influence of reference groups in the high-tech industry, Regis McKenna developed the concept of the *reference group infrastructure*.[12] The success of a high-technology firm depends on how they influence the reference groups located along the continuum that separates the supplier from its customer market. The more the firm gains positive written and word-of-mouth communication and endorsement throughout this infrastructure, the greater its chances of customers treating it as a preferred source of supply. Figure 19–6 illustrates two applications of McKenna's organizational reference group industry infrastructure.

Figure 19–7
Combining Lead-User and Infrastructure Reference Groups

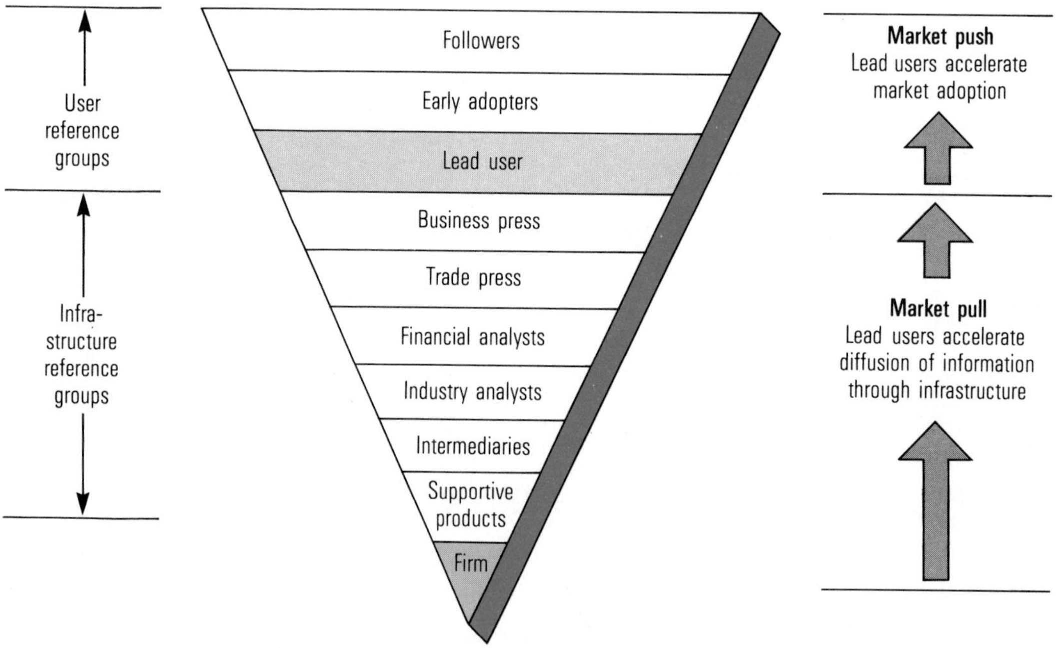

Source: Roger Best and Reinhard Angelhard, "Strategies for Leveraging a Technology Advantage," *Handbook of Business Strategy,* 1988.

If we combine the concept of lead users with the reference group infrastructure as shown in Figure 19–7, we have a more comprehensive picture of organizational reference group systems.[13] Since the lead users play such a critical role, their adoption of a product, technology, or vendor can influence the overall infrastructure in two powerful ways. First, a lead-user decision to adopt a given supplier's innovative product adds credibility to the product and supplier. This

Exhibit 19–4 Advertising Strategy That Accelerated a New Computer Purchase Decision

AD COPY

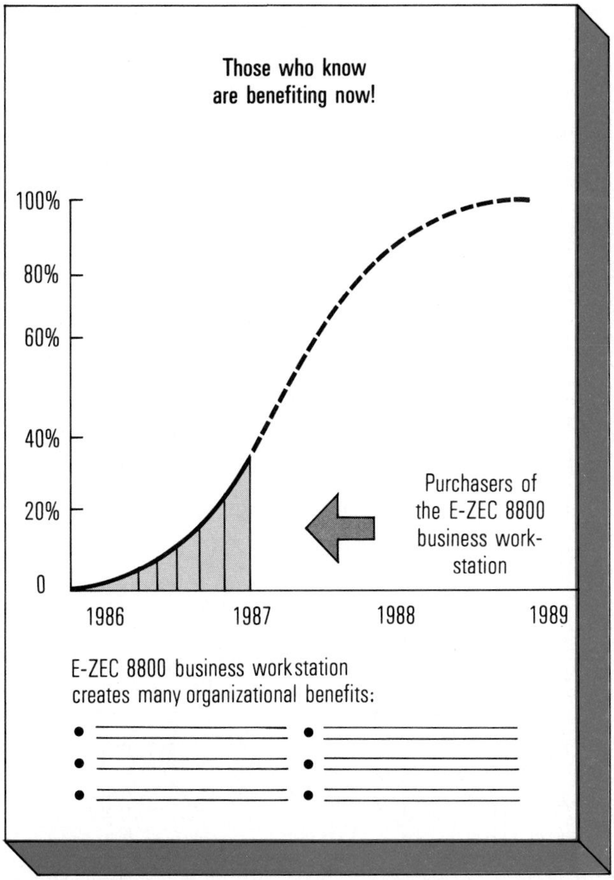

DESCRIPTION OF AD COPY

The ad copy for the computer manufacturer featured the names of lead users along the adoption diffusion curve shown in the ad copy. The intent was to communicate the value of this computer system by showing the reference group that already had adopted it.

Because these early adopters were well-known firms, the hope was they would create a lead-user effect and attract others to follow. Each issue of the periodical added new adopters to the ad copy shown.

RESULTS

The ad copy attracted customer attention and influenced decision making to the extent that some firms placed their orders early in order to be included in next issue's list of adopters. For lesser-known firms it was free advertising that conveyed a simple message: We're part of this well-thought-of reference group.

in turn has a strong positive impact on the infrastructure that stands between the firm and its remaining target customers. Second, a lead-user decision to purchase will have a direct impact on firms inclined to follow market trends. Exhibit 19–4 illustrates how a computer manufacturer accelerated the adoption decision by advertising the names of lead users that already had made a purchase decision.

Decision-Making Unit

Because of the nature, size, and consequences of some organizational decisions, decision-making units within organizations can become large and complex. Large, highly structured organizations ordinarily involve more individuals in a purchase decision than do smaller, less formal organizations. Important decisions are likely

Table 19–3
Issues of Importance in the Purchase of an Industrial Cooling System across Members of the Organizational Decision-Making Unit

Area of Responsibility	Key Importance	Less Importance
Production engineers	Operating cost Energy savings Reliability Complexity	Initial cost Field proven
Corporate engineers	Initial cost Field proven Reliability Complexity	Energy savings Up-to-date
Plant managers	Operating cost Space utilization Up-to-date Power failure protection	Initial cost Complexity
Top management	Up-to-date Energy savings Operating cost	Noise level in plant Reliability
HVAC consultants	Noise level in plant Initial cost Reliability	Up-to-date Energy savings Operating cost

Source: J. M. Choffray and G. Lilien, "Assessing Response to Industrial Strategy," *Journal of Marketing*, April 1978, p. 30.

to draw into the decision process individuals from a wider variety of functional areas and organizational levels than are less important purchase decisions.

The decision-making unit can be partitioned by area of functional responsibility and type of influence. Functional responsibility can include specific functions like manufacturing, engineering, transportation, research and development, and purchasing, as well as general management. Each function views the needs

Exhibit 19–5 The Decision to Purchase a Scientific and Technical Information Service

PURCHASE SITUATION (New Task): Three members of a chemical company were asked to evaluate and recommend for purchase a Scientific and Technical Information (STI) service. The decision-making unit included a scientist, manager, and librarian.

	Relative Importance of Criteria		
STI Purchase Criteria	**Librarian**	**Scientist**	**Manager**
• Speed of information recovery	20%	20%	30%
• Output documentation	10	5	10
• Output format	20	50	20
• Role of organization's library	40	15	10
• Price of service	10	10	30
	100%	100%	100%

RELATIVE IMPORTANCE OF BASES OF POWER

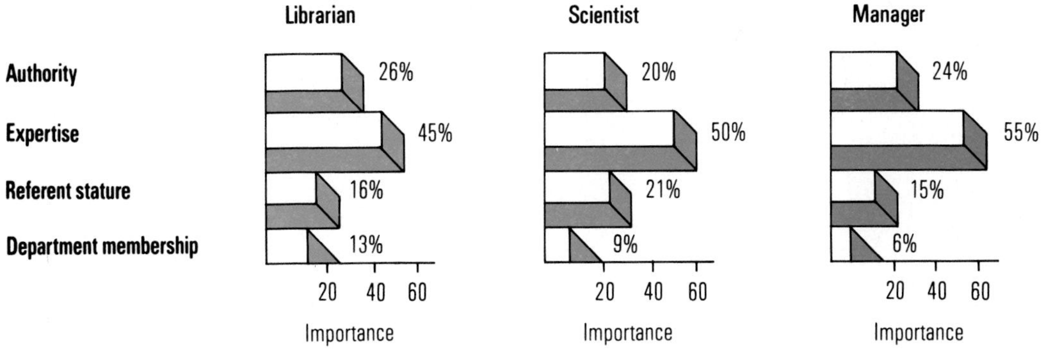

IMPLICATIONS: When a decision conflict arises, the conflict is most likely to be resolved on the basis of who has the highest level of expertise in the area of dispute. In the absence of expertise, the member with the highest level of authority would resolve the conflict. Other influences, such as referent stature and department membership, have a much smaller impact.

Source: Adapted from R. J. Thomas, "Bases of Power in Organizational Buying Decisions," *Industrial Marketing Management*, no. 13, 1984, pp. 209–17.

of the organization differently and as a result uses different importance weights or evaluative criteria.

In Table 19–3, we see that attribute importance in the purchase of a large industrial cooling system varies dramatically by area of functional responsibility. Each member of the decision-making unit has somewhat different needs. For a positive purchase decision to result, these needs have to be collectively met in some fashion. Energy savings are a key area of importance for production engineers and top management, but are a lesser issue for corporate engineers and HVAC consultants. On the other hand, being up-to-date is important to plant managers and top management, but is of lesser importance to corporate engineers and HVAC consultants. How the final purchase decision is made is in part determined by the degree of influence each functional area possesses in this

Exhibit 19–6 Marketing Strategy Based on Structure of the Decision-Making Units of Two Competing Pharmaceutical Companies

SITUATION

The decision-making units of two competing pharmaceutical companies are served by the same manufacturing organization. Both companies are multimillion dollar accounts and the product they purchase is the most critical component of the product they make and sell to hospitals.

DECISION-MAKING UNITS

As shown, there isn't much difference between the two buying companies in terms of information gatherers. However, in Company 1 the production manager and purchasing agent are the key influencers and also members of the decision-making unit. In Company 2, the R&D manager is the only real source of influence and he is also a member of the decision-making unit. Another key difference is the role of purchasing. In Company 1, purchasing is highly involved, while in Company 2, purchasing simply carries out the decision that is to be implemented.

Strategy

Company 1: Deliver needed information to each of the information gatherers, but dedicate efforts to production and purchasing since they are both key sources of influence and part of the decision-making unit. All key personnel in production and purchasing should be identified and efforts devoted to knowing both their organizational and personal needs. In addition, efforts to meet with general management need to be timed and orchestrated with purchasing and production.

Company 2: Deliver needed information to information gatherers, but target efforts on the R&D manager. The R&D manager's personal needs are very minimal but he needs a great deal of technical assistance. A technical person is personally assigned to work with the R&D manager and on several occasions makes emergency trips to help the R&D manager with an immediate problem. Purchasing is a paper function, but contact should be maintained.

Exhibit 19–6 *(concluded)*

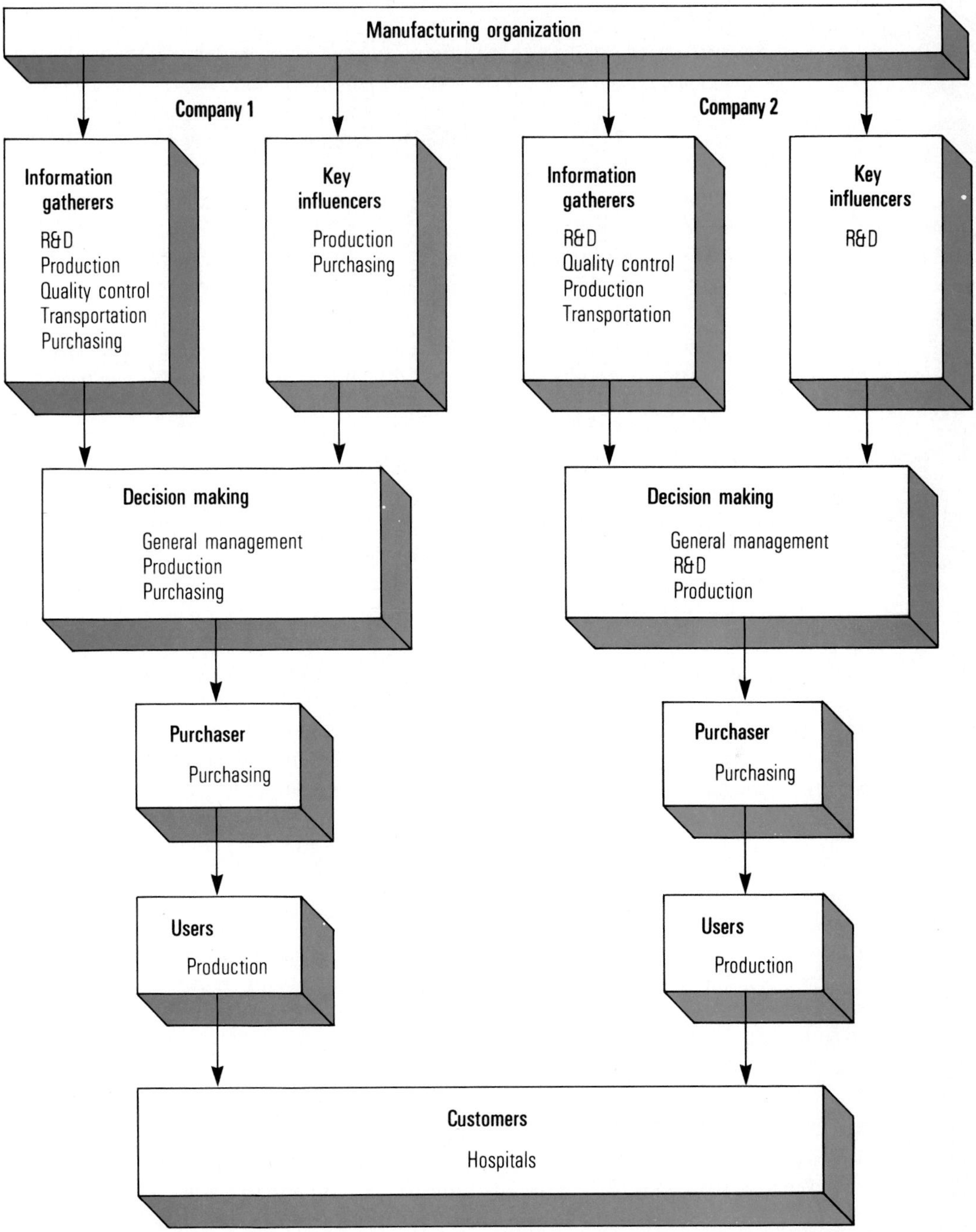

organizational decision and how the organization resolves group decision conflicts.[14] In general, degree of influence is derived from expertise,[15] as shown in Exhibit 19–5.

Members of the decision-making unit play various roles, such as information gatherer, key influencer, decision maker, purchaser, and/or user.[16] A plant manager could play all five roles, while corporate engineers may simply be sources of information. The role a function plays in an organizational decision varies by type of decision and organizational style. Exhibit 19–6 illustrates how an organization selling to two pharmaceutical companies has to vary its marketing strategy to meet the needs and structure of each decision-making unit. Their success is a direct result of recognizing these differences and developing separate strategies for serving each organizational customer.

Microsegmentation. Macrosegmentation allows a marketing organization to group customers with like needs and organizational demographics into market segments. Microsegmentation is the grouping of organizational customers on the basis of similar decision-making units.[17] Customer organizations which are heavily dominated by technical people might be segmented from those dominated by purchasing agents and finance managers. Recognizing these key differences in the structure of a decision-making unit allows the marketing organization to better customize its approach to organizations with different structures. Thus, microsegmentation may occur within a macrosegment or across macrosegments.

Decision-making units and microsegmentation strategies based on differences in their structure are also likely to vary over the product life cycle. Illustrated in Table 19–4 are changes in the decision-making unit that took place in the purchase of a 5K RAM computer chip by an original equipment manufacturer (OEM) over the stages of this computer chip's product life cycle. Early stages in the life of the new product presented a new task decision, and the size and structure of the decision-making unit resulted in a more complex decision process. As the product grew in its utilization, a modified rebuy decision evolved, as did a change in the functional structure of the decision-making unit. Finally, as the computer chip moved into a mature stage, it became a straight rebuy decision

Table 19–4
Changes in the Decision-Making Unit in the Purchase of a 5K RAM Computer Chip

Stage of Product Life Cycle	Type of Purchase Situation	Size of DMU	Key Functions Influencing the Purchase Decision
Introduction	New task	Large	Engineering and R&D
Growth	Modified rebuy	Medium	Production and top management
Maturity	Straight rebuy	Small	Purchasing

involving primarily the purchasing function. The introduction of a new, more complex computer chip started the whole process over.

Perception and Information Processing

To build a position with organizational customers, a firm must go through the same sequential stages of exposure, attention, and interpretation as required with consumers. A customer organization develops certain images of seller organizations from their products, people, and organizational activities. Like people, organizations have memories and base their decisions on images or memories they have developed. Once an image is formed by an organization, it is very difficult to change. Therefore, it is important for an organization to develop a sound communications strategy to build and reinforce a desired image or brand position.

Business-to-business advertising is one mechanism used to communicate information from seller to buyer organizations. Because electronic communications such as television and radio are less effective in reaching organizational customers and do not allow for details, print advertising and direct mail are more common. As shown in Table 19–5, over 75 percent of the organizations engaged in

Table 19–5
Direct Response Business-to-Business Promotional Advertising

		Company Sales		**Advertising**	
Direct Response Communication	Total Sample	More Than $25 Million	$25 Million or Less	$500,000 or More	Less Than $500,000
Channel					
Print advertising	76%	79%	75%	77%	77%
Broadcast advertising	6	11	3	13	3
Directory advertising	52	50	53	50	57
Direct mail	82	74	83	88	77
Outgoing telephone	17	6	22	12	17
Incoming telephone	32	17	39	25	34
Objectives					
Outside salesmen leads	37	26	47	31	46
Distributor leads	20	12	23	19	18
Internal sales leads	14	22	10	9	16
Customer service	8	7	4	13	0
Sales without sales call	11	16	8	14	9

Source: "Business-to-Business Direct Response Promotion," *Industrial Marketing*, September 1980, p. 60.

business-to-business direct response promotions utilize advertising, while over 80 percent use direct mail. Very few, primarily larger firms, use broadcast advertising, while smaller firms are heavier users of direct mail and the telephone. The objectives of direct response business-to-business advertising are also different. Smaller firms use it to generate leads for outside salesmen and distributors, while larger organizations use it to generate internal sales leads.

Unlike consumer advertising, organizational advertising is generally longer and more detailed. This is one reason print advertising is so heavily used. Longer advertising copy is more effective than shorter copy in business-to-business communications. Ads with less than 150 words are less likely to stimulate ad readership than ads with longer copy. However, this relationship is not linear, as ads with very long ad copy (greater than 200 words) are also less effective in stimulating ad readership. Thus, ad copy between 150 and 200 words seems to be most effective in stimulating readership.[18]

Ad size and repetition also have a positive effect on awareness and action. As shown in Figure 19–8, a 20 percent gain in awareness is achieved when two or more ads are placed in the same issue of a specialized business magazine. The size of the advertisement also affects action in the form of inquiries generated by the advertisement. Based on a study of 500,000 inquiries to ads run in *Plastic World, Electronics Design News,* and *Design News,* one can see in Figure 19–8 that the average number of inquiries increased with ad size. Thus, the combination of repetition and ad size have a positive effect on attention and interpretation. Exhibit 19–7 demonstrates the power of industrial advertising and ad frequency on the sales of an industrial safety product.

Figure 19–8
Impact of Ad Repetition and Ad Size

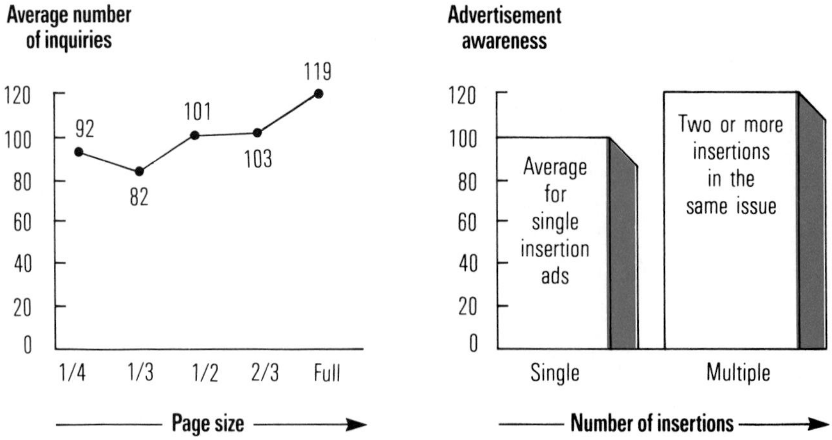

Source: Cahners Advertising Research Report, nos. 250.1 and 120.3.

Exhibit 19–7

Impact of Trade Advertising on Sales of Industrial Safety Product

The sales of a portable safety product sold to industrial organizations was tracked over a two-year period to evaluate the impact of trade advertising. As shown below a precampaign period was used to determine base sales without trade advertising. The first year sales increased almost four-fold, with advertising in one trade publication using an eight-page advertising schedule: six black-and-white ads and two color ads. When three color spreads were added to the schedule, sales continued to climb. When ad frequency was again increased, this time to 6 black-and-white single page ads and 11 color spreads, product sales rose to 6.7 times precampaign sales.

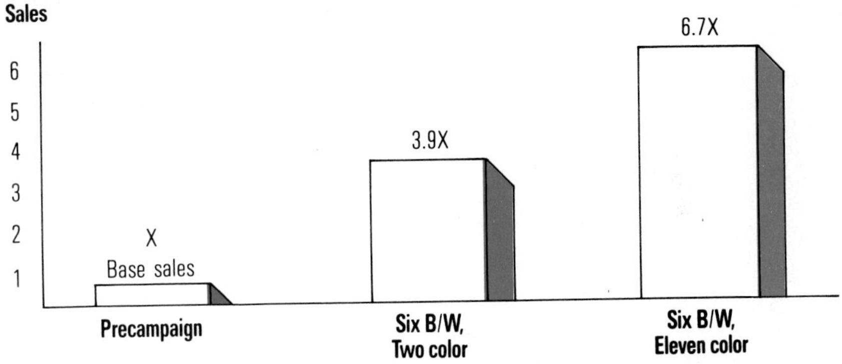

Source: "Study: Increase Business Ads to Increase Sales," *Marketing News*, March 14, 1988, p. 13.

Motives and Emotions

Organizational decisions tend to be less emotional than perhaps many consumer purchase decisions. However, because humans with psychological needs and emotions influence these decisions, this aspect of marketing to an organizational customer can not be overlooked or underestimated. Most organizations have as an objective to either improve their performance or lower their cost as a result of the purchases they make. Recognizing this fundamental organizational motive, Ball Corporation's Container Group utilizes the following sales strategy:

> In the glass container business it costs more to make a tall, slender jar than one that is short and squat. If an account is using a tall jar, the salesperson points out the economies in changing to a squat jar. If a prospective customer already has a shorter jar, the salesperson promotes the addition of a taller, more slender jar to appeal to today's weight-conscious consumer.[19]

However, the Ball Corporation sales strategy doesn't stop there. Developing a rational organizational benefit is the first step; the second is appealing to the emotions of individuals making the decision. With careful study of the personal motives, psychological needs, and emotions of decision makers and influencers, Ball Corporation gears its presentations to "excite" its buyers to take action in ways not possible with normal means of communication. Clifton Reichard, vice president of sales of Ball Corporation's Glass Container Group, points out:

> Businesspeople are human and social as well as interested in economics and investments, and salespeople need to appeal to both sides. Purchasers may claim to be motivated by intellect alone, but the professional salesperson knows they run on both reason and emotion.[20]

Quite often in new task decisions there is considerable risk. The risk of making a bad purchase decision can elicit feelings of self-doubt or psychological discomfort. These are personal emotions that will influence a new task purchase decision. IBM has used personal emotions to its advantage by selling the security of buying from IBM. The common expression, "No one ever got fired for buying IBM," is based on the feeling that no one would question the decision to buy IBM if something went wrong, whereas buying from a lesser-known firm and then encountering a serious problem could get you fired. Federal Express utilizes somewhat the same approach: "How do you explain to your boss that the important papers didn't arrive but you saved the company $5 by using a less expensive overnight mail service?"

Learning

Like individuals, organizations learn through their experiences and perceptions. In the sixties, a British manufacturer of headlights and automotive electrical systems was the supplier of this equipment to Jaguar. A new automotive lighting system for a new model Jaguar would simply stop operating at night after a certain period of operation time. The supplier company became known in the industry as the "Knight of Darkness," an image that persists today.

The negative consequences of an important organizational purchase decision are not easily unlearned.[21] Because of its greater importance, it is a high-involvement learning situation. And, when the experience is negative, unlearning is more difficult, as illustrated in Figure 19–9. For this reason, it is critical that the first time experiences in a new buyer-seller relationship be positive. A negative experience in a high-involvement decision could damage that relationship for an extended period of time.

Organizations also learn as they grow. Apple Computer had to learn a vast array of new behaviors as it moved from a small, informal, garage-based organization to a worldwide, formal organization. As an organization learns, it will develop a different organizational style and put in place different policies and guidelines to aid decision making based on learned experiences. Of course, learning can be cognitive as well as experiential as organizations process information and select vendors on the basis of information they have acquired and learned without the benefit of experience.

Figure 19–9
Unlearning High-Involvement Negative Experiences

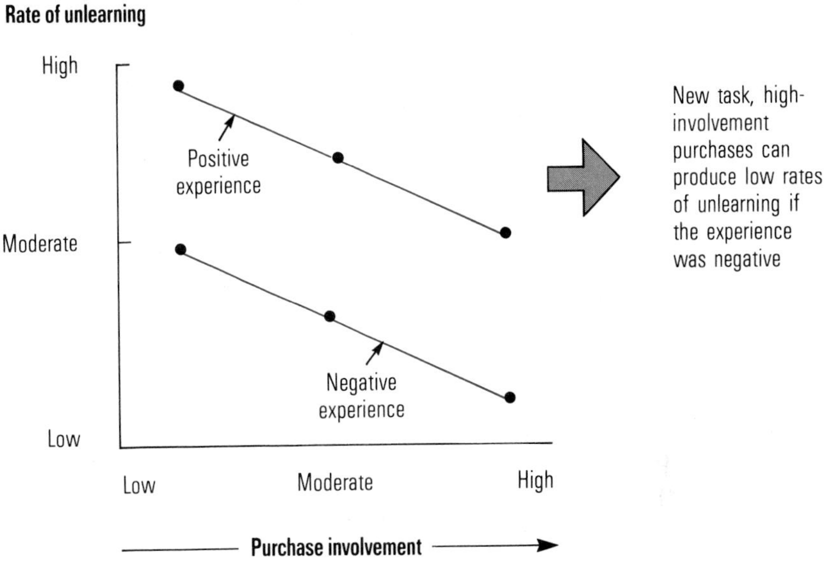

PURCHASE SITUATION

While the style of each organization may differ in unique ways, the buying process is also influenced by the complexity and difficulty of the decision task. Less complex, routine decisions are generally made by an individual or a small group without extensive effort. At the other extreme are organizational decisions which are complex and have major organizational implications. A continuum of purchase situations lies between these two extremes. A useful categorization of organizational purchase situations is Straight Rebuy, Modified Rebuy, and New Task.[22]

Straight Rebuy

Routine repurchase decisions are low-involvement decisions that may be made by a single person in the organization. Repurchase of copy paper under an annual contract, or commodity-type items used in manufacturing assembly are "straight rebuy" decisions typically made by one individual. The buyer chooses from suppliers on its vendor list, giving weight to his or her past experiences and the volume of orders placed with each vendor. Suppliers providing better service, quick response to problems, and reliable delivery are given higher priority in straight rebuy decisions. And, there are instances where the rebuy decision occurs automatically as part of an automated reordering system for items under contract.

Modified Rebuy

The modified rebuy decision requires that the buyer organization expend more effort and include more people because of an important modification to the product, delivery, price, or terms and conditions. When an automobile manufacturer modifies the dashboard design of a particular car model, it may require several alterations in the materials purchased as well as the sequence of assembly which could alter the time and sequence of purchase. Though the changes are not major, the modifications may impact engineering, production, quality assurance, purchasing, and ultimately vehicle availability and customer reaction. As a result, several individuals will be involved at various stages of the decision process. Some may simply provide information with respect to their own requirements, while others may want a say in which vendor is selected for certain dashboard components. The net result is a more complex buying process.

New Task

A third type of organizational buying decision occurs when the organization is purchasing for the first time a product or service of major importance. A weapons system, factory automation equipment, or a new computer or telecommunications system are new task-buying decisions that have implications which could adversely impact an organization's financial position, product quality, and corporate morale. In high-technology markets, new task decisions become a way of life as products and processes frequently undergo dramatic technological change. Yet investment in the wrong technology could wipe out many small and medium-size hi-tech companies. Thus, the number of individuals influencing and making the decision increases as does the involvement of these individuals. As illustrated in Figure 19–10, the level of organizational involvement increases with the

Figure 19–10
Types of Organizational Decisions and High/Low Involvement Processes

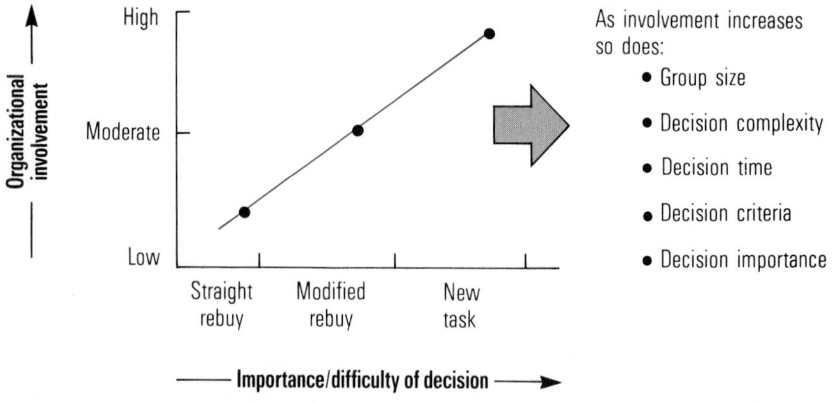

importance and consequences of a purchase decision. This in turn creates a much more complex marketing situation, where the needs and behavior of many individuals must be understood.

ORGANIZATIONAL DECISION PROCESS

Because organizational decisions typically involve more individuals in more complex decision tasks than do individual or household decisions, marketing

Figure 19–11
Decision Process in Purchasing Microcomputers for a Large Insurance Company

Stages of the Purchase Decision Process	Key Influences within Decision-Making Unit	Influencers outside the Decision-Making Unit
Problem Recognition	Office manager Sales manager	Field sales agents Administrative clerks Accounting manager Microcomputer sales representative
Information Search	Data processing mgr. Office manager Purchasing manager	Operations personnel Microcomputer sales representative Other corporate users Office systems consultant
Alternative Evaluation	General management Data processing mgr. Office manager Sales manager Purchasing manager	Office systems consultant Microcomputer sales representative
Purchase Decision	General management Office manager Purchasing manager	
Product Usage	Office manager Sales manager	Field sales agents Administrative clerks Accounting personnel Microcomputer sales representative
Evaluation	Office manager Sales manager General management	Field sales agents Administrative clerks Accounting personnel

efforts to affect this process are much more complex.[23] Shown in Figure 19–11, are stages in the decision process and sources of influence at each stage in a large insurance company's decision to add microcomputers to its office management function. At each stage, sources of influence both within and outside the decision-making unit were important. Altogether there were 12 separate sources of influence, each with different levels of influence and affecting different stages of the purchase decision process.

To have a chance to win this large office systems microcomputer contract, a selling firm must provide relevant information to each source of influence. This is not a simple task, given that each source of influence has different motives and different criteria for evaluating alternative products, as well as different media habits. To the degree a microcomputer company satisfies the information needs of each, it will improve its chances of winning this large contract.

Problem Recognition

In Figure 19–11, the sales manager and office manager were the first key influencers within the decision-making unit to recognize the need to add microcomputers to their organization. Recognition of this problem, however, could have come about in several ways. In this instance, a continuing problem between field sales agents and internal administrative clerks led the office manager and sales manager to recognize the problem. Aiding their recognition of the problem were accounting personnel and microcomputer sales representatives who called on the office manager. The combination of these sources of influence eventually led to an increased level of importance and the subsequent stage of information search.

Figure 19–12 demonstrates that in hi-tech markets, the head of a department is most likely to recognize a problem or need to purchase.[24] Perhaps more important is that purchasing managers are not a source of problem recognition. This points out the danger of salespeople only calling on purchasing people. As shown in Figure 19–12, problem recognition and determining specifications often occur without much involvement of purchasing personnel.

A business marketing to another business has to understand how their products or services will impact the client's cost of operations and performance. While the client's business is always seeking ways to economically improve its operations, it may not recognize problems that prevent them from improving. Thus, the task of the selling organization is to understand the needs of the client organization so that they can point out problems and solutions that the client organization has not yet recognized.

For example, a computer manufacturer pointed out to a large bank that their entire statewide banking system could be shut down if a fire or other disaster occurred in a given building. The bank literally could not function if the information were lost. This unrecognized problem led the bank to purchase a backup system and locate it in a building in another part of the state. While the need had gone unnoticed for years without loss to the bank and the cost of redundancy

Figure 19–12
Group Involvement in the Decision Process in High-Tech Organizations

Stages of Decision Process	Percent Involved in Each Stage of Decision Process					
	Board of Directors	Top Management	Head of Department	Lab Technician or Operator	Purchasing Manager or Buyer	Finance Manager Accountant
• Recognizing the need to purchase	7%	26%	70%	30%	0%	3%
• Determining product specifications	0	33	74	33	3	0
• Deciding which suppliers to consider	3	33	56	14	19	0
• Obtaining quotations and proposals	0	26	52	19	14	3
• Evaluating quotations and proposals	7	63	63	3	11	7
• Final product or supplier selection	21	48	48	7	11	0

Source: R. Abratt, "Industrial Buying in Hi-Tech Markets," *Industrial Marketing Management* 15, 1986, p. 295.

was high, in May 1988, six floors of the bank building caught fire and destroyed the original system. The next day, the bank operated as normal from its remote backup building.

Information Search

Information search can be both formal and informal. Site visits to evaluate a potential vendor, laboratory tests of a new product or prototype, and investigation of possible product specifications are part of formal information search. Informal

Figure 19–13
Sources of Information Use by High-Tech Organizations

Sources of Information	Awareness and Interest	Evaluation and Selection
Sales representative	56%	59%
Exhibitions/trade shows	70	37
Professional/technical conferences	37	30
Direct-mail advertising	36	0
Press releases	11	0
Journal advertising	22	7
Word-of-mouth	30	48
Technical consultants	0	15

Source: R. Abratt, "Industrial Buying in Hi-Tech Markets," *Industrial Marketing Management* 15, 1986, p. 296.

information search can occur during discussions with sales representatives, while attending trade shows, or reading industry specific journals.

Figure 19–13 summarizes the sources of information that influence awareness/interest in and evaluation/selection of vendors in hi-tech organizations. One can readily see the importance of sales representatives in both creating awareness/interest and influencing evaluation/selection. Trade shows and technical conferences also play an important role in providing meaningful information to hi-tech organizations. Word-of-mouth is largely derived from user and infrastructure reference groups as described earlier and shown in Figure 19–7. Thus, the combination of good sales representation and positive influence on information flow through reference groups can have a powerful impact on evaluation and selection.

Direct-mail and journal advertising are important influences but are limited to creating awareness and interest. A study of 674 leading retail chains showed that decision makers relied on trade journals to keep them informed.[25] They view trade journals as a prime place to get information on new products, product benefits, and special offerings. Sixty percent of these retail decision makers felt that trade advertising was a highly effective way to influence purchasing decisions for both new and existing products. More than 70 percent were influenced by a favorable product review in a trade journal editorial. Exhibit 19–8 outlines Harris/Lanier's extensive direct-mail effort to create awareness and interest in their office automation equipment among Fortune 1000 businesses.

Evaluation and Selection

The evaluation of possible vendors and selection of a given vendor can follow a two- and sometimes three-stage decision process.[26] The first stage is making

Exhibit 19–8 Harris/Lanier's Efforts to Create Awareness and Impact the Decision Process

"The selection of an information systems vendor in Fortune 1000 companies is based on a complex process. While the main decision maker is usually the director of information systems, there are numerous other 'influencers,' notably the chief executive officers and lower-level information systems managers."

Harris is well known in the field of information and telecommunications technology but needed to boost its recognition in the office automation marketplace since its acquisition of Lanier Business Products, Inc., a few years ago.

The strategy, "Make Another Great Decision" involved advertising and unusual and dramatic direct-mail materials (audio and videotapes) with multiple mailings to different decision makers in each Fortune 1000 company.

The campaign was implemented in four stages:

1. In February, a full-page teaser ad was placed in *The Wall Street Journal* listing the names of 500 firms that would be receiving the Harris mailings. The ad also encouraged other interested firms to request the material via a toll-free phone number.
2. Three packages of materials were mailed to the target companies. Package No. 1 went to corporate CEOs and included a letter from Harris chairman Joseph A. Boyd introducing Concept III, a brochure, and a 3-minute microtape presentation enclosed in a complimentary Harris/Lanier *Portable Caddy* portable dictation machine. MIS directors received a letter, a brochure, a 12-minute videocasette on the Concept III, and a gift flier describing the available incentives. Information systems managers received a letter, a brochure, an 8-minute audiocasette, a gift flier, and a business-reply card for requesting a visit from a Harris rep.
3. A Harris national accounts sales rep followed up with each MIS director a few days later to make appointments for product demonstrations.
4. Incentives, offered to MIS directors and information systems managers who agreed to a demonstration of Concept III, included Light Tech binoculars or a set of "The Excellence Challenge" tapes for the former, and a "Beep 'n Keep" key ring or a Braun Voice Control clock for the latter.

Source: "Corporate Purchase Influencers Target of Direct-Mail Campaign," *Marketing News*, April 25, 1986, p. 4.

the buyer's approved vendor list. A conjunctive decision process is very common. In this manner, the organization can screen out potential vendors that do not meet all their minimum criteria. In a government missile purchase, 41 potential manufacturers of a given missile electronics system were first identified. After site visits to inspect manufacturing capability, and resources, this list of 41 was

Table 19–6
Stage of Decision Process and Structure of Decision Makers

Decision Making Unit Participants*	Stage of Decision Process				
	Evaluation of Cooling Needs	Budget Approval	Preparation of Bidders' List	Equipment and Vendor Evaluation	Equipment and Vendor Selection
Plant manager	60%	—	50%	30%	40%
Top management	—	100%	—	—	20
HVAC consultant	40	—	50	70	40
	100	100	100	100	100

*Other participants who could have been part of the DMU but were not included were production and maintenance engineers, purchasing, architects and building contractors, and air conditioning manufacturers.

Source: Adapted from W. Patton III, C. Puto, and R. King, "Assessing Response to Industrial Marketing Strategy," *Journal of Marketing,* April 1978, p. 28.

pared down to 11. The remaining 11 all met the government's minimum criteria and from this group the government would eventually contract with two.

A second stage of organizational decision making could involve other decision rules such as disjunctive, lexicographic, compensatory, or elimination-by-aspects. For the government purchase discussed above, a lexicographic decision process was next used with the most important criterion being price. Using this decision rule, two vendors were selected.

Table 19–6 outlines how the decision-making unit varied from evaluation through selection of an industrial cooling vendor. In this decision process there were only three decision-making influences, two internal and one external. However, the relative importance of each varied at different stages of the decision process. Of particular importance here is how the mix of participants and relative influence changed from evaluation of need to selection of equipment and manufacturer.

Purchase and Decision Implementation

Once the decision to buy from a particular organization has been made, the method of purchase must be determined. From the seller's point of view this means how and when they will get paid. In many government purchases, payment is not made until delivery. Other government purchase agreements could involve progress payments. When a firm is working on the construction of a military aircraft which will take several years, the method of payment is critical. Many businesses offer a price discount for payment within ten days. Others may extend credit and encourage extended payment over time.

On an international basis, purchase implementation and method of payment are even more critical. One electronics firm with limited experience in international business found it very easy to sell its electronics system in Nigeria. However, they couldn't get paid. They later found out this is very normal and one needs to use letters of credit to get paid with any degree of certainty. Some South American countries prohibit the removal of capital from their country without an offsetting purchase. This led Caterpillar Tractor Company to sell earthmoving equipment in South America in exchange for raw materials such as copper which they could sell or use in their manufacturing operations. Another company signed a long-term contract at a very low price when the exchange rate favored the seller. This ensured the seller a good price when the exchange rate fluctuated, and provided the buyer a lower than average price.

Terms and conditions for payment—payments, warranties, delivery dates and so forth—are both complex and critical in business-to-business markets. One large manufacturer of steam turbines lost a large order with a 30 percent price premium to a foreign manufacturer because their warranty was written too much to the advantage of the seller.

Usage and Postpurchase Evaluation

After-purchase evaluation of products is typically more formal for organizational purchases than are household evaluations of purchases. In mining applications, for example, a product's life is broken down into different components such that total life-cycle cost can be assessed. Many mines will operate different brands of equipment side-by-side to determine the life-cycle costs of each before repurchasing one in larger quantities.

Exhibit 19–9 illustrates the life-cycle costs including postpurchase maintenance and operations for two competing brands. In this postpurchase evaluation, a brand that is priced at $1,000 more than the customer's current brand actually saves the customer $1,000 over the life of the product. In some mining applications the life of a product can be one week. Therefore, over the course of a year this type of postpurchase evaluation could save the buyer thousands of dollars. Unfortunately, many American firms consider only the initial purchase price and ignore life-cycle costs. Selling total value to such firms is very difficult even though it is in their best interest.

Ford Motor Company now evaluates all key suppliers on stated dimensions of quality. Winning Ford's Quality Award has quickly become an honor of great importance. As more firms strive to improve quality, postpurchase evaluations with stated performance criteria will become more common in business-to-business marketing. However, seller organizations do not have to wait for buyers to take the lead. One oil transport company tracked its stated and actual delivery dates over a two-year period for some 2,000 oil shipments around the world. Now when they submit a bid, they enclose their past track record on delivery for that buyer. Thus, postpurchase evaluation can be used as a marketing tool by seller organizations as well as an evaluation tool by buyer organizations.

Exhibit 19–9 Postpurchase Evaluation of a Product's Life-Cycle Cost

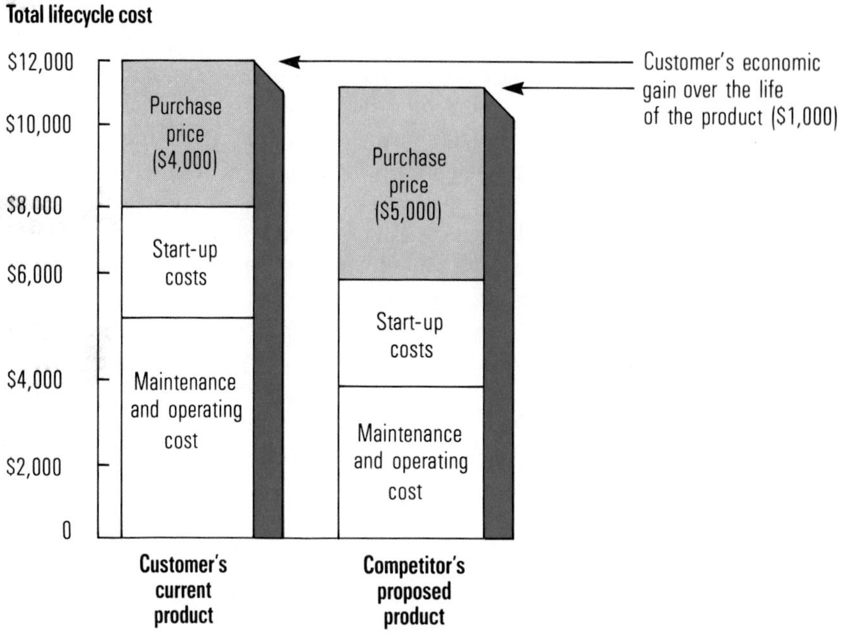

SUMMARY

Like households, organizations make many buying decisions. In some instances these buying decisions are routine replacement decisions and at other times new, complex purchase decisions. Three purchase situations are common to organizational buying: straight rebuy, modified rebuy, and new task. Each of these purchase situations will elicit different organizational behavior since the decision-making unit varies in size and complexity as the importance of the purchase decision increases.

Organizations have a style or manner of operating that we characterize as organizational style. The type of organization (commercial, governmental, non-profit, or cooperative) and the nature of their activity (routine, complex, or technical) helps shape an organization's style. Organizations can take on styles described as Competitive, Cooperative, or Command. Various combinations of buyer and seller organizational styles create mismatches where an equitable relationship cannot occur, as well as a variety of dependent, independent, and interdependent relationships.

Organizations hold values that influence the organization's style. These values are also held in varying degrees by individuals in the organization. When there is a high degree of shared values between the individuals and the organization, decision making occurs smoothly. Demographics also influence organizational style. Differences in location, industry, type of ownership, and composition of work force each plays a role in determining how an organization approaches purchase decisions. The process of grouping buyer organizations into market segments on the basis of similar needs and demographics is called macrosegmentation.

Reference groups play a key role in business-to-business markets. Reference group infrastructures exist in most organizational markets. These reference groups often include third-party suppliers, distributors, industry experts, trade publications, financial analysts, and key customers. Lead users have been shown to be a key reference group that influences both the reference group infrastructure and other potential users.

Organizations also develop images, have motives, and learn. Seller organizations can affect how they are perceived through a variety of communication alternatives. Print advertising and direct mail are the most common. Whereas organizations have "rational" motives, their decisions are influenced and made by people with emotions. A seller organization has to understand and satisfy both to be successful. Organizations learn through their experiences and information-processing activities. Negative experiences are particularly immune to extinction.

The organizational decision process involves problem recognition, information search, evaluation and selection, purchase implementation, and post-purchase evaluation. Seller organizations can help buyer organizations discover unrecognized problems and aid them in their information search. Quite often a seller organization can influence the information search such that they establish the choice criteria to be used in evaluation and selection. Choice decisions typically involve more individuals and the use of multiple decision rules. A conjunctive process is typical in establishing an evoked set and other decision rules for selecting a specific vendor.

Purchase implementation is more complex and the terms and conditions more important than in household decisions. How payment is made is of major importance. Finally, use and postpurchase evaluation are often quite formal. Many organizations will conduct detailed in-use tests to determine the life cycle costs of competing products or spend considerable time evaluating a new product before placing large orders. Satisfaction is dependent on a variety of criteria and many different people. To achieve customer satisfaction, each of these individuals has to be satisfied with the criteria important to him or her.

REVIEW QUESTIONS

1. How can an organization have a *style?* What factors contribute to different organizational styles?
2. Describe *competitive, cooperative,* and *command organizational styles.*
3. What is the outcome of different combinations of buyer-seller relationships when one combines competitive, cooperative, and command styles?

4. How would different organizational activities and objectives affect organizational style?
5. What are *organization values*? How do they differ from *personal values?* What is meant by *shared values?*
6. What are *organization demographics,* and how do they influence organizational style?
7. Define *macrosegmentation* and the variables used to create a macrosegmentation of an organizational market.
8. What types of *reference groups* exist in organizational markets?
9. What are *lead users* and how do they influence word-of-mouth communication and the sales of a new product?
10. What is a *decision-making unit*? How does it vary by purchase situation?
11. What factors influence the decision-making unit when a decision conflict arises?
12. How can a seller organization influence *perceptions* and *information processing* of a buyer organization?
13. What are *organizational motives,* and how do personal motives interact with organizational motives in an organizational buying decision?
14. How do organizations learn? Why is the rate of "forgetting" a negative experience slower than unlearning a positive experience?
15. How can a seller organization influence problem recognition?
16. What are the best means of influencing an organization's information search? How does each influence awareness/interest and evaluation/selection?
17. What is a *two-tier decision process*?
18. Why can purchase implementation be a critical part of the organizational decision process?
19. How does usage and postpurchase evaluation differ between households and organizations?

DISCUSSION QUESTIONS

1. Describe three organizations with distinctly different organizational styles. Explain why they have different organizational styles and the factors that have helped shape the style of each.
2. Discuss how IBM might vary its buyer style from competitive, cooperative, and command? What factors would influence IBM to modify its organizational style?
3. Discuss how an organization's decision process would change from a straight rebuy to modified rebuy and from a modified rebuy to new task purchase decision.

4. Discuss how the Red Cross differs from Apple Computer in terms of organizational activities and objectives. Discuss how these differences influence organizational styles.
5. How could an organization's values interact with an individual's values such that a purchase decision would be biased by the individual's personal values?
6. Discuss how the organizational demographics of a Pittsburgh steel mill might differ from Mary Kay cosmetics. How do these demographic distinctions influence organizational style and buyer behavior?
7. Discuss how IBM might use a macrosegmentation strategy to sell microcomputers to businesses.
8. Discuss how a small hi-tech firm could influence the reference group infrastructure and lead users to accelerate adoption of its products in the market.
9. Discuss the marketing implications of the decision-making structure shown in Table 19–6. Then using the information shown in Table 19–6 discuss how you would develop your marketing strategy for this purchase situation.
10. Discuss the effectiveness of different business-to-business promotional advertising described in Table 19–5 and how each differed by size of seller organization. Also discuss how the objectives of these promotion efforts differed by organizational size.
11. Describe a situation in which both organizational motives and personal emotions could play a role in the outcome of a purchase decision. What marketing efforts are needed to satisfy both types of needs?
12. Discuss the implications of the relationship shown in Figure 19–9 for a small start-up business that has a negative experience in selling an important component product to General Motors.
13. Discuss the marketing implications for the decision process shown in Figure 19–11.
14. Discuss how you would market to a hi-tech organization based on the results shown in Figure 19–12. What would be the dangers of a seller organization that typically only called on purchasing during sales visits?
15. Discuss how an organization would utilize two sets of decision rules in selecting a vendor in a new task decision.
16. Discuss Exhibit 19–9 and how this information could be used by manufacturers of the proposed product. How do you convince an organization that wants to lower cost to pay more money for your product?

PROJECT QUESTIONS

1. Interview a large and a small organization and for each identify purchase situations that could be described as straight rebuy, modified rebuy, and new task. For each organization and purchase situation determine the following:
   a. Size and functional representation of the decision-making unit.
   b. The number of choice criteria considered.

   c. Length of the decision process.
   d. Number of vendors or suppliers considered.
2. For a given industrial organization arrange to review the trade publications they subscribe to. Identify three industrial ads in these publications which vary in copy length, one very short (under 100 words), one with approximately 150 words, and one very long (over 250 words). Arrange to have these ads read by three or four people in the organization. Have each reader rank the ads in terms of preference (independent of product or manufacturer preference). Then ask each to describe what they like or dislike about each ad. Discern the role that copy length played in their evaluation.
3. Interview a representative from a commercial, governmental, nonprofit, and cooperative organization. For each determine their organizational demographics, activities, and objectives. Then relate these differences to differences in their organizational styles.
4. For a given organization, identify reference groups that influence the flow of information in their industry. Create a hierarchical diagram as shown in Figures 19–6 and 19–7, and discuss how this organization could influence groups who would in turn create favorable communications concerning this organization.
5. For a new task decision in an organization of interest to you, identify the decision-making unit and individuals that will influence the decision-making unit. For each, identify their purchase criteria. With this information, develop a marketing strategy for this organizational buying situation.

REFERENCES

[1] G. J. Coles and J. D. Culley, "Not All Prospects Are Created Equal," *Business Marketing,* May 1986, pp. 52–59.

[2] F. Nicosia and Y. Wind, "Behavioral Model of Organizational Buying Process," in *Behavioral Models of Market Analysis: Foundations for Marketing Action,* ed. F. Nicosia and Y. Wind (Hinsdale, Ill.: Dryden Press, 1977), pp. 97–120.

[3] F. Webster, Jr., and Y. Wind, *Organizational Buyer Behavior* (Englewood Cliffs, N.J.: Prentice-Hall, 1972).

[4] R. Moriarty and D. Reibstein, "Benefit Segmentation in Industrial Markets," *Journal of Business Research,* no. 14, 1986, pp. 463–86.

[5] N. C. G. Campbell, "An Interaction Approach to Organizational Buyer Behavior," *Journal of Business Research,* no. 13, 1985, pp. 35–48.

[6] D. Conner, B. Finnan, and E. Clements, "Corporate Culture and Its Impact on Strategic Change in Banking," *Journal of Retail Banking,* Summer 1987, pp. 16–24.

[7] G. Badovick and S. Beatty, "Shared Organizational Values: Measurement and Impact upon Strategic Marketing Implementation," *Journal of the Academy of Marketing Science,* Spring 1987, pp. 19–26.

[8] J. Hlavacek and B. C. Ames, "Segmenting Industrial and Hi-Tech Markets," *Journal of Business Strategy,* Fall 1986, pp. 39–50.

[9] J. Choffray and G. Lilien, "Industrial Market Segmentation by the Structure of the Purchasing Decision Process," *Industrial Marketing Management,* no. 9, 1980, pp. 337–42.

[10] E. Von Hippel, "The Dominant Role of Users in the Scientific Instrument Innovation Process," *Research Policy,* no. 5, 1976, pp. 212–39.

[11] A. N. Link and J. Neufeld, "Innovation vs. Imitation: Investigating Alternative R&D Strategies," *Applied Economics,* no. 18, 1986, pp. 1359–63.

[12] R. McKenna, *The Regis Touch: New Marketing Strategies for Uncertain Times* (Menlo Park, Calif.: Addison-Wesley, 1985).

[13] R. Best and R. Angelmar, "Business Strategies for Leveraging a Technology Advantage," *Handbook of Business Strategy* (1988).

[14] D. R. Lambert, P. D. Boughton, and G. R. Banville, "Conflict Resolution in Organizational Buying Centers," *Journal of the Academy of Marketing Science,* no. 14, 1986, pp. 57–62.

[15] R. J. Thomas, "Bases of Power in Organizational Buying Decisions," *Industrial Marketing Management,* no. 13, 1984, pp. 209–17.

[16] M. Berkowitz, "New Product Adoption by the Buying Organization: Who Are the Real Influencers?" *Industrial Marketing Management,* no. 15, 1986, pp. 33–43.

[17] Choffray and Lilien, "Industrial Market Segmentation."

[18] L. Soley, "Copy Length and Industrial Advertising Readership," *Industrial Marketing Management,* no. 15, 1986, pp. 245–51.

[19] C. Reichard, "Industrial Selling: Beyond Price and Resistance," *Harvard Business Review,* March-April 1985, p. 132.

[20] G. Reichard, "Industrial Selling."

[21] A. Isen, "Toward Understanding the Role of Affect in Cognition," in *Handbook of Social Cognition,* ed. R. Wyerand and T. Srull (Hillsdale, N.J.: Erlbaum, 1984), pp. 179–235.

[22] P. J. Robinson and C. W. Faris, *Industrial Buying and Creative Marketing* (Boston: Allyn and Bacon, 1976); F. E. Webster, Jr., and Y. Wind, "A Generic Model for Understanding Organizational Buying Behavior," *Journal of Marketing,* vol. 36, no. 2, April 1972, pp. 12–19; J. N. Sheth, "A Model of Industrial Buyer Behavior," *Journal of Marketing,* vol. 37, no. 4, October 1973, pp. 50–56; T. J. Hillier, "Decision Making in the Corporate Industrial Buying Process," *Industrial Marketing Management,* vol. 4, 1975, pp. 99–106.

[23] R. Abratt, "Industrial Buying in High-Tech Markets," *Industrial Marketing Management,* no. 15, 1986, pp. 293–98.

[24] Ibid.

[25] "Study Shows Frequent Four-Color Ads Attract More Attention in Trade Press," *Marketing News,* March 14, 1988, p. 13.

[26] R. LeBlanc, "Insights into Organizational Buying," *Journal of Business and Industrial Marketing,* Spring 1987, pp. 5–10; L. Crow, R. Olshausky, and J. Kammers, "Industrial Buyers' Choice Strategies: A Protocol Analysis," *Journal of Marketing Research,* February 1980, pp. 43–44; N. Vyas and A. Woodside, "An Inductive Model Industrial Supplier Choice Process," *Journal of Marketing,* 1984, pp. 30–45.

CASES

CASE 5–1 STEEL TECHNOLOGY, INC.*

The sale of engineered steel products to the heavy construction industry is complicated by a sequenced decision process.

The heavy construction industry involves construction of roads, dams, sewers, underground utilities, and so forth. Construction companies serving these markets utilize heavy-duty earthmoving equipment to accomplish many different earthmoving tasks. Various components of this equipment are subjected to harsh applications in which components can break or wear out at a fast rate. Because downtime is very expensive, these components have to have long wearlives and minimal breakage. Steel Technology, Inc. (STI) is recognized as a leader in the development and manufacturing of these steel components.

Because STI is able to combine steel chemistry technology with superior engineering design, they charge a price premium for their products. Though customers pay more, they get a better economic value in the long run since the STI product is less likely to break and it lasts longer due to a superior wearlife. However, only a small portion of the market purchased STI products for construction applications.

High price was often cited as the reason a potential buyer did not buy STI. While lowering price would seem like a natural thing to do in order to attract more customers, STI wanted to make sure this was the critical factor in not buying STI more often. To determine how potential buyers made this purchase decision, they conducted a purchase decision study of their existing and potential customers.

Construction Customer Research Study

Approximately 100 high-potential users were identified for the study. The first twenty were interviewed in person so that the survey could be improved before sending it out to the remaining 80 as a mail survey. While a variety of questions were asked, one critical set focused on what these customers considered in a

*Based on a proprietary project by one of the authors.

purchase decision and the sequence they went through in making a final purchase decision.

From the purchase criteria identified and the importance weight assigned each criterion, a general pattern emerged, although there were some differences across potential customers. Listed in Figure A are the purchase criteria and their respective importance weights. As shown, price was the fourth most important purchase criteria. STI was clearly ahead of competition on the three most important purchase criteria.

Their major weaknesses were in the areas of availability (was the product in inventory when the customer needed it?) and delivery (how long would it take to get it when it is in inventory?). STI design was also thought to be limited. STI's designs were excellent but were limited in number, given the many applications that existed. When ratings were assigned to STI and competitors for each of the purchase criteria and a weighted score computed, STI obtained the highest rating. This would normally translate into the highest market share, but this was not the case. They possessed only a small share of this market.

While the results in Figure A are similar to those reported in a construction-market trade association survey, they are dangerously misleading. The STI construction customer study revealed that a much more complex decision process was being used. Although the information shown in Figure A was indeed being used in purchase decisions, how and in what sequence revealed a completely different picture of where STI stood in this market.

Figure B summarizes the decision process used. The first question a construction customer asks is: "Is breakage or wearlife a problem?" In 20 percent of earthmoving applications, one or the other is a problem and STI is considered a candidate as are several of its competitors. However, 80 percent of the time, breakage and wearlife are not problems, and the decision maker turns to issues of productivity (time-related efficiencies), where design has a major impact. Because STI has a limited range of designs for different application environments, they are eliminated from consideration at this point 75 percent of the time.

The next screening criterion is availability. In the construction market, cus-

Figure A
Purchase Criteria, Importance Weights, and Competitive Position

Purchase Criteria	Importance	Competitive Position
Wearlife or product	25%	Superior
Probability of breakage	20	Superior
After-sale support	15	Excellent
Price of product	14	High
Availability	10	Very Poor
Delivery	10	Poor
Design	6	Limited

Figure B
Construction Customer Decision Process

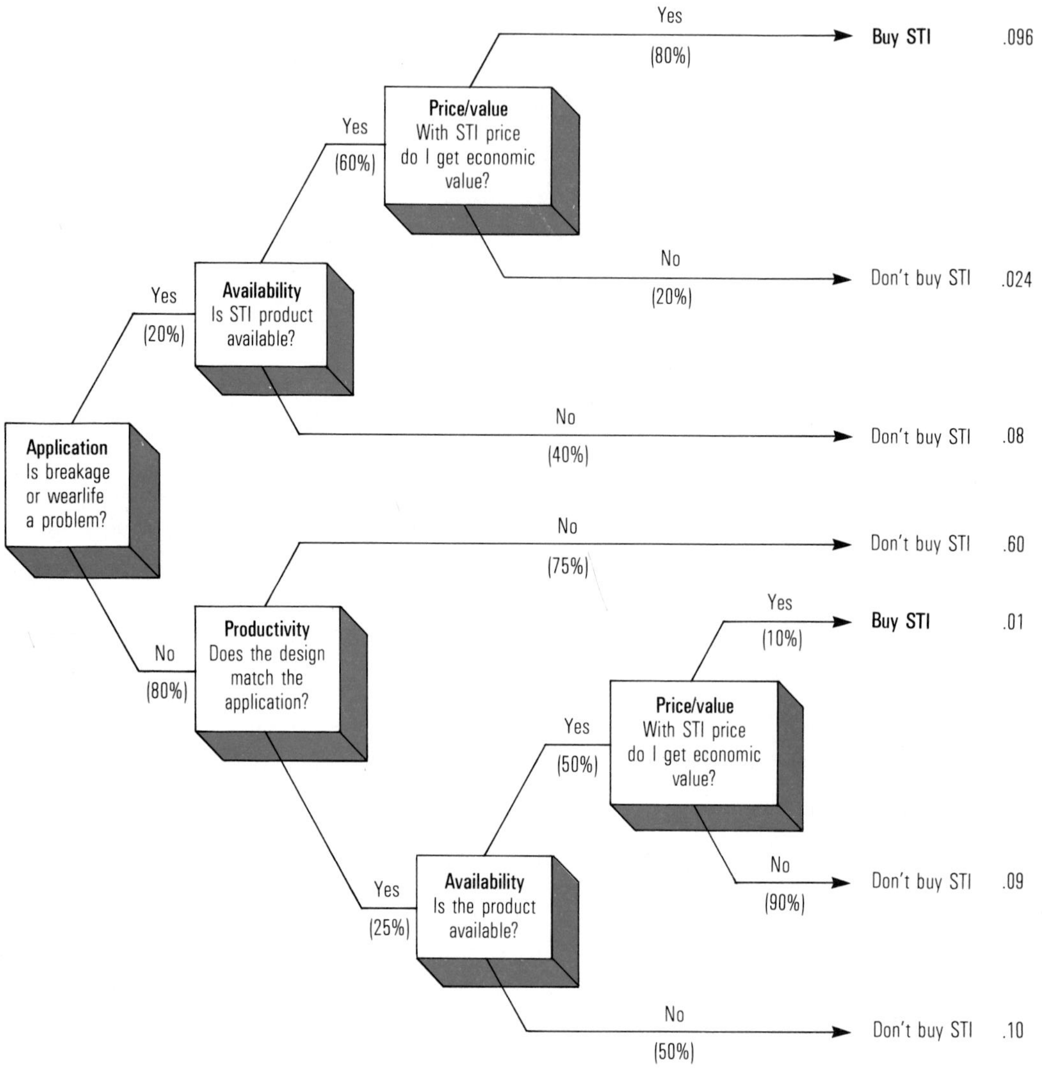

tomers like to maintain a minimum inventory and expect the manufacturer or its dealers to have the product they need at the moment they need it. In tough applications where breakage and wearlife are important issues, STI has the right product available 60 percent of the time. In productivity-driven situations where design is important, they have the right product available 50 percent of the time.

If STI survives these initial screening decisions based on application, productivity, and availability, the question of economic value is raised. In tough applications where breakage and wearlife are problems, STI delivers more economic value than competitors 80 percent of the time. However, in less demanding earthmoving applications where breakage and wearlife are not important, STI can win on the basis of value only 10 percent of the time.

When the entire decision process is taken into account, STI captures 10.6 percent of the market. The majority of this is in tough applications, where it has almost a 50 percent share. However, due to a limited range of designs (productivity), they cannot compete in 60 percent of the purchase decisions. And, due to poor availability they lose another 28 percent of market opportunity. Thus, while STI is recognized as the industry leader in steel technology, they can only serve a small portion of the market.

Questions

1. Describe the construction customer decision process and the decision rules that are being utilized.
2. What kind of information evaluation is the construction customer going through in order to determine if STI offers more economic value than a competing product? What kind of decision rule would the customer use in selecting the supplier with the best economic value?
3. Discuss the discrepancies between what construction customers rate as important in Figure A and how they use that information in making a decision in Figure B.
4. How would you advise STI to improve its market share position?

CASE 5-2 MOBILE-PHONE SYSTEMS, INC.*

How can a small cellular phone company increase the rate of adoption in a highly competitive environment with many substitute products?

The research firm of Frost and Sullivan estimates that the mobile phone market will be $6 billion a year in 1990. The business sector will account for 67 percent of this demand. More than 20 manufacturing companies have entered the market based on this expected demand, and many companies in large metropolitan areas have applied to the Federal Communications Commission (FCC) for cellular radio licenses. Licensed companies include small independent businesses, giants such as AT&T through its subsidiary Advanced Mobil Phone Service, Inc., regional phone companies, GTC, MCI Telecommunications, and Graphic Scanning. Mobile-Phone Systems, Inc., is a small independent company with an FCC cellular radio license for a metropolitan area of over 2 million people.

The need filled by cellular phone systems is currently met by mobile radios, pagers, and pay phones. Mobile phone systems have grown at the rate of 15

*Source: J. F. Cady and F. V. Cespedes, "E. T. Phone Home, Inc.: Forecasting Business Demand," (Boston: Harvard Business School, 1982), Case No. 9-583-121.

Figure A
Target Market Adoption Rate and Price-Demand Curve

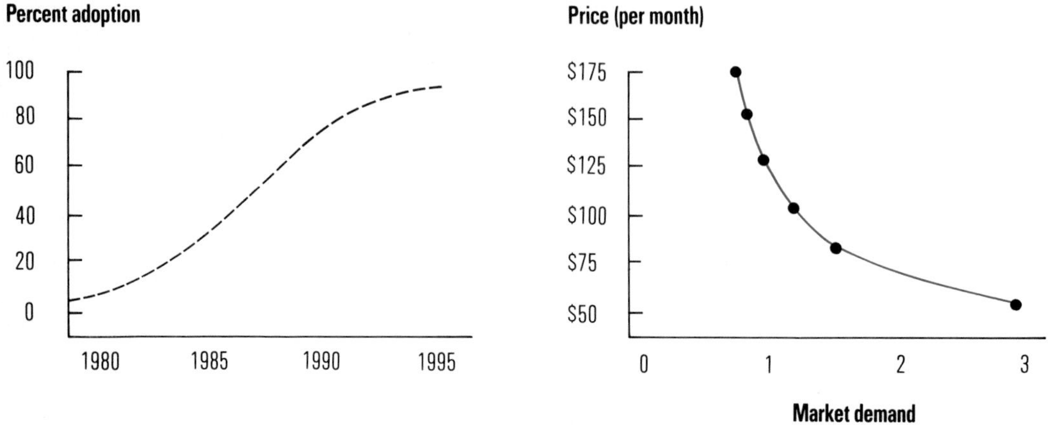

percent a year and pagers have been growing at a 30 percent rate. Because cellular phone systems offer even greater benefits to a wider range of potential users, their impact on the mobile communications market is expected to be enormous.

Figure A provides a projection of user adoption among potential customers, along with an estimate of demand at various monthly rates of service and equipment rental. By the year 1990, 50 percent of the target market will have mobile phone systems, assuming the price level is attractive. As shown, the market for mobile phone systems is price sensitive and could vary extensively, depending on the market price that prevails.

Mobile-Phone Systems (MPS) faces two very difficult challenges. First, how does it develop a portion of the market where it can survive among much larger competitors? And second, how can it aid in accelerating adoption and use of cellular radio phone systems? Cutting price is out of the question since MPS's larger competitors have a cost advantage and MPS may not be able to survive if prices go too low. Therefore, they need to pursue the market from an added-value point of view, where the benefits of what they offer customers exceed the cost, even perhaps at a slight premium over larger suppliers of cellular radio communications. To better understand how to approach the market and deal with these challenges, MPS conducted a study of existing and potential mobile phone users.

Market Research

Because 67 percent of the demand will come from businesses, MPS decided to focus its research on this segment. MPS management agreed with others in the industry that the consumer market would be slower to develop and more price

Figure B
Business Response to the Need for a Mobile Phone System

Degree of Interest if Offered at a Reasonable Price		Reasons for Not Wanting a Mobile Phone for Those "Not Intersted at All"	
8%	Very interested	92%	Have no need for one
23%	Somewhat interested	28%	A nuisance to carry around
9%	Not too interested	22%	Don't like to be tied to a phone
60%	Not interested at all	14%	Believe it would be too expensive

sensitive. The sampling frame included businesses and nonprofit organizations located in their market area. A total of 400 organizations were interviewed via telephone; 90 percent of those interviewed held managerial or administrative positions in their companies.

In rating various characteristics of mobile phone systems, respondents indicated that the most important features were "being able to receive and place a call at any time while in a vehicle," and having "a phone that is as easy to use as a standard phone." Of the 400 organizational users interviewed, only 8 percent said they were very interested in having a mobile phone, as shown in Figure B. Overall interest in having a mobile phone was low, and 60 percent stated that

Figure C
Mobile Phone Usage by Business Sector and Business Position

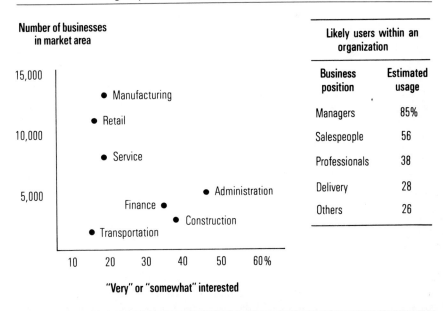

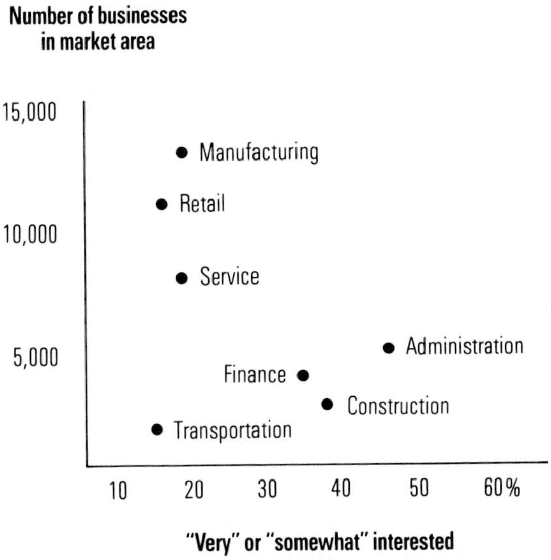

Likely users within an organization

Business position	Estimated usage
Managers	85%
Salespeople	56
Professionals	38
Delivery	28
Others	26

they were "not interested at all." Among those "not interested at all," the primary reason for not wanting one was their perception of having no need for one. This result led MPS management to conclude that felt need and the perceived benefits of a mobile phone were low.

In the MPS-served market area, interest varied according to type of business and type of user in the organization. Figure C indicates by business type the percent of firms indicating they were "somewhat" or "very" interested in cellular phones. As shown, manufacturing, retail, and service represent high market potentials, but their interest level is lower than that of organizations categorized as administrative in nature. Transportation represents both low market potential and a low interest level.

Within organizations, managers and administrators are estimated to be the heaviest users, with 85 percent stating they would use a mobile phone "often" or "occasionally." Salespeople were identified as the next most likely user group. An estimated 38 percent of other professionals in the organization would also use a mobile phone often or occasionally.

Questions

1. Describe the diffusion process for the mobile phone industry, and discuss how different factors that influence the rate of diffusion will impact market adoption of cellular phone systems. Why is the rate of diffusion expected to differ between the consumer and business segments?
2. Of the factors that influence the rate of diffusion/adoption, which can Mobile-Phone Systems, Inc., influence through their marketing efforts? Discuss how they would go about creating a positive impact for each of the factors identified.
3. Recognizing that MPS is much smaller than some of its competitors, develop a marketing strategy that would allow them to penetrate the market and build a sustainable competitive advantage with the customers they attract.
4. Develop an advertisement for MPS that will both impact rate of adoption (i.e., interest in mobile phones) and attract them to evaluate MPS as a vendor of this service. Indicate your intended audience and media. Will this ad have any positive or negative affects on nontarget audience members that are part of your larger target market?

CASE 5–3 LOCTITE CORPORATION*

Loctite takes a behavioral approach to position a new industrial adhesive.

---

*Source: Adapted form R. Alsop and B. Abrams, "Loctite Listens to the Marketplace," *The Wall Street Journal on Marketing* (Homewood, Ill.: Dow Jones-Irwin, 1986), pp. 281–83.

Figure A
Market Potential and Penetration of 15 SIC Industry Groups

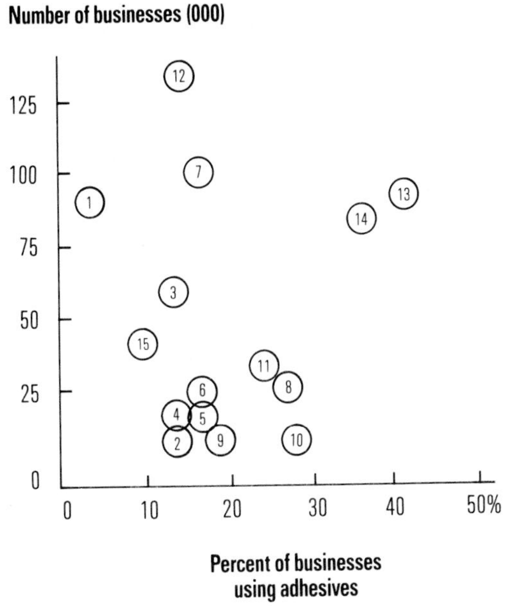

Industrial markets

Number	SIC	Industry
1	20-24	Food, textile, wood
2	25	Furniture
3	26-27	Paper and printing
4	28-29	Chemicals, petroleum
5	30-31	Rubber, plastics, leather
6	32	Stone, clay, glass
7	33-35	Machinery, metal products
8	36	Electrical, electronic
9	37	Transportation
10	38	Scientific and photo equipment
11	39	Jewelry, toys, sports
12	40-49	Utilities, communications
13	75	Motor vehicle services
14	76	Appliance repair
15	78-80	Entertainment and health

In 1987 Loctite Corporation achieved worldwide sales of $267 million. While Loctite is best known for Super-Glue, its big money makers are industrial applications for anaerobic adhesives, which form a tight bond in the absence of air. These adhesives are used in a variety of applications across many industries. To increase their sales, Loctite has had to develop new markets for existing products and develop new products for existing markets. This challenge has led them to adopt many of the concepts, tools, and techniques used by consumer goods companies.

In the late seventies, many industrial markets were beginning to use industrial adhesives where they once used other types of fasteners. Figure A summarizes by Standard Industrial Code (SIC) the number of establishments in each sector of industrial business and the percent using adhesives. The research used to prepare this figure revealed that only 16 percent of all firms used adhesives, and in only 14 SIC-industry groups did more than 10 percent of the firms use instant adhesives. Thus, the market potential was tremendous, but the marketing challenge was also enormous.

Industrial Organizational Buyers

To tap into the many industrial markets shown in Figure A and increase the use of instant adhesives, Loctite felt it had to understand better the needs of potential

Figure B
Preferences and Behaviors of Target Users and Influencers

User/Influencer Segment	Number	User/Influencer Profile
Equipment designers	20	Designers are risk-avoiders; they need to be correct in their work. They rely on charts, graphs, and known relationships in their equipment design efforts.
Production engineers	40	Production engineers are today-oriented. They need solutions that are reliable, perform well, and have minimal financial consequences if a problem occurs.
Maintenance workers	40	Maintenance workers are the fixers; they keep things running. They are uncomfortable with people in three-piece suits and are more influenced by pictures than charts and graphs.

users, decision makers, and decision influencers. Personal interviews were arranged with equipment designers, production engineers, and maintenance workers. As shown in Figure B, there are key differences between the three types of potential users or influencers.

The research study also revealed that maintenance workers are more likely to try an unfamiliar product than are the other two potential users. When the production line goes down, the maintenance worker can buy anything, anywhere, if he feels it will put the line back into production. For these reasons Loctite elected to focus initially on the maintenance worker. More open to trying unfamiliar products, they possess decision-making and purchase authority, and should not be price sensitive.

Quick Metal

Recognizing that most nonusers have the perception that an adhesive could not be as reliable as a metal fastener, Loctite decided to confront this misperception directly. The product, targeted at the maintenance workers in production businesses, was a puttylike adhesive that could be used to repair broken or worn machine parts. Rather than naming the product RC 601, predecessor of the new product, they selected the name Quick Metal to communicate both the speed and strength of the Loctite product in repairing broken machine parts.

Based on the psychographics of maintenance workers, Loctite management knew they had to communicate benefits with a direct and simple message. While advertising and promotion materials could have described the adhesive as a "nonmigrating thixotropic anaerobic gel," such technical language would not appeal to the maintenance worker. Cutting through all the unwanted technical jargon (which means little to the target user), they settled on a single slogan:

Keeps Machinery Running until the New Parts Arrive

Loctite management feel that Quick Metal offers substantial benefits to a user who possesses both decision-making and purchasing powers. The benefits derived from less downtime have direct economic benefits. Therefore, even at a premium price, Quick Metal could offer economic value to its users. Based on this logic, Quick Metal was priced at $17.75 for a 50 cc. tube. This produced an 85 percent gross margin. Cost-based pricing would have led to a price half that of the price selected.

Based on prior new-product launches of adhesives targeted at industrial organizations using more traditional industrial practices, Loctite estimated first-year sales of the new product effort to be $320,000.

Questions

1. Describe how differences in work within an organization create different attitudes, needs, and preferences for similar product types.
2. What risks would a maintenance worker perceive if he or she tried to repair a broken metal machine with "glue"?
3. Will this program be more or less successful than a traditional approach? Justify your response.
4. How should Loctite modify its strategy to market instant adhesives to equipment designers and production engineers?
5. Why would the marketing strategy created for maintenance workers probably fail with equipment designers and production engineers?
6. Develop an advertisement for equipment designers or production engineers.

APPENDIX

A Consumer Research Methods

In this appendix we want to provide you with some general guidelines for conducting research on consumer behavior. While these guidelines will help you get started, a good marketing research text is indispensable if you need to conduct a consumer research project or evaluate a consumer research proposal.[1] Figure A–1 summarizes the various methods of obtaining consumer information that we will discuss in this section.

SECONDARY DATA

Any research project should begin with a thorough search for existing information relevant to the project at hand. *Internal* data such as past studies, sales reports, and accounting records should be consulted. *External* data including reports by magazines, government organizations, trade associations, marketing research firms, and advertising agencies; academic journals; trade journals; and books should be thoroughly researched.

Computer searches are fast, economical means of conducting such searches. Most university and large public libraries have computer search capabilities, as do most large firms. However, computer searches will often miss reports by trade associations and magazines. Therefore, magazines that deal with the product category or that are read by members of the relevant market should be contacted. The same is true for associations (for names and addresses see *Encyclopedia of Associations,* Gale Research Inc.).

SAMPLING

If the specific information required is not available from secondary sources, we must gather primary data. This generally involves talking to or observing consumers. However, it could involve asking knowledgeable others, such as sales personnel, about the consumers. In either case, time and cost constraints generally preclude us from contacting every single potential consumer. Therefore, most

[1]This appendix is based on D. S. Tull and D. I. Hawkins, *Marketing Research* (New York: Macmillan, 1987).

Figure A–1
Methods of Obtaining Consumer Information

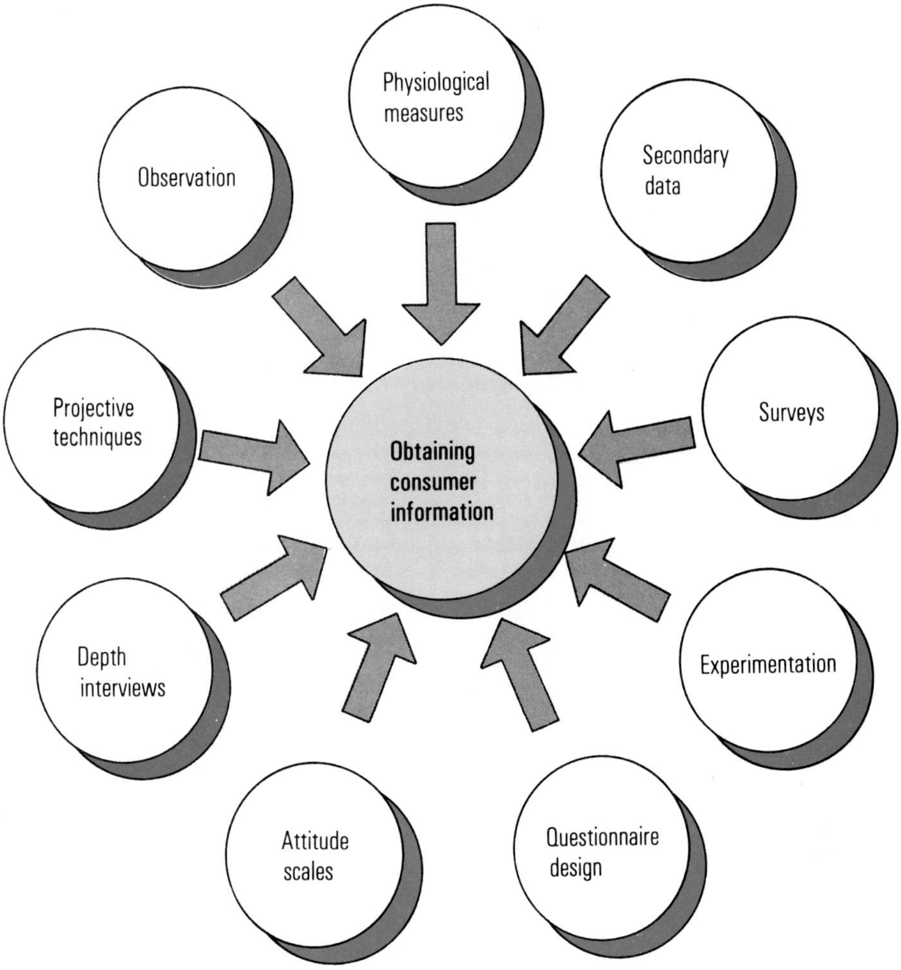

consumer research projects require a *sample*—a deliberately selected portion of the larger group. This requires a number of critical decisions as outlined in Figure A–2. Mistakes made at this point are difficult to correct later in the study. The key decisions are briefly described below.

Define the Consumer Population

The first step is to define the consumers in which we are interested. Do we want to talk to current brand users, current product category users, or potential product

Figure A–2
The Consumer Sampling Process

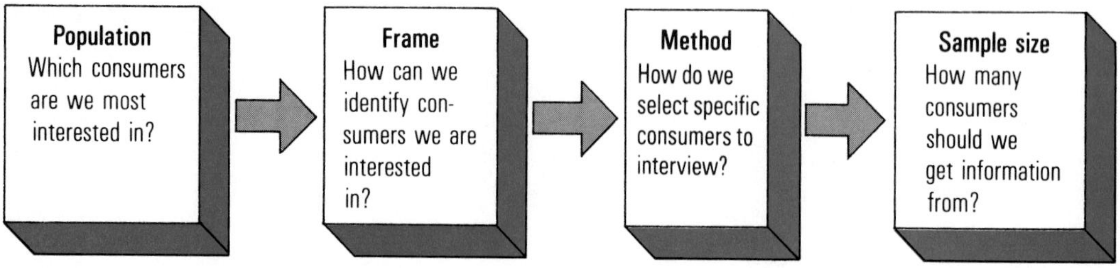

category users? Do we want to talk with the purchasers, the users, or everyone involved in the purchase process? The population as we define it must reflect the behavior on which our marketing decision will be based.

Specify a Sampling Frame

A sampling frame is a "list" or grouping of individuals or households that reflects the population of interest. A phone book and shoppers at a given shopping mall can each serve as a sampling frame. Perfect sampling frames contain every member of the population one time. Phone books do not have households with unlisted numbers and many people do not visit shopping malls, while others visit them frequently. This is an area in which we generally must do the best we can without expecting a perfect frame. However, we must be very alert for biases that may be introduced by imperfections in our sampling frame.

Select a Sampling Method

The major decision at this point is between a random (probability) sample and a nonrandom sample. Nonrandom samples, particularly judgment samples, can provide good results. A judgment sample involves the *deliberate* selection of knowledgeable consumers or individuals. For example, a firm might decide to interview the social activities officers of fraternities and sororities to estimate campus attitudes toward a carbonated wine drink aimed at the campus market. Such a sample might provide useful insights. However, it might also be biased since such individuals are likely to have a higher level of income and be more socially active than the average student.

The most common nonrandom sample, the convenience sample, involves selecting sample members in the manner most convenient for the researcher. It is subject to many types of bias and should generally be avoided.

Random or probability samples allow some form of a random process to select members from a sample frame. It may be every third person who passes a point-of-purchase display, house addresses selected by using a table of random numbers, or telephone numbers generated randomly by a computer. Random samples do not guarantee a *representative* sample. For example, a random sample of 20 students, from a class containing 50 male and 50 female students *could* produce a sample of 20 males. However, this would be unlikely. More important, if random procedures are used we can calculate the likelihood that our sample is not representative within specified limits.

Determine Sample Size

Finally, we must determine how large a sample to talk to. If we are using random sampling, there are formulas which can help us make this decision. In general the more diverse our population is and the more certain we want to be that we have the correct answer, the more people we will need to interview.

SURVEYS

Surveys are systematic ways of gathering information from a large number of people. They generally involve the use of a structured or semistructured questionnaire. Surveys can be administered by mail, telephone, or in person. Personal interviews generally take place in shopping malls and are referred to as *mall intercept* interviews.

Each approach has advantages and disadvantages. Personal interviews allow the use of complex questionnaires, product demonstrations, and the collection of large amounts of data. They can be completed in a relatively short time period. However, they are very expensive and are subject to interviewer bias. Telephone surveys can be completed rapidly, provide good sample control (who answers the questions), and are relatively inexpensive. Substantial amounts of data can be collected but it must be relatively simple. Interviewer bias is possible. Mail surveys take the longest to complete and must generally be rather short. They can be used to collect modestly complex data, and they are very economical. Interviewer bias is not a problem.

A major concern in survey research is nonresponse bias. In most surveys, fewer than 50 percent of those selected to participate in the study actually do participate. In telephone and personal interviews, many people are not at home or refuse to cooperate. In mail surveys, many people refuse or forget to respond.

We can increase the response rate by call-backs in telephone and home personal surveys. The call-backs should be made at different times and on different days. Monetary inducements (enclosing 25¢ or $1.00) increase the response rate to mail surveys as do prenotification (a card saying that a questionnaire is coming) and reminder post cards.

If less than a 100 percent response rate is obtained, we must be concerned that those who did not respond differ from those who did. A variety of techniques are available to help us estimate the likelihood and nature of nonresponse error.

EXPERIMENTATION

Experimentation involves changing one or more variables (product features, package color, advertising theme) and observing the effect this change has on another variable (consumer attitude, repeat purchase behavior, learning). The variable(s) that is changed is called an *independent* variable. The variable(s) that may be affected is called a *dependent* variable. The objective in experimental design is to structure the situation so that any change in the dependent variable is very likely to have been caused by a change in the independent variable.

The basic tool in designing experimental studies is the use of control and treatment groups. A *treatment group* is one in which an independent variable is changed (or introduced) and the change (or lack of) in the dependent variable is noted. A *control group* is a group similar to the treatment group except that the independent variable is not altered. There are a variety of ways in which treatment and control groups can be combined to produce differing experimental designs. One such design is illustrated in Figure A–3.

In addition to selecting an appropriate experimental design, we must also develop an experimental environment. In a laboratory experiment, we carefully control for all outside influences. This generally means that we will get similar results every time we repeat a study. Thus, if we have people taste several versions of a salad dressing in our laboratory, we will probably get similar preference ratings each time the study is repeated with similar consumers (internal validity). However, this does not necessarily mean that consumers will prefer the same version at home or in a restaurant (external validity).

Figure A–3
Using an Experiment to Evaluate the Impact of anIndependent Variable on a Dependent Variable

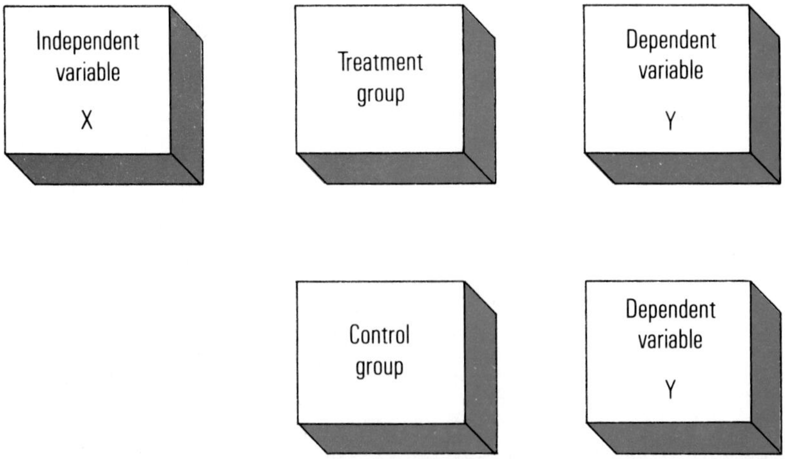

In a field experiment, we conduct our study in the most relevant environment possible. This often means that unusual outside influences will distort our results. However, if our results are not distorted, they should hold true in the actual market application. Thus, if we have consumers use several versions of our salad dressing in their homes, competitor actions, unusual weather, or product availability might influence their response (internal validity). However, absent such unusual effects, the preferred version should be preferred if actually sold on the market.

QUESTIONNAIRE DESIGN

All surveys and many experiments use questionnaires as data collection devices. A questionnaire is simply a formalized set of questions for eliciting information. It can measure (1) *behavior*—past, present, or intended, (2) *demographic characteristics*—age, sex, income, education, occupation, (3) *level of knowledge*, and (4) *attitudes and opinions*. The process of questionnaire design is outlined in Figure A–4.

Attitude Scales

Attitudes are frequently measured on specialized scales.

Noncomparative rating scales require the consumer to evaluate an object or an attribute of the object without directly comparing it to another object. *Comparative rating scales* provide a direct comparison point (a named competitor, "your favorite brand," "the ideal brand"). An example of each follows:

How do you like the taste of California Cooler:

Like it very much	Like it	Dislike it	Strongly dislike it
________	________	________	________

How do you like the taste of Gleem compared to Ultra Bright?

Like it much more	Like it more	Like it about the same	Like it less	Like it much less
_______	_______	_______	_______	_______

Paired comparisons involve presenting the consumer two objects (brands, packages) at a time and requiring the selection of one of the two according to some criterion such as overall preference, taste, or color. *Rank order scales* require the consumer to rank a set of brands, advertisements, or features in terms of overall preference, taste, or importance. The *constant sum* scale is similar

Figure A–4
Questionnaire Design Process

1. **Preliminary Decisions**
   Exactly what information is required?
   Exactly who are the target respondents?
   What method of communication will be used to reach these respondents?
2. **Decisions about question content**
   Is this question really needed?
   Is this question sufficient to generate the needed information?
   Can the respondent answer the question correctly?
   Will the respondent answer the question correctly?
   Are there any external events that might bias the response to the question?
3. **Decisions about the response format**
   Can this question best be asked as an open-ended, multiple-choice, or dichotomous question?
4. **Decisions concerning question phrasing**
   Do the words used have but one meaning to all the respondents?
   Are any of the words or phrases loaded or leading in any way?
   Are there any implied alternatives in the question?
   Are there any unstated assumptions related to the question?
   Will the respondents approach the question from the frame of reference desired by the researcher?
5. **Decisions concerning the question sequence**
   Are the questions organized in a logical manner that avoids introducing errors?
6. **Decisions on the layout of the questionnaire**
   Is the questionnaire designed in a manner to avoid confusion and minimize recording errors?
7. **Pretest and revise**
   Has the final questionnaire been subjected to a thorough pretest, using respondents similar to those who will be included in the final survey?

except it also requires the respondent to allocate 100 points among the objects. The allocation is to be done in a manner that reflects the relative preference or importance assigned each object. The *semantic differential scale* requires the consumer to rate an item on a number of scales bounded at each end by one of two bipolar adjectives. For example:

Honda Accord

Fast	X	__	__	__	__	__	__	Slow
Bad	__	__	__	__	__	X	__	Good
Large	__	__	__	X	__	__	__	Small
Inexpensive	__	__	__	__	X	__	__	Expensive

The instructions indicate that the consumer is to mark the blank that best indicates how accurately one or the other term describes or fits the attitude object. The end positions indicate "extremely," the next pair indicate "very," the middle-most pair indicate "somewhat," and the middle position indicates "neither-nor." Thus, the consumer in the example rates the Honda Accord as extremely fast, very good, somewhat expensive, and neither large nor small. *Likert scales* ask consumers to indicate a degree of agreement or disagreement with each of a series of statements related to the attitude object such as:

1. *Macy's is one of the most attractive stores in town.*

Strongly agree	Agree	Neither agree nor disagree	Disagree	Strongly disagree
___	___	___	___	___

2. *The service at Macy's is* not *satisfactory.*

Strongly agree	Agree	Neither agree nor disagree	Disagree	Strongly disagree
___	___	___	___	___

3. *The service at a retail store is very important to me.*

Strongly agree	Agree	Neither agree nor disagree	Disagree	Strongly disagree
___	___	___	___	___

To analyze responses to a Likert scale, each response category is assigned a numerical value. These examples could be assigned values, such as *strongly agree* = 1 through *strongly disagree* = 5, or the scoring could be reversed, or a −2 through +2 system could be used.

DEPTH INTERVIEWS

Depth interviews can involve one respondent and one interviewer, or they may involve a small group (8 to 15 respondents) and an interviewer. The latter are called *focus group interviews,* and the former are termed *individual depth interviews* or *one-on-ones*. Groups of four or five are often referred to as *mini-group interviews*. Depth interviews in general are commonly referred to as *qualitative research*.

Individual depth interviews involve a one-to-one relationship between the interviewer and the respondent. The interviewer does not have a specific set of prespecified questions that must be asked according to the order imposed by a questionnaire. Instead, there is freedom to create questions, to probe those responses that appear relevant, and generally to try to develop the best set of data in any way practical. However, the interviewer must follow one rule: he or she must not consciously try to affect the content of the answers given by the respondent. The respondent must feel free to reply to the various questions, probes, and other, more subtle ways of encouraging responses in the manner deemed most appropriate.

Individual depth interviews are appropriate in six situations:

1. Detailed probing of an individual's behavior, attitudes, or needs is required.
2. The subject matter under discussion is likely to be of a highly confidential nature (e.g., personal investments).
3. The subject matter is of an emotionally charged or embarrassing nature.
4. Certain strong, socially acceptable norms exist (e.g., baby feeding) and the need to conform in a group discussion may influence responses.
5. A highly detailed (step-by-step) understanding of complicated behavior or decision-making patterns (e.g., planning the family holiday) is required.
6. The interviews are with professional people or with people on the subject of their jobs (e.g., finance directors).

Focus group interviews can be applied to (1) basic need studies for product idea creation, (2) new-product idea or concept exploration, (3) product-positioning studies, (4) advertising and communications research, (5) background studies on consumers' frames of reference, (6) establishment of consumer vocabulary as a preliminary step in questionnaire development, and (7) determination of attitudes and behaviors.

The standard focus group interview involves 8 to 12 individuals. Normally the group is designed to reflect the characteristics of a particular market segment. The respondents are selected according to the relevant sampling plan and meet at a central location that generally has facilities for taping or filming the interviews. The discussion itself is "led" by a moderator. The competent moderator attempts to develop three clear stages in the one- to three-hour interview: (1) establish rapport with the group, structure the rules of group interaction, and set objectives; (2) attempt to provoke intense discussion in the relevant areas; and (3) attempt to summarize the groups' responses to determine the extent of agreement. In general, either the moderator or a second person prepares a summary of each session after analyzing the session's transcript.

Minigroups consist of a moderator and 4 or 5 respondents rather than the 8 to 12 used in most focus groups. Minigroups are used when the issue being investigated requires more extensive probing than is possible in a larger group. Minigroups do not allow the collection of confidential or highly sensitive data that might be possible in an individual depth interview. However, they do allow the researcher to obtain substantial depth of response on the topics that are covered. They also have a cost advantage over both focus groups and individual depth interviews.

PROJECTIVE TECHNIQUES

Projective techniques are designed to measure feelings, attitudes, and motivations that consumers are unable or unwilling to reveal otherwise. They are based on the theory that the description of vague objects requires interpretation, and this interpretation can only be based on the individual's own attitudes, values, and motives.

Exhibit 10–3 (page 367) provides descriptions and examples of the more common projective techniques.

OBSERVATION

Observation can be used when: (1) the behaviors of interest are public, (2) they are repetitive, frequent, or predictable, and (3) they cover a relatively brief time span. An observational study requires five decisions:

1. *Natural versus contrived situation:* Do we wait for a behavior to occur in its natural environment or do we create an artificial situation in which it will occur?
2. *Open versus disguised observation:* To what extent are the consumers aware that we are observing their behavior?
3. *Structured versus unstructured observation:* Will we limit our observations to predetermined behaviors or will we note whatever occurs?
4. *Direct or indirect observations:* Will we observe the behaviors themselves or merely the outcomes of the behaviors?
5. *Human or mechanical observations:* Will the observations be made mechanically or by people?

PHYSIOLOGICAL MEASURES

Physiological measures are direct observations of physical responses to a stimulus such as an advertisement. These responses may be controllable, such as eye movements, or uncontrollable, such as the galvanic skin response. Physiological measures are used for the same reasons that other observations are used—to obtain more accurate or more economical data.

The major physiological measures are described in Exhibit 8–8 (page 298).

APPENDIX

B Consumer Behavior Audit

In this section we provide a list of key questions to guide you in developing marketing strategy from a consumer behavior perspective. This audit is no more than a checklist to minimize the chance of overlooking a critical behavioral dimension. It does not guarantee a successful strategy. However, thorough and insightful answers to these questions should greatly enhance the likelihood of a successful marketing program.

Our audit is organized around the key decisions that marketing managers must make. The first key decision is the selection of the target market(s) to be served. This is followed by the determination of a viable product position for each target market. Finally, the marketing mix elements—product, place, price, and promotion—must be structured in a manner consistent with the desired product position. This process is illustrated in Figure B–1.

MARKET SEGMENTATION

Market segmentation is the process of dividing all possible users of a product into groups that have similar needs the product might satisfy. Market segmentation should be done prior to the final development of a new product. In addition, a complete market segmentation analysis should be performed periodically for existing products. The reason for continuing segmentation analyses is the dynamic nature of consumer needs. Figure B–2 provides an overview of this process.

A. External influences
   1. Are there cultures or subcultures whose value system is particularly consistent (or inconsistent) with the consumption of our product?
   2. Is our product appropriate for male or female consumption? Will ongoing sex role changes affect who consumes our product or how it is consumed?
   3. Do ethnic, social, regional, or religious subcultures have different consumption patterns relevant to our product?

Figure B–1
Consumer Influences Drive Marketing Decisions

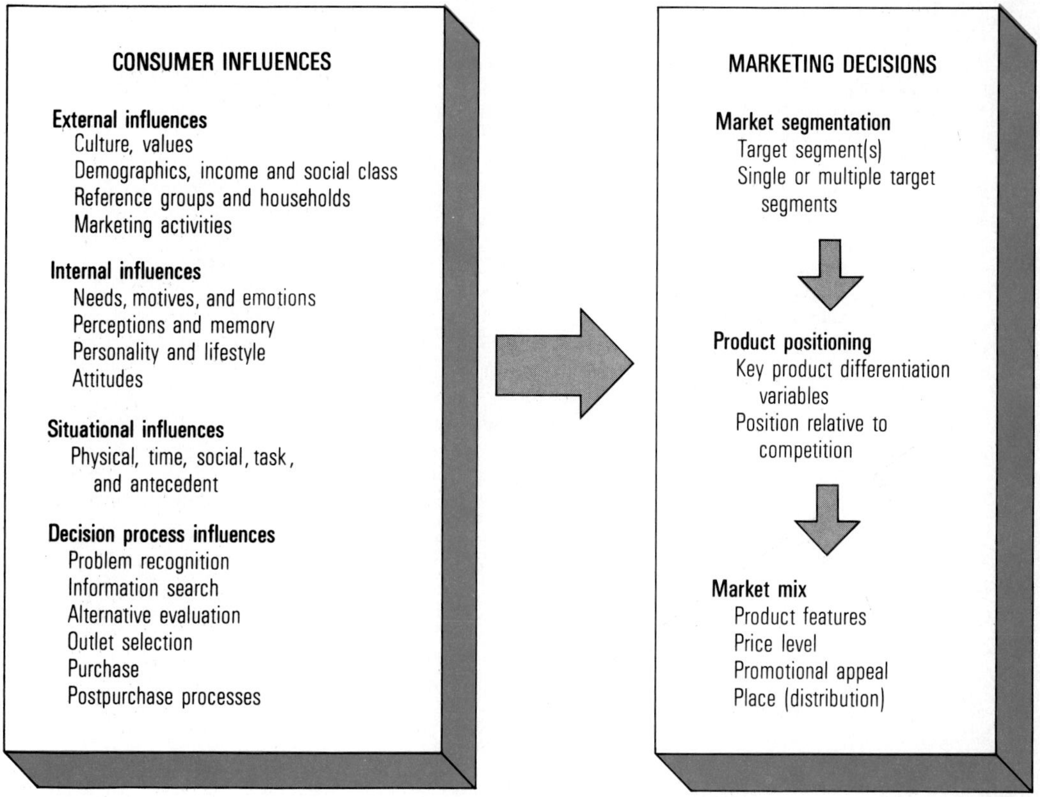

4. Do various demographic or social strata groups (age, sex, urban/suburban/rural, occupation, income, education) differ in their consumption of our product?
5. Is our product particularly appropriate for consumers with relatively high (or low) incomes compared to others in their occupational group (ROCI)?
6. Can our product be particularly appropriate for specific roles, such as students or professional women?
7. Would it be useful to focus on specific adopter categories?
8. Do groups in different stages of the household life cycle have different consumption patterns for our product? Who in the household is involved in the purchase process?

B. Internal influences

1. Can our product satisfy different needs or motives in different people?

Figure B–2
Market Segmentation

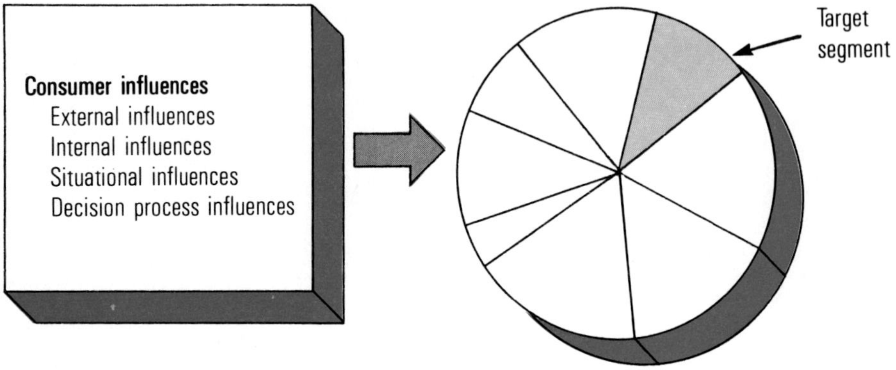

Which variables meaningfully differentiate consumers?
How do we describe the consumers in our target segment?
How can we reach them?

What needs are involved? What characterizes individuals with differing motives?

2. Is our product uniquely suited for particular personality types?
3. Is our product appropriate for one or more distinct lifestyles?
4. Do different groups have different attitudes about an ideal version of our product?

C. Situational influences
   1. Can our product be appropriate for specific types of situations instead of (or in addition to) specific types of people?

D. Decision process influences
   1. Do different individuals use different evaluative criteria in selecting the product?
   2. Do potential customers differ in their loyalty to existing products/brands?

PRODUCT POSITION

A product position is the way the consumer thinks of a given product/brand relative to competing products/brands. A manager must determine what a desirable product position would be for *each* market segment of interest. This determination is generally based on the answers to the same questions used to segment a market, with the addition of the consumer's perceptions of competing products/brands. Of course, the capabilities and motivations of existing and

Figure B–3
K mart Positioning and Desired Repositioning

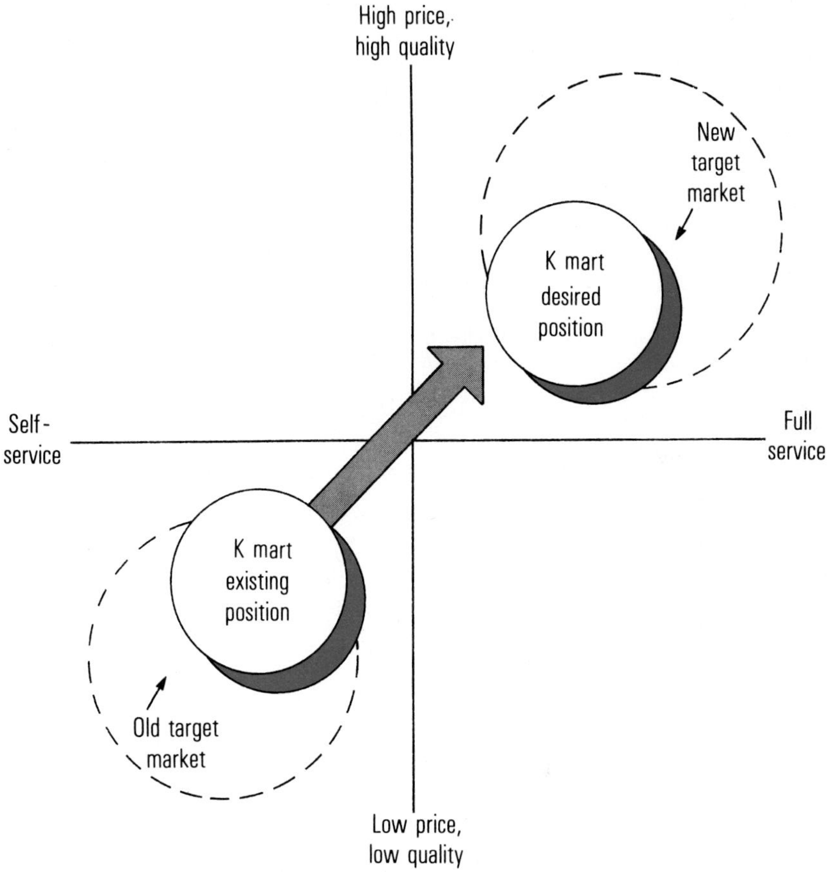

*Dashed circles are various market segments.

potential competitors must also be considered. Illustrated in Figure B–3 is how K mart is currently positioned and the market segment it currently serves, along with its desired positioning and new target market.

A. Internal influences
   1. What is the general semantic memory structure for this product category in each market segment?
   2. What is the ideal version of this product in each market segment for the situations the firm wants to serve?

B. Decision process influences
   1. Which evaluative criteria are used in the purchase decision? Which decision rules and importance weights are used?

PRICING

The manager must set a pricing policy that is consistent with the desired product position. Price must be broadly conceived as everything a consumer must surrender to obtain a product. This includes time and psychological costs as well as monetary costs.

A. External influences
   1. Does the segment hold any values relating to any aspect of pricing, such as the use of credit or "conspicuous consumption"?
   2. Does the segment have sufficient income, after covering living expenses, to afford the product?
   3. Is it necessary to lower price to obtain a sufficient relative advantage to insure diffusion? Will temporary price reductions induce product trial?
   4. Who in the household evaluates the price of the product?

B. Internal influences
   1. Will price be perceived as an indicator of status?
   2. Is economy in purchasing this type of product relevant to the lifestyle(s) of the segment?
   3. Is price an important aspect of the segment's attitude toward the brands in the product category?
   4. What is the segment's perception of a fair or reasonable price for this product?

C. Situational influences
   1. Does the role of price vary with the type of situation?

D. Decision process factors
   1. Can a low price be used to trigger problem recognition?
   2. Is price an important evaluative criterion? What decision rule is applied to the evaluative criteria used? Is price likely to serve as a surrogate indicator of quality?
   3. Are consumers likely to respond to in-store price reductions?

DISTRIBUTION STRATEGY

The manager must develop a distribution strategy that is consistent with the selected product position. This involves the selection of outlets if the item is a physical product, or the location of the outlets if the product is a service.

A. External influences
   1. What values do the segments have that relate to distribution?

2. Do the male and female members of the segments have differing requirements of the distribution system? Do working couples, single individuals, or single parents within the segment have unique needs relating to product distribution?
3. Can the distribution system capitalize on reference groups by serving as a means for individuals with common interests to get together?
4. Is the product complex such that a high service channel is required to ensure its diffusion?

B. Internal influences
1. Will the selected outlets be perceived in a manner that enhances the desired product position?
2. What type of distribution system is consistent with the lifestyle(s) of each segment?
3. What attitudes does each segment hold with respect to the various distribution alternatives?

C. Situational influences
1. Do the desired features of the distribution system vary with the situation?

D. Decision process factors
1. What outlets are in the segment's evoked set? Will consumers in this segment seek information in this type of outlet?
2. Which evaluative criteria does this segment use to evaluate outlets? Which decision rule?
3. Is the outlet selected before, after, or simultaneously with the product/brand? To what extent are product decisions made in the retail outlet?

PROMOTION STRATEGY

The manager must develop a promotion strategy including advertising, nonfunctional package design features, publicity, promotions, and sales force activities that are consistent with the product position.

A. External factors
1. What values does the segment hold that can be used in our communications? Which should be avoided?
2. How can we communicate to our chosen segments in a manner consistent with the emerging sex role perceptions of each segment?
3. What is the nonverbal communication system of each segment?
4. How, if at all, can we use reference groups in our advertisements?
5. Can our advertisements help make the product part of one or more role-related product clusters?

6. Can we reach and influence opinion leaders?
7. If our product is an innovation, are there diffusion inhibitors that can be overcome by promotion?
8. Who in the household should receive what types of information concerning our product?

B. Internal factors

1. Have we structured our promotional campaign such that each segment will be exposed to it, attend to it, and interpret it in the manner we desire?
2. Have we made use of the appropriate learning principles so that our meaning will be remembered?
3. Do our messages relate to the purchase motives held by the segment? Do they help reduce motivational conflict if necessary?
4. Are we considering the emotional implications of ad and/or the use of our product?
5. Is the lifestyle portrayed in our advertisements consistent with the desired lifestyle of the selected segments?
6. If we need to change attitudes via our promotion mix, have we selected and properly used the most appropriate attitude change techniques?

C. Situational influences

1. Does our campaign illustrate the full range of appropriate usage situations for the product?

D. Decision process influences

1. Will problem recognition occur naturally or must it be activated by advertising? Should generic or selective problem recognition be generated?
2. Will the segment seek out or attend to information on the product prior to problem recognition, or must we reach them when they are not seeking our information? Can we use low-involvement learning processes effectively? What information sources are used?
3. After problem recognition, will the segment seek out information on the product/brand, or will we need to intervene in the purchase decision process? If they do seek information, what sources do they use?
4. What types of information are used to make a decision?
5. How much and what types of information are acquired at the point of purchase?
6. Is postpurchase dissonance likely? Can we reduce it through our promotional campaign?
7. Have we given sufficient information to insure proper product use?
8. Are the expectations generated by our promotional campaign consistent with the product's performance?
9. Are our messages designed to encourage repeat purchases, brand loyal purchases, or neither?

PRODUCT

The marketing manager must be certain that the physical product, service, or idea has the characteristics required to achieve the desired product position in each market segment.

A. External influences
   1. Is the product designed appropriately for all members of the segment under consideration including males, females, and various age groups?
   2. If the product is an innovation, does it have the required relative advantage and lack of complexity to diffuse rapidly?
   3. Is the product designed to meet the varying needs of different household members?

B. Internal influences
   1. Will the product be perceived in a manner consistent with the desired image?
   2. Will the product satisfy the key purchase motives of the segment?
   3. Is the product consistent with the segment's attitude toward an ideal product?

C. Situational influences
   1. Is the product appropriate for the various potential usage situations?

D. Decision process influences
   1. Does the product/brand perform better than the alternatives on the key set of evaluative criteria used by this segment?
   2. Will the product perform effectively in the foreseeable uses to which this segment may subject it?
   3. Will the product perform as well or better than expected by this segment?

Name Index

I–J

K

L

M

N–O

P

Q–R

S

T

U–V

W

Y–Z

Case Index

Subject Index

B

C

D

E

F

J

K

L

T